TALES FRO

EDGE PLAY

One Woman's Post-Religious
Exploration of Family,
Non-Monogamy &
Psychedelic Healing

Rebecca Martinez

ZieBee Media
PORTLAND, OREGON, USA

Edge Play

by Rebecca Martinez

Copyright © 2020 Rebecca Martinez.

Cover Art & Chapter Numbers by
    Libby Landauer
    libbylandauer.com

Layout, Design, & Editing by
    ZieBee Media
    ZieBee.com

Dandelion Tattoo Art by
    Margaret Gallagher *(Margaret-Gallagher.com)*
    Digitized by ZieBee Media *(ZieBee.com)*

All Rights Reserved. No portion of this book may be reproduced, copied, modified or distributed in any form beyond Fair Use without the express written consent of the author.

Disclaimer: This story is based on real life. Names and certain identifying characteristics have been changed to protect the privacy of the individuals.

This story contains accounts of sexual experimentation, psychedelic drug use, police violence, and other mature themes. This book is not an advice manual, and does not equate to an endorsement of any behavior or activity detailed herein. Please practice discretion and common sense when participating in potentially risky behaviors. Be informed, practice consent, and stay safe.

This story invites readers to explore the edges of their comfort zones and question everything they think they know about.... everything. Side effects may include confusion, ugly crying, increased empathy, and an expanded sense of possibility and connectedness to oneself and others. Proceed at your own risk.

Discover more at EdgePlayBook.com

CONTENTS

AUTHOR'S NOTE 1

PART ONE

1. DESERT 7
2. FOUNDATIONS 10
3. FRACTURE 27
4. S-E-X 42
5. SHIFTS 53
6. BIBLE COLLEGE 60
7. IMMERSED 72
8. ADULTING 90
9. MARRIAGE 106
10. BEST, WORST 123
11. HELP ME 134
12. REBIRTH 142
13. DEATH & DYING 155
14. OPEN 163
15. TINDER SUMMER 184
16. MOTION 199

PART TWO

17. STARTING AGAIN 219
18. MONOGAMISH 240
19. SECRETS 250

20	FORWARD, BACKWARD	264
21	MEDICINE	279
22	RETURN	293
23	PARTING	307
24	INTERNATIONAL	317
25	FALLING IN MDMA	334
26	SOAK	346
27	LOVE EXPLOSION	363
28	BELOVED	376
29	THE FALL	389
30	AWAY	399
31	BREAK	413
32	VACATION	426
33	HOME	446
34	FULL CIRCLES	456
35	OFFERING	472
36	EPILOGUE	477

PERSPECTIVES 483

DEDICATION 525

This story is dedicated to
Sheila Maya Fadia.
I miss you.
Thank you for your love.
I am so glad you're flying free.

*Visit p. 525 for full story.

Acknowledgments

This book became a reality thanks to the collective efforts of numerous loved ones, mentors, and collaborators over the course of several years.

Thank you to my editor and designer Mackenzie Bakewell from ZieBee Media. You saw the merit of my story and took the project seriously when I was too drained to cross the finish line on my own. Your keen eye and open mind inspired me to rise to the occasion. I still can't believe we did it!

Thank you to my cover artist Libby Landauer, photographer Bria Bronwyn, and advisor Jeff Kellogg for offering your talent and expertise.

Thank you to my early donors and Kickstarter backers who provided the funds necessary to bring this project to life. Thank you to every reader who seeks out ways to support independent artists, writers and creatives. Please continue to amplify the work of underrepresented voices.

Indigo and Moses, you shared a home with me and helped me love this book forward. Thank you for the innumerable pep talks, quiet nights, pots of tea, and deeply meaningful reflections which fueled my storytelling.

Most of all, thank you to my family, friends and lovers whose lives intersect with my own (including the seven people whose perspectives are found at the end of this book). You've done so much more than fill an essential role in an entertaining tale. You've provided companionship, camaraderie, honesty and intimacy. You've created an environment in which I could heal. I hope I can bring as much depth to your story as you've brought into mine.

Becca

Author's Note

Perhaps it seems funny to pick up a memoir from someone who's just shy of 30. What could I know? I'm practically brand new here; just hitting my stride. And yet, there's a story in me that has to be told. She's been tapping at the door for several years, dropping hints, planting seeds, insisting. And she won't let me do much else until I put these words to the page and send them out into the ether as an ode to life.

> **This is an offering of thanks to the ocean of change that swept me up and hasn't stopped rushing for four years.**

It's a love song to the benevolent something that has whipped its wings through the air and swooped down to carry me across the improbable and unthinkable, into the irreverent and unconventional. I'm writing this book because I want to remember. I'm also writing because I want to forget. I want to lay some things down where I stand and walk forward a little lighter.

This story is an open-hearted, back-slapping hug to my whole generation. We've been living through massive cultural shifts and stumbling our way through.

There's sincerity among us.

There's depth.

There's self-involvement.

There's "what-the-fuck-am-I-doing-am-I-too-old-to-call-my-mom-for-help?"

This book is a snapshot of a moment in time and culture that we've shared: the unraveling of religious dogma, the questioning of social constructs around love, sex and race, and our expanding efforts to take responsibility for our own lives and the communities we are shaping.

Together, we're discovering that sometimes we're right on, and sometimes, in spite of good intentions, we're way off. We're shedding old baggage and stale conditioning, and doing the healing work of generations of trickle-down-trauma that came before us. No wonder psychedelics are coming back into mainstream consciousness.

I believe my story resonates with so many of us who have set out to "do the work," to show up for our individual healing and lean into our discomfort — our edge — whatever that edge may be. Doing the work has no room for perfectionism; it includes failing, sometimes publicly, and choosing to learn and grow from the experience. We've all made grand fuck-ups of good things and grown gardens out of wreckage. My hope is that by sharing this story with radical honesty, my raw, unfiltered truth can be an asset to the healing of others. Perhaps it will bring catharsis, raise questions, invite reflection, and extend permission for more of us to get really, really real with ourselves. This is lifelong work.

Within these pages, I share some of the deep healing and change that's taken place in rapid sequence over the last four years. These shifts revolved around my dysfunctional family of origin, my conservative Christian upbringing, my identity as a mixed race queer woman, and my relationship to love and sexuality, among other, more enticing things. The coming pages are replete with sex, romance, travel, irreverence, heartbreak, tears, incarceration, drug use and dialogue. I'll occasionally throw in an excerpt from a journal or break the fourth wall, just to shake things up.

When I began keeping a detailed journal in 2015, my intent was to write a book about my marriage and loss of faith. That was barely the beginning. Life played out very differently than I'd expected. I'm fortunate that I obsessively logged my life in pen and paper for years. Those journals were instrumental in the creation of this book. Many of the scenes and dialogue here are pulled straight from my real-time journals, aided by a nearly photographic memory, text threads, and Facebook history filling in the finer details.

Names and identifying characteristics have been changed, but the events in this story are otherwise true. It's been my aim to represent the story fairly and acknowledge that in telling my story, I am also touching on the stories of the many loved ones who surround me. I've set out to honor the truth of the events as they happened, as well as the subjective truth of my lived experience. Seven of my loved ones have added contributions, which can be found in the back of this book.

It's an important time. It feels like the world is spinning faster as it heats up and our society polarizes. Stakes are high, tensions are high, and it's a good time to put away our iPhones and start participating in the world in a fuller way. Healing this collective mess we're in starts inside each of us. This book is a piece of my attempt to move the needle.

An Examined Life

I've been on an unplanned path of reevaluating every single belief I brought into adulthood. I've discovered that that which is worthwhile can withstand scrutiny. I've had to let go of so much I held dear when it crumbled under my unwavering gaze. But first, I had to learn to trust myself. In a religious setting, I was never taught this skill. I was made to believe that my own mind and heart were susceptible to corruption from "worldly" influences, not to be trusted or allowed to lead.

May I make a suggestion? Find your center. Trust yourself. And then, shake everything loose.

Systematically, wildly, whatever it is, make space to EXAMINE the life you're in. Examine your default beliefs and move through the process of choosing the life you have on purpose, rather than blindly accepting whatever you came in with. We get to choose what we believe, and belief shapes reality. I believe the world can be a good, kind, abundant place that supports the wellbeing of all people and creatures. I recognize that it is our responsibility to bring this vision to life and dismantle the harmful beliefs that stand in the way of it.

I won't tell anyone else how to live. It feels important to avoid making sweeping generalizations based on my lived experience. I seek to avoid speaking for the collective "we" in this book. Sure, I have chosen an unconventional, emotionally grueling path and I am happier and more content because of it. High work, high reward.

I've chosen to create a life that is meaningful and hard and joyous. I don't believe my choices are necessarily better than others, but I do see that I have chosen my life on purpose, and that the thing which I have created is beautiful, expansive and full of possibility. I do believe that a life consciously created is better and more fulfilling than simply accepting the lives we were given by default. But I don't know what will be true for others. Life is contextual like that. Only you can know your context and your edges.

To me, self-work is activism. Or rather, it's a first step on the journey of activism and advocacy. And we can't stop at the trailhead. Self-awareness is the road map, not the end destination. This is a story about personal change. It is about becoming undone. It is about breaking down and rebuilding. What happens on an individual level translates to the shaping of our communities and society as a whole. How will we make a better future than our current reality, which has been formed by the forces of racism, classism, patriarchy and capitalism?

The winds are changing; the tides are turning. Around the world, people are taking to the streets. Are we ready? We the people have to change in order for our systems to change. We have to own our part. We have to peel back the layers of conditioning we didn't even know were there, wrapped around us like a heavy cloak. It's daunting, lifelong work.

The questions I've faced on a personal level within this book are the same questions we're facing collectively:

How do I know what I think I know about the world?

What are my blind spots?

What do I see when I look in the mirror? Am I receptive to feedback?

Do I recognize that beliefs are shaped by experience, and my experience is not the golden standard of truth?

Do I honor the validity of experiences I have not had?

Do I understand the history that I carry with me in every interaction, and how that history informs my movement through the world?

Am I aware of the impact of my conscious and unconscious choices?

What is my relationship with change?

Am I willing to practice being uncomfortable in order to grow?

Can I own my failures and shortcomings without losing myself in a spiral of shame?

Can I tolerate being wrong without making excuses for myself?

Am I willing to change my beliefs when presented with new information?

Am I willing to do what's needed to make things right?

And most importantly: Have I allowed myself to boldly, audaciously dream of the expansive possibilities that might actually be within reach?

It's a wild time to be alive.

Let's peer over the edge together.

Part One

1 Desert

November 12, 2016

Lake Powell, Arizona

I warmed a spicy pot of coconut curry over the flame of my Coleman camp stove, watching the steam rise in ribbons and disappear into the desert air. Behind me, Logan cursed loudly as she rummaged through her Subaru, searching for a hatchet. *A firecracker, that one*, I chuckled to myself. Who could have guessed we'd wind up here? Once, not long ago, I was an earnest college student, a mentor, tasked with looking after her as she grew from a child into a teenager, and leading her on the spiritual path of Christianity.

Now, she was grown; we were peers.

We'd spent a week smoking joints and drinking whiskey in the pristine wilds of Utah's Zion and Bryce Canyon National Parks. We came out here to celebrate my 26th birthday, but also to mend our broken hearts, share stories, and escape the terrifying realities of the recent 2016 presidential election. After dinner we chatted for a while, and only once we were ready, did I pull out the tiny, nondescript squares of paper I'd buried deep in my backpack. I slid them out of a small clear baggie and handed one to Logan.

"Okay," I sighed. "Here goes..."

"Here goes," she replied.

We set the paper on our tongues. Portals as small as confetti. We laughed. And then… we waited.

Logan, a scrappy, warm-hearted Native American skater punk, who managed a brick oven pizza cart in Portland, set about arranging the fire pit for later. I organized our essential supplies: water, snacks, cozy warm clothes, a speaker, twinkly LED lights, and candles. A quiet expectation had set in, the way one feels when sitting in a pew before a wedding or gathering around a beautiful meal but not yet partaking.

We wandered down to the water of Arizona's controversial Lake Powell, a man-made reservoir and bane to conservationists for decades. The low sun shone with a gentle grace. The air was still against the pastel sky, and a single boat floated lazily on the water.

I took in the scene: Glen Canyon's towering red sandstone walls all around, bearing fifty feet of whitened bathtub rings along its base, a marker of a bygone era when this full body of water represented power, tourism and economic opportunity. A marker of humanity's past attempts to bend nature to its will.

As we sat on the rocky shoreline, I explained to Logan that in our lifetime, the basin before us would likely dry up due to climate change, unchecked development and interstate water politics. It would be left obsolete, an embarrassing display of human arrogance.

"Hmm…" she nodded sadly.

Then I joked that in four years, we'd likely be saying the same thing as we looked back on an entire term of:

"P r e s i d e n t   D o n a l d   J.   T r u m p."

The words hung in the air awkwardly. She and I locked eyes, turned up the corners of our lips in restraint, then burst into uncontrollable laughter, gasping for air, doubled over, tears in our eyes at the absurdity and the reality.

"Well, shit," I said, wiping my eyes.

After we regained our composure, we rose to leave.

"W h o a." We both said in unison when we turned.

To the east, a massive, iridescent amber moon hung low over the water, larger than life. We stared at it in silent awe through furrowed brows.

"Is that… real?" I asked.

"I'd say. I read it's the Blood Harvest Moon," Logan replied. "Happy birthday, Becs."

"Oh right, that's today," I said. As I spoke, I felt like a fawn in a meadow: all senses heightened, aware something unusual was taking place.

"Do you feel that?" I asked.

"I feel… something," Logan replied, glancing around.

We walked back to our camp slowly, in giddy awe as the world around us began to shimmer and breathe into life.

2
Foundations

Handshake

I like to imagine what it would be like if I were to meet you today, dear reader. I would smile and say hello. I'd likely feel the urge to greet you with a hug. But maybe you're a handshake person. That's fine by me. Maybe I'd ask what brings you here today, or whether you live in Portland, too.

Within a few moments, you'd cross over the boundary in my mind between stranger and friend. The "mere acquaintance" section in my heart is quite narrow, you see. For me, with rare exception, to know you is to love you.

Who would be the first to make a witty retort that throws both our heads back in laughter? Would we discover that we share a mutual friend, or an interest in gardening, rock climbing, or irreverent comedy? What question would you ask me that compels me to grin, lean in close, and ask,

"Oh, boy. How long do you have?"

I'd like to tell you the basics here and now, since we're just meeting after all. I'm Becca. Short for Rebecca. I'm a 29-year-old, Hispanic, white-passing, able-bodied, non-monogamous queer femme and single mother to a six-year-old son. Wait. Was that too much, too fast? My apologies… I got carried away. Sometimes, the words just fall out of my mouth. Let me try another way.

Hispanic: of Mexican, Spanish, Portuguese descent.

White-passing: Some people perceive my ethnically ambiguous appearance as white, and I've experienced some of the cultural advantages of being fair-skinned.

Able-bodied: I have the privilege of an uneventful health record and very few physical disadvantages.

Non-monogamous: I often hold distinct relationships with more than one person at a time.

Queer: My sexuality deviates from heterosexual norms. I date men, women, and gender non-conforming individuals.

Femme: I am recognizable as traditionally female (on most days).

Single mother: I do not have a partner with whom I parent.

The Slightly Longer, Quick & Dirty Introduction

I arrived with a splash in Portland, Oregon in 1990, the fourth child to my mother Mary and my father Rocky. I practically tore my way into the world.

My two-hour birth, set against a cool November dawn, was rapid-fire and intense; the placenta detached before I came earth side, causing my mother's uterus to hemorrhage. The doctors who caught me said I was the bloodiest baby they'd ever seen. My mother once joked that I just about killed her getting here, and we've had a complex relationship ever since.

I grew up in St. Helens, a sleepy little historic town on the Columbia River where there seems to be as much religious dogma as there is methamphetamine. It's the place where the movie *Halloweentown* was filmed, as well as portions of the teenage vampire hit *Twilight*. I lived in the same home my whole childhood, a 2,000 square foot, split-level house built in the '70s with a sprawling yard and two calloused oak trees shading the front lawn. I became who I am there, alongside my six family members: my mother and father, three sisters and a brother.

All three of the town's schools were within walking distance from our house, as was my maternal grandmother's home. It was a safe, relaxed town with the underlying racist and classist attitudes one might expect from a predominantly white, working-class Oregon suburb split down the middle by a railroad dividing the town into the "wrong side" and the "right side" of the tracks.

My father, Rocky, was a first generation Mexican-American from Texas who spent his career working at a nitrogen fertilizer chemical plant just outside of town. My mother, Mary, born in Reno, Nevada, was "Betty Crocker white" as my sisters say, though she has Spanish, Portuguese, Irish and English heritage. She grew up in St. Helens too, in the same small, yellow, sunflower-dotted home where my grandmother lived until she passed in 2020. She graduated from the same high school as I did, thirty years before me.

We were a Christian family. And not just culturally: we were deeply, devotedly, Evangelical Christian. We belonged to a large Foursquare church and attended services every Wednesday and Sunday. We participated in youth retreats and summer camps, and all of my best friends were a part of our tight knit church community. Game nights, potlucks, barbecues, talent shows, Christmas and Easter plays, the works. I still cherish most of those memories, although so much has changed.

To simplify a complex family dynamic: my dad worked and my mom raised us. He was emotionally distant and under-involved, and she ran the household with a strict and controlling sensibility. I was the fourth out of five children. I was a reserved child, highly sensitive and observant. My sister, Kara, and I are two years apart and were together treated as the youngest. We reaped the benefits of being small and charming toward parents who had been around the block a few times and had less stamina to micromanage us.

Home life was quietly toxic.

For some people, core wounds are acute. Their cause can be pinpointed to a traumatic moment or series of moments. For me, they came more like overuse injuries — the ongoing strain of living in a home where both my parents had deep rooted traumas that went unaddressed, buried, and squeezed out sideways, like a low grade, ever present growl of impending chaos. We all felt it and dealt with it in our own ways.

Communication in my home was blocked and dysfunctional, marked with sarcasm, passive aggression and shutting one another down by speaking sharper, faster and louder. Occasionally, things were physically hurled at one another — shampoo bottles, shoes, toys, but more often the antagonizing looked like bullying and manipulating one another, vying ruthlessly for the attention and favor of our parents. Resentment between family members ran like a small, steady drip of poison in the water, nearly undetectable. I didn't notice anything unacceptable about this at the time.

Perhaps we all grow up believing on some level that the environment we are raised in is normal, standard, acceptable. How could we know any different until we are shown?

It feels important to acknowledge that between the challenging and harmful moments within our home were huge swaths of a circumstantially good childhood, for which I am grateful. I lived in a safe neighborhood. I had good friends. We always had food in the kitchen. I was treated with kindness, and I was not abused or taken advantage of as a child.

My core wounds come from unnoticed and ongoing harms that ran the length of my young life. They are a result of my dysfunctional home environment and the pressures of fundamentalist Christian religion. I adapted out of necessity, like we all do in our own ways. I developed a robustly independent and rebellious spirit, deep perfectionism and fear of failure, and what I now understand as a highly disorganized attachment style, marked by dismissive avoidance.

It's these adaptations that I'm continuously seeking to heal, unwind and unlearn now that I'm grown. I'm peeling back layers of armor that I never even noticed I'd put on. There's much more to be said about this. I'll opt for freeform to speed things along.

> When I was a child
> Home beat with chaos
> Not out loud
> But inside
> Noisy
> Suppressed intensity
> Loaded order
> Five siblings playing, fending
> Antagonizing
> Shouting to be heard
>
> Like the others,
> I was a tender, sensitive seedling
> In a harsh environment
> Feeling the buzz, the ache of old histories
> I tried to put my hands over my ears
> Shut it out
>
> My mother
> Depressed, resentful,
> Strictly grasping for control
> Wishing for a time machine
> Cold, distant stare in her eyes
> Was running from her demons
> "I should have stopped at three kids,"
> She said aloud

FOUNDATIONS

To me, the fourth
Both proud and ashamed
Of herself
Of her life
Of

My father
Ill-equipped
Son of migrant workers
Marred by loss and abuse
Oil stained coveralls, scrap metal trailer
Muffled voice, downcast eyes
Unsure

Sitting in lined pews
Ruffled dress
Unscuffed Sunday shoes
Well-behaved
I felt safe
Quiet
Maybe peace could find me
Just under the radar
Could I not rock the boat
Not draw attention
Live without sin
Live in the tension?

I learned that the worst thing I could be
Was wrong or mistaken
Smart child
Talented
Praised for perfection
Fast learner
Good girl
Appraising intention
I learned to hide fiercely
Preserve the space around me
Shielding myself
From suffocating shame
Mother's cold glare
Unattainable expectations
Judgment, criticism

Binding, biting words
From the anger of God himself

I willed myself to believe
That I didn't need
Anything from
My father, any father

His care and affection
Buried somewhere deep
Out of reach
Only an echo of what
Ought to be
To him
I felt invisible
Nothing special
Worthy or
Remarkable

My heart was bread soft
Drumming in my chest
But missing
Somewhere calm
Safe
To open my ribcage
And freely connect

Insulating myself
From imagined impact
From an impending, unkind world
Meant armored strength
Thick skin
Arms length

I became at once warm
Inviting
Yet elusive
Impossible to read
Just beyond reach
I lived like this for years
No.
Decades.

FOUNDATIONS

These adaptive mechanisms
Like a plant growing crooked
After being trampled
Are sometimes all we've got

Now.
A woman of 29
My warm distance
My self-preservation
My desire to draw you in
To hold and be held
And my impulse to run when you

Get too close
See too much
Witness my flawed imperfection
Could hurt you
Could cut you deep
It's happened before
It's not you it's me

I've seen the wounded lovers eyes
As I've shrugged them off
Pushed them away
"Why won't you just let me love you?"
They say

I'm so damn tired of hiding
Retreating
Bracing for impact that's not coming
This world is safe
These loves are free
Choice with power and agency
No strings attached
It's not a trap
But will I let myself believe?

I'm leaning in
The love I want
Dished up right in front of me
It's too good and it's true
Healing unfolding

Rebecca Martinez

Layers shedding
Moment by moment
Reviving, tending

For me
Safe means running
Scary means staying
Being imperfect and seen
I'm uncomfortable
But these days
I'm choosing to stick around.

SNAPSHOTS IN TIME: Moments That Shaped Me

Home

In the basement, the only cool part of our house on hot days, was the homeschool room. The shelves of our "school room" were lined with Abeka books, which were a Christian-based homeschool curriculum. My mom homeschooled us kids until late grade school, as was common in suburban Christian families.

We had loads of unstructured play time. The glory of the 90s. Tablets weren't a thing and we weren't allowed to play video games. My mom kept the home very orderly and was always up to something — house work, baking, watching a movie. One of her mottos was, "Only boring people get bored." So it was up to us to occupy ourselves.

I remember playing on the metal swing set in the big backyard. Over the years, the grass beneath the swings and monkey bars wore away, revealing bare dirt, prime mud pie material. Kara and I used our beach toys to mix up buckets full of wet dirt and pour it into molds, letting the mud pies dry in the sun for days. I loved to decorate them with grass, flowers, acorns, and leaves. After they dried, we would gift them to the neighbor kids or throw them against dad's metal sheeting and cheer as we watched them explode into clouds of crumble and dust. I used this dust for magic potions, naturally.

I remember the mysterious world beneath the huge wooden deck overlooking the backyard. Underneath was a labyrinth of my dad's tires, scrap metal, PVC pipe, and buckets.

One year, my parents stored a car load of five gallon buckets of white powder under the deck and told us we were not allowed to touch them. After a great deal of prying, my mom confessed they were sugar for my aunt's confection business. It didn't take long until we snuck down during a birthday party and tore into the buckets. We wanted to taste it. Sure enough — it was sugar. (And thank goodness it was. Otherwise this would have been a very different story!) For the rest of that year, I kept a small stash of the sugar to decorate my inedible mud pies.

Another time, I was startled to hear squeaks under my feet while drawing with chalk on the deck. We ran to retrieve our dad and showed him to the pipe in question. He reached for the large PVC pipe and lifted one end toward the sky. Out of the other side tumbled a pile of tiny, barely furry kittens. We spent the day pretending they belonged to us, begging our parents to let us adopt one. By dinnertime, we'd nestled them into a cardboard box and delivered them to the animal shelter across town.

I remember the food of my childhood: Top Ramen, Kool-Aid packets, Tillamook ice cream.

I remember my mom's scratch-baked desserts: chocolate wacky cake, apple pie, blueberry streusel muffins. I can still smell her signature recipes, and the family dinners she cooked every night when we were young: fried chicken, chili and cornbread, chicken cacciatore and ginger pork stir fry (the latter we simply called "good meat").

I remember "enchilada casserole," the one food that my dad made better than my mom. I still make it sometimes, and it's as saddening to me as it is comforting.

I can still see my mom's sterling silver jewelry collection on her dresser and my dad's closet lined with cowboy boots, hats and his black leather vest.

Mother

I remember the image of my mom striding down the porch to the car in her Sunday best: long velvet dresses with ties and buttons, curled hair and high heels. She was the image of beauty. Sometimes at home she'd let us use her St. Ives face scrub or maroon nail polish, what I considered the ultimate honor.

I remember going "Mega-Shopping" with Mom. Buying groceries for a household of seven was a significant task. It was often a feat if we could cross all the food off our list before the cart overflowed. Sometimes, we had to grab a second cart. If we were agreeable the whole time, Mom would let us pick out some candy to buy at the checkout.

I remember Star Trek. Or as my mom called it, "My Show." She recorded tapes of the episodes that aired during midweek church services and watched them eagerly when we returned home.

I remember when my mom went back to work after being a stay at home mom for fifteen years. She was the secretary at our church. The place seemed so big when it was empty. Kara and I, homeschooled, came along some days, and we'd do our school work while she perched proudly at her office desk like a queen in her empire. When we finished, we got to hang out in the big 200-seat sanctuary watching Veggie Tale videos on the big screen and eating snacks from the nursery. Sometimes we would help her fold and collate the bulletins for the weekend services, and I loved meticulously washing the windows and door knobs with the church cleaning lady.

Father

I remember riding in my dad's beat-up old pickup truck on scrap metal missions. We begged our mom to let us go with him. This often meant driving to the "bad" side of town or out into the country. Dad always had to clean out his car first — the cab was cluttered with coffee cups, Gatorade bottles, work gloves, paper receipts, and once or twice I even spotted a pack of cigarettes. One of the buckles was faulty, so Kara and I shared a seatbelt. (Known as "double buckling" back then).

Dad's friends, "Little John" and "Big John," were always friendly and nice enough, but I was scared of them. Scraggly Little John had a limp and had served in the army. Big John was massive and overalled with missing teeth. Once, Kara and I chased peacocks around a farm and gathered up fallen feathers while Dad and the Johns loaded up an old washing machine onto his trailer.

Every summer, Dad also took us to the county fair down on the waterfront and let us bring a friend for the day. It was a crowded, hot, sticky, dusty affair that my mother wanted no part of. Dad always carried cash in his ancient wallet. If I asked him for five bucks, he'd often give me a $10 or $20 bill. Dad knew a lot of people around town from the car races and his scrap metal business. People took to him, his mellow demeanor and neighborly generosity. These were not the same people we knew from church.

One year at the fair, we got to climb inside a food cart where Dad's Native American friends, Tim and Nadine, were making fry bread. They showed us the fryer and the huge bins of dough. They served them up to us piping hot, bigger than our heads, and buried in cinnamon sugar. We ate our fill, and all for free. One day, I went with Dad to their house, and Nadine showed me all of her Native American art, beads and garments. I was enchanted.

Sister

I have four siblings: three sisters and a brother, though most of my childhood memories included my little sister Kara, rather than my older siblings Krista, David, or Shana.

My first living memory is the day my little sister Kara was born. We were brought into the hospital room and someone lifted me up onto the bed where my mom was holding her. I was given a pink Velcro bow for her hair. I patted it onto her fuzzy head. That whole memory is tinged pink.

I remember the day our cat, Shadow, died. I was 14. My friend Doug had committed suicide the week earlier. The cat had been hit by a car. A neighbor came knocking on the front door, carrying a big plastic bag. Kara answered the door.

She called for me, a twinge of concern in her voice. I came outside and identified the cat. It was him, all right: black fluff in a yellow bag. Kara began to cry. We were home alone, so I decided to put him in a box until Dad could get home and dig a hole in the backyard. I found a big shoebox and I tried my best to be serious rather than sad — I wanted to be the strong one for Kara.

Then I got a firsthand lesson in rigor mortis. Shadow's body was as stiff as a tree branch, and huff and puff as I might, I simply couldn't bend him to fit in the box! I began to laugh hysterically. Kara looked at me in horror.

"Becca! How can you be LAUGHING at a time like this?!" she cried as she stormed inside, weeping.

I was numbed out from the recent loss of a friend, and the whole scene tickled me. I collapsed onto the front steps and took in the scene: my stiff dead cat, haphazardly hanging out of a bag and a box on our front porch. I couldn't contain my laughter. I must have looked mad. Finally, I gave up and plopped the box onto the back deck, opting to let Dad take the lead on the grave digging and cat burying business.

I remember sharing a room with Kara. We decided to push our beds together and make one giant bed. We soon discovered the gap between our mattresses made a prime trench for stashing snacks. We hoarded gallon boxes of Goldfish crackers, sleeves of Ritz, trays of Mother's brand sandwich cookies. Now I recognize where my late night snacking habit began.

Grandma

My grandmother passed a month before this book's completion. I remember countless afternoons at my grandma's house, the same house where my mother had grown up. My grandma, Arline, ran a daycare out of her home, so gaggles of us kids would spend our afternoons playing Barbies, watching cartoons on cable TV, and liberally eating Pop Tarts, Hot Pockets, and her flat homemade cookies.

I remember riding bikes with the neighbor kids to Sherlock's grocery, using pocket change to buy candy, chips, and inexplicably, pomegranates, which might as well have been from another planet.

My grandma was sweet to us… most of the time. She was plump and squishy and I loved sitting on her lap in her graying corduroy recliner. She gave us comfortingly long, indulgent hugs.

She had this upstairs room that was like a time capsule to the 70s, with framed photos of her as a teen and a mint green tufted bedspread. The adjacent room had boxes of artifacts from her life, and on the stairs hung a faded glamour shot of her on her wedding day, long red curls cascading around her shoulders.

I remember when she made me taste her cheap beer, even though I initially refused. She was not strict like my mother, so my cousin Brittany and I would often convince her to let us play with the neighbors down the street, watch MTV for hours, or cook up a small storm in the kitchen.

She slapped me once, right across the face while we stood on the front lawn. I'd been given a sparkly new baton for my birthday. It was pink and purple, with glittery tassels swinging from the sides. I refused to share it with the neighbor kids who had come over to play, insisting that it was special and brand new. Not at all for sharing; so much of my childhood had been shared with my many siblings.

My grandmother insisted that I give the others a turn. Still, I refused. She walked over and tried to yank it from my hands, but I gripped it harder, staring up at her defiantly. This inflamed her.

"Don't be a brat!" she exclaimed, and struck me across the face.

I stared at her in shock, humiliated and stung, as tears welled up in my eyes. Then I ran inside the house, rage-crying, and refused to come out of the spare room until my mom arrived.

I don't remember my mother handling it, or ever speaking of the incident again.

My grandma's serious, intimidatingly quiet husband was rarely around, and we're better off for it. I don't consider him a grandfather in any sense of the word. He abused numerous women in my family, and it's a shameful marvel to me that he was enabled for so long.

Life

One of the greatest gifts in my young life is the amount of time and space my friends and I were left to our own devices — to make art and music and explore the reaches of our epic, comical imaginations. We played in fields and creeks, attics and camping trailers, creating magical lands out of empty spaces. During grade school, my best friends and I created countless dance routines to Christian pop songs and performed them for our families. I felt graceful doing cartwheels and round-offs across the living room carpet, like for a brief moment I was channeling a courageous gymnast version of myself.

I remember my first secret boyfriend, Cory, also a fifth grader, and the blue lock and key journal where I wrote about him. He was the only African American kid in my class at school. He brought me a red fluffy teddy bear on Valentine's Day and gave it to me outside music class with a poem he had written for me. I was so thrilled and embarrassed, I shoved it in my backpack and didn't look at him all day. That red bear was on display in my bedroom until I left for college.

I remember playing computer games with my friends on Sunday afternoons. We played Put Put Travels Through Time, Cats, Smart Games. I spent hours making art on Microsoft Paint. My mom played Mist and Riven, mystery games set in a faraway land, and sometimes she'd let us sit by and watch.

I remember wetting the bed long after all my friends had grown out of it — years after. I had to wear absorbent underwear to sleepovers and was terrified my friends would find out. I'm sure they all knew. I had all kinds of medical tests done as a teenager to rule out underlying medical conditions. Even after all the blood tests and ultrasounds, there was no clear reason why it was happening. I was perfectly normal, it appeared. This was one lasting, deeply embarrassing source of shame for most of my young life.

I remember the first time I learned about sex. I was around eight years old. My neighbor friend Megan told me in hushed tones that she knew what sex was — her big brother had told her.

"It's when grown-ups go into dark places and lick each other's body parts!" she said naively. I was confused.

"Want to try it?" she asked.

"Okay!" I said, giggling. We closed ourselves in my closet, fully clothed, and took turns licking each other… on the elbow, on the ear, on the belly. It was completely innocent. We emerged, stared at each other with blank faces, and shrugged.

Grown ups, we concluded, were crazy.

I remember literally hundreds of sleepovers and playdates over the years. Almost every weekend, I was invited to a friend's house to play. Our tight knit church community had many families who all trusted each other and in many ways, the parents were helping raise one another's kids.

Gibson and Katie's moms helped homeschool me. Elizabeth's mom gave me rides to school. My mom splinted Rachel's arm when she broke it on the church playground. Mallory, Tori, and Chelsea's families hosted so many sleepovers I can't count them. Chelsea's dad took us camping. Gibson's dad taught me guitar. Paige's mom taught me how to thrift shop. Mallory's family brought me to Jamaica.

We were a gaggle of good kids with a zest for life and a reckoning of creative and musical energy.

Self

I remember videos of myself, age three or four, twirling and tumbling around the carpeted living room in a pink ruffled dress, completely entranced by motion and oblivious to my parents and older siblings watching a movie in the background. I loved moving. I loved fluidity. My relationship to my body in general, and dance specifically, has been a whole story of its own.

I remember my first theatrical debut as a fuzzy sheep in the church play. I was four and my costume was a full onesie with a hood and ears. My role was to sit in the manger by Mary and Joseph. I sang my first solo during a Christmas play years later. Silent Night. It felt powerful to sing into a microphone and hear my voice so loudly, so clearly.

I'll never forget my first day of public school in fourth grade. I was overwhelmed at the huge place, with all the different hallways and "pods" where different classes met. I was worried about getting lost. I made it through the first day, but after school I missed the bus to my grandma's house.

The buses all looked the same — how was I to know which one to get on? I saw mine rolling away as my neighbor friend banged on the window. Crying, I walked home from school, which was only four blocks away. The next day I cried again, this time to my teacher when I realized I had forgotten my first homework assignment at home. My mom said I wasn't ready just yet and decided to keep me home for one more year.

I recall carving out a lot of time to spend by myself. I was a little helper as a child. I wanted to be given a job, a project, a task. I loved pulling weeds in the garden and more than once I was mortified to discover I had pulled out my mother's flower bulbs thinking they were grass. I buried the evidence.

I also spent time folding our family's laundry. I got to spend time alone, a rare occurrence in our full house, and I felt I was learning about my family as I folded their clothes. It was a very intimate act. It felt loving. I remember my dad's 80s tank tops. One had Daffy Duck on it with a surfboard. Another was lavender colored and screen printed with a rainbow. It read, "Love is colorblind." I always wondered what that meant.

I remember the first time I stole something. It was an individually wrapped caramel from the Brach's candy bins at the back of the grocery store. It was so easy. I just slipped it into my pocket. Kara ran up to me, a concerned look on her face, and asked if I had just taken something. I lied to her face.

"No," I said, and walked away.

God

I had this cartoon-illustrated Bible that totally perplexed me.

"Did all these stories happen in Heaven?" I remember asking my mom. "It doesn't seem like they happened in our world."

My mom placated me with a hollow answer about Bible times. Even then, I had a sense for rationality and was puzzling over the impossibilities of what adults were telling me was true and real.

On Sunday mornings in children's church, we sat on rainbow colored wooden pews. The pastor's wife explained to us about heaven and hell, and how all humans were born sinful and needing to be saved by Jesus, lest we spend eternity separated from God. This terrified me, like being left alone in a dark room forever with no mom or dad or anyone I loved.

She had us bow our heads and asked who wanted to be saved by Jesus. I raised my hand every single Sunday for a month. Finally, she pulled me aside and assured me that the eternal fate of my soul had been secured. It truly mortifies me that we teach children things like this. Why is this okay?

I was very serious as a child. I felt the weight of the world, and I wondered why no one else was distressed by the starving, chocolate-skinned children on infomercial fundraisers or an injured bird fallen from its nest. I spent many nights lying awake, praying for all who were suffering, wondering if there was some way to sway the hand of God — who was all-powerful and all-knowing — to change the rules of the game and make a world where everyone had what they needed and could feel safe and be together with those they loved.

I didn't understand why God would rig the game so that a large portion of the world would never even have the option of accepting salvation from the Christian Jesus. It seemed cruel and cold, and the explanation that he "worked in mysterious ways" did little to comfort me.

This discomfort sparked my desire to become a missionary to the far reaches of the world. It felt like the most important thing I could do with my life — make sure that as many people escaped hell as possible. The cognitive dissonance between this deep fear of hell and the way Christian adults around me were living was noteworthy to me. It caused a deep fracture where doubt was able to set in. Was any of this actually as true as they said? But it was the foundation upon which my whole life and world was built, so it had to be true. Who would I be without it?

To me, this is a huge abuse of power, to teach a worldview that forces children to spend energy reckoning with existential dread rather than being kids and discovering the wonder and beauty of the world around them. I do feel that something was robbed from my youth due to the messages of Christianity.

For better or worse, I internalized my faith and had a strong sense throughout my young life that I was never alone. I felt I was in an active conversation with God, like he was a friend who hung out on my shoulder. He was different than the one I read about in the Bible though, or heard about in church — he was more of a Jesus friend going on nature walks with me than an old man on a throne in a temple. Because of this, I never felt alone, and I even craved my solitude.

Foundation

What I remember most when I consider my young life is the way I felt trying to navigate the world I found myself in. The structures were clearly defined within the two primary contexts of Christianity and our strict home life. I created for myself a world within that world, where through hiding my flaws and my shame, suppressing my deep impulses to forge my own path, and charming those in power and following their rules, I felt safe.

By doing this I could stay close to my parents, teachers and leaders while ensuring I would always have what I needed, whether that was attention, favor, support, protection or resources.

I grew up fast. Even as early as grade school, I remember looking at adults around me as though I was their peer, while watching my actual peers spin out with tantrums or meltdowns or helplessness. I would raise my eyebrows and shrug up at them.

Ooph. Kids, right? I seemed to say.

And they would smile in response or pat me on the head, and give me special projects, privileges and responsibilities. It was a foolproof formula that worked. In fact, it still works. The skill remained inside of me and it appears at times unexpectedly.

3

Fracture

Memories

My best friend Paige lived in the next town over. She was effortlessly cool — she read Vogue magazine and had a room decorated with thrifted goods and Urban Outfitters textiles. She was ahead of every trend. There were kids at my school who thought I was a style icon, photographing me for the yearbook and asking me where I shopped, but everything I knew about fashion I had learned from Paige. We spent long sleepover weekends at her house drawing in the tree house, playing cards, making weird teenager food, riding bikes and listening to music.

I was a grade ahead in school. I completed first and second grade in one year, so when I entered public school I was a year younger than my peers. This meant that when my classmates were turning 13 and becoming teenagers, I was turning 12. When they were getting licensed to drive, I was getting my learner's permit.

I was very embarrassed that I was younger, particularly because I didn't feel younger — if anything, I felt older than most of my classmates. I was still in advanced classes, found myself in leadership roles, and by middle school I was at relative social ease where others were struggling to settle in.

Middle school was a blur of crushes on bad boys, awkward body changes, and a lot of time spent at youth group. There were secrets kept from Mom — things I'd learned from my sisters like keeping makeup at school and sneaking the landline phone to our rooms to call boys late at night. I don't recall much else besides getting my period and learning to play guitar. Things became more vivid in high school.

In eighth grade, I started playing guitar and singing on stage for youth group. It felt totally natural to me, and I learned that I was good at leading a band.

Several of my best friends were also musically inclined — it ran in their families, unlike mine where I was more of an anomaly — so we started playing together more often, at church and on our own time, just for fun. Chelsea was a singer and played bass. Tori was also a singer and played drums. We wore trucker hats and pretended we were a chick band, going to make it big.

When I was 14, I smoked weed for the first time. One Friday night, my older sister Shana snuck a friend and I into the basement bathroom where she had fashioned a pipe out of an apple. She shoved a towel into the crease under the door. Then she showed us the weed and how to smoke it, instructing us to blow the smoke out the bathroom window.

I don't recall the rest of the night, but I must have enjoyed it, because in the coming years, I took every chance I had to smoke weed.

I remember the day I started my period. I was at school. I noticed droplets of blood in the toilet in the PE locker room. I made it through the day by improvising with a wad of toilet paper. I didn't know what to say or who to talk to about it.

When my mom picked us up from Grandma's house that evening, I leaned up to her in the driver seat and said, "Hey Mom, guess what I got today?"

"A black eye?" she retorted.

"No... I got my period!" I said.

She turned around to look at me.

"Oh yeah? Okay. We'll talk when we get home," she replied.

At home, in the dark hallway, she handed me a pack of pads and a handful of tampons.

"This isn't that big of a deal to you, right?" she asked plainly. And that was all I needed to hear. I shut down.

"Nope. Thanks." I took the supplies. It *was* a big deal to me. But I didn't feel it was allowed to be. I pored over the packages, hoping to learn the things that a mentor was supposed to teach me.

Young Love

I remember my first kiss. I did not consent to it. A boy named Trevor, a bass player on the youth group band, had been pursuing me heavily for weeks. He was always around and seemed to constantly have eyes on me at youth events and band practices. I could feel it. He cornered me after practice one night while I waited outside for my mom to pick me up and more or less forced his tongue down my throat. That was the first and last time — I kept my distance after that.

I met my first love at the end of eighth grade. It's such a precious, happy time in my memory. Our youth group went on a group trip to Tacoma, Washington for a water park concert called Big Splash. On the bus ride up, Paige introduced me to Jordan, who she knew from school. He was my dream boy: he was tall and strong with golden skin and swoopy skater hair. He played guitar and liked all the same music I did. The two-hour drive into Washington passed in a blink.

By the time we emerged from the bus, we had drawn silly sketches all over each other's arms and linked up as a pair. I wasn't allowed to date until I turned thirteen, but after meeting Jordan, my mom thawed out to the idea. That, or she realized I was determined to see him whether I had permission or not. My dad had no opinion on the matter, or if he did, it was not considered. This was sweepingly true in my mom's parenting decisions. They did not relate to each other as equals, and she modeled for me how to walk all over a man by acting smarter, dismissive, and ice cold.

Jordan and I had a sweet love for a year and a half; a large feat for young teens. He was affectionate, lighthearted, and thoughtful. We both played rugby sophomore year and watched each other's games. His family was warm and welcoming and seemed to love having me around.

We were in young love. We spent a lot of time in his basement pretending to watch movies but actually making out. Jordan wrote me poems and made me a wooden jewelry box and filled it with red Skittles.

I felt a natural pull toward him, an impulse to be more physically intimate. We gradually dipped our toes into the world of sexuality in a way that felt organic and welcomed. But I also felt very conflicted because I'd been taught, adamantly, that God had designed sex for marriage, and sex outside of it was a sin. This was the beginning of hiding and disassociating from my sexuality. I actually broke up with Jordan a year into our relationship at summer camp, after a preacher delivered a very compelling sermon about living in sin and God's call for us to be pure.

FRACTURE

A while later, I allowed my real desires to steer again and we got back together. His gregarious mother warned him to not let me kick him in the balls twice. Eventually, a year after that, I grew bored of the relationship and ended it. It was messy and emotional. It was my first glimpse into the way I respond when under pressure or facing complex relationship dynamics. I grew silent, hid away, and became distant and unavailable.

The many lovers who followed can tell you they've witnessed the same thing.

Rebellion

Age 14 and 15 bore an important deviation for me: I began sneaking around with higher stakes. Up until that point, the sneakiest I'd been was calling boys late at night from our landline phone and wearing the forbidden eyeliner that I stashed in my locker.

But as I grew, I felt a powerful urge to rebel.

I felt curious about all the things my mom was forbidding us access to. Music, movies and socializing were all censored. One day, as my mom was driving me to school, I proclaimed the following to her.

"Mom, I'm like a slippery bar of soap. If you keep squeezing me so tight, I'm going to shoot out of your hands to the scum at the bottom of the shower! Is that what you want??" Then I stormed out of the car and through the school doors. I don't know exactly when I decided it was acceptable to talk to my mother this way, but it felt effective. She backed off.

Something about teenhood had lent me a deeper realization that adults are people, and I had a keen sense that my mom had no better clue on how to raise me than I did. I felt like she saw a projection of her own vulnerable teenage self when she looked at me, and she was parenting me with the structure and tenacity she believed could have protected her from harm as a teen.

But I was a whip-smart, caged creature. Overconfident and hormone-riddled, I felt like an equal to her and had tossed aside all politeness and respect, opting instead for the dismissiveness and belittling I'd seen her use on my father for so many years.

My friends and I loved going to concerts. It was a way of participating in the "regular world" of teens, while still being super Christian. First, we saw Jesus-loving rock bands: Switchfoot, Kutless, and FM Static. (Who is choosing these names, anyway?) Then I began convincing my mom, one by one, to let me go to "secular" concerts. I damaged my rib while crowd surfing at a

Blindside concert at the Roseland Theatre and blamed it on rugby practice.

I knew how to persuade my mom into letting me go. We were playing a game, she and I.

I don't believe she honestly cared whether I went out or not, but she needed to save face, especially to the other kids who didn't always have the level of privilege I did. She seemed to accept that I was capable and mature beyond my years in many ways. So much so that, when I needed school clothes, she would hand me her credit card and say: "Just show some restraint, please." Which I did.

So, I knew what to do. I'd learned that charm and persistence were the simplest ways to manipulate. I would be the image of responsibility — making sure I was caught up on my chores and homework, and choose an opportune moment when she was relaxed and in a good mood to approach her. I'd make a case for why she should let me go out.

To some, this is pure manipulation, but I often struggled to see the line between manipulation and smart strategy. I'd show her the band or event in question and fabricate a whole story about the wholesome friends with whom I was going, who was driving, and what time we would return. She almost always gave in and allowed me to go. My siblings reference this as proof that I was the favored child.

Sometimes my dad drove my friends and me, letting us choose the music and giving us money for food. He would sleep in the parked car the entire evening until we emerged from the show. These simple acts were his way of showing love and support. I resented him for letting me down as a father in so many ways (in part because this was the story that my mom openly perpetuated every chance she got), but I couldn't help but appreciate his simple generosity and willingness to serve without expectation.

Girl Crush

I had my first conscious crush on a girl sophomore year. Her name was Brittany. She and I were guests on the Martin family's vacation to Jamaica, each of us invited by one of the sisters.

They were a close family from the church with an epic property in the country where many fun teenage memories took place. The four of us girls lollygagged around the Kingston Sandals resort unsupervised for a week, content to beach lounge and talk to cute boys and try, with limited success, to sneak alcohol and weed. (By this time, I hadn't begun to drink but I was quite interested in cannabis.)

I thought Brittany was *so cool*. She was a grade above me and had a lanky, androgynous frame, long straight hair and almond eyes. She talked me into joining the local club rugby team that was launching, promising to drive me to our practice in Scappoose three times a week.

How could I resist? I joined the team.

After school she'd scoop me up in her car and we'd stop at her house for snacks on the way. She called me Bex. Sometimes, she'd sit at her piano and show me a song she was working on. She was a brilliant musician with a preference for heavy metal.

Our team started calling us "Wheels 1" and "Wheels 2" for our speed and clever field antics. The fact that she thought I was cool and had a nickname for me and hung out with me after school enchanted me.

Nothing but friendship ever came of it, but it was a momentous relationship for me. I learned that I was attracted to women. I also learned that friendship and romance are not two separate things.

Drunk at the Roseland

I first drank alcohol at a concert. A parent dropped Elizabeth and I off at the battle of the bands at the Roseland Theatre. It was an all-day event, and we planned to hitch a ride home with friends. I donned baggy camo pants and a tank top. We promptly found some school friends in the crowd, who suggested we leave and find some weed. I was on board. We knew Sam could help us. He was the first cannabis advocate I knew; also my only known atheist friend, and he would later go on to help write the bill that legalized recreational cannabis in Oregon. Fifteen years later, he and I would work together on a political campaign to legalize the therapeutic use of psilocybin mushrooms in Oregon.

Our stoner plans changed to booze when weed became hard to find. The five of us walked down to the corner store and approached a homeless woman sitting outside, reading a small book. We paid her to buy us a bottle of vodka and some Dasani water bottles. Sam had clearly done this before. Inside the public park restrooms, we transferred the vodka to the water bottles and took off down the street, drinking it. I had no idea how much I was drinking, or how greatly it would affect me.

I was drunk by the time we returned to the theatre. I marveled at my ability to act normally as we went through security, even though I felt like my bones had dissolved. I felt great. I was grinning. For a while, we had fun. I felt sloshy and queasy, but I liked being surrounded by familiar faces from school who I didn't normally get to spend time with on the weekends. I sat on Sebastian's lap, a dreadlocked hippie dude who I shared an art class with. Cory, my only Black friend, the same one who had been my boyfriend in fifth grade, sat across from us. We laughed and joked as I begged him to let me wear Sebastian's patched vest. He refused. It was this age that I discovered my ability to work a crowd and raise the levity in a group of friends.

Then, my stomach started to churn.

I had barely stood up to excuse myself when I vomited all over the checkerboard flooring of the dining area, in front of a room full of friends and event staff.

"OOOHHHH." Everyone exclaimed, springing up to assist me.

I had overshot the liquor by… a bit.

Elizabeth walked me to the restroom as I apologized profusely to everyone. In the bathroom I locked myself in the stall and collapsed onto the toilet, immobilized. It must have been half an hour of Elizabeth and a female security guard speaking to me distantly, insistently, urging me to unlock the stall. Finally, I came to, and let them in.

I was escorted outside. My shirt was covered in vomit, so I sat on the sidewalk alone in just my bra and camo pants. The security guard told me I could come back in later, after I sobered up. I sat outside for what felt like a long while, watching bands load and unload their gear on the side of the building. Several men attempted to engage with me, and I gave off my hardest "don't fuck with me" vibe. Nobody gave me any trouble. This superpower has kept me safe during many vulnerable moments in my life. I carry an energetic armor akin to an armadillo, and it's readily accessible when I need it. The struggle is that I often feel I need this armor when I actually don't.

A friend from school, a quiet hardcore punk of Native American descent named Alex, came outside and offered me his sweatshirt. He brought me back inside with him. I was deeply affected by this kind gesture. It struck me that he had noticed and helped me in my moment of need, whereas Elizabeth was nowhere to be found.

Before long, my boyfriend Jordan arrived at the concert. He found me and laughed at my inebriation while we watched our friends on stage and swayed to the music. Later, on my way out, I apologized profusely to the event staff and thanked them for helping me. I was fortunate not to receive a MIP (minor in possession) citation.

The next day, I wrote Elizabeth a long email, apologizing for my behavior. I let her know that I had found my limits by crossing them, and promised not to put either of us in such a compromising position again. She received my apology and we moved on. That Monday, my friends at school all teased me about my initiation into drinking. I tolerated it with groans and laughs. Cory congenially remarked that I wasn't "as pure as he thought."

When I came home from school, my mother caught me by the front door and announced that I was grounded for a month. She had gone through my email and read my self-incriminating apology to Elizabeth. I was demoralized at her invasion of privacy and turned the blame on her. Isn't this called dirty evidence, anyway? (Perhaps I should have studied law.)

I reasoned that, clearly, I felt sorry and I was already changing my behavior. She reduced my punishment to two weeks. This grounding meant I had to attend adult church with her on Sundays rather than going to youth group with my friends. That was it. My older siblings were up in arms when they learned about this; they still tell stories about how much I got away with compared to the punishments they'd received.

My oldest sister Krista had been grounded for a month just for riding in a car with a boy. Birth order certainly shapes people, and she was the responsible oldest, while I was an opportunistic fourth child. I valued flying under the radar, self-regulating, and overall maintaining my independence for both self-responsibility and freedom. In the controlling environment around me, this made me feel like a human being with power of choice.

Privacy as Privilege

The worst part about the distrust in my home was the gross invasion of privacy. I had nowhere that was truly mine. No journal, no inbox, no room or desk or corner of the yard was safe from prying eyes. I felt that my autonomy and the safety of my inner world were illusions, constantly under threat. I'm a Scorpio, by the way. Privacy is extremely important to me.

My sisters and I had a habit of raiding each other's rooms, reading one another's journals and swiping clothes and make-up that we wanted for ourselves. My mother had a policy that once we had broken a house rule, we were now, in her words, "subject to random search and seizure" at any time she chose. This felt incredibly violating (not to mention the negative effects of using criminological terms on teenagers in a home setting).

My older brother David had already been in trouble with the law more than once, so perhaps that was where my mom had gleaned her vernacular. I remember him outside our house, scrubbing colorful graffiti off the newly poured cement sidewalk. His art was quite beautiful, but the cops didn't agree. Another time, I recall following the sounds of her shouting downstairs.

"Rocky, get down here," she called to my dad.

I ran down behind him, curious, and peered through the crack in the door. She held up a gallon Ziploc bag half full of dried mushrooms.

"Your son is selling drugs," she announced in disdain, not noticing my presence.

That was the first time I saw psilocybin. I was confused, as it looked like food to me, not drugs. Those mushrooms became so important in my life that I now have their image tattooed on my leg.

I have another vivid memory of hearing shouting downstairs, my brother in an altercation with my parents. I don't know what the argument was about. I snuck to the top of the stairs, peeking over the railing as my dad blocked the front door. He insisted David wasn't going anywhere.

My brother knew how to fight and began making threats. David had a flaming hot temper and it was common for him to kick a hole in the wall or knock a chair over and storm out of the room, or get locked in a shouting match, spitting words like daggers at whoever was in his way. This time, he and my father tussled out into the front yard until my mom finally called him off.

"Let him go," she called out to my dad. I heard a car start and saw headlights from my window as he sped away down the street.

Serve & Protect

My associations with the police were never positive. As a child, I watched my parents and brother struggle to navigate the juvenile detention system, which then became the prison system. David was repeatedly suspended from school, entangled in fights, and caught vandalizing public property. He'd had a fiery, powerful rage in him for as long as I can remember. One of the more memorable incidents was the day he and some buddies knocked over a school vending machine. *Why?* I wondered.

He and I both share a deep problem with authority (we sometimes joke about our similar Scorpio natures), but the way it showed up for each of us was like night and day. I worked the system by getting inside of it; he slammed up against it in a fury. He was whip-smart, articulate, creative, and angry. He raged against my parents, coaches (he was a gifted soccer and basketball player), teachers, pastors, bosses, and of course, the cops. He was reckless.

I remember stories of him leaping out of friends' cars and running from cops. Jumping fences. Hiding at my grandma's house until they gave up the search and my mom could safely retrieve him and bring him home.

I must have been in middle school when the cops came looking for him (on what suspicions, I can't recall). He was out of high school and living in another town, but had come to stay with us. It was after dinner when we heard a knock on the front door, and a surge of alert came over the whole house.

"Keep the curtains closed," my mom said in hushed tones as she rushed down the hallway with my brother. She shut him in a bedroom closet behind bags of clothes. My dad answered the door.

"Sorry, we haven't seen him," my dad told the police after they inquired about my brother.

"He doesn't live here," my mom added. I watched silently, peeking my eyes over the stair railing as they stared up, glancing around, then looked long and hard at my parents. Finally, the police gave up and left.

Low

I often think about a story I heard many times growing up, from before I was born. When my brother was two, my father came to my mother, dejected.

"I don't know anything about raising kids, Mary. I'm going to mess this up," he said. "From now on, you raise the kids and I'll earn the money. You can count on that."

He was attempting to do damage control. My mother felt abandoned and resented him bitterly. And yet, in spite of this, she proceeded to have three more children with him over the next ten years.

I sometimes wonder about the energetic shift that took place in our home, and in the family dynamic, when my dad made that announcement. David was a very sick child. He had severe asthma and was hospitalized numerous times. The doctor instructed my mom to bring him to the coast, where the ionized salty air was healing for little lungs. The beach became my mom's favorite place, and still is to this day.

My mom was very depressed. She had several suicidal episodes over the years. As I got older, I remember her depression worsening. Or perhaps my awareness simply increased. At best, she was functional with a propensity to chronically complain, criticize, and victimize herself. At worst, she was catatonic.

In a recent conversation, my mother said,

"My brain isn't very nice to me."

She expressed feeling tormented and resigned to life simply being hard for her from then on. During her episodes over the years, she would lie on her bed and stare out the window for hours at a time. She was checked out.

Mental illness never affects just the person suffering. Our home life was colored by my mom's struggle to cope. This manifested as emotional manipulation, guilt tripping, and disassociation. Family meals of my childhood turned into frequent "whatever nights" during adolescence, where everyone was left to fend for themselves. Affectionate hugs on her lap were tainted with her bleak outlook:

"When you're older, you won't love me like you do now," she would say, and feeling guilty, I would desperately try to reassure her otherwise. Like many of my peers, I entered into a complicated relationship with my mom as I grew older: I sometimes felt that I was the one mothering her and tending to her emotional needs.

She had a bad habit of speaking harshly about her body and her appearance to us kids, criticizing her weight, her face, her wardrobe. Shame hung around her like a heavy cloak. She was not comfortable in her body. She seemed disconnected from it. She felt unacceptable in the mornings before her hour-long beauty routine. I remember her in her fuzzy pink robe, apologizing for her breath and her hair and seeming distracted until she had primped herself into her idea of a presentable form.

As a child I loved brushing my mom's hair. It was the one thing my mom usually liked about herself, and she loved visiting her hairdresser. I often went to the salon with her, which had a massive technicolor ball pit. During her haircuts, Kara and I would play and screech inside the windowed room teeming with rainbow plastic balls. Sometimes at home, Mom let me brush her hair while we watched *Wheel of Fortune* or *Survivor*.

I remember noticing how crunchy and brittle it was — it had been dyed, and it took a daily beating with a blow dryer and curling iron. I sat patiently, brushing and brushing as the show rolled into commercials and back to the scheduled programming. I was willing it to soften and get healthier, if only I could brush it for long enough. I clearly knew nothing about hair. And I knew very little about damage. I didn't know that regardless of how much love and attention I gave to her hair, I couldn't repair the trauma it repeatedly underwent. I didn't know that it wasn't my responsibility to fix her.

FRACTURE

Cancer

Much of my mom's cancer experience is blocked from my memory. It happened when I was in middle school, and a combination of my own distance from her, emotional blockage, and her insistent independence, made the whole experience pass by under my conscious awareness.

The distinct memory I hold, is the image of her rushing into my bedroom to wake me up, holding a towel to her chest.

"Becca, get up," she said. "Get Kara ready for the day. I'm going to the hospital. Krista's on her way to come get you guys."

As she spoke, I watched a spot of bright red blood color the blue towel, and grow like paint water spilled onto a cloth. She looked ghostly. I sprung up, confused and asked what to do, but she was already out the door and up the stairs.

She'd had a series of perplexing breast health issues: cysts and growths requiring multiple surgeries, and the hemorrhage I witnessed that morning was a result of one of those surgeries. Eventually, the doctors found a cancerous lump. When I recently asked my mom about this experience, she expressed the feeling that there had been a margin of support for a short while, but that soon our family had expected her to "get back to normal" and she felt she was navigating the cancer alone.

I still carry guilt and must reckon with who holds responsibility for her feelings of isolation and victimization during that time. Whether she pushed support away, or we were self-involved and left her to fend for herself is not a binary question with a clear answer.

With multiple treatments, she recovered and has been living cancer free for over fifteen years.

High School

I enjoyed high school. I enjoy people; I always have. As a senior, I was voted "Friendliest" student by my class of 300. I had a knack for seeking out those who needed a friend and sharing my time with them. For the most part, I felt comfortable in my skin and secure. When others felt at ease, so did I. I sought to share that ease. I craved it, coming from the tense home life where very little felt easeful or light.

When I noticed a peer sitting alone or looking isolated, I felt a draw toward them. Sometimes curiosity motivated me. *Why were people avoiding this long-haired, eccentric, Goth kid wielding a yo-yo? Who was the silent girl drawing anime characters in the back of my art class? What motivated the kid offering to sell me OxyContin pills between classes, and what made him tick?* I felt unafraid of the dark in people. I felt like I had space for it, that it couldn't bring me down. Perhaps part of this was my Christian faith — I had internalized a deep and unconditional love for people. I also sincerely enjoyed them and craved a glimpse into the worlds of others.

The dichotomy of my double life in high school wore on me and was the start of an inner struggle of disassociating and compartmentalizing that I'm still exploring. I ran in two distinct circles, primarily — my church friends and my school friends.

My tight knit group of church friends were Chelsea, Tori, Mallory, Elizabeth, Rachel, Gibson and my boyfriend Jordan. We spent so much time together: in honors classes, in the halls between classes, at church multiple times a week, playing music and having sleepovers on the weekends. This was my community. I loved being surrounded by a swarm of friends who I loved and trusted. There was always a place to belong.

Our shared faith was foundational for me. I was not a half-assed Christian, though I was conflicted. I read the Bible in my free time. I prayed for my friends and family. I wrote songs to God. I believed that my biggest mission in life was to spread the gospel about Jesus to as many people as possible. I remember reading a fascinating and disturbing book my mother gifted me called *Jesus Freaks* — it was a long, horrific book detailing the abuses endured by martyred Christians around the world, and a call for young people to live so radically that we would die for our faith.

This was also happening in the wake of the Columbine shooting, when the book *She Said Yes* implored American youth to live with such devotion that they would literally die for the cause of Christianity. Still, I felt best when leading with radical love rather than trying to convince someone of a set of beliefs which, even then, seemed far-fetched to my rational mind.

Then there were my school friends.

I had my first couple of gay friends during high school. I also ran with a crew of mohawked, studded punks who hung out on the side of the building at lunch and had access to booze, mushrooms and pills. We liked going to parks after school and getting stoned. We would walk around town, eat junk food, play guitar and generally shoot the breeze. It was all fairly harmless.

I never once bought weed — I was always around people who had plenty to share. Several boys I dated had family members with Medical Marijuana cards. I started skipping class to watch movies or drive around with boys.

And yet, I continued to ace tests and keep up on my schoolwork. I didn't speak of my involvement with these kids to my church friends; I kept things separate. It was effortless to lie to my mom about the who, what and where of my days. All the moving pieces were steady. I felt I was managing it all.

I remember one afternoon, skipping school with a boy from the skate park. We smoked a joint and watched Cheech and Chong while fooling around all afternoon. Before I knew it, it was almost dinnertime and my mom would be returning home from work. As we were rushing along the train tracks on foot toward my neighborhood, I noticed my mom's Camry idling at the stoplight. We dove down and hid in the grass beside the road. I felt like a damn outlaw.

What was I doing? I ran home and made it inside a few minutes after her. I was clearly stoned. She wanted answers. She found a pipe in my backpack and I adamantly denied ownership. Finally, she rolled her eyes and dropped the issue. I shrugged in relief and headed toward the snack cupboard. There we were, attempting to co-exist.

Later that year, I was called a "closet slut" by a classmate who heard about my exploits with these skater punks from art class. I distinctly remember having a momentary upset, then thinking to myself, *Actually, yeah — that sounds about right.*

Even then, the notion of being shamed for enjoying sex seemed misplaced. I was just relieved to still be a closeted slut; I had a reputation to uphold.

I continued to develop a heavy, inescapable relationship with shame. I could feel that it wasn't coming from within myself. I didn't truthfully feel guilt for the choices I was making — I wasn't hurting anyone — but I could sense the judgment coming from the outside, and for that I felt a great deal of shame. Much of my self-punishment had come not from sensing that I had done harm or disappointed God, but the question of, *What will people think?*

What was happening within me was a deep fracture, a disintegration where I began to compartmentalize parts of myself into distinct containers that I could bring out only within their acceptable contexts. I felt that both parts of me were deeply, fundamentally me. But the dove-like love, levity and Christian faith was acceptable to one world, while my serpentine wiles and attraction to secrecy, disruption and rebellion had no place within the righteous community whose acceptance I craved. So I rejected these shadowy parts of myself and kept them hidden away.

Senior year, my final art project in painting class was to create a self-portrait. In the image, I am standing faceless in my school hallway with a large crack down the middle of myself. On one side are bright whites and golds, with hearts, music notes, golden keys, flowers and light beams radiating off of me. On the other side are dark shadows with spiked cast iron gates and spider webs and black wings and bones.

At the time, I didn't have the language for this disintegration.

I felt that I had boiled myself down into opposing forces and had no idea how to hold space for all the nuance of myself at once, or with whom I might be welcome to show up with all my light and shadow authentically. I didn't understand these forces as light and shadow then; I understood them as right and wrong, holiness and sin. I thought that this deep, shadowy part of me was fundamentally wrong and needed to be erased or transformed, and yet it was as integral a part of me as the eyes on my face or the skin on my chest.

So I held it, and hated it.

4
S-E-X

The Good, The Bad, and The Non-Consensual

Throughout high school, I kept on dating one person after another. Let's just name that right now. Eventually I learned the term "serial monogamy," which felt relevant, although I'm not sure I was all that monogamous. I was clearly seeking something — chasing some combination of personal freedom and an intimacy that had been lacking in my early life.

I'd been taught that affection was found mainly within romantic relationships, and I lived for the feeling of being wrapped sleepily in someone's arms. Accepted, wanted, held. It was deeply comforting; it fed a voracious hunger inside of me, albeit only temporarily. It didn't really matter to me who I was lying beside; I liked most people, and I liked variety.

This was Oregon in the early 2000s. Abstinence was the central safe-sex policy taught in our school. Purity was preached in my church. Yet I was running hot, from a young age. Before most of my friends had pointed a mirror between their legs, I'd mastered giving myself multiple orgasms. The company I kept with boys forced me to learn quick — I needed to keep up with their jokes and references, so I relied on UrbanDictionary.com for much of my sex education.

I'd had a fairly steamy and consensual relationship with Jordan in early high school, but I was insistent on not having sex with him. Sometimes he pushed things further, but I held the line, more out of guilt than lack of comfort with him. I didn't necessarily plan to wait to have sex until marriage (though I professed to), but I was very private and never felt the time or setting was right, what with parents upstairs and an open-door policy.

Jordan and I would feel each other up behind trees at the park or beneath blankets while watching movies. I became more selective about setting after the time I gave him a rushed, silent blowjob under a blanket while his best friend sat across the room downloading music from LimeWire. Finally, Jordan asked him to leave the room so he could finish. I left feeling embarrassed at our brazenness, though somewhat accomplished, a thickness in my throat signaling that a rite of passage had been fulfilled.

Eventually, I ended our relationship for the second time. Right after he shaved his hair off as part of an amusing school assembly... maybe I was just in it for his golden curls. Just kidding. Our relationship taught me a lot about love and communication at that young age. I am so grateful for the kind love he offered me early on in my relational life.

Side Note: I believe we need to teach our young people about sex, accurately and without bias, before the Internet does. We need to talk openly and often with them about enthusiastic consent. We need to resource them with accurate ways to stay healthy and prevent the spread of infection, and we need to create safe places for young people to process their experiences without fear of judgment. This would have changed my sexual trajectory and saved me, and so many others, a great deal of trauma and difficulty.

SEX

The first time I had sex was not by choice.

I was fourteen. I met a boy, Justin, whose last name I never learned, at a church trip to San Francisco. My youth group wasn't going, but a neighboring town was bringing kids, so I signed up with them. We piled into 14-passenger vans and took a road trip to an extremely intense rally called Battle Cry.

Battle Cry was an unforgettable conference, which I now find deeply disturbing. The event was run by preacher Ron Luce and his evangelical empire, Teen Mania. I had attended Acquire The Fire rallies every year in Portland, and this event was even more extreme. In front of a city hall, we attended a rally that was uncomfortable, to say the least.

We stood, praying and singing in the park while hundreds of protesters stood in the streets. These were people who lived in San Francisco and were against Battle Cry's presence in the city and the messages they were spreading. It was a tense scene. Kids in my group were walking up to the protesters and starting debates, always ending by saying, "Jesus loves you!"

The protesters were preaching tolerance, respect for the queer and non-Christian community, and calling out Ron Luce for being divisive, preaching hate. They stated that he was unwelcome in the city. I witnessed a parade of extravagantly dressed drag queens strutting their stuff in defiance. I felt connected to them. I found them beautiful and bizarre. I wondered if I was on the right side of the tension.

This was the first time I felt distinctly removed from Christianity, although I was very much within it.

Content Warning: Date Rape.

After Battle Cry, I remained in touch with Justin. At 16, he was a couple years older than me. We had chatted on MySpace in the weeks following San Francisco. He lived an hour away, toward the Oregon coast. One weekend, he invited me to his uncle's beach house, and I convinced my mom of a semi-believable story about where I was going and with whom.

Late that night, he arrived to pick me up with a buddy of his and another girl about my age. She and I squeezed into the back of his two-door Honda Civic. The two-hour drive to the coast was cramped and he chain-smoked the whole way. I stared out the window, thrilled at the rebellion, but otherwise having no fun. These people were not my friends, and I felt cold and alone.

When we arrived, we found that the fridge was empty aside from a few beers. The guys pulled some six packs of Mike's Hard Lemonade from the car and we began to drink, then kept on drinking. I was self-medicating to deal with the disappointment in myself for having lied and come here. It wasn't long before I was totally inebriated. I felt tired. I went into one room and changed into my pajamas and collapsed onto the bed, my head swimming. I left the lights on, still intending to brush my teeth.

A few minutes later, I felt hands rubbing my back. It was Justin. He rolled me over and started kissing me. Within a matter of seconds, he had yanked both of our pants down and pushed himself into me. It felt like a strange dream. I was numbed out from the alcohol. I could hardly believe what was happening.

I'll never forget the wood paneled walls that I stared at as I tried to catch my breath and feel out my options. I laid there perfectly still, in shock and afraid to move, feeling totally disconnected from my body, watching the scene play out from afar. He collapsed on top of me. I squirmed out from under him, eyes closed, and rolled over to face the wall.

"Well… I just got used," I slurred in a quiet mumble.

He climbed off of me and left the room without a word. We crossed paths in the kitchen the next morning.

"Not to be a dick," he said dismissively, "But... what happens at the cabin stays at the cabin. I'm in love with someone else."

The drive back felt charged and extremely long. Once home, I couldn't tell my parents about what had happened to me, because I had been breaking rules. I feared I would get in trouble or blamed for what happened. I didn't tell anyone about this incident for years.

Note to self: Consent is ongoing. Consent can be withdrawn at any time. It is not your fault you were violated by a drunken man. It does not matter what idea or expectations he had.

Patterns

My junior year, I dated a Filipino track star named Knight. He was a grade above me and had a jawline you could see across the field. We began playing music together, emo nonsense like Death Cab For Cutie and Dashboard Confessional, and putting it on YouTube.

If my memory serves, the only times Knight and I ever had sex were drunkenly at parties.

He brought me a huge bouquet of flowers on our first date. My mom swooned and said he was earning "major brownie points." Knight came from a big wealthy Catholic family. His mother and extended family had emigrated here from the Philippines. They owned a large, beautiful home on the river, where he was known for hosting parties that kids would talk about all year. It was mostly athletes from the cross-country and wrestling teams. Soon he was inviting me to join, and so I made up excuses for my mom and went ahead.

At his birthday party that fall, I got very drunk. I remember little of the night besides wandering around the house, through noisy and meaningless conversations, and excusing myself to the restroom any time I felt tired of socializing. I remember staring at my swaying reflection in the mirror and thinking, *Wow. You're fucked up.*

It was late. Or, probably, early. Soon, people were collapsing onto futons in spare rooms to sleep for a few hours before sunrise. No one would be driving home.

"Come on, we're going to bed," Knight said when he found me. His friends whistled and hollered at us as he led me up the stairs to his room. I rolled my eyes at them.

The door was barely closed when he started taking my clothes off, and soon

S-E-X

I was in his bed naked. We barely kissed and then we were having sloppy, sleepy drunken sex. I couldn't remember him putting on a condom. I laid beneath him, wanting it to be over.

Finally he rolled off of me and fell asleep.

I laid awake, staring at the wall in a haze, yet again, wondering why I'd felt I had to go along with it, and what might have happened if I had just asked him to stop. The social pressure was powerful. I knew this wasn't how sex should feel, and yet the alcohol I was partaking in seemed to be a trickster spirit, numbing me out and reducing me to a barely conscious body for horny boys to play with. I didn't want this experience, but the behavior loop of violating my personal agency through altered states was hard to break once in motion.

The underlying truth is that on other levels I did want to have sex, but I didn't want it in this way, and I wasn't honest with myself, or clear on my desires. Nor were most of my teenage peers, so conversations about sex and requests for consent went unspoken. The onus of communicating was deferred to the person on the receiving end, often young women, who within abstinence culture were no more equipped to speak up for themselves than pursuers were equipped to ask clearly and accept no as an answer.

Sixteen

On my sixteenth birthday, Knight arrived to my house with arms full of accessories he'd bought me at the mall — earrings, headbands and such — and drove me to a Thai restaurant for dinner. I was smitten, feeling spoiled.

He invited me to a friend's party afterward. We arrived late. The crowd was all men, like a small town frat party, and I could hear them making a ruckus before we reached the apartment. This was the residence of an older friend of Knight's who had graduated a couple years prior. The kitchen was cluttered with liquor bottles and the lights were low.

Soon, I was pulled into a circle taking Jaeger bombs and getting pats on the back. I was keenly aware that I was the only woman present and felt the weight of teetering, heavy-handed men demanding my attention.

I found these parties boring. Even at that age, I would listen to meaningless banter about bullshit topics and just wish people would get some real interests. I didn't feel safe here to talk about any of the things I cared about, nor did I believe these people would have anything meaningful to offer. To quell my social discomfort, I kept sipping on whiskey sodas. Again, I was soon very drunk and numbing out.

My birthday had taken a strange turn.

There was a room where Knight's friend said we could crash. For me, lying down was a strategy to avoid further interaction, but to him it was an opportunity. There was already some stranger passed out on the bed, so we had to sleep on the carpet. I went in alone, wadded up my coat as a pillow and tried to sleep. I woke later on, when Knight came in and started fooling around with me. I tried to mumble to him about it being late, and me feeling tired and not wanting to, but he repeatedly placed his hand over my mouth and shushed me.

"Shh. You'll wake him up," he said of the man in the bed.

He pulled up my dress and started feeling me up, then flipped me face down and climbed behind me. I laid there in resignation. Again. Waiting for it to be over. At one point, I noticed a stream of light on the rug and looked back to see several of Knight's drunken friends peeking through the door with their phone cameras pointed at us.

A few hours later, the sun was up and Knight drove me home. I stared out the window and against my best effort, I cried. He tried to hold my hand but I pulled away.

"What's up?" he asked, feigning ignorance.

"Let's talk later," I said to him before slamming the car door and storming across the yard toward my house.

That morning I was scheduled to lead worship at the main adult service at church. I stood on the stage, hungover and feeling like a huge liar.

Pastor Mike announced to the whole congregation that it was my 16th birthday — I had been leading worship for the church for four years — and he directed the 150-member congregation in singing Happy Birthday to me as I looked on, guitar in hand, laughing artificially.

After church, I called my sister Shana, crying, and asked her to help me get a morning after pill. She helped me, empathetic and supportive, as I told her the whole story.

Months later, she saw a photo of Knight and I from that night. Some guy had shown it to her and asked if it was me. It was circulating via text around our social scene. Every so often, I would hear a cheeky remark about my star printed underwear, which were visible in the photos. I still don't know if anyone filmed the incident, but the photos haunted me. Shame built upon shame.

S-E-X

Older

My senior year, when I was 16 to 17, I had a long distance Christian boyfriend, Adam. He was significantly older at 21 and I felt I had an adult relationship with him. His friends gave him flack for dating me, but only after they learned my age, which I usually had to confess when they asked where I went to college. My mom once told Adam that if he wanted to propose to me on my 18th birthday, she would give her blessing. That notion bothers me now. But I liked playing house: he lived with a roommate and, naturally, had his life sorted out more than I did at 17.

We would cook and take country rides on his motorcycle and watch weird indie films. We weren't having sex, but he would regularly undress me and get me off in one way or another. We didn't talk about it; it was sensed that if we had an open conversation, this would naturally result in us agreeing to stop fooling around. We tried to set rules to diffuse the sexual energy. It didn't work.

In our whole year together, I never saw him fully naked. I didn't push us forward, but it also didn't feel wrong to me. He always felt guilty after the fact, and eventually I stopped wanting to fool around because I'd grown tired of the emotional fallout.

Graduation

Around graduation I noticed I was orbiting with Cory again (my long time friend and fifth grade boyfriend) at parties and school events. Summer was approaching and we all knew we'd be going our separate ways soon. Cory asked me if I'd like to get lunch together. "Of course," I answered, not thinking twice about whether it would be appropriate for me to go on a date with him, given the fact that I was very much in a relationship with Adam. I went ahead anyway, simply because I wanted to.

We went on a couple of casual dates. After many years of friendship we had a natural ease. We laughed and chatted about life, family, resilience, and our plans for the fall. College was impending. I began to wonder how I was going to navigate the fact that I was essentially dating more than one person. I didn't feel I had cheated, as nothing physical had taken place with Cory, but it was obvious I was playing with fire.

Adam saw a Facebook post where a friend accidentally sold me out, noting that she'd seen me with Cory outside of a café. I played it off and told Adam we were only friends. But Cory had invited me to come to central Oregon for a big senior party after graduation, which I didn't want to miss. I lied again to my mom (it had become so easy) and to Adam about where I was going. I loaded up my Honda with two girlfriends, a couple backpacks, and we hit the road East. This short trip would stay in my dreams for seven years.

When we arrived in Sunriver, it was clear that our classmates had been partying for days. There was a pyramid of beer cans to the ceiling in a downstairs pool room. *Wow*, I thought to myself. *What am I doing here?* It was 2:00 in the afternoon and everyone was trashed. Cory saw me and greeted me warmly, but after that he was more or less unaware of my presence, being quite drunk himself.

My girlfriends and I downed a couple shots to get up to speed. It was a familiar sensation, that warm haze and swagger, though I hadn't drank alcohol in close to a year. Cory's best friend Casey lingered around me and promoted himself to being my date for the night. He pulled out his guitar and we took turns playing songs, a small group forming around the fire pit to listen. Then we made our way to the deck to share a joint. Cannabis was more my comfort zone. Casey took a slow drag. He pulled me close and exhaled the smoke into my mouth. Our first kiss. Even now, I think that was a pretty hot move.

I ended up sleeping with Casey that night. I cheated on the person I was cheating on my boyfriend with. This was a new level of guilt and complexity.

The next morning, Cory wandered into the kitchen and saw me slip awkwardly past the hallway wearing Casey's football jersey. Turns out, I'm not known for my tact. It was obvious to everyone what had taken place. My friends and I left soon after. On the drive home, Cory and I shared an ugly exchange. He stated that he'd thought I was different than all the selfish girls he'd dated. He'd been drawn to me because he saw more depth, more kindness in me, but it was obvious that this had been a mistake.

Instead of making a sincere apology, I deflected. I had no skills in apologizing or in owning my mistakes at that time. Humility was akin to humiliation in my mind. So I became defensive. I attempted to save face by pivoting the focus away from my actions. *Casey*, Cory's best friend of many years had hooked up with *me*, his new love interest. I felt it was unfair for me to take the whole blame when it was so clear that Casey had been on the prowl all night and was intent on seducing me since the moment I came through the door.

It was truly a hearty teenage mess, both of us too proud and lacking the communication skills to work through it. Silence was the solution.

Cory and I didn't speak again for years after that text exchange. We went off to college. Life moved on. For some reason, though, it continued to haunt me: both the guilt for my carelessness and the sense of being deeply misunderstood and rejected by our mutual friends, particularly for behavior relating to my sexuality.

Consent: A Breakthrough

The first person with whom I had enthusiastic consensual sex was Sebastian, the hippie punk kid from art class. He was two years older than me. We'd had a teasing, casually flirtationship over the years. The summer after my graduation, we crossed paths and continued to do so on purpose.

Sebastian had a lean, strong frame and dreadlocks and a smile that could kill. He was a fire dancer before I knew anything about the circus or festival scene. He'd ride his skateboard to the coffee stand where I worked and flirt with me through the window while I closed down the machine for the night. I didn't take him seriously, but I found his quick wit hilarious and laughed aloud at his jokes. We began to spend more time together and I noticed the attraction instantly.

One night, Sebastian stuck around after I locked up the building. He asked if I wanted to hang out. I did. His energy was refreshing to me. I certainly didn't want to go home. I handed him my keys and he drove my Honda up a logging road to a secluded park on the outskirts of town, which actually turned out to be a cemetery. The newest headstones were dated in the late 1800s.

It was nearly midnight. We wandered through the cemetery and settled under a big oak tree. Our surroundings were silent, save for the occasional rustling breeze or a car passing on the highway far below. We smoked some fragrant weed from his glass pipe and began kissing each other hard. We undressed gradually, unrushed, and for the first time, I realized that I was the one making each move. I parted my legs, welcoming whatever might come next.

He lingered there between them, grazing my legs and hips with his calloused hands and warm mouth. I laid my back on the earth and looked up at the clear, starry sky while he worked me over for quite some time. He paused and whispered, "did you come?" I wasn't sure, but I felt so enthusiastic about the situation that I nodded yes.

We had sex right there in the grass, under a shady tree, in a cemetery. It was the first time in my life that I chose to have sex. He was so comfortable with his body and mine, so at ease with our nakedness, and so confident in his approach that I felt I was allowed to be, too. The stars beamed down at us as he slid in and out of me, and I felt awash in bliss and freedom, like I was finally in charge of my life. It was sweet, delicious rebellion — young lust and vibrant aliveness dancing over crumbling bones in a forgotten graveyard. We fell asleep there in the grass some time later, and woke up at sunrise covered in dew, with terrible morning breath from coffee shop snacks, cannabis and sex.

That was the first time a partner ever had the consideration to ask me about my experience. Sebastian knew basic etiquette, was diligent about using condoms, and taught me a whole set of sex activities beyond just fucking in missionary position. We talked openly about STI status and using protection, agreeing on shared responsibility toward safety. It was as though he had learned about sex from actual mentors and real life experience, rather than from church, or porn.

"Alright Bec, it's your turn to buy the condoms," he said once with a wink. This led me into the public health clinic for the first time and empowered me to take charge of my sexual health.

. . .

That summer, we had sex any place we could: his bedroom, my bedroom, his back yard, my back yard. Friends' houses, the back seat of my car, parks late at night. It was all good to me. And I didn't mind being conspicuous; it added to the fun. His family was forever friendly and welcoming toward me, and treated us both like adults, offering us free reign of the kitchen and otherwise leaving us to our own devices.

Our relationship was friendly and trusting, but not romantic.

Our dynamic was playful, sensual and warm toward each other. Neither of us seemed to stray into emotionally complex territory. I was conveniently ignoring the fact that I was still technically with Adam, and he knew nothing of Sebastian. One day, Sebastian's close friend introduced me to another friend as "Sebastian's fuck buddy" and I realized that I was in a friends-with-benefits relationship. I hadn't spent much time deciphering what was happening, except that I enjoyed it and I didn't want it to end.

It was also the first non-monogamous scenario I explored, though we didn't have the name for it back then. Sebastian was still involved, on and off, with his ex and he knew about my boyfriend Adam (I didn't bother mentioning Cory). We approached the situation in a matter-of-fact way that was communicative and caring. It seemed to come naturally for us.

The other guys admittedly were not aware of my non-monogamy, and I only managed it well for a short while. I still wonder why I didn't feel guiltier about cheating. Perhaps one day a therapist will help me understand.

I do know that I felt incredibly sexy with Sebastian. For the first time, I felt fully free to express myself as a sexual being, after three years of a robust sexual life on my own and a destructive sex life with partners. I was finally unafraid to demonstrate how much I enjoyed our encounters, content to linger naked for hours after we had sex, and confident enough to see and be seen.

One night, Sebastian fell asleep in my bed after a particularly fun late night romp. I slept through the alarm I'd set to sneak him back out the window. When my mom came downstairs and found us curled up in my bed, she shook me awake and shooed him out; him trying his best to be polite (it was their first time meeting) and her hovering there, watching us get dressed like some sort of police officer. I walked him out and told him I'd call him later.

Back inside, under my mom's judging gaze, I lied and said we'd just been watching movies on my laptop, that nothing had happened, and I could tell that she wanted to believe me. Our partial nudity was a dead giveaway, but she seemed intent on ignoring that glaring detail. She was so worn out by my antics at this point that she didn't even bother to give me a consequence. She just stormed out of the living room, muttering,

"Oh for heaven's sake, Becca."

I continued to grapple with a messy blend of shame and sex-positivity, but thanks to these experiences with Sebastian, the scales were beginning to level out. Actively choosing to have sex and feeling good about my partner disrupted my previous narrative of sex being shameful and exploitative, a place where I was bound to be used and discarded. Now, it was a world of exploration, one with infinite potential that was enticing, creative and perhaps, the start of a lifelong unfolding in myself.

Recent curiosity inspired me to look Sebastian up online and see what ever came of him. I found just two videos: first, the image of him six years ago fire spinning on a beach, the doting camerawoman referencing his previous work as an erotic dancer. I grinned in knowing agreement. Then I saw a video from just a week earlier of him sitting on the rug playing catch with his baby son. There he was, smiling, laughing, glowing, proud and in love with his child. I was happy to discover this. I owe him a debt of gratitude for teaching me about consent and clarity through example.

5
Shifts

Leaving Home

Vishnu was a friend with whom I shared a deep and important bond. He appeared at a desk beside me late in high school. He was a reserved and handsome boy from a small province in southern India. In fact, he was one of the only Indian people in our school.

My close friend Chelsea took to him and sought to welcome him. Soon, the two of them were great friends and she brought him into our inner circle. He began to join us for lunch and attend our youth group. I wanted to break through his serious exterior and see what was beneath it. I wanted to crack him open, make him laugh, understand his world.

Vishnu was a talented photographer. This was back in the days of MySpace and Flickr.com. He began inviting me to do photo shoots with him. We drove in my 1989 Honda in search of abandoned houses and wide-open fields, vintage furniture and frosty roads. I was lucky enough to be his subject for a handful of portraiture shoots. Vishnu was friends with Knight, who I had a complicated romance with, and he joined us for jam sessions to film our music and put it on YouTube. The music was... only okay.

Months after the date rape incident on my birthday, I still hadn't considered walking away from Knight. Instead, I had blamed myself for the incidents and decided that I needed to be more responsible with my alcohol consumption (which felt true), as well as at protecting myself, because I didn't believe I could trust Knight to respect my desires or boundaries. I stopped drinking altogether. I had asked Knight to be my date to winter ball but felt unsafe going with his group due to past party experiences. I withdrew the invitation.

Finally, I ended the relationship altogether and made it very clear why. He responded by telling me that he had felt used and manipulated into having sex. I could not believe the words coming out of his mouth. I was shocked. I was confused. I was furious. I didn't have the words then for what it was: gaslighting. I swore him off altogether.

Hard To Get

I wanted to invite Vishnu to winter ball, so I came up with a bold, brilliant scheme. We had tickets to see a band called Cute Is What We Aim For at the Crystal Ballroom. The day before the show, I called the band manager (by digging deep on their website for his contact information) and asked if the lead singer would be willing to announce a message for me between songs. He said that yes, he would.

The venue was packed with eyeliner-adorned teens. During the show, I couldn't think about anything else. When the band stopped between songs, my heart started to race. The singer worked the crowd, meandering through witty banter, and finally said,

"Okay everyone, we have some family business to attend to. Is there a Vishnu in the crowd?"

Vishnu looked around, startled. He waved his hand. A spotlight found him.

"Vishnu, Becca wants to know if you will go to winter ball with her," the singer said.

He looked at me in surprise, then laughing, said, "Yes, of course!" We hugged, the crowd awwwwwed, the drummer clicked his sticks together, and off went the next song. I was elated. It was a bold move, and this reinforced my belief that in life, it truly never hurts to ask.

That year, in a touching series of events, Chelsea's family ended up adopting Vishnu, who had been in the foster system for years. They had just built a new house and serendipitously had a bedroom for him and everything. It was such a beautiful development to witness, and it meant he was part of the fold, for good.

Winter ball was a fun and wholesome night; eighteen of us packed into a limo and pretended we were adults for the evening. But I had attached too closely to Vishnu. He saw me as a good friend. There was no other energy between us, at least from him. We existed in this close-friend tension, and he was the first boy to ever be unavailable to my romantic interest. It threw me off. But it wasn't exactly romance I wanted with him; it was devotion. I wanted to belong in each other's inner circle, I wanted to spend large swaths of time together, and I couldn't make sense of his push-pull distance.

Meanwhile, at my house, tensions were rising.

My parents were in their first attempt at divorce, after a saga of infidelity, lying, and finally, a discovery that I had catalyzed by snooping through email inboxes and opening mail that had been returned to the house. I'd been the one to tell my father what was going on, and I could no longer bear the tension between my parents. Separate bedrooms, weighted silences, passive aggressive behavior; it was all getting to me. I'd started smoking quite a bit of weed, sleeping in until noon, and skipping school to cope. I felt that for my sanity, I had to get out of there.

Only Kara remained in the house, as all the others had graduated and left. Chelsea invited me to come stay with her. My mother barely resisted. Perhaps she was as done as I was with our parent-child relationship. Chelsea's family had always been like a second family to me: Her dad took us camping and boating on the Columbia River over the years. Both her parents had taught us to sing and hosted me as a guest in their home hundreds of times since childhood. They took me in and expected the same from me as the other kids. Chelsea, Vishnu and I were thick as thieves, together everyday, occupying the snack cupboard and household movie selections. Chelsea and I would set our alarms for 6 am and attempt to do Pilates, only to hit snooze and agree that we were healthy enough and could go back to sleep.

Chelsea and I, while close, had the challenges of being two teenage girls sharing a small space. I tend to take up a lot of space energetically, or so I've been told, and she had lived her life more or less as an only child. We had some growing pains as I inhabited a corner of her room with no end date in sight. But I was grateful to be welcomed in, and I made an effort to demonstrate that.

Vishnu often invited me to watch late night horror movies with him and straighten his hair before school (yes, that was a thing that teenagers did). We also watched Zeitgeist online one afternoon, and a week later he proclaimed he was throwing out his Bible.

"Just kidding," he said. Then, he handed it to me. "But seriously. Take it. Haha. I'm just joking… No. Seriously."

I furrowed my brow in response as we handed it back and forth. I didn't know what to make of it at the time, but I remember being just as challenged as he was by the doubts he expressed about Christianity and the points made in the film.

SHIFTS

I fell very hard for Vishnu, with his dry wit and giant brown eyes. Without realizing it, I claimed him as my person, the one who knew him best and always had his back.

When he developed a crush on a close friend of mine, I became territorial and proclaimed that she didn't care about him the way that I did — that she was using him for his photography skills to advance her own Internet reputation. My lack of support was enough to drive a wedge between us, which more or less ended our friendship. I was devastated.

This wound was formative for me. Before, I had a pattern that resembled anxious attachment, where I would move intensely toward the people I was attracted to, bonding fast and clinging hard. After this, I pulled away. I shifted subconsciously toward a pattern of dismissive attachment. I didn't want to be perceived as jealous, obsessive, overly available, or needy ever again.

So I armored my heart even further from people I loved.

I decided that the best way to avoid being hurt or humiliated was to remain hard to get, just out of reach, and be a fierce gatekeeper in deciding who to allow in close. I would always be the one to leave at the first sign of trouble, and the first to turn ice cold and move on from love without another word or a second glance.

At the time, I was making money working as a barista at Dutch Brothers, and felt like I was gradually easing into the impending pressures of adulthood. In my mind, I'd left home for good.

One day, perhaps a few months after I'd left the house, my mother called. She told me that it was time for me to come home, that people were starting to talk. I refused. I blamed her for the chaos at home and said I wouldn't be returning unless she forced me to. She let out an exaggerated sigh.

"If you aren't home by Sunday, I'll be forced to file you as a runaway," she said, matter-of-factly.

Hearing this, I hung up the phone in a rage.

That Saturday evening, I packed up my things and my mom came to pick me up. I waited near the front door and cried into Rita's shoulder, thanking her for taking me in, for being a second mother to me.

"You're a good person, Becca. You're going to be just fine. More than fine," she said. And I believed her.

I returned home, dragging my heels. Kara was relieved to have me back, but I made a point to spend as little time there as possible.

Justice

That year, I became very interested in social justice causes. I was particularly concerned with the problem of human trafficking. I'd attended a talk at a progressive Portland church hosted by an organization called One Voice To End Slavery. The speaker was a tattooed, graying man in his forties named Greg. He hailed from southern California and was running a non-profit that not only worked to educate folks of influence on the problem of human trafficking, they also worked on local projects to benefit people in need along the West Coast. One program was called Laundry Love, and the idea was to supply quarters and laundry soap at local laundromats, on scheduled days, in support of folks experiencing homelessness.

For my senior project, I asked Greg to come speak at my school. The talk was called "Sex and Chocolate," in reference to the human rights abuses within sex trafficking and the cacao industry. The title pleased me since I loved raising eyebrows and rocking the boat. I'd come to own the mover-shaker quality in myself.

I facilitated the event and introduced Greg. Straight out of the gate he led an eye-gazing exercise, which was designed to help students witness one another's humanity and drop into a state of compassionate receptivity. I was unsure how this would go with the macho jocks and giggling girls in the back. But to my surprise, everyone participated. It was only one minute long, but I could feel the energy shift in the room. I was impacted by how simple it was to guide a group of people into a more synchronized state where growth and understanding could happen.

Ten years later, I participated in a Solsara eye-gazing workshop at a festival and was reminded of that very moment: my first uncomfortable, unfiltered, raw witnessing of another human being, ever.

Greg narrated beautiful slides about the horrors of the cacao industry on the Ivory Coast using child labor for nearly all of the mainstream chocolate brands. He touched on Portland being one of the top hubs for human sex trafficking in the United States. These realities hit close to home and seemed to capture the hearts of my peers. I handed out samples of organic, fair trade chocolate, which I'd driven to Portland to find.

My teachers and classmates stopped me for several days afterwards to express how impactful it had been, and how it had stood out from most senior projects. This feedback reinforced what I knew of myself: that I was both a leader and a disruptor. It occurred to me that perhaps I was thinking differently from others and isolating as it could be, maybe it was a deep gift.

Shifts

I'd never had much challenge finding opportunity in life. In fact, it seemed to be around every corner, sometimes so abundant that I felt simultaneously exposed and smothered while out in the world. I was in a position of responding to interest and pursuit, rather than discovering my own interest and initiating pursuit.

Now, nearing graduation, I had a decision to make. I'd been accepted into a couple of state universities and intended to study either nursing or education. My school counselor, a family friend whose children I sometimes babysat, proclaimed to me one day in the hallway that I was his biggest disappointment of the year — I'd started strong, but barely graduated by the skin of my teeth after skipping so much school and flunking out of my missed AP classes. I felt ashamed at his remarks, but aware that I had so much going on at home which few people knew about.

Something was holding me back from registering for a state university. I wanted to be sure I'd examined all of my options. (By this point, perhaps it's clear that I'm reticent to make potentially limiting decisions of any kind.) My boyfriend Adam mentioned I might consider joining a local Bible College internship called ID (Immersion Discipleship). It was the same two-year program he had completed. I took some time to mull it over. I felt I was at a distinct crossroads, and I was conflicted.

Which self was the true one? Why did I feel like two people living in one body? What might happen if I went to U of O, a liberal hippie paradise in Eugene, Oregon and spent the next couple of years in a mainstream setting? I wasn't sure I could trust myself. I wasn't sure I could trust the world around me.

A couple of weeks later, I found myself once again on music staff at Camp Crestview, where I'd been every summer since childhood, and this time the programming director happened to be the pastor who ran the internship. It felt like confirmation. He was ecstatic at the idea of me joining and assured me there was still time. I thought that, after many years of living a double life, perhaps this could be my chance to get my act together. To gather myself up into one cohesive shape. To leave all the promiscuity and self-serving behaviors behind me, erase the slinky shadows with bright golden light and find God's will for my life.

The two years I spent working inside that church marked a huge turning point in my life, and not in the ways one might expect.

On the way home from summer camp, I stopped by Adam's house. I told him of my plans to join ID. He nodded as I spoke, realizing the implications of my decision. He was supportive and saddened. He understood that it effectively meant the end of our relationship; an infamous feature of the ID program was that dating was prohibited. That, plus about 100 other fun and enticing rules. Adam and I cried. We hugged. We prayed. We made out. You know, usual Christian stuff.

I confessed that I'd been partying in Sunriver the weekend after graduation, and I came clean about having dated Cory, too. He was unsurprised, and he forgave me; it was all water under the bridge, he said. I never mentioned Sebastian. Selective confession — just enough to clear my conscience, and not so much to do irreparable damage. I hadn't yet explored how radical honesty might feel.

A few weeks before the program began, I faced some serious doubts. I'd spent the summer with Sebastian, giving ear to all of his outlandish ideas about society, philosophy and religion. He insisted that Jesus, had he existed, would have used all kinds of transcendental plant medicines, as healers did throughout history. I was warming up to the notion that I may not have the ultimate truth about existence all sorted out; imagine that. I had cold feet. I was hesitant to dive into a path toward Christian ministry while feeling so unsure about the faith itself.

I rode up to a bluff in Scappoose one afternoon with Gibson, my close friend, and Jordan, my former boyfriend. We sat on a large log overlooking the rolling hills and rolled up a few spliffs to smoke. Gibson could tell something was on my mind.

"What's up with you?" he asked, looking over.

"Gibson," I said dryly. "Do you think God is real? Like... really?" I asked. I raised my eyebrows and stared out at the expanse.

He took a long drag from his spliff and was quiet for a moment. I chewed my nails.

"Becca. Look around," he responded, gesturing at the sweeping view before us. "How else do you think all this got here?" He seemed satisfied with his response. Apparently I was too, because that was the last time I allowed myself to ask that question for several years.

Without ever calling Sebastian again, I skipped town and moved in with the pastors of a large church an hour away, ready to turn my life around for good.

Bible College

Starting Fresh

I was eager for a new start. I was done with St. Helens, done with my family, done with the toxicity. My mom had called off the divorce and chosen to stay with my dad for reasons she wouldn't elaborate on. "It's just not worth it." Was all I can recall her saying of the matter.

I was tired of driving the same roads and shopping in the same grocery stores, seeing the same faces on the same mosquitoey Sauvie Island beach.

I looked to the small church internship for a fresh start. The second year students were four in total — three women and a man. These were indie-hipster Christian types who liked Sufjan Stevens and had skills in graphic design and locating Portland's best hole-in-the-wall restaurants. I effortlessly came to love them. They welcomed us newcomers, giving us the inside scoop and the lay of the land (the church campus was so large it had numerous buildings) and life hacks for managing our insanely tight schedules. My first-year cohort was also four in total — myself, two other women, and a man. There were eight of us altogether.

We started the year with an intense three-day retreat on the Oregon coast. On the drive to the church, I finished my last pack of American Spirit cigarettes.

Once at the retreat we embarked on a rite of passage called "The Walk." The Walk was an eight-hour solo excursion between each student and God, meant to set the tone for a whole year of devotion and sacrifice. To guide the experience, we were each given a multi-page Bible study packet to fill out throughout the day. Then, we would regroup for dinner.

I wandered the beach that day, finding metaphor and meaning in everything: the jetty, the bridges, the waves and stones, the charcoal in the belly of a cooled fire pit. It felt good to pause and reflect; I really did feel I was in conversation with the divine.

Somewhere toward the end of the day as the sun dipped low, I reached a question in the packet that discussed the symbolism and gravity of making a vow. A vow is an unbreakable bond, it said.

"What is one vow you need to make to God today?" the page asked. I thought for a moment, but I already knew my answer.

"I vow to never smoke weed again," I wrote.

Try and restrain your laughter now, would you? I know it's funny, and more than a bit ironic, given how my story progressed. But I meant it at the time. I'd felt a power in cannabis that could open up worlds that I found frightening and confusing from within my Christian context.

We gathered that evening for "debrief," a lengthy group circle that would become a cornerstone of the internship. Hannah, a second-year student who would later become one of my best friends, had a prophetic insight and a beautiful gift for painting. At the closing gathering that evening, she presented one-of-a-kind paintings to each of us first year students. Mine was a pink and orange watercolor, rolled into a scroll, a feminine figure standing in the center and reaching toward the sky. It read:

> "Warrior.
> You will be a voice for the voiceless.
> You will cry out for those in their depths and
> bring my light to their darkness.
> You are mine and your voice belongs only to me.
> Delight in me.
> You will seek me and you will find me
> When you seek me with all of your heart."

The following week I was placed in my host home. There were many affluent families willing to host a college student who was dedicated to doing "The Lord's Work." These were people who wanted to invest in the "next generation of leaders and world changers!" So I was taken in, not just by any family, but by the Maxwells, the head pastors of the mega-church and their 18-year-old daughter Bonita, who was also in my ID cohort.

She and I formed a strong, sister-like bond. The Maxwells housed and fed me for two years. They invited me into their family. In their home, I learned a weekly ritual of hours-long family dinners, which I've instituted many times with friends in subsequent years.

I steeped myself in my studies and service projects and was essentially cut off from my past life. I abided, more or less, by the cult-like rules imposed by the internship protocols. Among those rules:

> No dating.
>
> No jobs.
>
> No private conversations with members of the opposite sex.
>
> No Internet use at home or on our phones.
>
> No girl-guy hangouts in groups less than 5.
>
> No drinking, no smoking, or drug use.
>
> Always dress and act modestly.
>
> Schedule completely controlled by program directors.

Unable to hold a job under these constraints, I lived off occasional deposits my mom made into my bank account, $100 at a time, and the fact that I had free room and board and no free time in which to spend money.

The community of people at the church was truly remarkable. Many of these families had been tight knit for decades, some of them since the founding of the church in 1978. The town was an affluent suburb of Portland, and many of the patriarchs in the church owned reputable businesses: construction, farming, excavation and tech. Church gatherings functioned as much as a networking event as a spiritual one. I don't fault people for this: it's just good business sense.

Leading Worship

The mega church had a typical west coast Foursquare church band: elaborate sound system, drums, full band, upbeat songs — all the hits you'd hear on Christian radio from Hillsong United and Chris Tomlin. The amount of talent on that stage was astonishing. There were back up singers who had done voice acting for Disney and drummers who spent their free time in recording studios laying tracks. I spent an inordinate amount of time on stage during those years. I stepped seamlessly from leading worship in my hometown to leading worship at the new church.

Most of the band members had at least 10 years on me. Some were closer to triple my age of 17, but they backed me anyway. One woman said simply that I had the "X factor," which apparently was something you "couldn't teach." I felt imposter syndrome constantly, but I also received continuous feedback that both challenged me to keep growing and praised me for my efforts.

As a habit, I selected contemporary songs punctuated by a few timeless hymns, and I brought a soulful, feminine energy that remained upbeat. I wanted to keep the crowd engaged and make people feel something real. I wanted people to feel the divine rather than just ponder it. The vanilla congregation responded enthusiastically to this approach, which created a positive feedback loop such that service planners chose to add me into the regular rotation. I began getting stopped in the grocery store by church members who would proclaim that I had a gift from God, that I was anointed, and that I was called to lead. I didn't know about all that, but I was glad to feel like I belonged in this new city, new college, new church.

Over time, I noticed a striking correlation between a perfectly executed music set and people later proclaiming that they had "really felt the spirit moving" during the service. We managed to make heavily rehearsed three-part harmonies and carefully timed musical interludes appear spontaneous and spiritual. We had learned how to structure the series of songs in order to take people on an emotional journey with a clear start, middle, and end.

When people feel something powerful, something positive, they're more likely to give financially. Church is an experience. No one wants to think about it that way, but it's just the reality. A good band is good for the bottom line. And we needed to keep the lights on; those in-ear monitors were not going to pay for themselves.

Many of my memories from ID bear the image of myself behind a guitar in a dimmed room with a bright spotlight shining down in my eyes. I didn't resent it at the time, not usually. Though more challenging and higher profile than other roles, I knew I was cut out for it. I was filling a role that not many people could fill, and the music gave me life.

One ongoing issue with being on stage was that of the dress code.

It was loosely defined and built around the simple admonition to "be modest." What that meant was sometimes up for debate. Clothes were not to be tight, low-cut, short, or revealing. I had a habit of wearing tights and boots but was regularly asked to adjust my clothing choices because they were judged "too revealing." Skirts too far above the knee, dresses too form fitting. Generally, just too much allure.

I remember wanting to scream when I was sent home to change twice in one day. "This is really just looking out for *you*," I was assured by staff.

I cursed under my breath as I pulled items from my closet to appraise in the mirror. *If a grown man couldn't handle the sight of a 17-year-old in a church dress playing guitar, was that really my problem, or was it his?* There is so much to be said about modesty culture and the harm it does to women. It is a part of the much larger societal illness that seeks to make women responsible for the thoughts and behaviors of men. This attitude is an insidious undertone in rape culture.

Nevertheless, the church was a business and we had to run it that way; please the people. During my time there, we had nine pastors on staff. Yes, nine. The front office had at least four full time staff members; the college faculty was about half staff members from the church, plus pastors from other local churches. The administrative staff alone could scarcely fit around a dinner table.

Church was a production, and I mean that in every sense of the word.

The entire staff was required to pull off a church service of that caliber. Upwards of 1200 people attended each week. It might as well have been a community-wide theatre event. We had door greeters, parking attendees, ushers, sound, light and PowerPoint crew, musicians, emcees, pastors, speakers, custodians, hospitality staff and more.

One year, I got wind that the annual budget for the church was $2 million. I remember feeling indignant when I learned we were spending $6,000 on a new batch of in-ear monitors because some of the musicians were annoyed with our existing (top quality) system. *How was this connected to serving Jesus?* I wanted to know.

Yes, we had some noble non-profit extensions of the church, but they were few and far between. There was one well-intentioned woman visiting Rwandan prisons and providing prayer and Bibles. A group of ladies made sack lunches to hand out at the local high school. There were families every Sunday afternoon that brought food to houseless folks under the Burnside Bridge.

The town had a very rich Hispanic population, and yet the only Hispanic folks I remember from our church were the cleaning lady, Luisa, (who also cleaned our home twice a month) and the landscaper guys who tended the grounds. Sometimes on slow mornings Luisa would linger with me in the church café I oversaw.

"Como va tu espanol?" She would ask as she dusted. How was my Spanish?

"Tengo que practicar!" I need to practice! I'd reply. And so she would begin speaking Spanish, lose me, witness my puzzled expression, and, laughing, switch back to English. I loved her for these conversations.

Daily Life

Our weeks were packed, by design.

Mondays were our day off… unless you had been late during the week. For every minute you were late, you were required to come to the church at 7 am on your day off and perform one hour of menial cleaning and maintenance tasks. This punishment was simply called "Hours." So for example, if you were five minutes late one morning, you were required to come in for five hours that Monday. *How was this a thing that sane adults were willing to agree to? How was this something that I agreed to?*

I remember using a dull steak knife one cold Monday morning to shave down decorative candles and wondering what on earth my life had become.

In this world, people do all manner of strange things in the name of serving God. I had reverted to my childhood denial of self at all costs in order to survive the conditions.

Tuesday through Friday we had classes at the Bible college, which included numerous students from other churches. The curriculum included such classes as Prison Epistles (the letters written to the early church by Saint Paul while he was imprisoned), Ancient Hebrew, and Science & The Bible. On Tuesdays we had mentor lunches, a 90-minute slot where church leaders would take us to lunch one-on-one for quality time together. Women with women, and men with men… "naturally."

The youth department where we worked was responsible for the weekly programming for middle school through college. Brian, the youth pastor and program director, was flanked by his lanky and peppy assistant Katrina who had been one of the first ID students alongside my former boyfriend Adam. Katrina and I became quick friends, in spite of the dual relationship of her essentially being my boss.

Tuesday nights we ran the college group known as The Centre. This was a casual but deep-diving get together for folks ages 18 to 25, and it had its glory days during that first year I was there. There were 50 to 75 people in attendance on a given night. The leadership team, about eight of us, was bursting with charismatic, forward-thinking young people who were talented in event production, music, and public speaking.

We had a rotating series of speakers, and the format of the night was fluid and varied from week to week. We decorated the sanctuary with entire rooms worth of rich, ornate textiles, bohemian rugs, low tables and art and sacrament stations. The lights were dim and the music was vibey. We'd sip organic lattes in The Pour, the church's non-profit café that I was preparing to help open to the public.

The gathering began with a couple upbeat songs, then led into the speaker's sermon, and closed with a more evocative series of three or four throbbing worship ballads under dimmed lights and the ribbons of incense smoke.

I loved leading worship for The Centre. That talented group of people loved to sing. I was afforded a fair amount of creative freedom — something I've enjoyed at most of my jobs throughout my life — so I began bringing in new band members who toted instruments like banjo, mandolin, and cajon.

Wednesday nights were GEAR (an acronym for "Getting Equipped, Anointed, and Released). It was a mentorship event where teens were paired with interns to be raised up to be proper Christian leaders. I adored the small, ragtag group of teen girls in my group. I deviated heavily from the curriculum and often took them off site for snacks and chill time at my house.

Thursday nights were family nights with the Maxwells. Bonita's brothers and their families filled the home and we all enjoyed a feast of a meal. The babies would babble and doze off while we watched Survivor or The Bachelor, the pastors rolling their eyes and groaning, yet never changing the channel. I'd half watch while working on homework and nibbling on fruit and chocolate.

Friday nights were free, unless we had a mandatory "fun night," which I had a hard time considering fun in comparison to the rowdy shenanigans I'd gotten into during high school. When free, I'd ride with Bonita to the mall in NE Portland where several of her ex flames would spend time, or I'd go with Hannah to Hawthorne Avenue and dig through shop after shop of luscious textiles and vintage wall art.

Saturday nights were U-Turn, the teen church service. U-Turn was BONKERS. In my memory, it appears more as a satirical parody of a youth service than a real one. I'd actually visited U-Turn once as a teenager, several years prior, for a concert on Halloween. I remember hundreds of good-hearted, pimply, hoodie-clad teens playing in the arcade and getting into good, clean shenanigans.

Sunday mornings were the main church services, with their thousand-plus congregation. I'd be either on the worship team at "Big Church" as we called it, or on a monthly rotation through the youth program. I preferred Big Church. I enjoyed leading the band. It was a high-profile position, and I felt I was up to the task. It challenged me to constantly improve both as a leader and a musician.

It also pushed me to my edge. I remember many late nights writing term papers, only to finish and realize I hadn't pulled the set list for the next morning's chapel service. Many Thursday nights, while my classmates were at home and the Maxwells were having family night, I was at the church for rehearsal. Band practices in the youth building were sometimes easy, and sometimes maddening. Brian had a propensity for tinkering. I dreaded the nights when he was already on site before service. He'd inevitably wander past the sanctuary, pop his head in, furrowing his brow, and within moments, he'd make a beeline for the sound board.

He'd wave at us to stop, and I'd call "cut." Brian would begin fiddling with the knobs and make us run the entire sound check again, right in the middle of rehearsal.

"Something's not right," he'd say, unsatisfied. And I would sigh and sip my water, the whole team waiting around while he fiddled and tweaked. I'd will myself to keep a patient tone of voice and avoid making more frustration for all of us. Finally, when he was appeased, I'd eye my teammates, nod, and we'd get back to practice.

God... Bless... America

One Thursday at rehearsal for the weekend services, I walked on stage to find a printed copy of God Bless America on my music stand. I picked it up.

"What is this?" I asked the service coordinator, Diane. She explained that since it was Independence Day the coming week, we'd be celebrating with the addition of the song. She suggested I remove a mid tempo song from the set list to make room for it.

I was speechless as my bandmates filed in with their usual banter.

I followed her back to the sound booth.

"I'm not comfortable singing this," I told Diane, holding up the sheet music. "This seems really inappropriate. Our job isn't to boost patriotism. This is a place of worship."

She sighed, as though she had dealt with too many young idealists in her time. She explained that I'd need to talk with the head pastor if I wanted it changed, but that the easier option would be to simply sing the song.

At rehearsal, I had a backup singer lead the song. But I was on edge.

When I went to Brian for support, he made an appeal to me.

"That totally makes sense, Becca. But you have to remember who these people are. There are a lot of veterans in the congregation. Is it that big of a deal to you? You can't just bite the bullet and sing the song?"

I spent two nights thinking about it. Maybe I was overreacting? I sighed aloud as I thought about power dynamics within the church and the blurred lines between church and state.

No. Actually, I couldn't bite the bullet. I wasn't about to be coerced into using my platform to promote nationalism in this already white, upper class, conservative congregation. I had the backup singer sing the song, and I kept my jaw clenched the whole time. The memory still makes me cringe.

The upsetting and frustrating memories I have of these years are peppered with ordinary, profound, joyous and charming moments, too. Bonita threw me a surprise black tie birthday party when I turned eighteen. I made dozens of new friends. I regularly visited community gardens. I got my first road bike (I'd had my license temporarily suspended after receiving my third speeding ticket) and got to know the town on two wheels.

Dad

My parents divorced, for real, the first year of my internship. Before my mom left the house and moved in with her new flame, they remained in our childhood home. My dad made a habit of mailing me multi-page, handwritten letters. I wish I'd held onto them.

He had made the house basement his refuge, and he would write to me in long prose, lamenting his failures as a father and expressing his hope that maybe he could right his mistakes and win back my mother. He spent long swaths of paper referencing Bible passages and talking about his prayers for our family and my mom, or as he'd say with care, "your mother."

I sighed and rolled my eyes, feeling compassion for him but thinking it more likely for a single match to melt a block of ice than for him to thaw her out and talk her into staying after so many years of rigid resentment.

Every month or two, my dad would make the hour-long trek to visit my church for Sunday service. He'd arrive early and help with setup (a habit he'd had at church my entire life) and he'd stay for both the 9:00 and 10:30 morning services. I liked looking down from the stage and seeing him mingling with church members. Everyone loved him. I could tell when they were talking about me because my dad would wink up at me from where he stood.

After church, Dad would help tear down and wait around for me to finish my staff debrief, then we'd drive five minutes to La Hacienda, the Mexican restaurant in the strip mall situated beside a laundromat. We'd order enchiladas and tamales in Spanish and he'd chuckle at my fervent attempts at correct grammar. I felt like maybe this was the new normal, me and Dad eating rice and beans, everything seeming like it would work out okay. Maybe all he needed was some company and a listening ear.

Kitchen Time with Shari

With Shari, I learned to cook. She was married to Brian, the program director, and her deep, watery ways seemed to perfectly counter his fiery energy. I adored her.

I hadn't wanted to learn to cook. I'd decided this one afternoon during high school. A sullen, lanky vegetarian teen, I watched in disgust from the kitchen table as my mom deconstructed a whole raw chicken to roast for dinner. The wet snap of a bird joint.

"This is something everyone should know how to do," she said as she worked.

"Ew, Mom. That's seriously never going to happen," I said, turning back to my homework.

I did recognize I couldn't live off of burritos, pasta and cereal forever… but that was a problem that could wait.

And it didn't wait long. The expansion of my food life came during college. The very first week in town, I ate Thai food and sushi for the first time.

Tuesday's mentor lunches with Shari were a highlight of my week, though there was an initial awkwardness. It was daunting to sit down face to face with a near stranger and be expected to delve into deeply personal discussions about faith and spirituality. It sometimes felt forced. I was new in town, a familiar face from years at the regional summer camp, but still, no one knew much about my personal background or history. No one knew that I'd spent the summer fornicating in graveyards and public parks, or that I was still trying to kick my cannabis habit. I wasn't eager to open up.

Shari recognized this. She knew that I was a tough shell to crack. At our first lunch I'd been willing to discuss anything and everything besides myself and my life. Before our second lunch together, she texted me.

"Why don't we cook tomorrow?" she suggested.

"Sure. Sounds good," I answered. Better to busy our hands in the kitchen and see what might come of that.

We made Thai peanut tofu with cilantro rice. It was divine.

By the time I left, the house smelled like a restaurant and she sent me home with a dish full of steaming leftovers. I came to look forward to my cooking visits with Shari, and not just for the cooking lessons. She was different from the other women at the church. She'd had a rough life of poverty, trauma, and substance abuse, a path parallel to her husband Brian's, but they had both found their way to Christianity and believed that God had saved their lives. She was softer, more understanding and more edgy than the women who came from upper-middle class, white suburban Christianity.

Shari was beautiful.

She had tattoos and long dark hair. She drove a truck. She was serious and real, unwilling to play the social games and put on the bubbly church lady mask for gatherings. She didn't even feel obligated to show up at all. If she was having a rough go, if she was stressed or dealing with a bout of back pain, you knew it. She was real and raw, exuding the warmth of someone who knew pain intimately and understood that the world needed more love. More affection. More sincerity.

She was fierce.

She was a love warrior before Glennon Doyle made that a household term. The more she shared with me about her own life, I realized I was welcome. There were few things I could imagine confessing to Shari that would result in judgment or rebuke. Her realness gave me space to be real.

One day she picked me up and drove me to Barnes and Noble. "Pick out a cookbook," she said with a smile. We found one full of international cuisine — falafel, chicken vindaloo, mole, a whole section on spicy, fragrant soups. It was heavy and slick in my hands, the perfect shiny pages waiting for their inevitable splatters and oil stains.

I softened along with the salted onions and black beans.

My desire for a rich future home life, for stability and security, looked in my mind like a kitchen teeming with produce and lined with jars of dry goods and spices. My home would one day have a distinct smell, the smell of nourishing meals cooked with love. We talked about hope: about holding visions for our future and living with the patient expectation of their fulfillment. She asked if I had a hope chest, the old tradition of keeping heirlooms and domestic supplies in a collection for use after marriage. I told her no, there were no heirlooms in my family, but perhaps it wasn't too late.

My eighteenth birthday was a normal day at the office; we had services to plan and classes to attend. I opened my locker to find a large package wrapped with a bow.

It was heavy. A note was written in script on a small paper tag. "Becca- for your hope chest. Love, Shari"

I tore through the paper to find a concave, gleaming double-handled wok, a Chinese stir-frying pan made for high temperatures and large portions. This was the first kitchen item that was truly mine. It was the hope and promise of a life ahead.

7
Immersed

The One

I met Keaton on a wintry night at The Centre, our church college group. I'd been hearing his name for months from several peers at church, but at the time he was living in Mexico on a yearlong service project through an organization called YWAM (Youth With A Mission). His story caught my attention. My father comes from Mexico, and I had a dream of living in Central America and working with coffee and cacao farmers to support fair trade practices. Oh, also, Keaton was a talented drummer.

I was making name tags at the greeting table for The Centre, when my friend Danny hollered, "Look who's back!" and sprung from the seat beside me. I saw him greet a slender-framed man outside the main doors, and as they embraced I concluded that it must be Keaton. I made his name tag.

I watched Keaton as he walked inside. He had big blue eyes, swooping sandy hair and skin a shade darker than my own olive complexion. He wore a charmingly ironic argyle sweater and a pair of beat-up Vans on his feet.

"Hi Keaton," I said, extending the name tag.

"Hi. And you are…" He looked suspicious.

"Oh. I'm Becca. I've been hearing about you. Welcome back."

"Oh, right… thanks." He nodded with a slight smile and passed through the room.

Later on, Keaton told me that while he didn't recall the exact exchange, he did remember thinking that I was, in his words, "Some artsy neo-hippie chick," and wondering where I'd blown in from.

It was many months before we began orbiting each other's circles and taking note of one another.

Life As An Immersed Disciple

I am rebellious by nature (…or was it nurture?) so it is a wonder to me that I completed two years within this highly restrictive, structured, borderline cult-like environment. In the end, it was my stubbornness that got me through the final months; I was not inclined to resign and publicly fail after a year and a half of sacrifice.

Punctuating the years that would have otherwise blurred into the mundane were a series of retreats, camps, and service trips. We did know how to throw a damn good retreat.

In the space of those two years, I must have taken over a dozen flights and as many road trips. Atlanta, Los Angeles, Seattle, Denver, we made the rounds. The trips themselves were a mix of offering support at events, participating in church services, and a fair amount of chill time: the kind of free time when I normally would have smoked a bowl or gone on a date to wander the city.

Sure, I broke a couple rules — we all did.

I occasionally looked at softcore porn by using the neighbors' Internet connection. I masturbated frequently (which was the worst of *all* the sins, as everyone knows. Greedy pleasure-mongers, that whole lot of masturbators). I made out with an old friend on Thanksgiving break one year. I smoked a few cigarettes and drank a glass of wine one Easter, got my nose pierced, and texted with my guy friends and crushes all the time. I had numerous infatuations and mini-romances during the two years. Of course, nothing came of them, beyond late night phone calls and hopes of future entanglements.

Okay. So in reality, I routinely broke ID rules.

I did it to cope, to get through the oppressive nature of the internship with some semblance of my own identity and the freedom that my soul craved. I couldn't live inside a bubble. I didn't want to feel like a mindless Bible-thumping drone.

I knew that I had come into this program alone, and I'd be leaving it alone. I felt that I understood the heart of the rules, and I knew — let's be honest — that no one was truly following all of them anyway. It was a charade. I felt like God could see my sincere efforts and was unconcerned with the minutiae.

I'd grown up in a home with five kids and strict parents, where we routinely broke house rules and discretion became part of the culture. This sensation felt familiar during ID. I was in a repeat cycle of that which I had experienced during my youth: starting out with an eager desire to please my superiors and an intention to be perfect, to fit the standards expected of me.

Soon, I felt I was losing myself in the system and began to secretly rebel, again fracturing myself and my life into two disassociated halves: the acceptable one and the secret one.

Holy Land

During my first year, we traveled to Israel for a ten-day tour through the "Holy Land." It was a fascinating and challenging trip for me. I was met with a deep reverence for the history of the place and a potent discomfort with the Christian tour-bus context in which I'd arrived.

I remember aching for the freedom to escape the bus-tour cohort and get lost in the Old City for a few days, or a chance to see the *real* Tel Aviv. I recall a side street in Jerusalem where I enjoyed the best affogato I've ever tasted. And then there were the religious sites. They were awe-inspiring and engaged the imagination.

It was magical to float in the mineral-dense Dead Sea and hike through the lush oasis of En Gedi, where it is said that David hid from Saul and wrote many of the Bible's famous Psalms. I felt connected to a timeless Spirit while wandering through ancient olive groves and perching on the hill where it is believed Jesus delivered the Sermon on the Mount. I visited archaeological sites dating back to the times of Moses. I was baptized in the Jordan River. I led worship aboard a boat on the Sea of Galilee.

It was enchanting, but it was also troubling.

We had to endure our Jewish tour guide's political diatribes against Palestine, and it was equally jaw-clenching to overhear church members muttering harsh anti-Muslim sentiments when we visited the Temple Mount, also known as Haram esh-Sharif.

In addition to this, the far reach of commodification startled me in my naivete while in the "Holy Land." I witnessed the fact that tourism, and moreover, capitalism, is an unrelenting machine that will chew up anything, even the most sacred of things, in its path.

Witnessing all the tour buses, the Jesus-themed magnets and tiny bottles of holy water, watching the excitement over bargain souvenirs like Hebrew necklaces and knock off pashmina scarves made me cringe. And I wasn't totally immune. I did take the opportunity to ride an ornately decorated camel at one lookout point. While I didn't want to purchase a bunch of kitchy Jesus keepsakes, I did want to bring home an authentic Israeli hookah. Unsurprisingly, that idea was quickly vetoed by the trip leaders.

I have several friends now who grew up or lived in Israel, and a part of me is eager to return and discover their homeland, through their widened lenses.

Christianity for Hippies and Activists

That year, I was fortunate to meet a brilliant old man named Bill. He was tall and slim with a white beard and sandals. He reminded me of Gandalf the Grey. Bill had been a missionary in Uganda for many years, and as much as I lament the colonialist phenomenon of missionary culture, he's still one of the more respectable Christians I know. He's down to earth, pragmatic, compassionate, humble, and has a strong sense of the real world and the people in it. I see him as more of a philosopher than an evangelist.

For a school project, I set up an interview with him. We sat in his office talking about God, life, and culture.

"Sometimes you have to let go of the things you think you need," he said. "You have to find the end of yourself. And other times, you need to write a letter to a friend and have them mail you some chocolate chips."

Bill introduced me to a woman who lived with her husband in Tunisia, a country in Northern Africa, and ran a small church. She was earthy and spoke with a tone and cadence that put me at ease. She seemed cut from an entirely different cloth — a more worldly one, and it made me think that maybe there was a brand of Christianity, of alternative lifestyle within this faith, that could actually feel right for me. I'd been seeking this since high school, but still hadn't found it.

The mainstream church culture, the language (not-so-affectionately called "Christianese"), the fashion, the music… it felt like something I was putting on, and not something that was coming from within me. It was an adaptation to the environment, and not one that I could sustain much longer. As an intern and a Bible college student, I was often asked whether I intended to become a pastor, or better yet, marry a pastor, after graduating. The thought of leading a church made me cringe. It prompted mental images of cages and shiny shoes and trendy Jesus blogs.

I knew that wasn't the path for me… but what was? Why was I so damn restless?

IMMERSED

In some ways, I felt I was being ungrateful. I'd been given more responsibility and also more privileges. While some interns were busy lining up chairs and planning games for the youth group, I was rehearsing with the worship band and designing a community garden program proposal. That's not to say I didn't do my fair share of grunt work; if I'm ever asked to fold a hefty stack of bulletins again, I'll probably just stare blankly and laugh in response.

In any case, many staff members treated me more as a friend than as an intern, sharing things in confidence that were not disclosed to the entire group. It was a familiar feeling, the same feeling I'd had most of my life.

Irresistible

Late in my second year of ID, I bought a book called *The Irresistible Revolution* by Shane Claiborne. I drank it up. Claiborne was a "radical Jesus-follower," as he'd put it, and ran a Christian commune called The Way in Philadelphia. His story was like a glass of cold water to me. In his book, he called out the hypocrisy in the modern church and suggested that there was a better way to live out one's faith — radically, counter culturally, the way that Jesus had preached in the Bible.

As a rebellious and practical person, this style of faith made sense to me. Claiborne was more focused on the practicality of living out one's faith in this life, rather than the promised reward of heaven. He rejected the cultural emphasis on dogma that seemed to allow so many half-assed Christians in the modern world to justify their complacent lifestyles and sometimes harmful prejudices.

Reading that book was also the first time I witnessed a Christian speaking seriously about climate justice. He coined the term "Creation Care," which was cheesy, but held potential to attach spirituality to environmentalism for a whole sea of Christians. He'd invited a huge mass of devout folks to take climate change seriously, by removing the old standby excuses that had been made by patriarchal Christianity for generations: God had created the Earth as our dominion, he was going to create a new Heaven and a new Earth, and he hadn't created this one to last forever. I remember actually believing this; I even recall saying things like that at one point, in an attempt to comfort my bleeding heart about the sad Earthly state of affairs.

This is just one example of how radically we all can change. It reminds me to never attach my identity to a belief, because beliefs are living and evolving. They are and they must be. As long as we are alive, our beliefs about the world are being informed by new experiences and new insights. It's our responsibility to integrate those experiences and to stay flexible enough to allow space for being wrong. For admitting we were ignorant. It is an empowering choice to practice being adaptable and teachable throughout all areas of our lives.

But, I digress.

Claiborne wrote of "beating swords into plowshares," which is a reference to an end-times prophecy in the book of Revelation, where the chaos has finally ended and peace on Earth has come. Claiborne argued that it was possible to bring about heaven on Earth — in fact, it was our spiritual imperative to do the work of God here and now.

What a simple but novel concept! I allowed myself to dream of what the world would be like if Christians actually lived like they believed the messages of Jesus were true. I wondered what my life would look like if I did.

The image of beating swords into plowshares still brings me to tears. This is a dream of a world that I still hold onto — a world where wartime has passed, and all our weapons of war against one another can be re-imagined and transformed into tools that support life. I believe most world religions hold a vision like this.

I had a lingering tug in the back of my mind telling me that perhaps it wasn't possible for me to live as radically as Shane Claiborne, or even as the devoted peers around me. I realized that, maybe the reason I wasn't living as if Christianity was true, was because *I still wasn't convinced it was true*. Maybe my devoted displays of worship were an attempt to drum up a belief and emotional conviction that could override my growing and creeping doubts. Because no matter the depth of my devotion, I was coming up empty.

I also read a coffee book called *Uncommon Grounds* that gave me a deep dive fascination and passion for fair trade, farm-direct… well, everything. Coffee and cacao particularly excited me, with a passion for fair trade cacao reaching back to my high school days and the discovery of One Voice to End Slavery.

The who's who of Portland's craft coffee scene in many ways mirrored the who's who of Oregon's yet-to-be birthed recreational cannabis scene. Perhaps all industries have infighting, scandal and dirty players flanked by rock solid folks. I was interested in the behind-the-scenes nuance, the people behind the brands, and I wanted to know who the key players were, who the scary-smarts were, and whose coffee I could actually feel good about drinking. After all of that geeking out, I settled on a loyalty to Matt Milletto's coffee from Water Avenue, and I swore off Duane Sorenson's from Stumptown.

Doubt

Even as I was nearing the end of my internship, my doubts still persisted. What I had expected to be deep resolve and a fortified faith by now, felt more like dread at my continued uncertainty. I asked Brian if we could meet.

"I feel like I'm back at square one," I told Brian. I had been preparing a lesson about prayer for my GEAR discipleship students (five middle school girls for whom I was a sort of peer mentor) and I had hit a wall.

"I don't know how to teach this stuff, because my own questions are taking me down a rabbit hole. I need you to explain to me how prayer works," I said. I knew it sounded ridiculous, but I was desperate.

"What do you mean?" he asked.

"Well… I just, I don't get it. How important is it? If God is everywhere, all the time, and has removed all barriers to himself through Jesus, he already knows what I'm thinking, what I need, and what is best. Isn't prayer sort of… me getting in the way? It's using my human mind to try and tell God what to do. I feel like I'm treating him like an aging grandpa who needs a reminder to send me a birthday card with a $20 bill in it."

He looked at me and sighed.

"I know it's weird," he said. "I'm not sure if this brings you any comfort, but I have doubts, too. Every great person of faith has had doubts. And they don't always get resolved. You have to make the choice how you're going to live with those doubts, and lean on what you know to be real about God. He's not scared of your doubts. He can handle them."

Unappeased, I chimed in. "And also, I don't even see Jesus talking that much about prayer. He was talking more about how we were supposed to live than spiritual rituals. I feel like a fool just talking to the ceiling. I honestly can't feel if anyone's listening. What would happen if I never prayed again? Would that change how close I am to God? I feel like praying is connecting me more to myself, if anything."

He repeated what he had already said, gave me a hug, and sent me on my way.

For me, this was a big problem.

Yet I sensed that Brian believed it would blow over. I'm not sure what I was looking for — probably some sort of assurance that I wasn't crazy. Maybe I hoped that he'd had a different experience of prayer, that he knew something I didn't, and there was just something wrong with me. Something

I could change. But no, he had basically agreed that prayer felt like blindly talking to someone who never spoke back. That was of no comfort to me.

Graduation

Spring came soon after, and my class of six bible college students graduated. I had the esteemed honor of outcompeting my massive class and being selected as class speaker by the faculty. I delivered a speech which I can't now recall, though I remember they had asked me to put a personal message to God at the end. So, a prayer. I didn't know where to look during that part. Should I close my eyes on stage in front of 300 people, or cast my eyes up to the ceiling, the holiest place of the sanctuary?

Nonetheless, I got through the speech, and with that, I had a degree in Biblical Studies. To support my success, my mom and my sister Shana attended the graduation.

After the festivities, Keaton found me in the parking lot.

"Becca," he called from behind me. "I have something for you. A graduation gift."

I was surprised and touched.

He handed me a black book with a card on top. It was a leather bound Spanish-English Bible. We shared a long hug and that night, I read and reread his heartfelt card several times before setting it on my mantle and thumbing through my favorite passages in Spanish.

The translation of Psalm 23 impacted me. The famous line "The Lord is my shepherd; I shall not want." Was translated as "Dios es mi pastor. Nada me falta." Nada me falta. This phrase simply means: "I lack nothing."

Those three words, "I Lack Nothing," have followed me for the last nine years and become a tether to my center at so many moments when I thought I might become unhinged or lost in despair. I am grateful for the universal truths that find their ways to us, even through the filter of religion and cultural constructs.

And just like that, I was done with Bible College. Yet the internship had another month of trips and service projects before I would be *done*, done... I was beginning to check out.

Colorado

During this final month, we traveled to Colorado to work with a church that had a similar intern program called Masters Commission. Theirs was larger and had a residence set up where all the interns, about 20, lived together in gender-separated houses beside the church.

Our connection with this group had come through tragedy the year before.

It was November 12, 2009 (my birthday, I'll never forget) and we were working as temps at a large tech conference in Portland. We worked these jobs seasonally to raise funds for program expenses. We sipped our early morning coffees and straightened our uniforms as we waited to be briefed on the day's duties. I saw Brian get off the phone as he approached our group. When he arrived, he circled us up.

He told us he had some terrible news.

Content Warning: Car Crash

The interns who were meant to join us the next day had a tragic accident. They'd been caravanning from Denver toward Portland in several 15-passenger vans. It was early in the morning — most of the interns were asleep — when one van hit a patch of black ice and the driver lost control. In the process of flipping multiple times, almost everyone was ejected from the van. Two people died that morning. Fourteen others sustained serious injuries.

We listened to Brian in shock, grief stricken for these peers who we'd never met.

We decided to stay and work through the next week to fill their jobs at the conference, and to send them the money earned from those shifts. Afterwards, we maintained a relationship with the leaders of that program and I became connected with a woman named Leta, who was the coordinator.

It was a year and a half later, at the end of our internship, when we made the trek out to spend a week in Colorado with these interns, to whom we felt bonded.

In some ways, our time there felt like a normal church service trip. We had many prayer and study meetings, we helped put on youth events, I was asked to join the worship team for the main services, and we fit in some fun outings for good measure.

But the undercurrent of unaddressed trauma was thick in the community.

Only 18 months had passed since the tragic van accident. The subject came up every day. It was clear that the whole community was still reeling and permanently changed from the event. I roomed with the woman whose brother had died in the accident. I made friends with a man who had been airlifted to a Boise hospital. One night, as we snacked in the kitchen, he began discussing the event, then he lifted his shirt to reveal a back and chest marred with deep scars from the impact of the road. It was intense to witness.

I was affected by the resilience of the group and their faith in spite of tragedy. Any time they acknowledged their pain, though, it seemed to be an automatic impulse, like muscle memory, to turn the glory back to God, to express their trust in him and the belief that their lost loved ones were in a better place. In this, something of their grief and loss felt diminished.

In Christianity, the grieving process is truncated. I have seen it time and again. I have attended, and sung songs for, close to a dozen funerals: some for young classmates lost to tragedy, some for elders of the church, some for middle aged folks who ended their own lives.

The pattern I have seen is that people of faith do not often feel full permission to grieve their loss. The pain of loss seems to be eclipsed by the promises of the faith — that their loved ones are now in paradise, in full peace, living in harmony with God and self.

How am I supposed to allow myself to grieve and rage and deal with the trauma of loss, when being constantly inundated with well-intended platitudes about everything "working out according to God's plan" and the urge to "celebrate life" rather than grieve death?

Here in the West, we have a phobia of death. We are obsessed with extending life and outsmarting the process of aging. The topic of dying is taboo. Many other cultures are intimately acquainted with death and have ceremonies and rituals that are beautiful and weighty and last a long time. It allows permission and space for the nonlinear waves of emotion that come with loss. I believe we need to revive that in our culture.

As with any untended trauma, loss of a loved one can derail people for the rest of their lives. I am hopeful when I see the resurgence of death doulas in our culture as important guides in navigating the process of dying. I hope that people of all faiths feel permission to experience the grieving process fully, in all of its facets.

Pastor Problems

Immediately after our time in Colorado, we flew to Atlanta, Georgia for the annual Foursquare convention. The shift was jarring for me. This was the global gathering for all the pastors and leaders of the entire denomination.

Thousands of people poured into hotels and event centers for essentially the largest church experience I've ever witnessed. We were tasked with setting up and running the youth programs for all the "PKs" (pastors' kids).

I loved the vibe in Atlanta, and again, wished I could just break out of the group and actually experience the place. There was a Black heritage parade one afternoon, and bar none, it was the most vibrant, celebratory event I'd ever witnessed.

The Foursquare convention was always a bit of a culture shock. In the Pacific Northwest, we had a certain hip, laid back flavor of church. But the denomination itself is a Pentecostal one. Its four pillars are the beliefs that Jesus Christ is the "Savior, Healer, Baptizer in the Holy Spirit, and Soon Coming King." The church had a strong emphasis on the "gifts of the Holy Spirit," things like prophecy and speaking in tongues and acts of healing.

The history behind Foursquare is even more strange and fascinating — it's worth a quick read about Amy Semple McPherson, the eccentric Los Angeles woman who founded the denomination in the 1920s.

Attending the international gatherings allowed me to see the larger sampling of the organization of which I was a part. Sometimes, it alarmed and embarrassed me. I felt less and less like I belonged in any way.

I had been rolling my eyes all day as we constructed an over-the-top stage and sound system for this ridiculous pop-rock band called Press Play. I thought they were painfully cheesy — big fish in a small pond rocking spiked hair and leather bodysuits. They really seemed to think they were Christian superstars.

Children ages 5 to 12 began to arrive, and we were to look after them for several hours while their parents were away in the arena for the main church gathering.

After some age appropriate activities like group games, crafts and coloring, the kids were all gathered into the main floor for the "service." There was a brief performance by Press Play, which then transitioned right into a full blown worship service.

Earlier in the day, I had met the pastor who was facilitating the event, and he seemed, by my estimation, far too intense and intimidating to be working with kids. I was thrown off by the way he carried himself and didn't understand the staffing decision.

As the songs passed, this feeling became more pronounced. I noticed the event producers had gradually dimmed the lights as the music became more soaring, emotional, and heavy. As a worship leader myself, I was familiar with the strategy and knew exactly what was happening.

The preacher spoke during the musical interludes and gave an altar call for kids to be "baptized in the Holy Spirit." He was preaching about the gifts of the spirit and how the kids in the room could be given the gift of healing, prophesying, and speaking in tongues.

He began quoting intense, seemingly irrelevant scriptures about the End Times and going to war with evil, and that we would need tools to fight against "the attacks of the enemy." Then he demonstrated speaking in tongues. Even at the time, I noticed it didn't seem to be landing with a lot of the children. A lot of kids were just staring blankly or squirming around. An unusual number of kids requested to go to the bathroom. This confirmed that my discomfort wasn't solely based on my own personal bias against the situation.

Two little boys, brothers maybe 6 and 8, were clinging to me during the service. The little one kept pulling on my sleeve and saying, "Can we goooo? I want to go now." And all I could do was pat his shoulder and tell him his parents were coming soon.

I watched as a handful of kids toward the front of the stage cried and waved their hands in the air, as the pastor "anointed" them and commended them for their dedication to Christ, making them examples for the room full of pint-sized onlookers. I watched youth leaders pray over young kids, speaking in made up languages as the kids squeezed their eyes shut and extended their arms to the sky in earnest devotion. It reminded me of my own indoctrination.

My heart began to race and I ended up storming out. I stayed outside in the lobby until the service ended.

When I see something that's not okay, I can't keep my mouth shut. Injustice and abuses of power are intolerable to me.

My heart raced as old experiences from my own youth collided with the present moment, witnessing the same things happening to a whole new batch of kids, and all I could feel was rage. I felt like these kids should be protected from manipulation and lying and people in power who had an agenda to fill pews, staff churches and fatten revenues.

I fantasized about getting a flight back to Portland that very night and calling it quits: the ID program, the belief system, all of it. All I could see was the faith's disgusting flaws and blatant hypocrisy, glaring like the Atlanta sun.

IMMERSED

I guess I was triggered.

You see, I'd had some very intense experiences at summer camp that really messed with my idea of the divine and my trust in my own experiences as well as people in positions of power. In spite of my resistance, I was beginning to revisit and better understand some of these problematic childhood experiences.

The Holy Spirit & Me

Every year, from grade school until high school graduation, my youth group attended a week-long summer camp at Camp Crestview in the Columbia River Gorge. I loved and looked forward to sleepaway camp every year. It was $200 per child, and my mom insisted on coming up with the money for each of us, stating, "I can't afford for you *not* to go." She believed it was essential for our spiritual development.

Camp was festive and highly produced, hundreds of people from around the county working for months to plan the programming and coordinate staffing. Still, it left enough spacious time for open-hearted connection and new friendships to form. The last night of camp was unofficially programmed as "Holy Spirit night." I noticed this pattern after a few years as a camper, and then as a teen when I was on staff at kids camps, I learned this was in place by design. This was when the preacher would talk about the gifts of the Holy Spirit as tools from God to empower us to take what we had learned at camp and give it to the world.

Speaking in tongues and being "slain in the spirit" (falling down on your back) were promoted and encouraged. Staff and cabin leaders were brought to the front to pray for kids, and one by one, as the music surged on, we would all come up to the leaders, "as we felt called." They prayed over us to receive the gifts of the Spirit. It was all very moving and emotional. The lights were dimmed, the music was intense, and emotions were naturally running high after spending so many days in a new environment with all these new, wonderful people.

I remember multiple years, going up to the front to receive prayer for the gifts of the Holy Spirit. The pressure to succeed finally prompted me to start "speaking in tongues." It wasn't hard. I was simply mimicking the gibberish that I'd heard from the mouths of adults my whole life, just as all the kids around me were doing. My best friend Paige confided in me the next day that she didn't get it, that maybe God didn't want her to speak in tongues, and I felt so phony.

I wished I could tell her that I felt the same, that maybe we weren't the only ones for whom it "wasn't working." There was nothing wrong with us. But no, I had already told her that I could speak in tongues, so I felt forced to keep up the act.

This was a lot of mental and emotional labor for a twelve-year-old to deal with.

Don't Make This Worse

The morning after the children's service in Atlanta, our intern group gathered up for a debrief. I voiced my concerns and I didn't mince words. Brian shared that he'd heard similar feedback from others who were present, and that the preacher on stage had an unsavory history of pushing things too far. He said he wasn't sure why the pastor had been booked to lead the service and he'd look into it. He said he appreciated the feedback, in the tone I'd heard so many times in my life. It was a tone that seemed to say: "People are listening to you. Please go easy on us and don't make this worse than it already is."

His response did not satisfy me.

For two years, I'd been placated and dismissed when I brought up issues that needed attention. I felt like the contents of the church's toxic underbelly had been repeatedly exposed, and yet there was nowhere to put the knowledge, nothing to be done about it. I didn't believe that anything would truly change.

Men like that preacher would continue to lead churches and youth groups, creating little minions out of earnest, impressionable youth, who would have to unpack it all many years later, just like I did, once their brains had fully developed and they were removed from those influences. Well, those would be the lucky ones. The less lucky would end up filling their positions on staff as the previous generation aged out.

Still, I decided that this issue was not enough for me to sabotage all I had worked for over two years. I had to finish the program. I recognized that my anger would change nothing, so I attempted to move forward in spite of it.

I got through the final weeks of the internship with a severe case of senioritis and a loose plan forming of what would happen next.

Bonita and I had lived together for two years, shared a family, and in many ways our relationship carried the nuance of sisterhood. We laughed. We shopped. We irritated each other. We confided in each other. We swapped clothes. We counted calories. We shared secrets. And as graduation approached, we often discussed skipping town and traveling together.

I had a classic nineteen-year-old dream of being transient in Central America, living off very little money and relying on serendipity and the good will of strangers to carry us from one experience to the next. But by the time we graduated, the practicality of life urged us toward more conventional paths. She took a job at a mega-church on Hawaii's Big Island and I stayed in town to decompress for a while after the ID bubble popped. I needed to see if I could remember how to be a regular person in the regular world.

The last week of the program, Brian sat me down in his office.

"Becca, you are going to have countless opportunities in this life," he said. "You're a powerhouse. The world wants something from you. My sincerest advice to you is this: Do not say yes to every opportunity that comes your way. Be discerning. Some things… some people, are not deserving of your energy."

These words still echo in my mind sometimes, though nine years have passed since that day. He was right. I've seen it again and again — I experience the world as hungry and grasping at me much of the time. I've had to fortify my own boundaries to an extent I never anticipated. In some ways I've become hardened to the outside world, just to protect my own needs and inner resources — just to keep the clarity of my path and not get swept up into the dreams and ambitions of others. I'm only beginning to learn this. I've made a grand mess of this simple lesson a number of times.

That same week, there was the oh-so-scandalous fact that I had gotten my septum pierced on impulse, although the program had not quite ended. This was a thoughtless disregard for ID rules, which forbade tattooing or piercing during the program. I'd been thrift shopping with a friend one Saturday in Portland when she decided to have her nose pierced. The piercer then turned to me.

"Alright, your turn!" he said, jokingly. My friend looked up at me and smiled.

I was tempted. I thought that, with a couple weeks left to go, who would really care? I went for it.

Turns out, everyone on the pastoral staff cared, a whole... fucking... lot. This ring hanging from the center of my nose was seen as a very public rebellion and disregard for the elders who had set that rule. It seemed even more brazen because I led worship on the main stage that weekend.

Brian pulled me aside when he got wind of the situation.

"I'm going to level with you, Becca. I realize how ridiculous this is. You know I'm not worried about how people present themselves. And I'm definitely not worried about micromanaging your nose," he said. I believed this. He was a stocky, tattooed former addict with a teddy bear face who had been "saved by the grace of God," he always said. He sat back in his chair and crossed his arms, rubbing his chin in his hand.

"But listen. We've got to keep people happy. An unfortunate part of being in this ministry is keeping the machine running."

I recoiled.

"There shouldn't be a machine. This shouldn't be a business and there shouldn't be customers and stakeholders to keep happy, Brian," I retorted.

He was silent for a bit.

"Can you just give me one week? Take it out for the last week of the program. As a personal favor," he implored.

I sighed.

"Brian, I would, but they used pliers to put it in. It's not going anywhere. Sorry," I told him. This was a convenient truth.

Our program ended with our annual trip to Spokane to serve at the Union Gospel Mission, the shelter where Brian had turned his life around many years earlier. I spent most of the trip on stage doing music for multiple events. The week went by rapidly and as the days counted down, I was hit with a wave of preemptive nostalgia. I loved working with the teens who had become like my younger brothers and sisters.

In spite of myself, I'd grown to love sound check and leading worship and late night debriefs with the interns.

The last night in Spokane was highly emotional. Students and staff took turns expressing their gratitude through sniffles and tears to each of us ID students, naming specific memories and telling us of the impact we'd had on their lives.

One such tearjerker was a heartfelt outpouring from my dear friend Logan.

I was seven years older than her, and she felt like a sister and a wise peer all at once. We were kindred spirits — everyone recognized it and joked about it. She was passionate and scrappy and beautiful with an eye for art. She had a depth of compassion that usually only comes with age and a life filled with pain. She had seen a lot in her years. She operated, in many ways, as the adult within her family — one that had been surrounded by a deep level of dysfunction, mental health issues, and instability. I adored her family and I adored her.

I'll never forget the first night we had our GEAR mentorship class, two years prior. I'd asked Logan to offer an opening prayer to start our class together. She looked at me with an arched eyebrow and sighed, hesitant. We all closed our eyes and bowed our heads.

"Dear God… "

She took a long pause, unsure.

"'Sup?"

We all burst into laughter. Her comedic timing was impeccable. It always was. Here was a person as bewildered by prayer as I was. She was uncompromisingly herself, even amidst pressures from the outside to fit into many different molds during the years I've known her. We are still friends today.

Done

The drive home from Spokane to Portland took close to twelve hours. Bathroom breaks at rest stops take an eternity when you have 60 exhausted teenagers to keep track of. Herding cats, they say. I was literally hours away from a set of freedoms I hadn't had in two years. I alternated between feeling impatient and reflective.

As the kids snoozed, I watched the scenery pass outside the van window and thought about the fact that I'd made an impact on so many people — not just teens, but churchgoers who I'd never personally met but had shared in my music or heard me speak, or even simpler, all the new loved ones to whom I had offered my friendship and support, and received the same. I realized that this community was not what I'd come to this program to find, but it was a cherished outcome.

I had come into ID for two things: first, a radical shift in my lifestyle — a turn away from my freewheeling tendencies and rebellious spirit. Second, a renewed strength of faith that would prepare me for a life of service. I felt I had only accomplished the first of these goals, and I had a suspicion that this radical shift had been a temporary fix, not a foundational change.

Finally, we arrived at the church and I bee-lined it out of there. No more hugs, tears, nothing. I was FREE!

And I had someone on my mind: a certain blue-eyed drummer who I hadn't seen since band practice several weeks prior.

My friend and former ID student Danny walked with me to my Honda, helping carry my bags. I was mentally somewhere else, so close to leaving, debating whether to celebrate by taking a trip straight out of town or to smoke hand-rolled cigarettes 'til I was sick. Danny was waxing poetic about his favorite times we shared during the internship. It wasn't until I was climbing into my car to leave that I tuned into the words he'd been saying: he was asking me out on a date. I looked up at him, surprised.

"Oh. Um… yeah. Let me decompress for a while and we can talk about hanging out, ok?" I waved goodbye and went home, forgetting about the conversation completely.

I had done the impossible. My faith in Christianity had been cracked open in the process, but I had endured my skin-crawling discomfort and finished the mission I had started two years earlier.

8
Adulting

First Night

The evening my internship ended, I sent Keaton a text.

"What are you up to tonight? Want to go on a walk with me?" I wrote.

He called me a few minutes later, and within the hour I was parked in front of the house where, three years later, our son Moses would be born.

Keaton and I were up until 2:00 am talking about life, music, faith, friends and goals. I walked barefoot on the empty, still-warm roads under diffuse lamplight. We bantered. When the air outside grew cold, he invited me inside his family's new, unfurnished basement apartment. His parents were upstairs watching a Portland Trail Blazers game (the Blazers are a basketball team that manages to draw huge crowds of melancholy Portlanders straight through the winter in spite of the Oregon rains).

We sat on floor pillows in the empty space where we would one day live together. To me, the night felt at once perfectly ordinary and deeply significant, even familial. It wasn't electric, like I'd felt beside Jordan or Sebastian, but there was a quality of destiny, as though we were flipping a page of a story that had already been written.

At one point, Keaton's mom Kari knocked on the door. She popped her head down and we shared a casual introduction.

"I'm baking cookies up here. Do you guys want some? Feel free to come on up!" she said. She was relaxed and friendly and beautiful in an unfussy way. I felt instantly welcomed.

Young Love

Keaton and I spent a ton of time together that summer. We were pals. We went on bike rides around the rural edge of town, wandered through tree lined parks laughing loudly and eating picnics on grassy knolls. I was nineteen, he was twenty. We played music together in the little shed where he kept his keyboard and guitars. Kari loved hearing our music dance across the lawn toward the house. Our soaring harmonies were dialed in and we knew the songs by heart; we'd both been playing them for years. It was a stretch for me to play non-church songs, as my whole musical life had been consumed by church for eight years.

After several weeks of late night park dates and make-out sessions, I began to wonder what Keaton and I were doing. I was smitten, but it was a best friend kind of love, a kind of intimacy I hadn't ever experienced. It felt real, like something I wanted to keep in my life. He was steady and trustworthy. His energy was clear. There was something pure about him, different than most other men I knew — I didn't sense concealed layers to his care for me as though he had some ulterior motive and saw me as a snack to devour. I felt respected and appreciated.

But I wasn't totally clear. I had other interests to sort out. Another class member from Bible College, a charming, burly Californian lumberjack type with a noisy sense of humor had asked me out. I casually mentioned to Keaton one day that I might get dinner with him, and he barely batted an eye.

"Cool. Tell him hi for me," Keaton had said. He wasn't one to be competitive. He didn't seem jealous in the least.

Then there was Joe, an eccentric, soft spoken artist with whom I'd been highly infatuated for over a year. The memory of him still makes me grin.

Everyone in our suburban town adored Joe. He had kind eyes and a big beard and a charming, wispy, faux-hawk mullet that only he could pull off. He didn't fill the air with chatter. We made leather seed-pouch necklaces and hand drawn stickers and owl feather earrings together. We debated methods for pulling a pristine espresso shot. I came to his art shows and gave him haircuts in my kitchen. He lamented the burdens of modern budgets and time management strategies.

We had spent a fair amount of not-so-covert time together toward the end of my internship. I'd been holing up with him in local cafes since winter. We shared crafting afternoons on the weekends. Eventually, he invited me to attend another non-threatening art show, as I had before, and I simply panicked. I feared this innocent, secret love interest would be found out by the church staff. I approached him after The Centre one night and told him that I was excited to continue spending time with him, but that there was a lot on the line and it would need to wait until I'd finished my internship. He nodded in agreement.

"For sure. There's all summer to be had," Joe said with a wink before driving away.

Keaton and I gradually agreed that it seemed clear we were dating. But it wasn't without drama — our friend Danny, the one who asked me out on the last day of my program, was one of Keaton's closest friends. He was very interested in me and took personal offense at Keaton's involvement with me. He explicitly told Keaton that he felt entitled to a fair shot, and that "taking me" would effectively end their friendship.

When I heard this, I was disgusted. This young feminist was no one's for the taking.

"So, why is it between the two of you to decide who gets to *date me*? That's my choice. Only mine. I'm not going to date Danny, especially not after this. This whole thing is ridiculous," I insisted.

Keaton agreed. We carried on with our little love affair, and their friendship survived.

Keaton likes to joke that he had to fend off a sea of suitors to date me. That's not how I remember it. While it's true that I garnered the attention of guy friends during those years, the only one other love interest stands out is Joe. He and Keaton were stark opposites.

Even then, I knew that Keaton would help me lead the kind of life I craved — grounded, focused, and content. He was an extension of the things I'd been searching for when I arrived in town.

Joe, on the other hand, was an artist who had blown into town with an artsy experimental rock band from Bend, Oregon. The church youth group hosted a new band every Saturday and we'd hired the band to play at an event. Joe was known for live painting on door-sized canvases during the band's sets. He was immensely talented and had a thing for old-school sci-fi and Tom Waits albums.

These two men, Keaton and Joe, would become the polar archetypes for my future relationships: the pragmatic partner and the dreamer-artist.

But by mid-June, Keaton and I were enthralled. Everyone else seemed to disappear into the backdrop.

I went to Brian and Shari's house that week to let them know about my new relationship. I was lovestruck as I sat on their patio, soaking up morning light in my flowered sundress. Brian was wholly unsupportive. He recounted the numerous other people who I'd seemed to be connected with and with whom I was enthralled. He thought Keaton was the flavor of the week, an infatuation. Again, I didn't fully feel the mutual exclusivity of these many affections, though I had intent toward a monogamous relationship with Keaton. Shari stopped him.

"Brian. You're not saying she *can't* date him, are you? You realize you can't tell her that," she said with a look. He relented. They both gave me big hugs and wished us the best.

Adult Life... Lite

I stayed on staff at the church as a worship leader for a few months after I finished the program, but I was beginning to become unraveled. I was burnt out. I felt a magnetic pull off of the stage after so many years in the spotlight.

One weekend, I overslept on a Sunday morning, right through rehearsal, and scarcely made it to the church in time for sound check before the service began. The administrators were mortified. That had never happened, they insisted. This was the last straw — and my unsanctioned nose piercing, or as one conservative pastor called it with a grimace, "adornment," had probably pushed me most of the way out, anyway.

Diane, the service coordinator informed me that I was being offered a two month break from leading worship. I agreed that it was a good idea.

During this time, however, I notified them by email that I would not be returning. I was cooked. I had little left to give and I felt jaded by my experience within the church machine. It was painful to leave the team, to whom I had given so much for two years, especially without any recognition or appreciation. I thought perhaps I would take a year to work and then head south to pursue some WOOFer farm experience in Central America. I saw harmony with Keaton's path, and this felt significant to me.

With college over, I also no longer had a place to live. I needed to find a job, a roommate, a house. A start.

A friend put me up in her family's loft above their garage, and I alternated between the loft and camping trips outside of town with Keaton. Soon I roped a longtime friend of mine, Allie, into renting a little ranch style house with me. The house had a big kitchen, two living rooms, a decent yard and an out of commission hot tub in the back. Over the course of the year, we had between two and five women living in our four bedroom house. Allie and I were at the heart of the home, and developed a hilarious and deep friendship. I remember Mod-Podging empty wine bottles, hosting clothing exchanges, and binge watching *The Office* and *Friends* on DVD on the weekends.

I had been working as the manager of the church's newly established non-profit café after Brian had a small stipend approved for me from the main church. During my internship, I spent months researching fair trade ingredient sourcing, working on our branding and building spreadsheets of cost breakdown per menu item.

Unfortunately, funding was cut drastically for my position only a few months after I graduated. I was upset at the news, and I wasn't sure what to do next.

The Land of Oz

That afternoon, I drove to the next town over, a sleepy little historic town. On land originally stewarded by the Kalapuya People, the city of Aurora was founded a century ago by a Christian commune, but wound up inhabited mainly by woo-woo hippie families with big gardens and long hair. There was a bakery my friends had been raving about and it seemed like the kind of shitty day when you ought to eat a great cupcake at a new bakery. Naturally for the hippie town motif, the spot specialized in gluten free and vegan confections.

I pulled up and saw an attractive Hispanic man through the window. He was flipping the sign from "Open" to "Closed." We made eye contact. I climbed out of the car anyway and peeked my head through the door.

"Hi. Looks like you're all closed up for the day?" I asked.

He looked up from the counter. He was the kind of effortlessly lovely that stops you in your tracks.

"Ah! Yeah. Well, you know what? I'm ahead of schedule, come on in and have a look."

I requested a cupcake and a bag of the granola I'd been hearing so much about.

"How's the day been treatin' ya?" he asked casually as he rang up my order. And I was in no mood to bullshit, so I told him the truth. I explained how I'd just been informed the café I was running was closing and I wasn't sure what to do next. He sympathized. We chit chatted about coffee and the food service industry.

As he spoke, I noticed his subtle Spanish accent and his effortless style. He had on a hat and cuffed Levis and tattoos peeking out from his sleeves. Bob Dylan was playing on the speakers. The bakery had a Victorian psychedelic vibe — it was very Alice in Wonderland. I asked him if he owned the shop.

"I do! Yeah. Well, my wife Emily and I."

Damn, married.

I thanked him for the goods and said I'd return another time.

"I'm Becca, by the way," I said.

"Oscar. I go by Oz. Good to meet you, Becca. See you around."

The bakery became one of my favorite local haunts and the spot I'd bring friends from out of town. I was intimidated by the tall, waif-like redhead in the back. She was beautiful and thinner than I'd ever expect someone with her baking skill set to be. She was kind yet reserved, and I felt guilty for eyeing her husband the first time we met.

Eventually, we all became good friends. I'd stand in the doorway of the baking room and chit chat with them while they kneaded dough and piped icing. They were high school sweethearts. Oscar grew up in Mexico and Emily's family lived here. They had a little boy, age two, who I thought was the luckiest kid in the world to have these two beautiful souls as parents. He must have done something really good in a past life. Now he has two little siblings and their family is almost unbearably lovely. To this day, they're truly some of the best people I've ever known.

Still Adulting

I soon found a job at a new little café that was opening in the center of town. I was to be lead barista, training new team members on espresso best practices. When the owners lamented the female-only staff and whined that they needed more men on the team, I offered up that I knew someone. I got Keaton an interview and told him to smile and not cross his arms. They hired him on the spot, so he quit his retail job at Columbia Sportswear and joined the team.

We worked well together. Before long, I was promoted to shift supervisor and he was promoted to general manager. We saw each other all the time: at work, in our free time, on both the weekdays and the weekends. We spent as much of our free time as possible at each other's homes. We couldn't get enough.

Side Note: I wasn't familiar then with the concept of codependency, but looking back this is what we were heading toward.

And yet, we had agreed early on in our relationship to hold the strict boundary of not having sex.

"I don't want to treat you like a toy. You're not my toy," Keaton said one day.

We also never slept over at each other's houses. We'd taken a couple camping trips early on in our relationship, but those had all been uneventfully PG. It had been over two years since I'd had sex, and in some ways I felt starved for connection. I'd always been a highly sexual being, and there were moments during the internship when I feared I was shutting down a large part of myself to abide by the church's standards for sexual conduct.

A few months into our relationship, I began to wonder how long I could tolerate making out in my bedroom without pushing for something more to happen. But our resolve was clear (his more than mine), so I kept my sexuality to myself. This relationship felt different to me than past ones, and I took it seriously — we were dating with the intent to remain together long-term, and given our roots in the church, we wanted to honor God and start our relationship on the right foot. There was a certain dogma within the Christian belief system that God would not bless your ministry or your life if there was any sin hiding in the shadows. If we wanted to be missionaries, there would be no ungodly, enjoyable fornicating for us.

Farm Days

There was a multi-generational family at our church that seemed to make up half of the congregation. Everyone was somehow related to them. The oldest brother, now grown, managed his father's construction company and owned a gorgeous 5-acre farm on the edge of town. A friend and I agreed to go in on a farm membership. This was like a work-trade CSA (community supported agriculture) membership. Work parties were held once a month and members were required to participate. In exchange, members had access to you-pick produce all season long. It was a great model. On their farm I learned how to plant tomatoes, how to trellis beans, and how to know when watermelons are ready for harvest.

Until that time, I'd only worked in my mom's flower beds, pulling weeds and hoping that none of the plants I was yanking out were actually meant to be there.

At the farm, I also participated in multiple meat-packing days, which took place a week after slaughter, once the animals had cold-cured in a massive cooler down the road. The culture of mutual support between farmers in the area impressed me. It reminded me of a simpler time in history. These meat packing days were the most intimate I've ever come to knowing the animals that feed me.

Processing days always took place in the fall, and we kept our bundled up bodies nimble by hopping in place in the assembly line within the high-ceilinged garage. The patriarchs sliced cuts of meat with a saws-all and passed them our way to be wrapped, double wrapped, labeled, and chilled. We brined slabs of bacon with brown sugar, salt and pepper, where they would sit for several days before curing and smoking.

I began to think deeply about where our food came from, and why I was buying food at the store which had traveled from other countries to reach my humble kitchen.

Voices of Dissent

That same fall after ID, a friend organized a debate which was held in the main sanctuary of the church. Each side had two speakers. The debate was advertised all over town and well attended. The question: "Is There A God?" seemed simple enough. The stage was flanked by four people: On the right, a staff pastor with a doctorate who taught at my college alongside another instructor, a former atheist who now taught a course called Science And The Bible.

On the left were two atheists — one a lifelong nonbeliever and the other a philosopher and former pastor who had left the faith and become staunchly anti-religion.

As the night progressed, I remember thinking that I could have done a better job answering some of the challenges posed by the atheists. I felt I could get behind the logic of the atheists, and I wanted more satisfying answers than the appealing yet circular reasoning presented by the Christians.

It was a memorable night for me. I recall feeling sorry for the main debater on the atheists' side. Not because I thought he was wrong or foolish — his arguments compelled me — but because as I watched him standing among my church members after the event, witnessing their too big smiles and smug demeanor, I could practically smell their self-congratulatory attitudes.

The man had also worn a wrinkled t-shirt with an image of a giraffe on it, whereas most of the church members were well-coiffed and sophisticated in their accessorized ensembles. He didn't give a fuck. He also didn't seem concerned with convincing anyone. He was sharing the logic that had led him away from blind faith. It was as if the church believed they had won a fight which they had rigged and set up on their own turf. No one had proven anything. But in my view, as uncomfortable as it made me, the atheist side had posed far more thought-provoking questions than the Christians.

I recall the irony that I felt more understood by the nonbelievers. I felt they were being real. Not concerned with flashy appearances or tidy pat answers. They were intellectually honest. They weren't pretending to have everything sorted, but they were straightforward in why they believed what they did, and had the courage to discard that which didn't add up.

I couldn't help but imagine an alternate scenario: a debate hosted in a secular auditorium, where the pastors were the only believers in the room, and how comical and foolish some of their arguments would seem to me if removed from this comfort zone, and the supportive audience nodding within the church walls.

I set the thoughts aside.

Heathen Friends

One day I was buying groceries at the local Thriftway. The cashier, a petite, fine boned redhead about my age, perked up when she saw me in line.

"Oh, hey!" The adorable indie cashier said, straight to me.

"Hey!" I leaned in. "...Do we know each other?"

"Yeah... we met at the show the other night," she replied.

I looked on blankly.

"That WAS you, right...?" she trailed off, looking comically embarrassed. I noticed a black uterus tattoo on the inside of her wrist as she entered produce codes into the computer.

"Nope, I haven't been to a show in a while. But this is me!" I made a sweeping motion with my arms.

"Oh my God. Well you have a doppelgänger who likes to hang out at the Crystal," she said.

And that was the easiest friendship I have ever made. Her name was Margaret. I was totally enchanted.

I made a point to go through her checkout line whenever she was working, and after a few weeks, I finally asked her what time she took her lunch break, and would she like some company?

We sat outside the grocery store, discussing life and religion and what the hell people as rad as us were doing in this small, white, conservative town. She shrugged. She was bound for Los Angeles to finish her design degree, so she didn't have the urge to escape quite the way I did.

Margaret, along with Oscar and Emily, were the first non-Christian friends I'd made in two years. They were my tether to the outside world, a world I'd nearly forgotten existed during my time within the confines of Bible College.

Seedlings of Doubt

I had a great deal of spiritual baggage to unpack after I left the internship.

There was some bottled up feminine rage and repression within me which needed to work itself out. I didn't realize how cleverly I had avoided reflecting on my experience at ID during those early months on the outside.

Sure, I'd occasionally joke with Keaton about some crazy rule or quote a common Christian platitude in jest, but for the most part I kept my back turned on the highs and lows of the most emotionally and spiritually intense season of my life.

One spring afternoon, I took Margaret (who had been raised Catholic) to the bakery for lunch. As we sat there, I shared with her my recent decision to take a break from church. She listened intently as I opened up about my experience with the internship and subsequent leadership roles, and I told her that I could feel something shifting.

Inside, I envisioned I was moving toward a more radical, less church-heavy form of my faith. A little less Mars Hill and a little more Shane Claiborne. How she heard it was simply that I was leaving the church.

"Wow. Becca," she leaned over and hugged me. "I'm so glad to hear you say this. All this time, there's just been something that... didn't add up. I kept looking at you and thinking, 'She's too bright to be religious.' You're going to have such a great life. There's so much at your fingertips!"

We smiled. I chose not to correct her assumption. It was tempting to entertain the thought. An image flashed across my mind of a dense, lush fruit garden in which I was free to eat anything I pleased.

Family Ties

The year after ID was mostly uneventful as I juggled keeping a job, paying bills, and sorting out how involved I wanted to be, or not be, in the church.

I was more or less out of touch with my family — my siblings and I never spoke, and I only saw them in person on holidays. My dad had fallen out of touch; I hadn't seen him since before I finished ID.

Keaton began inviting me to weeknight dinners with his family. I adored them. They welcomed me instantly. In some ways, it felt similar to how Chelsea's family had taken me in during my youth and the Maxwells had done so again during college. These were wholesome, lovely families that made me feel like I belonged.

But Keaton's family was a different breed: they were Christians, but also Democrats. They liked Pink Martini and NPR and supported a woman's right to choose. Mark was a middle school principal and a cross country coach. He was soft spoken and pragmatic, a thoughtful and reasonable man who listened more than he spoke. Kari was a registered nurse. She was a congenial firecracker with a strong mama-bear vibe, as sensitive as she was sincere. Like me, she was a Scorpio and we resonated on a deep level due to our similarly passionate personalities.

I had a sense that I was a welcome addition to the family. Keaton, the middle of three sons, was the first to bring home a serious girlfriend. Kari loved having another gal around. She'd stop by the café on her way to work and get her morning lattes from us — she always raved that we made the best espresso in town. *(Which, of course, we did.)* Sometimes, Mark would stop by after his early morning run to pick up Kari's latte and a hot chocolate for himself.

We had weekly family nights and alternated between playing board games and watching Blazer Games or reality TV. I came to look forward to these times and began to imagine that these people would become my lifelong family.

Inside The Bakery

One evening, I stopped by Emily and Oscar's bakery for a scone on my way home from a friend's. Oz was closing up shop and the place was emptying out. We chit chatted like usual.

"Have you ever made focaccia?" he asked.

"No, I haven't. I've eaten my fair share, though," I chuckled.

"What are you up to right now? I'm just starting a batch," he said.

I grabbed an apron and washed my hands. What I felt first was hesitation. My church-conditioned psyche defaulted to suspicion: was it highly inappropriate for me to be there, after hours, baking with a married man who I found foxy? I'd had red flags go up every time I was alone with a man for two years straight, feeling on the verge of being caught by internship leaders. These days, the only man I was ever alone with was Keaton, my boyfriend.

And then it occurred to me, I actually trusted myself. I trusted Oz. There was clean and clear energy between us. There was inherently *nothing wrong* about what was happening: two friends baking some bread. And that's exactly what we did. I went home with a fluffy tray of focaccia and a renewed sense of connection to the nuanced world beyond the church walls. There was never so much as a questionable glance or suggestive comment, though we had some good laughs and a hearty hug on my way out.

That winter, it started feeling like Keaton and I were sharing an excessive amount of time together, so I decided to look for a new job. I mentioned it to Oscar and Emily, and they hired me on the spot to be their new counter girl.

I thrived with Emily, Oscar and Lenka, a crushworthy, no nonsense woman from the Czech Republic. This gorgeous, towering creature smoked like a chimney and had bright blonde hair and legs to write home about. She called me Becky through her thick accent, which I wouldn't have tolerated from anyone else, but I secretly liked it. And also, I didn't have the guts to correct her.

A lot of our time in the bake shop was spent philosophizing and sharing stories and witty banter. One day I had barely clocked in when Oz said, "Hey Becca. You're a Christian hipster, right?" I scoffed but relented. This prompted an hour long discussion about religion and church culture. I was fascinated. Oz had gone to Catholic school in Mexico. Emily had been raised Lutheran, but her mother was now much more new agey. Emily talked half seriously about the law of attraction and how she was experimenting using it to try to win a car. We all laughed.

"I don't get why it has to be so complicated," she said. "People add all these rules to something that's pretty simple. I know how to be a good person. Why can't I just do that? Why can't we all just be good? Sometimes, people ask me if I know God... I feel like I do."

I nodded. I was intrigued. I'd never heard a post-Christian person share their feelings with me. She continued.

ADULTING

"But of course, what they actually mean is, 'Do you have Jesus living inside your heart?' Why do they have to take it there? It's creepy," she insisted.

I laughed. I could relate, although I sympathized with her dreaded evangelizers, too.

The conversation further watered the seeds of doubt that had been trying to sprout and grow inside me for most of my life.

In the following weeks I thought of Margaret. I thought of Emily and Oz. These were lovely, caring people. They lived good lives. They were honest and hard working, loving parents and loyal friends. The community loved them. They did good by the folks around them. The fruit of their lives was vibrant. So, what good would Jesus do them? Was there anything real for them in faith beyond dogma and the approval of Christian folks?

I realized that, simply put, they were better people than many of the repressed, hypocritical people I knew at the church. I can't begin to list the number of bigoted, misogynistic men and catty, backbiting women I've met over the years who know the Word of God in and out yet didn't understand basic human decency. These are people I would never aspire to be like.

I didn't know how to reckon with this simple reality. If faith didn't make you good, that threw the whole system into question. God was bigger than Christianity. God was bigger than religion itself. God was everywhere, available to everyone. My churchless friends were in touch with the divine — in nature, in people, in art. They just didn't feel the need to tell stories about it or convince anyone else of anything. They were free.

I wanted to be more like that. I wanted to be free.

Falling Out

My roommate Allie and I had become more and more enmeshed as the year went on. I had many friends in town and a more active social life, but we had our home routines in place and loved spending time together. Simultaneously, Keaton and I grew more serious and had expressed intent to marry. I wasn't all that interested in other relationships; my friendships fell by the wayside.

One evening, Allie came home from work to find Keaton and I chatting and cooking dinner. She stormed in, keys still in hand.

"I think you guys spend way too much time together," she announced. She was visibly upset. We looked up, surprised.

"Allie. Hey. Umm… What do you mean?" I asked.

"Well!" she huffed. "It feels like every time I come home, you're here Keaton… no offense." She looked at me. "And we never have time to hang out anymore," she added.

I stared on, startled. And defensive.

"Well, Allie. We're in a serious relationship. I don't know what you want me to tell you."

"Good to know where your priorities are. I'll just go, then," she said. And with that she turned on her heel and walked right back out the door.

I rolled my eyes dismissively and got back to cooking. I didn't reach out or follow up with her. This was years before I was exposed to Non-Violent Communication (NVC) skills, a discipline which teaches how to effectively communicate and move through conflict with personal responsibility and openness.

I confided this messy situation to Shari, Brian's wife. I asked her if I could move into their basement apartment. In true form, my desired solution was to leave. She and Brian talked it over. They said it would need to wait a couple of months until their current tenant was out. For now, she encouraged me to just ride it out.

Eventually, I swallowed my pride and apologized to Allie sufficiently enough to repair the friendship for the time being. But internally, I was more or less checked out of the friendship.

A Ring On It

I'd gone into an antique jewelry shop with Keaton that winter to peruse. I can't recall when we decided we wanted to get married, but by January we knew this was our intent. I had actually visited the shop alone before picking him up from class at PSU and tried on one ring that inspired me — a 1940s engagement ring with stones forming a flower. It was a pearly moonstone dome surrounded by six petal-like diamonds. It fit me.

Not surprisingly, it still fit when I tried it on with Keaton an hour later. After that day we didn't talk about engagement again. We both knew his parents wanted him to finish his degree before tying the knot, and he still had a couple years to go on his Latin American studies major.

On a cloudy spring day in early April, Keaton and I had plans to go on a date after work. He was running late, something that rarely happened. I sat tinkering on our piano, and a thought occurred to me. I picked up my phone and called Allie. I reached her voicemail.

"I have a feeling Keaton's going to propose today," I announced. "You heard it here first."

A knock on the door. I hung up.

Keaton stood on the porch smiling.

"Ready?" he asked, barely greeting me.

"Yeah. What do you want to do? Will I need a warmer coat?" I asked.

"You'll see," he said.

He drove us to the boat dock at Willamette Park, a state park nestled beside the river. I looked around. He took my hand and led me down toward the ramp.

"Hop in!" he said. He was standing beside a little green rowboat.

"This is yours? What?!" I grinned. "We're going on the river?"

"Yep!" he answered.

Once on the water, Keaton was fully immersed in the act of rowing. I tried to make conversation and behave as one does while on a romantic date on the river, I really channeled my best Rachel McAdams, but he wasn't having it. That man was focused.

As we rounded the bend, I saw a dock upstream. I recognized the park — it was the place we'd had our first kiss the previous summer under a big oak tree. I looked more closely at the dock. He'd fashioned a canopy out of tree branches and lace drapes. There was a table set for two with steaming dishes placed on top.

Keaton tied the boat and we climbed out onto the dock. I raved about how beautiful it was and took in the scene. He reached out for my hands.

Oh my gosh. It's happening, I thought to myself. *This is that moment I'm always going to look back on.*

"Becca, I've known you for a couple years now, and I've loved you for nine months. You're as strong as you are beautiful. I'm a better person because of you. I want to spend my whole life with you. Will you marry me?"

I barely took a moment to think. "Yes!" I answered through clouded eyes. We hugged. We laughed. We cried. The whole experience was a surreal blur.

Up the road I saw two people emerge from the bushes. It was Mark and Kari! They came running down the road.

"Oh, yes! You did it!" They exclaimed as they approached. We all embraced, laughing and squealing and they welcomed me into the family. We had a good laugh at all the shenanigans they'd got into trying to prep for the evening. (I'd not yet noticed that the steaming dishes were fresh fajitas, our favorite meal.) Keaton had worked on the boat for a month, and a mutual friend nearly spoiled the surprise weeks earlier when he had asked Keaton right in front of me, "How's the boat coming along?" Thankfully, I was extra absent minded that day, because the comment flew right over my head.

We agreed to wait to set a date for the wedding. Perhaps we'd have a long engagement and Keaton would have time to finish his degree.

… A week later, we had settled on a date for that coming August.

It's unbelievable to me now that we moved so fast toward marriage — something which is designed to be legal, binding, and permanent. I was 20 years old; my brain was not fully developed. I couldn't legally drink, but I was allowed to be a wife.

Interestingly, my parents finalized their drawn-out divorce on April 6th, 2011. I got engaged on April 7th, 2011, a fact I only discovered when I interviewed my mom for this book.

Permission To Marry

In true respect for tradition, Keaton had gone to each of my parents and asked for permission to propose to me. He had met my mom once before, the summer we started dating, and he had never met my dad. He met up with my mom at the new Starbucks that had just been built in St. Helens. She was in enthusiastic support.

On a separate day, Keaton asked my dad to choose the meeting place. My dad took them to McDonalds. Keaton, not keen on eating food from McDonalds, ordered a salad. My dad laughed at him good-naturedly.

I was mortified when I imagined the scene. Keaton asked for my hand in marriage while my dad ate a Big Mac. He agreed wholeheartedly, hugged him, then stood up to refill his soda. Some moments, I feel like my life is a parody sketch. Perhaps that bewilderment is where my ability to find humor in everything comes from.

I was on the fast track to wifehood.

ADULTING

9
Marriage

A Place Of Our Own

A few months after getting engaged, I parted ways with Allie and moved into Brian and Shari's basement. It was early in the summer of 2011, and Keaton and I were wading knee-deep through DIY wedding planning.

The apartment was 400 square feet and had just one tiny window in the bedroom. I didn't mind; we were inseparable. *How much space would we really need?*

The plan was for Keaton to move in with me after the wedding. The main stipulation? No sex in the house beforehand. We agreed. I'd been gradually pushing the limits between us, but Keaton was committed to his boundaries and held a hard line.

On moving day, Margaret, the artsy cashier, volunteered to help me move in. She arrived early in her mom's pick-up truck. Later, she bought us Thai food and made us a makeshift dining table with moving boxes.

I was surprised again at my new friends' willingness to show up for me in practical, meaningful ways, an expression of love that I was growing to appreciate as I entered adulthood. It was the kind of love my dad had extended throughout my life — the kind I had underestimated as a young person — it was made up of more actions than words.

As I settled in, I lined the cabinets with my kitchen gadgets and cookbooks, hung up tapestries and quirky thrift store art on the walls, and resolved to make this new little space a warm and welcoming home.

Families Converge

My family and Keaton's didn't actually meet until he and I were engaged.

Looking back, I was never that close with my immediate family members. It makes more sense in retrospect; as a young child I had armored myself against intimacy, and the relationships closest to me were where I experienced the most hurt and betrayal, so I distanced myself from them.

Kara, my little sister, was my closest friend when we were small but we had grown apart over the years.

Krista, my oldest sister, was more like an aunt. She was my camp counselor and brought us to visit her college campus. She and my brother David babysat us when we were little, and soon they were teens in a foreign teenage world while we were content to draw pictures and ride bikes. I was often scared of my brother — his emotional volatility intimidated me. He could be funny and charming one minute, and irate the next. One day he screamed at me for putting his shirts in the dryer, as though my nine-year-old self should have known that screen printed textiles required air drying.

Shana, the middle child, was often antagonistic toward me and as I grew older, I felt that she saw me as a threat. She would call me a freak or say I looked chubby, even though I wasn't. She even insisted that I was adopted. We looked similar, both had interest in music and art, and liked the same kinds of boys. She'd instigate bullying with our brother David, picking on Kara and I, looking for ways to humiliate us.

Once, she and David lured me into her bedroom and pulled my pants down in front of all their friends, just to laugh and point at me. I was only six. I do appreciate that as a teen, she had my back when I needed to talk about sex or drugs, but I rarely confided in her out of fear that due to the power struggle, she may betray my confidence and snitch on me to our mom.

Still, I always admired my siblings, and at times wanted to be closer to them, but I relied much more on my friendships for companionship. I trusted my friends far more than my family members. And I wasn't the only one who operated this way; the tone in our house felt more like a group of roommates coexisting together than a mutually supportive family. It was not a nurturing space to exist; we were fragmented from each other and armored in our own ways.

Shana lived out of town and my brother David had been incarcerated earlier that year. Keaton had come with my family and I to my brother's sentencing, which happened just before my parents' divorce proceedings. It wrecked us emotionally. I can't erase the image of David walking in wearing an orange jumpsuit with handcuffs around his wrists. He looked so small standing before the elevated judge's seat, and he never once looked our way as the judge spoke. Felony conviction. Three years. After the sentencing we all filed outside and hugged without saying much, and then turned to leave separately. That was the Martinez way: repression as a way of coping. Alone while together.

Given all this history, I didn't invite my siblings to join us for dinner with my new in-laws.

The six of us met at a dimly lit McMenamins pub for dinner. My mom, upon meeting Keaton's mom Kari, remarked,

"Ah! You're so beautiful!" to which Kari understandably stumbled over her words.

As a side note, what if we collectively moved on from commenting on one another's physical appearances as a form of bonding?

My dad arrived separately in a shiny black Jaguar he'd just bought. He wore a bright Hawaiian print shirt. My mom scoffed. I gave her a look to imply that I was not available for comments about him or the car. My parents sat at opposite ends of the table. Everyone got on well enough; Keaton's family was a delight and I was just relieved to have the introductions over with.

Once the family meeting was accomplished, the months of planning were not particularly stressful. We wanted a simple wedding with a large wedding party. For us, it was all about the people. I knew who I wanted for bridesmaids. Tori, the drummer from my childhood, had been one of my hometown best friends since age three. Tasha was my closest friend at the end of high school. She had been with me that weekend at Sunriver after graduation. Hannah was my close college friend and mentor, Logan was like a little sister to me, and Krista was my oldest sister. I didn't ask my other two sisters. Kara volunteered to be the flower girl, and I agreed. Shana would sit with Mom during the ceremony.

For his groomsmen, Keaton chose his two brothers, who became like brothers to me, and a couple of his best friends and bandmates from school. We felt celebrated and supported.

He and I

The dynamic between Keaton and I was the same as it had always been — we were pals, best of friends.

We were doing normal life together — playing music, cooking meals, watching movies while cuddled up on the couch. Our relationship was still so young — we'd only begun dating a year before our wedding. I felt at ease with him, like we were family, but a kinder, safer sort of family. I didn't have to show up in a certain way in front of him; I didn't have to guard myself from antagonism with sarcasm and wit and defensiveness. I was welcome to simply be myself. His sensitivity and gentleness complimented my passion and drive, and together we formed a great team.

I have to admit, I also had moments when I felt unsure if this was how getting married was supposed to feel. There was an underlying sense of going through the motions. I think in many ways, I was.

Early on in the relationship, when I confided in Shari that I still sometimes felt conflicted between Keaton and Joe, she asked me what I saw down the line with each. With Keaton, I truly believed he would love God until the day he died. She nodded knowingly. That was the devotion I was looking for.

And yet, something about this relationship fell flat.

It lacked electricity, it lacked the kind of generative energy that multiplies on itself. I saw the thrill when my friends were planning their weddings. But with us, there was no sexual tension. I assumed he was holding back sexually because of his Christian faith. I was full of desire, but it felt like a one way stream. I reasoned that, as a virgin, he probably didn't know yet what he was missing. It scarcely occurred to me that this lack of heat would continue after we were allowed to have sex.

My tunnel vision was also a factor.

When I wanted something, it was impossible to deter me. I was decisive to a fault, highly unlikely to reconsider once I'd taken a stance. At this time in my life, I had a strong reactionary thread — a part of me was acting out of unrecognized behavior loops in order to feel safe in the world. The end of college felt very much like the end of high school. I was free falling into the unknown, and I feared my own wildness would take over unless I tamped it down, silenced it and tethered it to something tame. First, the tame thing had been Bible College. This time, it was Keaton.

Keaton was the most tame, safe and steady man I knew. On some level, my inner mania was clinging to him in hopes he could save me from my fractured self, that we could move forward and create a life together in which I could abandon my wild history yet again and live within the container of our wholesome, bright domestic little world.

MARRIAGE

Even after several sessions of pre-marriage counseling, we didn't yet see the red flags of my domineering forcefulness and his passivity.

I DO

Our wedding was adorably whimsical. It was more of a darling picnic in the woods than a formal event.

We gathered on August 7, 2011 at a scenic state park beside a meandering river. Everyone came. Between Keaton and myself, there were four church communities represented. We needed to accommodate 300 people, many of them rambunctious teens from the multiple youth groups we helped staff.

This was 2011 when Pinterest boards ruled the minds of suburban women everywhere. So naturally we had the ultimate DIY wedding.

I found a vintage dress on Etsy.com and had a seamstress from the church update it for me. She redid the skirt with a buttoned train and added deep hidden pockets, where I could keep a LaraBar for a post-ceremony blood sugar boost. Keaton and his groomsmen wore white button-ups with rolled sleeves, Levi's jeans with suspenders, and trendy leather shoes.

We thrifted 1970s floral pastel fabrics for the Polaroid photo booth and handmade fabric garlands. Brown glass bottles held wildflowers and foliage from local farms. Our friends and family helped with everything: set up, officiating, emceeing, sound, food prep, baking, décor. Katrina, the ID assistant, was our wedding coordinator. My parents even split the bill, which we kept minimal but greatly appreciated.

I asked Margaret to design our wedding invitations. The folk-art dandelion she drew for us is now tattooed twice as large on my forearm. Emily and Oz baked our cake, a lemon poppy seed cake with raspberries. It was truly a community event. Keaton's prior bandmates, four women, had formed a new indie folk band. At our reception, they played a sweet, hand-clappy rendition of "What I Wouldn't Do" by A Fine Frenzy, complete with three-part harmony. The song still gets me choked up; it reminds me of being young, naïve, and innocent in love.

When the ceremony was about to begin, Katrina, clipboard in hand, lined us up in pairs. I looped my arm around my dad's. He was subdued, chewing on a toothpick. I examined him.

"Dad. Take your sunglasses off! I'm about to get married!" I insisted.

"Oh. Okay," he said, smiling, and slid them into his pocket.

"The toothpick, too," I added.

"Right," he said.

"Geez," I said, with a teasing jab to his side. We both chuckled.

This is it, I thought to myself as I scanned the backs of the 300 people who had come to support us. *The start of the rest of my life.*

I held my emotions at bay until we reached the aisle. Keaton had recorded and produced the whole procession song, a beautiful layered instrumental that could have been written by Jose Gonzales. The song shifted in perfect timing when I was to enter. It slowed from cute and folksy to spacious and evocative, his expertly crafted melodic guitar drifting on the late summer breeze. My mother stood. Then 300 people stood and turned to face my dad and I.

I felt intensely loved and intensely seen. My eyes landed on Keaton, who was positively beaming at me, holding back his own tears. I grinned, my lip quivering. My vision was blurry when I arrived up front.

"Who gives this woman to be married to this man?" Brian asked.

"Her mother and I," my dad answered. I hugged him and turned to Keaton.

During the ceremony, Brian spoke for a few moments. I remember very little, though brief moments are as clear as still water. Brian said, "When I look at Becca, I see passion. When I look at Keaton, I see contemplation. You two are quite a match." The rest of the ceremony was brief, on purpose. I remember just one line from my vows: "I promise to keep our love sincere and exciting." I think I delivered on that promise.

Keaton and I laughed and grinned and kissed after we led the procession out of the field and toward the pavilion.

Alone for a moment in the adjacent cabin, we started to kiss. My hands wandered.

I fantasized about making love right then and there before the reception. Nothing complicated: just me tossing my expensive chiffon skirt over my waist and bending over for a quickie to seal the deal, with no one but the woodland trees watching from the window. Perhaps this sounds irreverent, and I'd agree that it is. But I was three years celibate, now finally married, and a highly sexual being to boot.

Keaton wasn't having any of it. *Ah well, worth a shot,* I thought. On some level, I took this as confirmation of something I feared: that marriage

MARRIAGE

wouldn't magically transform my partner into a more sexually aggressive version of himself. He was who he was. I would continue to be the initiator and the boundary pusher.

Rather than having a quick romp, we waited quietly for Katrina to announce the new bride and groom, and when she did we emerged, grinning.

The reception was sweet and traditional, if our own, somewhat ironic flavor of those traditions. We cut the cake. We threw the bouquet and garter. We had the father/daughter and mother/son dances. It was a tender moment, though slightly awkward as neither my dad or I were dancers. *I wish I would have taken this moment in, expressed my love and appreciation for him more. I wish I would have known that would be the last time I would see my dad for six years.*

Later, we exited through a procession of friends and family who blew bubbles instead of throwing rice, then we hopped into our Subaru, which was already loaded with bikes and bags. I watched our festive audience shrink in the rearview mirror and with that, we headed East toward Sunriver.

Honeymoon

On our honeymoon, I felt virginal in many ways.

I hadn't had sex in three years. I felt nervous, placing pressure on myself to make sure it went well. It was a wild sensation to be beside the person I intended to spend the rest of my life with, yet not even know what he looked like naked.

We spent our first night at a bougie hotel in Portland. The first thing we did? Order a room service pizza; we'd been experimenting with a vegan and raw diet for most of the year and in celebration, threw it all out the window.

After indulging in pizza, we slipped into our bathing suits to enjoy the Jacuzzi tub. It was nice to be sensual together, but it was clear we were both on edge. I remember Keaton remarking that he'd never seen me in a bikini. Meanwhile, my mind was wandering to the lingerie outfits buried in my bag; gifts from my girlfriends who had spoiled me with dozens of outfits as part of a lingerie bridal shower.

Neither Keaton nor myself seemed sure how the natural flow of the evening should go, and given the pressure of our first time together, whatever natural chemistry we usually had simply evaporated.

During our engagement, we had read a couple of painfully narrow-minded Christian books about sex within marriage, one called *Sheet Music* (cheesy,

I know). It had one chapter that was strictly intended to be read after the wedding, presumably because it was so explicit it would probably just lead these poor Christian kids straight down the road to premarital humping.

It's a marvel, the great lengths these religious institutions take in an attempt to control the sexual behavior of their parishioners. In any case, these books reinforced harmful gender roles and stereotypes and interestingly, also made it very clear that anal sex was a hard no. That raised my eyebrow. Even then, I wondered who these repressed writers were, why I was reading their books, and why they were so adamantly against innocent ass play.

When we finally did have sex, I experienced a lot of discomfort. I hadn't allowed enough time to prepare and I felt a shooting pain in my cervix as it went on. I asked Keaton to stop and we'd try again later. He was understanding. We ate a Kit Kat from the snack bar and went to bed, cuddling. I lay awake as he drifted off, shedding tears over the disappointment of a "failed" wedding night.

The rest of our honeymoon went better, thanks to a fair deal of wine and vodka. We explored with each other and had a fair amount of cautious sex. I never orgasmed. In the back of my mind, I carried a hint of guilt over being the more experienced one, never wanting to give pointers or make suggestions that would highlight my past with other partners.

Fortunately, my sexual past was never an issue for Keaton; it was something we laughed about at times, but he held no judgment or criticism toward me.

While he would sit out on the porch playing his guitar, I'd lounge around scantily clad reading the Christian sex books. In my mind, a honeymoon (or any great vacation) should be comprised primarily of great sex, punctuated only by necessary eating and sleeping.

Married Life

We received a ton of gifts, mostly food appliances, and opened them all when we returned home from Sunriver. I recall very little from our first year together. There was a lot of food. He managed the café. I worked at the bakery. I used all my new kitchen gadgets to keep my housewife game strong. I was obsessed with nutrition and baking, so sometimes I'd spend weeks perfecting French macarons and other times I was making huge batches of green juice tonics and fire cider.

Once while I was in the kitchen stirring a pot of caramel, Keaton remarked that he liked watching me cook. I asked why. He answered that whenever I stirred the pot, my ass wiggled. I felt so objectified! I rolled my eyes at him and told him to knock it off. Secretly though, I loved it.

Before we married, I had imagined us having sex all over the house. I wanted to defile the place. Whenever, wherever the mood struck. The problem is, the mood rarely struck. This expectation had been based on my past experiences with other people — I could barely turn and walk away without them getting horny. But in our case, I was nearly always the initiator. I figured that if I didn't, Keaton could probably go months without wanting sex. It didn't help that he was very underweight — truly the thinnest man I knew — and at 20 lbs heavier than him, I often felt like a linebacker beside him.

Once on the drive home from a Blazer game, I started rubbing my hand up his leg. It was late. I was frisky, fantasizing about giving him road head on the drive back to town. It was far fetched. He slid my hand away.

"It bothers me when you do that," he said.

"Do what?" I asked.

"When you touch me and we're not in a private setting. It feels like you're doing it just to get a rise out of me," he explained.

I was frustrated in more ways than one.

"Yeah. That's exactly why I'm doing it!" I said and meant it. "We're alone in our car."

"Well, please don't," he replied, looking straight ahead as he drove.

I was silent for a moment, stung.

"Fine, then." I stared out the window the rest of the drive home, embarrassed and wondering if this would be my sex life forever.

Rhythms

Later that year we moved into a bigger apartment the next town over. I'd grown bored of my job at the bakery, but not before farmer Mike, a handsome, long-haired, earthy Black man who Lenka tactlessly referred to as "Brown Jesus," asked me out. He had no idea I was married. We became friends instead.

I began selling vintage clothes at a quirky warehouse on Hawthorne Avenue called House of Vintage. I loved working for myself, whenever I wanted, perusing estate sales and back alley thrift stores for treasures, then selling them to Portland hipsters at a premium.

But that winter, I was depressed. I remember so many evenings Keaton would ask what I wanted to do, and I couldn't come up with an answer. I just wanted to lie around and not leave the house. I'd send him on runs to Dairy Queen up the road. I was disconnected from most of my friends; I'd let many friendships cool down since becoming so enthralled with Keaton during our engagement and wedding. We weren't consistently going to a church. We weren't seeing people. We'd sit around and watch Netflix and read books.

At night, we'd go to bed at the same time and read until we fell asleep. The air between us felt cool and empty, and I grew increasingly afraid to reach out toward him for more than a momentary huge or curt kiss goodnight. I didn't feel I could stand the rejection.

I bought two cats that year. Luna was the first, and six months later, I found a friend for her, Theo, who is now nine and quite furry and neurotic. I took so many unnecessary photos of cats and food in our first year of marriage. I also grew my first garden. I had Mark, Keaton's dad, help me build two raised beds on the side of our apartment building. I planted tomatoes and lettuce. I also began driving across the river several times a week for Bikram Yoga classes and working out again in general, in an effort to bring some life back into myself. I'd try to get Keaton to do the workouts with me, but he was mostly ambivalent.

That year, I also enjoyed playing a few café shows with Keaton. I began to embrace music again after stepping off stage and mostly ignoring it for a couple of years. We played simple singer songwriter covers, but Keaton was a great guitarist and I was a great vocalist, so people ate it up. Once or twice we opened for our friend ISABEAU, who now tours with Y La Bamba and is a role model, activist, and creative force of nature.

Just Fuck Me Like Danny

That March, for Keaton's birthday, I recorded a set of saucy, tasteful black and white photos and a couple of PG-13 video clips for him. It was fun for me to make, as seeing myself on camera was an edge I hadn't played with before. I sent them one by one to his email and marked them "NSFW." Several days later I had to text to specifically ask if he had received them. He responded with only a thumbs up emoji.

Huge fail… a swing and a miss. We spoke about it later that night.

"Hey. Did you not like what I sent you earlier?" I asked him.

"No. I did. But, I just couldn't get past wondering if it was awkward for you to take them," he answered.

"Really? Why… did I look awkward?" I asked, embarrassed.

"Oh! No! Not at all. They're great. I just mean, it's kind of a weird thing to do… taking pictures of yourself all alone," he said.

"Wow. Well… no. I didn't feel awkward. I do now, though." I didn't have the energy to unpack how wildly I disagreed with this attitude about sex. It felt obvious how much of his perception had to do with his own discomfort, but I felt impacted by it because we were in a committed sexual relationship, building a sexual — or not sexual — world together.

At that point, most of my sex life happened alone while he was away at work.

Before long, our first anniversary approached.

I wasn't sure what to do.

Our friends Sara and Danny lived downstairs. (This was a different Danny than the one who had tried to date me after college). They were a charming, edgy couple from church who had been married the year before we were. As the story went, at Keaton's bachelor party, Danny had drunkenly provided this profound marriage advice:

"Just remember to shave your balls, man," he admonished him with a pat on the back.

"What?" Keaton had asked.

"You gotta shave your balls. You want her to lick 'em, don't you?? Just shave 'em… trust me."

One day, I was home alone in the middle of the day sorting through a pile of vintage dresses for work. It was 1:00 pm on a Thursday and Sara and Danny were having loud, rambunctious, very fun-sounding sex downstairs in what I guessed was their living room.

I couldn't stand it; I was so jealous. I mulled it over for weeks. Finally one morning, I sat Keaton down on our couch.

"I want to connect with you more. I'm so unsatisfied with our sex life. I feel like… I'm starving. I want to know what we can do to make it better. Do you want to make it better?" I implored.

He agreed that he did. He felt awful that I was disappointed. It was a sensitive topic for both of us. I had taken this conversation so seriously that I prepared some written and discussion exercises that I'd read about online. I was literally self-facilitating a therapy session for the two of us. We discussed things we liked about our current sex life, fantasies we had that could potentially be realized, generally what we would like more of, and what a satisfying sex life would look like to each of us.

It was a tough conversation to have. I loved and trusted him, but I felt humiliated asking for something so desperately, especially something as intimate as sex. I knew on some level it would feel different knowing he was responding to an explicit, last-ditch request, which felt like me begging, rather than pursuing me out of his own desire. It's like when you tell a partner the words you need to hear from them, and then they repeat it back to you. It doesn't feel the same because it's not coming out organically.

But I was out of options. I would take begging for sex over no sex at all.

Lummi Anniversary

That month I stumbled upon an article in Sunset magazine. It was a write-up about a farm-direct restaurant and lodge in the San Juan Islands that hosted a James Beard Rising Star chef who was only in his twenties, like us. I convinced Keaton to take a food vacation with me for our anniversary.

We booked a weekend at The Willows Inn at Lummi Island.

When we arrived, I was instantly enchanted. Our suite was the nicest place I'd ever stayed — spacious and modern with a huge bed, gorgeous view, luscious linens and a massive tiled shower facing the mirror, the kind that's just asking for sex.

In those years I remember doing numerous bold things that made Keaton uncomfortable. He didn't always like my fashion choices — he thought they were too gutsy. That first night, we went to the most expensive dinner of our life and I wore a thin blouse without a bra (this was less common then) and silk floral ultra wide leg trousers with ankle boots. I liked to take up space when I had the chance, especially on the rare occasion we left the suburbs. We did turn some heads, and not only because at a sophisticated 21 we were the youngest people in the tiny dining room by several decades. I looked damn good and I was unashamed of it.

The dinner itself was one I will never forget. It was 20 micro-courses, a series of bodacious bites. Almost everything on the hyper-local menu was sourced from the gorgeous production gardens, which we had toured that afternoon.

In spite of myself, I'd hoped that maybe the change of scenery would be just the setting to rekindle our flame… or rather, kindle it properly for the first time. After the $300 dinner, we returned to the room rather tipsy and I half expected Keaton to make a move. Liquor usually helped our flow. But he didn't. I no longer had the patience to hint around.

"I'm going to take a shower. Want to come?" I teased.

"It's really late. I think I'm gonna' go to sleep babe," he answered.

"Are you sure? We only have two nights here... we can always sleep in tomorrow," I smiled at him, flirtatious.

"Babe, you saying it that way just feels like pressure," he snapped, not looking up at me.

I sighed and walked away. I showered alone, tending silently to my own desires, and couldn't tell if he was actually asleep when I finally came to bed.

The next day we went on a morning hike and were back at our hotel room by early afternoon. It was the second day of the Summer Olympics. We turned it on. I wandered around the room, restless, feeling irritated that this was how we were spending our anniversary weekend. Repeating the same pattern that seemed etched into the foundation of our relationship.

I climbed into bed. I tried making a move on him three times, nibbling at his neck, running my hand up his shirt, and he'd appease me for a moment, but his brake-pumping made it clear he had no intent on taking things further.

I gave up.

I laid there watching the high divers on the big screen and imagined all the people who would like nothing more than to turn off the damn TV and fuck my brains out right then and there.

• • •

After that weekend, I immersed myself in my own embodiment practices. Sex was an unpredictably rare event. I got serious about Bikram Yoga (this was long before I learned what a predator the founder was) and took classes most evenings after work. I would sometimes meet Kari there and loved having a mother-in-law who was so cool and interested in the same things I was. She simply called me "B". I loved when she would text me and say, "Hey B. See you tonight at yoga?"

That winter I took a new job in Northeast Portland. It was a full time nanny role for a 10-year-old girl with Asperger's named Lisa. The job was extremely challenging and super rewarding.

First off, I realized I didn't like spending time with kids, doing kid stuff. I also learned a ton about Asperger's and the lived experiences of folks who are neuro-divergent. We became quite close, and I was welcomed in as an extension of the family. I was entrusted with taking Lisa on fun outings as well as to occupational and behavioral therapy sessions and the homeschool co-op where she was a student.

Keaton had also gotten a better job. He'd left the café and was working at a non-profit boys' shelter that took care of teens who were picked up on the USA-Mexico border and were awaiting housing placement or legal proceedings. It was great that he finally had a bilingual job where he could use his Spanish.

We learned so much about the immigration system in the USA and had the unfortunate chance to witness the real life stories of some very lovely and very troubled kids from Central America. We heard terrible accounts of the way these kids had been detained and treated while within the system here. These experiences deeply informed the way that we both think of immigration today.

Surprise...?

In December, my period was late. At first I took it as a sign of my changed diet; I had just switched to a strictly paleo diet and thought perhaps it had thrown my systems out of whack. But the weeks kept ticking past, one by one, until I started to get concerned.

We were in the Burgerville drive through, rebelling against the paleo dogma, when I told Keaton.

"My period is three weeks late, babe. I think I might be pregnant," I blurted.

He looked at me. "Are you sure?"

"No. I'm not sure. But I'll go take a test tomorrow."

"I…" he paused. "I don't know what to think about that."

"Me either. We don't have our lives together. What are we going to do if I'm pregnant?"

"We'll figure it out. I'll get a better job or something," he answered.

That night, I laid awake imagining what it would be like to become a mother. Who that child might be and what they would mean in our life. I had vague, hazy dreams of a little brown haired baby. But Keaton and I had always agreed that the Earth was overpopulated and if we were ever to want a child, which we didn't, we would adopt one.

I took a pregnancy test the next day, convinced that our lives were about to change.

The test was negative.

I stared at that piece of plastic. I shook it. No, that couldn't be right. I felt like it was taunting me. Psych! My body seemed to say. Just messing with you. No baby. Go back to your regularly scheduled life.

Much to my surprise, I was crushed. I told Keaton that night, through tears. I hadn't realized that I even wanted to have a baby until I'd believed it was happening by accident. I'd opened myself up to the idea and something inside me felt right, excited, and at peace about it.

Looking back, I think I had found myself in a similar situation to many young married women, especially in the church. I had settled into a life rhythm that in many ways felt isolated and dull. I felt bored. I had lost myself in my marriage. I had done the thing: found "the one" and gotten married, made a home. I wanted whatever was next. I couldn't imagine this rhythm being my life forever. I was craving big, radical change.

To look at it in a more whimsical way, I believe there was a little boy knocking on the door of the ether and simply itching to be brought Earthside.

I was overcome with the dream of him.

When I expressed this to Keaton, he agreed that it might be good to talk about trying to get pregnant. That afternoon, I did some research. I texted Keaton.

"I just read that it takes some couples up to a year to conceive. I say we take our chances and just ditch the condoms now," I suggested.

"Sounds good," he said.

I was also pretty stoked for what this might mean for our sparse sex life.

Crisis

New Years came and went. One afternoon in February, I was at work folding origami animals with Lisa and noticed horrible stabbing pains in my side. Research from Dr. Google had convinced me I was going to die of appendicitis, so I left work early to get checked out. I let Keaton know on my way to the doctor what was happening, but my phone was about to die and I didn't have a charger.

I explained the symptoms to my doctor. She palpated my abdomen with her cold, fine-boned hands. My eyes squeezed hard, trying to shut out the pain. She was suspicious of gallstones.

"I think we should get some imaging done," she said. "But first, is it possible you could be pregnant?" she asked, routinely. I sat up.

"What? Yeah, I guess so… but I only had unprotected sex once and that was back on New Years Eve."

"Well, let's test just to be sure," she said. I peed in a cup and waited in the sterile exam room.

Five minutes later, she entered the room and announced that I was, indeed, pregnant. Clear as day.

I was shocked. We'd only had sex once since we decided to start trying! My mind was spinning. I thought she must be mistaken.

When I tuned back into my doctor's voice, she sounded concerned.

"I wouldn't start celebrating just yet," she said. "We need to rule out ectopic pregnancy. That's when the egg implants in the fallopian tube. These situations are very serious. I want you to go straight to the clinic for an ultrasound. Tonight," she instructed me.

It was dark outside when I left the doctor's office. I was alone, pregnant, and possibly in a medical crisis. My phone had 5% battery left. I took a screenshot shot of the directions to the hospital and texted Keaton.

"Getting more testing done. Call me on your break. Phone might die." I wrote.

My mind was spinning out. Finally, after a painfully long waiting room visit, I was called back for my ultrasound. Within moments, the technician found the source of the pain.

"There it is," she said.

"There what is?" I asked.

"You have a cyst on your ovary," she told me.

"I have a cyst? What does that mean?" I asked.

"It means you're pregnant. And you'll be just fine," she answered.

Like the good mommy I was, I sped the whole way home. I had to turn my phone on and tell Keaton! When I reached him he was on break at work. He had taken the residents to get burritos at El Pato Feliz.

MARRIAGE 121

"Hey. What'd you find out? I've been freaking out," he said.

"I'm going to be fine," I told him.

"Oh great. What was it?" he asked.

"I'm… pregnant," I said, grinning.

"Oh! ….. Wow!" he said through nervous laughter. "Wow. That was… fast." He turned from the phone for a moment and I could hear him speaking Spanish to the kids.

"I know. Okay… well, anyways… I'll let you get back to work. Just wanted to tell you. Everything's fine. I'll see you tonight," I said.

With that, everything changed. For me. For him. For us.

10
Best, Worst

A Break

Early on in my pregnancy, we moved again, this time into Portland to be closer to our new jobs. We also became more involved with Theophilus, a progressive Foursquare church in SE Portland, which gave us a much needed break from the suburban church community that seemed to permeate our small town. We rented a charming little house with a second bedroom, a space which somehow made the ever-growing bump beneath my T-shirt feel far more real.

Keaton worked a swing shift at the immigration shelter, so he'd bike to work at 1:00 pm and return home after 10:30 pm, when I was usually fast asleep. I worked full time as a nanny, so on weekdays, we hardly saw each other. This was a major shift from our first years as a couple, when we contentedly spent huge swaths of time working and playing together.

It was deep winter, when the sun seemed to tuck itself into bed before rush hour traffic could even subside, that I began to feel loneliness set in. As a married woman, I had fallen out of touch with many of my friends. None of my friends lived in the outskirts of southeast Portland, which made my sense of isolation even greater.

I spent most nights alone watching Netflix documentaries and eating whatever I could keep down, which mainly consisted of bland carbohydrates. My previously paleo self was nowhere to be seen. Meat, cold vegetables and avocados were all nauseating to me. I managed to make a human almost entirely out of pizza and cereal.

Keaton and I were always at our best when we had something to focus on together besides each other. The specifics didn't matter: running a café, making music, talking about social justice. We made great teammates and were great friends. Our main clashes were within our sex life. I wanted something from him that he just didn't feel he could provide. The news of the pregnancy was like a salve for our relationship and gave us a purpose outside of ourselves once again.

Near the end of my first trimester, we attended an Easter service at Theophilus. On the drive home, we had a frank discussion about how image-focused and extroverted the church community was. We felt that we were going to a hip social event each week, more than a spiritual one. It felt showy. Everyone there was pretty and young and almost painfully trendy. The music was perfect. The speakers were enticing. It was another church production, like the one we'd left in the suburbs, only this time, with progressive Christian hipster branding.

We decided to take a break from church altogether, in hopes of clarifying our beliefs before the baby was born.

Separation

That spring, Mark and Kari asked if they could come over for a visit; they wanted to talk to us. We were happy to see them, but curious about the unsolicited visit. Since we moved into the city, we were seeing less and less of Keaton's family and feeling the impact of the distance. When they arrived, we shared our usual hugs and hellos, but the air felt serious and a bit tense. I could tell something was out of sorts.

Settled in our small living room, Kari spoke first. She explained that things had been hard for quite a while, and that, as we knew, they'd been in marriage counseling for many years.

"It's just not working anymore. We've tried everything. We've decided to get a divorce," Kari told us.

All four of us held back tears as Mark and Kari described what would happen next — with the house, with Keaton's teenage brother, with family gatherings. In the meantime, Mark would continue to live in the downstairs apartment until they finalized the details of the divorce. They were civil. They had clearly spent a very long time coming to this decision. It was apparent how much they cared about each other and about our family. They'd been together for 25 years.

We reassured them that we just wanted them to be happy. We knew how hard they had tried to salvage their marriage and we respected their decision. As they drove away, I rested my hand on my round belly and thought about what this change would mean for our family and for our baby. A part of me cracked, learning that this family who had become my own, would be splitting at the seams just as mine had. Suddenly, a certain dream of wholeness seemed to be a naïve and unattainable pipe dream, not for me or the world I was to create.

Diagnosis

Winter and spring passed without fanfare. My belly grew from a small curve to an undeniable basketball beneath my t-shirt, and inch by inch, our identities as parents were beginning to take shape.

In June, we received a call from Kari. She was with Mark at the hospital. She asked us to come right away.

The previous night, Kari had returned home from work and smelled something burning. She called down the stairs, where Mark was now living, but heard no response. Then she saw Sofa, the family dog, walking past, dragging a piece of pizza in her mouth. Something was amiss.

When Kari went downstairs, she discovered a blackened pizza half spilled on the floor and Mark asleep on the couch. She woke him. He was confused and disoriented. Kari, a registered nurse, switched into caregiver mode and began to check him for signs of stroke. When he extended his arms straight out in front, his left arm immediately drifted toward the ground. This was a key indicator. She urged him to go to the hospital and, knowing something was wrong, he agreed.

Mark had been experiencing severe headaches for weeks but had chalked it up to allergies. He admitted that he'd been sleeping at work and the week earlier, he'd dozed off at the wheel multiple times during his commute home from the school where he served as principal.

At the hospital, Kari overheard one nurse telling another nurse she didn't understand why he was in the ER. Kari insisted that he be examined and something be done, explaining that she knew him and he wasn't acting normal.

When Keaton and I arrived at the hospital, they'd been running tests all morning. A CT scan revealed a spot on the brain. The doctor ordered an MRI.

I can't recall the exact moment we found out — I carry a blurred memory of us all sitting in his hospital room beside a big window. The doctor said tumor. More specifically, Mark had a large glioblastoma — an inoperable malignant brain tumor. His prognosis was 11 months.

Cancer. We were devastated. We returned home from the hospital that night and I watched Keaton cry in a way I'd never seen before. We were facing a dense cocktail of emotions, some toxic, heavy sea of shock, grief, and fear. We attempted to talk, and when words escaped us, we attempted to sleep. I stared down at my rounded belly in the dim moonlight and wondered if this baby would get to know what it meant to have a grandfather.

The dynamic at the hospital was complicated, and reached a head when a family member was needed to sign a consent form for Mark to undergo a biopsy. Before May, that person would have been Kari. It was uncomfortable for everyone to explain that she was newly his ex-wife. They received a few sideways glances from hospital staff that seemed to ask, "Why is the ex-wife here?"

"I couldn't sign for him. His mom had to sign it. I felt like an outsider," Kari had said. "We'd been together for 25 years. I knew that since I was the one who knew him best, I had to be his advocate. He tended to minimize his own pain."

No Cure For Life

Mark chose to put his faith in the doctors and nurses. He was scheduled for chemotherapy and radiation treatments five days a week, designed to shrink the tumor. A writer for a local newspaper approached our family to write a story about Mark's cancer journey, as he was a beloved public figure in the school district.

"The doctor said there is no cure for what I have. The best I can hope for is quality of life," he told the interviewer. "I wasn't upset by anything the doctors said. I realized something was going on with my brain. If the treatments were going to solve my headaches, then I was on board. I am a task-oriented person; I was ready to do what needed to be done."

"I don't want to know how long I am going to live," he told her when she asked about his prognosis.

"Those are natural questions; I just don't want to spend whatever days I have left worrying about stuff I can't control. None of us really knows how much time we have. We are born, and we are guaranteed to die. There's no cure for life. I've told Kari that if she finds out I only have a little time left, to rent a house in Sunriver and get the family over there so we can have some good days together."

Sunriver, a wooded vacation resort in central Oregon, was our family spot. It was the same place Keaton and I had spent our honeymoon. Prior to Mark and Kari's divorce, the whole family spent a week there together every summer. This would be our first summer since that shift.

At the hospital, once his pain levels were managed, Mark acted steady. He seemed to be at peace with the news and determined to remain optimistic. Kari, and the rest of us, experienced a spectrum of emotions — anger, disbelief, fear and doubt.

"I had gone through a hellish year coming to terms with our marriage ending," she said. "I asked God, 'Are you freaking kidding me?' I was really angry. I questioned: why this, why is one more awful thing happening to us?"

A few weeks after the "night Mark burned the pizza," as we'd come to know it, we had a treatment plan in place and settled back at home in the suburbs. Kari was a fierce advocate for Mark and stayed unwaveringly by his side from the first moment, even when spiteful family members met her devotion with skepticism. At first, he was guarded and hesitant to receive her care and attention — they had just been divorced, after all — but within weeks, something began to change.

To everyone's surprise, Kari and Mark were falling back in love.

Mark moved back upstairs into the main house and Keaton and I moved into the basement to be closer to the family. I left my nanny job in Portland so I could help with taking care of Mark, making food, and getting him to radiation appointments when Kari and Keaton had to work.

Keaton and his brothers planned our annual family trip to Sunriver — including a mountain biking excursion. Mark had purchased a gorgeous new titanium mountain bike and was eager to try it out. He was adamant that no one should feel pity for him because of his prognosis.

He even had a custom sign made and placed it on the porch by our front door. It read:

"This home is not a place of pity or sorrow but a place of laughter and friendship. Enter at your own risk."

He wanted to write, "If you see me feeling any pity toward myself, to go to the shed, grab the shovel, dig a hole and push me in." But the family members groaned at his morbid sense of humor. He winked at me and laughed. This dark sensibility was one of our many similarities.

BEST, WORST

I wondered often about how to support Keaton through such an unimaginably difficult time. Life had not prepared us to witness the premature death of a parent. There was no guidebook, no road map. I felt conflicted, torn between my own very real grief and his. The ache inside me felt at once unbearably heavy, yet also minuscule compared to a son's love for his father.

How could I have my own grief and create a just amount of space for the weight of Keaton's? I didn't want to compare my pain of losing this father figure, to Keaton and his brothers' experience of losing the man who had raised them from birth. I didn't know how to hold it all.

In times of tragedy, our earnest best is all we can offer. Fear of showing up imperfectly doesn't change the fact that we must show up. We must be courageous for those we love. So I relied on my strengths: holding a calm presence during times of chaos, organizing community support, and offering practical help to lighten the load.

And through it all, Mark and Kari rediscovered a long-forgotten love. Family friends who'd known them for decades said they'd never seen those two so happy. It was like they were young again. Soon, they decided to re-marry. We threw a jovial, tearful backyard wedding that summer, and together we found ourselves in what we remember as "the best of times and the worst of times."

Pregnancy

Once the shock wore off and we understood that Mark's diagnosis was a part of present life, the months passed with a new, less certain kind of routine. Mark's health was more or less stable while undergoing treatment. My belly bump was growing by the day. We had chosen not to learn the baby's sex, but based on my ongoing dreams and raw intuition, I was confident we had a little boy on our hands.

I'd always known I wanted to have a natural childbirth. It just felt like my approach. We found a midwifery center in Portland and I began reading books and watching documentaries about birth. I learned how backwards the maternity care system is in the United States, and how negative birth outcomes were often linked to unnecessary interventions. By and large, pregnancy and birth had been treated in this country like a medical emergency rather than a natural process.

I read two books by Ina May Gaskin: *Spiritual Midwifery* and *Ina May's Guide to Childbirth*. In the latter, she made a passing, critical remark about a large portion of the population believing that pain during childbirth is punishment from God rooting way back to the Garden of Eden. (As the story goes, Eve ate the forbidden fruit in the garden and gave some to Adam, too. Because of this, God punished her, and all women after, to have pain during childbearing).

Upon reading Ina May's critique, I felt immediately defensive of Christianity. I felt disappointed that I had so far been resonating with the book and then she had to go and take a dig at my faith. This knee-jerk defensiveness was a reaction I'd learned early in life; I'd been raised to believe that rational doubts were a tool of Satan to trick the world into not believing.

But as I read on, I couldn't get out of my mind what a solid, reasonable point she was making.

Did I really believe that childbirth was painful because God was being petty about some fruit disobedience bruising his ego in a past millennium? No. Childbirth is painful because it involves the human body accomplishing an unbelievable feat of physics. To say it another way, squeezing a cantaloupe through a sock would inherently be painful for the sock; no sock deity is punishing the sock.

I noticed my unprecedented willingness to explore my doubt around the topic and adjust my beliefs based on new arguments. It was at once invigorating and frightening. If I was so quick to abandon my old beliefs in this case, what about in other cases?

Meanwhile, I had been connected online with a friend from childhood, one who went to Camp Crestview with our youth group multiple times. She'd been posting on Facebook non-stop about having left the Catholic faith and adopting a humanistic worldview. I found it irritating, but not because I thought she was wrong. I was irritated because she was making valid points and I didn't feel I had the space or energy to consider all that new information, desire as I might.

Sex While Pregnant

I loved being pregnant and was fortunate to have a very straightforward and mostly comfortable pregnancy. My sex drive actually grew more intense, but given everything Keaton and I had been through in that regard, I wasn't inspired to attempt the same chase I had in the past. We had other demands in life that felt more important. Plus, our sparse sex life had become very monotonous and predictable, which left me unsatisfied, like an itch I couldn't quite scratch. Over the months, the topic of sex gradually faded to an undiscussed memory.

I ended up getting most of my needs met on my own, as I had for years. One particularly embarrassing day (or hilarious, for those who aren't me), I woke up from an afternoon nap feeling fiercely frisky. The house was quiet upstairs and glancing out the window, I saw no cars in the driveway and assumed everyone was away. I took my time getting down to business. Finally I began to climax. I came, again and again. Now, I am not naturally a quiet person. I can turn down the volume if I must, but in general there's a certain release I prefer that comes with making noise. So there I was, enthralled with my own fireworks, moaning my little pregnant heart out, when I heard a knock on the upstairs door. I froze, silent.

"Becca?" It was Kari's voice upstairs.

".... Yeah?" I answered, literally caught with my pants down. I wanted to crawl under a rock.

"Are you okay? I thought I heard crying," she said.

I held back laughter as my face reddened. I called up the stairs.

"Oh, I'm okay. I was just coughing. I'm fine now. Thanks." (Really… that was the best I could come up with on the spot.)

"Okay… well if you need anything, I'm here," she said.

I was mortified. I was convinced she knew and was judging me. Or maybe she truly didn't recognize the sounds coming from the floorboards. Either way, I find it hilarious now — both my brazen self pleasure inside the family house, and the fact that I was low-key caught in the act by my mother-in-law.

I was never open about my solo escapades with Keaton. We literally never talked or even joked about it, except me admitting I started as a teen and him admitting he had never gotten into it and felt he would somehow be perceived less of a man because of that fact. I never told Keaton that I often had solo sex while I was alone and had come to prefer it. It felt like some sort of betrayal or perversion — that's what you're taught to believe in Christianity. The closest I'd ever come to bringing this part of myself into our relationship was the sexy photos I'd taken for him, but they were not well received, so I kept this part of myself a secret.

Parents In The Making

Keaton and I took a Bradley Method birthing class for a few months as my due date approached. It brought us closer and helped prepare us for the birth. I read a book called *Mindful Birthing*, which was my first foray into the world of meditation, though I'd been doing yoga since I was 15. I began doing guided meditations as often as I could. As I learned about the human mind and the human body, and the ways they are intricately connected, I could sense that my worldview was beginning to shift beneath me.

I started to consider the ways we form beliefs. I realized that most of what I believed about the world was not based on my lived experience and active participation. Most of what I believed, I had been taught during a formative and receptive time in my life: childhood. I wondered if there were precepts that I would not believe if I were to hear them for the first time now, as an adult, with a (mostly) developed brain. (I was 22 years old during this discovery).

I knew this was a rabbit hole, so rather than diving in, I simply peered over the edge at the deep well of possibility. I spoke of these considerations to no one.

One important part of pregnancy was reckoning with what kind of parents we wanted to be. We knew we wanted to raise a healthy, loved, well-adjusted child, and we disagreed with many of the methods used by our parents' generation in raising us. I tend to have a counter-cultural, rebellious streak in me (as is probably no surprise by now), so I wanted to know what the undercurrent of alternative parenting had to say.

After reading several books, we settled confidently on the Attachment Parenting method as put out by Dr. Sears. Essentially, this philosophy states that children are whole people, and that the attachment styles that people learn during the first years of their life will form the blueprint for their whole relational life thereafter. This has to do with how we bond (or don't) with people around us, how we communicate, and how we get our needs met. So, basically the fabric of who we are and how we live.

It was painful to look at my own life through this lens. I began to understand the anxious and dismissive-avoidant attachment styles that I had developed early on in life because of my relationships of insecure attachment with my primary caregivers: my parents. Rather than being angry or bitter at something I couldn't change, I used this understanding as fuel for my efforts to do right by my child.

Keaton and I agreed that we would be a household which valued our child as an autonomous member of the family distinct from us, while honoring his extreme dependence on us. We would take his crying seriously, keep him close, guide him with structure and age-appropriate teaching. We would allow space for experimentation, play, asking questions, and discovering for himself rather than being told what is true about the world.

In the first couple months I was pregnant, we had a conversation about whether we'd bring our child to church. Or rather, as Keaton put it: "We're not going to put our kid in Sunday School, are we?"

"Ew... no," I said without thinking.

Our deeper feelings about the church were beginning to come through. We agreed that it was pretty strange to indoctrinate children from birth into a religion. We had both been raised in the church and were not exposed to other ways of thinking outside that Christian bubble. We both felt we were worse off for it.

It's obvious to me that by this time, we were no longer convinced that Christianity was inherently, objectively true. Most people refer to their faith as a relationship to God, most people don't call their personal experience of a faith "religion." But to us, religion was more and more what it had become. It seemed we understood Christianity more as the culture we had been born into, and saw it as equally valuable to other faiths. Ours just happened to be the flavor of our geography and demographic: progressive hipster Christianity.

Keaton and I also agreed that I would be a stay-at-home mom for our first year. We agreed to tighten our budget and live off Keaton's non-profit income so the baby could bond with us as primary caregivers.

Crash

When I was eight months pregnant, I was rear ended at a stoplight. I was on my way to meet Keaton at the midwifery center for my bi-weekly checkup. Sitting at a red light, I suddenly felt a huge slam from behind me and my car was shoved forward into the intersection. The driver, a man in a small pickup truck, had been texting while driving and didn't see the light turn red. He hit me at a full 35 miles per hour.

I was in shock. I pulled over and I climbed out of the car. The man's color drained out of his face when he saw my swollen belly and realized I was very pregnant. I stood there, disoriented, knowing I needed to take his insurance information, but unsure how to go about that.

A silent, peaceful person appeared, seemingly out of thin air, and handed me a stack of paper and a pen. When I turned back to thank him, he was gone. That's one of the only moments in my life that I could have been convinced of real-world angels.

I wrote down the man's insurance information, checked out the damage on my car, and decided the best thing I could do was go straight to the midwives as I had planned. I made no effort to ease his worries or minimize his massive guilt. He received a silent and unforgiving stare from me through the whole exchange.

The eight miles into Portland was excruciatingly long. True, I probably had a concussion, but my biggest concern was checking on the baby. I couldn't feel him moving at all. I poked and prodded at my belly, I chugged the iced lemonade I'd brought along, I tried everything to feel a kick or a sign of life. I called the midwives and let them know what had happened.

When I arrived, I was rushed straight to the exam room and our midwife, Kori, placed a Doppler on my belly. Keaton was already there waiting.

Searching…

Searching…

Heartbeat. Da-dum. Da-dum. Da-dum.

The underwater, percussive heartbeat on that little speaker was the most beautiful sound I could have imagined at that moment. It was as if he was saying, "I'm here. I'm okay." The whole room breathed a massive sigh of relief.

After that, I underwent many months of physical therapy to recover from whiplash injuries. As I researched bodywork specifically for pregnant women, I came across a woman named Barbara who did womb work and Maya Abdominal Massage. I scheduled an appointment for her the following week.

This was only the beginning of the most intense summer of my life.

BEST, WORST

11

Help Me

Unraveling

I hadn't heard from my father, Rocky, in several years. I'd mostly tried to block thoughts of him from my mind, because I wasn't prepared to deal with the reality of his absence. The last time I had seen him was at my wedding two years prior. In the space of those two years, he had in many ways unraveled. It seemed the unrelenting structure my mom provided to his life functioned as a container to hold him together. Without her control, for the first time in decades, he was lost.

My sister Kara, who was a senior in high school when they split, had stayed with him in our childhood home, having chosen my dad's side in the divorce and, in a way, stepped up as lady of the house. My mother quickly remarried and moved across town. A new house, a new man to blame for her unhappiness.

My dad became enmeshed with a woman named Sy who he'd met at a local dive bar. She was on disability benefits for fibromyalgia and had intense mental health issues. She claimed she was a Native American princess and was very paranoid about him having connections to us kids. She became extremely controlling over my dad, and he allowed her to be.

Soon, Sy had replaced my mother as the boss of his life. The two of them married. She moved into our childhood home with my dad and Kara, who was trying her damnedest to make the best of a trying situation. Within a few months, Sy had worked to systematically turn my dad against Kara, instigating more and more conflict between them until he kicked her out and she was forced to go live with my mom.

Once, while visiting town to see a friend, I drove past the old family house and as I approached, I noticed there were "No Trespassing" signs all over the front lawn. The red letters stunned me, sending a surge of shame and confusion through my body. I turned my eyes away, making a mental note to avoid that street in the future.

As it happened, my sisters had made several attempts to contact my dad during those two years, with the excuse that they needed to retrieve furniture and boxes of personal items which were stored in the basement. Each time he turned them away, and stated simply that they were not welcome on his property. Several front porch arguments ensued.

He went so far as to have a certified letter sent to one sister, claiming that if she set foot on the property again, he would call the police and have her hauled off. He was losing his grip. That same sister also had a friend who claimed they saw my dad spending time at a known meth house. When she brought it up, I didn't believe her words.

My brother David was absent from this saga, living out several years of blurred days in the Oregon State Penitentiary. The incident which landed him there took place while he was trying, after multiple attempts, to get off of opiate painkillers. Anyone who's ever tried to quit an addictive substance recognizes the toll that withdrawals can take on a person's body, mind and spirit.

In his case, a heated confrontation escalated to the point of violence. I point this out not to excuse what took place, but to highlight how intricately social injustices are connected. These issues are like spokes on a monstrous wheel. Predatory pharmaceutical companies design, market and overproduce highly addictive drugs. Doctors participate and financially benefit by over-prescribing. These drugs, legal and not, often begin as methods of medicating then create conditions in which people's ability to cope with life is hijacked, making it near impossible to get sober.

Addiction often leads to broken relationships, financial ruin, and mental health crises. There is money to be made. Police, prisons, and the corporations that resource them profit from punishment for drugs, mental health breakdowns and drug-related violence, among many other things. We are living in a punitive society that commodifies human life and raises revenues from addiction.

My brother's story intersects with mine, as do all of my family members'. I still wonder how to speak on my experience of our lives together, while honoring the individual experiences of those around me and not speaking

HELP ME

on their behalf. It is soil on which I must tread lightly.

Having a brother who was locked up multiple times throughout my life was formative. The incidents, the legal process, and his deeply felt absence were traumatic for all of us. We witnessed firsthand the abuses of the prison-industrial complex, a beastly matrix of capitalism and politics and white supremacy that is built on the backs of black, brown, and poor people.

We watched him work as a barber for obscenely low pay, twelve cents an hour, while paying real-world prices for basic goods like soap and shoelaces and notebooks from the commissary. In many states, inmates aren't paid at all. This is modern day slavery, a loophole in the thirteenth amendment which made it illegal to keep human beings captive and force them to work… except as punishment for a crime.

My sisters and I sat with David one day at visitation, eating snacks we'd bought from the vending machine and listening to him spit rhymes about resilience and personal power. We weren't allowed to hug him when he came in. The cold, thick-walled cement cafeteria felt oppressive to me, heavy in more ways than one. I looked around and imagined what it would be like to live inside a cage like this. I often struggled to go through security without crying, passing by the irritated workers and loud-mouthed officials who held absolute control over my brother's daily life.

"When I get out of here, I'm going to find him and beat him up. Set him straight," David said of my dad as we discussed what had been happening. I rolled my eyes.

"And what do you think that will solve?" I asked. He rolled his eyes back at me — we were operating from such opposite scripts about the world that we each saw the other as naïve.

As much as I could, I kept all of this family drama at arm's length. I didn't visit David in prison as often as I felt I should. I always tried to answer when he called me, though. The shame of our family's circumstances was intolerable to me. This wasn't the family I remembered, my dad and sisters arguing on the front lawn like a reality TV show, my brother sleeping for years on a bunk bed inside a large human cage.

Being connected with my sisters, who were more connected with my parents, was deeply painful for me. I did not feel I could hold space for my family's discord and unraveling while trying to build a new, more functional life for myself. I didn't feel that my dad's actions toward my siblings had to affect me directly. The dad I remembered loved me and was kind and considerate; he took the time to visit me at college and write me letters and danced with me at my wedding. Whoever this new person was, he was not my dad. My dad was gone. I didn't know the person in that house anymore.

I wanted to hold onto the memory of him, arm in arm with me at my wedding, calm, chuckling, chewing his toothpick in his crisp button-up shirt. My family compared this response to the disassociation that I'd displayed when my mom first filed for divorce; I had responded by moving out at age 16 to get away from the tension and toxicity.

Leaving had always been my automatic solution to emotional and relational chaos. I got by, reciting to myself a narrative that I didn't need any of it — that I was better off with no family at all, or creating a new one, than staying involved and being repeatedly wounded by my broken one.

Help Me

It was the weekend after my car accident when everything truly collided. I was eight months pregnant, living in the suburbs and helping take care of Keaton's dad. I woke to a great deal of pain in my body — my back and shoulders were locked up from the whiplash and the concussion was still healing. I sat up and rubbed my neck with one hand as I reached for my phone. I saw a missed call and a voicemail from my mother, a rare occurrence. *Great*, I thought.

"Your father's been shot. He's in the hospital in critical condition. The police are there," she said through a tense voice.

I stared at my phone and shook my head, as though to erase her words. I replayed her message once. Twice.

"Fuck," was all I could think to say. Emotions evaded me; it didn't seem real. I wasn't sure what I had just heard or what to do about it. Should I go to the hospital? Should I care? Shouldn't I be feeling... something? The pain in my body was pronounced, but this shock to my system left me numb.

The cognitive dissonance rattled through me as I grasped for something to feel. Thoughts of him from my youth played through my mind.

I saw him mowing the lawn in his navy blue coveralls, adorned by neon orange earplugs and safety glasses. He waved a hand casually to neighbors as they passed, as he always did.

I saw him sitting across from me at the dinner table, all those ordinary weeknights, and us kids teasing as he mixed his piles of meat and vegetables and mashed potatoes together.

"It's all going to the same place," he'd say unapologetically. No fuss.

"Your dad's so chill. Rocky's not like other dads," I remembered all my friends in high school insisting. I resented them for that — no, he wasn't like other dads. He was emotionally absent. But he was also never misogynistic or condescending like other dads I knew. He was never domineering or overbearing. He let us be. He was benign. Passive. Safe.

Content Warning: Police Shooting

The following is what I have gathered from police reports, news stories, and a firsthand account.

It was well past midnight. My dad and Sy, his new wife, had been drinking and gotten into an out-of-control verbal altercation. Sy called the police in hysterics and told them she felt in danger. When she hung up the phone, my dad stormed from the house, a bottle of liquor in one hand and a large kitchen knife in the other. He began walking down the street toward the highway.

If that sounds insane and out of character, it's because it was. He was having a mental health crisis.

A short time later, four police officers arrived, including the chief of police, a family friend who we knew from my grandmother's daycare. They found my father wandering across the parking lot of the Best Western hotel. The police tried to reason with him and ordered him to drop the knife, but he was despondent. He showed clear signs of intoxication and emotional distress. He would not drop the knife.

An officer attempted unsuccessfully to subdue him with a taser stun gun. They tased him multiple times. But he would not fall. He charged toward them.

Three shots were fired.

My father was shot twice in the abdomen and once in the arm. The police rushed to his aid as he bled out on the cold pavement.

"Help me... help me... please help me," he was heard saying through slurred speech.

There was some speculation by the judge, and my own mother, that he was attempting suicide by cop.

I didn't know how to process this information as the day progressed. The forceful mental image of the scene doubled me over. It made my ears ring.

It made me physically ill, but by the time I explained the situation to Keaton that afternoon, I'd become rational and detached. I had subconsciously blocked the emotions from surfacing, feeling they might break me in two.

I did not go to see him. I didn't even have a working phone number to call. I didn't know that man who was lying in a hospital bed. The Rocky I knew was earnest and gentle and hardworking. I had never known him to be violent, not even rough. He was someone who used his strength to break up bar fights, not threaten people. Yet here, at his unraveling, deep pain and desperation had caused him to abandon all reason, all regard for life, all regard for us. He was lost in the pit of his own trauma, out of reach.

My mother later emailed us his mug shot. I still can't understand why. It seemed vindictive and cruel. My family members called him a fool and a coward.

I turned away.

Solar Plexus

The following Monday, I drove to Portland for a massage. At eight months pregnant, whiplashed, and facing a family crisis, I was holding so much tension that I felt like I was living in someone else's high-strung body. I was relieved to settle onto the table to relax, an opportunity to shut out the world for an hour. That was my intent, anyway.

Barbara had healing hands. Equal parts brilliant massage therapist and intuitive energy worker, she paused when she reached my solar plexus, a nerve center just beneath the sternum.

"Becca," she said softly. "Have you had something very upsetting happen this week?"

"Hmm? Oh. Yes. I was rear ended..." I answered. I wanted to roll my eyes; we had spoken at length about the crash and she knew why I had come in.

She kept her hands resting softly on my belly. I laid there, silent, and we both knew I wasn't saying everything. Steady and patient, she moved her fingertips over my solar plexus, barely pressing and then releasing, drawing my attention to the soft spot beneath my ribs, the most vulnerable area of my body, now more so with my unborn child sheltered within. There were no bones to shield it, no reactive limbs to push her away.

Then I cracked.

"... And my father was shot by police..." I broke down, sobbing, and drew a hand over my eyes.

Salty hot tears poured from them as I lay there, gasping, realizing the truth of my words and allowing the crushing weight of them.

I trusted Barbara; her presence was safe and unpressured. She didn't seem startled or put off by this huge surge of emotion. Yet I was bewildered, like I'd been caught under a riptide and had no choice but to swim through it and wait for air.

It felt like a shattering of my defenses. I felt a deep loss, like something fundamentally human had been snatched away — the last semblance of my family's dignity and stability. I swam in confusion about my place in the world, my identity, and the family I thought I knew. I felt the sting of public humiliation. I raged at the whole town reading news headlines about the shooting, this private, life-altering moment in a man's life, and those who mocked and condemned him from a distance as a deranged man on the loose.

I didn't rage at the police or their use of force. I could find no alternative to what they'd done. I raged at a deeper injustice: that of racial disparities, lack of access and generational trauma, the injustice which left people of color like my dad walked-on by this country's power structures, which reduced him and his kin to uneducated laborers trying desperately to stay out of the way and dig themselves out of poverty.

I raged that after never missing a day of work or taking a vacation, he had lost 35 years of hard work in the wake of divorce. That he had resorted to medicating with booze like his father, and his father's father, and that he had become so hopeless, feeling so insignificant to the world, that he believed the only relief was to spiral out of it.

My father. The man who made me, whose DNA is inside my cells. This was a broken man, a gentle man, a man desperate for help. A man who was dealt a hand which doomed him to fail from the start.

That was the moment I came to believe that we store trauma in our bodies. That the events of our lives leave imprints on us which will find their ways to the surface eventually, either with our conscious awareness or in messy, often terrible ways without our permission.

Perhaps I couldn't have believed it until Barbara unearthed it, hiding right there under my ribs. It was undeniable. My body was shouting what my mind was denying — that a traumatic event had occurred which shook the sparse foundations of my sense of safety and belonging. My abdomen, a place where I usually brace for impact, as though an invisible punch is headed toward my midline, was tender and buzzing and begging to be tended.

In the years since, numerous bodyworkers have found emotional blockages stored in my body — things I was hardly aware I had tucked away, as though ignoring them would simply make them evaporate. Sometimes there is a cramp or an inexplicable pain or extreme tenderness in a muscle which, when accessed, results in deep emotional release.

I believe that sometimes, strange symptoms or unexplainable diagnoses have roots in our personal histories. I have cried, laughed, groaned, and wailed during bodywork sessions. Totally sober, I have taken dreamlike, metaphysical-seeming tours of my own body in which I was able to walk through different joints and muscles, old injuries and stagnated energy, and unearth the deep wisdom and memories stored within.

I left Barbara's office feeling relieved and unbearably raw. I wasn't used to having such access to my emotions. I had no idea where to put them now that they'd surfaced. I didn't feel I could talk with my family about this, or that Keaton's family could understand.

I chose not to attempt to contact my dad. I recognized that I was in a very tender time, preparing to give birth. There was so much going on in my own health and that of Keaton's dad; I couldn't take one more thing, not now. I considered that my dad hadn't made any effort to contact me in two years. I saw no benefit in allowing this event to have any practical implications on my life.

I wanted to insulate myself as much as possible and bring this baby into a safe and peaceful world. I wanted to shut out whatever chaos I could.

Mark was diagnosed with brain cancer in June.

I was rear ended in July.

Mark and Kari remarried in July.

My father was shot by cops in July.

It was one hell of a summer.

12

Rebirth

Ready

By my 38th week, the glow of pregnancy had worn off. I was done. My clothes were all uncomfortable. I had endured a hot summer and I felt like a manatee. We had gathered the necessary baby items: cloth diapers, baby carriers, a beautiful sidecar cosleeper bed that Keaton's brother had built out of Cherrywood. We'd also collected our home birthing supplies: sheets, pads, towels and tarps to put beneath the pool, which the midwives would bring.

I was ready to see our baby's mystery face and start our life together. I'd been walking several miles each morning, receiving prenatal massage and acupuncture from Barbara, doing squats and fetal positioning exercises every night. I used evening primrose oil and drank a quart of red raspberry leaf tea and other herbs every day.

Each night, Keaton and I would talk to my protruding belly and say, "You can come tonight if you're ready. We are! We want you here!" And each morning I would wake up, still pregnant, and think, *Okay... one more day of this.*

On Sunday, September 22, I felt fluish. I had a keen sense that the baby would be coming any time. So while Keaton was at work, I spent a quiet day alone with the baby — I journaled, baked bread, prepped our bed for the birth, and organized the house. When we went to sleep Sunday night, I could feel period-type cramps, but fell fast asleep.

I woke at 5:45 am on Monday morning to a contraction. As I climbed out of bed for a glass of water, our cat Luna came running wildly after me. She was a fluffy, lazy creature who almost never ran. She followed me around the house, meowing loudly and pawing at my legs. I suppose her feline senses were signaling that something unusual was happening. My contractions were seven minutes apart when I went to the bathroom and noticed some blood in the toilet, a common sign of labor. As I washed my hands and stared at my rounded reflection in the mirror, reality began to set in: this baby was coming Earthside.

Keaton called into work. I sent a text to our lead midwife, Kori, to fill her in. She instructed us to try and have a normal, restful morning, as there was a big day ahead. We milled around the house like usual: I ate breakfast, took a shower, and got dressed for the day. I called through the house to Keaton each time I felt a wave of tightness spreading throughout my abdomen. "Here's another one!" I'd holler, and he'd write down the time.

The baby wiggled around in my womb. I wondered if he could sense that today was the day. The sun had just risen and it was raining hard outside, yet I wanted to get some fresh air while I still had the energy. I barely managed to zip up Mark's large rain jacket around my belly before we headed out on our normal route toward the city park.

As we walked, I felt like I had a big secret — while the rest of the world was carrying on as usual, getting ready for work and school, I was in labor and this was the day Keaton and I would become parents. My contractions were still tolerable, allowing me to walk and talk normally. I thought to myself, *This is how I imagined labor would feel. This shouldn't be too hard.*

I was comically naïve.

We returned home and spent the cozy morning drinking tea and watching reruns of *The Office* on Netflix. My contractions had picked up the pace. Every five minutes, I could feel an intense tightening, which began deep in my back and spread like a Charlie horse cramp across my whole belly and down between my hips, as if a powerful cosmic fist was squeezing me in its grip. I stayed on the floor, draped over a bouncy yoga ball, rocking and breathing with every contraction.

Later, it became too painful to laugh at Michael Scott's antics, so we turned off the TV. As the morning wore on, I shifted from breathing, to sighing, to humming through each contraction. Staying silent seemed to make them much more painful.

Keaton called Kori at 1:00 pm since we knew things were moving along. She said I should lie down and try to nap for a while. She sent our midwife Kathy to prepare the tub and arrange the supplies. I turned on a birth meditation and went to lie down on the bed, resting a heating pad on my belly and trying to focus on Keaton's calming hand on my side.

Open

I began to weep, and soon tears were streaming uninhibited down my face. I could feel a huge, energetic opening and with it, a wave of emotion like a tidal wave. Within a moment, I completely left my body, zoomed way out into space, and from afar I could hear the sound of desperate sobs.

I could feel my mother there, and her mother, and my father's mother, and all of their mothers far back into history. I could feel the pain and the strength of women I've never seen or met. I was wading through a new, foreign place. When I returned to my body, I realized the sobs I'd been hearing were coming from me. They were sounds I had never made before.

Something was unleashed. It was like I'd crossed through a gateway and was welcomed into a sacred space to do the work of bringing forth life, as though all the women in history were supporting me in this hard, terrifying rite of passage.

I remember this as my first psychedelic experience, prompted not by a mushroom or a tab of acid, but by the altered state of labor and the alchemy of giving birth.

We dimmed the lights and made a nest in a dark corner on the floor. I heard blues piano playing in the other room. I liked focusing on the music's complexity. Each contraction, Keaton pressed on my lower back while I rocked on the yoga ball. I now needed to close my eyes and vocalize to get through each wave. My focus was closing in; I began to shut out all awareness of the world outside my body.

Distantly, I heard the door creak open, followed by footsteps through the apartment. Kathy had arrived. She checked my cervix and found that I was 2-3 cm dilated and about 80% effaced. I was in disbelief; I had been that far along at my last checkup, before labor even started. That couldn't be. She must be wrong. I wanted to know how I had been working so hard in labor for nine hours and not made any progress. I had expected to be halfway there, at least. This news pulled me out of my body and into my head. I began to feel hopeless.

I continued laboring for several blurred hours, while Kathy set up the tub and arranged all the birth supplies. I moaned and cried with each contraction, Keaton staying constantly by my side. I stood in the hot shower, which helped a bit. I vomited four times onto the shower floor, the nausea a response to the increasing pain in my body. The sensations had become so intense that I felt like I was being consumed and turned inside out by each contraction.

Any sense of control I'd had was gone. I felt trapped in my own body. I wanted to escape, to tap out and trade places with someone — anyone — for even a moment of relief. Facing surges of intense pain and tension every few minutes for a whole day was beginning to leave me unhinged. I fantasized about transferring to a hospital to numb out and relish in the relief of an epidural. Just considering the thought made me feel like I had failed at childbirth.

Kori arrived around 5:00 pm. I was in full blown labor. I felt like a hot mess. I must have been a sight to see. Before she checked my progress, she said she'd be satisfied if I'd reached 4 centimeters, I thought that was crazy. (Apparently I was 5 centimeters at that time, but she chose not to give me an update.) I was soon distracted by the next contraction.

I climbed into the birthing tub — and was able to get some relief from the warm water. I continued to cry through each contraction.

Kori asked me why I was so sad. But I wasn't sad; what appeared to be mourning was the only way to release all the intensity taking place inside of me. I've always been a crier... watery Scorpio vibes, I suppose. Something within me was changing and opening, in more ways than one.

I began to dread each contraction rather than resting during the breaks between them. I felt as though I would be in labor forever and that somehow, there would be no part of me left at the end of it. It was the most out of control I have ever felt in my life.

There was nowhere to escape, no way to avoid the confrontation with my own embodied experience. For once, there was no option to disassociate; my body and my life were demanding my full attention. I wanted out. I wanted to go to the hospital and get an epidural. I asked Keaton if he would still be proud of me if we had our baby at the hospital. Of course, he said he would.

Great, we are going to the hospital, I thought to myself. *I just have to convince Kori.* Thankfully, she was not easily convinced. She had seen this maternal crisis countless times.

Kori assured me that my feelings were totally natural and every mother goes through them — the fear was a sign that I was making progress. Nothing was wrong, I was safe and progressing perfectly at my own pace. She asked me what I was afraid of. I couldn't answer.

My midwives reminded me that it would be a long hard drive to the hospital, and that there would still be a delay for pain relief once we arrived. By the time that was all done, I would probably be having my baby. I wasn't willing to accept that outcome. Kori asked me why I had passionately wanted a homebirth. I answered that I wanted our baby to be born into a gentle and peaceful world. I wanted this on so many levels. My resolve was strengthened.

With no other options, I accepted that there was no way out, and no going back — I simply had to go through this. I could not trade places with anyone. I couldn't run away from what was happening; there was only one way to get to the other side. I told my team what I needed: help staying in the present moment. I recall saying out loud, insistently, "I just have to do this."

We decided that Kori would break my water to help things progress. I was 7 centimeters dilated by then, and after that, Kori had me changing positions every few contractions. Labor stayed at about the same intensity, but it felt much more manageable because of the simple shift in my perception.

I had stopped using my energy to fight against it and committed instead to acceptance and trust in the process.

Kori, the midwives, and Keaton were watching me do the very thing I was afraid of. They knew all along that I would have the baby at home. All the fear and suffering was inside my own mind. (Isn't that often the way it is?)

Our third midwife arrived around 8:00 pm and joined Keaton and I at the tub to relieve Kathy. I glanced up to see her knitting calmly on the couch while Kori sat nearby doing some charting. *How can they be acting so normal when all this is happening?!* I thought. But their calm presence and silent support helped Keaton and I know that everything happening was perfectly normal.

The sun had long since set by now. Suddenly, my contractions changed. It felt like my whole center was trying involuntarily to expel something — which, I suppose, it was — in the same way your body convulses when you throw up. It wasn't an urge to push, my body was simply pushing without me telling it to. I felt inside my body with my finger and there was a wrinkly head only half a finger length inside. I gasped with excitement and looked around, wild eyed.

The midwives rushed over to the tub where I was squatting beside Keaton and began to shower me with encouragement. With low hums, they vocalized with me through each contraction and told us that our baby was almost here. Kori instructed me to try holding my breath and pushing three times with each wave. This made the baby move down significantly faster. I could feel the head just at the surface, partially coming out more and more with each push.

It was a maddening game of two steps forward, one step back. The baby would slide back up a bit between every contraction, which I found extremely frustrating. I had my hand on the baby's head during the rests and would talk to him, half saying and half crying desperately, "Come on out, just please come on out… I need you to get here…"

I asked Kori how many more contractions were left. She didn't answer; who was to say?

"Just estimate! Is it two? Is it twenty??" I demanded, a crazed expression covering my sweat-sheened face. She guessed I had about five contractions left. "Okay," I said. "I can do this in five."

I pushed with all my might. Kori checked for his heartbeat, but it was very faint. She took my hands in hers and locked eyes with me.

"Becca. You need to push this baby out, NOW," she urged me.

I pushed harder than I ever thought I could. I screamed. I raged. I cried. And finally, at 9:59 pm, our child was born.

"Oh my God," I said as his head finally came out and stayed out. I quickly leaned back from squatting and pushed again as Kathy guided out his first shoulder, then the next, and finally he was here. She pulled him from the water and handed him to me.

It was the most breathtaking moment of my life.

Time stopped. Sound vanished. I just looked at our baby in my arms. I looked up at Keaton and we cried together with waves of joy and relief. The child was intensely quiet and alert — just looking around silently with his big, dark eyes. He didn't even cry. We stayed together in the tub while we waited for his cord to stop pulsing, taking in the moment through disbelief. I'd been waiting all day, yet somehow, his arrival seemed sudden.

After a minute we realized we hadn't checked the gender. We already knew, though. He was a boy just as I'd suspected. Moses was here.

Keaton cut his cord and I delivered the placenta (no one mentions that your work isn't over when the baby is out). The midwives gave Moses to Keaton and he lied on his chest while they tended to me. I had minimal bleeding and no tear; I couldn't believe it. I had made it through childbirth in one piece.

I took Moses back in my arms and nursed him for the first time, letting it sink in that I was a mother holding my child. Kathy weighed and measured Moses in a hammock-style cloth fish scale while we all looked on and chuckled. We couldn't believe how big and juicy he was! I'd made a 9 pound 6 ounce baby, 20.5 inches long.

Around midnight, Keaton's mom Kari came downstairs to meet Moses. We wept together. She shared how she and Mark had been upstairs cheering us on all day, listening through the vents for the sounds of a baby, their first grandchild.

The midwives gathered up all their supplies and left us to spend our first night together. I couldn't believe they were leaving us amateurs alone with a baby! Moses slept on our chests in contentment after his long day; he had taken his time in arriving, quiet and unrushed, in contrast to my cannon-fire entrance into the world. I already had a sense that his earthy quiet would temper my hurricane energy.

The time afterward was a blur of nursing, resting, eating, and crying whenever I looked at Moses or even thought about him for too long. He became the most precious thing to us. As consumed as I felt going through the power of labor, it diminished when compared to the all-consuming, relentless love I now felt for my son. This love, motherhood, was the transformative force that would devour me and reveal something new where I'd once stood.

Mother to Mother

My relationship with my own mother was complicated and difficult for me. I'd hardly spoken with her in recent years besides occasional, brief phone calls — we weren't the type to have lunch together or chat on the phone, like some friends I knew.

Neither my mother or I were willing to move toward the discomfort of our relationship; I felt that the responsibility of repairing our connection should not fall to me, and the fact of my having a baby did not solve the years of history we had to reckon with.

We had never cleared the air of what happened in the divorce, let alone the years leading up to it. Whether from fear or shame, she never owned the fact that she'd had a spiteful edge toward my dad and tried to turn us against him for decades, that she'd had at least one romantic affair and lied to us all about it continuously, or even that she had allowed her mental health to suffer and repeatedly refused help from therapists she didn't like. She never owned the fact that her actions and inactions had caused us significant pain with lasting repercussions.

What she did do, over time, was talk about how much she hated herself and had regrets about the past. But indulgent self-deprecation does not amount to an apology or repair. It does not feel the same as looking someone in the eyes without excuse and saying, "I am deeply sorry for my actions. I was wrong. I understand they caused you to suffer in these ways. I wish I had known better and done better for you. Here is what I am doing to change, so that I can do better moving forward."

Apologizing in this way is extremely humbling and hard to do. It can also be a step toward radical healing. It's a muscle I'm just beginning to familiarize myself with, after a lifetime of avoiding being wrong.

It is very challenging to move forward in a relationship without moving through conflict in a meaningful way. My family had always dodged confrontation, and I felt that I was waiting on both my parents for apologies and conversations that would never come. So, unable to move through the difficulty alongside them, I felt compelled to move forward without them.

During my pregnancy, my mother did support us by bringing meals for the family during Mark's cancer treatment, which we all appreciated. Kari and Mark tried repeatedly to have her stay for dinner and spend time with us. But each time, she insisted on leaving right away, even though she had cooked food for us all afternoon and driven an hour to deliver it. They looked at me, puzzled, as she drove away, and I shrugged to them in response.

In spite of all this distance, she was the first person I texted after Moses was born. She was still my mom, after all. She came out to meet him the next day and hung out so that Keaton and I could shower, eat, and rest. She told me to let her know if I wanted help again, any time.

But I didn't ask her for help with the baby. It was too difficult for me to spend time with her.

There was always a weighted and unaddressed history hanging heavy in the room. I felt that she had an uncanny ability to center herself in every conversation we had; having had five children herself, she positioned herself as an expert on parenting. She made a point to highlight that I was a novice, discussing her (more experienced) stance on cribs, vaccines, breastfeeding, and a number of other topics about which I hadn't asked.

I felt the urge to argue, to show her my stack of child psychology books, and to highlight all the ways I was purposefully parenting differently than she had. But I knew it wouldn't serve me to put my energy there. So over time,

I conserved my energy by keeping her at arm's length and she sadly only received updates through social media and text messages.

This wasn't spiteful on my part. I was insulating myself from unnecessary difficulty and emotional labor as I tried to move forward and build my life. Space was my solution. She didn't attempt to reach out, and didn't once offer to babysit. I likely would have accepted her help, but I wasn't willing to ask. I was sick and tired of the family's relational politics. This was the beginning of a two-year-long awkward silence between us; I felt that if she was too proud to even ask to see her grandchild, it shouldn't fall to me to make it happen.

Family

After Moses was born, Keaton took a month of paternity leave. He was amazing with Moses; we made a great team, as we expected we would. We didn't leave the apartment for two weeks, except to take short walks, at the encouragement of our midwives. The world was all Moses, all the time. Everything else faded into the backdrop.

Over the coming months, we spent a great deal of time upstairs in the house with Mark and Kari, plus Keaton's brothers for family meals and lazy afternoons watching sitcoms. Mark's health was declining, but he was still well enough to get around, and he loved holding baby Moses and chit-chatting with him on the couch. As Moses began to crawl, Mark would settle down onto the rug with him and pretend to be baby cougars, a game he had played with his sons when they were babies.

I celebrated my 23rd birthday a couple of months after Moses was born. In my birthday reflections, I noticed my newly discovered appreciation for my physical body and a deep sense of positivity toward it. I felt comfortable in my skin, transformed by motherhood as it was. I was proud of what I had accomplished in making Moses and nourishing him, day in and day out.

It felt important to me to advocate for my needs as a mother and a woman, so I took to nursing Moses whenever and wherever he needed to eat. The whole household, the whole neighborhood really, became accustomed to seeing me breastfeeding. And I chose not to put a scarf over him, because who wants to eat under a hot blanket?

I was unapologetic, feeling no need to manage others' discomfort around seeing breasts in their most natural element. "Modesty," as Christians put it, was so far from my radar that it scarcely occurred to me as a factor to consider. The deeper shift that I felt was a willingness to assert myself and take up space, and a refusal to treat my powerful body as inherently shameful or sexual.

Unknowingly, I was discovering a gradual comfort with not only nudity, but with holding court and being seen. It became increasingly significant as the years passed.

Past Into Present

Around the time I became pregnant with Moses, I began having recurring, troubling dreams about Cory, my fifth-grade boyfriend and post-graduation flame. These dreams had happened a handful of times in past years, but now they were becoming regular. I finally told Keaton about them and they evolved into a running joke.

"You see Cory last night?" he'd ask me with a wink over our morning coffee. I'd respond with an embarrassed sigh and muse curiously about why on earth I was dreaming of someone I hadn't seen or spoken to in five years.

In the dreams, I was back at that house party in Sunriver where I had last seen Cory. I walked toward him and called his name. Through the dream and through the house he was elusive, keeping his back turned to me. I could never see his face, never find the moment to stand still and connect with him. I'd weave across the building, up stairs, through throngs of people, trying to apologize, trying to set things right, but his distance implied that I was invisible, or he couldn't hear me.

These dreams went on for months. I didn't think about him in daily life, and I believed I had long forgiven myself for my drunken teenage mistakes. But something deep in my psyche just would not let him go.

Faith, Unraveled

Throughout my pregnancy and the months after Moses' birth, my faith in Christianity had been deteriorating. I was especially aware of this disconnect during conversations with Mark and Kari. I was perplexed by Mark's refusal to try some Turkey Tail mushroom capsules I'd ordered for him, which were a groundbreaking supportive therapy for brain tumors.

He said he trusted God and didn't feel like he needed to try and control the cancer. He said all this while undergoing chemotherapy and radiation. I was confused. Did he trust God, or did he trust the doctors? What role did he believe God played in all this? Or in life and death in general? And, why didn't more Christians trust natural remedies like mushrooms, if God was the creator of all the brilliance of nature?

I struggled with the cognitive dissonance, and Keaton confided that he did as well, but there was nothing to be done. At this point, we just wanted Mark to feel comfortable and supported.

But God's role in people like my mom and Mark developing cancer was just the tip of the spear. I continued to turn over numerous doubts in my head one by one, and they grew within me like an untamed garden of free thinking. First, I finally acknowledged that I had an attraction to women, and I didn't believe that was a sin. Why would God want men to be attracted to women, but not me?

I realized I no longer believed in Hell as a literal place where nonbelievers would be punished. The notion which, as a child, had kept me awake at night in distress, now seemed comical. I thought of my non-Christian friends who were beautiful, generous, loving souls doing actual good in the world. I thought of all the Christians I knew and saw on TV who were misogynistic, prejudiced and greedy. I thought of everything I'd learned during Bible College about the origins of the Bible — the forgeries, the councils voting on what would be included, the changes made by scribes over the years. Something wasn't adding up.

One night, I woke up to feed Moses. As he fell back asleep, I grabbed my phone and typed "ex-Christian pastor" into the search bar. I hesitated for a moment, feeling guilty to be peering over the cliff-like edges of my faith.

I tapped "Go" on my glowing screen.

I had just leapt down the rabbit hole and there would be no praying my way back out.

I found books and blogs, entire YouTube channels even, made by former ministers, preachers, and priests who had left the church. I took a deep dive. It was as if there was a whole underground movement confirming that, no, I was not off base for questioning Christianity. I read articles and listened to podcasts where people put into words the exact questions and problems I had with the belief system. They examined not only the holes in the logic, of which there were plenty, but also the clear ways within society that Christianity failed to demonstrate the reality of a good and perfect God who was actively transforming lives.

Christians were just people. People with a belief system, like practitioners of all other religions. The unbelievers on my screen saw what I saw when they examined the church: well-intentioned people who believed a set of strange, unbelievable and sometimes harmful things, within a welcoming and close-knit community.

One night, a few weeks later, Keaton, Moses and I were out on our evening walk. Moses was wrapped in the baby carrier, asleep on my chest. As we crossed through the city park, I confessed my unbelief to Keaton. My heart pounded. I was so worried he would feel betrayed, like I was no longer the person he had married. I had gone from a worship leader to an agnostic in the time it took me to cook up his child in my belly.

"I want to tell you something," I said, unusually timid. "I… I don't think I believe in God anymore. And I definitely don't believe Christianity is true," I told him. He was quiet for a minute. We crossed the street in silence "…. Maybe you saw that coming," I added.

"Yeah. You know what? I don't think I do either," he said, looking over at me.

"Wait — what??" I asked. I was shocked.

"Nope. I think we needed to be away from the church to figure that out. I'm not really sure what I believe anymore. I think I believe in God, but not in the way we were taught. I think we should just live and let live," he explained.

I was truly amazed, and deeply relieved.

Deep Dive

For months after that, I went on a deep dive, deconstructing the Christian faith, brick by brick. Keaton was the only one who knew. I read books by Bart Ehrman, Sam Harris and Christopher Hitchens. I gorged myself on the Godless in Dixie blog.

I began cautiously talking with friends who had left the church and had similar experiences. Two of my sisters and my brother had already left the church. Kara was agnostic, Shana was Buddhist, and David seemed to believe that he was God and the actual center of the universe. I watched documentaries. I studied cult mentality and the ways people come to form beliefs and groups to reinforce them. I found it both fascinating and troubling.

I already knew more about the Bible than the average Christian. I had read it front to back, and studied it for two years of college. I knew the context in which different texts were written and which texts had unknown authors or massive issues with translation. I had known since college that the Bible was a flawed and patchworked document, the content of which was voted on by a group of old men at the Council of Nicaea, 300 years after Christ was said to be crucified.

I viewed the Bible as a flawed historical document, not a divine one. It baffled me that anyone professing to have intellectual integrity would call the book anything else. Those who claimed the Bible was divine after having studied it must have some skin in the game, I concluded.

The more time passed, the angrier I became.

I felt like I had been duped. I had devoted my entire young life to something that was comically unbelievable. The only way to continue believing it was to surround myself with the people who also did. As soon as I had removed myself from those influences, I felt I could hear myself more clearly and see the world around me with clarity. It had more dimension, more color, more nuance than the appealingly over-simplified story about the world that I had been spoon-fed since birth.

There was also grief.

I felt like God had died. My invisible, lifelong companion, the one I talked to when I was all alone or fearful or hopeful, wasn't actually there. Or at least, God wasn't what I thought he was. I was relieved to no longer be talking in my head to an unresponsive ceiling, but I was angry that I had been taught stories that supported judgment, prejudice and separating myself from entire groups of people who Christianity deemed as wrong and sinful.

I realized that the internal tension around my natural sexuality, and the shame I felt projected onto me for so many years, was a construct. It occurred to me that — obviously — sex was more than reproduction for married couples, as Christians claimed. It was a vehicle for pleasure and release and connection, and the church's attempt to control it was exactly that — vying for control. I felt I had been robbed and harmed by something with no other purpose than to control people's behavior and ensure the survival of the faith to the next generation.

I was stirring the pot. It felt terrible, and it felt good.

This courageous exploration at the boundaries of my comfort zone, this unbridled inquiry and that nervous thrill in the pit of my stomach as I teetered on the precipice of new and unknown territories: this is the experience I've come to know as Edge Play. This discipline has shaped me into the capacious person I am today, someone who can tolerate discomfort, even find a thrill in it, and stay present with it long enough to be transformed.

13

Death & Dying

Best & Worst

Whenever Kari talks about that year with Mark and the family, she says, "It was the best of times and the worst of times." It truly was. It was as if the volume had been turned up on every emotion and every experience. The house seemed to become a nest. Friends, family members, and church members turned up frequently to bring us food or take care of the landscaping. Family nights became more and more frequent until shared dinners and cozy evenings in the living room were the default.

Mark and Kari were more in love than ever and shared countless little and big moments throughout the year. I'll never forget them lounging on the back patio around the fire pit or eating lemon curd crepes together on lazy mornings.

Mark's condition steadily declined as the year went on. Several rounds of treatment and one brain surgery contributed to the day to day rollercoaster of unknowns that come with a cancer diagnosis.

We made several sweet family getaways, including a couple trips to the beach, one of Mark's favorite places. We had game nights. Mark and I set out to bake all the things he had never baked. We made crème brulee, pull-apart monkey bread, apple muffins, donuts. Mark bought a recumbent bike — I had the privilege of taking him to the bike shop across town to pick it up — and he grinned as he rode it around the neighborhood on good days.

We kept up our annual holiday tradition, Express Christmas, an idea we'd borrowed from the sitcom *Modern Family*. To launch the month of December, we would split up into teams and allot just two hours to put up the tree, decorate the house, and create a wintry holiday feast. We did it every year. It's still one of my all-time favorite holiday memories.

There were also moments that I believe we'd all rather forget. There's a certain loss of dignity that comes with losing agency over your body and mind. I'd rather remember Mark mountain biking, returning from his morning runs, building with his sons. That's who he was. Toward the end, there were several falls and some broken bones. There were personality changes due to the brain tumor. There was family conflict. Times were hard.

Fear

We loved watching Moses grow from infant to baby. He brought beams of joy into the home at a dark and heavy time. But even this was tinted with hardship. When he was six months old, Moses began having seizure-like episodes. At first, we thought they were fever related, but then they continued. They were usually triggered by motion, like swinging or bouncing.

During these episodes, he would go into a blank and unresponsive state and then become extremely lethargic and spend the next 12 hours vomiting. It was painful and terrifying for a mother and father to witness. We didn't know how to comfort our baby who was so confused about what was going on. We had some truly awful ER visits that involved long waits, blood draws, CT scans, EEG's, and all manner of things no baby should have to endure.

He had such a negative association with the emergency room that for the next year, he would scream in terror any time I laid him down on a changing table or a floor in a new environment.

All of Moses' tests came back totally normal. The doctors couldn't explain what was happening or why. His neurologist didn't seem concerned, since he was developing normally and otherwise seemed to be a happy, healthy baby. We watched and waited. The episodes happened almost like clockwork every 28 days. I felt crazy when I started theorizing that perhaps they were connected to the moon cycles. We were plagued with worry — was it epilepsy? Had something traumatic happened while he was in the womb? Was it related to the car accident? There were no answers.

The doctors theorized that it was Cyclical Vomiting Syndrome, something we had never heard of, and surmised that he may be at risk for migraines later in life.

Around his first birthday, Moses had his last episode and nothing like it has happened since. By his second birthday, we finally let ourselves relax. I feel so grateful to have a healthy child, but his seizures and hospital visits robbed us of a great deal of joy and peace during his infancy that we can never get back.

Afterlife

During the year Mark was sick, the contrast between spiritualities became messy.

Keaton watched as his father, thinking more about the end of life and concerned about the eternal fate of his sons, tried one by one to evangelize to them and ensure their place in Heaven. He begged Ty, the eldest son and a known atheist, to watch a Christian film called *A Case for Christ*. He confided in Keaton that it felt like the most important thing to him, at the end of his life, to know that his sons would be in Heaven.

It was painful for Keaton to witness this after having left the faith himself. None of our family members knew that we were no longer Christians. He chose to simply tell Mark what he needed to hear — he didn't want to add unnecessary stress by voicing his own loss of faith at such a sensitive time.

Mark asked us if we would play a hymn at his memorial service. We were honored that he would ask. For months, we were conflicted: should we give a dying man his wish, or might he feel betrayed if he knew the song wasn't sung from a heart of devotion to God? We didn't know.

A Father

Mark had become somewhat of an honorary father to me, too. He was someone who had earned my trust and respect. I felt accepted around him. He asked good questions and wanted to know how I saw things; our analytical brains and comic sensibilities worked in similar ways. He gave tight hugs and complete presence; he was devoted and steady. During his last year we had the opportunity to share a lot of one-on-one time baking, taking walks, and driving to his radiation appointments.

Before all the cancer and appointments, Mark had taken me to a Blazer game, just he and I. (And Moses, who was only a twelve-week old belly bump at the time.) As we walked down the night's cold, bustling streets toward the Moda Center, surrounded by commuters and basketball fans, Mark asked me about my family. How were they? He wanted to know. This caught me off guard. People in my life didn't know or ask much about my family. I offered vague updates about my mom and sisters, the little that I knew, and then glossed quickly over the fact that David was still in prison and my dad, well, we were out of touch.

"Why don't you call him?" Mark asked.

"Hmm… it's complicated," I answered.

He looked at me and furrowed his brow.

"Why is it complicated?" he asked.

"Well, a lot has happened between the wedding and now. I know I haven't talked much about it," I said. "I'm not even sure I have his number anymore. Truthfully, I have a feeling the next time I see him will probably be on his deathbed… sad as that is."

At this, Mark halted.

"Oh, Becca," he said, visibly distressed by my statement. "That just breaks my heart. I can't imagine having my kids say that."

"Well, that's because you're an awesome dad, Mark. They would never have a reason to say something like that," I replied. I was uncomfortable with his sympathy. The sense of pity reminded me why I rarely spoke of my dad.

When the streetlight changed, we continued walking. But Mark stopped again, this time in the middle of the crosswalk.

"Becca. Please call your dad. I don't know what he did, but I just know that someday you'll wish you'd reached out to him."

I nodded with a half-smile and continued walking, not wishing to discuss it further.

"Becca," he said, insistent.

"Okay. I'll call him," I said, urging him to get out of the street. "Come on," I said with a wave and a chuckle.

He stood, staring at me.

"Seriously," he said.

"I'll call him!" I said again, amused and touched at his insistence. No one else in my life had so readily witnessed the inherent value of my relationship with my father.

• • •

It became clear in the spring that Mark would not get better. He was sleeping around 20 hours a day. Our prayers for a miracle shifted to plans for comfort as breakthrough therapies were ruled out and hospice workers were brought in. We were drained. We felt suspended in an unresolved state of grief. He was still with us, but not really... a lot of him was already gone.

Kari and I shared many tearful moments, trying to deal with the slow, grueling process of grieving someone who was gradually fading out of this life.

During Mark's final weeks, Keaton and I took to sleeping upstairs on the living room floor adjacent to the bedroom. Moses slept on the floor between us. We shared some sweet moments and good laughs together toward the end. We celebrated Mark's birthday in June. That morning Keaton and I came in to check on him.

"Did you hear the news?" Mark asked us.

"What news?" we asked.

"I died last night," he answered. He was totally serious.

"You... huh? You died?" We looked at each other, perplexed. We weren't sure whether to laugh or cry.

"Yep. I died last night. I'm dead." He looked on, dreamily, as though this were the most normal thing in the world.

"It seems like you're still here with us," I replied. "Um, what did it feel like?"

He smiled sleepily.

"It felt like chocolate," he answered.

That night, we filmed a home video singing happy birthday to Mark and eating ice cream in the bedroom. We passed around a tin of Almond Roca, his favorite. The boys cracked jokes. Moses cooed. It's a memory I'll cherish for all of my days. It felt like family. Deep, true, hell or high water, family.

Mark passed a week later, surrounded by all of us. We each had a moment alone with him during his last days to say goodbye. It was a surreal, heart-wrenching relief to have the dying process over with. It felt final and sudden, as perhaps all deaths do. We gathered in the backyard, where Mark and Kari had remarried the summer before, as the hospice team carried his empty body away. It was a bright July day. We noticed an expansive, marigold-colored butterfly fluttering around in the poppies and blueberry bushes. Kari later had its image tattooed on her arm.

Mark's memorial was packed with people from the larger community whose lives he had touched. As I sat in the front row beside Keaton, remembering Mark's life, I thought of what makes a life. I held Keaton's hand as we watched vintage photos of Mark's childhood stream across the big screen. I saw Keaton and his brothers, little blonde haired boys, laughing and playing with a young, strapping Mark. I felt grateful that Keaton had learned about fatherhood from this man. This person who showed up. He tried. He asked questions. He gave of himself.

I squeezed Keaton's hand, tears spilling tenderly down our cheeks, and we smiled down at baby Moses who bounced and crawled contentedly on our laps.

Of all the father figures who I had lost in recent years, Mark's death hurt the most. He had truly loved me with an unmatched care and respect and confidence in me, in a way no other mentor or leader or family member had.

Two summers earlier, Chelsea's father, Tim, who had housed me when I left home at 16, had died suddenly of a heart attack on a family camping trip. My college pastor, Brian, was no longer in my life since I had left the church and the faith through which he mentored me during college. My own father was on house arrest and awaiting trial.

It didn't seem like men were set up to be lasting fixtures in my life.

A New Normal

Life changed after Mark passed. We took our annual Sunriver trip, straight from the memorial service, and spread Mark's ashes on the Deschutes River Trail where he had spent so many sun-soaked days mountain biking with the boys.

Once we were home, life met us with difficulty. Kari learned one afternoon that I was no longer a Christian due to a post I had "Liked" on Facebook. She was upset and wished to talk about it, right then, at length. She felt betrayed and disappointed, and was confused on whether Keaton felt the same, or it was actually me behind this wholesale rejection of the church.

What began as a discussion escalated into a heated argument. She took personal offense at our rejection of God. I felt distressed, trying to navigate these nuanced talks about spirituality and personal beliefs while Moses climbed all over me and cried for attention. He could feel the tension building in the room and was beginning to whine. I felt cornered and attacked.

Ultimately, I blew up, stating simply that her being mad about us leaving Christianity was like being mad at someone for no longer believing in Santa

Claus. We weren't rejecting Santa Claus, we just didn't believe there was a Santa Claus to reject. This really upset her. The talk ended abruptly and awkwardly.

Kari began having side conversations with Keaton about the issue while I wasn't around. I felt disrespected and distrusted. Our relationship was sorely damaged by the rift, and a few months later, we moved out of the family house and rented a place of our own.

We also started an organic micro-dairy.

Micro-Farming

During my year as a stay-at-home mom, I'd gotten it in my head that I wanted to be a farmer. I had been reading books and researching for most of a year. As with most other passions of mine, I was adamant, and I roped Keaton into it. We leased some land across town, from the church family with whom I'd learned to grow vegetables and slaughter animals for meat, and used our tax return to buy a cow and two goats.

For a year, we milked those animals. Twice a day, every day, holidays and weekends alike. We sold out of the milk and Keaton was able to cut his hours at the boys shelter since the milk sales were mostly supporting us financially.

That year I discovered that I'm much more of a plant person than an animal person. Those fickle, messy, lovable creatures sometimes got under my skin.

It was a crazy time to try and run a business — Moses was barely a year old when we bought our first cow. It was a lot to juggle, and some family warned against it. In truth, it added extra strain to our already taxed marriage. He and I had been through so much in just a few short years together: several moves, several jobs, family crises, pregnancy and childbirth, neurological issues with our baby, the death of a father.

I was willing Keaton to be someone he wasn't — a scrappy, outdoorsy farmer dude. I thought he just needed the encouragement. I sometimes saw a blank canvas when I looked at him, as though I was waiting to discover what he might become. He agreed to the farm project to support me and my dream, but it was never his. It's comical to consider that I convinced my drummer, social worker husband to start a farm and milk cows with me.

For better or worse, I think I could have convinced him of just about anything at that time. I was charismatic and domineering and he was passive and wanting to please, a power dynamic I knew all too well from my own upbringing.

Running a micro-dairy was all about systems. There was distinctly one right way to do things, and it was imperative that we do things correctly, every time, for quality and safety reasons. We were soon unhappy. I was way too sporadic in my interests and fluid in my rule-following to do the same thing every day. And especially not something as high-stakes as micro-dairying, with all its lab testing and quality control and safety considerations. We began to dread milking every morning and every evening.

We should have taken our first cow dying during birth as a sign to let it go. But, virtually overnight, our friends and family crowdfunded $2,000 for us to buy a new cow. We named her Vida. That crazy cow caused us ongoing distress and, within months, convinced me that the dairying life was NOT for us. I did love the goats; they behaved like some sort of cleaner, sassier dogs, and it was hard to give them up.

A year into the project, we sold the animals and moved on with our lives.

Through this I learned how much I love the sweet relief of quitting. Ending. Open space where there was once an obligation. I guess these endings represented freedom to me. I hadn't yet learned (and perhaps I still haven't learned) how to gracefully adjust directions and pivot — I've been known to take more of a pendulum swinging, all or nothing, "knock the whole thing down and begin again" approach to life.

Home

After the farm, Keaton and I bought a small, butter yellow house two blocks east of the home where Moses was born and Mark had passed away. It was a charming place, the first spot to call our own. One evening as we lounged in our living room, he commented that he'd be happy to still live in that house after we'd paid it off in thirty years. I was in disbelief.

The thought of staying in one place for that long made me feel physically ill.

14

Open

We Need Weed

After we closed the micro dairy, Keaton got a job at a music education non-profit and I persuaded Farmer Mike (also remembered as "Brown Jesus" from the bakery) to create a position for me at his vegetable farm. I learned how to prune acres of tomato plants and pick crates of zucchini and ride on a lettuce transplanter. I delivered CSA shares and boxes of produce to hip Portland restaurants, flirting with the chefs in their kitchens as they sliced radicchio and sharpened knives.

I enjoyed being out in the world in a new way. After years of church, marriage, small town life, stay-at-home motherhood and farming, it was refreshing to meet new people within other subcultures and witness how they responded to me with warmth and curiosity. I fit into the world around me.

Mike was very challenging to work for. He was always stressed about money; vegetables have a very narrow profit margin, and next to nothing at wholesale pricing, and he transferred that stress to the team. I would often come home from my days in the field physically wiped out. But I couldn't relax once I got there. There was housework to be done and my baby to play with and meals to make.

"You need to learn how to chill," Keaton said one night.

"What I need is to smoke some weed," I replied, half joking.

Keaton hadn't used cannabis before, but it was 2014, and now that recreational use was legal in Oregon, he was totally open to the idea.

So I made it happen.

Preferring the old school style, I got a small baggie of homegrown weed from Farmer Mike. Soon, Keaton and I created a new routine: a couple of times a week, we'd put Moses to bed, pop a bowl of buttery popcorn, queue up *Saturday Night Live* on the TV, and smoke some sticky cannabis from my swirly glass pipe on our back deck.

This may seem like a small ritual, but these stoned evenings were a catalyst toward the rest of my life as I now know it. I owe a massive thanks to the cannabis plant for making the life I have today seem possible. Not once did I feel apologetic to my seventeen-year-old self who had made a "vow to God" at the beginning of Bible College to never smoke weed again.

Keaton and I had a hay day hanging out stoned in our living room. We laughed and joked and shared deep talks and had a fair amount of stoned sex. The cannabis helped erode the guardedness I'd built up toward him. It was more fun than we'd probably ever had together.

Face To Face

Summer slipped into fall. It was 2015, a year since Keaton's dad had passed. I had transitioned to a job on a cannabis farm tending to plants and stuffing joints. Moses was almost two.

One thing hadn't changed: I was still having dreams about Cory. After enduring two years of these ongoing dreams, I was at a loss. Keaton suggested a novel concept: what if I just talked to him? The thought terrified me, but I was willing to do whatever I needed to bury the hatchet and get on with my life.

I sent Cory a Facebook message. I explained that he'd been in my dreams recently and asked whether he'd be willing to meet with me. I offered no further explanation. He replied the following day, sounding sincerely surprised and curious. We decided to meet at a park in a neighboring town where, as it happened, he was now a firefighter.

It was a warm Sunday afternoon. On the drive over, I thought my heart might pound out of my chest. I wondered what I might say, what it would be like to stand in front of this man who I had known most of my life, and who had occupied so many hours of my dream life that I was unsure I could even separate my imagined version of him from the real one. I felt droplets of sweat collecting on my forehead as I rounded the sunny bend to meet him.

There in the parking lot, he climbed out of his red truck and smiled his warm familiar smile at me. I was transported back to my youth. We wrapped each other in a long, warm hug. He was exactly… Cory. The tall, strong, gentle bear of a man I'd remembered. As we walked to a grassy knoll to settle for a while, he stared at me, an incredulous smile on his face. I could see his wheels turning, clearly trying to piece together the reason I'd brought him there.

Sitting on the hill, talking over the sounds of children squealing on the nearby play structures, I brought up the dreams I'd been having and my unresolved feelings about our past. I didn't go on for long, and I didn't tell him the dreams had lasted two years. He listened graciously, nodding as I spoke.

When I was finished, Cory told me that he'd let it all go a long time ago — chalked it up to a drunken teenage drama. He shared that he had always thought highly of me and wished me the best. I breathed a sigh of relief. Well that was… easy. Anticlimactic, even. I almost felt silly. But alas, my dream self had forced me into it. I acknowledged aloud that many years had passed — I was a mother now, he was a police officer turned wildland firefighter — and it seemed silly to hold onto such a youthful mistake from the past.

I could feel an energetic shift, a settling, after I said my peace and Cory received it with simple grace. I wondered why I hadn't had the courage to come here and have this talk years ago.

I could have left after that fifteen minutes, but I chose not to. We stayed at the park together for three hours, surprised at how naturally our conversation flowed, as though no time had passed. We caught up on the past several years — college degrees, relationships, careers, shared memories. We both seemed to be looking for reasons not to leave. There was a clear heart connection between us, an electricity. I sensed that the people we had become shared even more in common than our younger selves.

We stood to leave. Before we parted, I asked Cory what he had been expecting when I reached out. He told me that he'd had no idea, but his friends had joked that if I was a married woman having dreams about him, Keaton and I must be swingers!

I laughed it off.

"Ah! Well, we're open minded, but we're not quite that far out," I said, growing hot and averting my eyes.

We hugged tight, lingering slightly, and went our separate ways. I walked a little lighter in the following weeks, relieved to have finally sorted through things. I thought I had moved on, until the dreams came back in full force.

OPEN

Only this time, they were romantic dreams.

Fuck! I had made things worse.

Be Normal

I felt like I'd used my one chance to sort out this hang-up with Cory and still be perceived as a sane, loyal person. I couldn't imagine Keaton adjusting well to the notion of these continuous dreams. I felt guilty for feeling the way I did, like my subconscious self was betraying my husband.

I tried to set it aside, wanting so badly to have this saga resolved; Keaton had been gracious and understanding for years now, but still, I couldn't seem to let Cory go. I had a deep attachment to him that I couldn't explain. If it wasn't the hang-up about how our connection ended, then what was it?

Every few months, I'd casually exchange a few texts with Cory just to say "hey" and check in. It thrilled me to see his name appear on my phone. I felt an excitement I hadn't felt since college. I didn't mention any of this to Keaton, and I never wrote anything I wouldn't want him to read. I was walking a fine line. At times, when the guilt overcame me, I was disciplined enough to stay out of touch with Cory, but then the romantic dreams only became more frequent and lusciously detailed.

About six months after I saw Cory at the park, I experienced an internal tantrum that threw my life decisions into question. In many ways, it was a long time coming.

I was at home doing yoga one afternoon while Moses napped. Keaton was gone at work. I laid on my mat in pigeon pose, reliving a sex dream I'd had about Cory the night before. I was feeling sexually frustrated, yet again.

Is this seriously going to be my life... forever? I thought to myself. *Until I die... just me and Keaton? In this house? In this small fucking town where he grew up?*

The thought terrified me.

I felt like a part of me was starving to death. Keaton and I were close friends and getting along well enough, but there was nearly no heat between us anymore, not that there really ever had been. We had endured so much together, and our relationship was taxed to weakness by the pressures of work, grief over Mark's death, and beautiful Moses receiving most of our attention.

I had become bossy and bitchy toward him; he was inattentive and distant.

This naturally led to a cold, hollow energy in the bedroom. Backs turned to one another, together but alone.

Keaton was the recipient of my stinging words and careless comments, and because he didn't feel emotionally close to me, he didn't want to have sex with me. This was a toxic cycle where neither of us were getting what we needed. I recognized that opening our relationship wouldn't make us happier, that we needed to heal the existing problems between us.

With some long, cannabis-assisted talks and a hefty dose of humility, we felt we were getting to the heart of the struggle. We tried to be humble and candid with each other and ultimately, we identified the negative feedback loop of my emotional distance and his sexual distance. Over the next several months, our relationship drastically improved. We felt much happier together and more prioritized. We found a peaceful rhythm in the midst of busyness and hard work.

Still, steady as the shore, the romantic dreams with Cory went on.

I found myself waking up from indulgent dreams with a sinking feeling in my stomach — realizing that it had all been imagined and bore no resemblance to my actual life. The romance, the affection, and the sex were all products of my mind, not a reality. And this made my heart ache. My mind was stuck in a loop that had begun on my yoga mat: *Is this my life now?* And furthermore, is this desire even about Cory, or is he simply representing an unmet need?

I had always sensed undertones of affection from Cory, but wasn't sure, because he clearly respected the obvious boundaries of my marriage. I was his friend and a married woman; even if he had an attraction to me, he would never have expressed it.

One morning, I broached the topic while cracking eggs and stirring vegetables in the kitchen.

Keaton was stacking blocks with Moses in the living room and seemed nearly unaffected when I told him that my dreams about Cory had grown more intense, not less. I had never explicitly told him that they were romantic. I explained how I felt guilty and conflicted, like I was cheating on him in my sleep. I also felt guilty for staying in contact with Cory without Keaton's awareness; I'd been totally monogamous and loyal to Keaton for five years, and I'd never had a secret attraction that I hid from him, beyond the fleeting and playful crush.

He asked me what I expected him to do with that information. I didn't know, I just needed to get it off my chest. I expressed how I wasn't sure how long I could live in the tension between my dream life and my lived reality. I wished that I could have two lives, so that I could keep our happy family life just as it was, but also experience what I felt I'd missed out on with Cory.

"Is… that even possible?" I mused, tiptoeing carefully. These were uncharted waters. I felt I was handling a bomb.

"Well… I'm sure there are people out there who have done it," he said dryly.

I stared at him. "What, like an open marriage?"

He just looked up at me and shrugged.

"Not sure what else to say, Babe. I'm not sure what you're asking for."

I wanted to find out if my dreams were based on a real connection, or an idealized version of who Cory was and how things could be. I wondered if polyamory, being in multiple romantic relationships at once, could even work. In some ways, I'd learned during high school that I had a capacity for this complexity, but a lot had changed since then.

Options

Over the next few weeks, I hashed out my options: I could try seeking therapy and see if this would help me uproot Cory's presence in my dreams. I could talk to Cory again, and see if he had any interest in dating me experimentally. I could do nothing and live with the current reality indefinitely.

I decided to make an appointment with a local therapist; her soonest opening was five weeks out. I called around to numerous others and encountered the same issue. The thought of therapizing myself out of these desires felt forced, and not like a true solution, but when I imagined what my friends and peers would suggest I do, it seemed almost mandatory.

From the outside, it probably seems like the obvious "right decision" would have been self-sacrifice. Most of society would tell me to cut off the source of temptation and remain faithful to my husband. *Don't feed the connection with the outside man.*

At the time, I was thinking very little of Keaton's needs and desires; in many ways, I'd spent the last five years adapting to the expectations of our marriage and suburban life, which he was much more suited for than I was. I'd begun to lose myself in my role as a wife and a mother. I felt bound to society's standards for marriage and motherhood, not out of deep personal values, but out of obligation.

This was an important crossroads in my life.

Would I continue in a status quo, nearly sexless relationship, in a life that felt small and established, and possibly find myself miserable in a few years? Or would I rewrite the script?

I wanted to rewrite the script, to find a creative way to have it all. But I also felt afraid. How might this situation harm my relationships at home? How would my stepping out affect Moses, and what would the cost be with Keaton? I knew that I was playing with fire. Still, I felt that I would always regret letting this deep, visceral passion, this willingness to explore the corners of life, this adventurous spirit which was so essential to my identity, continue to shrink and die. I'd been losing touch with her for years.

Keaton didn't have a desire to explore outside of our marriage. He was content with the life we'd built and had no interest in dating. This disparity of desires further pronounced the distance between us. I felt that the power was all in my hands, and he felt like the only way for us to stay married was to give me the freedom to explore with Cory. I wanted to be married to Keaton. I loved our family and our life, but I also felt trapped and unhappy within its monogamous restraints.

While I never gave him an ultimatum, I was beginning to feel I was out of other options. I'd tried to repair our sex life so many times. I'd made numerous changes in my work and daily life to scratch the itch for adventure. We'd been working on the other aspects of our relationship. I was lined up to see a therapist.

In simple honesty, what I wanted was the experience of being with a new person. It was about Cory, and it was also about more than Cory. When I sat beside him at the park that day, I felt an energy between us that made me feel like a woman in every sense of the word. It seemed almost visible to me, like a matrix of flashing electrical impulses, magnetizing us and swirling around in a silent exchange.

Because I could foresee no end to the vivid, ferocious dreams, I took the moment as a signal from something deep inside of me. My soul was unwilling to cast the rest of my life as a woman, on the altar of lifelong sexual exclusivity that I'd promised my husband when I was 20.

I knew that I needed to flip the script.

Open

We discussed all of our fears and the risks involved with opening our relationship, even experimentally. The worst-case scenarios frightened us the most: what if I fell in love with Cory, or came to believe that I was better off with him? What if I fell out of love with Keaton and abandoned our family? What if polyamory drove an irreparable wedge between us? Would we always look back on this decision as the beginning of the end?

Through tears, I explained to Keaton that I simply could not imagine any of that happening. He was my family, the closest family I'd ever had. We'd been through so much together. Even on our worst days, I loved him immensely. I enjoyed his friendship and felt grateful for his presence in my life. We had become adults together. I couldn't envision wanting to build a life with someone else.

I also knew that, even in another life, Cory and I were incompatible long-term. He was a free spirit, go-with-the-flow type, prone to heavy drinking and lack of foresight. He had deep wounds from a turbulent childhood and racial injustice that he glazed over with a smile and positive attitude. I couldn't fathom building a life with him, but I also loved his heart and held a deep connection with him that felt unresolved. I felt this exploration was a safe bet, because Keaton and Cory occupied totally different arenas of my heart. I knew with certainty I would never leave Keaton to be with Cory.

Keaton agreed to me meeting with Cory.

I texted him nervously. *What was I supposed to say?* I had never done any of this before. Should I just casually mention that my marriage was now open, and ask this man on a date? Well, that's exactly what I did. I asked if he wanted to meet me for coffee or go on a hike. A part of me almost wished he would say no, effectively shutting the door and saving me from my wild self.

Cory was surprised and delighted. He said he'd love to see me, especially with the new knowledge of my open relationship.

When I told Keaton that night, we both became emotional. Shit had just gotten very real.

Keaton asked me again what I was expecting and hoping to get out of this. Did I want to fall in love? Did I want to be affectionate? I wasn't sure. I'd envisioned making dinner with him, having hours-long conversations, holding hands, kissing. Potentially more? I trailed off, unsure how much of my fantasy life to disclose.

Keaton nodded soberly. He explained that I may have to prepare for emotional distance on his part. He didn't want to keep me at arm's length, but he couldn't tell how this dynamic would affect him. He said he needed to protect himself. It seemed the honesty of our decision only partially relieved his sense of betrayal. In hindsight, I can see that this wasn't true consent —

he was agreeing because he felt he had no other options.

The next morning, I texted Cory in an attempt to cancel our plans. I was panicking. Cory was understanding but didn't quite grasp that I was having second thoughts. He explained that he was hesitant too, having never dated someone in an open relationship. He understood the risks and said he would feel awful if our seeing each other caused problems between Keaton and I.

Ethical Slut

Cory sent me a picture of a book that would end up changing my life: *The Ethical Slut*. Had I read it? He wanted to know. At first, I was offended. Was he calling me a slut?? I would later learn that a slut is defined in this book as a sex-positive person who incorporates sex into their life in an abundant and positive way. That description felt like me, or at least the aspirational me who hadn't yet found herself.

That evening, I sat down with Keaton and explained that I was reconsidering. I knew it wasn't fair to ask him to embrace an open marriage when we had agreed to be exclusive. I was the one whose desires had changed, so I should be the one to adapt. There was no middle ground that I could see; there was only monogamy or non-monogamy. I thought that it would be better for me to suffer the pain of letting Cory go, however I might make that happen, than to bring Keaton and Cory and Moses into it and potentially hurt everyone in the wake. Better for one person to hurt than four. Right?

But Keaton was skeptical. He wasn't sure this was a true solution, though he seemed relieved at the idea of finally putting all this behind us and getting back to normal.

Later that night, as we lay in our bed, he rubbed my back and I sobbed into the darkness, shedding tears for all the love I would never know. I felt regret for signing so much of myself away at age 20. It hurt me that all of this had hurt Keaton. It hurt me that there was no easy answer.

For the next few weeks, I did my best to put the issue away. I didn't reschedule with Cory. I worked and played with Moses, had tea with my friends, and embraced my life.

But I felt dishonest and phony, doing the textbook "right thing" while fostering resentment. I had been so close to a freedom my soul craved, and I'd gone about it in what felt like the ethical way, while so many couples were lying to each other and having secret affairs.

I sat on the couch with Keaton one night and explained all this to him. We were going in circles. I didn't ask if I could see Cory. I just wanted Keaton to know that I hadn't moved on. I was still working at it and willing to try, but I was not willing to hide away in shame, as I had for several years of dreaming.

I ordered two books: *Open* by Jenny Block and *The Ethical Slut* by Dossie Easton and Janet Hardy. When *Open* came, I read it within 24 hours. I felt for the first time that I wasn't alone in this relational tumult. The author was a highly sexual woman who had seemingly found a way to make an open marriage work, after originally committing to monogamy.

Cut To The Chase

Later that week, Keaton told me that he knew where this was all going. Could we just cut to the chase, already? He told me to go and see Cory. At least then I would know if there was something there worth pursuing. He later told me that there was a part of him that hoped it would be over and done with soon and we could return to our normal lives.

Perhaps one or two dates would heal this broken thing inside of me, get the impulse out of my system, and enable me to be a content wife.

I met Cory in early March at a Whole Foods. I was happy to be there, and also keenly aware that I was on a date, in public, with a man who was not my husband. We talked for several hours and walked around the outdoor mall until sunset. I kept my hands in my coat pockets. I'd spent several years learning how to engage in a non-flirtatious way with men; those habits were ingrained and difficult to unlearn.

We candidly discussed the nuances and expectations of our situation. It seemed we were on the same page; he knew that this was a detour for him, since he ultimately wanted a family: wife and kids and monogamy. We agreed that however and whenever this ended, we would be prepared and move apart with respect. It felt refreshingly clear.

The afternoon sped past. I needed to get home. When we reached the parking lot, I stopped and turned to Cory to say goodbye. He looked at me and smiled in silence for a moment too long, and I thought he might lean in to kiss me. I deflected. I dug for my keys awkwardly, muttering, "Alright... I'm going to go," through nervous laughter. We hugged tight.

On the drive home, I felt invigorated and very freaked out. My phone buzzed in my purse. I knew it was him texting. My heart swelled when I read his message: He was all in. He was excited to see where this might go and grateful for my courage in reaching out to him.

It's understandable that Keaton and I struggled when Cory came into the picture.

It was one of the hardest periods in our already taxed relationship. We were undergoing a fundamental shift in the structure and paradigm of our marriage, so challenge was a certainty. Not to mention that this shift was fully initiated by me and not something that Keaton, who identifies as monogamous and demi-sexual, would ever have asked for. *(A person who identifies as demi-sexual can experience sexual interest within emotionally bonded and trusting relationships, though sex is less of the focus. Demisexuality exists on the spectrum of asexuality.)*

This relational shake up led to several more weeks of late-night discussions to lay out all our fears, hopes, ideas, and expectations. I have to admit, our nightly cannabis usage enabled us to work through these scary topics with open minds and the ability to zoom out beyond our own egos and immediate impulses to react. It would have been a messier and more drawn out process had we been stone cold sober throughout these talks.

Note to other couples: Think about sharing a nice joint before getting into it… If that's your thing.

N.R.E.

I placed a lot of pressure on myself at home when I first started seeing Cory. I wanted to make sure that Keaton didn't regret giving me this freedom, so I went into relational overdrive during that first month. I fully committed myself to making sure that Moses was happy and well cared for, and that Keaton felt prioritized emotionally and sexually, but not overly doted on. My mind was on Cory throughout each passing day. We were in the buzzy, early phase of our relationship.

In the world of non-monogamy, this is known as NRE or New Relationship Energy, and it can take a toll on one's existing relationship.

I was in happy disbelief to be experiencing this new relationship with Cory and I felt free and relieved knowing that Keaton had lent me his support. But the infatuation was palpable, overwhelming at times, and Cory seemed to permeate all my waking thoughts. Interestingly, the dreams stopped as soon as we started seeing each other and never returned.

I allowed myself to escape the present and lose myself in daydreams of heat and connection and pursuit with Cory. But, juggling all of this, I was tired. I felt like I was running on empty all the time. I hadn't blocked out time for any days to myself, and as an introvert, I needed time alone to reflect and recharge. I'd been squeezing in moments for myself during Moses' nap times and late nights, but I knew that I was running myself into the ground.

Every morning I woke up still feeling exhausted. My sleep quality declined. I had chronic neck pain, headaches and body aches. I lost my appetite. But I continued on, dusting myself off after each emotional mountain and valley, too stubborn and excited to admit that I needed to slow down.

It helped to remind myself that for me, the initial phase of a relationship usually lasted for just a few weeks. I knew that the chemical cocktail in my brain would soon subside, as it had in all my past relationships.

The infatuation with Cory lasted about a month. Our first date (if you can call it that) was our coffee date at Whole Foods. He asked me to go bouldering with him the following weekend. I had never done any rock climbing, but had committed myself to getting out of my comfort zone and trying new things; that was half of the thrill of this, anyway. I can see looking back that this craving for new experiences was a primary driver in opening my marriage.

So, I agreed. We had a fun and terrifying time bouldering. It came naturally to me, and Cory was a relative beginner as well, so we divided our time climbing routes and sitting on the gym mats, sharing stories. He shared a story about the "It's On Us" campaign, which he helped lead on his college campus. It seeks to build culture around consent, bystander intervention, and survivor support. He told me of a time he physically intervened to protect a drunken mutual friend from an unwanted sexual encounter at a party. Given my history, it was moving to me that he felt passionately about the issue of consent.

A week later, on a cloudy spring day, Cory took me to a hip neighborhood in northeast Portland for food and beers. We spent our evening on outdoor patios around fire pits, drinking beer and looking into each other's eyes, marveling at the fact that we were together.

"Wait. Am I actually sitting here with Becca?" he would ask with a laugh. And I would squeeze his leg and reply, "Yep, I think this is real."

Visits

Keaton had agreed to let me invite Cory over to our house once a week on the evenings when he worked late. Of this whole experience, this fact blows my mind the most; not only that Keaton agreed, but also that I had the brazenness to ask. There was a three-hour window between Moses' bedtime and Keaton getting home from work. Moses was a great sleeper; he almost never woke up once asleep, and I knew Keaton's schedule like clockwork.

The first time Cory came over was strange for me — I don't think I relaxed the whole time. Seeing Cory sitting at my kitchen table drinking tea, or on my couch where I usually hung out with my husband and child, was complete cognitive dissonance, worlds colliding. I felt like I was going to get caught. I forced myself to be present, reminding myself that this was an honest experience which Keaton knew about.

We began a regular rhythm of seeing each other twice a week: one hangout at my house and one date on the weekend. Both Cory and Keaton had agreed it would be good to meet at some point, but not one of us was quick to initiate that meeting.

When Cory and I finally kissed, I knew I was done for. I hadn't kissed someone other than Keaton in seven years. We stood in my kitchen one night, lingering close to one another while we munched on chocolate chip cookies I'd made.

"I wanted to kiss you that first day we hung out," he told me.

"I did too… I just, it was a lot to take in, you know? I think my brain was playing catch up," I said honestly.

He stepped closer.

"Well. Do you still want to?" he asked.

Of course I did.

"Yeah," I grinned.

"Come here, then."

Cory slid his chocolate arms around my waist and pulled me in slowly. I was swept into the moment with him. Tossing my arms around his neck, I let myself feel what it was like to be desired. I lost myself in the sensuousness of his hands moving over my body, the fullness of his lips against mine, and the weight of his muscular frame drawing me closer. I could feel all our history and friendship and trust, accented with the thrill of new discovery and possibility. It was nourishing to a part of me that had felt neglected.

It was hard for Keaton to hear that Cory and I had kissed. He confessed that up until that point, he'd thought that perhaps we were just friends, and hadn't found a romantic element. It was an exercise in radical honesty for me; I didn't want to tell him. I knew it would be hurtful to hear, and thinking of taking things further with Cory seemed almost insurmountably difficult for my relationship with Keaton.

On our fourth date, Cory and I spent a whole day together. I packed a picnic

OPEN

and we drove into the Columbia River Gorge to hit a few hiking spots. It rained most of the day and we wound our way through the trails, stopping to embrace at the viewpoints as the rain ran down our cheeks and brows. He told me of his hopes of relocating to Hawaii. I asked him about his time fighting forest fires.

We finally talked about our sexual history and health practices, and it became obvious that we were both thinking about when and where we might be able to find enough privacy to connect. I hadn't thought about the logistics of trying to get away from my "default" life long enough to have sex with Cory. A part of me hadn't given myself permission to go there. We finished our evening in Portland, sharing Thai food and drying off around a fire pit on a patio bar.

That week was difficult. Keaton and I were clashing at every turn.

I knew that I was distracted and being extra irritable. Moses needed extra attention too, and all I wanted was some time and space to process everything that had transpired in the last month. That's the catch about open relationships, and all relationships, really — life carries on, regardless of what you're going through with the people you love. Responsibilities and expectations don't go away, and you have to find a way to work through your shit while tending to your life.

In non-monogamy, there's always a possibility that you could hit a rough patch in one, both, or all, of your relationships. And you still have to buck up and go to work and show up for your family and find a way to deal. Polyamory means more on every level — more potential for love, affection, and connection, yes, but also more effort, difficulty, and communication.

Grounded

That week, Cory called me to ask how things were.

"Hard," I answered. "Keaton and I have been clashing all week. I can't seem to switch back to my normal life after this weekend. I feel like… I'm starting to wish that *you* were part of my normal life. I didn't realize how hard it would be to balance two relationships and stay grounded."

"You're in the hardest position Becca," he replied. "You're a mom and you're juggling two relationships. This experience is a challenge and it's something we all decided to take on. But the present moment is all we've got. So find a way to be present with your family. If I was a part of your regular life, well, we would be having our own challenges. I'm confident you guys will get through it," he insisted. I knew he was right. He continued.

"I'm chasing happiness, and right now I've caught it by being with you. We have to remember that things will change eventually. If we expect them to be a certain way, we're all going to get hurt."

It was exactly what I needed to hear, but not what I wanted to hear.

His response showed me that he was going to be the one to keep the reigns in the relationship. I had allowed myself to fantasize about how my life would look with Cory and he was imploring me to keep my feet steadily on the ground. He reminded me that our relationship was unique, but I was married and going to stay married. He was never going to get swept up in emotionally dangerous territory with me, and I am so grateful to him for that. Never before had I recognized my ability to do such rapid and risky emotional gymnastics.

I felt more grounded in our relationship, knowing what it could and couldn't be, and seeing a clear line in the sand. He wasn't going to allow himself to think or plan beyond the present moment with me, partly because planning was not in his nature, and partly because he needed to protect himself from getting entangled in our dynamic in a way that might leave him high and dry. In other words, we both knew that if the going got tough, my loyalty was to my marriage.

After our first month together, I settled. I worked with the practice of being present, and gave myself permission to fully be wherever I was, trusting that both of my relationships were solid enough to be sustained without constant effort and attention. Keaton and I found our groove again, and the fact that I was also seeing Cory became less charged and more of a logistical topic than an emotional one.

A few days after our conversation about how things were going, I texted Cory an alluring photo of my butt in some lacy underwear. He was so enthralled that he wrote me a short, cheeky poem in response. I'd so rarely had the experience of initiating a sexual exchange and having the energy multiply.

We shared many more dreamy dates together over the coming months: hiking, camping, park dates, dinners, snuggling on my couch, and eventually, going to his college roommate's wedding together. I was experiencing romance, in a way that I never really had before. There was a warmth, a candor, and a refreshing magnetism toward each other.

During our ritual cannabis-laced chillout, I talked with Keaton about how things were going. He didn't want our friends or family to know about what we were doing, but he said otherwise, he was feeling fine; now that the initial shift had settled, things felt mostly the same. I broached the topic of taking things to the next level with Cory; his birthday was approaching and I thought I might take him to the beach. I truthfully can't remember the discussion, but Keaton agreed.

I went ahead and booked an AirBnB for a night on the coast.

Heating Up

Cory's birthday weekend was the happiest time of our relationship.

Before the trip, I wrote Keaton a long letter of appreciation and bought him some gifts for the weekend: beer, snacks, weed, and a hobby magazine. I made sure to have sex with him that week, hoping to leave on a positive note. I stocked the fridge with enchiladas. I drew a funny picture for Moses (who was too young to read a note) and left two cupcakes for them to enjoy while I was away. Internally, the line between gratitude and guilt felt like a blurred one.

The car was running and packed for the weekend, and I stopped on my way out the door for our routine hugs and kisses. As I hugged Keaton, I burst into tears. I hadn't seen it coming. This was the first night in five years that I would spend away from Keaton. It was the first night in Moses' whole life that I would spend away from him.

I felt free and supported, yes. But I also understood the weight of what was about to happen — it was simultaneously no big deal, and earth-shatteringly important. I had a deep sense that I was about to do something irreversible. When I came home, I would likely have slept with a man who wasn't my husband. Keaton smiled and told me to have a great time, and to get going so I wouldn't be late.

I always appreciated the 20-minute drive between my house and Cory's apartment. I needed that time to switch gears; to switch off the mom-wife talk in my mind and switch into friend-girlfriend mode.

As things became more serious with Cory, I found myself sometimes wishing that the drive was actually longer. Going into this experiment, I believed I could be "on" all the time, switching effortlessly between family time and time with Cory, giving my undivided attention to whoever was around me, wherever I was. I wouldn't allow my two lives to overlap much or talk excessively about one person in the presence of the other.

But I had discovered within a week of dating Cory that this would be impossible. I couldn't compartmentalize my life in the way I'd expected. I wanted to share openly with everyone, and it didn't help that I was a verbal processor, needing to talk things out to understand them. I learned to respect boundaries by asking before divulging information or processing my emotions aloud. I learned to lean on my girlfriends rather than Keaton for this support, though only three of my best friends knew about Cory at all.

Cory and I could not spend time in certain towns for fear of being seen. I had to censor myself when family members would ask, "What's new with you, Becca?" I couldn't exactly tell them that I was having an affair which Keaton knew about and supported. That would rock the boat more than even I wanted to. We were shattering a whole paradigm, but doing so in secret.

It was a sunny April day on the Oregon Coast. We wandered Rockaway Beach hand-in-hand and I felt like I was living a surreal second life. I realized that if anyone who knew me saw me on the beach with him, kissing there with our feet in the surf, they would assume I was having an affair. Although I was acting in full integrity toward my husband, the social pressure to be monogamous existed outside of our private lives. It's still the dominant culture, by a long shot. Nobody seemed to notice us, just another pair of young lovers meandering on the sprawling coastline.

That night was the first night Cory and I slept together.

It happened organically, and sober as a Sunday morning. I found him irresistible, with his muscular body and tightly coiled hair and rich skin. We tried to lie down and watch a movie, but within minutes the tension between us took over and Cory reached for the remote to turn it off. He was my first partner besides Keaton in eight long years.

I felt wildly feminine. He must have had forty pounds on me, and he moved me around effortlessly, flowing with me in a way that felt present and deeply connected. I felt wanted, beautiful and powerful. The experience of him shook me loose. I cried that night, feeling like I had been fed on a fundamental level after years of starving for true, out of control affection and desire.

I rested my head on his chest as we drifted to sleep.

"Cory," I whispered through the dark. "I love you."

Silence.

"I love you too, Becca." He kissed the top of my head. "But I know where my place is."

I came home feeling simultaneously depleted and sated. Keaton greeted me warmly and asked how it had gone.

"It was great. Thanks again for helping me do that, babe," I answered, and abruptly steered the conversation elsewhere, as I scooped Moses from the floor and cooed at him.

Over the next few days, Keaton cracked a few kind-spirited jokes about me sleeping with Cory, and I knew that our relationship had weathered the storm. In truth, it seemed barely a blip on our radar. I began to recognize the ways that I had friend-zoned my own husband over the past few years. I was able to talk to him like a friend who had next to zero sexual interest in me.

Well, that's a simplification.

Keaton was attracted to me and wanted to connect, but we preferred different vehicles. We'd been attempting to meet in the middle, a balance of emotional intimacy and physical closeness, for years. But he was comfortable going months at a time without having sex and could do so without feeling pent up.

My baseline orgasm quota for general wellbeing was far on the other end of the spectrum. Our sex life picked up, in my estimation, to the best it had ever been, around the time Cory came into the picture. Still, our dynamic felt more like best friends and co-parents who sometimes had practical sex, than lovers or husband and wife.

Deeper

The month after our beach trip, Cory and I stayed at a cabin at a local state park to spend a weekend playing disc golf and sitting around the campfire. We laughed, ate homemade food, and meandered through light and heavy conversations.

He offered me a glimpse into a world that I'd only previously witnessed from a distance: the world of racism. He told me about his experience as a Black police officer in an all-white precinct in our predominantly white hometown. The experience was so difficult, from the daily racial slurs and microaggressions, to witnessing the antagonistic culture of police toward the public, that he ended up leaving the profession altogether.

I felt humbled and trusted as he shared these raw accounts with me. He spoke of his brother who, as he put it, "blamed a racist society for his problems," and contrasted it with his own commitment to self-responsibility and rising above. He believed our society was a meritocracy, a world in which people get ahead based on their individual accomplishments, disregarding factors like social class, wealth, race and gender.

I had to bite my tongue. I wanted to say that society was responsible for a lot of his struggles and an unjust distribution of opportunity and resources. I wanted to agree with his brother, to talk about systemic racism (as though, after a lifetime in his Black body, he didn't already know) and invite him to get mad and look hard at the leaders and systems in this country that have fucked him over and made Black peoples' lives so much harder. But here I was, a white-passing Hispanic woman. Who was I to tell a Black man about his own lived experience in the world?

The candid conversation (along with our building sexual connection) deepened our bond and brought us closer. As if perfectly timed, the drive home from the cabin also brought our first argument. He told me that he'd changed his mind about meeting Keaton. A friend of ours had suggested how weird it would be, asking: "What are you going to say to the man who knows you're fucking his wife?" A fair question, I agreed. The whole dynamic was pretty unusual.

Since the beginning though, we had all agreed it would be healthy and productive for the two men to meet. As my feelings for Cory deepened, it felt even more important for them to know each other, even if they only met briefly. Without that, I had come to feel more and more like I was living two separate lives. I compared it to a weak triangle with only two lines drawn. I felt that if they would just meet, the situation might feel more secure and perhaps the transition back and forth between the two relationships would feel less jarring.

On the other hand, as Cory's feelings toward me deepened, it had become difficult for him to reconcile the fact that he loved a married woman who would never be fully available. He said that seeing Keaton would just intensify that reality. I was taken aback when I heard this. I argued that if the two of them were unwilling to meet, it was a sign that the situation really wasn't healthy or sustainable. I didn't want there to be a sense of competition or rivalry between the two, a feeling that came more from my own projections than their actions.

Playing Out

Keaton would later tell me that facing my emotional exploration with Cory was scarier for him than the sexual aspect. For both of us, sharing someone's heart felt like the big risk, knowing that a beloved has deep love and attraction for another person.

The physical act of sex on its own didn't hold much weight for either of us — we were two of the least jealous people who could end up together —

for us, it was the context, whether love, betrayal, or pure lust, that would determine the weight and meaning of a sexual encounter.

As the months carried on, something shifted between Cory and I.

We grew distant. It felt as though we'd filled the limited container for our relationship and, having nothing more to discover together left us wondering how to proceed. He accepted that he was dating someone with whom he couldn't have the relationship he ultimately wanted. He also started seeing another woman, a kind and lovely athlete I'd met once before.

Cory's schedule began to fill with other commitments to friends and family, and so did mine, so that we were seeing each other less and less. We rarely had sex due to lack of privacy and a gap in our sexual chemistry. Connecting sexually became a smaller piece of our relationship than I wanted it to be. I felt I might end up in two sexless relationships.

As the summer reached its peak, Cory was hired as a wildland firefighter in a small town toward the Oregon Coast. He called me one afternoon to tell me. He wanted to know if I'd be able to come out and stay with him at the fire tower on his days off.

For me, it was nuanced. Loving someone who's continuously in danger in their line of work is emotionally taxing. Moses was becoming a full-blown toddler and required increasingly more energy to look after, and Keaton wasn't keen on me devoting swaths of time traveling to and from the coast.

I didn't believe I could feasibly continue to devote what was needed to make the relationship with Cory work. His moving effectively meant the end of our time together. I was the one to call it off first, and his response summed it up best.

"I'm feeling every emotion right now," he told me over the phone.

I clung to pragmatism and I felt grateful that he had reminded me so many times during those months that the value of our relationship was in the present moment, for however long it might last.

I've come to believe this is true of all relationships — that their value is not defined by how long they last, but by what they are made of while they're breathing, and as an extension, the way they are entered into and stepped out of.

Cory and I lived out the third iteration of our lifelong affection for four rich months. What had begun in fifth grade with a poem and a red teddy bear, resurfaced as a false start after high school, trailed on with years of tenacious dreams, and against all odds, found us in an unlikely open romance at age 25.

My adult experience of him burst forth with complete and utter, all-consuming infatuation, but soon settled into deep care and love for one another. His presence in my life, his energy, his sexuality, woke me out of a haze. I hope that I brought as much happiness and satisfaction into his life as he brought into mine.

As complicated as Keaton's role was, he set himself aside and acted as a brilliant support during the whole experience. We became closer through the act of being real with each other. We learned that central to making an open relationship work was the discipline of meeting our relational needs at home first, and ensuring that we both felt prioritized, treated fairly, and heard.

It was a fulfilling and thrilling time in my life, this new uncharted territory, feeling the electricity of new love grounded by the stability and deep intimacy of my family at home. Satisfying these fundamentally opposing needs had seemed impossible to me before Cory came into my life.

Cory and I closed our relationship amicably through tears and gratitude. That was the last I ever spoke with him, and the dreams were finally laid to rest. I hope he is somewhere healthy and happy and loved. In fact, I heard recently that he made good on his plans to relocate to Hawaii.

15

Tinder Summer

Matches

One secondary result of my connection with Cory was that it allowed me to see that my relationship with Keaton could withstand outside sexual endeavors. In fact, my sex life with Keaton was soaring. The element of an outside partner added a friendly sense of competition, but it also nourished me and opened me up to bring more emotional availability and appreciation when he and I were together. This was a positive feedback loop. We ultimately agreed that our relationship needn't be non-monogamous just in Cory's case, but philosophically we both felt curious about maintaining an open marriage as a baseline.

About a month before Cory and I parted ways, I had told Keaton that I was fantasizing about sleeping with a woman.

"Babe, you've been talking about this for like three years," he said. "Just do it. Honestly, I don't think there's much that I'll say no to at this point," he added with a dry laugh.

And with that, I had a Tinder account.

Once I saw all the babes on Tinder, I asked him if he would ever consider dating people he met online. He said yes. He made an account too, just for fun. I gave him my full blessing to have a connection — whether casual, dating, something deeper — I wanted him to have the option to enjoy the freedom and excitement that I had experienced.

I dated a couple femmes during this time, but I don't think I was ready. I had so much pent up sexual energy from five years in my marriage and I was craving a masculine presence with which to work this out. I'd been in a more masculine, pursuer, alpha role throughout my entire marriage and wanted more of what I'd tasted with Cory. I wanted the opportunity to be receptive, to co-create, to lure someone in and entice them and drive them crazy.

Later, I would realize that this dynamic is fully possible with a partner regardless of the body they're in. The "feminine/masculine" binary simply does not tell the whole story of who we are as sexual beings. This attitude held remnants of the straight-laced church culture in which I had been raised, where men are framed as dominant pursuers and women are expected to be demure responders.

In any case, I wanted to explore, and pursue, and be dominated. I just needed the right person. When I expressed this to Keaton, he agreed that it was only fair that I have a pass at casually dating men since he was on Tinder to casually date women. Keaton was so accommodating, I wouldn't believe it if I hadn't actually lived through it.

Keaton calls that summer my Tinder Rampage.

I matched with a man named Samuel. We spent several weeks talking at length, neither of us in a rush to set up a date.

I matched with a guy named Ryan on a Thursday, confirmed his STI status and established ground rules on a Friday, and on Saturday after our family morning at the farmer's market, I got a babysitter for Moses and drove into Portland to meet him. At a hotel. Keaton was headed to work and had given me the OK, but expressed surprise and hesitation at my zero to 60 acceleration. I texted Keaton his name, contact information, and where we would be, plus his identifying features (I listed tattoos, blue eyes and a shaved head. I did not include "pierced penis" or "armpit pizza tattoo" in the description, though those were equally true.)

Well, I got what I was looking for: friendly chit-chat, followed by rowdy, sweaty, hair pulling, no frills fucking. Then he ordered us a pizza and we laid on the plush hotel bed while he told me a tragic story about his last girlfriend who had died of a heroin overdose. I left that hotel room a more worldly, well-fucked woman, with a slice in my hand for the road. He and I are still Facebook friends. Most of what I know about him is his love for advanced yoga and preference for New York style pizza.

During this time, Keaton had a few conversations with women, but was still trying to decide how interested in Tinder he was. As a one-person-at-a-time kind of guy, he found it exhausting to spend a week talking with someone, only to have her ghost him, and to be back at square one looking to form a new connection.

Meanwhile, I had 47 matches and my inbox was bubbling with conversations. In my profile, I had more or less listed "Sex positive, non-monogamous mother, age 25. Nothing serious." And I guess that pretty much sealed the deal.

I dated around a bit, enjoying casual hook ups with a handful of people, most notable a witty Korean surfer, a German bartender, and a toxic, articulate journalist.

There were just a few people I matched with who stood out to me. These were folks I admired and with whom I shared interests and values. By this time, I sensed that I could take my pick of dates, so I wanted to be around someone with whom I not only had undeniable chemistry, but who I also sincerely enjoyed and could connect with on many levels. I didn't need many more pierced penis, pizza-tattoo dudes.

Samuel, Part One

Samuel was that person — a sincere, serious man with piercing hazel eyes surrounded by deep smile lines that defied his age of 33 and told of a life under the sun. He looked like a younger, more hip Robert Downey Jr. He was a landscape architect from the Florida Keys, who seasonally taught permaculture courses at an eco-village in Costa Rica.

I knew instantly that we'd have a ton to talk about. I was working as a landscaper for a friend's farm, and with my background in organic farming, I was eager to hear more about the work he was doing in regenerative agriculture. We shared intimate details of what we were looking for in a connection and why, and I voiced the desire to expand my sexual experiences and have more cyclical, spacious, and creative erotic encounters with someone who I could trust. He replied that he couldn't have said it better himself.

We met for dinner at a famous taco joint. I'd known he was short, but I was thrown off when I realized just how short 5'3" feels to someone who is 5'8". I felt like a tree with trousers on. Once we were seated eating dinner, though, I settled in and forgot the disparity. We had a lovely summer evening together. He asked me about my family and my work. He wanted to know about my experience in the church and wondered aloud how I had made it out of something so formative and into an open marriage.

The sun was low in the sky when we left to wander through the neighborhood and he showed me several yards he had designed, giving me a walking tour of the native plants we passed along the way. I found him incredibly attractive. His hands were rough and bore the marks of years of hard labor. They reminded me of my dad's. I sensed a mutual respect between us, as though we were witnessing each other with a deep understanding of what it meant to live with passionate attention to one's life.

While we were out, we ran into three friends he knew; he seemed to be well known and well loved. When we were finally alone, he stopped me on the street corner and pulled me in for a slow, hard kiss. There was heat between us, and more than just a little.

As we walked on, I asked him his Zodiac sign, as much to gain clues about his worldview as his personality.

"Aries, April 1st," he said with a smirk. "I have an April Fool's Birthday."

I stared at him as he smelled a Camellia flower.

"Seriously? That's my dad's birthday," I replied.

"Oh, really? How weird. Hey, do you have time to hang out a while longer?" he asked. I did.

"I have an idea," he continued, stepping closer. "Want to go to Everett House for a soak?"

That sounded lovely, but I didn't have a bathing suit with me. He informed me that it was a clothing optional spa. I hesitated for only a moment before agreeing. I was intent on sleeping with this person, after all. I checked in with Keaton and let him know I would be home at the agreed time.

What followed was the most intensely erotic date of my life.

I was in a completely new setting with a completely new person. The spa had a no-touching rule, to keep the environment non-sexual. The tension between us was palpable as we undressed in front of each other and walked, naked, to the sauna, and then out to the open-air soaking pool. He was hung. He was almost comically large given his short stature, as though nature had put all of its resources for this man into creating the perfect oversized cock. I hadn't skinny dipped since high school, yet being outside naked, surrounded by strangers, felt like the most natural thing in the world. There were dozens of people milling around, chit chatting in groups of friends or sitting alone meditatively. But my eyes were fixed on him.

During our visit, we touched each other far more than was acceptable, given the environment. He got a massive erection while we sat alone in the sauna and we grinned at each other through the tension. I reached over and stroked him silently for a few moments until the door began to creak and a group of chatty friends walked in. He casually tossed a towel over his lap. The whole scenario was wildly inappropriate, which made it that much hotter.

When I returned home, my hair was wet.

"Where did you guys go? Why is your hair wet?" Keaton wanted to know. The room felt tense, reactive. I explained about Everett House and the spa, but left out the explicit parts. He was convinced we'd had sex. I assured him that wasn't the case. Finally, we diffused the conversation and went to sleep.

The next morning, tensions were still high. Keaton said things were changing too fast. First, I had wanted to date Cory, then I wanted to casually hook up with women, then men, and now I had a meaningful new friend with whom I seemingly wanted to create an ongoing sexual relationship. It was too much for him to keep up with.

Keaton was right: I was changing my requests based on each new connection. I was taking advantage of his accommodating nature; I had tasted freedom and developed an insatiable appetite for it, as though I needed to make up for the lost years I'd spent repressing my sexuality. I had no idea where this left our relationship, or what it would take to keep it healthy in the midst of all this newness and unpredictability. I felt like I was on a train headed down a steady incline, gaining momentum at a rapid clip.

I told Keaton I would slow down and asked him to be gracious with me and keep communication lines open. I asked if I could continue seeing Samuel, who was also in a committed partnership and as such, seemed like a non-threatening person to explore with. Keaton agreed.

Samuel spoke with his existing partner as well. She was in support of us connecting, but like Keaton, requested that we pace ourselves. We both needed to get an updated STI test before either of them would be comfortable with us having sex. He was about to leave for a month-long trip to Costa Rica anyway, so we arranged for him to come over once for a low key visit before his trip.

Keaton was working the overnight shift at the shelter. He agreed to me hosting Samuel. Moses, two and a half now, was asleep in his bedroom (as he always was when I had company — never once did he wake up and find someone there with me).

This was a season of firsts and mosts. That night, Samuel and I shared the hottest, most sensual, most paradigm-shattering encounter I had ever had… and while we didn't have sex, it was extremely intimate.

We spent three intense hours together, free of clothes and free of assumptions.

Not for one moment was I bored or overwhelmed or exhausted. He showed up with full presence, expecting the same from me. He moved slowly and asked questions. He looked at me and allowed me to see him.

There was no rush, no destination besides sharing pleasure. We talked in relaxed tones as we ran our hands and mouths over each other's bodies, experimented, and responded to one another with words and sounds and heated breath. It was the cyclical, explorative encounter I'd been craving.

Samuel wasn't a fuck buddy or a friend with benefits. He was a lover, through and through. We had taken each other to new heights.

"Can I tell you something?" he asked me as we sat upon my bed at midnight, stoned, eating a bowl of fruit.

"Of course," I answered, allowing my hand to trail mindlessly over his leg.

"I don't think I've ever had a season in my life that I felt sexually satisfied. I always felt that something more was possible. Becca, I believe I could find that limit with you."

I might as well have melted. I'd hit the erotic jackpot, like some sort of cosmic reward for my five years of monogamous near-celibacy. And it seemed I'd be making up for lost time, ten-fold.

Then, Samuel boarded a plane for Costa Rica.

On our initial dates together, I'd seen Samuel as confident and capable, bordering on arrogant. He took himself very seriously and wasn't at all silly, light-hearted or even particularly affectionate. He was kind and wise, but there was some subtle block on an emotional level. I didn't fully believe he saw me as an equal. At 33, he was seven years my senior and frequently pointed out how young I was, how much life I still had ahead of me.

At moments, I felt like a caricature to him — a beautiful, free-spirited, naïve 25-year-old who enjoyed having abundant sexual encounters. And sweet. Always "Sweet Becca," which threw me off because, though I am a warm, kind person, I'd rarely in my life been described as sweet. Usually passionate, strong, intense, driven, wise or friendly... but not sweet.

For knowing me very intimately, he also barely knew me. And I didn't know him very well either — he was as earthy as they come and had a very zen attitude toward life, which in his case meant he didn't waste words. Everything out of his mouth seemed measured and well-considered, never particularly free-form or candid, whereas I am particularly verbose. When I sincerely inquired about his viewpoints or opinions, his most common answers were:

"I think it depends how you look at it," or "I can't tell you how to live your life, it's really up to you."

I couldn't get much out of him. I wanted candor. I rarely knew what was going on inside his head, let alone his heart. I did manage to glean that he had reservations about the number of people I was dating and wondered about my ability to safely track my potential partners and protect myself from contracting an STI. I agreed that safety was the top priority, and we decided to reconnect once he returned home, and feel out how to best approach our connection then.

Tinder Friends

It was almost June. I must have gone on twelve dates in a month. Many of those connections later became friends, and a handful were fun repeat hookups over time. I didn't connect with anyone as intensely and deeply as I had with Samuel.

There were a few weekends that were so packed with back-to-back dates and one night stands that it might as well have been a comical sped-up movie montage of me greeting a man, eating food with him, sharing a sweet walk, then driving across town, changing clothes in my car, and doing the whole thing again overnight with a different person. It was too much, and I loved it. Keaton didn't seem to mind as long as I did it on my two free days. He had freedom to go out before or after work while I was at home with Moses.

In my journal that month, I wrote the following:

> "I've felt so depleted lately and at times on the verge of tears. I feel like the lack of rest has mixed strangely with all the sex chemicals in my system. Between Jesse, Mike, Winston and Keaton, I have had so much sex in the past week... Too much... which is something I didn't know was possible. The sheer number of condoms I've used is just wasteful. And I call myself an environmentalist!

> "I need a few sexless days between these events. I want my body to myself. I want to enjoy the more subtle pleasures — fresh air, good food, taking a walk with Moses and Keaton. I dove in the deep end but I'm ready to find balance again."

Andrew, Oh Boy

Andrew was at the apex of this huge transition in my life. He was a catalyst and didn't intend to be.

I'd slowed down on my dating pace but felt that maybe meeting one more person wouldn't hurt. It was early June, when the days were long, the dresses were short and the cocktails were strong. We'd had some sweet, sincere interactions over text and I was taken by his big blue eyes, his climber physique and a certain boy-next-door charm. He owned a bike repair company and looked like he'd hopped right out of a Patagonia ad.

Our first date was in Northeast Portland, just up the street from where I now live. We met in a classy little high-end Italian restaurant and ate cured meats and fresh pasta. I sipped on a gin and tonic and he clanked the ice in his empty tequila glass. Our comedic chemistry was perfect. I love when I can make a man laugh, and he got a kick out of my antics. But we also connected more personally. We were each on the tails of monogamous committed partnerships and confided in each other about the struggles of loving someone when the fire has gone out. We strolled through Alberta Park and soon we were entwined with each other beneath the trees.

"I'm thinking I'd like to invite you over," he said.

"Oh yeah?" I smiled back at him, massaging the muscles of his shoulders while we spoke. "That sounds nice."

Andrew later told me that we had more sex that first night together than he'd had in the last year of his relationship. There must have been six or seven condoms strewn around the room by sunrise. Our chemistry was multidimensional. There was closeness, heat, humor, and immediate trust. I felt a more open-hearted connection than I had with Samuel, and more sexual chemistry than I'd had with Cory. Damn… this man was the whole package.

It was also the first time I'd slept so comfortably beside someone new. I drove home, exhausted and exhilarated, early the next morning.

We continued seeing each other often, mostly for late night hookups and sleepovers. He was out mountain biking or summiting peaks most weekends and I was occupied with family life, so I prioritized my available evenings for him. One by one, my other casual connections fell by the wayside.

I became totally enchanted by Andrew. He was the month of June, personified. His sunny, Gemini charm seemed to compliment my watery, sensual depth. He was the first person with whom I'd developed an ongoing, deeply satisfying relationship that held sexuality and emotionality. The sex was always great, like some sort of carnal alchemy. I brought passion and heat; he brought stamina and play. It was more than the sum of its parts. When we had sex, I could feel his heart and his doting affection as much as his stiff cock.

Out on the town, walking under street lamps and dining in little neighborhood haunts, we were clearly a pair enthralled. There was an uninhibited innocence in how we related that felt authentic. Unprecedented. I could find no fatal flaw between us, no safeguard that might keep me from seeing him as the "real deal" and falling into something more serious. This unnerved me.

Samuel was still in Costa Rica, a connection held in suspense.

The Fight

One weeknight in late June, my Tinder friend Jared came over. He was an androgynous, anarchist cyclist in an open marriage whose wife had recently gone on a date with Keaton. They had a son about Moses' age. Keaton knew Jared was coming over, with the usual agreement that company leave before 10:30 pm. I had a routine of airing out the bedroom, changing the sheets when necessary, and smudging the house with sage before Keaton got home; it was more for my own sanity than necessity.

Jared and I spent a few hours in the usual way — snacking, cuddling, laughing. We ended up having sex. It was the first and only time. We had fun. Afterwards, we shared a strong joint that Jared had brought before diving into a tray of snacks. I became way more stoned than I had intended.

As we laid in my room talking and riffing on each other's dry humor, it occurred to me that I had no idea what time it was. I'd left my phone in the living room and we were tied up in some conversation about cult classic films. Moments later, I heard the front door. I froze. Jared's eyes got huge.

Shit.

The door slammed. I got dressed and rushed out of the bedroom. Keaton wasn't there. I looked out the window and saw his truck parked out front.

Jared followed me out, apologizing profusely. I assured him that everything would be fine and that it was my fault for not watching the time. He gathered his things and left.

I called Keaton's phone several times. No answer. I texted him apologizing and asking where he was. I paced the living room, tidying up, restless, still very stoned, until he came back. He'd been out on a walk.

"Hey…" I said.

"I'm so furious right now, I can't even look at you," he said as he walked past me through the living room.

"I know. I fucked up. I'm sor—"

"I don't even want to hear it, Becca. I've given you so much freedom. I've been so fucking gracious and accommodating and you can't even seem to hold up your end of the deal. All I want is to not come home after work and hear some other dude laughing in our bedroom."

I realized that must have felt pretty shitty.

"You're right. We got really stoned and I lost track of time. I'm sorry," I began. He cut me off.

"All I hear is excuses. You always have a good explanation for pushing the limits," he said, finally looking straight at me.

That was an exact line my mother had used many times toward me. He had struck a nerve. I should have bit my tongue and apologized. Instead, I became defensive and let out my scorpion stinger.

"Keaton. I didn't keep Jared here on purpose. Do you think I want to be in this situation right now? This is as awkward for me as it is for you. And, to be fair — you knew he was going to be here. So maybe you should stop blowing this out of proportion and acting shocked as if you just caught me having an affair. You're trying to fuck his wife, for Christ's sake!"

"Are you serious right now? That's your apology?" he demanded.

"Whatever. It was an honest mistake. If you can't believe that, there's no use trying to apologize to you," I snapped back.

I'm pretty sure one of us slept on the couch that night. I was too stoned to remember.

The Last Vacation

That same weekend, Keaton's older brother got married. His new wife Megan was a perfect fit for the family — she had been present for Mark's cancer journey and death, and she and Kari were two peas in a pod. They spent loads of time together, baking and shopping, just like I had when I was first with Keaton. I adored her and, in many ways, felt like I had been replaced by her.

The backyard wedding was beautiful and, behind the scenes for Keaton and I, quite tense. Keaton hung out with his friends and I wandered around with

Moses, trying to make small talk with his entire extended family. A couple of friends gave me the cold shoulder while playing yard games, and I sensed that they knew some element of what was going on between us. I was happy to have Moses with me; adorable toddlers are always the life of the party and deflect attention away from the parents.

Immediately after the wedding, we headed out on our annual trip to Sunriver. Keaton and I kept our private struggles to ourselves.

Megan had bought Kari a sweet gift to commemorate Mark's passing two summers earlier and thanked her for renting the house for our family that week. I felt like an asshole; it hadn't even occurred to me to get her a gift.

As I was unpacking my bags in our upstairs bedroom I overheard them downstairs chatting. I noticed how they laughed and hugged and shared tears, and I remembered the bygone times when that was a part of my relationship with Kari. I thought about how unfair it was that Kari and I had a falling out over my loss of faith, whereas Megan was an outspoken atheist, as was Keaton's brother Ty, and no one seemed to have a problem with that.

Mark and Kari used to tell Keaton and I that the day we married was one of the happiest days of their lives — that I was like the daughter they never had. But by now, I felt like my value in the family had been reduced to the mere fact that I had brought Moses into the world. I was not invited to go on the annual memorial mountain bike ride, for obvious reasons — I had a toddler to look after — but this just further distanced me from feeling like an integral part of the family the way I once had.

Achingly, I wasn't sure how much I wanted to be there anymore at all. Keaton and I had grown cold. Kari and I had grown cold. I couldn't stand her creepy new husband who had joined the vacation. I adored Keaton's brothers and sister-in-law more than my own siblings, but otherwise, I felt isolated and pushed out. I wondered how much I actually had in common with the people surrounding me, and how long I could grasp at our common threads.

Why?

On the drive home from Sunriver, Keaton and I got to talking. The anger from our fight had cooled off. So had our attraction; we hadn't had sex in several weeks. Moses snoozed in the back of the truck while we crossed over Mt. Hood. At my request, Keaton described to me what he would look for in another partner if he were to have one (he'd been on a few dates but nothing, not even a kiss, had come from them so far).

He described someone gentle, loyal, sweet and nurturing. As he continued,

I realized he was essentially describing the opposite of the way he'd experienced me in the last year: fiery, inconsistent, harsh and self-serving.

He asked me the same question. I refused to answer, believing I had already done enough damage to our relationship. In my mind I listed words like: confident, passionate, initiator, adaptable, loving.

I hadn't paused to zoom out in a very long time. Perhaps I never had. I began to recognize how poorly matched we were. I recalled friends over the years asking what I loved about Keaton, why we were together, how our relationship was going. And I never really stopped to think about how we fit together, beyond being great friends who happened to have gotten married.

I replayed our six shared years, remembering how we had tried so many times to become what the other person needed. I had tried to be soft, steady, consistent, and humble. He had tried to be willing, open-minded, courageous and capable. Ultimately, though, I was passion. Keaton was contemplation. Our true natures had always snapped back into place like rubber bands, regardless of our efforts otherwise. When left to my own devices, my shadows would skew toward fierce and unpredictable and his leaned toward passive and unmotivated.

With our Christian faith gone, the Venn diagram of Keaton and myself had very little overlap. What did we share?

Mostly, we shared the incredible two-foot tall person sleeping in the back seat. He was such a gift in a small package; his presence had pushed us out of the nest and catalyzed our journeys toward self-actualization. Already, Moses had brought out balance in each of us, smoothing out our jagged edges and filling in our gaps. He had softened me, made me more gentle and patient and nurturing. He had brought out Keaton's strong and protective side.

"Damn," I remarked. "You're basically describing the opposite of me. I'm not sure what to make of that."

"Yeah, well... we're not the most natural match," he replied. We both chuckled dryly. "No surprise there."

We sat silent for a mile or so.

"Hey. Has divorce ever crossed your mind?" I asked him.

"Yeah... once or twice," he said, glancing over from the driver's seat.

"Keaton... why are you still married to me?" I asked him.

I wasn't sure I wanted to hear the answer. I stared out the front window at the passing landscape.

"I guess, because divorce seems really complicated and hard," he answered.

I nodded, speechless. We were together because it was the easiest, most convenient option. I found this intolerable.

Inevitable

I spent July 3 at work digging weeds out of a flower bed. I'd been at it for hours, alone in the soft sunlight, reflecting on all that had taken place in the past year. I mulled over Keaton's remarks about divorce. The reason he was still married to me wasn't because he had hope for our future, or because he loved me and wanted to make it work, or he couldn't imagine his life without me. He was with me out of complacency. I felt disgusted by this. It highlighted the parts of him that I had struggled with most over the years — a desire to stay comfortable. A tendency to keep things the same when given the option. I realized then that divorce was inevitable.

And of course, it would be me to drive it forward... the same way I had with every other major decision since we met.

I began to weep bitterly into the soil as I pulled out the crabgrass, blade by blade, root by root.

I had pursued Keaton the night I finished my internship. Even before that, I had invited him into the band and asked him to play countless times during those final months of ID. I had given him an ultimatum that resulted in our starting to date. I had taken him to the jewelry shop and shown him the exact engagement ring I wanted.

I had led our sexual and romantic life and taken initiative over and over through the years to plan special occasions, getaways, vacations, date nights. I had pushed him to the doctor when I suspected health issues could be affecting his sex drive. I hired him a personal trainer when he showed the slightest willingness to try and put on some weight.

I had led our walk away from the church (yes, I admit it). I had affirmed his own doubts and encouraged him to continue pulling at that thread.

I had decided we should have pets and picked out both of our cats on my own.

I had urged us to try and get pregnant. I had decided what kind of birth to have and bought Keaton the parenting books to read. I had decided everything: how long to breastfeed, what foods Moses could eat, when to have him immunized, what kind of schools he would attend.

It was me behind the farming endeavor. I pushed forward the decision to buy our house. I had asked that we open our marriage. And now… I had brought up divorce.

I'd been running the ship. I'd been in near complete control of our life since the very beginning. It was lonely. I'd been acting like my mother, and Keaton had been acting like my father.

Fuck. *How had I never seen this before?* I had spent six years acting out a dysfunctional cycle, completely unaware. I wanted to hate myself for it.

I needed out.

That night, we sat together in the backyard as Moses used a stick to chase the chickens around. (Oh yeah, I had urged us to raise chickens, too.) The tone was resigned as we agreed, exhausted, that at this point, divorce was inevitable. We had no desire to seek counseling or try to rekindle our flame. Moses was two, almost three — he wouldn't remember much of our time together at this house. We knew it would be better to make the transition now and get settled into a new rhythm before he got much older.

That evening, there was an air of relief between us. After I put Moses to sleep, we put our phones away for the night; Tinder could wait. We rolled a joint and watched SNL together like old times, appreciating the steady camaraderie between us that had existed through the years. It hearkened back to before I'd brought in the upheaval of non-monogamy that had shaken our marriage loose at the foundation.

It was obvious we could, and would, be friends.

Independence Day

The next day was the Fourth of July, and I woke up under a gray cloud of the looming divorce. We took Moses to the town parade and tried to play nice, but it was unbearable. We cooked burgers on the grill and set off fireworks in the driveway. Moses wore out early.

"Keaton, I need to get out of the house," I told him. "I can't be here right now. I can't pretend everything's fine in front of your family tonight."

"You want to leave? Where do you want to go?" he asked.

"I was thinking I'd go into Portland and hang out with Andrew and some friends. Is that okay?" I asked.

TINDER SUMMER **197**

"So… you're just going to abandon me here in all this turmoil, then."

I thought of conversations I'd had with family, all the times I'd been called out for leaving during a crisis.

"Well… there's nothing I can do to make this better or easier right now. Staying is too intense. Please. I just need a night away. I think it will be best," I pleaded.

"Fine. I'll just tell my family you weren't feeling well."

I went into Portland and waited around for Andrew to be free. He didn't call till after the fireworks. I arrived at his place around 11:00 pm.

As he unpacked from a camping trip, I shared the news about my impending divorce, as nonchalantly as I could. I realized how jarring this might be, having entered into a connection with a sex-positive married woman, who was suddenly becoming a single mom. I was keenly aware that this could change or end our relationship.

He was easygoing and understanding — many of the problems I'd had in my marriage were mirrored in his last long-term relationship.

We stayed up for hours, entwined in our usual way, until sleep finally caught up with us. *I could get used to this*, I thought.

There was a momentary red flag in my mind — perhaps I was leaning too hard on this man at such a vulnerable moment. *No*, I told myself, *it really is as good as it feels. Right?*

Mother

The following weekend, I invited my mom to come by the house so Keaton and I could tell her in person about our decision to separate. She expressed sadness along with support; she knew how hard it was to make a marriage work, she said, and she wanted us to be happy.

"I know we've been distant," I said matter-of-factly, "But I could really use your help with Moses going forward. I know he would love it."

Tears welled up in her eyes.

"Honestly, it's been really soul crushing to miss out on seeing Moses grow up. I'd love to be more involved," she said.

I assured her that I would appreciate it. We hugged and she left shortly afterward. It was a small step, but a step nonetheless.

16 Motion

The Golden Hearth

Two weeks after Keaton and I agreed to part ways, I moved into an intentional community, or as some people might imagine it, a "hippie commune." I found my new family there. It was a vibrant urban farm just south of Portland. Twelve people lived on site. It was three mothers including myself, all of our children, and a handful of single people residing in various dwellings around the property: a yurt, a geodesic dome, and a tipi. It featured a massive vegetable garden, a fruit orchard, and a big chicken yard with happy hens clucking about and nibbling on dandelion greens.

There was a hot tub, a cob oven, and a massive treehouse suspended in a Bigleaf Maple tree with a trapeze and two sky swings hanging from its limbs. There was a trampoline, a zipline, a slackline, and a seasonal pool.

This was a place of play and food, family and community. I loved it here.

It was here that I met Tess, who would become my best friend. I'd never had a best friend before, just many good ones. The first time we met, she pulled a crispy wad of moss from my hair and I knew we were going to look after each other. She reminded me of all the things I liked about my mom and none of the things that I didn't. I can't imagine who Moses or I would be without her. She stepped in as an honorary aunt, a sister when I needed one, and was present for all of my heartbreak, fuck-ups, and big life wins between then and now. I've attempted to be there for hers, too.

At the Golden Hearth, I also met Jack. He showed me a whole world that I didn't know I was missing.

Pickathon

On August 7th, my fifth wedding anniversary, I was not with my husband. I was bare-skinned and rhythmic in Andrew's bed, until the soft Saturday morning light began to stream in bright stripes across our bodies.

He stood still before me, a sweet softness in his voice as he watched me get dressed.

"Becca, you're lovely," he said. I let my white tunic drift down loosely over my dainty flowered bra. We smiled at each other in silence for a long moment.

Later that day, we smoked a joint and rode bikes up a rural road to Pickathon Music Festival, an event teeming with hipsters, talent, and sticky, late summer energy. We spent the day drinking microbrews and twirling in the dust amid the sweet tunes of bluegrass and ambient rock. I was hopelessly smitten. No one had ever wooed me the way he did. Not Keaton, not Cory, no one. If it was romance I wanted, I'd found it: in the way he slid his hand along my back, the wily lift of his brow when trying to amuse me, and the weight with which he pulled me close to him and stared long into my eyes.

Over and over throughout the day, friends would call our names across the crowd and we'd meet them with congenial introductions. Andrew seemed proud to be seen with me, letting our worlds collide with ease. We gallivanted between stages and stole tender moments between dances. The next morning, we slept in late then dragged our tired bones to a power yoga class at the rock gym. I caught a glimpse into what my life with him could be like. I was falling: hook, line, and sinker.

It wasn't all dreamy with Andrew, though; when we were apart, I was perpetually anxious about our connection. I checked my phone obsessively to see if he had texted. Neither of us were seeing other people, though it wasn't clear whether this was by choice or coincidence. But what truly disarmed me was his periodic aloofness, which always seemed to dissolve before I arrived on his front porch. Still, I had begun to fixate on our relationship in a way that didn't feel like me.

I was attaching hard to him, a fact that we both could feel.

The Build Up

The Golden Hearth, as a community home, was a gathering place. Stay in the kitchen long enough and a worthwhile conversation was inevitable. Mealtime was a sort of free-for-all to discuss anything from philosophy, gardening, politics and nutrition, to the nature of time and space. You know, normal chit chat. This summer, many housemates were experiencing transition in their love lives, so relationships were a common topic as we sliced and sautéed.

"That sounds exhausting," Jack said as he swept the floor one afternoon. I'd been whining to him about Andrew's mixed messages. He had recently told me he could see a future with me, and he wanted to spend more time together. He had even begun planning a trip to Arizona for my birthday that November. And yet, he would regularly disappear for several days at a time, unreachable. I didn't understand it.

"Yes. Thank you. It is exhausting," I said. "I'm on the opposite end of the spectrum — I say exactly what I mean. Well... I try to... I actually don't always know what I mean." I huffed and tossed the potatoes into the hot cast iron skillet.

"Sounds like sexual politics. A lot of people feel the need to play games. It's part of why I've stayed single; it's super difficult to find people who are seeking a real connection," he said as he scooted me to the side to sweep the floor beneath my feet.

We locked eyes for a moment longer than expected.

"I know... you're right. We'll just have to see what happens. Thanks for making me feel sane again," I chuckled.

"Good chat, Bec," he said as he snatched a Brussels sprout out of the sizzling pan and popped it into his mouth. He cruised out of the kitchen, whistling.

Jack was one of a kind. He had southwestern vibes, although he'd been raised in upstate New York. He came from a progressive family, the son of an architect and an art teacher, and he truly had the world at his fingertips. He was acutely aware, even ashamed, of how much privilege he'd experienced in life, and he seemed actively bent on choosing an alternative path. He was outdoorsy and unfussy, with rough hands and a scruffy beard, and one pair of broken-in Carhartts which seemed to be an extension of his own legs. He had lived in his truck as a ski bum in Colorado, guided countless rafting excursions, and now lived in a tipi on the urban farm.

Radio Room

It was a weekend in early September, and I had a date with Andrew planned for that evening.

I had just returned home from a rocky, sun-baked hike with my close friend Lori, who happened to know Andrew from college. She and I had spent a good deal of the day discussing my relationship with him (I was obsessing, as you'll recall). I aired my grievances and explained the ways I felt conflicted — I wanted something real and consistent, which in hindsight is somewhat surprising to me, given that my divorce wasn't even finalized. Or... perhaps that makes perfect sense.

In any case, he had been going around the same indecisive circles for weeks. Every time we saw each other he had a different tune and a different mood. Sometimes, he wanted to make plans to spend more time together; other days, he wanted to keep things the way they were: "casual." The unpredictability was wearing on me.

"Fucking Geminis!" I lamented. "I should remember how much trouble Geminis are for me. He's probably the fourth one I've dated from Tinder... I can't resist that unpredictable charm."

"Some guys just take a while to open up," she told me. "Give him some time and don't stress about it too much."

I agreed that at this point, that was all I could do. She reminded me that my life was in a major transition and my situation could be complicated for a lot of people, most of all me.

At home, I showered and changed into my favorite dress — a high-necked denim sundress with pockets and a bare lace-up back. I felt beautiful: sun-kissed and at ease. Lori's words had settled me. I'd come around to simply letting Andrew be himself. I resolved to enjoy our time together and not lay unspoken pressure on the relationship, the same resolve I'd reached with Cory. I would give it time to breathe and enjoy the connection. Wasn't that the whole point, anyway?

I climbed Andrew's porch steps and greeted his roommate before knocking on the front door.

"Hey there," I smiled as he came over to greet me. "Ready to go?"

As we strolled through the neighborhood, the sun warmed our backs and he swung his arm over my shoulder sweetly. He recapped me on the wild weekend he'd had on the coast. It was largely a reunion of college friends and, as expected, they'd had a hell of a time: yard games, an enormous slip and slide, a late night costume dance party. His present lack of energy made more sense when he recounted the amount of alcohol, weed, and magic mushrooms that he'd consumed throughout the weekend. Thirty-year-old entrepreneurs and young parents could still turn up, evidently.

We arrived at Radio Room, a local bar, and found a table on the rooftop patio. The small handful of patrons lent a relaxed and intimate tone, a soft murmur of clinking and chuckling as the late sun settled lower. I perused the menu.

"Is this place okay?" Andrew asked, looking around. "We can go somewhere else, if you want." His comment seemed strange to me. I assured him that this was perfectly fine. Our server brought two glasses of red wine as we spoke.

As Andrew reflected on the weekend and his time with loved ones from school, he brought up the fact that there was still a lot we didn't know about each other. So we shared about our youth and college years, reminiscing about our best friends growing up and the dreams we'd had. We spoke about our goals for the future. I told Andrew that, after such a crazy year, I felt called to settle in and find some balance in my life. No radical changes or pushing the envelope for a while. My goal was to set down new roots on my own. Just live. He smiled and nodded in acknowledgment.

Our meal was winding down. The waiter brought us new glasses of wine.

"So, I've been thinking about us," Andrew said.

His words hit my ears and for a moment, everything went still. I couldn't read the expression on his face.

Finally, he's figured something out. Why does this feel sudden? He is either going to end things or dive in, I thought, preparing myself.

I pulled my hand away from his leg and turned to face him.

"Yeah? What are you thinkin'?" I asked.

"Well. You know I've been in a rut for a while. And it's made things hard. I'm sorry I've been so confusing. I know I need to pull myself out of this funk." He set his wine glass on the table. "I've been going around in circles... but I think I know what I need to do."

"I'm glad to hear that. What do you need to do?" I asked, truly interested in his answer.

"Becca, I think I need to stop seeing you," he said.

Silence. My eyes began to blur. I nodded, but my mind felt blank. He continued talking, and I determined not to make a scene on the patio, which was humming with relaxed diners. I tuned back in.

"...And I really want to be ready like you are. I want to be the partner you deserve. Consistent and committed. I want to meet Moses and be involved in his life, not some absentee boyfriend. But I'm not there, and I don't know if I'll ever be. Knowing that you want that feels like pressure. I need to get my own life sorted out. I'm still not over Em and it's been half a year since we split up."

He paused and searched my face for a response. I looked away, fixing my eyes on a colorful mural full of waves and jovial figures.

"Well, I can't say I'm totally surprised," I said, unable to look at him. "I knew you were conflicted for a while. I've made it clear that I want something real with you, more than just sex, and lately, I've felt like we've been in limbo."

"So have I," he said.

"I get that," I replied. "I think we've both been trying to sort out whether we could meet in the middle. I really thought we could...." I took a sip of water and continued.

"Well… I know I don't need to tell you all the reasons this is worthwhile. We both know." I ran my hands over my neck, looking up at the sky, overwhelmed. "I haven't found something great like this before. I don't think you have either, right?" I searched his eyes. "There's really not a lot more I can say." I was torn between the desire to fight for him and the urge to stand up and walk away without a second glance.

He reached over and put his hand on my leg. He said nothing, so I continued.

"I hope you know I wasn't asking for you to come over every weekend or call me every day. That was never something I wanted."

"It wasn't?" he asked. He seemed truly surprised.

"No! All I wanted was for you to be *in this*. I wanted you to be present like a lover who really wants to be here. I wanted to have something clear, instead of this confusing mess we've been in. I see you once a week and it's so great; we connect and laugh and share from the heart… we both do."

I stopped, feeling my frustration with him building.

"Plus… we have crazy good sex. So, there's that." I added to diffuse the tension.

He smiled.

"But then when I leave… I barely hear from you. It makes me question your intentions. The distance feels… unnatural." I couldn't believe my honesty as it flowed from my lips.

"I know. It's fucked up. I'm sorry I've been that way," he replied with a sigh.

"That's not how I want it to be either, Becca. I really love having you in my life. When you're away and we're not in touch, I miss you. But something's holding me back. I just can't get there. I can't be all in," he said.

We pushed our food around on our plates quietly and waited for the server.

"Fuck. Okay," I said. "Well, if we're going to leave this restaurant and never see each other again, I just need to know that now."

"No!" he replied. "No... that's not what I want. I just need to figure things out. I honestly feel like I need another year, or two, to go live my life. I still have things to do, places to go. I have goals to meet, you know? And I can't ask you to wait around for me."

"You're right. You can't. I mean, I'm not going to just hop back on Tinder; I'm done with all that. But if this is ending, I have to move on. I don't want to feel like I'm burdening or distracting you."

He took his glasses off and rubbed his face. "I know I'm going to kick myself for this. You're such a catch, Becca. God. I think maybe it's just a timing thing? If it were down the road and your divorce was finalized… or maybe if we'd met a different way… I don't know. I'm confused. I'm just trying to do what I need to right now."

The server quietly slipped the check onto the table. Andrew reached for it mindlessly and pulled out his wallet as he spoke.

"You're so perceptive. So lovely," he sighed. "Thank you for understanding."

But I didn't understand. I couldn't imagine a tomorrow where he wasn't my person. I couldn't fathom why he felt his life would be better without me in it. I finished my second glass of wine and looked around while he signed the check. Couples everywhere. Chatting… touching…. laughing. Sipping and munching absent-mindedly. Walking down the sidewalk hand in hand.

And there we were, shutting the door on our future. All I wanted was to blend in and get the hell out of that restaurant.

"Ready?" I asked, standing to grab my purse.

We stopped in the restrooms on the way out and as soon as I latched the stall, it hit me. A forceful wave of emotion came on, which I could barely keep at bay. My life was crumbling from all sides. I had no one steady in my life to hold onto.

The one solace, the person who had distracted me from my life's chaos and soothed me with hair strokes and midnight embraces, gone. I sensed that

MOTION

this was only partially about Andrew. I thought of everything that had shaken loose and fallen out of my life in the past month. I allowed myself one tear.

I lingered in the dimly lit bathroom, fussing with my hair, washing and drying my hands twice. I stared blankly at my reflection.

There is sometimes a brief moment between our world being fractured and our acknowledgment of it. If I stay right here, we think, or keep my eyes closed, or don't take the next breath, perhaps I can stay frozen in this moment in time. Maybe, just maybe, I can preserve the world as I know it and fend off the new reality that has been unceremoniously thrust upon my life.

But we don't get that option, do we? Denial never pans out. Heartbreaks continue to crush us. Losses remain gaping, vacuous holes. Failures shake us to our core and bad diagnoses suffocate. Reality can be relentless like that. And here, I had a new reality. So I took a deep breath and I walked out the door.

Andrew stood there, smiling softly. He took my hand and I leaned into him as we walked back to the house.

"I'm really sorry, Becca. I wish things were different. I'm going to take some time. I need to talk to Emily and get some closure… figure out what I want." We stopped outside my car and kissed hard. Then, instead of pulling away, he stepped closer to me and wrapped his arms around me.

"I'm wondering if it would be a bad idea for me to invite you inside," he said.

"Probably," I said dryly. "It won't make this any easier, Andrew. Here, let me grab your things out of the back."

I had borrowed some camping gear from him for a recent trip. I fiddled with the sticky lock on my Subaru's trunk, frustrated. Andrew chuckled. He was the only person able to coax that damn lock open, so I handed over the keys.

"I'm going to miss that the most," I joked as I pulled his camping pad and sleeping bag out of the car.

"Actually, I want you to have these," he said, tossing them back inside. "Maybe it will make me feel better for doing this," he added. I thanked him.

Nothing more to do now. We both sighed as he wrapped me tightly in his arms. We stayed steady like that as several cars passed us by, his hand in my hair and my head on his shoulder.

"Are you sure… about this??" I asked him.

He was silent.

"No," he mumbled into my neck. "I'm not." I pulled away.

"You'll hear from me, this isn't it," he assured me.

I climbed into my car and watched in the rear-view mirror as he walked up the steps, disappearing out of sight.

As I drove away, I let the tears come, but only for a moment. I'd made it around the corner before swerving and realizing I was too buzzed to drive.

Fuuuck.

I pulled over, unsure what to do.

I called Andrew and explained my predicament.

"Just come back here. You can hang out with me while you sober up," he offered. "It's better if you're here, anyway."

"Okay. I promise not to seduce you," I said, and he laughed.

The front door opened as I walked up. Andrew's eyes were as red as mine.

"Thanks for this," I said, settling awkwardly on the couch. "I wouldn't have had that second glass of wine if I'd known where the evening was headed."

We'd rarely spent time outside of his bedroom. I leaned back on the couch cushion and closed my eyes. Andrew pulled my legs up to rest across his lap, running his hands over them affectionately.

"Want to hear something weird?" he asked.

"Sure." I opened my eyes.

"Right after you left, I got a text from Emily. We haven't talked in over a month. She asked if I'd meet her for coffee."

"Wow, that's wild," I said, and I meant it. "Talk about timing. It'll be good for you guys."

Bye Beauty

After a few silent moments we were hot and heavy again. There was no stopping us. At that point, I felt it was more for comfort than pleasure. His hands began to wander up my dress. I paused, considering, then looked him in the eyes.

"Well... do you want to go upstairs?"

"Yes."

And up we went.

Things came as naturally as they always had. The weight of our relationship ending didn't seem to diminish our desire for each other; if anything, it magnified it.

"Is this okay?" Andrew asked as he untied the back of my dress.

"Yeah. This is good."

The evening turned into a kind of sexual Last Supper. We were all over that damn room. We took turns giving and accepting, initiating and responding.

"Know what we haven't done?" he asked as we stood naked, embracing, our faces inches from each other and my arms around his neck. Andrew took hold of my legs behind the knees and in one motion, effortlessly lifted me off the floor and slid into me once again. I gasped. I wrapped my legs around his hips as we moved. There was no nervousness, no self-consciousness, only rapture. After a while, we collapsed onto his bed, freed of all tension.

"Damn. You were holding out on me — where was that little trick all along?" I teased.

He shifted closer to me and I nestled against him. The sun had long since set, cool moonlight and a soft breeze pouring in streams through the windows. He propped himself up on one elbow.

"There, now I can see you," he said. His hands mindlessly wandered over my hair and face, neck and shoulders while we caught our breath. I felt numb.

He bent to meet my lips, barely brushing them with his. Then he kissed me harder, wetter, and pulled me toward him. Round two; I knew the drill. Always more languid and relaxed, more tender and intimate than the first time. It was always raw, full of passion and saturated with emotion. My favorite round. I held his face in my hands and wrapped myself around him tight as we moved slowly in unison.

Then the reality hit me full force. This was a goodbye.

I threw my hands over my head and pushed against the wall.

"Make love to me," I whispered.

He grabbed hold of my hips and we moved, the tears welling up in my eyes until the floodgates finally broke. I cried silently as waves of pleasure and pain crashed over me and then receded, then crashed again. I let myself feel it all. This was a new experience — I'd never cried while climaxing before. It was almost too much to bear. Andrew slowed his pace and continued to hold me.

"You're beautiful," he said, looking straight at me in the moonlight. "Come here."

He rested beside me and I laid my head against his chest. It was the worst: the sex had cracked me open. The tears kept coming, and I let them, gasping, crying, and wiping my eyes over and over.

After a minute, I felt emptied out. We laid together in the stillness. I wasn't ashamed of my tears. I ran my hands across his chest and neck. Lost in thought, I stared blankly at a photograph of a field of sunflowers on the wall.

My mind bounced from my divorce, to Mark's death, to my dad sitting in a prison cell. And now, Andrew. It had all been too much. I couldn't be with the men I loved.

Andrew started to shake. He brought his hand up to his eyes, and I looked up to see him crying with as much abandon as I had. It was a heavy comfort to see him undone. He shook and moaned and cursed.

"You know how this feels?" I asked. "It feels like one of us is about to leave the country... like neither of us actually wants this to happen, but it's inevitable."

"That's exactly how I feel," he replied after a minute.

We both sighed.

"Do you... want to stay the night?" he asked me.

"No," I said. "I mean... I do, but no, I can't wake up here. It's too much." I sat up. "I should actually get going."

After we'd wiped our eyes and retrieved our clothes, we sat on his bed, hugging.

"Goddamnit," Andrew said as he helped me re-lace the back of my dress.

We shared about a dozen more embraces between his bedroom and the front door.

"Bye, beauty," he said, still pulling on my hand.

"Take care, Andrew." I closed the door behind me and forced myself not to look back.

MOTION **209**

New Normal

At first when we moved to Golden Hearth, Moses struggled to get used to the new schedule, crying for me on the nights he was at Keaton's house. He was still so little, only approaching his third birthday, and he didn't understand why I wasn't there with him. We tried our best to stay consistent and wait the transition out.

Even with this challenge, I loved my new home and the folks in it. The two other single moms, one Black woman and one white woman, each had preteen kids in the house. There was an ongoing air of play and shenanigans, with family and food at the center. A single dad lived downstairs. Tess and her partner Matt lived out in the geodesic dome, an Instagrammable orb of white tarp and PVC pipe that became a dreamy little abode with the addition of rugs and twinkly lights.

The landowner, Che, lived in a big ornate yurt with space for several friends to do yoga. Jack lived in a canvas tipi that smelled like a campfire and was packed with outdoor recreation gear. The house itself was full of sunlight, trailing houseplants, musical instruments, and cursive handwritten notes reminding everyone to hand wash the kitchen knives and water our designated garden areas.

That first summer on my own, between parenting and dating, I had become *obsessed* with hiking. I was working four days a week as a nanny and brought Moses with me. On the other three days, Moses was with Keaton, so I spent every spare morning I could in the Columbia River Gorge.

I mostly hiked alone or with just one other friend, preferring the quiet of the woods and the solo pace that I'd set for myself. It was a place to set everything down — I'd march right up to the mountain with my heavy burden of angst and grief and confusion about my life and just hammer it out beneath my feet, letting the wind whisk it from my skin. It was a holy place. My breath was a confession and my effort was an offering.

I'd sit on the summit and let the tears come, which they always did, and I'd descend a little lighter.

This nature therapy kept me sane as I waded through the loss of the entire life I had known. Keaton, Cory, Andrew... all gone. My home. My farm. My faith in God. The embodiment of the "normal" life I had craved after my dysfunctional upbringing. My father. Keaton's father. Some of these I had left behind, others had left me. I was peeling back layers that I didn't know I could lose, unsure what would be left of me at the end of it. Still, the weight of grief was no match for the mountains.

The Gorge, unafraid, bound up my wounds.

One weekend, as summer was becoming fall, I hiked up Dog Mountain alone. I wrote a poem as I sat at the summit. It captured the way I envisioned myself coming out of this season of chaos, whenever I might finally emerge.

> A woman has found her roots.
> She is strong, grounded
> Sun-kissed, wind blown
> Salt on her brow, earth on her feet
>
> Her pain is her power
> One foot before the other
> Patient
> Unhurried
> Steady
>
> An embrace of belonging
> A heart like the mountains
> A mind like the tides
>
> Her touch is a breeze unfettered
> Her body a glory garden
> Her passion an untamed forest fire
>
> She moves with ease and purpose
> Alone and unafraid
> A wolf on the bluff singing to the open sky
>
> She is an elusive creature
> Seen by many
> Found by few
> Rarely known
>
> She cannot be contained
> For she is wild.

Dealing

Summer had slipped unnoticed into fall. I drifted through the first few weeks without Andrew feeling hollowed out. I had made Andrew my tether to love and connection during a time of chaos in my life. I knew that wasn't fair to him, to the nature of our bright summery romance.

MOTION

I understood his need to step away, and I coped in the healthiest ways I knew how. A new haircut. Reorganizing my closet. I got a shitty guitar and restrung it, lulling my frayed nerves with heartbreak songs.

Lacking intimacy, I felt cold and alone. I frequently broke down crying on the highway and in the aisles of the grocery store. I continued to hike — farther, faster, harder. My body became stronger and leaner until I hardly recognized it.

I also set to work on kitchen projects to distract myself from the heartache: fermenting kombucha and kim chi, baking quiches, processing all the beautiful produce from the community garden into ready-to-eat delights. I crafted homemade soap and body butter. Kitchen work always has been a place to find my flow.

I was stripping basil, lost in thought one afternoon, when Jack shuffled into the kitchen. He'd been traveling most of the summer and just returned from a birthright trip to Israel. We had been introduced only a week before he'd left.

"Oh, hey. How are you?" he asked as he filled a glass of water.

"I'm... okay," I answered, tentative.

"Okay," he repeated. "Want to talk?"

"I don't know that I want to bore you with it. Just going through a breakup… alongside a divorce. Not something I'd recommend, by the way. It's… a lot all at once." I tossed a handful of basil in the bowl. "Definitely hurting right now," I said. I was weary.

"Damn, Becca. I'm sorry to hear that," he said with disarming sincerity that invited tears. But I wasn't about to cry into my pesto.

"It's okay. Thanks for asking. How are you?" I asked, turning the attention around on him.

"Well, I've been better too," he said. "I'm laid out with food poisoning, so I'm staying near the bathroom. I feel awful. Just…. don't get too close."

"Ugh! Food poisoning is so rough. Do you need anything?" I asked. I was tempted to go into full mom-nurse-mode and start smothering him with natural remedies and essential oils.

"I think just rest for now. Thanks though," he answered.

The following evening, I sat facing Logan on the couch by the fireplace. Logan, who I had mentored as a spunky teen at the church, was now a grown-ass woman living in Portland. She was capable and wild and free, covered in artful tattoos and burns from manning the brick oven at Pyro Pizza. She always arrived bearing cheap beer, tight hugs, and a pack of American Spirits. I needed her wit and company.

Jack was still sick. He'd been in and out of the living room, but passed through and assured us we weren't stealing his temporary sleeping spot on the couch.

"So. I've decided to take a vow of celibacy," I announced, before taking a long swig of beer. Logan burst out laughing.

"Right, Becca. Sure you are." She looked at me incredulously.

"I'm serious! I'm on day three, I'll have you know!" I insisted.

She continued to laugh. "I'm sorry, it's just — you're the last person I would ever expect to give up sex."

"I know. And that's exactly why I need to. For sixty days. And I'm not getting myself off, either," I insisted. "I need to figure out how sex is connected to everything that has happened this year. It's not going to be fun."

"Well, I respect that. Good on ya." She raised her beer in salute.

"Not to mention, any sex I have will just remind me of Andrew and make it that much harder to get over him," I added.

"True. You guys had it pretty good there, didn't ya?" she asked.

"Oh my God. You have no idea, Logan. It was like… another level. Like all the best sex I'd ever had. Combined. Well, besides Samuel." I made a vulgar motion between my legs. She laughed. "The night we broke up, Andrew and I had so much sex. At one point he picked me up and we just kept going and going like it was nothing. Sometimes he makes me come faster than I can. He's like a fucking mind reader."

"Well, damn!" Logan stared at me speechless, grinning. I sighed.

"Ugh. And his body — well, anyway, don't get me started. I just don't know how to move on from sex that good. Even if I can accept that we shouldn't be together, how do I give up the sex? I feel like I'm never going to have it that good again…"

"Hey now!" Jack walked out from behind the couch, startling us. He'd been lying on the rug across the room and overheard our whole conversation. "Give the rest of us some credit!"

MOTION **213**

I debated whether to feel embarrassed that he'd been listening to my candid remarks about my sex life.

"Fair enough," I laughed. "But hey, I'm *grieving* here, you guys. It was sooo good!" I threw my head back orgasmically for comic effect.

We all chuckled.

After we finished our drinks, Logan gave me a long hug and left. It was getting late. I turned to Jack, who had returned to lying on the floor.

"Hey, sorry you had to hear all that. You were so quiet I didn't realize you were there," I said.

"It's all good. Free entertainment," he replied. I shot him a sideways glance. "Not to make light of your situation… just saying, it's interesting."

"I'll take that as a compliment. I'm gonna turn in. Working early tomorrow. Goodnight." I slipped off to my room.

"Night," he said with a chuckle.

I smiled to myself that evening over the friendly banter. I knew Jack's teasing was rooted in sincere friendliness. It struck me how lucky I was to be in a home full of grounded, warm people, as I navigated the many transitions of my personal life.

It was subtle, but I began to sense that the pain I associated with our breakup went far deeper than just losing Andrew. It shouldn't have shaken me or broken me as much as it did. I set out to understand what had conspired in my own history and the dynamic between Andrew and I to create the perfect storm. The heartbreak that summer was the catalyst for some huge, foundational changes in me. It took me months to make any sense of the experience and in fact, it's taken years to truly reach the heart of it.

Alone, Alone

Keaton and I still had final paperwork to file for our divorce. We met in a little tea house, Tea Chai Te, to hash everything out. This was only a week after my breakup with Andrew. I felt wrung out and hollow, but we managed to plow our way through the stand of forms and negotiate the finer details of our divorce in just a couple hours, with almost no disagreements. Somehow, we laughed and teased quite a bit. There was no tension between us, but there was a certain tone of formality coming from Keaton that I wasn't accustomed to.

We signed the last of the papers.

"You hungry? Want to grab lunch and hang out for a bit?" I asked.

"Sorry, I better get going. I have to pick up Moses from my mom's."

It caught me off guard. I wasn't used to him refusing me... anything.

"Alright. Thanks, Keaton. I'll see you soon."

We hugged goodbye and went opposite ways down the sidewalk. I stood, considering what to do next. I was hungry. Exhausted. And I was alone. Alone, for the first time in my adult life.

Utterly, completely... alone. Alone, alone, alone, alone, alone.

The word rang and reverberated in my mind — a mocking and menacing word that bounced around my skull until I literally shook my head to clear myself of it.

I crossed the street to order some sushi, then wandered to Blue Star Donuts. A while later, I sat in my car with a dragon roll and a chocolate ganache donut in my lap and began to laugh-cry. I had no appetite. I sent a text to Logan.

"Well. Looks like I've hit rock bottom," I wrote. "I'm eating sushi alone in my car. Divorced, dumped, and somehow I've got fucking chocolate ganache in my hair." Her laughter and words of comfort pulled me back up to Earth. Silly girl. I wasn't alone; not by a long shot.

I sighed and drove home, opting to leave the radio off, lest I hear a lovely, nostalgic song and have a meltdown on the interstate. *I have a good life*, I thought to myself and believed it. *Nada me falta... I lack nothing.*

I was in uncharted territory. I'd spent my adult life avoiding aloneness and, more so, loneliness. I had only a vague sense of what lay underneath my manic need for control and my urge to bond so fiercely to others. But for the first time, I wanted to know. I trusted myself enough to feel safe excavating my own inner workings. I knew I had within me the strength and resilience to rebuild a life that was truly my own.

As isolating as it was to have severed myself from Keaton's family and the life I knew, it was also invigorating. Freeing. I had the sensation of emerging from a warm, sleepy climate-controlled house into cold, fresh winter air.

For the first time, I had no one to answer to but myself and Moses. I realized that he would be the person beside me after all the dust settled.

I'd been distracted from motherhood while cracking my life open and cathartically fucking my way across the Portland metro area. Yet he had been

MOTION

gracious and wise and adaptable through it all. So, I resolved again to be the kind of mother I had needed as a child: strong, soft, open, warm. The kind of person I would have trusted and admired. I resolved to heal my past. I resolved to write a new story for myself and my tiny family, one that stretched beyond the limitations set for me by generations of trauma, brokenness, and dysfunctional family history.

I would learn how to be my own, to embrace the personal agency which was my birthright, that self-possession which I had given up, first to religion during childhood and romance not long after. I would tend to my intense emotional life and learn to relate to men in a new way, no longer allowing old fears of scarcity and rebellious impulses to steer the ship. All this heartbreak and chaos had lit a fire under me.

This felt like a do-over, a fresh start after playing house and mimicking adulthood for five years. Maturity isn't about jobs and houses and cars and biological age; it's about self-responsibility.

Whatever was coming next, I was paying attention. I would advocate, first and foremost, for my healing and do the hard work of the heart myself. I would seek out the sweet spot between the freedom and grounding that my soul craved. I would unshackle myself from the layers of conditioning which were weighing me down. I would trust my ability to take flight and land with intuitive grace.

We watery Scorpios live for change, and we love looking darkness in the face. *This will be right up my alley*, I thought to myself.

This unshackling would also be long, drawn out, and fucking painful.

I don't remember anyone mentioning that part.

Part Two

17
Starting Again

Natural Love

I was lying awake one night in my empty bed, thinking about a conversation Jack and I had shared in which we lamented our low-touch society. It seemed the only acceptable context in which to have physical closeness was within romantic relationships. We spoke of our desire to foster higher-touch communities and discussed how isolating it felt to be single and deprived of intimacy.

As I wrapped my body around my spare pillow yet again, I cursed myself for committing to sixty days sex-free. What I needed was touch. So I took a risk and texted Jack. As nonchalantly as I could, I pitched the idea that, perhaps, we could be platonic snuggle buddies once and in a while. You know… for our health and wellbeing.

Well, he was into it.

A few nights later, Jack invited me for a visit to his tipi. Barefoot, I snuck outside, as subtle as I could, not eager to cause a stir within the house by the appearance of a budding romance. He built a fire in the center fire pit and tended it effortlessly as the night grew darker and the crickets began their song. Our chemistry was instantaneous. The quality of his touch was strong and purposeful. It felt natural, like salve on a wound. With his strong frame encircling me, he joked that in normal circumstances, we'd be making out by this point. However, he was in full support of my dramatic vow of celibacy.

A couple weeks after that, I invited Jack on a hike. The sky was bright blue that day, and the orange leaves were crisp on the trails. We wandered through Powell Butte, a rocky cinder cone formation on the outskirts of the city, and took turns telling adventure stories, examining spider webs, and petting strangers' dogs. We found a perfect picnic log and sat upon the moss, sharing the sandwiches and kettle chips he'd brought.

I told him about my family… even my dad. Not everything, but more than I'd expected. More than I'd told Andrew or Samuel. We spoke about all the things I found most important: philosophy, environmental activism, gender and race issues, understanding and deconstructing privilege. At one point, I reached out and took his hand. He squeezed it. By the drive back I couldn't seem to maintain any physical distance from him.

• • •

The pinnacle of my hiking season was Mount Defiance, the highest point in the Columbia River Gorge. It was a grueling day hike covering 12 miles and 4,800 feet of elevation gain. I'd gathered up some die hard, experienced hiking friends and invited Jack to join at the last minute. It was the hardest hike I'd ever done. I fantasized about quitting multiple times. Somehow though, we made it. We shared chocolate and salty snacks at the summit.

As I looked out over the expanse, I felt content. I was also humbled and impressed by the fact that Jack fared just as well as I had, though I'd been logging miles on the trail diligently all summer to prepare.

During our descent, four of us branched off from the group to scout a hidden waterfall. We heard it before we saw it, and our sun-baked impulses demanded we go skinny dipping. We squealed in the frigid water and laughed at our antics as we dried our dripping bodies with scarves and T-shirts.

On the drive home, we fantasized about cooking up some hot curry for dinner, and I loved the fact that I was going home with Jack. I realized that I had never had a man with whom I could adventure. I felt challenged by him, but also appreciated and witnessed. That night, as we curled up in his bed, I felt a deep love forming. I was magnetized toward him. I wanted to seduce him… bad.

Well, I tried for hours. But he wasn't having it. The heat between us seemed enough to warm the late October night. I made myself irresistible to him, I threw myself at him, but he refused.

"Nope," he said, matter-of-factly, exhaling his own sexual tension as I writhed next to him invitingly. "You made a commitment! Sixty days, remember?" He seemed to almost be enjoying the refusal.

"Fuck the commitment! I went 27 days. That was plenty! Besides. I'm a grown woman. Aren't I allowed to change my mind?" I breathed my hot breath down his neck. I was playing dirty.

"Sorry, lady. No can do." He squeezed me tight as if appeasing an indignant yet adorable child.

"Hmph. Alright then." I fell asleep in a huff, making sure I was backed right up against his hips to let him know just what he was refusing.

Early in the quiet hours of the morning, when the light was barely rising, we slid out of our clothes. There was no conversation about it; we had both decided some time while we were sleeping, that it simply had to happen. Our connection was alive, bursting through the seams.

And one thing is certain: it made me forget all about Andrew.

Afterwards, I dozed back to sleep. I awoke to Jack wandering around the tipi getting dressed and preparing for an interview he had that day. Like a fly on the wall, I witnessed his rituals — buttoning his shirt, slipping his watch on, winking at me with a warm smirk, and finally kissing me goodbye and whistling on his way out. I laid in his bed for an hour after he left, looking at the artifacts of this man and his life, and marveling at the fact that we had collided with such simple harmony.

The First Song I Wrote

> There is a man
> Salt on his brow
> Sun on his skin
> Feet on the ground
> Heart like a mountain
> Hands hold the weight of the world
>
> He met his match
> Her voice is the breeze
> A face like the moon
> A mind like the seas
> Soul is a forest
> Passion a fire untamed
>
> Freedom for her wild things
> A place to land his open wings

Root and soil for the seeds

I'd rather be cold
While he's gone
Than warm in someone else's arms

Rolled into town
Covered in dust
Smile on his face
Raft in the truck
Talking of canyons
Tall groves of Aspen in June

She drew him in
Welcomed his gaze
They camped the fire
Hiked on the plains
Dreamed and delighted
Sparked and ignited a flame

I'd rather be cold
While he's gone
Than warm in someone else's arms

Something Real

Halloween in Portland is one hell of a party. I went with Jack to a ravey costume party called the Bacon Ball, and a week after that we attended the Portland Erotic Ball. I dressed as a siren and he was a very sexy cowboy. The erotic ball, a Portland classic, was a delightfully naughty event. Around midnight, he and I nearly had sex in an ornate elevator as a crowd of rousing onlookers egged us on.

Our level of freedom and sex-positivity was wildly invigorating to me after the five years I'd just experienced. It became routine for us to have sex in semi-public places. He'd sweep me off to empty hallways, kitchen tables, restaurant bathrooms (only the classy ones, of course), and I couldn't get enough. We had a special skill for nonchalant quickies, which were outshone only by our skill for having afternoon-long languid lovemaking sessions punctuated with lightness and laughter as well as ropes and bite marks. There was a shadowy fire inside of me that came alive with him.

Our housemates were in full support (besides a brief hiccup with Tess, who also had an attraction to Jack). Three-year-old Moses knew Jack first as a housemate, playing cars with him in the kitchen and picking raspberries out in the yard. They had a spacious ease, and most of my time with Jack happened while Moses was sleeping or away with Keaton. I never stopped to consider whether something that felt so good, this new love with this trustworthy dream of a man, might not be well-timed. I rationalized it by reasoning that one shouldn't question the timing of life. Jack and I were right for each other on so many levels. He brought with him the deep friendship of Keaton and the sexual prowess of Andrew.

As equinox marched toward solstice, we did everything together.

We went rock climbing. We made sauerkraut and cooked brunches worth writing home about. We played John Prine duets on the guitar and banjo, and we laid awake at night reading Ed Abbey and Mary Oliver books to each other. We went to films and potlucks and farm work parties, integrating effortlessly into each other's lives. We were smitten.

I felt like I was gathering up a free, wild part of myself that I had abandoned after my post-graduation summer of gallivanting around with Sebastian. I was welcoming her back into the fold.

That November, I planned a road trip to Utah with Logan to celebrate my 26th birthday, a replacement for a Grand Canyon trip with Andrew that was no longer going to happen. Jack had a work trip to Minnesota scheduled the week before, so the timing meant that we'd be apart for several weeks.

He had a sneaky Gemini way of enchanting me with thoughtful surprises: bars of chocolate, little notes, and hand-folded paper flowers. I came home from work on the day he left to find a gift on my bed, alongside a love letter that is still tucked into a box in my closet. Inside the package was a pair of ornate rainbow earrings shaped like suns. He had bought them while in Israel, unsure who they might be for, and I had settled into the Golden Hearth while he was away on that very trip. I opened the letter.

> "Becca — I don't have the words to describe how I feel about you and the joy you bring into my life. It transcends any love I have felt thus far for a person. I bought these earrings in Jerusalem, knowing full well I had no one back home to give them to… there was just an energy of potential that I recognized in my life. You are a manifestation of that potential.
>
> "You have changed my life in so many wonderful ways and I know that the timing is perfect. Any gift I give you will pale in comparison to what you have given me and continue to give me every day. I want to be a partner who will cherish and love your whole being for exactly what it is. A friend

to help you grow and a helper to get through the hard times. Someone who is there whenever you need them: me. With so much love, Jack."

I sighed and wiped a tear from my eye. I was absorbed in him, falling deeply in love, yet still swimming in deep heartbreak from my failed marriage and Andrew's subsequent rejection. It was a lot to hold at once.

Andrew, Again

In early November before the road trip, Andrew and I exchanged a few messages over text. We confessed to missing each other terribly and decided together that it would be nice to meet in person.

On a dark, rainy Sunday evening we met for Thai food. I arrived early, trying not to sweat when I considered that I was about to see him again. He had become one of those people who always set my nervous system into a frenzy. From afar, I felt wistful love toward him, but in person I often felt anxious and unsteady.

We had gotten together for beers back in September, a few weeks after the breakup, and it felt almost too nice. We sat close together in the booth, legs touching, as he examined the newly formed calluses on my rock climbing hands and I noticed he let his beard grow in. We talked lightly about how we were doing, but it was obvious that we were both too tender to say much. I drove him home after an hour, lingering in my car for an extra moment before saying a weighted goodbye.

This time, our dinner together was sweet and the attraction was as palpable as it had always been. We laughed over Halloween stories, and he shared that he had gotten back together with his ex, Em.

"Oh. Good for you guys," I said, and I half meant it. *There's no way it's going to last*, I thought to myself. "You two aren't open, are you?" I smirked.

He looked up from his curry at me, wide-eyed.

"Nope. Damn Becca, you're trouble. Why you gotta do that to me?" he asked.

"Hey, I was just asking," I grinned, knowing exactly what I was doing.

The temperature seemed to rise in the restaurant.

He insisted on paying for my food. Outside, sheltering ourselves from a downpour, we shared a long, drawn out hug. Then he took me by the waist and kissed me urgently, in the same juicy way he always had. I was startled. We pulled back and looked at each other.

"I... probably shouldn't have done that," he said, looking down.

"No, probably not," I replied. We hugged again tight, then turned to go our separate ways.

That same weekend, I was house sitting with Jack. I came through the door, tossed my rain dampened coat on a hook, and curled up on the couch with Jack and the dog.

"So. How was the dinner?" he asked, tentative.

"He kissed me," I said, grimacing at the truth.

"Really? And he had just told you he got back together with his ex? Pfft. That guy." He rolled his eyes. Jack and I had been existing in a very loving conversation about how to be sustainably non-monogamous, but this scenario was still plenty irksome to him.

"Thanks for not being mad," I said. "I'm not sure what I was expecting out of seeing him."

· · ·

The day before my Utah trip, I sat in Keaton's living room, the same living room where so much of our shared life had been redefined over fragrant cannabis joints and buttery popcorn. Moose played with matchbox cars. Keaton and I had a routine of hanging out for an hour every week during drop-off, to catch up on each other's lives and stay connected. We'd become comfortable friends in the months after I moved out, and the transition was truly a relief more than anything else.

Our divorce had been finalized earlier in the week. It was official. He handed me an envelope with the documents of our dissolution, and with that, we were both ex-spouses. I thanked him. I told him of the latest with Jack.

Tears began to collect in Keaton's eyes. He'd always been compassionate and soft hearted.

"Sorry," he said, gathering himself. "It's just really nice to see. Seems like you two are in real love. You make me believe in it. What you had with Andrew was like… dumb, blind love. But this seems like the real deal. I'm happy for you, Becca. Really."

I'll never forget such sincere, supportive words coming from my ex-husband, right on the heels of our divorce.

STARTING AGAIN

So much had happened in rapid sequence and left me in survival mode with very little bandwidth to process it all. In recent months, I had ended multiple relationships, moved out of the house, left one job and began a new one.

Then there was Moses. The first few months of our new parenting schedule were gut wrenching and guilt-ridden for me. I had constant, low-grade anxiety whenever I was away from him, feeling like a part of my identity as a mother was crumbling. He and I had been inseparable for the first two and a half years of his life. We spent every day together. He came to work with me, he slept beside me in our bed, he played with me in the grass while I gardened.

I had been the gatekeeper on where my baby went, who held him, who played with him, what he ate, how he slept. Moses and I were wildly sweet and silly together, and he was held in our arms more than most babies are fortunate enough to be. Alongside Keaton, I took care of his every need. We almost never had babysitters and when we did, it was Keaton's mom who helped us. Friends and strangers in the grocery store often remarked at the deep bond and secret language our little family seemed to share. The longest we'd ever been apart was that one night when I was away with Cory.

And suddenly, we were in different cities for three nights every single week.

It did help me to see the mothers I lived with successfully co-parenting, but Moses was still so small. There were moments when I feared we'd create irreparable damage to Moses' bonding and attachment by separating during such a formative time. It took years to forgive myself and recognize that two healthy, happy divorced parents are far better for a child than two miserable, bitter, married parents.

Election Day

It was the day after the 2016 presidential election. Like many across the nation, I was filled with dismay and dread at the coming four years. Logan and I reckoned with disbelief as we loaded up her Subaru with camping gear. I brought a hatchet from Jack, a sleeping bag from Andrew, and some vintage cooking gear I'd inherited from Mark, Keaton's late father. Logan and I were both riding on the heels of huge breakups and life transitions. Although I was deeply entangled with Jack, Andrew's absence still weighed heavily on me every day; I hadn't let him go.

Logan and I headed east to spend two weeks trying to leave the world behind.

As we drove toward Idaho, she shared about her desire to go to North Dakota and support Standing Rock, but to truly help, and not just be "another little half native chick with a backpack." We sang our hearts out to "A Change is Gonna Come" by Sam Cooke and hummed over the humble voices and plucking strings of Townes Van Zandt and John Prine. We ate homemade weed cookies. We watched the sun go down. I cried. Logan cried. We saw distant Nevada lights through the dark open landscape, and kept on driving.

It was deep night when we arrived in Utah. I could almost make out the silhouette of towering black that rose high into the starry sky, blocking out the light. I woke up inside our little rented house at the base of a red rocky mountain. Zion National Park: a place mighty and sturdy and wild. A place that could unwaveringly hold all the pain of the world and transform it into cold nights and flash floods and desert sand.

It was mid-November. We'd planned for cold days, but the sun greeted us instead. We spent the next two weeks hiking through canyons and scouting the best hideaway camping spots on nearby BLM land. My comedic chemistry with Logan was on point, and our ability to make each other laugh buoyed our post-breakup propensity to make each other cry. When we'd had enough catharsis, we numbed our pain with simple cocktails and tangy cannabis joints.

Zion had a timeless, otherworldly quality. The night skies were vast and unafraid, and the sunrises were kind and gentle.

It was my first taste of desert medicine. It's almost as if the harsh conditions had cleared the land of energetic clutter allowing for only the strongest, purest, most concentrated parts of life to exist there. As if the veil had been thinned between the spirit world and the physical world. There was nothing said or done while we were in the desert of Utah that didn't feel rich with potency. Our laughter came deep from our bellies. Our tears were made of pure grief and regret. Our songs sung within the canyon walls ricocheted off the stone and multiplied into choirs. Even our slow-cooked food satisfied deep hungers within us.

26

The day before my 26th birthday we hiked Angel's Landing, a notoriously breathtaking and dangerous hike in Zion National Park. I could feel a deep shift happening within me as I stepped into the first day of my late twenties. By process of elimination I had become my most free self — untethered to a spouse or obligation or life plan that might propel me in any particular direction. Jack's presence in my life was new, delightful and undefined, welcome as it was.

It seemed that the spectrum of life possibilities was laid out before me and I had the thrilling and bewildering task of choosing a course.

The past year had cracked me apart, and now I was bursting open in the blink of an eye like a hatchling emerging from a shell. I remembered that tearful day, alone on my yoga mat, when I had wondered if married suburban life was destined to be my lot forever. And now, I was here. I wasn't ready to start dreaming yet, but I reveled in the freedom of choice.

Later that day, we drove up to a frigid and cloudy Bryce Canyon National Park and I played Nina Simone's *I Wish I Knew How It Would Feel To Be Free* on the speakers. As we climbed curve after curve on the long mountain highway, with no plans or responsibilities or ought-to's, I was reminded how wildly fortunate I was to have the agency to claim my own life. I had begun to boldly break so many conventions, with very little consequence, thanks to my cultural, racial, and socioeconomic context. The depth of that privilege was not lost on me. As I peered out at the expanse of hoodoo formations, I felt responsible to honor the opportunity life had afforded me.

The following morning, we packed up and bid Utah farewell; Arizona was calling. We drove along winding roads carved into the mountainside. It seemed that every few miles, there was another natural marvel to behold. When we entered the Grand Staircase Escalante National Monument, I gasped. Logan pulled the car over and we stood beside the road in awe. In reverent silence we took in the landscape, which defied the imagination on all sides.

For miles and miles, the landscape was covered with cliffs and canyons in layers of white, gray, brown and vermilion. The sky was joyously clear and blue, and the midday sun had chosen not to rage. Witnessing the layers of rock standing thousands of feet into the air, unwavering, and imagining the millennia they spent forming, gave me pause. I thought of the deeply disruptive tectonic shifts that had forced these layers up and out of the earth and birthed the monument before us.

I felt a familiarity with this place and its power, but I also felt smaller than I'd ever felt. I had the sensation of being a grain of sand on a vast beach. It was a comforting thought. A grain of sand's biggest problems and most dramatic meltdowns don't stop the beach from forming or the tide from coming in. They won't stop the fragile dunes from turning to stone and becoming something ancient and timeless.

We crossed into Arizona, a state neither of us had visited before. I had expected Utah to be the place to break me open, but in many ways, its trails and red mountains simply held me. And here was Arizona, quiet and foreboding, as though it had been waiting for us with something unnamed still in store. We stopped to witness the magnificent Horseshoe Bend, seeking a quiet moment on a rocky edge as flocks of tourists took selfies.

The longer we sat, the more emotion arose until we were both weeping bitterly. Logan was thinking about Billy. I was thinking about Andrew, imagining how different things would be if I were sitting on the edge of the Grand Canyon beside him at that very moment.

There was something quietly heavy about the city of Page, and a desolate feeling hovered on the quiet, empty campsites along Lake Powell, a man-made lake which activists say never should have been created. This place held so much tension: between thousands of locals and millions of tourists, between Navajo Nation sovereignty and the intricate pressures of capitalism and assimilation, between the natural beauty and exploitation of its richness.

Logan and I toured the otherworldly sepia-toned Antelope Canyon, one of nearly a hundred slot canyons in the area, marveling at the meandering network of narrow passages formed by powerful flash floods. We both held the discomfort of the experience, as the tour guide, a member of the Navajo Nation, demonstrated the best photo filter to use and stopped our small cohort along each Instagrammable photo op. We witnessed the busloads of tourists taking in this natural marvel through the lens of their iPhone screens. I wanted to breathe in the place, to feel the wind and imagine the rushing water, to absorb the beauty of the bright blue sky winding a snake pattern across these orange-red ceilings, but I found myself judging tourists instead.

"Wow, people suck," Logan said to me as we emerged from the canyon. I agreed, and felt in many ways that we were no better, having paid to come here and having snapped a few photos ourselves.

Our campsite on Lake Powell was scattered with sagebrush and wild rabbits hopping from one bush to the next, in the same way squirrels scurried around tree branches back home.

That first night a massive, glowing full moon rose over the lake, the Blood Harvest Moon, as I'd heard it called. We built a fire — Logan was the designated fire builder, thanks to her brick oven pizza prowess — and I heated our curry and rearranged our camp as dusk set in. I called Keaton for the first time in a week. Moses was still doing perfectly, he said, same as he'd been every day that I'd texted to ask about him. I should go enjoy myself, he said. I hung up.

I had permission to let go.

STARTING AGAIN

Open

I had carried two illicit substances on the adventure with me besides cannabis: LSD and MDMA. Many people see these simply as Schedule 1 substances, lumped together with other drugs like cocaine and heroin. Others call them psychedelics. And to others, they're medicine. I brought them along because I wanted a breakthrough. I understood that this time in the desert, this mark of a new year, was a chance to pause to reflect. I wanted to carry on the deep inner work I'd been treading through, to understand what had led me to this point in my life — to my first birthday as a single, agnostic, broken-hearted woman with a beautiful and terrifying world at my fingertips.

I'd spoken with my brother at length over the phone about psychedelics in previous months. He'd been released from prison and was creating a new life in Portland. He spoke about how many great thought leaders, scientists and artists had used psychedelics, specifically LSD, which I had never used. He explained something I later confirmed against the research: that psychedelic drugs enable regions of the brain to communicate in novel ways, enhancing creativity, promoting a sense of openness and receptivity, and for many people, catalyzing transformative and sometimes challenging cathartic experiences.

As I learned about MDMA, which I had never used either, I realized it was more than just "Ecstasy," the party drug which I associated with all-night dance raves. MDMA is an empathogen — it increases pleasure, yes, but it also deepens one's sense of connectedness to self and others. It was my brother's suggestion that I use these two substances in tandem. This was his second nugget of life advice, after his old mantra: "If you're going to do something illegal, don't get caught."

This move toward psychedelics felt like peering over an edge, peeling back another layer of old stories I'd internalized about the world. Why would these drugs, which worked as medicine for so many people, be wrong or "sinful" to use? Why didn't I have a say in what I put inside my own body?

Here I was in the desert with Logan, a friend who I had mentored in the church since adolescence, and who had been a bridesmaid in my wedding. And now, we were about to drop acid together. *What a moment*, I thought to myself.

After being raised in the anti-drug 90s, where mentors wore D.A.R.E. shirts and told us to "just say no to drugs," plus the Christian church environment, where drugs were "tools of the devil" used to control our minds, there was a significant edge for me to overcome. But I was curious.

This was before famed journalist Michael Pollan published his book *How To Change Your Mind*, which thrust psychedelics into mainstream consciousness, and Gwyneth Paltrow's stylish "Goop Lab" sent employees to a beach house in Jamaica to take psilocybin mushrooms with white woo-woo journey guides.

As I peered over this new edge, I was thankful for Logan's presence. She was a close friend from the church who had also left the faith, and she had been experimenting with psychedelics for the last year. She explained that simply having a body sometimes feels difficult while "tripping," or riding out the effects of the drug. Through laughter, she'd told me about the very real struggle of simply going pee or changing a jacket while tripping on acid (LSD). She laid out her process of creating a space, gathering comfy clothes and arranging soft areas to nest down in. She suggested having snacks and water and tissues available, plus anything else that might make one feel safe and at ease, such as a trusted and experienced friend who might provide support.

I dug out the LSD and MDMA, which I'd buried safely into a secret pouch in my backpack. She and I talked about our plan and intentions for the evening and I relayed my brother's instructions. Each small square of paper had one full dose of LSD. We were to place it under our tongues and wait. I dissolved a single MDMA capsule into a jug of water for us to sip on, a pro-tip courtesy of my big brother (*what else are older siblings for?*) and marked it with a hair tie to prevent confusing it with regular water. The idea was that a steady, mild dose of MDMA would help keep us in a warm, positive and open space, offering some added protection from a telltale "bad trip."

I did some additional research before leaving Portland. I learned that one major predictor of how a drug experience will go is "Set and Setting." This term refers to the context in which the drug is taken. "Set" means the mindset, mood and intention of the user; psychedelics can be non-specific amplifiers of emotion, so difficult and repressed feelings can often surface during a drug trip.

The other factor to consider is "Setting." Where is the drug being taken? Who is the user surrounded by? What is the sensory environment, and is it a place that feels safe and supportive, if intense experiences begin to surface? These are major factors to seriously consider before taking any drug. The other essential piece is quality and purity of the drugs. Many drugs are laced with contaminants and fillers, and some are entirely different substances than what they're sold as. It is important to know the source of your drugs, as mistaking a substance or dosage can be deadly.

Author's Note: Please trip responsibly. My awesome friends at Double Blind Magazine have a variety of offerings, including drug testing kits, harm reduction resources, informative articles and post-trip support available at DoubleBlindMag.com.

I pulled the papers from the bag and handed one to her. We paused for a quiet moment. Eyeing each other and grinning, we each tucked a full dose under our tongues, chuckling and wondering how long to wait before spitting out the small bits of paper.

We went about arranging firewood, organizing our belongings, and choosing the perfect playlists, then we walked down to the edge of the lake. Its pastel hues and the silhouette of a single boat out on the water carried a kind of melancholic beauty. Settling on the shore, we talked about everything and nothing: water rights, politics, human nature.

"I never imagined I'd be here," I said, and I meant it in more ways than one. As we walked back up to camp, the visual effects of the LSD began to set in. I noticed a dreamy shimmer covering every surface — the path, the leaves, my own skin. I turned to Logan.

"Do you feel something?" I asked.

Logan stopped walking and looked around.

"Oh yeah. I feel something. Let's get back." The night was beginning to come alive.

Logan and I snapped happy, eager photos under the expansive, amber full moon. We began sipping on the MDMA water and carried on throughout the night. We'd gone through a portal. This place, this night, was pure magic. Everything, even inanimate objects, seemed to vibrate with its own life. My focus became hyper attuned to the present moment — wherever my eyes landed became the most incredible thing in the world.

I marveled, childlike, and thought to myself, *How have I never paid attention to leaves before? Or rocks? Or beetles?!* I felt like I was stepping through a gateway, entering into another world where I would be met with unnerving and unknown wonders, and perhaps even meet a different expression of myself on the other side.

Dusk turned to night; sunlight was replaced by moonlight, starlight, and firelight, a welcome and comforting shift. Then, the evening began to sparkle and warp intensely. Logan started the fire. Soon, we stopped talking altogether and stayed quiet for what felt like hours, hearing nothing but the sounds of crackling firewood. I stretched out atop the picnic table and gazed up at the sky, lost in the dancing specks of white light and the way they seemed so personal and familiar, so close to me in this strange here and now.

"You know," I whispered, looking over to Logan. "I feel like I'm floating. Like there's something carrying me. At first, when I left everything, I felt like I was just, adrift… but this is different. I don't actually think I'm lost in life. I think I could float like this for a while. It's not that scary."

She nodded with care, smiling, and gazed back at the fire.

I returned my attention to the stars. I began to forget that I had a body at all. As this notion settled in, I continued to let go, first in my body and gradually in my mind and my heart, too. The more I let go, the more I encountered my own sense of risk and resistance. I was worried I might lose myself and become too open, too easily swayed by wonder and mystery.

I wasn't tethered to anything. I wasn't sure I could discern what was real and what was an illusion. I didn't feel confused, though — it was just my strong sense of self grasping for control. It was fascinating to witness such an obvious yet invisible phenomenon: an inner conversation with oneself. I had the sensation of my chest opening, as if my heart had forced my whole rib cage apart and splayed it toward the sky to make space. Something inside of me was unwinding, and I didn't know what.

I felt a sensation of being held inside a large, warm hand, or perhaps tucked under a wing.

It was getting late. I allowed my trains of thought to meander in and out of focus. We threw another log on the fire and nestled our chairs closer to it. Entranced by the dancing flames and glowing rainbow embers, we mused aimlessly about life.

> *What is pain?*
>
> *Why does so much bad, ugly shit happen in this world?*
>
> *What does it mean to be someone powerful inside a vulnerable, flawed vessel?*

We wore out our hearts and our attention spans with these questions and many others.

Craving a distraction, we let a few songs play on the speaker. The music poured out on us and mixed with our young, tender heartache, our angst and our regret. I watched the smoke rise and thought about the way fire can be so many things at once: energy and heat, destruction, transformation, ending. I thought about Andrew. A part of me still believed we might find our way back to each other. It occurred to me for the first time that perhaps that wasn't the goal.

"What was it really like with you two?" Logan asked me. "You know… besides all the great sex."

"Ooph." I thought for a moment. "It was like… a summer long interview. It was sweet a lot of the time, romantic. But I was anxious. I was so desperate for him to accept me. He was the only person I was seeing after the divorce and so I started clinging to him, and I was totally at his mercy all the time." I picked up a stick and poked at the fire. I continued.

"I never knew which of his moods I was going to get or whether I'd leave our dates feeling lit up or destroyed. I wanted him way too much —I think maybe I still do — and he knew it."

We burned through all our logs. Logan told me about her heartbreak and the ending of her first real love, which had lasted several years and been scrappy and deep, an endearing mess soaked in liquor. When the fire fell low, we scrounged up twigs and branches to burn for warmth.

Finally, the last ember had given up and we retired to sleep in our tents on the cool, hard ground. I slept like a worn-out child, still afloat on the sparkling LSD sea.

Acceptance

Morning came late and I woke to the sun high in the sky. Logan was still fast asleep. Emerging from the tent, I felt like I was waking from a long, vivid dream. Everything still had a shimmery, picturesque hue: the forest green Coleman camp stove, the blue milk crate, my tangerine puffy coat… all of it was washed in iridescence.

I boiled water for the French press; extra strong today. My mother, who I rarely thought of, was on my mind. It felt as though something in me had softened, thawed, cracked open in the deep hours of the night.

I sighed heavily as I oiled the warming cast iron and cracked eggs into a bowl.

Last night's medicine had invited me to move toward the deep pain I'd spent so long avoiding, a sore ache under my ribs that had made its home in me as a young person and intensified after my breakup with Andrew. It felt odd to me that I'd risen with my mom on my mind, rather than all the other pains that had been stirring in me recently.

I stirred the coffee grounds and allowed myself, for the first time, to fully feel all the grief of being raised in our home. Memories flashed across my mind of all the times I'd felt pure shame, guilt, rejection and neglect when what I'd needed was a warm, safe place to land.

And then it hit me. It was so clear. It came on like a flash of lightning.

My grief over Andrew wasn't about Andrew at all. I was reliving the pain from my first relationship in this world — the one with my own mother.

I turned toward the lake and ran to the edge of camp. In the wave of emotion I doubled over, certain that it might actually knock me to my knees. I heard the sound of sobs, a familiar and forgotten voice escaping my lips. I hadn't heard these cries since the day I labored to bring Moses into the world.

I let the tears come. Love had not been guaranteed. I had lived bracing on the edge, holding the tension of never knowing whether my mother would be stable or deeply depressed, supportive and bright or intent on tearing me down because of her own shame. I felt that her love and approval were conditional, that she and I were forever at odds, and this belief had held me in suspense for my entire young life.

My deepest desire as a child was to please her, to be accepted by her. This evolved into a desire to please God and be accepted by Him. I'd seen my friends with their parents and wished for that kind of closeness and trust. When I realized this was impossible, I sought other ways to be acceptable. I became charming and congenial with an unparalleled candor. My deeply magnetic qualities came out to play, at the expense of my multifaceted, imperfect self.

I sat and wept fiercely onto the sandstone shore, my head in my hands.

My deepest fantasy was to be fully seen and accepted, and yet I didn't believe it was truly possible. So, I hadn't allowed myself to be seen. I had always withheld some part of myself from others, for fear that there was something objectionable, forbidden or unworthy in me. I'd never been fully free in the presence of anyone: not my family, not my friends, not my husband or my lovers. No one.

Andrew abruptly ending our relationship that summer had torn open a very old, very deep wound of rejection that I'd buried under those layers of charm and comfortable distance.

LSD and MDMA, these medicines, these "drugs," which have been so vilified in our country, gave me a deep gift by tearing me open. They offered important insights and catalyzed a receptive openness within me necessary to begin the healing of my oldest wounds. They offered a gateway back to the beginning.

Home

The trip home was... rough. Our moods and energy levels were extremely low. Our systems were depleted from the travel, drugs, and emotional processing. I laughed on the Utah highway when Logan blurted out:

"Do you have any good gossip or something? I need a fucking distraction, I feel like shit!!" and I completely resonated.

I ached to hold Moses, and when I thought of Jack or played his favorite John Prine songs on the radio, tears of gratitude welled up in my eyes. I couldn't wait to return to the new life I was forming.

I felt like I had been transported across the universe and back again, through time and space and the uncharted depths of my own soul, in the space of two weeks. The desert had offered a pause, a respite from life's demands, and a space in which to look hard in the mirror and explore my own path toward healing.

I returned to Portland tender and torn open. I was willing to do the work before me, but aching and worn from the constant labor of it. I would fill an entire leather-bound journal with prosaic outpourings before the approach of the new year.

Moses stayed extra close in the days after my return, and I also noticed he became more comfortable spending whole weekends with Keaton. My leaving had been good for all of us.

The community home was a sweet and gentle place to land, and Jack's company and support brought me periods of joyous relief from the intensity of my own self-reflection. We made a habit of taking an overnight date once a month — usually booking an indie hotel room or an AirBnB.

His intentionality and passion toward me was a sharp contrast to what I'd become used to for many years, and I felt a thrill and intimacy within our romance that I'd never experienced. It was steadier than the flash in the pan I'd shared with Andrew, yet it shone with an even brighter fiery chemistry. Still, I was only partially present.

Perhaps I could have embraced all this intimacy more fully if we'd met at a steadier time when I wasn't spread so thin, trying at once to sort myself out and hold myself together.

. . .

Perhaps thanks to a new openness that began in Arizona, I picked up my guitar again. I'd left my musical self behind with Christianity. When I was 25, shortly after my confession to Keaton that I was no longer a Christian, I went public. I'd created a blog unpacking my experiences within the church and my reasons not only for leaving, but for my disbelief.

I tore down the central tenets of Christianity one by one, in a way that was well informed (I had a degree in Biblical Studies, you'll recall) and irreverent. It was a cathartic experience, and in the process of reflecting, I'd grown disgusted with my distorted relationship with music and abandoned it altogether, much to Keaton's chagrin.

So, in this new place and time, I began plucking the strings again and reclaiming the voice in my throat and the melodies on my strings. I devoted myself to bouldering (rock climbing without ropes) and became physically stronger than I'd ever been. I pulled out my art supplies and spent snowy afternoons painting watercolor landscapes. During long nannying days at work, I let the kids play for hours while I sat watching nearby, deeply absorbed in my own inner landscape.

It seemed that embodiment was where my healing wanted to happen. The acid trip in the desert had offered a reminder of somatic experiencing, the reality that moving through personal blocks does not only happen in the brain. It reminded me of my bodywork with Barbara, where she found a traumatic block in my belly, the same place my father had been shot. I resolved to not just understand myself in my mind, but to experience the sensations of finding my way through this messy, stirred up, important moment in life.

Perhaps the process of healing, lifelong as it would be, required a depth of presence that I couldn't intellectually bypass by conceptualizing and analyzing from a comfortable distance. Perhaps I needed to feel it all.

I began seeking out opportunities to get out of my head and into my body. I was in the best shape of my life, in a body I barely recognized, and I felt a duty to invite all of my senses to the table to participate in my healing.

Why Flow Matters

Sometimes, it's wise to take a break from all the talking, processing, and overthinking that we associate with doing "the work." Our bodies need to integrate our healing as much as our minds do. During this time in my life, I turned to singing, rock climbing, cooking and gardening to let those insights and questions settle deeper. These activities connect my frantic mind with something more tangible and grounded. On one level, it makes sense that I'm intensely practical — I need hands that can tether me down to earth like a weight for the helium balloon of my mind. Doing settles my thinking. This physical practicality invites my mind back into a balance with other, more subtle ways of knowing. So do practices that embrace and seek out mystery — when in the presence of unknowable and indescribable phenomena, my mind stays in its rightful place, where I can set out to admire rather than grasp.

I also came to realize that a well-spent day is best sealed by the underestimated delight of preparing a nourishing meal. Chopping vegetables, mixing sauces, and moving swiftly between sizzling cast iron and wooden cutting boards brings me solace. I don't have to think about what my hands are doing. The ingredients come together fluidly, and I know from years of practice, how hot, how long, how chopped, how sweet, how salty and acidic to go. I hover over the pan and my mind goes quiet. Raw ingredients meld into meals and take on a life and story of their own.

Nourishment

The alchemy of this transformation never gets old, inspiring my awe at the magical elements of blade, salt and fire, and my ability to wield these forces that sustain not only my life, but my daily peace.

There's another place that moves me into flow: the garden. There's a profound peace that can be found in the midst of living plants. In the garden, I feel held — I sense that I am a part of the whole, and I'm reminded that the same energy of life that flows between my own cells is buzzing within the seedling and the honeybee. We are together warmed by the sun and washed by the rain.

I have been fortunate to have access to land and space to cultivate these sacred earthen experiences. The pace of nature is patient. Steady. Unapologetically true to its own timeline. Seed by seed, I fill the trays with future food — kale, heirloom tomatoes, summer squash and fiery peppers. I fill them with beauty — zinnias, sunflowers, and nasturtiums. And I fill them with medicine — calendula, chamomile and cannabis. Then, I wait. I feel the provision of the Earth. I feel the extravagant generosity poured out on humanity, in spite of our continued brokenness and greed. It is cleansing. It is humbling.

As the soil warms, there is more to be done. My Boggs and Carhartts hang near the door ready for the next task.

Some days are all toil: ruthlessly pulling up wheelbarrows full of unwanted weeds and vines before they grow unmanageable. Turning steaming mounds of compost (three cheers for everyday magic). I break up soil and prepare beds for Spring planting. And I pause, hour after hour, to stretch my shoulders and wipe the sweat from my brow. I pour out my earnest effort as an offering to the earth that feeds me, a prayer of thanks to the plants that sustain me. As I step back and survey the work of my hands and feel the relief in my bones, I know I have accomplished much more than my busy mind could.

Some days are all hope: planting seedlings by the light of the moon, tucking them into the soft soil as if they're my own sweet small children. I watch, transfixed, as they sprout their true leaves and later, begin to flower. They never rush ahead, never skip a step. Wise in their patience.

Some days are lush with gratitude. I smile toward the sky as I snip sunflowers and pluck the fruits that hang heavy on the vine. My baskets overflow so I drift to and from the kitchen, arms bursting with bounty and abundance, and I dream up ways to save and share it all.

The garden provides a task for my hands, but the wisdom of the plants themselves, the pace with which they move through cycles of life, is what truly moves me. It slows me down. Everything is simpler here in the garden.

Physical labor is work with deep, immediate rewards. There is something in my cells that thirsts for this satisfaction. My very genes seem to carry the imprint of generations of native Mexican migrant workers who labored in the fields, bent beneath the hot sun, fighting to feed their families and live another day. Doing the work of my ancestors feels like redemption. A full circle. A moment in my lineage where this work with the earth is finally done by choice.

I recognize this freedom and agency as the huge privilege that it is. I get to toil with a spirit of joyful participation, rather than enmity. Labor no longer reflects the power of an oppressor, a landowner, a boss who holds control over whether I eat or starve. The barrier between myself and my sustenance has been removed, and as I commune directly with the source of my nourishment, as I watch my son digging up potatoes and plucking raspberries from the vine, I feel at peace and safe in the world.

To this day, growing and preparing food are some of the most grounding, recalibrating ways I can spend my time. The garden and the kitchen are tactile places where I can work out my healing, a long exhale for the soul.

18

Monogamish

Monogam...ish?

My relationship with Jack continued to bloom, although we lived in a state of ongoing tension as we tried to sort out whether we were monogamous or not. At the end of fall term, he moved out of the tipi and into a house with some grad school students to be closer to campus. This newfound distance added a layer of complexity to our relationship.

Neither of us were philosophically aligned with monogamy, and I had just finished reading *Mating in Captivity* by Esther Perel and *Sex at Dawn* by Christopher Ryan and Cacilda Jetha. After my marriage, and with this deeper understanding of human psychology, I didn't believe I could ever be monogamous again.

This time, my desire for non-monogamy was built not out of desperation for a solution (as in my relationship with Cory) or desperation for sexual satisfaction (as in my Tinder Summer). It stemmed from a desire to retain agency over my life and the freedom to love as I felt called, things I didn't believe I could do within monogamy.

In Esther Perel's widely referenced TED talk "The Secret To Desire In A Long Term Relationship," she highlights the dichotomy of two fundamental human needs: on one end is the anchoring need for safety and security. On the other end is the thrill of adventure, newness and risk. These core desires exist on a spectrum. Reconciling these two core needs into a relationship is a paradox to manage, rather than a problem to solve. This is the basis of her book, *Mating in Captivity*, which helped shape the way I understand love and relating.

Perel doesn't believe, and I tend to agree, that there is one solution to this paradox. For some people, opening a relationship can be a healthy way to meet those lasting needs. For many others, simply acknowledging attraction and allowing space for flirtation can relieve the tension. And still for others, doing new things with an existing partner and tricking the fickle mind into seeing them with new eyes again and again can stoke the fire of desire while honoring the parameters of an exclusive commitment.

Because of the unique circumstances of my own life, religion, and marriage (and perhaps in reaction to it), I felt most drawn to and excited by non-monogamy as a way of honoring my own needs for stability and variety. I wasn't interested in locking myself down in a serious commitment; I'd just gone through the painful process of prying myself free from the last ones.

Jack and I had numerous inconclusive conversations on the topic, which always seemed to end with us musing about threesomes, getting hot and bothered, and forgetting all about our discussion in the midst of foreplay and sex.

In general, Jack and I agreed that we would take other connections on a case by case basis. I insisted that any other connections I had would be mainly about sex — I couldn't imagine holding the kind of love I felt with Jack, plus deep love for another person.

Testing the waters, I connected with one woman during that time, a southern dream boat named June, who showed me the world of femme sexuality in a way that puts mainstream porn to shame. But there was a subtle, well-concealed jealous streak in Jack whenever her name came up, and this left me unconvinced that my connecting with other people in any form would ever be conducive to our relationship. It seemed like a pipe dream.

In truth, I was still very hung up on Andrew. I already *was* holding love for multiple people, but I was suppressing it beneath the weighted pressure to move on.

When we first started connecting, Jack expressed his reservations about getting involved with me in such a brokenhearted state. But I assured him that he was not a rebound — this was the real deal. We made so much more sense together than I ever had with Andrew or even Keaton, and I felt this in my heart as much as my reasoning.

What would I have done as Andrew's monogamous partner? Did I really believe I belonged in a community of affluent, self-employed mountain bikers and marathon runners? How long would that have lasted before I felt I had abandoned my textured, multi-dimensional self and become completely miserable, in a haunting parallel to my marriage?

With Jack, I could already see how our life could take shape.

We both loved the Earth and the people in it. He'd been an outdoor guide in Steamboat Springs, Colorado and was studying Leadership for Sustainability Education. I was interested in organic farming and permaculture. We were scrappy, hardworking and easygoing. We even looked right together — his stocky frame and worn-in Carhartts alongside my tattoos and Blundstone boots. We spent a lot of energy thinking about how to leverage our skills and passions to do some real good — individually, and together. I felt understood in this way.

But I was still connected with several men I had dated before, and I wasn't ready to let go. I was nervous about the unavoidable day that I'd have to ask Jack for the green light to revisit my steamy past.

Samuel, Part II

Samuel, the dark and earthy permaculturist from my Tinder Summer, had remained in touch with me, although he had taken a big step back when my marriage collapsed and my whole life was thrown into flux. I was so preoccupied with Andrew at the time that I'd let him go without a fight. By winter we were simply exchanging friendly, appreciative texts but there was clearly still an energy between us.

It was early December when I flippantly mentioned my plans to have tea with my old friend Samuel. Jack inquired further.

"Wait. Is this the same Samuel you used to have insane sex with?" he asked bluntly.

"Yeah… well, hey now. That's not what this is." Okay, it had certainly crossed my mind, but based on Jack's reaction, I knew not to push.

"I thought you two never had a very deep connection and ended things on weird terms?" he asked.

I fought the urge to roll my eyes. His defensiveness was off-putting.

"Well, that is one way to look at it. But, it was a weird time. My marriage was ending. I just want to circle back around now that some time has passed and see what's there. If nothing else, he's a good contact to have in the plant and farming world. We have a lot of mutual friends… according to Facebook." I looked at him. "I haven't seen him in six months. It's no big deal."

• • •

The morning I was supposed to meet Samuel, Jack called me in a huff. He was on his way to guide a cross country skiing trip, but couldn't get my meetup with Samuel off his mind.

"For some reason, he just bothers me more than the other guys you hang out with," he explained. (I had remained friends with three of the Tinder connections I'd had the previous summer.)

"I know most of your guy friends are exes… and I'm not really phased when you spend time with Keaton, Andrew, Max… but I woke up thinking about you seeing Samuel today and it's getting under my skin. I don't know why," he told me.

It was obvious to me why. On our first date, as we hiked through Powell Butte, I had carelessly mentioned to Jack that I'd had a fling with this brilliant, arrogant, hobbit-short landscape designer who was hung like a horse. He was the man who had introduced me to the world of permaculture. I had simultaneously sung his praises, remarked on his massive penis, and left it all in the past. Yet, I rarely spoke so highly of people, and Jack hadn't forgotten it. It was obvious I had a soft spot for him that was built on deep respect and affection. He was a shiny human, as I put it.

Understandably, Jack seemed guarded and jealous with this knowledge. If I had heard him speak so highly of someone from his past, filled with respect and lust for them, I would feel threatened, too. I assured him that there was nothing to worry about. Even as the words came out of my mouth, I wondered if they were true.

On his front porch, Samuel greeted me with a wide grin and a tight hug.

"Hey, Becca," he said in his gentle voice, with a familiar lift at the end as if asking a question.

Something had changed with time; the space between us felt easier and more natural. He was upbeat and warm, even funnier than I'd remembered him. He didn't feel as distant and guarded this time, either. The dust had settled now and we were both in much less complicated moments of life.

We drank Puerh tea at his kitchen table and then wandered through the expansive garden he maintained. Even in the depth of winter it seemed somehow bursting with life. There was no shortage of things to discuss. We touched on regenerative agriculture and community building, food and politics. The tea ran low. Finally we tiptoed into the way our connection had

MONOGAMISH **243**

faded that summer.

"Yeah, you had a lot going on..." he said with a wink. "Maria and I had reservations about getting tied up in the middle." It was understandable. I felt a little embarrassed about the manic season of life in which he'd met me. I wanted to explain how steady and solid I had been for eight years before that — to somehow prove to him that I knew what it meant to be grounded.

He opened up about how, in August, a month after we'd parted ways, his partner of five years abruptly announced she was moving across the country with her children. In a rage, he'd screamed "FUCK YOU!" in her face and shattered his iPhone against the wall. It was strange to imagine him so raw — this man who had always seemed so zen and carefully considered. So he was human after all. Of course, he'd made amends and felt awful about letting the fire out like that. And away she had gone. I was surprised to be hearing so candidly about it now. It felt like a deeper, uncharted emotional territory between us.

Samuel stared at me across the table.

"You're beautiful," he said. I smiled back at him and kicked his leg playfully.

"Actually," he continued, "I think this is the first time we've ever hung out and not fooled around…"

I laughed it off as we locked eyes, in an effort to keep things platonic and not say something inappropriate. I left a while later, feeling positive about his restored presence in my life, albeit different, and curious about how our lives might overlap in the coming months and years. I knew he was significant to me.

I was proud to report to Jack that I'd had a nice time with Samuel and nothing had happened. He was less enthused to hear that I intended to stay in contact with him this time around.

"I think there's something there worth talking about… when we're up for it." Was all I could muster. This made Jack uneasy.

Ice Storm

A few weeks later, I was stuck at home in the middle of an ice storm.

Samuel called to see if I wanted to come over. I had the day free — Jack was guiding a snowshoe trip on the mountain and wouldn't be back until nightfall, and Moses was with his dad. But I wasn't about to drive, so Samuel came and picked me up in his Tacoma. I gave him a tour of my community house and then we left, skidding around on the icy side streets.

"Damn, I love driving on this stuff," he said, grinning.

Back at his house, he fed me homemade pumpkin pie and steaming oolong tea. I remarked that I didn't know he could bake. He shrugged it off modestly. We picked up where we'd left off a few weeks earlier, discussing the usual themes: family, work, plants, food, travel, politics. We laughed as we shared stories of our best and worst psychedelic experiences. I told him, glowingly, about my recent time spent in Utah. How the desert had stolen a piece of my heart and ignited a series of breakthroughs that had nothing to do with camping and hiking.

We shared a few hits of bright sticky cannabis from his glass pipe and reclined on his small couch, legs entangled, sharing our fears and hopes for the community as the country moved into a dark and uncertain time. Much like discussing stormy weather, grappling with politics with like-minded friends is a connecting point. It is a shared experience that we struggle through together. It bonds us to one another. I lowered my guard as we went beyond current events to our individual struggles of holding the vision for justice while growing more aware of such heavy, starkly corrupt times.

"I'm cold. I think I need more tea," I said.

"Or, we could just snuggle," he smiled at me.

That was the moment. It was the first line in the sand where I could have paused and said, "No, thanks." But I didn't want to; I didn't even hesitate. I inched closer.

"Alright, come warm me up then," I said. Jack barely crossed my mind; he barely even existed to me inside Samuel's home. That has been a flaw and a superpower of mine over the years — a disassociation, a compartmentalization that allows for absolute presence with the moment and the person in front of me — flanked by disregard for others to whom I have made commitments of time, loyalty, or exclusivity.

We climbed into his bed and he turned on some music — Sean Hayes, an old favorite. The soft basslines of "Low Light" washed the room in an easy, self-assured atmosphere. It felt familiar and comfortable to be up against him, listening to him breathe. We'd been here several times before.

Samuel was aware of my involvement with Jack, but he also knew that Jack and I had long discussed being non-monogamous. He must have assumed by my consent that everything in my personal life was aligned and in support of us inching closer. I understood where this was headed and made the enthusiastic choice to participate. As I'd done so many times before, I chose to be fully present in the moment, to remove from my mind my entire past and future, with all its important relationships and considerations.

We began to kiss, slowly, purposefully. He stared into my eyes, pressing his strong hands against me and running them over my body. We breathed hard. I slid my shirt off and let him kiss every inch of my skin, undressing me garment by garment as he went. And it all felt delicious and familiar and good to the core. Finally, he reached for a condom out of his drawer.

"Is this okay?" he asked me.

"Yes," I said. I clung to this moment, this man, refusing to think of anything but arriving fully for the hot, sticky energy in the room.

We had sex… really, really good sex.

I felt very little guilt during the act and afterwards. Since my Tinder days, casual sex with people to whom I wasn't committed had become such a common pastime that it barely registered as something I should be hung up about. I no longer had the church-driven cultural guilt surrounding sex that I'd carried as a younger woman. I'd worked hard to reframe my understanding of what nakedness and connection really meant. In fact, once we were dressed again, I felt like nothing out of the ordinary had happened at all.

"How are you?" Samuel asked as he flung the curtains open.

"Good. I'm getting hungry," I answered, stretching languidly and regaining my breath.

"So am I. We could make something? Not sure what I have on hand," he said. I checked my phone.

"Hmm. Let's cook. It's only 5:15, I have time." Jack had said he'd be getting back around 7:00 pm.

We returned to the living room. Samuel lifted a fifteen-pound Cinderella pumpkin from its decorative space on the floor and plunked it down on a cutting board.

"How's curry soup? This pumpkin's kind of a two-person job."

"Sounds perfect," I said.

We turned up the music and set to work chopping, seeding and steaming the enormous pumpkin. It was an undertaking. I sautéed onions and garlic in bacon grease and watched as they melted into their sweet, savory magic.

It took forty minutes before the damn pumpkin was cool enough to handle. I carried the pot outside and nestled it in a snowy corner of the porch to expedite the process. When I came inside, my phone buzzed. It was Jack.

"Hey! I just got back to campus. You hungry for some dinner?" he'd written.

Fuck. I checked the time: 6:30 pm.

"How long 'til we eat, Sam?" I asked. He guessed fifteen minutes.

I was perplexed — Jack was never home on time. In truth, I expected he'd be home after 8:00 pm. In our three months together, I had lost count of the hours I'd spent waiting for him. He was a brilliant, professional, talented man with a tendency to over schedule himself.

Of course, this first time I'd made an assumption, he surprised me and returned home on time, early even. Now I would be hypocritically late, bearing the weight of another man's sweat on my skin. When I remembered his mixed emotions about me spending the afternoon with Samuel, my stomach dropped.

I wrote back.

"Hey! I'm still at Sam's. We're making soup and it's taking longer than I expected. He drove me here though, can I call you when I'm home and heading your way?"

"Okay. So, I should eat then?" he asked dryly.

"Yeah, go ahead and eat. I'll see you tonight," I answered.

Ugh, I was the worst.

We scraped the steaming pumpkin flesh from its skins and blended everything together. Samuel made an amusing spectacle of tasting and seasoning the soup to perfection. Curry paste. Coconut milk. A splash of vinegar. More curry paste. A little more salt?

I was exasperated.

"I'm sure it's perfect! Let's eat, yeah?"

His pureed masterpiece was piping hot and he served me up a giant bowl of it with crusty bread. Even eating seemed to take longer than I would have liked. We discussed skiing and he offered to teach me, which only served to remind me of Jack and made me more eager to leave. I washed dishes while he packed the remaining soup into jars, then he finally drove me home.

He kissed me on the cheek and I went inside.

Hurriedly, I showered, changed and drove to Jack's. Most of the ice on the roads had melted. He let me inside without a greeting, and it only took moments before we cut to the chase. He was upset that I had skipped out on our dinner plans and extended my visit with Samuel.

I rested my hand on his leg.

"I'm sorry, Jack. That was my fault. I shouldn't have assumed you'd be late."

"Well, I understand *that* part… I know historically I haven't been on time," he admitted.

I squeezed his leg.

"And I know part of it is my own jealousy about you hanging out with Sam. Which I'm not putting on you… I'm working through those feelings. I support you spending time with your friends. I trust you."

A pang in my gut. There was no way to fend off the guilt now. He was hurt and upset that I'd prioritized spending time with Samuel. Yet, he had a right to be immeasurably more hurt and upset with me for breaking our agreements and having sex with him. He just didn't know it. *Done is done. This doesn't have to change anything*, I told myself. I put it out of my mind.

We ended up having a lovely night together. It was a relief to be with him. Two glasses of wine later, he began sharing dreams with me. He poetically laid out his vision for our future — a home on acreage and a family. We mused about how the years might look between now and then, and it made my heart swell. I shared in his vision, more than he realized, and I was again convinced that he was the person for me. At the time, it didn't seem crazy to be talking about these things three months into dating, let alone hours after sharing intimacy with someone else.

We enjoyed some mellow cannabis and watched an episode of *Planet Earth 2* together. Then we got ready for bed, smiling at each other in the mirror as I splashed my face with water and he brushed his teeth. This was my real life, my real partner. Where I wanted to be.

"Come here," he said urgently as he shut the bedroom door. He turned me around by the waist and pushed me against the wall. *Here we go*, I thought to myself.

He kissed me with force and bit my ears and neck and grabbed me hard by the hips. I wanted him to. I knew why he was being rough, and I surrendered into it, but with an edge of resistance to fuel the fire.

He was working out his emotions from our conflict, and sex was our preferred outlet. The noise of our interactions, the pushing, pulling, rolling, slapping, and thrusting up against walls and furniture must have carried through the house. It went on for at least an hour.

We collapsed into each other, sore, exhausted, and a little worse for wear. As we snuggled under the sheets I remarked on his extra dose of intensity.

"Well, that was new. I know it had something to do with earlier…" I said.

He looked caught.

"What? Well... okay. Yeah," he smirked. "You know it's hard for me to be rough with you. I just love and respect you so much. I haven't been able to get to that really primal state and just let everything go. Not gonna lie, it helped to be a little frustrated tonight."

You don't know the half of it, I thought to myself, but didn't say it aloud. I envisioned how out of control the make-up sex would be if I ever told him the truth of what I had done that afternoon. I'd be done for.

"Well, glad we're making progress then. That was pretty wild…" I said, and reached to turn off the light.

We drifted to sleep. It was the deepest night of sleep I'd had in a while. Being thoroughly banged twice in a day will do that to you.

19

Secrets

Secrets are For Keeping

The week after I stripped down with Samuel, I sat with my friend Lori in the climbing gym, sporting chalked up hands and throbbing muscles. In between routes, I mentioned to Lori what had happened. She was a close confidant; we'd met working together at Farmer Mike's vegetable farm, and she'd been present for the entire saga of my open marriage, Tinder Summer, divorce, Andrew, Jack, Samuel… all of it. I'd been out hiking with her the day Andrew broke up with me. She was understanding and nonjudgmental toward the swirly and unpredictable mess of my romantic life.

"You want my honest opinion?" she asked. I nodded. "This is Becca just… being Becca," she stated simply, as if my impulsive neurosis was the most natural thing in the world. I raised my eyebrows.

"Well, I doubt others will see it that way," I replied.

"Do NOT tell Jack," she continued. "What good is that going to do? If anything, it's going to ruin your relationship with him. Is that what you want? If I were you, I'd just let it go." She stood up to climb a route.

"But I'm keeping a secret. What if he finds out?" I protested. She turned to me.

"You're Becca. You fuck people. It's a part of being with you. You've been pretty clear about that, right? If he can't make space for that, what did he honestly expect to happen? Unless it's going to keep you up at night, it's better to just leave it in the past."

I pondered that for weeks. She did have a point — I'd been making a concerted effort to be clear about my desire for non-monogamy.

Yet, I hadn't sorted out how to reconcile that with my desire for a life with Jack, and when it came down to it, he seemed intent on preserving our exclusivity. I had been afraid that, if I radically asked for what I truly wanted — freedom to safely have sex with any friend, lover, or acquaintance when the moment was right — he would judge me, say no, or worse, end our relationship. This fear, and my subsequent inaction, had led me straight into Samuel's arms and out of my agreements with Jack.

I felt I had no choice but to leave my secret in the past. I felt, as I had in my marriage, that I had to be monogamous in order to have the kind of life and love that I wanted. I also believed that, based on recent events, I was terrible at monogamy.

Going Back

It was mid-December. A few weeks earlier, I'd sent Andrew a handwritten letter. I wrote it on actual paper and mailed it with a stamp and everything. After my experience with LSD in the desert, I'd had time to process my unraveling. While I recognized that Andrew wasn't responsible for all my deep heartache, I did feel I'd deserved more consideration than he'd offered me while we were together.

In the letter, I shared all the things I felt I had left unnamed: how I had been hurt and confused, and how I felt I had deserved more clarity and respect. I didn't feel it was fair that he'd strung me along, knowing full well how swept up I was in our connection. I didn't expect to hear anything back, but I felt hugely relieved to have it off my chest. I walked forward a little lighter.

A week later, he sent me a simple text.

"Hey Becca. Thank you so much for your letter. I've been doing a lot of thinking lately. I can see that I have a long way to go in becoming a more caring and considerate lover. I wish you well. Have a lovely Christmas."

Christmas with Jack

A couple weeks later, Jack and I took a Christmas trip to Bend, Oregon. Moses stayed home with Keaton and they celebrated a traditional family holiday in my absence. It was the first time I'd driven Highway 26 East since July. As Jack and I crossed over Mt. Hood, I relived in vivid detail my drive home from Sunriver with Keaton. So much had happened in such a short time frame. Five months earlier I was married to my son's father, spending family holidays on out of town trips with my in-laws. This highway was the place that I first sensed that a whole era of my life was ending — one which I had believed was fixed and permanent.

I exhaled. I looked out across the hills at the evergreens and the snow tipped peaks. Then I looked over at Jack, with his beard and beanie, his puffy North Face jacket, his jovial whistle, the crate of maps in the back seat of his truck. His hand rested effortlessly on my knee. This man was capable, open hearted, and deeply in love with me. A new chapter.

Our AirBnB was a quaint little cabin outside of Bend. It had a massive bed, a cozy kitchen, big windows overlooking the white hillside and a wood stove. We always insisted on having a wood stove on these getaways. The first thing Jack did was build a fire. The next thing he did was take off half my clothes and nibble on my neck.

I don't remember much from that weekend, besides the sexual breakthroughs that came one after another. Ironically, our trust in each other was deepening dramatically. Every time I took a sexual risk, tested a limit — asking for something I wanted or initiating a new way of connecting, he was there for it. We were tuned into each other, receptive and willing in a way that I had never experienced. For us, there was no such thing as too much sex. One day we didn't leave the cabin at all. We took naps in between lovemaking and ate our meals naked in bed. When we thought we were worn out, we laid by the fire to read our books. Soon our books were tossed aside and our bodies entangled once again.

The next afternoon Samuel sent me a text. Jack saw my phone light up.

"Babe you have a text. It's from Samuel," he said. I carried my phone across the room to look at it.

"Whoa, secretive much?" he said.

I laughed.

"Well you never know with people… I just don't want you to see anything you don't want to see," I half joked.

It was a simple Christmas greeting with some emojis, but I could feel Jack's eyes on me as I responded.

"Hey now. Are folks sending you dick pics?" he inquired.

"What? No. Nobody's sending dick pics. That's not what it was," I placated him, regretting turning my phone on.

On Christmas, we snowshoed Tumalo Mountain together. We were exuberant in the fluffy snow (though he lamented the fact that we weren't on skis). I felt deeply in love. I so appreciated the way Jack could bring me into his world — he'd been a ski instructor for many years — without mansplaining or giving off an air of condescension or superiority. I was thankful that I had someone with whom to share Christmas, who truly felt like my person, my family. It was the first holiday I'd spent away from Moses, and Jack was a salve for the pain of that change. I felt one step closer to a more aligned life, inching nearer to a life in which I didn't have to pretend.

After our Christmas getaway, we celebrated the New Year together, too, cozy around the fireplace at my house with friends and talk of resolutions.

Women's March

January, with its looming Inauguration Day, brought the first national Women's March. The day of the march was bone-cold and waterlogged in Portland. We met with friends beforehand to make signs and drink hot toddies. I felt more love for Jack than I'd ever felt for a man in my life, like I'd found my match. We cared about the same big, heavy things. To us, justice mattered, the experiences of people of color, women, and queer folks mattered. I didn't have to temper my passion or my anger; I felt supported in it. Jack locked eyes with me amidst all the noise and chanting and activity, and all I saw was love. Pure, huge, unadulterated love.

It seemed that the final piece of our puzzle had fallen into place — seeing each other in this last context, a time of fear and anger and uncertainty, made me believe that we could weather just about anything with grace and resilience. I knew that if the world had a frightening future, I wanted to be by Jack's side (and not just because he had a truck-sized camo tarp and knew how to bow-hunt).

We were ready to work. Or move to Canada. Yes, we researched it. His unshakable love was a force powerful enough to temper the palpable fear that was flooding in from all sides in light of the election. He made me believe that, not only was a better world possible for us, Moses, our society and beyond, but we were capable of helping cultivate it. We were a team.

• • •

That evening, I made grass-fed steaks for dinner. Jack made a salad and herb roasted potatoes. Moses played with Play-Doh while we cooked. Jack hovered over the stove, slapping my ass several times and swooning at the

SECRETS **253**

perfect sear on the steaks and sampling the rosemary basting butter as it sizzled in the pan.

While I supervised the cast iron, I overheard Jack's conversation with our housemate Che. They were discussing Che's love troubles, and considering what role honesty plays in healthy, lasting relationships.

"I know for me," I heard Jack say, "I need to be able to trust the person I'm with. I feel like being lied to is a huge deal-breaker in a relationship."

I had my back turned to them and listened nonchalantly as they spoke, melting butter over the steaks. I might have looked relaxed, but I felt like a spotlight was on me. *You have to tell him, Becca. Soon.* I thought. But I forced the idea out of my mind as quickly as it came.

After dinner, I tucked Moses into bed and Jack and I shared spoonfuls of cashew milk ice cream straight out of the pint. He looked blissful, silently smiling at me as we leaned facing one another on the wooden kitchen island. He took on his familiar speechless grin, then walked over and took me in his arms.

"Thanks so much for today," he said. "It meant a lot to me to be there with you." After a moment I heard him sniffling. He took my face in his hands.

"I love you so much. Just… yeah," he trailed off.

I deflected. "Is this about the steak?" I asked with a grin.

He rolled his eyes at me and swatted my butt.

"No. This isn't about the steak. Geez Becca, gotta ruin the moment…"

"I'm sorry!" I laughed. "I couldn't help myself."

"Okay. Maybe it's a *little* bit about the steak. But it's also about the other, bigger things. I'm too tired to talk about it right now. Let's talk tomorrow. I just… I love you."

I got choked up, too. We stood, quiet in the kitchen for a long while, wiping our eyes. It was the most certain I'd ever felt of my desire to share my life with someone. I wanted to throw myself into him, to ride the wave of knowing and being known in a new way.

My love for Jack was grounded in friendship, yet gripped with passion. I'd seen him in many elements. I knew him up close and from afar. I knew his quirks and his dreams, the ways we were compatible and the ways we clashed. It didn't bring up giddiness or fear to think of choosing him. To envision him by my side as the years passed and the world changed around us felt like the vision of a clear and true future.

But I had a secret. It was decided then and there — I would tell Jack the truth about Samuel.

The Truth

Four weeks had passed between that evening with Samuel and the night of the Women's March. I'd exchanged a few texts with him, but more or less moved on from the connection, not wanting to play with fire any more than I already had.

During that time, as in previous months, Jack and I had several more half-joking conversations about opening our relationship, usually on the heels of a discussion about our conflicting schedules and limited time for each other. He was in grad school; I worked full time and had Moses during the week. The inconclusive conversation was beginning to wear on me, like the notion was being dangled just out of reach. A carrot on a stick. A part of me subconsciously hoped that my guilt about Samuel would be absolved when Jack and I finally opened our relationship.

We wondered aloud how long we could both get our needs met within monogamy, and we tried to identify exactly what we needed and wanted from one another to begin with. When he asked who I'd get together with on the side, I skirted the issue. We'd get into the weeds of emotionally complex territory; Jack hated the thought of me having sex with another man, and I hated the thought of him falling in love with someone else. Ultimately, we decided, more than once, that our relationship was too young to complicate with non-monogamy.

One evening, I told him that I wished I felt more monogamous at my core, lamenting my tendency to chase variety and novelty. The search for newness and the desire to rebel had been powerful forces throughout my life — and though before the ice storm I hadn't cheated since high school, I'd pushed boundaries over and over with Keaton toward the end of our marriage.

"Just so you know, that's my one big deal-breaker," Jack said simply. "If you were to go behind my back and be with someone else without communicating about it first, just… please, don't do that to me." My face must have gone pale. I heard him loud and clear: if I wanted a future with him, which I unequivocally did, I would have to bury my secret at all costs. He could never know that I'd had sex with Samuel.

I had spent those four weeks holding my secret, cycling through all the possibilities in my mind. Forget about it. Tell him. Wait until some time has passed. Don't wait any longer. Acknowledge how huge this is. Don't make it a bigger problem than it has to be. I was unable to just erase it from my mind. It was maddening.

The night of the Women's March, after dinner had been enjoyed and our bodies had collided to our ultimate satisfaction, we gave in and let rest take over.

Well, he did. I lay awake, watching his chest rise and fall while he slept. He was a beautiful man — his strong brow, nose and beard tempered by long lashes and blue eyes. His lean, muscular body had been sculpted by years of intense activity. Logan had once remarked that Jack was like the warriors from mythology who were summoned to palaces to sleep with queens and goddesses. I smiled at the thought.

But his beauty ran deeper — he was pure-hearted, unwaveringly good to the core in a way that didn't bore me, but made me feel secure. There was simply no hint of callousness or greed in him. I saw love and incredible patience. Even at his worst, in his most exhausted, raw form, he was driven by good intentions. I'd never known a man like him, who cared so deeply and so joyfully appreciated the fullness of abundant life.

Jack had been so sincerely good to me since the day we met, always treating me as an equal, appreciating my talents and supporting me in my pursuits. He truly adored me and believed I would accomplish anything I set out to do. He was generous with his affection. Sincere with his words. Moving through life with the knowledge that he was my partner had drawn out the best in me, and I knew those feelings were reciprocal.

I felt guilty that his love wasn't enough for me — it couldn't satisfy my appetite for variety and diversity. No single person could. I noticed that this depth of love was able to coexist within me alongside attraction to others: past partners, new flames, even dear friends. One attraction did not negate the other. I watched him stir in his sleep with the knowledge that tomorrow, I would have to break us apart at the foundation and ask him to help me rebuild.

I had no idea how it would play out. I was terrified. There were no words to soften, mitigate, or diminish the fact that I had unapologetically had sex with Samuel. I wondered: *If I could go back — would I do it again?*

And I thought that truthfully, I might. The reality startled me. My personal freedom was of comparable importance to me as my relationship with my beloved partner. I wondered if I would ever be able to reconcile the two.

Get some sleep, I told myself. *Tomorrow's coming.*

I curled myself against his sleeping form and he unconsciously pulled me closer. I wished to preserve this moment in my memory, imprint it on his restful heart: my sincere desire to love him fully, to reconcile the hidden parts of myself. It was, in fact, this desire that made me willing to bring my hardest truths to light.

Confession

This was the first high-stakes confession I would ever make. Until now, the word "confession" had simply meant an earnest prayer seasoned with a few tears. A promise to change my ways.

Confession was a secret between myself and an invisible God whose love and approval of me was unshakable. There was no accountability or restitution; there was only absolution.

But this time, I would have to truly own the consequences of my actions. With Jack there was no Savior to rescue me and no slate to simply wipe clean. All I could do was own up to my actions and hope that Jack would allow me to remain in his life long enough to repair the damage. Jack held the power, but no responsibility, to forgive me. For a moment I missed quick-fix Christianity with its simple solutions. I drifted off to sleep with images of church altars and tunes of old hymns swirling around in my mind.

We parted ways early the next morning as Jack left town to guide another cross-country ski trip. Keaton picked up Moses for their weekend, and I spent the day resting. I'd been sick with a chest cold for three long months. It must have been the eighth time that I felt a tickle in my throat, just as I was on the upswing of recovering from an earlier wave of sickness. Was the virus mutating?

The constant motion of my life was wearing on me. I'd been fighting to keep these illnesses at bay with an avalanche of natural remedies — Echinacea, garlic, Fire Cider, vitamins, Emergen-C, Neti-Pots, soaks and steams and essential oils. All the while continuing my intensely active, low-rest, low-recovery lifestyle. I practiced positive thinking and popped supplements as I blindly complained of muscle soreness from my bouldering and hiking habits. But now, feeling my swollen tonsils yet again, I finally understood that self-care was not optional.

This forceful approach had only made me sicker and on the brink of burnout. So, my new strategy would be rest and space. It had to be. I would stop all my healing remedies and all my compromising activities. I would take a difficult but much-needed break from climbing, socializing, Internet use, and late nights. I would rest, *actually* rest, and let this thing take over, whatever it was, and empower my body to fight it off. I would regain and protect my health, for real this time.

I wasn't sure how Jack fit into all this, but I knew I would be telling him. Tonight. Sick or not. I forced myself to sleep the afternoon away in my dark bedroom instead of obsessing over the situation. I woke to a text from him.

"Heading back now! Want to go to Everett House tonight?" he wrote. I stared at my phone. It sounded delightful, but it also felt like a cruel sign. Everett House was the nude spa where Samuel had taken me on our first date. Another reminder of my mandate for the evening.

Instead, we had a cozy and restful night at home. We shared leftover steak and salad, munched on a bar of artisan chocolate and drank local wine. We stood hugging in the kitchen and I asked him to finish telling me what he'd wanted to say the night before.

"Well… no. It's going to sound weird. I don't want to say," he looked bashful.

"Tell me!" I persisted.

"Okay, fine, but you're making it a bigger deal than it needs to be," he replied.

"Just. Tell. Me." I smiled, squeezing him harder.

"Okay. So we were standing there in the kitchen last night, and I was just looking at you… and I brushed your hair out of your face. Remember? And right then, I had this crazy flash forward to doing that exact thing on our wedding day. Brushing the hair out of your face in the middle of some beautiful field." He shrugged. "…and that's it."

It was sweeter and more touching than anything else he could have said. I felt like the envy of women everywhere. What lottery did I win to have the privilege of loving this person?

We dipped into my homegrown high-CBD weed, which made us feel warm but clear-headed, while we challenged each other to a round of Settlers of Catan. I was thankful for the opportunity to relax together for a while, but the evening passed quickly and before we realized it, it was late.

We had hot and explorative sex, as we often did. In fact, it was one of the best nights we'd had together in that regard. Later we settled into each other, relieved, and Jack reached to turn off the light switch.

"Damn, I'm tired," he said, adjusting the covers. "What a long day."

The wine had given me the needed courage. I felt sober enough to bring it up.

"Hey Babe, there's something I want to talk with you about, but I wonder if it might be better to wait until tomorrow," I whispered.

"Oh yeah? Is this a good or a bad thing?" He asked.

I paused.

"I can't really say."

"Well, now I'm too curious to fall asleep," he said. He flipped the lamp back on. "What's up? Your heart's pounding."

"I know," I said. I held his hand to my heart, hoping that the pressure would ease it back to a steady pace.

This was it. I knew that once I spit out the words there would be no going back. I'd never be able to reclaim his unfractured love. There would be only forward motion.

"Jack, I fucked up," I said. "I slept with someone. A month ago."

A pause. He turned away. I stared at his profile as he looked up at the ceiling.

"Becca…." His voice sounded more disappointed and ashamed than angry. He clenched his jaw. "Who was it?"

"…Samuel." I answered.

He nodded, unsurprised, then took a deep breath, blowing it out through his lips. I started rambling.

"And it's not going to happen again… but as time went on, and the more you and I talked, I realized I couldn't just leave it in the past. You said your two deal-breakers are cheating and lying. I knew I had to be honest if I wanted even a chance at fixing this," I said desperately.

Silence.

"Well… thank you for telling me. Really." He looked over at me briefly. "Why now?"

I was amazed that he was responding so calmly. I was amazed we were in a civil conversation, and that he hadn't up and left the room.

"Last night. Something about yesterday, marching with you, made me sure that I want to be together. It was like another piece fell into place. And I knew we couldn't move forward, talking seriously about our future like we were, without addressing this first."

"And yet, this happened a month ago? Why did you wait a whole month to tell me?" he asked. It was clear his frustration was growing. *Lori!* I wanted to say.

"I was scared. Once I realized how serious this was. That it wasn't a gray area to you. And I just didn't know if you would want to know... or how to tell you."

"Of course I want to know," Jack said. "But what I really don't get is, why did you go behind my back? We talked about this so many times, Becca. You could've just asked."

I wanted to protest. I didn't at all believe that was true; after he had expressed feeling anxious about my connection with Samuel, what were the chances he'd simply give me the go-ahead if I asked for a green light to be sexual with him? Still, that was beside the point.

"You could've gone about it the right way. Sure, I would've been jealous, but I probably would have given you the okay. And instead, you decided to make your own rules. Did you even use protection?" he asked.

"Yes," I told him, honestly.

"Okay. Well, let's assume *that's* true. I want to believe you... but the problem now is that it feels like anything out of your mouth could be a lie."

"Jack," I pleaded, wide-eyed.

"I know it's not. But you understand why it feels that way, right? This adds a whole layer on top of the last month we just had. Wait, was this before Christmas?" he asked.

"It was during the ice storm. That day I was late for dinner," I confessed.

"Are you serious? It was that night? Fuck, Becca!" He sat up and threw his legs over the side of the bed, turning his back to me. "I'm really pissed right now." He ran his hands over his head.

"I know. I'm sorry." I sat motionless, understanding that there was nothing else I could or should say.

"So, we went to Bend and had this amazing Christmas together... I spent New Year's Eve with you... I've given you so much of my time and my heart this past month, and you had just fucked another dude and weren't even going to tell me." He sighed heavily.

I could hardly muster a nod.

"But what scares me the most, is that you hid it *so well*. I had no idea that anything was out of the ordinary. You could be lying to me or hiding things right now and I'd have no way of picking up on that. This throws everything into question."

"Please don't think like that," I pleaded.

"Well it's how I feel right now. You can't tell me how to feel after dropping a bomb like this."

I paused. He was right. It brought back memories of arguments I'd had with Keaton. I wanted to be different than I'd been back then.

"You're right. I'm sorry. I can't tell you how to feel. I need you to know that this was my only lie. And that's why I'm telling you, because I need to get back to complete honesty. I don't want to hide things." Against my will, I started to cry. "What's been so good about this relationship is how safe we are with each other — we've let our guards down and let each other in. I haven't had that before. And I need it to be real again. I want to be someone you can trust."

He hugged me.

"Fuck, Becca. This is… a lot," he told me.

"I know," I agreed. "Maybe I should have waited until morning to tell you."

"No. I'm glad you told me," he said. "There never would have been a good time. But I appreciate you being honest."

I nodded.

"We should try to sleep," he said, turning off the lamp yet again.

We lay there in complete, wakeful silence for a long time. He rolled toward me and slung his arm over my hips.

"What are you thinking?" I whispered.

"Just how I thought you were perfect," he replied.

"Well, that's sort of an unfair expectation to put on someone," I retorted. The word perfect had struck a nerve in me.

"No, not that kind of perfect. All these months, I just kept asking myself if this was too good to be true. I finally let my guard down and believed that you really were *that* wonderful. When you choose someone, when you get to know and love them, you see their good sides and their flaws, and that shapes your idea of perfection. I knew everything about you… well I thought I did, and I loved you so much. You were perfect for me." He removed his arm from my hips.

"And now there's this huge piece of you that I never knew was there, never signed up for. I really didn't think you were capable of hurting me like this. I don't know how to reconcile something so painful into my sense of who you are. And I have to decide if you're still the right person for me."

At that, we both fell apart. Everything ached. We lay beneath the covers, wrapped up in each other, and wished for relief. He cried at the betrayal. I cried for what was lost and the work ahead, should he choose to take it on. I couldn't bear to think of the alternative.

"I'm so sorry, Jack. I wish I had some way to show you."

"I know," he said.

It was 3:00 am by the time we drifted off into a fitful, restless sleep. Jack had dreams of us fighting. I woke several times, heart pounding, and had trouble relaxing again.

Morning came too soon. Once the sun had risen, I couldn't sleep any more, though I felt totally exhausted. I lay with him in silence, his head on my chest as he drifted in and out of sleep. There was no anger or passion or connection between us — just a hollowed out, numb space.

"I can't sleep anymore," I whispered as I climbed out of bed and gathered my clothes. "I'm going to take a walk, I'll be back in a while." As I kissed his shoulder, he opened one eye.

"'Kay. Lock the door behind you."

It was a damp, gray Portland morning. I called Logan as I walked. No answer. I called Tess. Pick up. Pick up. Her sleepy voice was a refuge for me. Without invitation, I told her everything.

"…And now it feels like everything is broken. I'm so helpless, I hate it. I don't know how to fix this. I don't think I can."

"Well I'm proud of you for telling him the truth, Becca. You did the right thing. I know it's crazy now. That's so hard. But you guys are strong, you'll find a way through this. Remember to take deep breaths."

I exhaled.

"Right. Breaths. But, what else can I do? What should I do?"

"He's the one with the work ahead of him. He has to make the choice to forgive you. Try to forgive yourself. And do what you need to, to make sure this doesn't happen again," she urged me.

"Damn... Okay. Thanks, Tess. I'll keep you posted," I said.

"Please do," she replied. We hung up.

I wandered into a coffee shop and ordered an Americano. I sat by the window, willing my heart to stop pounding, and pulled out my journals. Jack had asked whether I'd written about Samuel at all. He knew I processed everything on paper. Even if he didn't feel he could trust what I said, he knew my written words would be honest. I told him he was welcome to read through them.

I dug through the pages. The unfortunate truth was that I'd barely written about Samuel. I'd made a passing reference to him only once, shortly after Jack and I returned home from our Christmas trip.

> Had a perfect weekend with Jack. I'm feeling so at home with him... our roots are going down deep. Even after what happened last week, I'm confident in what he and I have and I'm really believing in our future. He's my person. I don't think I want to pursue being open right now. I've realized it might only be a temporary solution. Maybe it would feel more natural to me... but why? I'm not sure yet.

20

Forward, Backward

Moving Forward

After my confession, we took some space for a couple weeks. I was held in suspension and Jack knew it, and by his own admission, he chose to draw it out. January and February were a string of long talks and tense exchanges. Ultimately, Jack agreed to work things out.

In some ways, the breach of trust seemed to make us stronger, deepening our understanding of each other. He saw the event as a warning of what I was capable of when I felt constrained, yet to me, it felt too soon and too raw to ask for what had become clear to me: I wanted to be in a committed, open relationship. I was acutely aware that we had barely made it through the upheaval, and I wouldn't have other chances to fuck up like that again.

Around that time, I asked Andrew to tune up a new bike for me. It had been a few months since we'd seen each other, and I was curious about how it might feel. When I arrived at his house that icy morning, he greeted me out front in his slippers with a mug of coffee in hand. He looked smaller and meeker than I had remembered. In his garage, I perched on his work bench and we caught up on life while he tinkered effortlessly on my bike.

He shared that his partner Em had been shopping for houses. Meanwhile, he was dealing with commitment aversion. I nodded in mutual understanding, as I'd been grappling with my own questions about freedom and commitment. He showed me a nice road bike he was planning to sell and wondered aloud if I'd want to buy it for a deal. I politely declined, but only after deliberating about what he could really be trying to say by offering it to me.

I left that day on friendly terms with a shined up bicycle and without a line-crossing kiss. Perhaps we were finally learning how to be friends. He texted me while I was driving away.

"Good to see you, Becca," he wrote. "I was really tempted to ask you to stay for tea… but thought better of it."

Despite all of my strongest resolve, and even in light of the recent upheaval with Jack, it's possible that I would have stayed. Messy, heated things would have ensued. Andrew texted me a few days later.

"Hey, B. Emily wasn't happy hearing that I had you at the house. She asked me not to do that again. Sorry. Hope you understand."

Fuck. Yes, I did understand. Was I gaining an unwanted reputation? Was the notion of me as a sexually wild, uncontrollable free agent becoming more than just my own self-critical projection?

That Valentine's Day, Jack and I had mostly settled back into our rhythm. He bought us tickets to a Shibari (Japanese rope bondage) class put on by SheBop, the local femme-positive sex toy and education shop. It was fascinating to see the numerous pairs in the class — think you know what the kink scene is like? Wrong. It's far more multi-dimensional than leather chokers and pigtails. There were young and old, straight and queer folks, and bodies of all shapes and sizes.

We shared a bright, fun, and sexy evening together. What a transformation in the space of a couple years. How was this my life now? Kid-free weekends and date nights learning to tie up my partner? Shopping for sex toys? We went home with a couple of new purchases to try out. Jack already owned several Shibari books demonstrating beautifully elaborate knots to practice at home.

We had an insane amount of sex that spring; it put my Tinder Summer to shame. Every month or so, either Jack or myself would float the idea of a threesome, half-joking, and mention an attractive friend who may be into something like that. We actually never pursued it. We did, however, film a great deal of homemade sex tapes that expanded my sense of my own sexuality even further.

But while our bedroom shenanigans are a key part of *this* story, most of what I remember from that season was the other 80% of my life: working in the garden with my housemates and Moses, bouldering with Jack at the Circuit, and making music with Tess. I began finding my deeper identity as a mother, one who is honest with Moses, who admits when I need help and make a mistake, one who plays and asks questions and really listens. These abilities permeated every other relationship in my life, too.

Parenthood is full of sacrifice. I had two housemates who had children, but no other friends who did, let alone single moms. Naturally, I missed out on many gatherings and events, and when I did choose to socialize with people during the week, my focus was divided, with one ear on Moses and getting him what he needed. This was sometimes a challenge in my connection with Jack; the way I show up when I'm parenting is starkly different from my weekend self.

Part of growing up is learning how to set oneself aside, how to dig a deeper well when there's nothing left to give. Parenting has been a crash course in this. It is a radical shift in priorities that constantly demands the best of me, decentralizing me from the throne of my own life and requiring that I let the small things go. Motherhood calls me to be radically present, lest I miss a single moment of the magic and pure joy waiting to transform me at the hands of my weird, twinkly-eyed wonderchild.

Bamboo Sushi

Before long, summer meandered our way. A year earlier, I had been a wife with a house and a toddler and several lovers. Now, I was a partner who lived on an urban farm, perpetually trying to keep up with my busy three-year-old.

In June, out of the blue, Andrew called me and asked if I would have dinner with him. I was surprised. The last we'd spoken, it was clear that for Emily, us seeing each other was a hard no. But I was curious, so I agreed.

Enough time had passed that the dull ache of his rejection had begun to wear off. I felt like I was in a steady enough place to see him. Yet of all my loves, he had been the only one to break my heart, the proverbial "one who got away." He was the one who made my palms sweat, whose opinion of me mattered, almost at all costs, not because it was rational, or because he treated me better or was more attractive than Keaton, Cory, Jack or Samuel, but because he had rejected me, and I still wanted his approval.

For me, there was a snag, a stuck spot, a skip on a record.

But more than that, he held a particular kind of power over me. From the beginning, I had associated him with the way out, the bigger, cooler, braver, freer life that I wanted after my marriage. He represented a more worldly world, one that wanted me in it, and I had made him the gatekeeper to say that I belonged. I felt anxious and uncertain every time we spoke, tempering my words and measuring my actions.

And yet, when he was sincere with me, when he pulled me in close and held me tenderly and sung my praises, it stroked my ego in a way that no one else did. He was the cool kid who had turned me down, and now, a year later, he was asking me to dinner.

At the time, I lacked awareness of these dynamics; all I could feel was the magnetic pull, the powerful impulse to go toward him, and it blinded me from all else. I wanted to believe this powerful draw represented something meaningful and worthwhile between us, and my 26-year-old self lacked the maturity to see it for what it was: an unhealthy infatuation with a perfectly ordinary man.

He was bright and giddy when I arrived, squeezing me long and hard and slinging his arm around my shoulder as we walked toward Alberta Street. His texts had been peppered with smiley faces and enthusiasm. We causally caught up as we wandered to Bamboo Sushi, just a few blocks from Radio Room where he had broken up with me the previous summer. I tried not to relive it.

We sat outside on the patio beneath twinkly lights, nibbling on edamame and sipping sake.

He gazed at me. I smirked back.

"I'm sorry, Andrew. It's just… this is really bizarre," I confessed. "Sitting in this restaurant with you. It feels like we've gone back in time."

"I know. It's crazy. But we've both had a whole year to grow. How do you feel being here with me?" he asked.

"I don't really know," I said. "To be honest, it's kind of unsettling. I mean… you broke my heart last year. Like, hard. I know you know that. We don't have to dig it all up now…"

"I broke up with Emily," he interrupted.

I set down my sake and looked at him, searching his face for clues to what might be coming next.

"…What?" I choked out. It was all I could muster.

"Becca, I love you. I did then, and I still do." He took hold of my hands. *Was I in a sappy rom-com?*

I stared at him in shock. He had never once said he loved me when we were together; not once.

"I made a big mistake in ending it with you," he continued. "I wish I hadn't

FORWARD, BACKWARD **267**

done that; I regret it all the time. Do you think there's still something here?" he implored.

I was truly stunned. I didn't say much; what could I say? This was what I had wanted most a year ago. The dream come true. I muttered something about Jack and my life now, how I felt happy and clear. But underneath, I was undone, reeling from his confession. We finished our food, sitting a little closer as I attempted to digest the words that had just spilled from his mouth.

Andrew bought our food and we walked back to his house, hand in hand. Beside me he felt smaller than I had remembered, having become used to Jack's stocky frame and assertive demeanor. I looked at passersby smiling at us and nodding hello, as though we were just another couple out for a walk in the neighborhood.

I didn't allow myself the time to check in, to explore how this change of heart actually made me feel. I was swept up in his narrative, thinking perhaps he felt clearer than I did, or knew something I didn't. Perhaps I knew that if I slowed down, I would have found a "no" inside me, and my scorned ego was intent on overriding it.

I had to look back into my journals to remember what happened next. "Oh. Shit." I said, when I came upon the entry from the next morning. In shame and fear of the consequences, I had pushed the memory deep into forgotten history, and never told anyone about the rest of that night. That is, until sharing it with the contributors of this very book.

Once we arrived back at his house, Andrew took my hand and led me straight upstairs. All bets were off. I had new information: Andrew loved me! He had always loved me. This knowledge possessed me, tipping the weights of all my priorities into his favor. I felt a deep impulse to relive our connection, piece by piece, inch by inch, and pit it against the new life I had formed with Jack. Was our relationship as fiery and magical as I remembered? Who was I in the midst of these two men? Where did I fit? I felt I was being asked to make a fundamental decision on the spot, and I was going to make an informed one, goddamnit.

It scarcely occurred to me that I might slow down and rationally consider what was happening. Andrew asking for me back felt like a blip on the radar, a crack in the ether; like a passing moment that may never come again. This scarcity drove me closer to him. I was still committed to being exclusive with Jack and yet, even after all we'd been through, after how close we'd come to falling apart that winter, I was willing to betray everything we'd rebuilt for just the notion of being with Andrew.

Jack doesn't have to know. He'll never know. This never happened. I comforted myself before even kissing Andrew. Something deep inside of me resented how easily I could rationalize away my guilt by preemptively resolving to bury it.

Unfortunately, the sex was great. It felt like a throbbing, juicy declaration of love and an earnest apology for the wrongs of the past. I stayed the night, and I slept great too, which made me feel like a heartless person with a rotten soul. The next morning, waking up beside him and wandering barefoot through his house felt surreal in the deepest sense.

He had to get to work. We shared a brief breakfast on the front porch: eggs and avocado toast with black coffee. It was the first time he cooked for me.

"You never told me you loved me," I said between bites. He ran his hands through my hair.

"You knew though... didn't you? I must have told you," he insisted.

"No, Andrew," I replied. "Believe me. I would have remembered. I was hung up on you all that time. I could never tell whether you were infatuated, or in love, or just stringing me along as a fun rebound. Or all three, for that matter."

"I wasn't clear either. I was still getting over Emily," he said. He sipped his coffee, then turned to face me. "Things could be different now, though, couldn't they? Are you happy? I feel like we could be happy."

I thought of the conversation at Radio Room, how he had surmised that maybe someday he'd come groveling back to me and it would be up to me to decide if I still wanted him. Well, he had called it. I hadn't believed him at the time; now, it felt like a cruel joke. I didn't know whether to cry or slap him. It was all such a fucking mess.

But it didn't take long to sort out. Two days later, I came to see Andrew again. I came straight from the climbing gym, not bothering to tame my frizzy hair or change my clothes. It was a contrast to my old pattern of needing to look, seem and act perfect with him. We sat on his front porch in the fading daylight.

"I can't do this, Andrew," I told him, shaking my head. "It took me a year of hell and an acid trip in the desert to get over you the first time. I don't want to be your rebound. I can't put myself through this again."

Was I sure? He wanted to know. No. I wasn't sure, but I felt something true in my gut. He was saddened, with eyes downcast in their familiar way, but unsurprised. He quietly wished me the best and leaned in for a lingering hug, and then I excused myself for what felt like the last time.

I was almost disappointed he didn't fight for me harder; perhaps it had been a test and he had failed. Perhaps I was testing my own resolve. Yet again, I came to recognize how deeply I loved Jack and believed in our future.

Just... not enough to tell the truth; I told Jack a lie. I told him that Andrew and I had shared dinner, made out in the heat of the moment, and that was it. I told him what I felt mattered: how Andrew had tried to win me back, but I declined. Again, I justified my dishonesty and felt the truth about my choice to have sex with him would serve no purpose and had no real-world benefit. I never told Jack, or anyone, not even my closest friends, about that night. I erased it, along with Andrew, from my memory.

Hell's Canyon

In July, Jack took me on my first multi-day rafting trip. We joined a group of 10 for a week on the Snake River in Eastern Oregon. This was the first time Jack had ever invited a partner to join him on a rafting trip. Rafting was like skiing for him — his first two loves, the ones that no partner could ever compete with. He often said in jest that he was married to the river, and he was only partially joking.

He brought me a gift the week before the trip: a turquoise PFD (flotation vest) and a matching dry bag for all my belongings. He wrote me a note, expressing how significant it felt to be involving me in his world in this new way. I understood what it meant to him; river life was a huge, formative part of his identity. To share his deepest passion, joy, and enthusiasm with someone for an extended trip felt like committing to a deeper sharing of our lives together.

Packed into the truck, we headed East toward Idaho. Jack showed me his organizational systems and made it clear that being a first mate meant contributing like the most seasoned river rats. I helped fasten the boat frame to the top of his truck, loaded tote after tote from the vehicle to the boat, learned how to secure metal cam straps to every loose item so that the boat, affectionately named "Los Dos" was "rigged to flip." The fact was, Jack had never flipped a boat, and didn't intend to start now, but the thrill of possibility terrified and excited me as we approached each set of Class IV rapids.

I soaked up every moment of that trip. It was one of the happiest weeks of my life. We were completely removed from society — just our tiny caravan of boats, floating like a transient community through the meandering, lazy, roaring Snake River. Watching the massive cliffs on either side framing the clear blue sky and hearing nothing but rushing water and Jack's jolly whistle hearkened to a simpler time, a time before cell phones and digital marketing ruled the world. I felt settled, undistracted, and at peace.

Early mornings gave way to easy afternoons drinking beers and lounging on the riverside. The men fished along the shore, hoping to snag a sturgeon. Our kitchen crews took turns cooking pasta and stir fry. Entertainment was made up of campfires, guitars, wrinkled books, and brush hikes. Some days were intolerably hot — they don't call it Hell's Canyon for nothing — so river dunks were many and close between.

Jack and I slept outside on an inflatable mattress on the sand. One night, I awoke to find him awake beside me in the deep hours of the early morning. The sky was rich black and sprinkled with huge, boisterous stars oozing pearly light.

"Wow," I whispered. Jack climbed on top of me and I opened to him. I watched the starlight on his skin and took in the cool night air, allowing myself to be washed in a deep contentment that I hadn't afforded myself before. I was immersed in nature, in ease, in a simple and whole love that for once didn't feel intolerable to me. It felt irresistible.

The river shore wasn't the only place we had sex. We were ravenous for each other. I like to think that my willingness to work hard and my adaptable, positive river attitude made me extra enticing to Jack. We lured each other up to a sunny lookout point one afternoon during a beach layover day. Within moments our bathing suits were off and Jack had me up against a massive rock face. If we hadn't been so enthralled with each other, I might have noticed the hundreds of prickly plants covering the stone, depositing their hair-thin spikes into my entire backside.

By the time I noticed, we had enough pleasure chemicals coursing through our veins to find the whole scenario hilarious. We laughed loudly and took our time picking them out of my skin, one by one. Lesson learned: protect your backside. Nature sex is best done from behind.

We upped the ante the next day on the river. Jack and I were alone on our boat, opting for each other's company without ride-alongs from the other eight in our group. He confessed that he held a fantasy of one day having sex on the river — that this would be the ultimate culmination of "living his best life" as he put it. I perked up and arched my eyebrow at him.

"Well..?" I shrugged.

"Are you serious??" he asked, glancing around. "...Now?"

"Of course I am," I answered.

"Goddamn, Becca," he grinned. I slid my knees apart teasingly.

Jack rowed with fervor. A simple bend in the river was all we needed to eddy off out of sight for what felt like the fastest and naughtiest quickie on record. I leaned over the edge of the raft and told him to hurry. We both laughed and sighed as the boat rocked. Our view of the American Flag waving proudly from the stern, plus the fact that we were both bare-assed but still wearing flotation devices made for a comical sex scene. We finished just as the blue tip of the next boat in our group came peeking into view. By the time they reached us, all appeared normal aboard Los Dos, though the dripping between my legs held our cheeky secret.

We returned from Snake River deeply bonded and glowing with gorgeous new memories that felt like art pieces we'd crafted ourselves. We wept bitterly when we returned to the city, sitting constricted in traffic among stoic urbanites. We discovered that we thrived together in the wild. Jack had brought a fire, a texture, and a richness into my life that I'd been hoping to find. In only one year since I'd left my marriage, I found myself sexually saturated, deeply in love, and drinking up an exciting life adorned with new experiences.

Shift

But in the weeks after we returned, I began to feel a disconnect between the practical facets of my own life and Jack's. Whereas we'd been carefree during our summer adventures, Jack had another, more anxious side that came out with work and grad school. He felt crushed under the pressure. He was completing a Master's Degree and thinking about what might be next for him; for us. He had come to Oregon for school and wasn't interested in setting down roots here. We spoke in vague terms about what this might mean for us. I was willing to explore possibilities, yet I also felt deeply tied to Portland.

We spent more and more time together with Moses and I began dipping my toe into moments that resembled co-parenting. But I was very guarded, and I always had been. I didn't trust anyone else to meet Moses' needs and be as gentle and firm as he needed. At three, he was still incredibly small. I was a fierce gatekeeper, particular about the way Moses was looked after and the messages he received from the world around him. I felt that no one besides Keaton could fully love Moses the way I did, and anything less felt inadequate or tainted by obligation.

In my mind, any love Jack felt toward Moses was simply an extension of his love for me. I didn't believe the two of them could have a sincere, deep connection on their own; he hadn't been particularly interested in children before I came along. While he loved that I was a great mother, it was also never in his plans to date someone with a child and all the complexity that comes with that. I was his first serious relationship, and as a wild hearted 26-year-old man, he was far from wanting to settle down.

The tension reminded me eerily of the dynamic I'd shared with Andrew. I laughed to myself at their shared Gemini natures — the ongoing duality of wanting depth and wanting to blow with the wind. So, I walked the line, craving time together as the three of us, but also not entrusting Jack with Moses' care. I wasn't ready for a co-parent, nor did I want Jack to feel that pressure. When we were all together, I was not at ease. I felt unsure how to divide my energy without feeling guilty toward either my child or my partner.

I also wondered whether Jack wished I were a different version of myself, one with less responsibilities and commitments demanding most of my attention. A version of myself who could go on adventures like our river trip at the drop of a hat, untethered to any place or person. This fear, and my deep knowledge of the sacrifice involved with raising a child, held me back from taking my relationship with Jack more seriously.

Pickathon, Again *(New Year, New Man)*

Jack and I bought weekend tickets to Pickathon, the music festival where a year before, I'd spent what would have been my fifth anniversary dancing in the dirt with Andrew. Now, I danced to folk tunes with Jack and let Moses snooze in a makeshift wagon bed after the sun went down. (Hard to believe he still fit comfortably in a wagon back then.) I also remember all three of us being grouchy and tired when an argument erupted between Jack and I about personal space as I tried unsuccessfully to get Moses to sleep in our tent.

That weekend was eye-opening for both of us.

It shattered our illusions and opened Jack's eyes to the realities of traveling with family and breaking routines with small children. It opened my eyes to my propensity to mother, or rather, control, situations and take on more responsibility than is fair or helpful. At one point, I realized that I'd be more relaxed if I were there alone with Moses, because I couldn't tolerate the pressure I was placing on myself to be the perfect partner and the perfect mother all at once.

Doubts about my longterm compatibility with Jack began to grow harder to ignore.

Meeting The Family

I'd been hearing about Jack's family for a year and was excited to meet them. They flew to Portland for a wedding and filled two weeks with festive summer plans. Unsurprisingly, they were wonderful. His father, Gary, was an architect with short hair and smart glasses, and his mother, Joy, was an eccentric artist with a down to earth whimsy about her. Jack's older sister was a graphic novelist living in Boston and we had many overlapping interests and a shared sense of humor. We all had an easy time getting along. His parents simply adored Moses and he took to them right away. Moses was particularly enchanted by Jack's mom.

Seeing this natural relationship made my heart swell. We felt instantly like family. We went together to his cousin's wedding and I was brought into the fold even further. It was a beautiful, functional, well-read group of people with progressive values, open hearts, and critical thinking skills for days. I felt the way I had with Keaton's family, except these people were even more "my people."

That weekend, we attended Northwest String Summit together and camped there for the weekend. It was the first music festival where I saw a gaggle of onesie-clad millennials stumbling past on their way to wander in the forest. I was totally perplexed and wondered what they might be tripping on at such a nice, low key event like this. I had some hunches. *Kids these days*, I thought.

We set up home base at the main stage and watched the live acts one after another, made complete by the crowd of swing dancers, blues dancers, and hoop spinners adorned with their twinkly lights and festival garb. Little Moses was mesmerized. One afternoon, he perched on Gary's lap while the music played and Jack and I dozed. The two of them drew race cars together, Gary's effortless sketches were frame-worthy pieces of art (perks of being a skilled architect). Those three sketches, two race cars and a VW van, are still on display in Moses' room.

One night, Jack's parents stayed at the campsite while Moses slept soundly. We were free to drink and dance to the bumping beats of the late night headliner, Turkuaz. It was a roaring time and a completely surreal experience for me to feel so confident trusting someone to look after Moses, and trusting their generous intentions in offering me support. It felt like they had seamlessly stepped into the grandparent role I had dreamed of for Moses, and I was equal parts elated and guarded.

How could I accept Jack's parents' role in Moses' life, when I couldn't make sense of Jack's role in his life?

The following night, Moses went to Keaton's for the weekend and I enjoyed the rest of the festival kid-free. Jack's parents were award-winning swing dancers; they'd actually met dancing swing in their 20s. His dad gave me a quick and dirty swing lesson on the grass: basic steps, then twirls and tricks. I remember grinning and laughing as he reprimanded me warmly, "Eyes up here! What are you looking at your feet for?" before sending me on a spin and pulling me back again. Once relaxed, I took to it effortlessly and laughed so hard I developed a headache.

That was the first time I remember easefully dancing in public. I felt graceful and embodied in a way I never had before. It helped to have a strong leader and a glass of wine in my belly. I felt welcomed, accepted, and celebrated in a deep way by Jack and his family, with no pressure to be anything less or more than I was.

I wasn't sure how to accept this. It felt almost more than I deserved.

Coastal Doubts

During their July visit, Jack's whole family, aunts and uncles and cousins and girlfriends, rented a house on the coast and we joined them for the weekend. Each morning, I woke before everyone and went for a quiet run on the beach, enjoying the solitude and space to clear my head. I felt positive about Jack's family, and also a bit overwhelmed at how real our relationship had suddenly become.

We played on the beach and Jack's mother and I split off from the group for some one on one time. We had a lovely heart to heart in which I shared about my background, my dreams and goals, and how I saw the future playing out. She wondered aloud whether my path and Jack's were aligned, noting that he was intent on owning land and raising animals. I echoed my own personal background in farming and my resolve to never farm for a living again. She mused that Jack seemed to be idealizing the lifestyle and perhaps didn't quite grasp how the day to day grind of farm life felt.

She thought perhaps we'd be a good fit and a compromise in our lifestyles would serve us both.

That afternoon, I drove home alone to return to real life in time for the work week. On the drive, I reflected on the days I'd just experienced. This family was truly beautiful, and so was the way I fit into it. I could imagine holidays baking with Jack's mother and ski trips in Colorado with the whole family, Moses included. I daydreamed about how it might feel to visit upstate New York and see Jack's childhood home.

There was something unsettling about the thought. It felt uncannily wholesome, just as my marriage had, and the thought of joining another family who I adored and shared a bond with was terrifying to me. I didn't feel ready to decide my whole life again. A year earlier, I'd left a marriage in pursuit of... what?

I was in pursuit of my own life. Something larger and freer and truer for me than what I'd chosen in blind, young love.

Then that week Samuel called from Costa Rica. We'd been speaking every couple of weeks. I told him he'd caught me at a weird moment, telling him of the ways I was freaking out at the sight of a beautiful family and sensing that I might self-sabotage.

"I'm sure on some level, you know what you want, Becca. Let that find its way out," was all he said.

He was more confident than I was.

Peru

It was late summer, and Jack was finishing his Sustainability Education degree. Part of his Permaculture Design Certification included a trip to Peru. He intended to stay beyond the course to do some exploring — why go so close to Machu Picchu and miss seeing it for yourself? It crossed both our minds that in other circumstances, perhaps I would fly down and join him. It just wasn't feasible with a three-year-old and a tight work schedule. We prepared for a month apart with love letters and gifts and long languid mornings in bed when we could.

Before he left, several of us living in the intentional community began plans to move to a new house — something smaller and more settled, a place where we could co-create the vibe and house agreements from the start.

Tess and I found a dreamy two-story cabin by the river with a big, shady yard and a long driveway. We talked the guys into joining, including Jack, five of us in total. Jack and I were discussing living together with separate bedrooms, like we had at the Golden Hearth before he'd moved closer to campus that winter. It felt simultaneously like a huge commitment to cohabitate again, yet also like no big deal. We had lived together in groups before, and we spent most of our evenings together. But choosing to share a home after a year of dating was different. Whether we liked it or not, it would mean something larger to us and to Moses, too.

Even with this plan laid for the future, we agreed to relax our "monogamish" status while we were apart. It seemed like the right time to finally make good on our year-long philosophical exploration of non-monogamy. We finally trusted each other. We were both highly sexual. It felt like a safe container, a free month, to consciously explore other connections if they arose. And with the defined time frame, we felt safe to return to our more exclusive agreements when we reunited, if we so chose.

"Who would you want to get with if we were open?" he asked me one day during a picnic in the treehouse.

"I don't know. I'm not really interested in meeting people. For me, it's the people who I already know and trust, who I have deep friendships with," I answered. "Obviously, Samuel comes to mind…"

I braced myself as I awaited Jack's response, knowing he'd never think favorably of Samuel after the ice storm. He held a straight face as I spoke.

"Or Matt (who was Tess's very monogamous partner), or Michael."

Jack had met Michael at the climbing gym one day and found him friendly and nonthreatening. The three of us had even grabbed food and beers together a few weeks later. He expressed that he would feel comfortable with me enjoying that connection while he was away.

Michael was a hip and musical Korean surfer who was working on his PhD. We had met on Tinder during my open marriage, and he'd been a brilliant and sincere support to me during those life transitions. Our connection was all witty banter and lo-fi tunes as the backdrop to extremely saucy sex. Damn, that man could kiss. He was as funny as he was emotionally intelligent, a true friend with benefits.

His becoming a psychiatrist was a major perk — we'd lounge around in his hammock and drink wine and talk humorously about my daddy issues. But he also asked great questions and created a candid space where I was more than willing to talk. Good sex and free therapy? No complaints.

With Jack traveling, my weekends were freed up. I spent a great deal of time writing and reflecting. I could feel the texture of my life on its own, and found that I truly enjoyed it. I also began to examine my doubts. Was it really best for Jack and I to move in together, now? Did our futures align? How did my status as a mother fit into Jack's life and his plans?

Underneath it all, I wasn't sure I was willing, able, or ready to lean fully into the relationship and all the potential it held.

ID # 21

Medicine

Forest Fire

It was early September. Jack had been gone for a month, and life had been full of farmer's markets, garden work, and berry picking with Moses. I'd seen Michael a couple of times on the weekends and enjoyed the fresh but familiar connection and the chance to visit his world. I also appreciated the ease of returning to my own world without lingering expectations from either of us.

I cherished my time spent alone with Moses. The family I nannied for was taking multiple vacations, which meant he had my undivided attention for the first time in a long time.

We had a special flow, a secret, unspoken language. When it was just he and I with nothing to do, our nervous systems were settled, our humor was dynamic, and we found ourselves wrestling in the grass, staring up at the clouds and making up silly songs. I'd form the chord shapes with my fingers and he'd strum the strings of my guitar and sing about painting and kites and dogs. We were content.

I also craved time, alone, in nature.

One weekend, while Moses was with Keaton, I stuffed some gear in my backpack and headed east to Mt. Hood National Forest to spend a few days backpacking at Timothy Lake. It was freeing to feel so anonymous out there. But it was Labor Day weekend and there were families camping along all the designated sites. So, I went rogue and cut deeper into the forest for some primitive, leave-no-trace camping.

I holed up in my disguised, woodland home between three large trees, spending a great deal of time just lying on the forest floor and staring up at the sky. It was hazy and the sun at dusk was red hot. I wondered why.

On Sunday morning, I awoke just before dawn and set out to hike the perimeter of the lake, a twelve-mile loop. I had an introspective and magical few hours. Evidently, everyone had been up late the night before, because the lake was quiet and sleepy well into the morning. The first five miles of my hike, I saw no one, aside from two fishermen in the distance, perched lazily on the calm waters.

I could hear the pine needles crunching beneath my feet and birds flitting in the branches. It was just me and the forest. As I rounded the bend, I saw a man step drowsily onto the path a few yards ahead. *Ugh. Humans*, I thought. As he meandered, he zipped up his jacket, scratching his head and rubbing his face as though he had just emerged from a deep sleep.

It was his feet that caught my attention, his flip-flopped bare toes peeking out from loose sweatpants. I realized I knew those feet. At that moment, he stopped walking and turned around. We stared at each other in disbelief.

"Becca?" he asked.

It was Samuel. I grinned.

"Hi! What are you doing here?" I asked as I walked toward him.

"I'm… camping," he answered.

I rolled my eyes. Sarcasm, so typical.

"I thought you were in Costa Rica," I marveled, still in shock at the coincidence.

He looked me up and down and smiled. Then he glanced to the path behind me.

"Wait, are you here alone?" he asked.

"Yeah, I am. Just getting some nature time. Jack's been in Peru," I told him.

"Where are you camping?" he asked.

"Oh, far away… probably five miles from here, up on the north edge of the lake," I answered.

We chatted about the ecology course Jack was taking, and Samuel introduced me to his friend and co-worker who was camping with him. They were out on their annual psilocybin mushroom vision quest to prepare for the coming year of teaching in Costa Rica. He apologized with a shrug for his distance the past six months, and I did the same, telling him not to worry. I didn't feel like dredging up everything that had transpired after our wintry tryst.

We paused to take in the moment and laugh.

"This is really wild. I have not seen another person all day. I'm kind of amazed that you just walked out on the path right in front of me," I said.

"Life's funny like that," he replied. We shared a long hug. I could feel a mutual desire to stay longer, to extend an invitation or offer something up, but the moment didn't make sense for it, so we parted ways. I stepped forward on the trail while he returned to the lake's edge.

I spent the next couple miles mostly alone, besides sharing the path with a trio of equestrians atop their massive, stoic horses. A couple of miles later, I was greeted by the biggest raven I'd ever seen. I heard it before I saw it.

First there was a loud whooshing from behind. Flap... Flap... FLAP right behind my head. The hairs on my neck stood up. I ducked. On the path before me swooped a huge, black shadow with a wingspan as wide as the trail, shrinking as it moved up and away into the trees. I looked up. There, perched in an evergreen, was the jet black raven. It looked out over the lake and let out several deep croaks.

I stood still for a while, allowing my heart rate to return to normal and wondering why crows and ravens get such amusement from dive bombing humans. I thought about their brilliance and the way they get into mischief simply because they're smart enough to and seem to enjoy exerting their power over cats and dogs and unwitting hikers. I remember reading once that, thanks to their intelligence, crows spend only a small fraction of their time feeding and caring for themselves. The rest of the time is theirs to do with what they please: socializing, pranking, and general tomfoolery.

I looked down at the tattoos on my forearms: A dandelion on one side. A blackberry bramble on the other. It seemed I had an affinity for misunderstood and underappreciated creatures.

When I left Timothy Lake that afternoon, I reached the parking lot to find Samuel's truck parked right beside my Subaru. I recognized it instantly; he had a trademark bumper sticker that read "Keep Narwhals Real!" and some work gloves and tools tucked into the back. I jotted down a short, affectionate note, tore it from my notebook, and tucked it under his windshield wiper.

I drove away. *What a wild, magical day*, I thought to myself as I traversed the winding mountain roads back toward the main highway.

I noticed a red truck coming from the opposite direction, and recognized it immediately. It was Cory's.

Impossible. Seriously?

As he approached, I saw his familiar smiling face beside another person in the passenger seat. He was unmistakable. What were the chances there was another handsome Black man driving the exact red Tacoma? I waved as he passed, but he didn't notice.

I laughed out loud, thinking to myself that, if I ran into Andrew today, this whole thing must actually be a dream. (I didn't run into Andrew.)

That evening, home at the Golden Hearth, I sat out in the garden beside the fire pit and called Logan. I explained the day's magical happenings to her.

"So I went into the woods to be alone and I ended up seeing two past flames. Seeing Samuel was crazy enough. What are the chances? But then the raven, and then Cory… what is happening, Logan?" I paused and looked up. There were white flecks falling from the sky. It looked like snow. I reached out to catch one, but it crumbled in my hand: ash.

"That's weird. There's a bunch of ash falling from the sky. Seriously… what in the world is happening?!"

She chuckled darkly.

"Must be from the fires. Eagle Creek. You haven't heard?" she asked.

"What fires? No, I've been in the mountains all weekend," I replied, alarmed.

"Oh… yeah. Some kid lit a firework down by Punchbowl Falls and now the whole fucking Gorge is burning," she said plainly.

I hung up the phone. News report after news report confirmed what she'd said: the Gorge was on fire. A place that had meant so much to me and thousands of others over the years, up in flames. The home of Camp Crestview where I'd met God as a child, and Dog Mountain where I'd grieved my divorce, and Mount Defiance where I'd fallen in love with Jack.

All told, 50,000 acres of Oregon's forest were torched by that fire, the result of two small firecrackers and a thoughtless, immature impulse.

Medicine

A deep undercurrent of personal healing had been steadily moving through my life at an unpredictable and meandering pace like a creek in the woods.

I marked the beginning of this exploration distinctly at the opening of my marriage. It was like something in me had woken up. I'd chosen to take a huge, audacious chance and open myself up to life, to its greatness and risk. And in some ways, the past year had been me posing one long, open-ended question to the invisible powers that be:

What terrifying, marvelous wonder is possible in this life?

Intricately linked to this process was my willingness to explore the far reaches of my own consciousness. This had begun in a lasting relationship with cannabis, and after my LSD experience in the desert, felt more like a universal awareness than simply the deeper workings of my own psyche.

Yet, I noticed that discoveries and insights were rarely "Aha! Moments" which integrated themselves on their own. With Andrew, for instance, I'd gained a deeper understanding of the pain he'd caused me, but on its own, that insight hadn't been enough to prevent me from abandoning myself, and my agreements with Jack, to be with him again.

My housemate Mali, a fellow mother at the Golden Hearth and a mentor of mine, had been a spiritual guide for many years and was diving into offering support for psychedelic ceremonies. She invited me to participate in a mushroom journey of my own. It seemed like the perfect time — I hadn't interacted with psilocybin since a single instance of casually eating mushrooms while drunk at a high school party.

Now, at 26, I was in the midst of a profound transition in life. I was finally gaining my bearings after a year of single motherhood. After a month without Jack beside me, I felt clearer than I had in a long time, maybe ever. I was interested in deepening my relationship with psychedelics, yet I wanted more support in understanding the experience than I'd afforded myself last time around. I agreed to work with Mali.

The following week, I cleared my schedule for two days. Moses was with Keaton (as all my seemingly "free" time took place on the weekends, in pockets of time between work and parenting). It was a Friday, and everyone was away from the house, a rare occurrence. I ate a small breakfast and tidied my room, throwing the windows open and meticulously dusting every nook and cranny. I swept out the treehouse in the Bigleaf Maple and prepared in it a cozy nest of pillows and blankets.

I created an altar in my bedroom with sacred objects — stones and shells from significant moments, a crow feather, dried plants from my corner of the garden and hikes in the gorge, and Jack's turquoise bolo tie.

MEDICINE

Mali brought in a teapot with a handful of delicate dried mushrooms resting inside. Psilocybin Cyanescens. We sat together on my bedroom floor for a quiet moment. Then, she burned sage and called in the four directions, opening the space and inviting in whatever guidance might be available to me.

As I poured the boiling water over the mushrooms, I set my intent for the day: to be open and willing, a brave and clear listener.

Mali blessed me and stepped out of my room quietly, leaving me to find my way, as I'd requested. I wanted someone to hem me in, but more than that I wanted time alone with these wise, earthly forces, the kind of quiet and solitude I'd craved during my labor with Moses and my dance with LSD.

I took my time drinking the tea. When the pot was emptied, I chewed the softened mushrooms, one by one. Their taste was earthy and medicinal, and it lingered in my mouth after they were gone. I felt slightly queasy as I wandered through the garden and gradually made my way up to the treehouse.

Within minutes, I needed to lie down. It came on hard and fast. I felt the effects settling in as my vision became distorted and my stomach began to swim. There was a lot happening all at once, in my body, mind and emotions. I needed to ground. So I curled up in my makeshift bed with my back up against the massive tree trunk. I lay there in the fetal position for a very long time as the mushrooms began to carry me, covered in blankets and staring up at the green leaves and the clear blue sky.

I spent all afternoon up in that tree. A flock of crows came and perched in the branches, more than just a few. But they made no sound. I thought that perhaps I was imagining them, their eyes dancing in a kaleidoscope swirl with fluorescent green moss and white marshmallow clouds.

Source

Something so ineffable, so otherworldly happened to me that day. I hesitate to even try describing it. It was the most profoundly spiritual experience of my life. It was the day I met my maker. I was yanked from my atheism with the realization that everything — and I truly mean everything — is divine. I witnessed all of existence as an expression of the imagination of God.

First, I felt myself dissolve from the edges, molecule by molecule, and evaporate into the atmosphere. I saw my cells as bits of ancient stardust returning back in time to their original source. I was gone. There was no longer a self. There was only a watcher, zoomed way, way out, beyond humanity and Earth and our galaxy altogether.

There was just… one. All of life a part of the whole. Here, nothing mattered. Everything was truly, deeply, irrevocably whole.

Then I was drawn deep into the belly of a dark pit, a place made of shadows and void and forceful obscurity all at once. The shady birthplace of everything. There was no fear here, but there was depth and mystery; there was quiet; the great unknown. I was far from my body, as though in another world altogether.

A massive, sweeping motion yanked me (or whatever I was) out of the deep and I was blasted into a glistening place inside of sunlight. There was all spectrum of color and yet no color, only a bright glowing. Pastels and rich hues encompassed me from all sides, and vibrant rainbow fractals began dancing on the light in unending patterns and configurations. It was the most beautiful vision I'd ever seen, like the brilliant, gem-encrusted, sparkling sea set against a warm sunset, only the whole sky, all of space in all directions, was made of this patterned shimmer with its dancing motion.

It was the pulse of life. Aliveness expressed as art before my eyes.

I was visited by Source. Or I was taken there. Or was I the Source? I can't quite say. But I was all of it, and it was all me. There was no me, and there was nothing that was not me. It was as real and tangible and convincing as this book in your hand

I drifted further and further out, with the familiar sensation I'd had in the desert of simply being afloat. Something was holding me up and nudging me along. Was there a tether for me? I opened my eyes, thinking perhaps I could shake the visions loose and come back to Earth. But in the trees and the bark I saw the swirling kaleidoscope of life: there were the tree's cells and the multitude of insects and microbes all coexisting there, out of human sight. Zooming way in and zooming back out again I saw the tree's tenacious roots reaching deep into the soil, through rocks and clay, with the invisible colonies of life and webs of mycelium bursting into activity as I beheld them in stillness.

All went quiet. There was nothing. Silence. I thought for a moment that perhaps I was back.

And then I heard sobs. It was a sound I had heard before, and I recognized it as the voice of a woman. I saw her lying on her bed in the throes of childbirth. I saw her doubled over on the edge of a lake in the throes of heartache. And here she was again, in a tree, shaking something loose. Opening to the next deep, wide, unrelenting wave of expansion. I knew her.

Witness

I drifted off into a dreamlike state. First, I saw only a dark, thick red. This vision expanded like an organ growing into a heavy orb above me and finally enveloped me altogether. I lay sobbing, enclosed inside this maroon womb. It was beating like a heart and I floated in a pool of thick, sticky, warm blood.

My mother was there. Then I was with her, and then I was her, all curled up, as an unborn baby. She disappeared, and I was my familiar grandmother. Then I became my unmet grandmother, giving birth to my father. And then I was her mother, and her mother's mother, and all the mothers, moving rapidly back through time and around the world, within a thread of the wombs and women who had birthed me into existence, into this moment in a tree. Women I didn't know and couldn't know.

In a singular moment, I was burdened with everything these women had endured since time immemorial. These were no longer only my family; these were all women. I was taken through a coursing, whiplashing rollercoaster of unspeakable despairs and abuses: the shame and humiliation of being crushed and exploited and silenced and killed. Their blood was crying out, screaming. This soft, fluid energy, this birthplace which had brought forth all of creation, trampled by the forces of boots, fists and weapons, hunger and misplaced rage.

I was consumed by a tremendous, searing pain, both sharp and dull, an ache so deep I wanted to stop existing. I couldn't bear the weight of it. I couldn't heal it. I was helpless, like being in labor again.

But it occurred to me that I didn't have to hold it, and I didn't have to heal it.

So I bore witness. I looked right at the pain and the injustice. I saw that it was real. I acknowledged its weight.

I continued to let the grief pour out as deep, guttural sobs until I was emptied of breath and tears, and the blood was no longer crying out in tumult. Witnessed and acknowledged, it began to rest as I did.

All was quiet, finally. I opened my eyes and my vision swayed. I wondered if I could move. With caution, I made my way gradually down the wooden steps of the treehouse and back through the garden. I heard music coming from inside. Mali was in the living room, humming and sweeping, doors flung open.

"Hey there," she said as I entered. "How ya doing?"

I just stared at her. I must have been a sight to see.

"I am… somewhere else right now," was all I could muster. She opened her arms for a hug and I buried my tearful face in her shoulder, allowing myself a moment of relief from the intensity.

When I returned to the tree, I felt emptied out. Again, I let go.

I was afloat on a raft in a calm river, staring into the leaves and sky above me and watching as the green and blue became black and white and returned again to color. Their patterns danced and orbited in breathtaking beauty, and at moments it seemed almost too much to behold. I felt thrilled to be alive. What a wonder, a fortune, to be a conscious being, my cells and neurons aglow with that same colorful, shimmering light that danced around me on its sunset shore.

I smiled like a fool. I opened my eyes to see a quivering, nervous squirrel staring at me, just inches from my face on the trunk of the Bigleaf Maple.

"AHH!" I squealed in surprise. It squealed back and scurried away with a start.

I began to laugh hysterically. I laughed and laughed and laughed and laughed.

"Everything okay up there?" I heard Mali call from the window, chuckling.

But all I could do was laugh. Louder and harder and longer than I ever had in my life. Just thinking of it brings a grin to my face.

It occurred to me once again that everything was so marvelously beyond me. It seemed almost too good to believe: the notion that I am simply a tiny part of this human and earthling ecosystem as it conspires toward wholeness and repair in the face of daunting forces.

I am here to be alive, to fill my role, and to bear witness. What if full presence is the only guidebook we need, and our divine mandate lives within our guts and beneath our feet? This place or being or state that we call God, gave me a profound gift that day in the tree: peace. Repose from the craving for explanations. What freedom it is to trust one's intuition, and to know that what feels most alive is often the next step forward.

I felt freed from the pressure to save or change anyone, and also understood that my passionate fire, my crow-like wit, and my dandelion tenacity are offerings to this world, not liabilities.

The spirit of freedom that I embody is one that wants to multiply. There is a courage in my bones that wills me to go deep into the shadow, witness untold pain, and come out the other side. It's the courage to take a stance and hold a vision. To carry a torch.

Might I simply trust these powers, instead of living comfortably in my head? What if I refused to cling to the rational reasons that no one can heal the world in a single lifetime, so we may as well never begin the work? What if the outcome was not at all the point of any of this, but the process and the ways we are each called to heal ourselves and hold one another along the way?

I watched the crows and squirrels in the tree, coexisting amidst their profound differences. I stared up at the crows holding court and I saw myself. I saw Samuel. I saw a dark knowing and magic that is rare to come by. These crows were brilliant, with an ease in their mischief and self-assured pace. I had always tried to be good: bright, fresh, perfect, gentle. But these birds were dynamic, sardonic and regarded with distrust. Like it or not, they were my guides.

I watched the squirrels with their nervous, scattered energy. They were diligent, thorough and unendingly committed. They didn't have time for mischief; they were preparing for winter. It seemed so foreign to me, the effort, the trying, the scurrying about.

I thought of those I loved who were busy and industrious and good to the core: Jack. Tess. Those who draw me out of my brooding and intensity and inspire me to compromise with the daily demands of life and participate in the world.

I realized I need both: I need my soul family, those who are built from the same clay and fed by the same damp, dark forests. And I also need the balancing energy of the bright and good and practical ones around me.

As my thoughts wandered, I heard someone speaking Spanish down below. Or a language older than Spanish.

I felt ready to be indoors, before the kids all returned home from school and regular activities resumed. I returned to my room where the journey had begun earlier in the day (though it felt like a decade had passed). Lazily, I sprawled on my bed, plucking the strings on my guitar and staring at the ceiling. What a ride. Outside my window, I heard the voices speaking Spanish yet again.

Mali came to find me in my room. We checked in. She held quiet space and asked me gentle, open-ended questions. But I didn't feel quite ready to talk.

"Who was here earlier?" I asked.

"Besides us?" she replied.

"There was someone speaking Spanish. Outside." I told her. "Did someone have guests over?"

"We're the only ones here," she smiled at me. "Well… *you* might have had someone over," she winked.

I was mystified. I had been *convinced* that the voices belonged to physical people, standard issue human folks. What had they been saying? Was I meant to know? By the time I posed the question, I recognized the answer was irrelevant.

Mali closed the gates of the four directions, with their corresponding elements, and invited me to share with her what I could, whenever I was ready. We embraced. I chose to do some writing alone, and she gently shut the door as she left. But before I could write much, I dozed off into a dreamless sleep. I can only imagine the communion with ancestors, plants, animals and fungi that continued behind my closed eyes and somewhere else entirely.

Family

The next morning, I woke up with a crystalline knowledge: I needed to call my dad. After six years of silence, I was ready to revisit the past and tread on the paths I had abandoned. I had come out of my mushroom journey knowing that I could stare into that which was messy, painful, and unresolved and, simply allow it to be so.

For years, I had refused to get back in touch with my dad out of pride. Tess had asked me once if I saw any value in doing so, and I said that I did.

"Why don't you want to, then?" she asked.

"Ugh. It's just so cliché. Daughter comes of age and reconciles with her estranged father," I rolled my eyes. "It's like a plot point for a sappy book."

I had long ago given up the idea that I could help or change either of my parents. For the most part, I'd removed myself from relationships with my family altogether. My sisters and brother would often take trips over state lines to party in groups. Being the only one with a child, it was easy to opt-out, though in reality, I didn't enjoy the antagonistic group dynamic when we congregated. They also went out to lunch with my mom and had tried in earlier years to reconcile with my dad. But not I; I had chosen a new life on a separate path.

I had refused to reconcile with my dad because I believed it would probably just cause me pain and frustration. I had no clear goal in mind; I didn't feel the need to say my piece and I wasn't holding out for my family to say the things that I believed needed to be said. Things like:

> "I'm sorry."
>
> "You deserved better."
>
> "I respect you."
>
> "I want you to believe I can change."
>
> "I wish I had _____ differently."
>
> "I am growing and healing myself in these ways: _____."
>
> "My love for you is not conditional, and I am sorry for the times I made you feel like it was."

I didn't believe I'd ever hear any of these things, from any of my family. I had, in many ways, let the past go. I had accepted that my mother and father, my sisters and brother, were all just… people. People with pain. Like me, they had worked it out in healthy and harmful ways. This understanding made it really hard to resent or condemn them, because doing so would also mean casting judgment on myself.

I developed empathy for my parents and siblings after seeing the ways my own unconscious behaviors had hurt the people I loved, like Keaton and Jack. I had even begun to recognize the ways I had formed disorganized attachment: I'd become dismissive and avoidant early in life due to the experiences of smothering scrutiny and emotional neglect.

This adaptation, this sense of guardedness, meant holding a strong boundary and not allowing toxic behavior close to myself or Moses. I didn't feel I owed my family members my time or energy. My brother's assertion that "blood was thicker than water" meant absolutely nothing to me. I never consciously kept my family at arm's length, but their natural distance was comfortable. Moses barely knew my siblings, which amazed me. While they would swoon over him on Instagram, they made little effort to spend time with us. My mom sometimes watched Moses for me, but our interactions were brief and impersonal. I held my family members to the same standards of relationship as I held everyone else, and the way I felt leaving family holidays — frustrated, misunderstood and depleted, was not something I wanted more of.

Now though, I knew that reconnecting with my dad wasn't about having a specific purpose or expectation. I had opened myself up to a deeper current of growth and healing. I was riding a wave over which I had no control, and this family work was where it intended to take me next.

The Crows

After my mushroom journey, I saw three dead crows on our street in the space of a week. The first one seemed like a sad and rare occurrence. The second one was cause for pause. And the third one was tucked under the sage plant in the corner of the garden I was responsible for tending. Thoroughly startled and almost irritated, I called Mali.

"Mali. I'm getting some crow visitors and I feel like they're going to keep dropping out of the sky until I do something," I huffed.

"What do you feel you need to do?" she asked. I stalled, then answered.

"I need to make a fire."

"Well, there you go," she replied.

Before our call ended, Mali told me about raven medicine. Raven represents magic, mystery, creation, transformation, cunning, adaptability, fearlessness, and voice.

I felt slightly uncomfortable setting up a ceremonial fire. These were some witchy-ass shenanigans taking place in the suburbs, in broad daylight, on a Tuesday morning. The fire pit was situated in the main garden between the raspberry vines and the Swiss Chard. We'd had many full moon fires around this pit, but I'd never stood here alone, with an unspoken cosmic mandate to burn a bird.

I prepared the fire and used a large spade to scoop up the crow. I placed her in the center of the generous platform of kindling and branches.

What did all of this mean? Why were the crows dying? I could speculate, but there were no answers. One thing was clear: they were asking me to pay attention. I thought of the saying, "small deaths prevent big deaths."

Something was shifting and transforming inside of me, and perhaps a part of this shift meant the end of things to make space for whatever was new. My eyes were opening to the reality that the dark, heavy, hard, mysterious parts of life didn't deter me like they often did others. Darkness wasn't inherently wrong or bad or broken. And now, I was readily present for it.

I lit a match and tucked it under the crow's finest feathers.

As I watched the flames rise, I made an agreement with the cosmos: I would embrace the shadows as a welcome part of me, and I would dance on that scary and invigorating edge of the unknown for all the days of my life. I would find my joy there.

In earnestly nudging outward the boundaries of my own perceived limitations, I would become expansive. I would be unafraid to take up space when necessary. And I would become someone who could hold space for others, too.

This is the experience of Edge Play.

22

Return

Jack Comes Back

A week after my mushroom trip, my treehouse adventure of a lifetime, Jack returned from Peru. I was giddy to pick him up from the airport, to share with him about the breakthroughs I'd had and hear all about his time in the mountains. I felt that the time apart had been good for us. Even so, I still had more questions than answers about our trajectory. In many ways, I had grown accustomed to being without a partner during the month he was away, but this was overshadowed by the sheer craving I felt for him and his presence.

I waited outside the airport, where I had waited for him several times that year, listening to a CD he had made for me featuring love songs by John Prine and Elephant Revival. The music brought up tears of warm affection. Usually, he emerged from the revolving airport doors donning a puffy coat and ski bag, but this time he wore a sun hat and hiking sandals.

I had expected an enthusiastic and warm reunion, but Jack was subdued. I chalked it up to the long day of travel. That night, lying in bed, Jack told me that he was feeling distracted. He had met someone while in Peru, he told me, and formed a strong connection with her. He used the word love. I hadn't seen it coming; not at all.

Over the coming days, I did my best to listen as Jack wistfully told me about his time with Julia, a European earth worker and flow artist who was living at the permaculture base in Peru.

Instead of visiting Machu Picchu, he had spent his extra travel week with her at the base, helping repair a water catchment project. They went bouldering and hiked the local area. They shared a deep bond and felt connected on many levels.

They didn't have sex, he said, but it wouldn't have made much difference to me. Love was love. Heart pull was heart pull. It was challenging for me to take in. I was unsure how to lean into this reality and not pull away from him. I felt like a hypocrite, given the ways I'd unapologetically embraced my own entanglements with Andrew and Samuel.

It seemed to me, and perhaps him as well, that she represented a world of freedom that I did not. She had lived in several countries and was untethered to anywhere, while his partner at home was deeply rooted and a mother of a four-year-old child.

My mind turned to criticism and rationalizing.

Of course he was drawn to the wispy, dreamy hippie chick living the life of his dreams. I rolled my eyes at how obvious it all seemed, like a cliché. He was at a crossroads and she and I represented the two archetypes — freedom and novelty pitted against safety and security.

It was hard for my ego to admit what I already knew to be true from past experience: that it was completely possible to meet and fall in love with someone while still very much in love and committed to someone else. The gravity of the wild heart holds little regard for monogamy.

Yet at the same time, I found myself believing that Jack might actually leave to move to Peru and build a permaculture life with Julia.

The following weeks consisted of numerous discussions attempting to sort out our emotions and next steps. Jack was unsure if he felt ready to live together, and I reminded him that we had done it once before. Plus, it would be in a group setting with friends and not a nuclear family scenario. I was earnestly holding onto him and conveniently pretending Julia did not exist.

Jack's trip to Peru sparked an unraveling of the magical year we'd been living in. Realities had begun to set in.

You see, Jack had come to Portland with the intention of staying just long enough to complete his Master's Degree. Now, he had only one term left, but was intimately connected to me and our possible life together. Come winter, the world would be wide open to him again. I couldn't ignore that Portland's long, wet winters and hipster culture wore on him.

In truth, he wanted to live in the foothills of a mountain somewhere or along the edge of a river, not in the city. I, on the other hand, loved Portland and intended to stay, at least until Moses was much older.

Even as we continued our tentative life together, I was unsure whether Jack was ready to be partnered with a parent, and whether I was willing to be the kind of partner he wanted. I wanted to be both deeply committed and fantastically free to explore. I also wasn't sure we shared the foundation or the relational wiring for non-monogamy. We were both powerfully afraid of outside forces pulling us apart.

Jack mused that perhaps he just needed some time to "get his wiggles out," and then he would be ready to settle down. Maybe there was a way to pace ourselves and continue to build the individual lives we wanted. He wanted to travel. He wanted a job where he could work seasonally and be free to recreate the rest of the time. We argued about whether this was a practical goal, and what maturity and settling down would actually look like for us.

More than once, he pitched the option of moving together to rural towns nearby. I fantasized about it, but in my guts I knew it was not for me. I had my community, my son's father, and a life I loved in Portland.

It was obvious to us that something would need to be decided, and sooner rather than later.

Through all of this, our connection was still there, and Jack intended to move into the house. We agreed to have our own rooms, and his would be a protected, kid-free zone, per his request. And due to lease commitments, he would move in a couple of months after the rest of us.

Dad

By now, it was early October. Jack had been home for a month, and it'd been six weeks since I'd awoken from my mushroom journey realizing I needed to reconnect with my dad.

I was at work one morning watching the three kids happily raking up piles of leaves and rolling around in them. I decided to see if I could track down a phone number for my dad. Skeptically, I called the last number I'd had for him. It went straight to a generic voicemail message.

"Hey, Dad. It's me…. Becca. Is this still your number? Anyway, just wanted to say hey and see how you were… I know it's been a while. Call me back when you have a chance."

I set my phone down. *What had I just signed up for?*

Not a minute later, my phone rang.

"Hello?" I answered.

"Hello? Someone from this number just called my phone," a voice said. It was a voice I'd known my whole life.

"Hey, Dad. It's me, Becca," I managed.

Silence.

"Ahh, Becca… is that really you? Hi, dear…." his voice cracked. I burst into tears. I could hear him doing the same.

We spoke for a few minutes. It was a brief, weighty catch up. We both attempted to ignore the fact that we hadn't spoken in many years and that so much messy shit had transpired between then and now.

"I'm just about to head into an AA meeting," he said. "Can you give me a call later tonight? We'll catch up."

"Of course," I said, and we ended the call.

That night after I tucked Moses in, I called my dad back. It crossed my mind that he may not answer; that he may not want to catch up or talk to me again. After all, he'd had my number all those years and had chosen not to call. This didn't deter me, though; I called him as I'd agreed I would, with him and the Universe, and he picked up after the first ring.

Who He Was

I spent the next two hours on the phone with my dad, and I came to know him better than I ever had, even after sharing a home with him for 17 years. I updated him on my life — how I was living outside of Portland, my son was now four, and I was recently divorced.

"Oh, that's too bad," he said comfortingly. "I always liked Keaton. But sometimes, things just don't work out. At least you figured it out early and spared yourself years of grief," he added.

I knew he was speaking from personal experience.

I told him about Jack and his years spent in Colorado. My dad had lived there before meeting my mother in Oregon. His mother, my grandmother, still lived in Colorado, in a small tumbleweed town east of the Rockies. My dad was one of 11 children, yet due to sickness and poverty, only 6 children had survived past their first birthday. In sixth grade, he had dropped out of school to become a migrant worker.

My father told me about his journey from Texas to Colorado, then to Montana, and finally, to Oregon. He was in the Job Corps and worked building roads and bridges. He shared memories from his time spent in Missoula, Montana, and I told him about my recent trip to Utah and my newfound love of the American Southwest.

Eventually, we broached the topic of his incarceration.

He was quiet for a moment. I wondered whether I had pushed too soon. Then he spoke.

"It was a bad time. A real hard time," he said humbly. He recounted the whole incident with his wife Sy, from the argument at the house to the police shooting and the trip to the hospital. I wandered around my home as he spoke, watering plants and keeping my hands busy as I heard the unimaginable pain in my father's words. I willed myself to witness it. My housemates went about their evenings, cooking dinner and doing yoga.

I stopped in the dark hallway to lean against a door jam, attempting to breathe as he described the sensation of hitting the pavement. I could see him there clear as night: losing blood and begging for help from the police officers whose bullets were in his body.

The weeks and months after the shooting were horrendous. The shot to his abdomen had caused organ damage which resulted in a portion of his colon being removed. He was in critical condition for weeks, but after he stabilized, he was taken to jail. Later, he was taken to prison in Portland to serve out his sentence.

He couldn't get access to the medications he needed in jail. His requests were dismissed numerous times. Ultimately, his wounds had burst open and become infected. He had internal bleeding from his colon and was re-hospitalized only after he proved grimly to the prison guards that he was, in fact, losing massive amounts of blood. His healing was dramatically slowed due to the stress of being jailed, the terribly poor food quality, and the lack of access to sufficient medical care.

This negligence is so common within the prison system, it's shameful. As I listened, I tried to temper my rage at the system as a whole, this punitive machine that chews up human beings with lives and families and traumas and reduces them to criminals with case files.

This rage was multiplied by my deep grief. Watching my brother go through prison was one thing — he was strong, young, arrogant and resilient. He had spent the time inside those walls dreaming of his life afterwards and preparing to beat the powers that be at their own game.

I felt angry at my mother for emailing us kids a photo of my father's mug shot shortly after he was arrested. She knew better; it was an ugly and spiteful thing to do. In it, he looked old and tired. I felt deep shame when I saw it, an image of him at his lowest, which I'll never be able to erase from my mind.

It made me physically ill to imagine my father, frail and mild, disabled by gunshot wounds which permanently damaged his body and the nerves in his hand and arm. This was the man who had once been so strong and sturdy, who spent his best years, day in and day out providing for his wife and five kids, now completely alone in the world, forgotten within prison walls, being pushed around by guards and threatened by inmates.

While we talked, I recalled a time during my first year of college when I went home to visit for the weekend.

My parents' divorce was in process but not yet finalized. My dad was struggling, so deeply depressed at the proceedings that he was losing weight and growing emotionally distant. He was outside raking leaves one afternoon and I called him in for lunch. I'd made him a big turkey sandwich with chips and orange slices. Double mayonnaise, hoping to get some calories onto his thinning frame. He thanked me. He left the oranges on his plate, uninterested.

As he ate, he asked if I'd be willing to give him a haircut. I felt awkward in the kitchen as my mom sat in the adjacent living room, watching a movie. I used the same hair scissors and comb that she'd used on our whole family's hair for years. Now, I was in my mother's role. I was the caregiver, the parent. The mother. I combed out his wiry, wavy gray hair and cut it short, hoping to return to him some of his fading dignity. Hoping to defy the fact that he was exiled to sleeping in the basement of the house he had spent decades paying for, while my mother slept in the ocean blue master bedroom she'd recently remodeled for herself.

I remember realizing then that parents were just people, and people with pain. People with pain can be really shitty sometimes. I recognized at that moment that I had become the adult in my relationships with my parents. My adaptable nature gave me more power in those relationships than I realized. I wasn't stuck in the ways that they were stuck; there was still hope for me.

And now, I was a parent too, on the phone with my aging father. I listened to him speak about the times in prison when he wanted his life to end. He spent a year and a half inside those walls, after a year on house arrest during court proceedings.

I remembered my dad, young, strong and capable, playing with us in the carpeted living room.

"Again, Dad! Again!" Kara and I would squealed, hanging onto my dad's flexed arms above the elbows.

"Ready?" he would ask. We'd nod eagerly.

He'd hoist his arms upward, lifting us off the ground. She and I would hang from each arm like giant ornaments from the bows of a Christmas tree, clinging for dear life as he spun around. He'd spin and spin until we screamed in delighted terror, then we'd all fall down, dizzy and laughing.

He described life now. He had lost most of his savings. He was in his sixties and couldn't hold a job due to the nerve damage in his arm preventing him from doing the work for which he was skilled. He was living in a mobile home on the back acreage of a friend's farm.

"Just taking things one day at a time and trying to keep busy," he told me.

He'd been enjoying working on his little Honda.

"Any chance you need an oil change?" he asked.

"Actually, yeah. I do. That would be great. Maybe you can teach me how it's done," I said. "You know what? I'm moving this weekend. If you're free, do you want to come hang out for the day and help me out?" I surprised myself with my own words.

"I'd be happy to, dear. It'll give me something to do. Thank you.... thank you," he said.

We said goodnight and hung up.

The Move

The night before the move, Jack and I went to see Rising Appalachia in concert. The Crystal Ballroom was warm and crowded. We draped ourselves over one another as we swayed to the bouncy harmonies, punctuated with hammer claw banjo and djembe drums. We sipped on mediocre tequila and I felt happy and at ease. We laughed and bantered together, playing off one another's energy in a way that had been nearly forgotten in recent months, and especially in the weeks since his return from Peru.

After midnight we shared a pint of gooey chocolate ice cream and collapsed our tipsy, tired bones into bed.

Somehow, our tiredness always seemed to drift to the periphery amidst the electricity of warm bare skin on cool sheets. *Such are the perils and pleasures of sleeping naked.* We tore at each other in our familiar way. Breathing hard and humming involuntarily, I bit his neck and he pulled at my hips. Within moments, I was atop him. We rode the cascade of sensation and intensity until we'd had enough, and then we had a little more.

Beads of sweat cooled on my neck as the warmth of the tequila brought on a fuzzy, sleepy stupor.

Before I drifted off, I made a mental note to double check the calendar. I had recently had my IUD removed, and was still getting used to having to pay extra attention to my fertile days of the month. For years, I've had a distinct pain in my ovaries every month, right on schedule, making it easy to tell when I was ovulating, aka "in the danger zone." Now, lying awake, I hoped my estimation was correct.

Morning came too soon. We were hungover, but it was moving day. Not just that, my dad was coming over to help. It would be the first time I'd seen him since my wedding six years earlier, and adding to the pressure, Jack was along for the ride at this very weighty moment in my life.

We nibbled on scones and I sipped my coffee, piping hot and black, on the drive to the Golden Hearth. He expressed that he was preparing to hold space for me as emotions came up throughout the day. As much as I appreciated the sentiment, I didn't intend to turn to him for support, as many months earlier, he'd made comments which led me to believe that my intense emotional waves were taxing to him.

And besides, I felt surprisingly centered and calm about the unfolding situation with my dad.

The move was simple — a blur of boxes and bags, and long hours without eating because I was in the zone and had things to get done. My dad was helpful and low key. He had arrived in his little red two-door Honda, wearing some sort of waterproof camo pants and a matching jacket. They hung loose on his thin six-foot frame. His health was clearly in decline. He'd lost so much weight that he looked like a fragile, emptied out shell of the man I remembered. He quickly became winded carrying my smaller boxes and armfuls of dresses and jackets, and had to sit down frequently to take cigarette breaks. Jack and I wordlessly moved my bed and furniture.

My housemates were gracious and welcoming to my dad, calling him by his name, Rocky, and making friendly conversation. I unpacked the kitchen and stacked books on the shelves. He went out to his car and when he returned, he held out a box of organic food for me that he'd saved from the Oregon Food Bank. He'd set aside the best foods from his haul, knowing I was picky about organics. Here was a man who had nothing, *nothing*, offering me the best he could muster. That simple, humble extension of love touched me and broke me more than I could cope with at the moment.

Throughout the day, Jack and I clashed repeatedly. While I was unpacking the kitchen, he was complaining about not being able to find all the ingredients for a salad in my tangle of bags and boxes. Tired and hungry, he was centering on his own experience, and his low blood sugar seemed to make him completely forget about the paramount importance of the day I was navigating. I snapped at him and told him to "fucking figure it out."

Why is he even here? I thought to myself.

When the move was finally complete, I walked my dad out and thanked him for the help. We hugged several times. He promised to come visit again soon. Tentatively, I stepped inside.

"So…. that's my dad…" I said, shrugging, and looked around at my friends. They made kind remarks about his easygoing energy and natural helpfulness.

"I just couldn't get over the cigarette smell," was the first thing Jack said. "I'm wondering about his health, too. He had to stop and take a lot of breaks. What was that about?"

I looked down at the floor, feeling ashamed by association and lacking energy to explain to him why his remarks were so hurtful.

"Also, does he… hunt? I was confused by his camo outfit," he said coolly.

"No, not that I know of… it's just what he was wearing, I guess," I answered.

"Don't you think that's kind of weird for someone to wear camo if they're not a hunter?" he asked.

I wanted to slap him. I wanted to explain that today was completely, utterly not about him and his feelings or his discomfort or petty opinions.

Well, in his world, it was. Turns out, Jack was wrapped up in his own emotions about the move and his place in it. He was concerned about financial stresses and an upcoming job interview in the Columbia River Gorge. He was thinking about a farm that he had invited me to manage with him and facing confusion about where he might be in a few months, and what it would mean for our relationship.

RETURN

Adding insult to injury, he later flippantly called Eastern Colorado (where my dad and his family come from) a rural wasteland of ranching and poverty.

"During my years in Colorado I always avoided going east of the Rockies. There was nothing worthwhile there," he added nonchalantly as he bit into his pizza, seemingly unaware of the barely concealed dig at my family.

I was hurt and frustrated by his comments and lack of sensitivity throughout the day, yet I lacked the energy to bring it up. That night, we slept together lazily in my new room, opting again to forgo protection since I was past my fertile window for the month. I hoped the sex would bring me some comfort, but as I held him close, I couldn't get his heartless comments out of my mind.

The next morning, I couldn't see Jack leave soon enough. I took some time for myself after he was gone, needing space to breathe and take care of myself. I needed to process all the emotions that had surfaced — emotions about my family, belonging, change, shame, healing, and heritage. I was mentally and emotionally wiped.

Plus, I had woken up with a familiar, heavy ache in my left ovary. It was radiating throughout my hip and centrally toward my uterus. If I hadn't just ovulated the week earlier, I would've been certain this was it.

Wait... how certain was I? I began to panic. Last time I'd had full-on, brazen, unprotected sex during ovulation, I had become pregnant with Moses on the first try. I was dangerously fertile, and at the moment I had a sea of Jack swimming inside my body looking for something to fertilize. *Fuck. Fuck, fuck, fuck*, I thought.

We drove to the Golden Hearth to clean out our old rooms and scrub the fridge shelves. Tess and Matt went inside, and I stayed in the car. I took a deep breath, and out came weeping, gasping, and sobbing. The tears came in stages. First, there were the tears of frustration over the chasmic disconnect between Jack and I, which was either growing or simply revealing itself faster by the day.

Then came tears of catharsis: I had invited my dad back into my life and after everything that had transpired, it felt mostly like old times. He was simple and easy and helpful, as he'd always been.

Finally, came the worst of all: the weight of grief over what his life had become and all that he had lost, and the weight of anger at the deep-rooted systems that caused such pain.

I was overcome with white-hot hatred for seemingly unending injustice humanity poured out on itself: Racism. Colonialism. Poverty. Trauma begetting trauma. Survival mechanisms. Coping. Addiction. Alcoholism. Overpolicing. The prison industrial complex. It was all a part of the same sinister machine. I raged against all of it.

Matt opened the trunk a few minutes later and witnessed the sobbing, snot-covered mess I'd become. I looked back at him, surprised. He was another crow like me; he was soul family. He was someone who recognized the dark side and didn't flinch at it.

"How ya doin' there, Becs?" he asked gently.

Coming around the car, he squeezed into the passenger seat beside me and took me in his arms. I only hesitated for a moment. There was too much to hold, so I dropped my guard, and let myself cry into his shirt.

"It's hard being so strong all the time, isn't it?" he said with compassion.

Those were the simple words of acknowledgment I'd needed to hear.

Baby Bird

That day, I enlisted multiple remedies intended to prevent implantation or end early pregnancy.

I went into Planned Parenthood for emergency contraception and took it immediately, knowing I was still within the 72-hour window. I returned to the Golden Hearth in search of Queen Anne's Lace flowers, double and triple checking that it wasn't poisonous hemlock, water hemlock or yarrow. I found one hidden, seedy stem that Tess had missed a week earlier while weeding. I chewed the fuzzy seeds to a pulp and swallowed them down, thanking them for their help and their medicine. I double and triple checked the seeds again, thinking of what irony it would be if I had just poisoned myself in trying to end an unconfirmed and not-yet taken hold pregnancy.

The next morning, I sat in the sun at work as the kids rode bikes along the deck. A windstorm on Saturday evening had knocked loose a fluffy layer of branches and pinecones. I was clearing off the debris when I noticed a dead bird lying on the deck.

It was beautiful — charcoal gray with pumpkin colored streaks on its wings and head, chest and back. A creamy white belly. I called the three kids over to help create a burial for her. They gathered their plastic sand shovels and each searched for one beautiful item to bury her with — Mia chose a red leaf, Silas found two gold leaves, and Moses found a wet stick covered in furry moss. I found three yarrow leaves growing beside a rain gutter.

Eloise, the neighbor lady, appeared in the driveway holding a plate of cupcakes to deliver. When she noticed the bird on the end of my shovel, she asked if she might take it next door to show her mother, a lifelong birdwatcher. I handed over the bird on a piece of cardboard. She handed me the cupcakes in exchange.

Meanwhile, we dug a hole in the wet dirt on the edge of the property, not far from the grave where we had buried Rainbow, the family's neglected fighting fish, gone too soon.

Eloise returned and explained what her mother had shared: the bird was a female Varied Thrush. She spread its wings to show us the intricate feather designs. The kids ran their fingers over the bird's tufty chest. "Whoa," they whispered.

As we tucked the bird into her makeshift grave, I saw another live thrush in the grass across the yard. It hopped around for a moment before flitting up into a tree. The kids helped me take turns gently scooping soil onto the cold, still bird. Tears sprang from my eyes.

I saw this female bird and thought of all the conversations Jack and I had shared about family: how we had each envisioned having a daughter someday, how maybe we would do so together — we'd name her Madrone or Lupine. We'd teach her to rock climb and ski and bake and play banjo. She'd live immersed in snow and soil and local ecology, able to tell you which plants were safe and which were poisonous. She'd hum Johnny Cash songs under her breath and read fantasy novels. Maybe she'd have her dad's barrel laugh and her mom's dry wit.

So I held on to Jack, as I had committed to so many times, with open hands. And now an open womb, too, allowing the seed of our shared potential to pass gently through me and away. All the potential within my body that could permanently link us together — was it just a vivid dream, or could it be our DNA was trying to merge within me at that very moment?

I was lovingly saying no. I asked the medication and the Queen Anne's Lace to help me let go of our future in exchange for my own future.

Salty tears dropped into the hole and soaked the already wet soil. This was letting go. It was time to accept the shift in my trajectory and the necessary split between Jack and I. At once, I felt a powerful sense of both saying no and saying yes. No to a future bound up with a man, a false security launched by a pregnancy, a move motivated by a partner's opportunity. The parts of me willing to make that kind of personal compromise for Jack were dying and being buried.

It felt like the first time that I was fully saying yes to myself and my own path. Yes to the pursuit of my own goals: entrepreneurship, owning land, unapologetic independence, and a robust family and friend life instead of an intensely bound partnership.

It was equally terrifying and freeing. It was the very thing I'd intended to do a year earlier after Andrew and I had split up: build my own life. But I hadn't been ready. I had more to learn and more to heal before I could build a life on my own with resolve and clarity. I didn't feel I had those things now, but I knew I was closer than a year prior.

Two weeks later and five days late, my period finally came. It was a relief and a loss.

Like a Wave

Two days after the move, Jack and I had plans to see First Aid Kit together. But I was incredibly depleted. I hadn't realized how much the transition of moving, plus the emotional upheaval of reconnecting with my dad had demanded of me. I was feverish and exhausted and sad.

It was a cold and rainy Tuesday night, so I blasted the heater and the windshield wipers in my Subaru, cursing the Oregon weather and wishing to be home in my bed. On the drive to his house, I listened to First Aid Kit's new album.

Their song "To Live a Life" hit me like a rough wave. I continued driving through evening traffic along the usual route, but I was somewhere else entirely, immersed in the timeliness of the lyrics dancing in aching harmonies within my car.

Sitting at a stoplight on Hawthorne Boulevard, I was overtaken. It was obvious then that I would not be going to a concert. And I would not be a partner either. There was no deliberating, no thinking. It was something I just knew. It came from somewhere else. For that moment at least, it was clear.

I asked Jack to come out and meet me in the car. I blurted everything out in a graceless, tearful, sputtery mess.

"I'm so exhausted, Jack. In every way. I honestly don't have anything to give right now. I barely have energy to say all this. I've never felt this worn down. I need to go home and rest. I need some time to think through everything. Can we just take some space for a week or two? I'm sorry. I love you."

I didn't really leave space for him to speak.

He stared at me and nodded, watery eyed and confused as I spat out the words. We hugged stiffly and I cried as I watched him climb out of the car and walk back across the rainy street and into the house, the place which had been like a second home to me all this time.

23

Parting

Halloween

Halloween was my favorite holiday, by a long shot, and we had tickets yet again to attend the Portland Erotic Ball. Even though our relationship was in limbo, we decided to keep the tickets and go together as a couple.

Despite my declaration four weeks earlier, our separation did not happen all at once. It filled most of Autumn, and for every moment of clarity, I had another moment of total fear and doubt, driving me to write him letters and make calls musing about whether this was really the end, or just a time to reset and start again? Our love and desire for each other was pitted against the obvious disconnect with our lifestyles, plans, and even the inner work we were each doing at the time.

I'll never forget the moment when Jack and I both knew our relationship was ending. It was a clear, dry afternoon, and we stood in his side yard taking turns applying layers of latex paint to each other's bare bodies. I was perched on his picnic bench, bent over with my hands on my knees while he stood behind me with a paintbrush and applied golden paint to the crevices of my ass.

He leaned around to see me.

"Hey babe," he said. "Do you want to talk about things before tonight?"

No, I didn't. *Why ruin a great night?*

"Right now? I'd rather not, babe. Can we just enjoy this evening?" I implored with a laugh.

"Okay. Yeah. Just as long as you're not going to break up with me tomorrow…" he pleaded.

I turned and looked over my ass, giving him a gentle, incredulous look.

"Babe! Why are you being like this?" I asked.

In recent times, Jack has pointed out that in that moment, I did not reassure him or answer his question. In fact, I recall actively choosing *not* to.

On the bright side, our costumes were impressive.

Jack dressed as an elaborate dragon with wings and scales and a mask, and I was the dragon's gold. We both wore latex body paint from head to toe. I wore golden contacts, a golden blonde wig and a studded bikini. We looked fantastic.

He and I were the darlings of the erotic ball. Tipsy, sexy urbanites went bonkers for our barely-there costumes and we were recruited for the famous costume contest.

Twenty-five couples were invited to compete on stage for a $5,000 cash prize. We paraded across the platform. It was surreal to be on the stage of the Crystal Ballroom, the same venue where, ten years earlier, I'd had the lead singer from an emo band ask my high school crush Vishnu to be my date for winter ball.

I'd been on many stages in my lifetime, but never like this, nearly nude and cheered on by a crowd of debaucherously horny city dwellers.

Jack and I stirred up the crowd and showed off our costumes with a cheeky blend of suggestiveness and restraint. The crowd cheered so loud for us that we were selected in the top three couples. Everyone else left the stage. Again, by a show of cheering, the three remaining pairs were ranked. We beat out a set of rainbow unicorns, but we were overtaken by an older couple in traditional Irish wedding garb.

We placed second in the Erotic Ball costume contest. Prize value: $0. It was a disappointment. It had honestly crossed my mind that the best-case scenario would be splitting a $5,000 cash prize with Jack to ease the blow of our impending breakup.

That night, we peeled the paint off our bodies with laughter and had rowdy sex on Jack's kitchen table. I looked at him and felt fondness and love, and preemptive nostalgia for times like these that would soon be ending.

The following morning, in the clear light of day, we sat at the same table and I told Jack how I truly felt. It wasn't the right time or circumstance for us to continue trying to push our relationship forward. Even though our shared values and chemistry were obvious, there was just too much disconnect in our life seasons, plans and goals. On a deeper level, we had known this for a while. We agreed to step away from each other and live separately. Jack would not be moving into the cabin with the rest of us. It was a teary affair, but for me, it also bore some relief to have chosen a course and no longer be wondering. I kissed him hard and left.

Surreal with Andrew

Like stray magnets in a bowl of beads, Andrew and I had gotten back in touch yet again during my separation with Jack. Staying out of contact with him was like paddling upstream. I entertained the idea of meeting him for lunch, unsure of my intent, and when I asked him, he suggested we set the whole day aside later that week. It fell on the day after the Erotic Ball. I agreed, feeling guilty and curious how we might fill a whole day.

Leaving Jack's house, I barely gave myself enough time to shower and scrub the paint from my nooks and crannies before driving to Andrew's.

These roads were memorized. What was I doing revisiting the past yet again, after so much cat and mouse between the two of us? Did I actually want to be there, or did I simply have something to prove? What might that something be?

Neither of us seemed particularly relaxed when I arrived. We sat on his couch near the front door as he drank his second coffee of the morning. We chatted. He ran his hand over my leg. I could feel the ways I was muting myself and presenting a more contained, polished version of me yet again. There had been so much back and forth, and so little comfort or substance, between the two of us. I couldn't even sort out how I felt. I was bewildered and guarded, and just beginning to see past the pedestal I had set him on, to recognize the ordinary, confusing Gemini man who sat before me. How well were we really matched?

Before long, and I don't even remember making the decision, though I'm sure I did, we were upstairs in his bed. My body became feverishly hot. This is something I've noticed numerous times throughout the years. It's a stress response. When I am in a close embrace and things begin to move faster than I can emotionally keep pace with, I become undeniably flushed. My back grows damp with sweat. It's as though my body is trying to send out a warning sign that my mind and heart are ignoring. The subtle pressure from a lover to get lost in the heat of the moment too fast, makes me feel cornered and disembodied.

But I let it continue, witnessing the moment from afar, as though I was not participating. I tried to convince myself that this was what I wanted. It was a repeat of many times in my younger life when I'd gone along with sex out of politeness. I hadn't yet integrated the knowledge that I could pause and come up for air, pump the brakes, just say no altogether. And this time, with Andrew, I wasn't clear enough with myself on what I even wanted to begin with.

So, we had sex. It was nice and familiar. It wasn't exciting.

Later, we drove a couple of hours to a small, pristine lake. The conversation was sweet, if a bit constricted. I felt no flow or ease with him. This was clearer after a year lovingly entangled with Jack, with whom I had felt more celebrated and accepted than any other person. Now, sitting in my Subaru beside Andrew, everything I said went through a filtering process. I still didn't know how he regarded me or what he really wanted from me. And, in spite of myself, I still cared.

And, why was he taking me out on a day trip on the lake with his friends?

The six of us cruised around the lake and took turns wakeboarding. I cozied up beside Kaylee, a peppy and beautiful snowboarder chick.

"So, how do you two know each other?" she asked. Andrew and I looked at each other.

"Ummm…" I stalled.

"It's a long story," he smiled.

While Andrew was in the water, Kaylee and I nestled under a blanket and ate chunks of baguette and creamy brie.

"Alright. What's the real story?" she asked me with bright eyes.

"Well… we met on Tinder last June," I told her. "We dated all summer. But we were both getting out of serious relationships… and I have a son. He's four. It just wasn't the right time, I guess."

She nodded. "Do you think it's the right time now? Are you going to try again?"

I glanced at his grinning face, gliding effortlessly on the water.

"Honestly? I don't know if it will ever be the right time with us," I answered.

Andrew climbed out of the water, winking at me as he peeled off his wetsuit.

"Gettin' cozy over there, you two?"

We smiled.

"Seems about right. Everybody loves Becca," he mused.

We got home late that night. I stared at my ceiling feeling hollow, I hadn't allowed myself a moment to deal with the huge decision I'd made with Jack just that morning. Instead, I'd gone back into the arms of Andrew, who brought me only temporary, surface level comfort.

Done, Done.

A week later, I got clear… again. *(Why was clarity such an elusive creature to me?)* I simply didn't feel good around Andrew. I didn't fit into his life, and he didn't fit into mine. I reached out and asked if he had time for lunch.

We sat on his porch eating chili and chit chatting about business and plants. He made a fart joke as he refilled his bowl with beans. I got to the point.

"So, I wanted to talk in person about all this," I said, motioning between him and I.

"What's up?" he asked nonchalantly, in what felt like a role reversal from our breakup the previous summer, and a familiar echo of the June conversation we'd had on that same porch.

"It was really nice to spend the day together last week. It just… it still doesn't feel right," I told him. "We're both single and available, and a part of me thought when our lives were more settled, it would just work. But, it doesn't, I can't lean into it."

"Hmm," he put down his food and looked at me. "Why are you here, then?"

"I'm here… to have this conversation," I became irritated. "I think it's best if we don't see each other. I'm still heartbroken about Jack. I really don't have any business being here."

We let the conversation meander through what-ifs and might-haves. After so many partings, they were beginning to sound trite. I stood to leave and he rose to hug me goodbye.

"There's definitely a pattern here," he said into my neck.

"What's that?" I inquired.

"Becca's on my porch and she's heartbroken. Happens every few months," he shrugged, looking smug.

PARTING

That pissed me off.

"Hey, now." I stepped back and looked right at him. "Who was the one hung up on Emily last summer? And if I recall, it was you who took me out to dinner this summer after breaking up with her a second time. We were both out looking for some comfort, Andrew. I was just the only one to own it."

"Yeah, maybe…" he said with a subdued chuckle.

"Bye, Andrew," I said. I turned on my heel, hopped down the porch steps and walked to my car without looking back.

Birthday

It was over with Jack. It was over with Andrew. I was a free woman, and I felt a tired, quiet peace with it all. My birthday was coming, and there was an exciting quality of newness within all this change and loss.

For my birthday, Tess helped me host a ladies-only celebration dinner. The night before my birthday, I stayed up until 1:00 am baking myself an epic birthday cake and decorating it to the nines. Three layers of Mexican spiced chocolate cake with dark chocolate ganache, salted caramel, and espresso whipped cream. My soul in confection form.

I made a single matching cupcake in the process and ate it on the couch while watching feminist Latinx comedians on Netflix and thinking about my life. Satisfied, I scrubbed the dishes and put the ornate cake on display on the table. I looked around at the spacious log cabin with its floor to ceiling windows and the row of sneakers by the front door reminding me of the friends and adorable child with whom I shared a home. I marveled at the beautiful life I had created for myself and let a few tears go. It had all been so much.

I felt proud, exhausted and totally worked over.

It had been one year since my birthday trip in Utah, one year since the psychedelic breakthrough that had catalyzed this season of unfolding and unlearning, and I had just experienced the fullest year of my life in its wake.

On the morning of my birthday, I woke up early and wrote in my journal while Moses played Legos and tried to sneak tastes of frosting.

> "I'm 27 today. I'm coming into the next year of my life with a patch of gray hairs, more smile lines around my eyes, and a joyful sense of resolute ambition. This has been the richest, most challenging and rewarding time of my life. I'm bursting with anticipation for the

things ahead, but learning to show up and stay present for the valleys between each peak.

While I was 26:

I finalized a divorce.

I fell in love.

I broke my own heart in order to heal, more than once.

I lived in community.

I went on countless outdoor adventures.

I blossomed in physical, mental, and emotional strength.

I grew the biggest vegetable garden yet.

I raised Moses with a deep well of patience, affection and hope.

I reconnected with my father after six years.

I started writing a book.

I formed bonds with the most important people in my life.

I made huge missteps. I practiced taking responsibility for them.

I took the high road.

I took the easy road.

I started fasting.

I lived on the edge of my comfort zone and reaped the benefits.

I'm stronger, more resilient, bigger-hearted, and more willing to learn because of the inner work I've done this year.

I'm ready for more."

I invited a dozen of my closest girlfriends, sisters and mentors of all ages, sizes and colors over for a feast of Mexican cuisine. Not everyone would want to cook their own birthday dinner, but I did. I felt in my element serving up locally sourced, slow-cooked carnitas and laughing loudly with my sisters and friends.

Tess was irreplaceable by my side. I don't know how I would have weathered the heartbreaks of those years without her care and understanding. She knew how to listen, and I never felt judged, not even when I told her that evening after my party that Jack was on his way over for a visit. She just raised her eyebrows and said, "You're the birthday girl!"

He and I were still in the throes of grief, trying to accept our relationship ending. The chemistry and deep love between us created extra difficulty in letting go. I was in denial. He had become my comfort zone, and each day I seemed to have a different understanding of what was happening and why. Perhaps it was just a season apart?

That September, on our anniversary, I had sent him a black and white photo of us at the coast, smiling. In the caption I wrote,

> we
>
> return to each
>
> other
>
> in waves.
>
> this
>
> is how
>
> water
>
> Loves.
>
>   - Nayyirah Waheed

Mosier, Oregon

Months earlier, Jack had reserved a yurt on AirBnB to celebrate my birthday in the Gorge. Even after deciding to step back from the relationship, we chose to keep the trip. Life had been moving non stop for both of us, and we needed time to slow down and reflect. We wanted to honor the year that we'd shared, and clarify our expectations for one another as we transitioned out of romance and attempted to stay in community.

We planned for a standard romantic weekend together like all the others we'd had — full of food and sex and exploring the outdoors. Only this time, there would be tears and hard talks instead of daydreaming, and hopefully some semblance of closure. It seemed as painful to share the trip together as it would be to skip it.

It was the first time I'd gone into the Gorge since the Eagle Creek forest fires. Driving through the blackened Cascade Locks area was so devastating I had to turn my eyes away. When we arrived in Mosier it was early evening.

Jack made a fire and heated curry for dinner like old times while I dozed on the bed. We had agreed ahead of time to connect with each other however came naturally, without arbitrary physical boundaries reflecting our change in relationship.

The steaming bowls of curry and mugs of tea finally warmed my chilled bones after several cold weeks at my drafty new log cabin home. Jack and I discussed our goals and visions for the coming year, wondering aloud at the possibility of reconnecting in the future. I expressed hope, but it was punctuated with strong doubt, citing what I believed were fundamental incompatibilities in our lives and career paths. Who was to say that we would ever sync up and be willing to move forward together? I didn't know how to simultaneously hold space for an ending and an open door.

Could he really "get his wiggles out" in one year after grad school, and then be ready to build a life with someone who was a mother and as such was tied to her place and community in a concrete way? How could he know now, whether this need for adventure, space and freedom were things to "get out of his system," or a core part of who he was, to be honored?

It reminded me uncannily of the conversation I'd had with Andrew the summer we split. The identity crisis and the outstanding dilemma was the same: his deep care for me, at odds with the question of whether he truly wanted to "settle down." Was he just not ready, or was his path more fluid and dynamic, requiring greater freedom than traditional partnership and family life could accommodate?

Then there were my own contradictions: like Jack, I also needed ultimate freedom, but for me it wasn't about geography or lifestyle, it was about the world of the heart. I wanted a grounded, committed relationship from which I could branch out again and again, for many years. I still believed that commitment and non-monogamy could coexist, though I hadn't seen it in reality.

I didn't want to play house.

I didn't want a family dynamic that felt forced.

I didn't want to sacrifice my dreams and ambitions to advance the goals of a partnership.

I thought of the chorus of the song I'd written him a year earlier:

> *Freedom for her wild things*
>
> *A place to land his open wings*

Root and soil for the seeds...

That night, we lay by the fire for hours, drinking each other in. He was like a cool, shady garden bed on a harsh summer day. I didn't want to leave him.

He lifted my shirt and kissed my ribs, grazing my belly with his warm lips. He rested his head on my body and stared up at me through crystal clear eyes. I kneaded his muscled shoulders and drew him in closer.

Wasn't this connection, this deep knowing and intimacy what I'd been craving all those years? Moments like these confounded me. It wasn't until we found physical distance that I was able to trust the more pragmatic voices assuring me we were in fact growing apart.

We made love again for the hundredth time, with less urgency and more emotion. We couldn't seem to hold one another tight enough. It felt like our last hours together were ticking off at an accelerating rate. We waxed and waned in that bed numerous times before I finally stopped him — feeling him reaching so deep inside of me, seeing him above me, was too much to bear. The weight of our intimacy stood in sharp contrast to the lightness of his coming absence.

He cried and cried, letting out sounds that I'd never heard from him. My chest was soaked with his salted tears. They had mixed with my own, and as I wrapped around him, with my whole heart and body, the lines were blurred where one person ended and the other began. It was a familiar sensation with him. Intimacy previously unknown. Intimacy we were trying to let go.

24

International

Winter

Fall completed its descent into winter and I tried to find a new normal after that weekend in the Gorge, making my best efforts to let go of Jack and embrace my own life. I enrolled in an online permaculture design course through an Oregon university to pass the time. Samuel was written all over it and I knew that the course instructor was a friend of his. At one point, in fact, I even saw a slide in which he stood examining a demonstration garden in Key West, Florida.

Other than the program, winter for me was long and bleak. The holidays had been sweet enough — most of my housemates stayed in town and didn't have family around, so we threw a festive Friendsgiving and a similar event on Christmas. Moses was with Keaton for most family holidays, a tradition that all three of us felt comfortable with.

Unsurprisingly, I was still pulling Jack around here and there; I could be selfish like that. We were separated but couldn't seem to stop having sex. All our friends were asking what the hell we were doing, and to that we had no answer. We were bathing in our heartache, dragging it out for months and comforting ourselves with orgasms, that's what.

Jack joined us at my house for Christmas. We made a massive sweet and savory waffle feast at and spent the morning with friends. That evening when everyone left the house to look at Christmas lights, I found Jack in the hallway and asked if he wanted to make a sex tape with me. I was an opportunist; I loved the thrill.

"Right now? I mean, I'm pretty waffley," he explained.

I just grinned at him and shrugged.

"Well, only if you want to. We could do it…" I looked around. "Right here!" I said, motioning theatrically to our gorgeous, big living room with the toasty fireplace, fur blankets and massive floor-to-ceiling undraped windows.

"Seriously?" he grinned back. He thought for a moment. "I mean… yeah. Duh. Yes."

And so, we did. We came away with an hour of footage documenting creative, passionate, and damn good-looking sex, set to the stage of a crackling fire and twinkly Christmas lights. You can see in our language toward each other how in love we still were. It was like an offering to our whole connection and everything it had meant to us.

Don't ask me if I still look at it from time to time. You already know the answer.

After that, Jack and I tried clumsily for several more weeks to wrest ourselves from the magnetic connection pulling us toward each other's beds.

She Crow

For Christmas, I bought myself a new tattoo. Perched on the front of my leg is an eight inch tall crow looking over her back. She is holding a cratered, moon-like coin in her mouth and surrounded by Psilocybin Cyanescens mushrooms, Juniper branches and Mexican-native Dahlia pinnata flowers.

She is a reminder of the power I began to discover that season. It's a power that's available when I step beyond my own agenda, my own ego, and experience my place within the whole. She is a reminder of my affinity for the shadows and the deep magic that rushes through me like a river — a magic that wants to be expressed. And she is an anchor to the lives that came before me — the mothers especially, who I will never meet in this lifetime, but who live inside my cells, in my very DNA. They are the wind at my back and the catalysts for my healing.

For the next year, it was a challenge for me to express any of this when friends would see the avian imagery peeking out from the hem of my shorts.

This is because I was not yet ready to lean into the truth of the crow's meaning. I was still possessed by the idea of being good; I wanted to find a way to be acceptable. A part of me believed that my true healing would look like a shift in my fundamental nature; a transition from an affinity for the shadowy, hard places I'd seen on my mushroom journey to the beckoning call of the iridescent, sparkly ones.

Ghost Ship

Over the winter, I had taken a second job as an overnight in-home caregiver. I was looking after a woman in her 90s with late stage Alzheimer's. Back in her glory days, she happened to be one of the first female stock brokers in Oregon. It was an easy and uneventful role I filled, like caring for a child, only much easier. She slept for 20 hours a day. It was my task to feed her, change her, put her to bed, and keep her company with guitar tunes and sitcoms.

One evening at work, I laid awake after changing and turning her.

Samuel had been on my mind. I still held these warm and unresolved emotions toward him — the nature of our connection was more like a tide that ebbed and flowed than a door that opened or closed. It was never clearly defined and our stretches without contact were never charged or uncomfortable, but understood as a part of life's natural rhythm. I sent him a short message asking how his time in Costa Rica had been. As I waited for him to respond, I let my mind wander back through our days together and considered all of the weight he had held in my life.

He'd introduced me to permaculture, for one. He had catalyzed the unwinding from my marriage by cracking my sexual life wide open; he was still the best sex I'd ever had. He had catalyzed a rift between Jack and I by holding space for our connection at the moment when I was most fed up with monogamy. In both instances, his presence pushed me toward realizing that what I desired in a relationship did not conform to the relational agreements I had made. Just his presence had the power to highlight the disparity between who I was and the containers I was creating for myself.

My phone buzzed.

"Hey, sweet Becca. I'm happy to hear from you. Actually, I'll be home next month," he wrote.

"Amazing. I'd love to see you. How long will you be back this time?" I asked.

I considered the depth of our understanding toward each other. It occurred to me that we knew each other far better than we should, given the short periods of time we'd shared in the past 18 months. I wondered about past lives.

I recalled the familiar way I felt wandering with him in his garden, watching him work with his hands, eating fruit off the vine and drinking in his body and his sweat after dark, as though we'd done these things before, in other times and other places.

Could it be that he was my true match? This had never occurred to me before. I still wanted to believe in such a thing — that the rhythms of life were conspiring to help me find my singular person — the one with whom I could build a life, a home: not a birdcage, but a nest to leave and return to for the long haul. *Why was there such a natural, uncomplicated power between us, and what might it be like to be more than occasional lovers?* I surprised myself when tears welled up at the notion. I was discovering something inside of me, a deep trust and affection that had been there all along.

My phone buzzed again.

"Just a couple months. Then I'm moving down here full time!" he said.

A drop in my stomach. As quickly as I had entertained the fantasy of exploring a relationship with Samuel, the possibility dissolved. He was leaving the country for good. I allowed for a few bitter tears and thoughts of missed chances. A Cheryl Strayed quote came to mind:

> "I'll never know, and neither will you, of the life you don't choose. We'll only know that whatever that sister life was, it was important and beautiful and not ours. It was the ghost ship that didn't carry us. There's nothing to do but salute it from the shore."

"Oh! That's wonderful," I wrote, but I didn't mean it. "Call me when you're here and we'll make some time."

Meet Mindful

It was a frigid Saturday night in February. I had just begun a second job at a hemp farm, which was keeping me busy alongside working my caregiving job, spending time with Moses, and completing my permaculture course. Tess and I often stayed up late making nachos and I smoked a fair amount of weed. I lamented the fact that I was single again, becoming pickier and more jaded with every ending. I joked about the possibility that I would never find a man.

"Like... *A MAN*," I insisted. "And yet, I can't resist all these softhearted Gemini man-children," I told her.

I continued.

"You know what I want, Tess? If I could just find, like... a tall, mature, mixed-race man who runs a tech company... well, that'd be great." We looked at each other and laughed. I knocked on wood.

"Good luck with that, Becs," she said. "Find one for me too, while you're at it. Have you thought about just going back to dating ladies?"

"Yeah, but I'm craving masculine energy these days," I answered.

I was sure this faceless dream person didn't exist. And if he did, he and I would likely be very poorly matched. But I was so curious that I downloaded a dating app called Meet Mindful. My friends and I simply called it "Hippie Tinder" — a dating app for people trying to live consciously and form sincere connections. *Just to see what's out there*, I told myself.

I matched with Omer the next day.

I took in the image of a tall, thin, extremely fit man doing a handstand on the beach. I learned that he was a computer scientist from Ankara, Turkey. He had kind eyes and a sweet smile and head of gray, well-tended hair. He looked age-indeterminate; his face had a sweet youth to it, but his gray hair and wrinkles suggested time had passed. On his page he wrote that he was looking for friends or casual connections.

He was a rock climber too, and a musician. He sent me a message. Would I like to go climbing the following week?

Yes, I would. And why in the world not? I was single and neither of us were looking for anything serious. Jack and I had broken up in November, and while were still occasionally sleeping together, it was happening less and less. I thought that perhaps a new connection would help me break the habit.

We chatted over text throughout the week and when the weekend rolled around, I found myself snowed in at work. I ended up working a 39-hour shift at my caregiving job because my co-worker couldn't get her car up the icy hill.

Omer called while my client slept in her arm chair.

"Would you like to join me for a dance party tonight? It's put on by Black Rock Café, they're a Burning Man camp. The party is called White Out. Everyone wears all white."

I was so exhausted, I'd barely slept. But I had also been cooped up for almost two days straight with only a nonverbal, dozing woman for company. I was eager to meet him, so I agreed.

INTERNATIONAL

We met at the Doug Fir Lounge. I wore a flowing white robe with waves printed on it and sat at the bar, chatting up the bartender in an effort to diffuse my nervous energy. I saw Omer as he walked in. He was taller and thinner than I expected, with a beaming smile, broad shoulders, an olive-colored puffy coat and a soft spoken voice that complimented his Turkish accent.

"I'm not really using any substances for a while. It's been a rough winter," he told me, after we both had ironically ordered cocktails. "Well, one drink won't hurt," he smiled.

I felt an instant draw toward him and an insatiable intrigue. He had a metrosexual appearance in his shiny, white R2D2 leggings, a satin white vest, and sneakers. He was the most physically fit person I'd ever seen outside of a magazine, truly — with every motion I could see his defined muscles rippling under his skin. It was equal parts attractive and fascinating.

We made small talk and gradually moved to more serious topics.

"It's probably best to start with a disclaimer," he said abruptly.

"A disclaimer? Alright… that's a new one. Lay it on me." I set my drink down and turned to face him.

"I'm pretty unavailable," he said. "I am still heartbroken from my serious relationship that ended in the fall. And since then I have really hurt a couple of lovely people… I got involved before I was ready," he added.

"Thanks for filling me in. I hear that," I replied. "I'm in a similar position. We can keep it casual… no pressure from me," I said, letting my leg brush against his.

"Thank you, Becca. Well, shall we go next door and meet my friends?" he asked.

On the walk over, Omer took my hand and mentioned that most of his friends would be rolling.

"Like, on Molly?" I asked.

I wasn't deep in the Burner scene (artists, hippies, scientists and free spirits who attend and help create Burning Man every year). My friends and I didn't make a habit of going out on Saturday nights and dancing into the wee hours of the morning with the assistance of fun, mind-altering chemicals.

"Yeah. But I'm taking a break," he said. "It's not good for me when I'm already in a low place."

I respected his self-awareness. I was also relieved he didn't intend to take party drugs on our first date! Once inside, I found myself surrounded by five of Omer's close friends and we were instantly laughing and hugging and bantering loudly. We squeezed into a photo booth as though we were old friends, and as the photographer clicked his camera and one woman kissed me on the cheek, I wondered what in the world it was that I had just stumbled into.

Omer and I found the dance floor and shared an instant chemistry. He had decades of background in Tango, and I certainly didn't have any formal training, but I knew how to move my hips and keep a beat. He pulled me in close and jokingly remarked his regret for wearing such tight, revealing pants. I laughed. We started to kiss. He paused for a moment and stepped back to look at me. We grinned at each other.

"What's up?" I said with a smile.

"I have a feeling I'm going to remember this night," he said.

"Me too," I echoed.

Easing In

There were a few cultural differences between Omer and I that took some getting used to. Our lifestyles were very different. The fact that he went out to Burning Man community shows, dance events, and house gatherings on most nights after a long day designing computer chips was all foreign to me. I was at home at night. While he was partying, I was studying companion plants and writing web articles for the hemp farm while Moses slept in my bedroom.

Omer's home was studded with techy gadgets: a set of Google Home speakers which invoked my strong suspicion, an electronic cat door, a robot vacuum, and upstairs in his man lair, a huge and impressive recording system with several screens and mixers. The adjacent wall displayed the countless stringed instruments he'd collected around the world over the course of his travels.

I looked at the photos of kiteboarding trips he'd taken around the world and I thought of my humble home, with my single bedroom's worth of belongings for myself and my child. I thought of the fact that he earned three times my salary and I wondered for the first time, whether there would be a complex power dynamic to navigate.

The first couple of months with Omer were hot and cold. His mother was visiting from Ankara and staying in the guest bedroom. My house was home to not only Moses, but four roommates. There was nowhere to find privacy, which necessitated a slow burn. Our connection was forming on many levels — we enjoyed talking about family histories, human nature, culture, friendship, goals, and memories. I felt cared for, and I appreciated our warm interest toward each other. We'd been walking in parks and meeting for tea, but it was obvious we were both craving more.

He asked me if I would be receptive to a splurge of a date; he could get us a spot in a nice hotel by the river and we could share a night out on the town.

I said yes enthusiastically.

I cringed only once, when he suggested we start our evening with a soak at Everett House. I did not want to think about Samuel while out with Omer. I knew he'd be back in town soon.

"How about cocktails instead?" I countered.

Our first real night out together was blissful. I felt like a different, more sophisticated version of myself. And in truth, I was bringing out a different version of myself. I wore a black tunic dress (with my crow tattoo just peeking out the bottom), ankle boots and my white, tailored, wool Ralph Lauren coat which still held its tags, featuring an original price that would have made Jack shudder. Omer looked like he was simply built to wear sleek button-ups with sport jackets and stylish, understated shoes.

I couldn't decipher whether I was intimidated to be seen with him or proud. I think I was proud. I remember heads turning to look at us as we entered the posh cocktail lounge. We are a hot pair with smiles for days.

Who wouldn't want to be us? I thought.

We nestled in a dimly lit corner booth and ordered olives and charcuterie. Omer shared with me about his terribly bitter and abusive father who had died years earlier of cancer. He was intent on not becoming someone like him, someone who blamed the world for his unhappiness. I had met his mother by surprise already (since she was staying in his house). She was lovely — a strong, independent artist with a round face and kind eyes. She seemed fond of me.

I tried to follow along as he, in his most amusing professor voice, explained in oversimplified terms the principles of supercomputing. I nodded attentively, my mind blank, and marveled at the complexity of this man's brain. He had spent 11 years in DC earning his PhD.

The hotel where we stayed was possibly the coolest hotel I'd ever been in. I was briefly distracted when the young man working the front counter glanced at us several times, a flash of curiosity across his face. We were an attractive couple, yes, but also there was a clear age gap; seemingly more than our 11-year difference. I appeared a sophisticated 25 and he looked more like a spirited 45. I tried not to overanalyze.

In any case, our room was pristine and beautifully decorated with a giant, lush bed and a rain shower just oozing sensuality. I had a flashback to my first anniversary on Lummi Island, when I'd been such a sex-hungry young wife, thrilled to be in a lush hotel yet thoroughly disappointed at the lack of lovemaking.

I leapt onto the bed and looked up at Omer, grinning. We locked eyes as I kicked off my boots. He dimmed the lights and began to unbutton his shirt. It didn't take long for us to heat up, although neither of us seemed to feel rushed or nervous. Omer and I fit together effortlessly. He was equal parts attentive and assertive, and by the time we were finally naked, I was eager for a ride.

We were brilliant together. Perfect in many ways. Afterwards, I fell asleep easily beside him, bare and buried beneath the cloud of Egyptian cotton, breathing him in. I felt small and soft nestled up against his towering, statuesque form.

Late the next morning, we lazed in bed and he read me the room service menu theatrically. I laughed and remarked that literally anything would sound sexy coming out of his mouth. We bought all the breakfast foods we wanted, and more that we couldn't possibly fit. I thanked him profusely. I wasn't used to this kind of treatment; so far, I hadn't paid for a thing — the dance party, the hotel, our meals, drinks… nothing. I wondered if it was too good to be believed.

. . .

As I was getting to know Omer, I continued seeing Jack on occasion, until I revealed to him that I'd begun seeing other people and we finally took some true space. I had also been awaiting Samuel's return that spring. Between those three connections, there was a lot of deep, complicated love commanding my attention. At one point, I mentioned to Omer honestly that he was the only person I was dating. He told me the same. This wasn't an agreement to be exclusive, but it was true, nonetheless.

INTERNATIONAL

Soon after, Omer pumped the brakes. It was a Monday morning and we were lying in bed discussing plans for the coming weekend. I asked if he wanted me to come over, as I usually did, but he blew me off, seeming rude and aloof. I was stung. He left the room to shower, and I slipped from the house silently, hearing him harmonizing loudly to Bohemian Rhapsody as I closed the front door behind me.

I whined to Tess that I was dealing with another Gemini man-child who couldn't decide what he wanted.

"What is it with you and Gemini's?" she teased.

"I don't know. I'm over it. I wanted something simple and straightforward, and now I'm just confused again. Let's be honest, I have better places to put my energy than dating more confusing people. Right?" She nodded in solidarity.

I chose to let it lie. Later that week, he came over and apologized. He expressed that he could feel his walls going up, and that he wasn't used to my disarming level of comfort and intimacy.

He asked if we could continue dating but remain non-monogamous. The words soothed me. He was nervous about diving into another committed relationship so soon, and hearing these words made me feel safe. I agreed that it would be best to stay open.

I have to admit, I felt conflicted in my desires. I felt a powerful draw toward him (a magnetism which, I'd begun to recognize, was *always* how love felt to me at first). I wanted to deepen our connection and the overlap between our lives. I also didn't want to give up my freedom.

In the past, I had never found a dynamic where that was possible. And it seemed that in Omer's mind, like others I had loved, non-monogamy was spacious and casual, something to be enjoyed early on in a relationship, while monogamy was entangled and intimate, and some inevitable destination.

We decided to take our time.

Samuel, Part III

In late March, much to my delight, Samuel landed back in Portland. I didn't mention this to Omer, but I did let Samuel know that I was dating someone casually. We spent several afternoons together, making the usual rounds: soaking at Everett House, afternoon tea in his kitchen, laughing and teasing beside a sushi track. The ease between us had deepened once again, and it seemed that after two years, we finally had a sense of each other and how we fit together.

I kept him company as he practiced his Spanish on DuoLingo and organized his belongings in preparation for his permanent return to Costa Rica. I brought Moses over to Samuel's farm, as I often did, to feed the chickens and pick flowers while we visited.

"Is he still growing?" my four-year-old child asked me when he noticed Samuel's short stature. I laughed.

"We all are," I answered with a wink.

Even after a couple years of friendship, I still couldn't predict how I might respond to Samuel from one day to the next. We had certain edges that grated on each other. Or rather, I allowed his edges to grate on me. One day, I may feel warmly open to him, and the next day I would be rolling my eyes in irritation at his coyness and arrogance.

One weekend, Samuel invited me to spend the evening with him at a friend's home that he was house sitting. He had just rebuilt their patio and redesigned the backyard. It was stunning. While I felt a flicker of annoyance that he sometimes seemed so intent on being impressive, I was also truly amazed at his craftsmanship and passion for his work. The next morning he was flying back to Costa Rica to teach, so I offered to stay the night and drop him off at the airport.

We wandered around Cully neighborhood and wound up at a little joint called Old Salt, a deli that transformed into a classy supper house in the evenings. Next thing we knew, we were laughing with each other across a candlelit table.

"This place is…. super nice," I said with an approving nod.

"Well, I guess this is a date now," Samuel said with a smile.

"Wow…. we've never actually had a sit down dinner date before," I teased back. "It's usually just flowy pants and nudity with us."

"I'm buying, Becca. Just, don't go crazy and get the ribeye or something," he said, winking at me.

We shared a sweet and lighthearted meal together, arguing about the curing methods for beef tartare and giggling at the server's theatrical mannerisms as he walked away.

Back at the house, I sidled up beside him and gazed at the whimsical, winding garden through the front window. He pointed out a handful of his favorite plants and mused about the landscaping tasks that still needed to be done, lamenting that he wouldn't be here to do them all. Such a workhorse. His attitude constantly reminded me of my father's.

As we pondered the garden, Samuel loaded his pipe with Critical Mass, his favorite strain of cannabis flower. Soon we were pleasantly stoned and retired to the couch to watch stand-up comedy. We argued about whether Jim Gaffigan was annoying or funny, he showed me his hysterical impression of Keanu Reeves as a puppy dog, and we drank steaming mugs of Kava tea.

The banter and touch between us came easy and without hesitation, as it often did. When we were in a room together, it felt as though the external volume was turned way down and a buzzy friction could be felt filling the empty space. Not an uncomfortable friction; it was more like the rubbing of two hands together. This reactivity appeared in our teasing and wrestling and suggestive glances during long walks and car rides. It was a constant current of electricity, which charged us, both our big egos and our tender hearts.

In fact, it was a challenge for us to be in such close proximity and focus on anything other than closing the space between our bodies.

Before long, we paused Netflix and haphazardly pulled the curtains closed. I was craving him — we hadn't yet shared a private moment since he'd returned stateside and my body nearly ached for it. I reminded myself that he was leaving the country soon, as a way of fortifying my own expectations and honoring the moments that we could share. Same time zone, same room, one body... if only for a moment. He was still the ghost ship.

Healing

With Samuel, beneath the teasing and bickering, there was a sensation of total ease. Groundedness. Like walking through the forest. As we felt one another's skin and each turned our attention toward the other, I didn't feel I needed to do anything at all. His pace was slow and methodical. He studied me like a garden. I could truly lie languid and writhing, finding it enough to receive and enjoy whatever impulse he had toward me.

He got off on taking the lead and reading me like sheet music, which freed me to fully let go and lose myself in the experience. *Take a load off*, his body language seemed to say. *Let me take care of you.*

There was no rush between us — we knew from past experience that we could be naked together for hours without the heat waning or exploding. His fire and my water, sustained at their boiling point.

It was one of those nights where I felt amazing in my body to begin with: strong and soft and light all at once. I wanted his hands all over me. The last time we'd had sex was the night I cheated on Jack the previous winter. The memory was heavy in the recesses of my mind. This time was different, though. Now, I could fully let go without any thought of disloyalty in the mix. His body inside mine demanded my full attention — he was so much to accommodate that for both our comfort, I simply had to relax into it.

There was something otherworldly about the expansiveness of our sex, and even the way our two bodies fit together, that invited me to open in ways other partners didn't.

It reminded me of the transformative experience I'd had giving birth. Birth and sex, like my experiences with LSD and mushrooms, were times of deep energetic opening. This time, our deepening trust in each other, plus the assistance of cannabis, made me receptive to a cellular level of unwinding that I may not have otherwise been able to receive.

A moment of wild, unexpected healing found me that night while our bodies were entwined. It was like nothing that had ever happened before. I reclined on the couch with Samuel towering over me, and suddenly he paused. His eyes danced over me. Moving slowly, he slid the hair away from my face. I saw only a profound love and affection in his eyes as he ran his fingertips over the contours of my forehead, my eyebrows, and my lips.

"Te quiero," he said. I love you. I want you.

He wrapped his arms around my waist and pulled me in close, never close enough. Then he cradled the back of my neck in his strong hands and kissed my forehead. He held me there for a long while and continued to move slowly and deliberately inside me.

It was the most nurturing, safe, and deeply loving moment I had shared with another person. I felt a whoosh and with a blink, it was as though energetically, I was someone innocent and he was the protector. Sex was the vehicle, but the emotional experience had nothing to do with sexuality. I was a child and he was a father. He was providing me with an experience of being held, witnessed, treasured and protected that I'd never embodied before. It was a salve on my oldest wounds — of feeling invisible to the first man in my life, my father, the one who was supposed to hold and treasure and protect me.

I felt as though, in this open space, I could rewire old circuits and return to a long-forgotten belief in the existence of deep, safe love. Yes, I had been deeply loved and treasured by many people in my life, but this time, my body, my brain and my soul all felt it long enough to believe it.

I invited all of my senses to join the moment with Samuel. I watched as the dimming firelight danced across his strong form, marveling at the way our smooth skin and dark hair and eyes swirled together into one being. It called to mind a vision of the last moments before sunrise. I was rapt with attention toward the wave of healing crashing over me and the man who was carrying it along and holding space for me.

A tear sprang from my eye. Then several more, gently and freely until my temples were soaked.

"Don't stop," I urged him. He listened.

Healing integrations in my life have looked a lot of ways, but I have to say that night was one for the books.

Later on, when it was dark outside and the tea had grown cold, we wandered lazily to the bedroom and I slept soundly beside Samuel for the first time. Dawn arrived all too quickly with his flight back to Costa Rica.

Surprise

I woke with a start. It took me a moment to orient myself to this new bedroom beside a new person; I'd never spent a whole night with Samuel.

We were sweet with each other when he woke a few minutes later. To me, this morning felt like the end of an era. I thought about the last two years and turned over some of the common threads that had emerged. He had been a catalyst in my life, an unintentional guide toward my own deeper truths. Through our relationship, I'd realized that I was not monogamous and I had come to discover and embrace my tantalizing sexuality. And just last night, I had received a first wave of somatic healing over my deepest wound — the feeling of invisibility.

"Thank you for last night. What a sweet send-off to share," I said to him. Sleepily, he pulled me tight and replied with a quiet "Mmmmm," kissing the top of my head.

On the drive to the airport, he reached over and entwined his hand in mind. He wore the expression of a sad, sleepy puppy.

"Thank you for letting me fuck you," he said with total sincerity in his disarmingly large eyes.

It occurred to me that I would probably want to slap anyone else who made a show of thanking me every time we had sex. But something about his earnestness charmed me.

"I wish we'd had more time together, Becca," he said.

I'd wanted that too, but hadn't allowed myself to feel emotions like longing and regret with him. I had managed my expectations, so I felt satisfied and willing to release him to his dream life in Costa Rica.

We hugged tightly and then he disappeared through the revolving doors. I drove away from the airport with a suspended sense of conclusion. So that was it, then. I had finally bid Samuel farewell after being locked in a lovely, frustrating push-pull dance with him for almost two years.

Falls

An hour later, I got dressed in my hiking clothes and met Omer at his house. We had a date day adventure planned. *(It may be apparent that I'd been spending much of my weekend free time in bed with men. Why? Because I was a hardworking single mama and deserved to feel good, goddamnit!)* The two of us sat sipping coffee at a corner café in the Hollywood district and thumbed through the pages of a well-worn hiking guide.

"So, I've been thinking," Omer said. I glanced up from the book, alarmed. Those were the same words Andrew had used the night he ended our relationship at Radio Room.

He continued.

"I really missed you while I was kiting in the Outer Banks. I was telling my friends and my brother about you. It made me realize that I want to be with you, more than we have been."

I was surprised. My body grew hot. I nodded with a smile.

He reached over and took my hand in his.

"How would you feel if I called you my partner?" he asked.

I smiled. I didn't think. "That would feel good to me," I said.

We beamed at each other and kissed sincerely, nearly knocking our coffees over. I wondered if I needed to mention that I'd been with Samuel the night before. I chose not to. It seemed fitting to me, almost too perfect, that I had just sent my last love away on an airplane, and here was a fresh new love in its place.

There was no conversation about exactly what our new commitment would

INTERNATIONAL

entail, but it seemed those things would work themselves out as they needed to.

That day, Omer and I hiked a spot called Fall Creek Falls. After we'd climbed the forested path for miles, we scrambled up a wet rock face beside a waterfall. We laughed in the spray of the water and turned back when the conditions looked too dicey.

I remember choosing not to be annoyed when Omer made remarks about burning calories and wondering how many miles we'd covered. To me, the forest was a sacred place where I could find respite from human concerns like numbers and waistlines. Hiking in the Gorge had gotten me through the darkest moments in my life. To Omer, nature was an outdoor gym. I wondered if I would be able to share my deep communion with nature alongside him, or whether this was a part of myself I'd rather protect from outside influence.

Motherhood

In some ways, I kept my dating life and family life compartmentalized. I didn't want to form a nuclear family dynamic with someone I was dating. I was fundamentally different from other mothers I knew, and as such I didn't surround myself with friends who had kids. I allowed Moses, who was four, to meet the people I was seeing, but referred to them as my friends or in Jack's case, my "special person." I never implied to Moses that people could only have one special person at a time.

After Jack and I separated, Moses knew that we weren't seeing each other as often, and when he asked, I explained to him that we'd decided not to spend so much time together. I considered what messages I wanted to imprint on him about life relationships, not just in my words but in my way of being. As the saying goes, so much is "caught, not taught." A few things rang true for me.

First, I wanted him to see what an independent, self-determined woman looked like in the context of a hetero-normative world which still worshiped partnership and marriage. I wanted him to see that deep, committed love could take on many forms: friends, housemates, partners, and lovers of all genders. I wanted him to see that parting did not mean one person was wrong and one person was right, but that people have differences and sometimes adjust their relationships to accommodate those differences.

Second, I wanted Moses to understand that, while he was a huge priority in my life, my identity didn't revolve around him. As an only child, with lots of aunts and uncles and doting grandmothers, I wanted him to understand his place as a part of this family ecosystem, as an important and valuable member of our community, and not the center around which we all orbited.

So, I shared with him about the adventures I took while he was with Keaton. I planned adventures to take him on, too: camping, hiking, and road trips. (Jack and I had taken him on his first backpacking trip that summer.) I let him see me as a three dimensional person with passions, desires, responsibilities, and play of my own.

Finally, I wanted him to know that there wasn't one "right way" to be a person in the world. I knew he'd see plenty of traditional models of how to live: get an education, get a good job, make money, find a partner, buy a house, get a dog, paint the fence white, consume entertainment, and live complacently ever after.

I wanted him to witness the joy, struggle, and creative opportunity of forging one's own path. I committed to being honest with him and let him see when I was unsure of myself, considering a decision, choosing an unconventional way forward, failing at my attempts, or breaking social norms. I wanted him to know that adults don't have all the answers, and that it is good to question those who pretend to.

This was a season of life simply packed with opportunities to explore the many ways to be a person in the world, and Omer's presence in my life had set the stage for the bigger, braver, and more fantastical experiences to come.

25
Falling in MDMA

Meeting MDMA

Omer's best friend, Eneas, a charming Greek man he'd met during grad school in Washington D.C., was flying up from San Francisco to join us for a festive weekend at an event called Down The Rabbit Hole. Omer couldn't wait for Eneas and I to meet; they'd been friends for over fifteen years, and he thought we would get along swimmingly.

Down The Rabbit Hole was a huge, counter-cultural Alice in Wonderland themed party for burners, hippies, and the DJs who got them dancing.

I assembled a fantastical, understated Queen of Hearts outfit: a low cut, barely there black swimsuit, topped with a cartoonishly buoyant, high-waisted satin skirt that reached to the floor. It boasted hidden pockets, vertical black and white stripes as thick as my thighs, and crimson red roses the size of dinner plates. I wore red contact lenses and a sheer red bohemian scarf draped whimsically over my head. For good measure I wore my lace-up platform ankle boots. I felt like a hybrid of an alluring little red riding hood and an enchanting queen of hearts. My lean rock climbing limbs and tall frame, combined with soft fabrics and bare skin to form the very picture of mysterious, feminine power.

When I arrived at Omer's, everyone stopped their activity and turned to greet me, grinning. They were primarily middle-aged tech engineers from Europe, so I stood out in the best way. They doted on me as I made the rounds of hugs and introductions. I played along as they twirled me around and examined me with approval, showering me with "oohh's" and "aahh's" and, "Omer! How did you snag this one?"

I sipped LaCroix, watching in amusement as the four men painted each other's faces jovially, tried on top hats, and strung LED lights through their tights and sequined jackets. There was a sweet innocence to the scene of these grown, hetero, six-figure earning men playing dress up and laughing affectionately with one another. Only slightly less innocent was the scene of Omer, dressed as a psychedelic Mad Hatter, as he stood in the kitchen dosing made-to-order capsules for everyone in our group. We had all agreed it was the perfect night to take MDMA together.

Omer, a comfortingly careful soul, sourced only the best and purest drugs. I had never taken MDMA on its own; I had only used a partial dose once during my acid trip in Arizona, so I was very excited to feel it fully, in a festive setting. I knew that I felt safe with these people and had spoken at length with Omer about what to expect, as this was a departure from my previous relationship with psychedelic experiences as a form of medicine.

After a shared moment of intention-setting in the kitchen, we all clinked our tiny capsules together like champagne glasses and down our throats they disappeared. It disrupted the anti-drug paradigms of my youth to be partaking with these healthy, responsible professionals who took their drug use seriously and spoke about it openly. I wondered how many other people like them had been under my radar all these years. *(Turns out, a lot. Just attend Burning Man to see for yourself!)*

I squeezed into a Lyft between Omer and Eneas and we laughed loudly as our driver watched us struggle to fit our tall hats and big skirts inside. By the time the driver parked outside the Crystal Ballroom twenty minutes later, the drugs had begun to kick in. Eneas and I sat melted in the back seat, grinning, luxuriating in the untold wonder of holding hands. Omer laughed and led us out of the car, remarking that he'd known we would get along.

I had explored many altered states by this point in my life, but MDMA was something else entirely. It felt like being submerged in a delightfully warm cloud of plush velvet and soft sunlight. Everything was wildly pleasurable; everything was *THE BEST*. It was better than the best sex I'd ever had, plus the best meal I'd ever had, plus the best joke I'd ever heard. But it was more than a surge of serotonin and dopamine. I also felt open to the world and connected to everyone I saw. Everywhere my eyes landed was a world unto itself, and I felt I could tap into the experience of each Alice, Mad Hatter, and White Rabbit I linked eyes with.

As we came up, we each became very social and interested in how the others in our group were feeling. It was an exaggerated version of my normal baseline: high touch, highly connective, preferring open-hearted conversation rather than bullshit small talk. Omer had disappeared onto the dance floor and I hung back to take it all in. Soon, Eneas was beside me. Our chatting became hugging, which became dancing, which became laughing, which became kissing.

As soon as our lips met, there was no dissuading us. We were captivated. We must have stood on the edge of the dance floor kissing for close to an hour. Some friends found us, laughing too, and I was temporarily pulled out of my oxytocin-fueled indulgence and lured by the music. Omer was lost in a dancing frenzy. He hugged Eneas and I, laughing at our antics, kissing us both, and returned to dancing. Another friend, Javier, inexplicably wore a fuzzy hooded Elmo onesie and wanted long, tight hugs from everyone. We ended up kissing for a while, too.

The scenario was funny for a couple of reasons: First, these were Omer's closest friends, and he didn't seem to mind my intimate proximity to them at all. Or if he did, he didn't show it.

Second, I had met them all very recently and by midnight we were romping around like the best of friends. Omer and I had not discussed boundaries in a while, and in true Becca form, I was exploring the edge by dancing along it and seeing what might happen. Based on his response and his continued openness and warmth toward me, I took it as a sign of one thing: I could be my full, free self with Omer. Our unspoken agreement was one that was open and trusting.

I took to Eneas effortlessly. There was a flawed charm to him that reminded me of many people I had loved over the years. He was pragmatic and lighthearted, with the good looks of a classic film star from the '40s, his olive skin and thick Greek accent softening his deep gravelly voice and barrel laugh. He had a big-eyed, boyish grin and haphazardly swooped back hair that made even his chain smoking seem innocent. He was a good friend, too — he and Omer had known each other for more than a decade and managed to stay connected through frequent phone calls and seasonal kiteboarding trips around the world.

I soon felt overwhelmed by the depth of our sudden connection and excused myself to find some water. I felt fantastic, but a part of me, my "default self," was aware that I was very high. I was witnessing my experience from afar and paused for a moment to check in and assess whether I was behaving in a way that felt safe and aligned to me.

I placed a hand over my heart. It was racing. My jaw was tight, and I searched my pocket for the gum Omer had given me to deal with the "grind" that sometimes accompanies a high. I sat on a bench and drank my water, reminding myself I was probably peaking and wouldn't be this high all night.

I reminded myself that I was safe, and that I could do whatever I needed to in order to manage my experience. I committed to giving myself breaks, listening to my body, and spending time around the people I knew and felt comfortable with.

I went to wander on my own for a moment, feeling a wave of memories from the Crystal Ballroom surge through me. In this very room I had asked Vishnu to Winter Ball as a 16-year-old. I had brought Keaton here to see Death Cab for Cutie as a birthday surprise when he turned 22. Just six months ago, I had paraded half-naked across that very stage with Jack, adorned in powdered gold and latex body paint.

My thoughts were interrupted when I ran into Tommy, Omer's closest Portland friend. Tommy was a chatty Puerto Rican chiropractor, well-versed in rock climbing, acrobatics, and Capoeira arts. And he was a brilliant dancer to boot. I couldn't resist the music. We found a flow as effortlessly as I ever had with a dance partner. It was all hips and turns and low-down grooving. People circled around us and watched. We laughed loudly, wide-eyed and amazed at our synchronicity. It seemed even we were surprised at the flow unfolding before us.

I'm sure I shared some sweet moments with Omer, but that night lives on comically in our collective memory as "The night Becca made out with everyone."

Bump

Around 3:00 am we all began to feel sobriety approaching. We took a Lyft to the after party and we bumped up our levels with a second, smaller dose of MDMA. This propelled Omer and Tommy into another wave of dancing, and Eneas, myself and Javier retired to an ornate tea lounge where we reclined on plush daybeds and chatted lazily between cups of steaming oolong tea.

Every so often, we would wander out to the main foyer where licensed massage therapists, chiropractors and acupuncturists were performing energy work and body work. We especially liked the buffering station, where people could take turns having their bodies buffed by a practitioner wielding a large, fuzzy, vibrating power tool.

Back in the tea lounge, Javier, disguised as a now drowsy, mustached Elmo, drifted off to sleep beside us. I became aware that Omer was away dancing, and Eneas seemed equally aware. Glancing around, I realized I didn't know anyone in the room. Anonymity plays well with MDMA. Eneas pulled me in close and we got hot and heavy in the corner of the tearoom.

"Jesus woman, I am like a prisoner to you!" he whispered.

Only once did his hands begin to wander south, and I promptly moved them away, feeling aware that even under the influence, there were clear lines not to cross. For me, kissing was affectionate and flirtatious, rather than outright foreplay. I could only hold that perspective for myself — how others experienced our connection was up to them. His remarks, similar to other men in the past, caused me to wonder about the seductive powers I held over the male psyche and whether I was working these powers out with care and consciousness.

We dozed off to sleep around sunrise, and later, when we finally emerged from the venue, it felt like waking up groggily from a fantastical dream. The sun was low in the sky and the light was still diffuse and pale. We dragged our heels and zipped our coats up tight, huddling for warmth until our ride arrived to take us home.

Using MDMA has been compared to swiping a credit card on your brain. The surge of chemicals means a subsequent depletion which must be managed later. When we arrived home, we took 5-HTP, an over-the-counter supplement that is a precursor to serotonin. It is intended to help the body manage chemical depletion and avoid the deep, depressive slump that often comes after using MDMA. Again, I marveled at how proactive these recreational drug users were, and I took notes on their practices.

Sauvie Island

After a much-needed and too-short morning nap, we all reconvened on Omer's couches and voted to spend the day soaking up the sun on Sauvie Island, a beachy little patch of land situated north of Portland along the Columbia River. The cars were packed with kiteboarding gear and the forecast looked windy.

First, though, was the necessary post-party meal: a heavy brunch at Radio Room to replenish our bodies after a sleepless night of dancing. I sat on the sunny rooftop beside Omer, facing Tommy and Eneas and we all laughed about the previous night, then moved on to discuss life and love and technology. We were situated next to the very table where Andrew had broken up with me almost two years earlier. I didn't feel the need to mention it.

As I glanced over the menu, I remembered the entire year in which I avoided driving down Alberta street, as it was too charged with the memory of Andrew. Now though, I felt nothing. It was an effort to conjure the memory of emotional turmoil at all.

I noticed how I felt here and now. The contrast between past and present was dramatic.

Omer and his best friends simply adored and embraced me. I recalled the way I had felt beside Andrew, self-protective and hesitant to speak. Not only had my chosen company changed, but I had changed, too. Now, I was surrounded by educated, big mouthed men and I effortlessly held my own space and occupied my own seat at the table. In the space of one night, Omer's friends had become "our friends."

Feminist as I was, though, I still let Omer pay for my food, as he always did. I hadn't paid for much of anything since we met, beyond the token coffee date here and there. It softened my hard edges to receive his support in this way — I'd never been in a relationship with someone who was financially stable and generous. I felt cared for, free from pressure, and protected by him. It was a new experience that challenged me at times, but I welcomed it and wondered whether it was something I could relax into.

When we made it to Sauvie Island, it was a blindingly bright and windy afternoon. Omer gave me an introductory kite lesson on the beach with a small boomer kite and praised my natural abilities.

"You'll be on the water by summer," he said like an adoring father.

He had been intent on teaching me to kiteboard since before we met, mentioning it during our first conversation on the dating app. I was less convinced; as a weak swimmer and only newly comfortable with outdoor sports, it seemed like a big jump to be out on the river playing with the wind and waves, on a board, with a 12-meter kite attached to me by rope and harness, and no flotation device in sight.

I don't recall him ever asking me directly if I wanted to learn, but it was such a huge part of his life that it felt like an unspoken part of the agreement. His free time and vacations mostly revolved around the sport. To be with Omer was to be a kiteboarder. It helped that I love learning and I can't resist new challenges. I was generally willing to lean into my discomfort, to dance on the edge of my abilities and stay present rather than self-sabotaging. That was the deal I had made with the Universe, at least. Plus, kiting looked fucking fun.

Later, I sat on the dunes chatting with a mutual girlfriend who had just come

FALLING IN MDMA

in from the water. I roughhoused with our friend's drowsy puppy dog while we chatted about love and unconventional motherhood. We both had sons about the same age and held similar lifestyles. We were single moms, free on the weekends, and occasional partiers, who still took our roles as mothers very seriously. Yet, neither of us ascribed to the traditional script of martyrdom and loss of identity that our culture venerates as good motherhood. It was refreshing to speak on these topics with her.

She asked me about Omer. I glanced over at him. He stood near the shore, at ease, as though he was surveying his tiny empire. I looked out at our friends dappling the water, gliding back and forth in the breeze like small specks beneath giant butterfly wings.

"Things are good. Really good," I told her, grinning. I stood to brush the sand from my legs.

"Though I haven't really had a moment alone with him this weekend. I'll be back," I said, leaving. I jogged over and wrapped my arms around him from behind, burying my face in his back.

"Hey," I said.

He pulled me around beside him.

"Hey honey," he smiled, wrapping me in both arms. "What a beautiful day."

We spoke for a moment about the wind conditions and how lucky we were to have friends like these. We giggled as Eneas attempted a complicated flip, which quickly became a harsh-looking wipeout on the water. He was fine.

Omer turned to face me. "I want to tell you something."

"What is it?" I looked up at him. His sunglasses were obscuring his face. "Hang on, can you take those off? I feel like there's a barrier between us."

"Oh. Right," he smiled and removed his glasses. "Remember the other night, when you told me you were falling for me?"

"Oh, I remember…" I smirked. "I felt like I made you uncomfortable. I've got to stop pouring my feelings out after sex when I'm all juiced up and open hearted…"

He stopped me.

"No, you don't need to stop. I'm sorry for not responding. You know I have been guarded."

I stood silently and waited for him to continue.

"I am falling in love with you, too," he told me.

Spring

Spring was a fun and hopeful time. Omer and I brought a lot of joy into each other's lives. In May, I decided to have him meet Moses.

We'd been together consistently for three months and we were in a place that felt steady. We were still non-monogamous and not speaking on it often, but partners none-the-less. I knew he'd had one long-term relationship with a single mother in the past and I felt confident that having him and Moses meet would enrich the connection without adding pressure to it. I was excited for the two most important people in my life to know each other.

We played together at Sauvie Island, that same beach where Omer had confessed his love to me two months earlier. I set up a picnic while they ran along the beach and splashed their feet in the water. Moses, usually so quiet and reserved, was laughing and shouting, chasing Omer with a piece of driftwood. Omer had that effect on people — he made them feel safe enough to come out of their shell.

They raced each other down the shore and Moses proclaimed that Omer deserved a special "tropee" (trophy) for winning. On the drive home, I asked Moses if he had fun.

"I had fun with the sticks," Moses said. I nodded. "Ooh! Mom!" he added. "Maybe after we're done living at this house, we can live at Omer's house!" he said innocently.

I didn't know how best to respond. A tear sprang to my eye. I thought of Moses' last bond with Jack and wanted to do right by him this time around. Jack and I were still amicable, and I always spoke well of him to Moses. (This has always felt like an important part of dating as a parent, honoring the connections Moses makes with my partners and moving through transitions with love and respect.) I imagined Moses and Omer forming a bond — what would that be like? It was a lot to consider. I looked back at him.

"Oh yeah? You think so?" I replied simply.

He nodded and stared out the window at the passing river, chewing on his dried mango.

It felt to me like Moses had sensed the rightness of the relationship before either Omer or myself were prepared to admit it.

A week later, Omer and I were wandering the produce section of the local co-op.

"So, I got tickets for Beloved," he said. "The music festival."

"Sweet." I hesitated. "Wait... I'm wondering whether you're telling me to brag, or whether this is a subtle invitation."

"Neither," he said coyly. "I think we can decide when we get closer, but just know that I have two tickets."

"Okay, then," I said, swatting him playfully.

"Oh, also, I got tickets to SOAK," he continued matter-of-factly.

"The Oregon Burn? Those are hard to get. I have the same question as before. Omer, why are you sharing this with me?" I set a bundle of bananas into his shopping basket and looked up at him.

"Well, it has crossed my mind that it would be fun for us to go. I bet we'd have a great time. But also, festivals can be really challenging for couples. I'm not sure I want to put us in that scenario quite yet. As you know, I haven't had the best experience in those situations…" He trailed off.

I considered his background. Omer had endured a very heart-wrenching, in-your-face break up while he was at Burning Man the previous fall. It was a messy and painful time that he wanted to forget, and he and I had met only a few months afterwards.

He once told me that the times we spent together in those early months brought him happiness in an otherwise dark time. I chose not to read that as a red flag, as a sign of a rebound or potentially misplaced attachment. I wanted to be a bright spot for him. I wanted him to experience the love that he clearly deserved. I had learned from a young age that I had an ability to bring brightness to others — I'd seen this quality come through with my own mother, with friends, and now with Omer. I wasn't scared by depression or darkness. I was able to meet people in it and shine a gentle light.

I thought about how Omer's 39th birthday was approaching. *What could I give the man who already had everything?* He was thinking about buying himself a Les Paul guitar that he'd been dreaming about for years. I couldn't give him something material. I didn't want to give him something sexual (even though that did cross my mind). I wanted to give him something meaningful.

I sat on my deck overlooking our big garden while Moses dug in the sand box. I watched the last of the morning's rain sparkle on the tips of tree branches. I grabbed my guitar, and a song poured out of me without excess thought. It was a spacious and melodic song in the key of E. I tucked the lyrics away and decided I would know the right moment to share them with him.

Past Haunting

An ongoing struggle in my relationship with Omer was the question of how to deal with the pasts that neither of us were totally ready to release.

It seemed there was a great deal of relational residue that neither Omer or myself had allowed the space and time to sort through. It didn't help that Andrew lived in our neighborhood too, and we'd run into him in the grocery store and the climbing gym every so often. Even though I had moved on, the sight of him always made my heart race and our brief exchanges were awkward and forced.

Omer was still holding deep, bitter hurt from Nora, the ex who had ended their three-year relationship at Burning Man while in the arms of another. But as we grew closer, layers of good seemed to cover over the cracked foundation of his heart and the unstable foundation of mine. He was burying Nora beneath our life and love and pretending she had never existed. We sometimes ran into her around town, and it was often so upsetting to Omer that the encounters would throw off the course of our days and darken his mood beyond repair.

While I had emotionally let go of Andrew and Jack, I had not moved on from Samuel.

When I drove him to the PDX airport, I had thought I'd sent him off for good and truly let him go. But every few weeks, his name would appear in my WhatsApp with a photo of a glistening rainforest flower set against the blue Costa Rica mountain sky, and I felt pulled in his direction once again.

In a recent message, he'd told me that he would be returning for a couple of summer months before the "big move" as he called it. He had chosen to move in phases, and now that he was done teaching his spring course, he wanted to enjoy one last Portland summer. I felt the desire, as I always had, to stay open to our connection.

Party Life

Omer began inviting me to more and more events as spring marched toward summer. It seemed that every weekend I was staying out into the wee hours of morning, dancing in event halls and relying on small doses of mushrooms or cocaine to fuel the habit. My roommates noted their surprise at the shift.

"I haven't been seeing you much on the weekends," Tess said one evening, while Moses slept and we lounged on the living room floor by the fire. She and I used to take Moses to the farmer's market every Saturday morning, but that habit had fallen to the wayside with my new social circle and my late Friday nights.

"I never knew you were that into partying," she added.

"I'm not," I replied. "Omer definitely is, though… and I kind of feel like I'm getting sucked into his world. I know I should be paying closer attention. I just can't keep up with those guys," I admitted.

"You have a lot more responsibilities than he does, Becs. You have Moses, school, work… your whole life. It's good to keep an eye on all that," she gently reminded me.

"You're right," I looked over at her. "Ugh, you're right."

Matt chimed in from the kitchen.

"What's this guy's deal, anyway? Isn't he like, way older and loaded?" he asked, the criticism clear in his voice.

I looked at him, incredulous. "That's an exaggeration."

"Well, from the outside it kind of seems like you're bringing the sex and he's bringing the drugs and money," he shrugged.

I felt judged.

"Wow! You have no idea what you're talking about, Matt. You barely even know him. Maybe you could actually spend some time with us before passing judgments." I felt self-conscious hearing Matt's assessment, as though I was under an interrogation light and didn't actually know what the truth was.

East West

Matt and Tess's feedback reminded me to stay grounded in my life, even while falling fast in love and exploring worlds unknown. So that spring, shortly after I completed my permaculture design certification, I enrolled in massage school and my whole life rhythm changed dramatically to accommodate student life. I had an insatiable craving to learn and expand my scope of knowledge and abilities. I felt drawn to bodywork after meeting several massage therapists who had aided in my own healing.

Quitting my part time job as a nanny, I took on more weekend shifts as a caregiver on top of my communications job at the hemp farm. I enrolled Moses in a local preschool. He had an awful time with the transition, crying and wailing during drop-off every single day for a month. I felt like an asshole parent.

On the long tram rides to the college, I wondered whether I was doing the right thing. I wondered how I was going to keep everyone in my life happy — *Would Omer be content to meet me for lunch between classes and hang out with me after my long shifts on the weekends? Would Moses have enough time with me when I sometimes couldn't even get him from daycare until 5:00 pm? How many hours would I have to work in order to afford all this? How and when would I find unstructured time alone to recharge? When would I study? Would this all be worth it in the end?*

I wasn't sure.

Calvin

On the day of college orientation, I met Calvin, a tall and sun-kissed man of few words. I stood behind him in line for headshots, and taking him in, I immediately had the sensation of having found "my people" as they say. As we chatted in line, I gathered that he lived in the Gorge and had worked at the Pendleton wool factory. He was into exploring nature, surfing, and cultivating mushrooms.

His long golden hair and crystalline eyes contrasted surprisingly with the pair of beat up Crocs he wore almost every day. He could have been a model, except that he gave zero shits about presentation. We passed each other in the hall once or twice and he always caught my eye, but otherwise we were in separate worlds. I smirked and thought to myself that only a man that attractive could get away with wearing Crocs.

I didn't know then that he'd become my acro-yoga partner and so much more: he'd be the man to teach me to Salsa dance, swim in fast waters, and show me what connection free from attachment could look like.

FALLING IN MDMA **345**

26
Soak

Into the Burn World

Omer and I had been dating for three very concentrated months. I had just started massage school and was experiencing massive transitions in almost every area of my life. I rarely saw my friends other than Tess, who I lived with, and others who I naturally crossed paths with at the farmer's market. Yet Omer and I were finding ways to fit together. As a team lead for engineers, Omer often worked from home, which was near my school. He would pick me up for lunch breaks between classes and have study-work sessions with me on the weekends.

Some evenings, he would meet Moses and I at the climbing gym for a bouldering session and take us out to eat afterwards. Other times, he'd surprise us at the midweek farmer's market where I ran the hemp farm's booth, slinging organic CBD products while playing Legos with Moses and nibbling on vegan chocolates from the adjacent vendor. I had so much going on. Omer took it in stride; Moses did, too.

I felt that the added structure and demands on my life would safeguard me from diving too deep into Omer's world, but I was only partially right.

• • •

It was very difficult to get tickets to the regional Burn, called SOAK, though not as hard as getting tickets to actual Burning Man. Omer had invited me to attend with him less than a week after bringing it up in the grocery store. I felt excited to go. As a low-key person, I wasn't sure how I'd feel camping around thousands of energetic festival-goers for a whole weekend, but I was curious about the new experience and thrilled to have the quality time with Omer.

These were the kind of big, uncharted experiences I had craved while living in the birdcage I'd made of my marriage. I hadn't taken a significant trip since my rafting adventure with Jack the summer before. While I was relieved to have a break from all the responsibility of daily life and cut loose in the woods, I also realized I was compartmentalizing my life in a way that might not be sustainable in the long run.

To avoid messing with our work/life schedules, we decided to go Friday night through Sunday night. Omer didn't have any friends going and I certainly didn't either. However, I did know that Jack would be attending. Recently, he'd gotten more involved in the poly/kink community and was part of That Fucking Camp, the folks who hosted consent education classes at the ornate "Orgy Dome" which was constructed every year at the top of the hill.

I texted Jack to let him know I'd be there. At first, he was irritated. He was leaning fully into his new life and the last thing he wanted was to be faced with the woman who broke his heart, attending with a new flame, no less. We agreed to meet up and say hello, but to otherwise give each other space.

Those 48 hours at the Burn felt like a lifetime of their own. It was like entering another world, deep in the countryside of the Columbia River Gorge. Most of the attire we brought came from my ever-growing costume box and Omer's basement full of festival garb coated with Burning Man playa dust. *("Playa" is the inexplicable term for the festival zone where the annual event takes place.)*

Arrival

When we arrived, I was coaxed out of the car by greeters to ring the "Virgin Bell" for first timers. Everyone cheered theatrically. We had no designated camp, but within minutes we were adopted by a crew of friendly characters into a camp called "Grandma's House," which featured a fully decked-out cabin with furniture, décor, and a resident granny offering butterscotch candies and storytime snuggles.

We set up camp in the dimming sunlight between two trees. By dark, our tiny home was established and we were ready to cut loose.

Nestled into a valley with mountainous cliffs on several sides, the technicolor field of stages and art installations stood out like an alien landscape. Voices of laughter and rowdy shenanigans mingled with wompy beats coming from the stages throughout the rolling acreage. One cool principle of Burning Man is the decentralization. It's totally citizen-run, so registered camps set up activities, entertainment and offerings for the crowds.

The Gorge gets very cold at night, so we bundled up in fur coats and warm boots as we took our first tour of the place. We had split a hit of acid and wandered aimlessly, waiting for it to kick in.

Having felt the effects of LSD before, I was confident in sharing the experience with Omer. At the same time, I felt aware that I was partaking in an important substance that had been deeply meaningful to me in the past. I wondered whether I was losing respect for these powerful agents, the further I stepped into festival culture. I didn't see anyone honoring them as medicine the way I'd been taught.

> *Was it okay for me to enjoy recreational drugs for their light and playful effects as much as their healing benefits?*
>
> *Was it possible that lightness and play were healing effects?*
>
> *How did I feel about the way people around me were relating to these substances?*

People moved about, laughing and chattering in small pods, bundled with furs and outlandish costumes. I noticed a pervasive theme of cultural appropriation, which is common at events like this. I didn't see anything as blatant as a white woman wearing a Native American headdress, for example, but I did see countless people donning tribal-style face paint and jewels, kimonos, traditional Indian and African textiles, and an unending sea of printed harem pants on the dance floor.

There seemed to be a lack of awareness, or an unwillingness to acknowledge this behavior as problematic. Once or twice when I mentioned it, I was met with dismissal by my peers and told that folks here were "good people" with "good intentions." What I heard was: *Don't ruin the fun.* I found this response unsettling.

We found our way to a space-age themed stage and I soon noticed a familiar lit-up cowboy hat across the dance floor. I had followed it like a beacon during last summer's World Naked Bike Ride. It was Jack.

He was twirling with someone in a hilarious cow costume. The LSD was just beginning to kick in, washing a golden shimmer over the whole scene, and I wasn't inclined to greet him in this altered state.

I wordlessly slipped back toward the path, and Omer followed.

Wanderer

One thing I've learned is that psychedelics give me the urge to wander. They bring out my need for complete agency and it often becomes challenging to collaborate on decisions and activities. We agreed to surrender to the night: we would wander freely for a while, letting the LSD guide the adventure, and reconvene at a chosen meeting place if we (inevitably) became separated. Not five minutes later, I turned to point out an installation to Omer and couldn't see him in the dark, technicolor crowd. I spent most of the night wandering around dancing and looking at art comfortably, feeling Omer's warm and protective presence around me, even in his absence.

I made several friends while I explored. One petite, gregarious woman spotted me and decided instantly that we were going to be friends. She and her crew became our festival mates for the rest of the weekend. Omer was unsurprised when I returned to our meeting place in the wee hours of the morning and exclaimed, "Babe! I made us some friends!"

We spent the next morning naked together in the tent until the sun was nearly overhead. I relaxed there for a long time, staring at my inverted silhouette in Omer's clear eyes and marveling at the wild way my life had unfolded. My son was hours away in the care of his father. I was deep in the Gorge, exhausted, taking delightfully strange drugs and dancing all night with the man I loved, plus a whole field's worth of potential friends. There was no agenda but silliness, open-mindedness, and connection. It was more freedom than I'd realized was possible in adulthood.

Another layer of my previous worldview had sloughed off. Again, life was showing me that there was always *more* possible: more ways to live, to love, to connect, to be a thoughtful and present human being. I wished Omer could know what a gift he had given me by inviting me in. I wondered if I was at risk of getting lost in the expanse of this bizarre, wonderful world.

Morning at SOAK was sunny and serene. Partiers were generally sleepy and easygoing, and I had woken up feeling groggy, with the afterglow of LSD encouraging me to move slowly and be gentle with myself and Omer. Our little camp site was a simple and well-organized home base, complete with a hammock, a guitar, and two coolers full of fresh food, kombucha, and coconut water. I had offered to be in charge of meals since Omer had bought the tickets. We enjoyed Greek yogurt with fruit and granola, homemade curry, and an unending supply of hippie-dippie snack bars.

"Wow, honey. I'm just imagining if I had food this good on the Playa," he said.

"Well, that's a good sign. I'm glad you like it. Not sure I'll ever go to Burning Man though….let's just take this one festival at a time," I winked at him.

The daytime festival environment was like a hilarious dream. We wandered through workshops like "Design Your Own Recycled Space Suit" and "Twerking 101."

That afternoon we passed by the Orgy Dome and I spotted Jack again. I waved. He greeted us warmly and we all shared an easy and light conversation outside the camp. Many hugs were exchanged. There was one awkward moment when a friendly, flamboyant stranger emerged from the porta-potties and began swooning over a shirtless Jack.

"Well look at you, mister cowboy!" he exclaimed. He turned to me. "Quite a catch you've got there, missy!"

I debated whether to correct him, but I thought that pointing out that Jack was my ex and Omer was my partner would make the scene unnecessarily awkward. We all laughed it off and moved on.

Omer noticed a sign for a "Ten Hand Erotic Massage" workshop on Sunday and we made it our imperative to show up for it.

Saturday night was the temple burn. Crews had built a full-size, ornate wooden temple where visitors could leave notes of love, loss, pain, hope and devotion, and then the crowd of thousands would surround it and watch it go up in flames. I don't remember much from the night; time seemed to change and it both went on forever and also disappeared in a flash. I do remember burying myself in a fuzzy pile of new friends beneath a color-shifting art installation inside a room of mirrors.

It was there that I took a Whip-It for my first and only time, which was a strange experience. I was curled up in the cuddle puddle beside Omer and already rolling hard with the amount of MDMA and mushrooms in my system. John, a yogi friend dressed as a sassy train conductor, was fiddling with a metal whipped cream canister.

"Alright, who wants one?" he asked. I watched hesitantly, with no idea what was about to happen. I felt like a teen again, learning about drugs on the spot. It had been a long time since I felt so in the dark about a party substance. I turned to Omer.

"What is it?" I asked him.

"It's nitrous oxide. A Whip-It," he said. He turned to the group. "Last time I took one I fell flat on my back. Probably got a concussion."

"What?! Why would someone do that?" I asked him.

"Because it gets you high," he laughed. "It's a dissociative. It's hard to describe… it only lasts a few seconds, but it's safe. It's the same stuff they use in dentist offices," he explained.

I had heard this before, that "laughing gas" used to be a substance enjoyed at high society parties as far back as the 18th century. But I had no way of confirming my hunch in real-time. I already knew from research and personal experience that MDMA and psilocybin played well together, a term known as "hippie flipping," and around me, I saw people mixing all manner of more questionable drug cocktails inside their bodies, so I was inclined to trust Omer.

"Oh," I said.

I watched as they passed the canister from person to person. One after another, they sucked air through the contraption and proceeded to have theatrical reactions, laughing hysterically and waving their arms and legs toward the sky.

I watched as Omer inhaled and lost himself in the euphoria. We all laughed too. It was a wild and disorderly affair. John held it out to me, "Want one, Becca?" he asked. I turned to Omer.

"Should I?" I turned to address everyone. "I'm a mom. So, I'm pretty risk averse." They chuckled with me.

"It's up to you," Omer answered with a shrug.

I thought for a moment.

"Alright, why not," I answered.

I was too curious to refuse. It was a departure from my usual planned and well-informed drug consumption. I had John guide me through the breathing technique. What happened next was a strange and indescribable rush. I felt like I was in a chaotic circus. I inhaled the gas and held my breath for a few seconds. Then, everything became drastically distorted. I was pulled deep into my body and though I could see, I was witnessing the scene from far, far away, as if through a distant portal. It was much akin to the "sunken place" in Jordan Peele's movie *Get Out*.

Through my distant eyes I saw my own feet kicking above me and heard distant hysterical laughter, including my own voice. The faces surrounding my field of view were at once friendly and grotesque.

A few moments later, I was lifted out of the sunken place and back into the mirrored cuddle room of color and chaos.

"So?" Omer asked.

"...Whoa." I said.

A short while later, I excused myself from the crowded tent and wandered off on my own. I wasn't totally keen on the vibe of these folks, and the mushrooms were making me extra sensitive to peoples' energies. I wasn't up for complex new people; I wanted to feel safe.

Heart

I wandered around on my own for a couple of hours. There were moments when I felt very lonely and wanted to connect with someone — MDMA is a highly connective drug, and rolling while alone can be very strange. I continuously nestled my cheek into the large fur blanket I was wearing as an extra coat.

Other moments, I was relieved to feel anonymous. I twirled around a pole on a stripper platform, I met dozens of new people, and I felt open to the world. Finally, I hung around by a flaming installation at the Tektonic camp for a time, as the night was becoming cold and the fire made me feel safe in the dark. I decided to set out and find Omer.

I began walking across the field and not half a minute later, there he was — twenty yards away and gliding toward me with arms swung open. He looked like a beacon — tall and strong, draped in fur and face paint and an inviting demeanor. We both grinned. As I approached, I felt giddy and proud to be with him. He was truly a good, safe and lovely soul. The embrace when we reached one another felt like we'd been apart for years. He wrapped his coat around me and we settled into a delightful and emotionally charged hug. We didn't speak for a minute. My heart was so incredibly open and it had been looking for a safe place to land.

"How are you, honey? What have you been up to?" he asked.

"I'm good. I've been… I don't know. Around. Doing stuff… wandering," I smiled. "It doesn't matter. How are you?"

"I'm good. I've been staying warm dancing. I'm feeling great. I was missing you, though," he answered.

"I know! I was just setting out to find you and then… well, here we are!" I said.

He stared at me and smiled. I stared back, pleased at the way the amber firelight flickered on his cheekbones.

"There's so much I want to say to you," he said.

I listened intently. "Like what?"

"Ahh. I don't know if I have the words. Let me try." He took my face in his hands and exhaled deeply. "Hmmm. Wow. You are so good."

I rolled my eyes at him, deflecting the pure sincerity in his stare. I felt insanely vulnerable as the object of his focus and adoration.

"No. Listen to me." He leaned in even closer. "You. Are. So. Good. I've been around the block. I know a lot of people. And you have the biggest heart of anyone I've ever met. You are filled with more love than you know what to do with. You could probably fall in love with every person at this festival and still have more."

I blinked back tears. His words rang true. It was overwhelming to feel so deeply, simply witnessed by someone with whom I was trying to be my whole and unfiltered self. I felt understood in a way I hadn't before.

"No one's ever said that to me," I replied. "I mean... I *do* feel so much love, sometimes more than I know what to do with..." I looked away, feeling exposed beneath his unwavering gaze. "But, I don't always believe I am *good*."

"No one's ever told you how big and wonderful your heart is? How can that be? It's the first thing I saw when I met you," he proclaimed.

"I feel like I've spent my life trying to change and become good," I said.

As a steady stream of tears came, I let them fall freely. He stood with me, looking into my eyes and wiping my tears with his fingertips.

"I love you so much," I told him earnestly. "Thank you for seeing me as I am and loving me. I want to feel free like this with you. I want to be good. I want to grow this."

I motioned my hand between his heart and mine.

"Well you've got me, honey," he said.

There was something in his voice during our exchange that I began to notice every time we used drugs together. It sounded higher than usual: a lighter, brighter, almost constricted quality. Over time, I began to recognize that it meant a great opening was happening, but we were accessing depths of

SOAK **353**

intimacy that would almost certainly be out of reach in times of sobriety.

We must have stood in that field together for over an hour. We alternated between hugging for long stretches of time, staring wordlessly into each other's misty eyes and musing about the lucky circumstances that led to our meeting. In that moment, I truly felt as though I'd found my person.

Finally! A partner with whom I could be fully honest, fully myself, for the long haul. I didn't have to sacrifice my affections or connections with others — he was like a steady tree that I could fly out of and return home to, over and over again. For a moment, I feared he had no idea what he was getting into.

This fear diminished when I remembered how it felt when he looked at me: he trusted me. He saw a good, big hearted, powerful person. And I saw the same in him.

"Well... wanna dance about it?" I eventually asked, wiping my eyes.

The Dome

We laughed and tromped out of the field to carry on with our night. Morning was coming fast. On our way up the hill we saw the Orgy Dome and discussed going in. Omer had never been in a place like that. I hadn't either, but I'd been on camera enough times with Jack and fooled around at erotic balls so blatantly that I felt unabashed about being seen.

"Why don't we just check it out, and then we can decide what we're comfortable with? I'll let you take the lead," I suggested.

Inside the first lobby, the door staff offered us condoms and lube and gave us a no-nonsense discussion about the rules of engagement. Each bed had fresh sheets; there were adjustable signs above each mattress which read "open" and "closed," used to indicate whether or not we were open to company.

There was nothing especially shocking happening inside. Perhaps eight beds were arranged throughout the circular space, and a suspended net provided an upper level for folks who wanted a bird's eye view of the action. I noticed two men on a couch together in the middle of some very fun looking sex. I realized I knew one of them — he was the person who invited us to camp at Grandma's House. I smiled at the realization, and how normal it all seemed to me. There were a few other couples in various states between undress and explicit fucking. Omer and I cuddled up in a quiet corner.

We were relatively mellow. We did end up having sex in the Orgy Dome, but it was more because we could, almost felt we *should*, than anything else.

The environment didn't especially turn either of us on, and while I was mostly comfortable, I was very aware that it was his first time in an exhibitionist setting, so I was preoccupied with making sure he felt at ease and had a positive, low-pressure experience.

Now, if there had been a rowdy, attentive audience watching, that might have been something different for me. I found over time that it was the act of display itself that turned me on.

We emerged from the dome smiling, and off in the distance Omer heard a DJ he wanted to check out. I was ready to rest, so we parted ways and I took a long, meandering route back toward camp.

I rarely felt unsafe spending time alone while tripping or wandering through the paths at night. I had discovered that I trusted individuals who were exploring altered states of consciousness much more than I trusted people who were inebriated with alcohol. The culture here seemed friendly and mutually supportive, and the unspoken community agreement was that everyone treat one another with respect, look out for each other, and lend a hand whenever possible.

Strangers would smile and say hello as we passed. I never got catcalled and rarely received unwanted advances. Every so often, an overly friendly man would try to engage with me, and I would remind myself of the "Two Foot Rule: If you don't feel good about something, use your two feet and carry yourself elsewhere." This isn't to say consent violations and harmful incidents don't happen in these settings — in fact, festival culture can be rife with abuses that go unaddressed, but it was not something I was privy to at the time.

Sunday Morning

I finally made it back to our empty tent sometime in the deep dark of early morning. The sun was still a little ways off, so I slept soundly for a couple of hours, sprawled out on our inflatable mattress.

When I woke to check the time, I had received a WhatsApp message from Samuel.

"Thinking about you," he said, adding a heart for effect. He was online. I wrote back.

"Hey, Samuel :)" I wrote.

"How are you, B? It's been a while."

"I'm good. I'm at SOAK this weekend, so… festive, happy Molly vibes over here, you know."

"Mmm… sounds amazing, I wish I could be there with you. I miss you."

I snapped a fully nude photo of myself, staring straight into the camera with my wildly blissful eyes. I thought for a moment, but chose not to send it, given my altered state.

"I miss you, too," I replied. "When will you be back stateside?"

"In July," he wrote. "Will I see you at Beloved?"

I grinned at the thought.

"Of course! Can we spend some time together?"

"Yes. I can't wait to see you. I have to go now. I'm on the mountain. But I will think of you. Te quiero."

"Te quiero tambien."

I put my phone away, got dressed, and left camp. Jack had invited me to check out his new bus, which he'd been in the process of converting for many months. This seemed like an ideal time to check it out without having to explain my outing to Omer. I headed straight back up the hill toward That Fucking Camp in search of Jack. When I wandered in, the smell of bacon wafted through the small crowd of sleepy, glittery residents sipping strong coffee. I asked around for Jack and one woman told me he was alone in his bus.

I knocked, thinking that my being there could either be a really nice surprise or an awkward mistake.

"Well, hello there!" he said with a chuckle. "Would you like to come in?"

I nodded. We settled down inside his bus and it felt like old times, except for the weighted distance between our two bodies as we sat formally beside each other. Usually, close proximity meant touch and affection, mindless hands wandering over rough skin.

Our conversation was light and warm. Looking around, I complimented his bus retrofit. He complimented my new haircut, running his hand over the bare nape of my neck warmly. I told him I'd taken MDMA the night before, and he told me he was still floating on mushrooms.

"Do you want to cuddle for a few minutes?" I asked him with a laugh. A full circle moment: Jack and I, attempting to be friendly and platonic, and me attempting to get closer.

"... Yup. Course I do. Let's cuddle," he replied.

We plopped onto his bed and within moments we were grinding on each other, rolling around with abandon and tearing at each other's clothes in a way that hearkened back to our earliest days. We were trying not to kiss, breathing hard into each other's ears and biting each other's necks. The tension felt equally powerful for both of us. It felt naughty, secretive, to be here with him, and yet I didn't want to take it further.

If there was one thing I'd learned, it's that an impulsive pleasure is rarely worth the cost of betraying an agreement. Once we finally came up for air, we laughed together. I shook my head rapidly, as if to shake the lust free.

"Whoo," I said with a wide-eyed grin. "Just like old times."

"Ha, dang Becca," he said. He took hold of both my hips and squeezed hard. "Any chance you and Omer are into a three-way? We can meet at the dome..." he said with a wink.

"Well, there's a mental image I can enjoy for a while," I laughed. "Sounds like a shit show that would *almost* be worth it!"

We hugged and he gave me a pat on the bum on my way out of the bus. I felt pulled in so many directions. This deep love and commitment to Omer, this international connection with Samuel, this warmth and history with Jack. I wanted it all. Usually, I could keep it controlled. But with my guard lowered, enabled by MDMA, I felt like water poured out onto stone, slipping off in all directions and letting gravity decide.

When I returned to camp, I heard Omer snoring in the tent and could tell by the haphazard way he had crawled into bed that he'd had a wild night. Soon he woke up. We lounged around camp and shared stories from our evening. I admitted I'd made out with Jack a little bit. He laughed.

"Oh, honey," he said in a teasing tone, unbothered. Then I told him Jack had solicited us for a three-way. That really got him laughing.

"That depends. How is he in bed?" he asked. I waved him off.

After breakfast, Omer and I sat in our camping chairs and swooned over the night we'd had. I told Omer I had a birthday present for him that I wanted to share early.

As I tuned his small travel guitar, I made several disclaimers about not having performed in quite a while. He shushed my fussing and told me to just let out my beautiful voice already. So I did.

Soft harmonic notes rang out in the key of E.

> *He is the pause in the chaos*
> *The sun casting shadows in late July*
> *He is crashing waves upon a beach*
> *The heat before arrival*
> *The sweetness of sleep*
>
> *How can it be?*
> *He's flown the world and crossed the sea*
> *How can it be?*
> *Still so full of mystery*
> *So many things at once to me*
>
> *How does he stay kind*
> *In a world so spiteful?*
> *How does he stay young*
> *In a world so bitter?*
> *There's magic in his eyes*
> *I'd be a fool to pass it by*
> *See how love, it multiplies*
>
> *How can it be?*
> *To feel at home and flying free*
> *How can it be?*
> *Baby we could be the moon and sea…*

I let the end ring out, and finally we grew silent.

His eyes glistened, brimming, as he reached over to set the guitar down and pull me in for an embrace. A sweet older lady from the camp next to ours popped her head out of a tent.

"Was that you singing, honey? My, you have a beautiful voice!" she exclaimed. I grinned.

"She wrote the song, too," Omer replied.

The two of us sat knee to knee, facing each other in our humble camping chairs for a calm, quiet while. Our locked eyes might normally have unnerved me, except that I was so intimately entwined with him in that moment that I couldn't access a thread of our separateness. I had found my person. He wiped a tear from one eye.

"Thank you honey," he said. "No one's ever done something so beautiful for me. Please record that. I want to listen to it over and over." I bristled at the thought, perfectionist as I am, but agreed to do so. He tossed his head back, relaxed, and stared up at the sky. I ate my granola without a care in the world. Then he looked straight back at me.

"What is your plan for when your lease is up? It ends in October, right?"

"Yeah, October. I don't know yet… I know I need to be closer to Portland for school, I can't keep commuting like this," I said.

He stared at me, lips slightly parted, as if he was holding back from speaking.

"…. Why do you ask?" I stared back at him.

"I mean, I do have an extra room…" He shrugged nonchalantly. I leaned in closer.

"Don't tease me like that, Omer. Are you saying what I think you're saying?"

"It's crazy, I know," he said. "But, I really love you."

"And I love you. So much," I said, smiling. "I mean, there's Moses to think about. I'd need to talk with his dad. This is a big deal." I was stating the obvious, as much for my benefit as his.

"I know it is," he repeated. We paused and let the notion hang in the air.

Then he continued.

"Listen. I've spent my whole life making calculated decisions. And look where it's gotten me. Maybe it's time to take a chance for once and do something crazy. I want to follow my heart this time. I love you. And I love Moses."

I grinned. I didn't even hesitate. I knew it was what I wanted.

"Well… what if we lived together?" I said, seeing how the words tasted on my tongue.

"What if we lived together?" he echoed.

"Yeah. Yes. Okay. Let's take a chance!" I said. We both grinned and sighed, raising our eyebrows in surprise at our own audacity, then kissed each other hard to seal the intention.

We had built such a deep bond of trust that deciding to live together only eight months after meeting didn't seem impulsive to me at all. (Granted, I was someone who had gotten engaged after nine months of dating, so it was par for the course). I could see a future with Omer. He had struck the balance of freedom and stability that I'd been seeking. He and Moses were at ease together. Omer felt like a man, not a boy. I believed that my passion, drive, and enthusiastic love would enrich his life as much as his devotion, forethought and adventurous spirit would enrich mine.

And to think that I could share all of this with someone, without being restricted to monogamy seemed almost too good to be true.

Ten Hand Massage *(Or, the Fastest Orgasm I've Ever Had)*

That very afternoon, we found ourselves at the Orgy Dome again, this time for the highly anticipated ten hand massage workshop. To this day, it was one of the most unforgettable (and most organized) sexual experiences of my life. It also made me appreciate the value of excellent group facilitators. *(Always thank your facilitators.)*

The line to get inside was long. The staff stopped accepting participants shortly after we were allowed in. We dressed down to our comfort level — myself in my plunging one piece swimsuit and Omer in his leopard print boxer briefs. Inside, the dome was full without feeling crowded and comfortably warm. There was an air of flirty, anticipatory energy coloring the low voices and an occasional eruption of giggles.

We were instructed to gather into groups of 5 to 7 people and choose a bed. Omer and I linked up with two other couples, all of them very attractive to me. They were sexy in an authentic, counterculture, non-airbrushed kind of way.

The educator explained the concept: Each person would have a turn receiving. During your turn, you were to first express your boundaries to your group. For example, did you want an erotic massage or a platonic one? Were there zones of your body that were off limits, or areas that you wanted only your partner to touch? Everyone would then confirm they understood the receiver's boundaries. There were hand wipes and hand sanitizer available for everyone to use before each new person's turn.

The receiver would then lie down on the bed and get comfortable (facing up or down — their choice, with an option to flip over halfway through). Once the facilitator turned on the music, we had eight minutes to give the receiver our complete attention. Everyone's hands descended onto the receiver's body and began massaging attentively.

The air was heavy with sensuality as the music played. Laughter turned into sighs, then moans which ricocheted throughout the room and seemed to add fuel to the fire of givers and receivers alike.

As we massaged one another's bodies, sore from the long nights spent dancing, we givers would lock eyes, enjoying the sight of so many relaxed, barely dressed, grinning friends in the periphery. We synced our movements — working together up someone's legs and then back down, mirroring each other's strokes and speeds. Several people in our group were open to receiving an erotic massage, so I had the opportunity to give several hand jobs.

Best of all was collaborating with one man's enthusiastic partner. I've never sucked on so many nipples or tickled so many testicles in such a short amount of time. It was awesome. And more than a bit surreal.

I volunteered for my turn about halfway through the workshop. I stood and slipped out of my swimsuit, then perched on the mattress fully nude to discuss my boundaries with my new and very intimate friends. I requested that my butt be left alone; more distracting than sexy to me in that context. Otherwise, I was an open book.

Well, I'm converted. I want everyone on this green earth to know the pleasure of a ten-hand massage. Within moments, I was flooded with feel-good chemicals. I closed my eyes and attempted to take it all in: the surface of my skin, the music, the temperature. The variety of sensations around my body all at once made me writhe in delight.

Two people sucked on my nipples, another kneaded the tension out of my neck, and one ran her strong, weighted hands over my hips and thighs. Within a moment, I felt the heat of Omer's mouth between my legs and was practically coming by the time he arrived there. He expertly carried me over the edge. I grinned and laughed and began to moan loudly as I rode the waves of climax after climax, the sound of my own voice dancing with the other receivers in the dome.

I felt blissed out and intoxicated from the experience, but also loved, received and celebrated. It was the most natural thing in the world, yet the kind of moment my devout Christian self could never, ever have fathomed.

There was a special kind of intimate gratitude we extended toward one another after being in the center. It was all juicy sighs and giddy giggles and hugs all around.

I slipped out between massages to use the restroom. Two women about my age were leaving at the same time, for the same purpose.

"I'm not going to bother getting dressed," I said, motioning. "The restrooms are just across the way."

"You're not? Okay! Then we won't either!" they agreed.

"Great! Let's all run together! Ready?" I asked.

The three of us took off running naked through the field in broad daylight as costumed campers wandered wearily along the path. We laughed loudly when we arrived at the restrooms and realized there was a line to get in. We stood there in the nude, chit chatting casually. Jack walked by and did a double take when he realized it was me standing there — an image he had seen countless times, now completely out of context. I grinned and waved. What else could I do? He laughed audibly and waved back, shaking his head at my antics.

I made it back just in time for Omer's turn. Watching him settle into the middle, totally naked, was enticing for me. I was practically drooling at the sight. I had his body memorized, but seeing him in this context, beneath the admiring gaze of so many new people was like discovering him all over again. I felt I had a special privilege as his partner and his one request was that only the women touch him below the belt. Everyone agreed.

The music started. I worked my way up his thighs, kissing and massaging as I went. One new friend returned the favor from earlier by helping me go down on Omer, just as I had with her partner.

As we worked him over in tandem, running our tongues up and over him and squeezing our smooth hands around him, I thought to myself that this whole scenario was so much sexier (and more interesting) than most of the porn I'd seen in my life.

An hour or so later, Omer and I emerged into the bright sunlight, hand in hand, grinning and chuckling and feeling very relaxed indeed. It was a delicious, unbelievable way to wrap up an expansive and unruly weekend.

27

Love Explosion

Summer

Spring with Omer burst forth into summer in a blur of sexy sleepovers, café work dates, rock climbing nights, and weekends visiting friends in other cities.

When we actually chose to stay in town, I was buried in homework for massage school. We still managed to make time for low key evening hangouts with friends after Moses had gone to sleep and Ecstatic Dance on Sunday mornings. Ecstatic Dance is a worldwide movement of dancers who gather for freeform group dances that I love for their equal parts' meditative movement and festive get downs.

In June, Omer turned 39 and I cooked him an elaborate birthday dinner to celebrate. I had already shared his main gift, the song I'd written for him, at SOAK. I brought Moses along, who helped me shop and prepare veggies. He played in the backyard, watering the kale and marigolds I'd planted in Omer's garden beds, while I did the cooking.

That weekend, we had a small gathering with friends at the house and I imagined what his next birthday might feel like; he'd be turning 40. He had been speaking often about the approach of his 40th birthday and what the landmark might represent for him.

He felt pressure to finally make certain decisions about his life: Was he happy in this city? Did he want to settle down and have children? Could he reconcile his responsibility toward his aging mother with his desire for fun and freedom?

Calvin

Omer called me from work one afternoon asking if I'd like to meet him in the park that evening for an acro-yoga jam. Essentially, this was a group of folks from the local acrobatic/partner yoga community who would set up in the park and practice their sequences and stunts before heading off to a local class. I agreed. I'd done a bit of acro-yoga before and was eager to learn more.

When I arrived, Omer was running late. I scanned the scene, feeling apprehensive. Then I saw a familiar face. It was the tall, handsome surfer acquaintance from massage school. The one with the Crocs. Out of context, it took us a moment to recognize each other.

"Hey! I know you!" I smiled.

"Oh! Hey!" he said, walking toward me. We reintroduced ourselves and chatted about classes. Then he held up his yoga mat.

"So… do you wanna try some stuff?" he asked.

"Oh. Yeah! Let's do it," I said, following him toward a flat patch of grass.

Acro-yoga is unlike other kinds of yoga. Essentially, one person is the base, lying on the ground with their hands and feet extended toward the sky. The second person is the flyer, who balances on the base's hands and feet in a series of poses that are then linked together into a sequence of (eventually) graceful moves. These sequences are called washing machines.

Calvin had been active in acro-yoga during his years in Chicago. He took my hands in his, rested his feet against my hip bones and muttered, "Ready? Keep your body straight like a plank."

Then he effortlessly popped me up into bird pose. We began touring a round of poses, me balanced in mid-air on his feet, and he remarked that I was a fast learner. I explained that I was a rock climber.

"Oh, yeah? I could see that. How's your handstand game?" he asked.

By the time I saw Omer approaching up the hill, I was suspended upside down in a shoulder stand, the tops of my shoulders balancing on Calvin's feet and my toes stretched like arrows toward the sky. I introduced the two of them and we all took turns trying different poses together until the mosquitoes came out and the air became cool.

Before leaving, I made sure Calvin had my phone number and we agreed to meet up again. There was an obvious attraction between us, which I willed myself to believe was unnoticeable to Omer.

Ari

By summer, I had left my caregiving job and was working full time for the hemp farm as Director of Communications; I'd even dropped out of massage school to focus on the work. This was 2017, before the big CBD boom, back when no one outside of the cannabis industry really knew what CBD was. I was being interviewed on podcasts and writing articles for websites and magazines about its potential for therapeutic use.

Because of this role, I spent a fair amount of time networking at cannabis industry events and quickly became friends with some heavy hitters in the scene. The world of Oregon cannabis had quite the cast of characters, like old school underground growers boasting decades of experience, amateur scientists turned industry leaders, eccentric hipsters, and scary-smart executives.

In July, a journalist, who I had worked with on a couple of articles, invited me as her plus one to a hip, invite-only party in Chinatown to celebrate the launch of a new women's cannabis business incubator. I gravitated toward a couple of familiar faces and soon I was sipping on cannabis cocktails and craft beer and being introduced to some of the biggest names in the world of recreational weed.

I noticed I didn't see these folks as celebrities. I wasn't star struck and didn't give them extra airtime just because everyone in the industry referred to them by only their first name. It helped that I was new to the industry and frankly, I didn't really care about who was a big shot. I'd watched so many privileged men in my life (big shots in the progressive Christian community) as they waved their proverbial dicks around, that I was more interested in cutting through the social posturing and discovering who was behind the movement. I got a sense that I was in a room full of people I couldn't trust, and perhaps just a few who I could.

As the evening wore on, I began to feel like the darling hemp socialite newcomer. I was surrounded by middle-aged men who either wanted to orbit with me because I was a young attractive woman or wanted to collaborate with my company because of our hemp licensing.

I escaped outside for a breath of fresh air.

When I walked back into the room, I saw her.

There, in a sea of mingling executives dressed in chic black and distressed designer denim, stood a woman my age enveloped in a candy-red plastic trench coat. I tried not to stare. She had short, banged platinum blonde hair that peeked out of her black velvet cap in wild waves. Around her dainty neck was a gaudy rhinestone necklace, the kind I used to worship from my grandmother's ornate box of costume jewelry. I caught her eye. We looked at each other twice.

She was standing silently between some men I knew, so I walked over.

"Hey," I said.

She stared up at me, a dreamy quality in her eyes. She was so instantly open to me that for a moment, it crossed my mind that she might be high on MDMA.

"Hey," she replied with a smirk.

Time stood still. Everything went quiet. For a moment there was no one else in the room.

Without thoughts or words we instinctively moved toward each other. I wrapped one arm around her and brought her close to my side. She leaned into me. Our bodies fit together like they were built for it.

"I'm Becca. Becca Martinez."

"I'm Ari."

One of the men chimed in.

"Wait — you two are just meeting?!" he asked.

We looked over at them and grinned.

"Doesn't feel like it," I answered.

Later on, she left with a few people while I stayed at the party, engrossed in a conversation with a friend of questionable sobriety as he lamented his marriage problems and inquired about how my child fared in the divorce process. Ari had invited me to come along, but something in me held back. I think I wasn't ready, or clear-headed enough, to deal with the simple fact of her. She was enthralling to me, all-encompassing.

Caught Up

That evening, I wound up at Roadside Attraction, a quirky dive bar in SE Portland, with five of the first-namers who I'd only previously read about in magazines. One such person, Jamie, an exuberant, tall and wiry scientist of international renown, was tipsy and intent on discussing cannabis genetics. A few of us played along. He asked for a ride home, and since it was on my way, I offered. I was the soberest of the bunch, by quite a bit.

On the drive home, he lamented how isolating the work sometimes felt and confessed that there were moments he wished he could turn back the clock and choose a different path, one outside of the spotlight. As I listened, I witnessed the familiar, lifelong phenomenon: people immediately sensing they could confide in me and be received with care and understanding. (I consider this my superpower and an occasional liability).

"I haven't been touched by another person in months. Well, more than a handshake," he said, as I pulled up in front of his high-end apartment building.

"Becca, it has been a true delight to meet you," he said.

"Yeah! It's great to finally meet you, too. Thanks, Jamie," I replied.

I unbuckled and leaned over to hug him warmly. It took him a moment to relax into it, and I sensed that what he'd said was true — he was deficient in human contact. So I stayed a moment longer, then another. I pulled away and held onto his arm, examining his face under the light of the streetlamp.

Then I leaned forward and kissed him.

Why did I kiss him? Honestly... I just felt like it. It seemed like it would be nice for him and interesting for me. There was no deeper motive than that. He swooned and sighed and said my name wistfully like a lovesick poet before finding his way inside.

I returned to Omer's house around 1:00 am and found him dozing in bed. I told him I'd had an amazing, unexpected night. I'd been brought to the inside. These connections would be good for work and good for life. I wondered whether I'd be able to keep them separate.

Well, I couldn't.

The following week, I found myself on Jamie's sailboat. I say "found myself" because I had developed a habit of offering a big, hasty, less-than-conscious YES to anything life offered. I've had the repeated sensation in the past of "coming to" after one of these enthusiastic impulses, be it a week or a year later, only to then realize the weight of the marvelous, frustrating, bewildering things I'd agreed to.

This time, I "came to" on the boat, but not right away. Jamie wanted to discuss hemp and potential work collaborations, he had said. When I arrived, he whisked me away theatrically onto his sailboat and fed me charcuterie and rosé as we sailed around the marina. Sailing was a remarkably athletic skill for someone of his constitution and reputation. I was impressed. I wasn't attracted to him, but I wasn't one to squelch my curiosity by mere vanity. I decided to let it play out.

However, I was subtly aware of the power differential. We docked the boat and enjoyed a nicely curated picnic, hanging our feet off the stern into the cool water. He sat smotheringly close. As Jamie pulled item after item from his picnic basket, I accepted that this was not at all a business meeting. It was a date.

He recited Rainer Maria Rilke poetry to me and compared me to Rilke's brilliant lover, Lou Andreas Salome. She was a wild, uncompromising woman who also held the affections of Sigmund Freud and Friedrich Nietzsche. She was considered the muse of many great thinkers, a force behind their brilliance. I scoffed at the compliment, but he insisted.

"And how on Earth did my good fortune find us here, on a boat, on a beautiful night such as this?" he pondered aloud. "Come, I'll give you a tour of my sea home."

How much could there be? It was a boat, after all. But I followed him. We descended into the belly of the vessel. Within minutes we were kissing, and soon he was peeling my clothes off. It happened almost urgently. Well, for him.

Surreal

I was compelled only by a faint curiosity, as if watching the event unfold before my eyes, and yet he was moving at a pace as though we were long lost lovers finally reunited, consumed by the heat of passion. I was in a receptive role that reminded me of being an adolescent again. I did not actively want anything to happen, so I mostly kept my hands to myself as he explored my body like a wild specimen.

At that moment, I felt as though I came to. I'd been lost in my own thoughts, noticing, as if from the outside, what a bizarre life I had: that I was here, in this intimate situation with Jamie Clay on a weeknight, while my son played at a babysitter's. That I had a lover, a partner to come home to. And that when I arrived at the marina, I had naively thought I was going on a work date.

I don't remember if Jamie ever asked whether or not what he was doing was okay. I don't know how I would have answered. The whole scenario was just…awkward for me. And yet, I allowed it to happen. He seemed to be having a great time.

It baffles me that even after so much work peeling back the old stories in my psyche about sex and pleasure, when put in a situation with a male in a position of power, my response was to freeze and please. I had learned how to embrace sex and celebrate my own sexuality, but when a man wanted to take, I gave. I hadn't practiced saying no or slowing down enough to check in and become aware of what I actually wanted.

Instead of slowing down, I had made a habit of convincing myself I was into it, disassociating from my body, and making the best of the situation rather than having to simply say no.

I hadn't just wound up on the boat; I had made choices. Rushed, unconscious choices, but still, they were my choices. This realization was foundational to beginning to take responsibility for my own life.

I lay on my back staring at Jamie's ceiling. He asked if I wanted to talk about sex. I didn't. I told him I felt we had gone far enough. I checked the time and said we should head back.

I texted my babysitter. She said Moses was asleep and I could feel free to stay out longer. "Come over!" he exclaimed. And I did, even after what had just taken place. I felt a vulnerability hangover, and perhaps I hoped that an exchange in which I had more control would make me feel less gross about the whole experience. Plus, I was curious to see what the infamous Jamie Clay's home was like.

The entire evening was surreal, in part because he had transitioned from a powerful, geeky stranger to a man who had touched me naked in the space of a week. Somehow, though, the power dynamic was complex. Yes, he was the famed cannabis researcher, but I was the powerful, beautiful woman, barely out of reach.

As I drove, I imagined his awkward years in high school, and recalled my socially joyous and easeful years, and reminded myself that our inner children don't just go away when we are adults. Those dynamics were perhaps still playing out. If I'd had my voice on the boat, the power would have truly been mine and I would have been more than my younger self.

His apartment was gorgeous, modern and colorful as I'd expected. His dog flopped lazily at my feet as we ate blueberries and wispy crackers. Everything was meticulously chosen, from the art to the books and the food. We stood out on his balcony overlooking Portland.

LOVE EXPLOSION

"Wow. This is beautiful," I said.

"I know," he said, staring not at the skyline but straight at me. Yes, as if he was in a romantic comedy. I half expected some cheesy music to queue in at that moment.

I tried not to roll my eyes. There was something so cloying, so over-the-top earnest about the way he'd been engaging with me since the very start. I sensed no ease, and a particular type of effort. It was as though he had learned all his romance skills from movies. It crossed my mind that he was either putting on a great act, or truly just this much of a helpless romantic. Either way, I found it unsettling.

"I have an idea," he took my hands in his. "Becca, do you want to take a shower with me?" he asked. "That's a fantasy I'm having."

Every cell in my body cringed. I felt so uncomfortable. I was keenly aware that I was in his home, on his balcony, and no one knew where I was. My phone was about to die, and I did not want to be undressed with him again. Not now, not ever.

"No… thanks. That's more of a third date scenario for me," I answered. He nodded humbly and suggested we remember the idea for next time. I knew there would not be a next time. We had a few snacks and talked more about cannabis science, and then I excused myself.

I never told Omer that Jamie Clay had gone down on me in his sailboat that night. I felt so awkward about the whole scenario and was more than tempted to erase it from the record of my memory. Yet, I made a deal with the universe to include my real and unfiltered stories, as truly as I can recall them, within these pages.

Knowing Her

The one person I'd met at that cannabis party and been totally smitten by, Ari, was also sincerely interested in sourcing CBD for her popular confections company. She emailed me about pricing and I offered to bring her down to the farm for a tour.

We met at Townshend's Tea. She had her assistant in tow, who barely spoke a word the entire day. I was curious whether Ari was all business, as her successful company seemed to imply, or all freeform artist, as her whole energy seemed to imply. Well, she was just as charming as I recalled, and much chattier than she'd been beside the men at the party.

On the hour-long drive from Portland to the farm, she sat cross-legged beside me in the passenger seat, interrogating me with question after question about the fine and the paramount details of my life. Our conversation flowed like juice from a pitcher.

In between questions, she'd talk playfully and offer up a variety of snacks that she'd brought along.

"Dolmas are healthy…. right?" she implored and flashed a cheeky smile.

"Oh yeah. Definitely. You can eat that whole can and feel good about it. Nice, healthy… oily… rice," I assured her with a wink.

"Okay, good. What about rice crackers? Healthy, yes?" she asked.

"Yeah, rice on rice. Pure starchy nutrition goodness!" I replied.

We both giggled. The banter was effortless. We had barely left Portland, yet were already playing a game, just for fun, that neither of us could name.

Ari told me about her years spent in Buenos Aires and Barcelona. She'd intended to study fashion, but found her way out as fast as she'd entered. She ended up working at a cultural center, and over the years had worked as an art director and consultant, and now entrepreneur slinging cannabis sweets to hundreds of dispensaries.

Somewhere along the way, she had married a close friend, the woman who was still legally her wife. They lived apart and hadn't spoken in a while.

"We'll probably get divorced eventually… I'm not in a rush to hassle with it," she said nonchalantly. "We actually had our wedding on a sailboat. Do you know Jamie? He was our officiator."

"Oh yeah, I know him. Small world," I chuckled, not wanting to mention my recent experience on the same boat.

We marveled at the fact that we'd both grown up in Oregon, 30 miles apart, and even bought our school clothes at the same shopping mall. She asked sincere questions and stared out the window, listening intently as I answered. She wanted to know all about Moses, amazed that I was a Mom. She asked about Omer and teased me when the first thing I thought to say was "He's a kiteboarder." Eventually, we talked about our families and our strained relationships with our fathers.

I barely remember the farm visit. I just remember driving down I-5 beside her and feeling like no place had ever been so lovely. The traffic was bad and Ari's assistant sat scrolling on her iPhone in the backseat, but to me it was perfect.

LOVE EXPLOSION

Naked Falls

The cascade of romance seemed to continue all summer. Impulsively saying yes to life had brought me regret in some instances, as with the night on the sailboat, yet more often it brought me deep joy and connection. I felt surrounded by gorgeous souls who were worthy of my love, people who made my life rich and challenged me to be my best.

To celebrate the longer, honey-hued days of peak season, Tess and I decided to host a big barbecue with our roommates. Among our guests were Calvin (this was the first time we saw each other after our acro-yoga meeting at the park), Omer, several of his friends who we often went dancing with, and Jen, an artist with whom Omer was forming a connection. She was polyamorous, spunky, and easy for me to talk to. I felt good about her presence in Omer's life. *Same team*, I often thought about her and I.

We all sat around the fire pit, and two beers later, when I perched contentedly on Calvin's lap and watched Omer and Jen dancing together in the firelight, I thought that perhaps an open relationship could actually work for us.

I was relieved Omer hadn't asked me to choose him exclusively over Ari or Calvin — I believed there was space in my life for everyone. It just meant I needed to be present for what time I did have with each person. Between work and being with Moses, my margins for lovers were fairly narrow to begin with. Omer and I didn't identify as polyamorous, though "open" felt like an apt descriptor. I wasn't sure of my end game; all I knew was that I felt more longevity in a relationship with open doors, one where I had space to move toward Omer and space to be an individual with my own life and loves, too.

• • •

After our connection at my party, Calvin and I spent a day hiking in Washougal and playing at the river. I clarified with Omer that it was a date, and he agreed in support of us connecting. We spent the afternoon sunning our wet bodies on the rocks and jumping into swimming holes. Calvin had a hilarious "White Jesus" impersonation. "I am the way, the truth and the life," he preached as he emerged, glowing, from the sparkling water. "Now send me money!" he said. Our laughter echoed off the rock faces.

He beckoned me to swim further from the shore. I confided in him that I was uncomfortable in deep water. I felt inept at treading it.

"Get over here, then," he insisted. "I'm all water. I won't let you drown."

"No," I said.

"Come on…." he ducked under the water and came up again while awaiting my response.

"Seriously? You're not going to let me refuse, are you?" I lamented.

"Nope!" he splashed me playfully.

"Ugh. Fine," I said. I pushed away from the rock and swam over to the middle of the pool. When I reached him, I hovered above the surface, treading water, albeit tensely.

"Hey, you're doing it. But you're not breathing. You're telling your body to panic," he said.

"Oh," I said. I slowed down my movements and filled my lungs. Instantly, I felt more at ease. I felt safe.

"Alright. Now let's swim over there," he said, motioning across a deep, calm expanse of water which appeared to me ten times bigger than it actually was. "You go first."

I haggled back and forth with him again, until he reminded me that I only had so much energy and it would be better spent swimming.

Resolve. Or, resignation.

Either way, I started swimming slowly, pacing myself. He stayed by my side, completely at ease, pleased to witness the situation unfolding. As it happened, I didn't die. I was fine. We reached the other side and I perched on a warm rock. He pulled himself up once I was contentedly on land. I leaned over and kissed him through dripping, river-soaked skin.

"Ahhhh, see," he smiled. "I knew you could swim. Just had to let go of that other story."

"Thanks," I said. "I appreciate you. Seems like I'm making friends with my lungs lately." And when I said lungs, what I really thought was voice.

The day was hot but not scorching, so we wandered up the creek and found a rope swing. Calvin showed me his favorite stunts while I picked and arranged wildflowers on the shore. Later on, when the sun began to soften, we lay down on a giant warm log, dripping, and Calvin slowly, sumptuously devoured sticky fresh figs from my belly and the inside of my thighs, each bite an excuse for a kiss.

The feeling of his cool lips grazing my skin sent a surge of desire through me. The company of such a sensual man — one who thrived on sounds, textures, flavors, moments, sensations, pulled me into my own senses. My pulse quickened and I felt myself craving more of him.

In the months that followed, I made a habit of going to Washington once a week to do acro-yoga with Calvin. Or that was our excuse, anyway. In truth, I made the long drive so I could lie around with him, eating garden fruit and talking about love, philosophy and social justice. Our connection resonated on many levels. It was physical, but it was also emotional, intellectual and soulful.

I was insatiable toward him. Before long, he was tying me up with ropes, something I hadn't experienced since dating Jack, and pulling out gleaming metal sex toys to experiment with. We had a fantastic time exploring our darker sides together. He was naturally dominant, and I was naturally submissive, and our appetite for each other was an outlet for me.

Omer and I had great, connective sex together, but it was without the power play. It was all love and lust and athleticism. With Calvin, it was a trusting exploration. He made a habit of seeking out my edges and dancing along those lines. It turned him on. He taught me a great deal about communication, enthusiastic consent, and how sexy a psychological connection can be.

I was lured in by the contrast of his glowingly handsome, boy-next-door appearance and the mischievous look in his eyes when he'd ask: "Want to try something?" before running ice down my spine or doing other, dirtier, things to my willing body.

We'd have all the sex, and then retire, worn out, to his garden day bed under the summer sky to talk about Carl Sagan and eat fruit out of each other's hands. He was a garden educator and a mushroom cultivator (and soon to be massage therapist; he hadn't dropped out of school like I had). There was a steadiness in him. He talked often about his dreams of an old age spent tending to beehives and fruit trees. A deep love for nature was something that bound us together, as though we had been cut from the same cloth or grown from the same seeds.

In his company I felt known, treasured, and free.

Calvin also identified as uncompromisingly non-monogamous. He had been around the block in many ways, and had packed a ton of life experience into his thirty something years here. He was quick to connect with me, yet slow to attach. This spacious dynamic between us, one that was open-hearted, willing, and communicative, without grasping at each other, made me feel safe and understood in a whole new way. He didn't just mentally understand why I wanted to be non-monogamous, he felt it too.

Calvin was deeply supportive of my relationship with Omer and asked often about how things were going. He smiled sincerely when I shared fond stories, and he taught me the term "compersion," which means vicarious joy in acknowledging someone else's romantic or sexual happiness. The three of us sometimes did acro-yoga together and went on nature outings in groups of friends.

Omer seemed trusting toward Calvin, and his main request was that I prioritize our time together and use protection with other partners. This felt like a balanced dynamic, as Omer had a love interest, Jen, who he'd begun to spend time with.

Inside of myself, I wondered again whether polyamory would work for me. It felt supportive to meet my soul-deep desire for understanding with multiple love interests: Calvin, Samuel, and Ari, (not to mention many friends) while freeing Omer to be himself and not willing him to be different than he was.

There was so much beauty within our own heart connection, even if it was more practical and lacked this deeper personal understanding that I craved. I felt I could be passionate and sensual with Calvin. I could be earthy and fiery with Samuel. I could be playful, weird and unfiltered with Ari. Omer brought out my steady, more domestic side. And all of these were parts of me. But where was I fully myself?

I was still forming a clarifying sense of self, and each person in my life seemed to hold a mirror with which they could reflect the Becca they knew back to me. Through these heart connections, layers of understanding and acknowledgment were building on each other like soil and sediment. They were affirming that I wasn't alone in the world, that my desire for justice, freedom, creativity and expansiveness were shared desires, and that my true nature as a bold, open, free-spirited, and intensely loving person was undeniably felt by those around me.

28
Beloved

Beloved

Omer had gotten us tickets to Beloved, a delightfully earthy music and arts gathering tucked away in the forested Oregon coast range. It featured a life-giving blend of self-care opportunities like yoga, and sound healing, plus had protected affinity spaces for members of the BIPOC and queer communities. There was one central stage showcasing a global array of music throughout the day, and through the hours of the night, famed DJs and illicit medicines kept eager dancers moving and connecting until sunrise. I had never been, but knew many friends who attended every year.

After my experience at SOAK, I was looking forward to another festive weekend, this time less wacky Burning Man and more earth-groove.

Omer would be arriving late due to work, so I was connected with some friends in the community to carpool with. I thank my lucky stars for this! The four people who I traveled with to Beloved became close soul friends, and we wound up naming our little cohort "Moth Lounge" (an inexplicable inside joke) and having weekly Moth Lounge dinners together at my home for the better part of a year. It felt like family. One of the women I met took a backpacking trip with me in Canada the following summer. These are just a few of the deep soul-friends that Omer indirectly connected me with. Many of my close friends today are people I can trace back, one way or another, to Omer.

Once our camp was set up and thoroughly decorated with tapestries and LED lights, I had a whole afternoon to myself to wander and explore since Omer would be arriving after dark. I romped down the path with my new friends through larger-than-life art installations built with branches, flowers, shells and stones. There was a maker's market where artisans peddled their wares. An entire side stage was devoted to live art and smiling faces caught my eye wherever I looked. Introductory hugs abounded. Yep, home.

The indigenous land acknowledgment made me feel more at ease in the crowd. I saw the faces of people who seemed to care about these issues. There was a somber awareness of the land on which we stood, which called for an acknowledgment that we were not there with permission from the Alsea, Siuslaw and Kalapuya people, stewards of the land who had long since been displaced due to colonialism. The speaker also acknowledged that naming these tribes was not a solution, but a call to our communities to begin the humbling work of making amends.

I thought of my ancestors to the south, the native Mexican people who had been there for millennia, and the alchemy within my own blood between colonized and colonizer. Mexican, Spanish, Portuguese, Irish, English. Victim and perpetrator alike coursing through my veins.

Afterward, I wandered up the hill, feeling content, and heard someone call my name. The cannabis in my system convinced me I'd imagined it.

"Becca!" I heard again, in a low, clear voice.

And there was Samuel, standing on the path ahead of me, just as he had been a year earlier at Timothy Lake. I grinned and leaned over to my campmate and said, "Go ahead without me."

I ran up to greet Samuel and we stood in a long embrace in the middle of the path. My friends walked on with winks and waves.

It was a very emotional afternoon. I was so relieved to be beside him, reunited after months. And I hadn't expected it — I had prepared, or almost willed myself, to be distant and casual with him. But that was no longer the nature of our relationship. Once again, my connection to him had grown deeper in our time apart.

In earlier conversations, Omer had made it clear that he had reservations about my connection with Samuel. This had become a familiar theme. Just as Keaton and Jack had done, Omer sensed that I held a deep bond with Samuel. He voiced that he felt unsure of us getting involved again; that it felt different than new connections like Calvin and Ari, which didn't seem as likely to subvert the foundation of our own relationship the way someone from my past could. He had a point.

Samuel and I spent the day dozing in his hammock together, staring up through the conifer trees and talking about life. His best friend wandered over and fed us mouthfuls of cardamom CBD tincture as we laid there like baby birds. Then she gave the hammock a gentle swing and went on her way.

Te Quiero

There was a tension between us. He spoke first. He wanted to relive the last night we'd shared. Did I remember that moment on the couch? He wanted to know. Of course I did. His attentive presence had been healing for me. He wanted to know what was happening in my life now, and whether there was space for him in it. I told him about my not-so-new love with Omer and my plans to move in with him in a few short weeks.

Samuel's eyes widened.

"Wow. Are you happy? Like, really?" he asked.

It reminded me of the night Andrew had questioned me about Jack. What was it about me that gave off the sense that I was willing to be convinced, willing to be stirred and swayed like water in a bowl?

"Yeah. I am. Things are good." I nestled closer against his chest. "I mean, they're different than this, but you and I were kind of a flash in the pan anyway," I said.

"Not totally," he countered. "We've known each other for a while. So, are you guys open?" he asked.

"Yes… and no. I'm seeing a couple of people casually. But I've told him a little bit about you. He's hesitant about the connection because of our history. Maybe it feels more threatening because you were in my life first," I explained.

"Is he here? Can I meet him?" he asked. He was earnest, not combative.

"He'll be here later. But, why do you want to meet?" I asked.

"Well, he's a part of your life, for one. And I want him to know I'm not trying to take you away. I just want to connect with you. I just want to share. Sharing's nice, right?" he asked, nuzzling into my neck irresistibly.

"You make it so simple, Sam. Yes. Sharing's nice. I do like sharing." I slid my hand under his shirt and rested my forearm on his warm chest, dragging my fingers over his tufts of hair. I imagined what it would feel like to be around both of them at once. I wasn't keen on the idea. My mind conjured an image of oil and water trying to mix.

He kissed my forehead and let his lips rest there for a while.

"Te quiero," he said.

The longer I lay there, the more drawn to him I felt yet again, back inside our little world where everything was simple, sometimes frustratingly so: nothing but skin and food and breath and fresh air and lust.

I thought of the irony of having abandoned myself again, having agreed to a restricted dynamic with Omer because I felt it was necessary to preserve the relationship. I had done this very same thing with Jack and was now having a parallel situation present itself with Samuel. I loved Omer and wanted to be with him. For him, that love didn't seem to have space for my connection with Samuel, even though I had budding connections with Calvin and Ari that he seemed to support.

As we laid there, I could feel myself getting lost in his eyes. I felt like a timeless, aimless version of myself. Like the rest of my life had halted in his path. I felt an urge to pull away and clear my head, so I promised Samuel that I'd find him later on and climbed out of his warm hammock to make my way back toward the main stage.

As I wondered about self-responsibility, agreements, and my capacity for love, I could feel that the past and present, once-separate parts of my life were approaching a convergence.

Shake

That night, I was shaking my body on the dark dance floor when Omer found me. I lit up. I introduced him enthusiastically to all our new Moth Lounge friends. We meshed well. Everyone seemed jazzed to know each other, and throughout the weekend we periodically stopped mid-activity to group hug and laugh giddily at our great fortune of having crossed paths. We knew good people when we found 'em, and these were damn good people.

It was an unforgettable weekend. In the mornings I went to yoga and Solsara mindfulness workshops, then spent the afternoons dozing on the concert lawn or snacking at our campsite.

I felt a strong urge to seek out Samuel whenever I had a free moment. I only briefly mentioned to Omer that I'd seen him. Knowing he was somewhere on the same acreage all weekend, and not in another country, was a lingering knowledge that felt like a good itch I wanted to scratch. Omer and I went to workshops and shared meals together, but otherwise freed each other to wander around when we felt called.

Saturday night, our group took a combination of MDMA and MDA that intensely defied my previously conceived notions of pleasure and indulgence.

I laugh just thinking about the extremely fun, hilarious, open-hearted, and sumptuous night we shared. I'll probably never be that high again in my life; it was overwhelming. I thought my heart was going to beat out of my chest, with electricity, but also with absolute love.

About an hour into our adventure, we all found each other on the dance floor and placed our hands over one another's hearts, as if to keep each other on the ground and avoid floating away into an intolerably big, love-drenched dreamland. We reminded each other to find the breath and to drink water. Always more water than we thought.

Omer pulled me aside, his eyes wide.

"I think I just got all our friends *way* too high!" he exclaimed.

I began to reassure him. Just then, we noticed our tall, lanky, long-haired friend nearby dressed in a furry onesie, absolutely beaming, truly ecstatic, imitating an inflatable tube dude (you know, those dancing wind-blown caricatures installed outside of car washes and furniture stores?). I was overtaken by hysterical laughter. We all were.

I took Omer's hands in mine.

"Okay, maybe we overshot it by a bit…" I shouted over the music. We kept laughing. "It is what it is. Let's just enjoy. We're safe. We're here," I told him. We both exhaled heavily, overwhelmed and grinning.

I looked into his eyes and placed my hand over his heart. He put his hand over mine.

"This is us," I said.

"This is us," he said back.

We hugged. We danced; we danced so fucking much. There was no stopping. My body actually found dance sequences and ways of moving through space that I had never discovered while sober. Parts of my body were unlocked and stayed unlocked to this day.

Later on in the night, once I felt the MDMA set me down gently and I began walking with my own two feet again, I took a solo adventure to ground down for a while.

Closer

Near the stage, I saw Samuel leaning against a tree in a sweet mossy alcove that he was in charge of tending with a group of friends. It featured ornate chandeliers, bohemian rugs, pillows, logs, and little altars adorned with natural and found objects. He waved me over. There was a large, live python slithering around near its keeper, and people clumped in pairs, talking softly with one another.

I greeted Samuel without words, nestling against his chest and letting the weight of the Earth and his solid form hold me up. I lost track of time against that tree, tucked in beside him and musing about life and love in our usual way. There was no future-tripping. He told me he'd had sex with a stranger the night before but wished it had been me. When he told me this, I didn't feel jealousy or competition. I felt recognition of our unique connection. I felt wonder. I wanted him to have love and connection, whether it was with me or someone else.

An hour later, I saw Omer walking the path slowly, looking around. I guessed that he was searching for me, and for a moment I intended to let him pass by.

"Hey, isn't that Omer?" Samuel asked me. Caught.

"Oh yeah — it is. Still want to meet him?" I asked tentatively. He nodded.

"Omer!" I called, waving him over. He came and squatted beside us. As he approached, I subtly shifted my body away from Samuel's to create at least a small semblance of space between us.

They were kind and congenial toward one another as we talked about the night, the festival, the music. After a couple moments, Omer excused himself and said he would catch up with me later. I was relieved that Samuel hadn't invited more serious conversation in that moment — I didn't want to talk about sharing and non-monogamy on the spot.

After Omer left, Samuel asked me if I had ever tried San Pedro, a hallucinogenic cactus native to Peru. Its active ingredient is mescaline, the same medicine found in peyote. I hadn't, and as usual, I was up for a new experience. We ate just a bit, given the night I'd been enjoying, and embraced the gentle glow that set in as night approached morning.

"Did I ever tell you about the first time I took DMT?" he asked as we relaxed under the trees. The music was slowing and the dance crowd had thinned to a tired few.

"No. I'd love to hear," I told him.

He dropped right into his story and I was transported. He was with his men's group, a few close brothers, sitting in ceremony. Each man had a turn to partake in DMT in the center of the circle, while his brothers surrounded him in support. After the first couple of puffs, he could use a hand signal to indicate whether he still felt tethered to this world. If he did, he was given more, until he was completely lifted out of his body and away to another place.

While he was with the medicine, Samuel had a vision that he was holding the Earth in his hands. At that time in his life, he'd been working in Costa Rica and feeling hopeless. He was experiencing debilitating grief about the state of the natural world and its ongoing destruction by humans. Standing there, he gathered the world in his arms and allowed his love to heal it, bit by bit, cell by cell, until the whole earth was made complete and harmonious again, as it was intended.

His account was healing to hear. I witnessed his fierce love and knew that I had felt those same qualities emanating from him in our own way. I lay beside him, listening, and allowed tears to run from my eyes. I spoke no words. It was a rare opportunity to witness his raw emotion and his passion toward that which he cared about most. His passion often manifested as angst, so to witness such tenderness and depth of love felt intimate. I also felt deeply understood in my own grief toward the suffering of the Earth and those living here.

"That day changed me," he said. "It freed me. In my vision I was still me, but I was also the medicine. Or, a part of the medicine. It made me realize that I'm not the hero. The Earth is healing itself, and all I have to do is know my place," he said, a wistful glimmer of resolve in his voice.

"So that's what I've been trying to do ever since," he concluded. "And for me, my place is in Costa Rica."

I listened silently, envisioning the journey he'd described, imagining the weight lifted from his earnest shoulders while still feeling it on my own: an urgent drive to fix this broken place we were in. I attempted to absorb through proximity some of the relief he'd experienced. I felt understood by his words, and envious of his ability to move beyond the burden.

Yet, what a fitting moment to try and embody that relief. Perhaps in this moment, there was nothing I had to change, fix or save. Here, in the arms of a lover, while my partner was off dancing gladly, and Moses was far away in his father's care.

I looked around and saw harmony — hundreds of people moving as one organism to the DJ's offerings, others on the ground nearby sipping tea with loved ones and strangers alike. I nestled toward Samuel and gazed up at the sky: tree branches swayed in the soft breeze and stars shimmered far above them. I breathed it all in, silencing the chattering voices in my mind claiming I was unworthy of such a perfect moment.

The only discomfort I felt was the growing magnetism between myself and this man that I had been grappling with for two years now. Our souls were tied. I couldn't have him, and I couldn't shake him.

Sunday

Sometime around sunrise, Omer and I wound up in a hammock back at camp and slept most of the day away. I woke feeling sweet and raw. We were to leave that evening. I spent many hours wandering alone, inevitably meeting familiar faces along the path and stopping for serendipitous encounters.

At one point, I skidded on some loose gravel and badly tore up my knee. (I was completely sober, I'll mention; the problem was a combination of loose rocks and a deeply flawed impulse to protect my kombucha from spilling rather than brace my own fall.) My filthy knee began gushing blood down the front of my leg, and I kept walking. Passersby stopped me by the arm, asking with concern: "Do you know you're bleeding?!" *Yes, thank you* — I was well aware.

Once I was all patched up, I set off in the general direction of Samuel's camp. I peered inside the adjacent tea cart, a cozy, dimly lit train car adorned with ornate eastern artifacts and the smell of Darjeeling. I waited for my eyes to adjust.

"Hey B." I heard a voice say through the dark. There he was.

"Oh. Hey." I smiled.

"What are you doing? Want to have some tea?" he asked. I did. Strangers shuffled to make space for me in the corner beside him. He gawked at my knee and urged me sweetly to be more cautious. After a while, the cart was mostly empty and we sat quietly, staring at each other. The tea server, who happened to be a yoga instructor Omer had a crush on, continued to fill our small cups over and over in silence.

Samuel ran his fingers over mine, sighing periodically but never breaking contact. I rested my chin in my hand, face to face with him for what felt, comically, like another "last time." Words danced through my head on repeat, all the things I wanted to say, but wouldn't allow to escape my lips.

"I love you."

"You are my soulmate."

"I'm so sad we missed our chance."

"Take me to Costa Rica."

"I'm not sure this will ever be over between us."

I allowed these words to stir in my mind until they were replaced by a simple marvel: how could one man's hazel eyes be so many colors at once?

On the drive home with Omer that night, I cried. I squeezed his hand tight, feeling intolerably confused, tender, and hopeful for a vague, whole future alongside a yet undefined love.

Panic

The following weekend, Omer took me to Hood River for another kiteboarding session, this time on the actual board. He was satisfied that I had passed my first water lesson. In the coastal town of Manzanita, splashing in the cold ocean waves, I had succeeded at body dragging: pulling myself through the water along the shore by maneuvering the 36-foot kite in the wind.

That morning on our drive east, I blurted out a request.

"Alright, babe. I'm moving in with you in *two weeks*. We need to talk about some hard things. We need to talk about sex, and we need to talk about money. So… you choose." I exhaled rapidly, eager to clear the air.

First, we talked about sex. I repeated my need to remain non-monogamous and expressed my desire to continue sleeping with Calvin and to revisit our unclear agreements about Samuel. He skirted the topic of Samuel, yet he was in support of my being with Calvin. I wondered aloud about how to meet these needs while protecting our shared home space.

We agreed that the second bedroom could double as a guest room when Moses was gone on the weekends. Friends from out of town could stay in there, and if one of us had company over, that was a place where we could spend time with them as well. No guests were to be in our bedroom, which was a protected area for our energy only. We both seemed to feel good about the agreement.

It crossed my mind that the only time I might have romantic guests in Omer's house would be while he was gone traveling. I doubted I would ever use the option, but felt relieved to have finally established a clear agreement.

Then we talked about money. He had given me a credit card with my name on it to use for household expenses like groceries and décor, and asked me to help him spruce up the place; ever since his ex Nora moved out a year earlier, he had left it cold and barren, opting to stay out of the house whenever possible. It wasn't a place he wanted to spend time.

I imagined bringing it back to life — hanging art on the bare walls and tucking big plants into the sunny corners. I wanted to reorganize the kitchen into a place where we could cook together on wintry nights. I thought of garden projects out front that would make the pathway feel vibrant and inviting, and I envisioned the garage which we had decided to transform into an aerial yoga and meditation space.

We agreed that on trips I would pay my own airfare, but other expenses would be case by case. He understood that I had limited financial means, and desire as I might to contribute more, I had bills to pay which occupied most of my income.

"And also, honey, please stop calling it *my* house," he insisted. "It's *ours*," he said. He repeated this request many times in the following months.

I sighed. He smiled over at me, squeezed my hand and turned his eyes back toward I-84.

I was relieved to have talked things through. By the time we unloaded the car in Hood River, though, my nervous system was totally fried. I felt as though I was swimming in big, dark, uncharted relational waters. I wasn't sure I was safe. Something didn't feel quite right. There were complex power dynamics here, which I felt I was more aware of than Omer was. I had the sense that we were both bending toward each other, in a way that felt strained. I was nervous we were about to start making sacrifices we weren't prepared for. It reminded me, in some ways, of the rushing into commitment Keaton and I had done.

The beach at Event Site was crowded with beginner and veteran kiteboarders that day, and the wind was rushing through in strong gusts that threatened to launch me into the air and out of control. I wasn't confident that I had the kite skills to remain safe on my own. I felt rushed. Omer assured me that I was ready and reviewed the multi-step safety sequences for if something were to go wrong while I was out on the water.

He had me run through our routine land and launch drills, which went normally until, in an instant, with one wrong move, I popped his best kite. I watched as the massive piece of gear deflated on the sand. A thousand-dollar error.

I was mortified. He assured me it was a common mistake and ran toward the car to retrieve his backup kite. I'd been taking CBD drops all day, but there was only so much CBD could do for the all-encompassing anxiety I was experiencing. This was about kiting, yes, but it was also very much *not* about kiting.

My wetsuit was hot and sticky on my skin. Sweat dripped down my back while I waited for Omer to return. By the time I was strapped into the harness, helmet on, and jogging the unpredictable 36-foot kite back and forth on the beach, I could physically feel the panic rising in my chest. I'd never had a panic attack before, but I was sure it was happening. A surge of wind came and yanked the kite, along with me, forward with a jolt. "Sheet out!" he shouted. (If I were to react and tighten my hold on the bar, the kite would gain more power and launch me into the air and out of control.) I released the handle.

"Omer, take the kite. NOW." I shouted back to him. He ran up and clipped the kite into his harness, releasing me from its pull and regaining control.

"You're okay," he said.

I turned on my heel and ran off toward the river, tearing out of my wetsuit in the process and diving into the cool water. I splashed my face and bent into the shallow waves, letting tears stream from my eyes. I felt a distinct loss of control that I couldn't pinpoint, but I knew it had to do with this place, this day, this man... this life.

He kited for a few hours while I wandered the beach and talked myself down from the total emotional spin-out I was having. We ate mediocre fish tacos and drove home without much to say. He mused about getting a dog and buying a vacation house in Hood River.

Home

August ended, and many weekend evenings were spent keeping Omer company as he packed and prepped for Burning Man. Moses and I were doing our own packing, as our move-in date was set for the week he was away. Calvin had volunteered to help me move the larger items with his camper van.

There was something I so loved about our home life; by now I was basically living with Omer on the weekends. We had our flow, and we knew each other's daily routines and quirks. It was understood that it was always a good idea to buy Greek yogurt and a large supply of fruit. We could sense without words when it was a good day to have friends over and when we'd prefer to lie around half naked watching Netflix on his big screen TV. I loved falling asleep together. One of my favorite moments of each day was climbing into his giant bed beside him, under the cool, smooth sheets and plush comforter. He'd pull me in close, his tall form enveloping me.

"Okay, Google. Turn off all lights," he'd mutter sleepily through his soft Turkish accent. Instant darkness, quiet, skin. I was both irked and impressed by our strange robot roommate.

Moses took to Omer effortlessly, and the three of us sometimes spent time together rock climbing or playing at the park or farmers market. I was touched by the ease Moses and Omer had with one another, and I marveled that Omer had chosen not to have kids. They were so natural together. Their personalities were similar, too — like two slender, solid trees with an affinity for order and consistency. And then there was me, all water and fire and tenacity, looking for something to transform.

We often hosted dinners and barbecues at the house. Our social circle was big-hearted and engaging. By now, Omer and I were functionally in an open relationship; he was casually dating Jen, the artist, who had become a casual friend of mine. Once, we spent a day at the local nude beach with her and her close friends to celebrate her birthday.

Another time I had Calvin over to practice Salsa dancing in the living room. We had such fun that I suggested we make it a weekly hangout: either salsa or acro-yoga at the house. This was often before Omer returned home in the evenings, but sometimes he'd arrive mid-session, his furniture rearranged to make space, and I think we all wondered whether it was a comfortable scenario. It felt bold, even for me, to be taking up space in this way.

I wondered sometimes whether Omer was actually okay with it, or simply wanted to be. Those two were always warm and friendly with each other. Calvin was rooting for Omer and I, and was truly glad we were together. He was the king of compersion.

I loved my days spent with Omer. We rarely fought, and our communication lines were open. I tried to tell him what was true for me often, and willingly. He walked the line between holding clear views and hearing out other perspectives. I felt like I could probably tell him anything and he would at least be willing to have a respectful conversation about it. Where we did differ was spirituality and magic. He had a pragmatic view of the world. He thought it was a beautiful place, but not one studded with synchronicity and enchantment like I did.

"Life is just creatures responding to their environment," he once said. While true, it felt like a short-sighted and limited way of viewing the world. It confused me, though, because whenever we took LSD together we would end up watching Alan Watts videos and marveling at the wonder of all things.

One day, I was rambling on about the wild variety and sheer quantity of birds that had been visiting me and demanding my attention for several days in a row: crows, ducks, hawks, hummingbirds, even an owl. I waxed poetic about the parallels between the presence of all these birds and the deep life lessons that had been unfolding for me. He rolled his eyes and smirked condescendingly. I felt foolish.

"What, you think I'm imagining it?" I bristled. "You have to admit, that's a lot of fucking birds."

"I didn't say that," he said. "I just think humans are very good at finding patterns," he added nonchalantly.

I realized then, that there was a deep magic, a felt sense of rhythm and attunement to the Universe or Spirit or Divine, that I would likely always feel, yet would struggle to share with him. We were built differently. We saw things differently. I decided to save those wonders for the people in my life who experienced the world's subtleties in the same ways I did.

29

The Fall

Falling

Ari and I met for lunch a couple of times that September. It was always electric. One day, she showed up to the restaurant wearing a head-to-toe light-wash denim ensemble that made her look like the lovechild of a ragdoll and a train conductor. Because, *why not?*

She seemed to bop her way through life everywhere she went, but she wasn't airy at all — as a Virgo artist, she was all Earth and focus and design. She was articulate and savvy and had a laugh that could end a war. She was a breath of fresh air to me, a reminder that social norms are actually playgrounds upon which to do as you please.

"People love Halloween so much," she said once, munching on a salad. "But, I don't know... I play dress up every day. I don't wait around for Halloween," she grinned. I watched her pop the lid from her kombucha. Fuck, I adored her.

She's this way because... art. Just, art, I thought to myself. I'd known a lot of over-the-top hipsters in my day who put huge energy into their appearances to seem unique or counterculture. But I saw none of that in her. On the outside, she was capital "C" Cool. But in truth, she was past all that. She was all play. Uninhibited creativity. I imagined a brighter world in which everyone staring at us simply recognized and appreciated freedom when they saw it.

I was at home one afternoon with Omer, swooning about how much I adored Ari. I told him about the natural chemistry between us and the way we could talk and talk for hours.

"Sounds like you've got a new best friend on the horizon," he said, smiling. I looked up. It occurred to me that perhaps he was unaware that this connection went far beyond friendship.

"Yeah… but I think I want to kiss her. Just so you know," I confessed.

"Oh. I see," he said. "Wow. There's really no limit to how much you can love, is there?"

"No, I don't think so. My schedule's another story, though…" I lamented.

Stoned

Our first date was a witchy cannabis party for women. It went comically poorly. I picked Ari up at her house and we drove downtown to the venue. Within 30 minutes of arriving at the event, I smoked way too much off a stranger's joint and became incredibly high. While standing to get a glass of water, I fainted. (I hadn't fainted since Thanksgiving Day of 2006, when I was an anemic vegetarian teen refusing to eat the holiday food). Everything closed in from all sides and I felt the world spin for a moment. I landed flat on my back with a loud crash.

When I came to, friends and strangers surrounded me in a halo of concerned faces framing my view of the ceiling. Ari had rushed over from across the room. She and Lori, who I'd coaxed into coming as well, helped me sit up and schemed to move me to the couch where I could eat some food and get my blood sugar up. I found it surprising that, of all the powerful substances with which I'd experimented: LSD, psilocybin, MDMA, MDA, San Pedro, Ketamine… it was good old cannabis that knocked me down hard.

On the slow walk across the room, I passed out *a second time* and opened my eyes to see Ari laughing, bewildered. She and Lori had lowered me down gently when my legs gave out again.

"Geez Becca, you're so close! Come on, now," Ari said.

I was mortified. Ari laughed it off and told me that next time we ought to have a non-cannabis related hangout. I called Omer.

"Hey Babe… I'm okay….. I'm having a Lindsay Lohan moment. Can you come pick me up, please?" He headed straight over.

By the time he arrived, the CBD and beta-caryophyllene supplement had kicked in — the event staff kept them on hand for situations of overconsumption — and lowered my high substantially. I hugged the girls goodnight and they walked with me down three flights of stairs to Omer's car. He had no idea that I'd been so altered. I seemed totally capable and had a completely coherent conversation with him on the way home. On the other hand, I was convinced Ari would never go anywhere with me again.

Luckily, she was unruffled and a few weeks later we met for a make-up date at CloudForest chocolate. She arrived in a leopard print fur coat and platform boots, with a little blue box in her hand. We hugged long and tight.

"I brought you something. It's silly," she smiled up at me.

I cocked my head to one side and resisted blurting out, *AWW! YOU LOVE ME, TOO!*

"Ahh, what? For me?" I said instead. I squeezed her hand and grinned foolishly, restraining myself. "You're amazing. Okay, let's see what's in here…" I said, untying the satin ribbon with a flourish. She watched, smiling.

I lifted the lid from the box and there, lined up in a tidy row were three fat, juicy figs, fastened to the inside of the box with gobs of thick amber honey. We both laughed at the surprise. My eyes lit up and my mouth hung open. It was at once so intimate and thoughtful, and yet totally unexpected and weird. It was such an Ari kind of gift. I felt a deep appreciation for both.

"How are you so… indescribable?!" I asked as we hugged. She brushed it off modestly.

"I'm just glad you're not laughing at me for using the box from my old glasses," she said.

Leisurely, we shared a whole bar of chocolate and the three figs, which mirrored our juicy, unrestrained conversation. At one point she paused mid-sentence and exclaimed that she could see my aura clearly — it was like an orange and pink cloud around my head and shoulders. I liked the sound of that. Our tea ran out too quickly, and parting ways came too soon.

Burning

Not long after our giddy chocolate date, Omer left for Burning Man, leaving me alone in the house for a couple of weeks. The first thing I did was buy a car load of house plants and ceramic pots in which to plant them. I bought a beautiful new rug and a bedspread, and local art for the bedroom, as he'd requested. I framed photos from our favorite hikes and memories and displayed them around the house. I set out a little notebook for us to jot down our funniest inside jokes and a running list of inventions to create. I had our handyman come over to hang shelves for photos and spices. All told, I must have spent $800.

We settled in easily and Moses loved having his own room, in addition to the porch hammock and a cat to play with. He adjusted nearly effortlessly, which no longer surprised me since he'd now moved homes with me several times and had casually known multiple partners: Jack, Samuel, Calvin and Omer.

When Moses went to Keaton's for the weekend I had the whole house to myself. I loved it for a few hours. But soon, I felt like a teen who had a house to herself and should really be hosting people and making the most of it.

So on Saturday, I invited Calvin over for dinner. I cooked pasta and confided in him about an ongoing struggle I'd been having. I'd met a very domineering Lithuanian man at Beloved Festival who was wildly enthusiastic (nearly manic, I'd say) and in the process of becoming a new-agey life coach. At a recent party, he'd cornered me in a cuddle puddle and verbally attacked me. He accused me of bringing "low vibes" and negativity after he overheard my conversation with a Black friend about festival culture and the dominating forces of privilege and cultural appropriation.

It was classic gaslighting and silencing tactics: he claimed that I was the one making the problem, and it was only a problem because myself and others *chose to focus on* it instead of just allowing us all to get along. Finally, I'd gotten up and left the party because it was such an intensely frustrating and alienating experience.

I stood at the stove, passionately recounting all of this to Calvin while I chopped vegetables and boiled water. I knew he had lived on a social justice commune in Chicago and done many years of inner work around race, gender, and privilege. He was one of the most humble and aware white men I'd ever met. Finally, I stopped my rant and looked over at him in a huff. He was tearing up.

"Ugh. I so appreciate you right now," he said, walking over to hug me. "I hear you. Thank you for being someone who cares. You are paying attention. I haven't had someone in my life who I could talk with about these things with in a really long time."

We sat out on the back deck eating pasta, drinking wine and sharing stories until the September night became too cold. I invited him to sleep over and we made use of the guest bedroom, which he'd helped me move into and set up earlier that same week.

I wasn't used to waking up beside him; most of our rendezvous had been set in the middle of the afternoon and I was home before dinner. But it felt natural and comfortable to be situated beside his inviting form as I slept soundly in his arms.

The following weekend, I had Samuel over for an impromptu evening together. He helped me assemble Moses' new bookshelf and we argued with the glitchy Google Home speaker while trying to get it to play songs by Femina and Dogon Lights.

"So, who all lives here?" he inquired.

"Just Omer and I. And Moses, part time," I said.

"Oh. Wow. Wait, we're in Omer's house right now? And he's cool with it?"

"Well, I can't bring you in there," I motioned down the hallway. "That's off limits, it's our room. But you can hang with me in the guest bedroom."

"Wow, you guys are really doing the whole evolved non-monogamy thing. Good for you. Seems like quite a change from last we talked at Beloved," he said.

"Yeah… we had some conversations," I explained vaguely.

"Does he know I'm here?" he asked.

"No. I don't think so…your name didn't come up." I felt embarrassed at my lack of communication on stark display. "But it's fine, it's good that you're here with me," I added.

We shared as sweet a time together as we'd ever had. It felt natural and overdue to reconnect with him, almost inevitable. After that, Samuel and I began talking more frequently, in spite of the fact that he was preparing to move to Costa Rica… this time, for real.

Homecoming

Omer returned from Burning Man with lovely stories. He had discovered that his "spirit animal" (his words, not mine) was a baby dolphin. He'd connected with a Californian woman, Aurelia, who we'd met on a trip to San Francisco, and felt very emotionally invested in their connection. I let him know that I'd had Calvin and Samuel over while he was gone. He didn't ask for details, and I didn't offer them up.

The evenings were getting dark earlier as the weeks settled deeper into Autumn. Omer and I had developed a keen interest in acro-yoga and partner acrobatics. He was taking classes and relaying all the skills to me. One Friday evening, I waited at the climbing gym to meet him for our routine climbing and acro session.

I was sitting on the mat stretching when he arrived.

"Hey honey," he said brightly.

"Oh, hey!" I smiled up at him.

"You're very smiley today. How are you?" he asked.

"Oh. I'm good. Really… so good," I answered, grinning.

"Wow. Sounds like it. So, you had a great day off, I take it?" He settled beside me and began stretching.

"Yeah. Actually…" I trailed off. I'd had a profound experience that afternoon and was coasting along in the afterglow. "I feel like you might judge me for this. But I took DMT today."

"Wait, what? Today? Like, this afternoon?" he asked.

I laughed.

"Yeah. Just before this, actually. I was hanging out with Samuel at his place and he offered. It was pretty incredible. I can't really put words to it right now… but don't worry, I feel great now. I'm definitely up for climbing," I replied.

He stared at me, surprised. It seemed he didn't know what to do with this information.

"Hey." I reached a hand over, "How are you?"

"Wow. I'm just… I'm kind of surprised you did that on the spur of the moment," he said. "DMT is a big one. It doesn't seem like something you'd take lightly."

"I know that. But, he and I have been talking about it for months and we finally had the chance. Plus, he's leaving soon. It just seemed like the right moment for it." I looked at him, searching his face. "I felt good about it."

"I have to be honest. I feel a little jealous. I've never done it. I thought maybe that was something we would share," he said.

I felt guilty. I scooted closer to him.

"Ah fuck. I'm sorry, Babe. I didn't realize that was something you wanted. You're right, it was kind of impulsive. But it felt right to me. And it was really, really beautiful. Can I tell you about it another time?" I asked.

"Sure. Let's climb," he said.

As I buckled my climbing harness I realized that I wouldn't have, perhaps couldn't have, chosen any other person besides Samuel to use DMT with for the first time.

Samuel, Part IV

Samuel was preparing to live in Costa Rica full time. We discussed leaving town together for a weekend while still we had the chance. There had been numerous times when he'd tried to sweep me away on a camping trip and I'd cancel at the last minute because Keaton, or Jack, or Omer, had a problem with me going. So I was eager to spend this time with him, yet I had no idea how to frame it to Omer. I think by this point, he and I were both very tired of talking about my relationship with Samuel and getting nowhere. I wanted to move closer toward him without giving up Omer. Meanwhile, Omer would have been satisfied if he never heard Samuel's name again.

It felt like an important time, though. Samuel's years of back and forth travels were about to end. We would be living in separate countries for the foreseeable future. I wasn't willing to sacrifice our last chance at time together. I tried to be honest.

"I know you're tired of hearing about Samuel," I told Omer one evening as we finished dinner. "Here's the thing. There's just something... unresolved. I feel like it's going to be there until I make enough space for everything between us to come to the surface," I said. I had a flash of memory from three years earlier, of talking to Keaton about my desire to explore things with Cory.

"Okay," he answered dryly. "So, what does that look like to you?"

"Well we were talking about taking a camping trip," I told him. "Maybe taking some mushrooms together? I don't know... there's just something with the medicine between us that I still want to explore."

"Honey, I want to support you. I hope you can understand why this is challenging for me," he said.

I nodded. I didn't reply. It was a familiar and complex pang of guilt in my stomach. On one hand, I felt relieved for being honest. I applauded myself, even. Over time, it was becoming easier for me to ask clearly for what I wanted and needed, and not feel so emotionally responsible for the reactions of others. At the same time, I'd seen how Keaton and Jack had both felt challenged by the way I spoke of Samuel and the weight he carried in my life, along with my ever-evolving feelings about him.

"What does he mean to you?" he asked me. "I need to understand."

How could I explain in words something so powerful and so enigmatic? I knew what my truth was. So I chose to be as radically honest as I ever had been about Samuel, aware that I wouldn't be able to take the words back once they escaped my mouth.

"He's everything. Not *my* everything. Just… everything. All the things," I shrugged with a sigh. We stood in the kitchen facing each other, unsure where to go from there. I'd found myself in a relationship with Samuel that had its own magnetic agenda. It seemed at odds with my life and with Omer. I couldn't see a clear path forward. Perhaps this is what happens when you invite plant medicine into an already powerful connection steeped in sex and magic — it takes on a life of its own.

He just sighed and nodded in acknowledgment, asking me to let him know what days I planned to be gone.

I felt at once guilty and thrilled. I had never spent a whole weekend alone with Samuel in our two and a half years. We chose a weekend later that month.

The Wedding

In early October, all the concerns I had about my romances with Samuel, Ari, and Calvin were set aside when Omer and I boarded a plane for Washington, D.C. As early as high school, I'd been an expert at compartmentalizing, so by now it came easily. Omer's only brother was getting married and I was invited to come along for the week. As usual, I traded parenting days with Keaton to make the trip possible.

We stayed with Omer's brother and fiancée in DC, and the four of us fit well together. We had a natural camaraderie and I felt instantly welcomed by the entire group: friends, family, extended relatives. I was part of the fold. Omer and his mother took me to their favorite Turkish restaurant in DC. I adored her. She was a fiercely independent feminist and stained-glass artist who walked miles every day and said men only brought limitations.

In many ways, I felt understood by her. She and I were close, despite the language barrier. She was going to be staying with us in November and she was eager to spend time with Moses, asking about him often. I couldn't help but entertain a fantasy of her speaking Turkish with Moses and teaching him to paint with watercolors.

On the morning of the wedding, Omer and I rose early and took a five mile run through the National Mall, stopping at the Lincoln Memorial and Washington Monument. We passed by the White House and stood outside, wordless. It was much smaller than I had expected. I felt a visceral fury, standing outside and considering the despicable man at the center of its affairs.

Omer asked if I wanted a picture out front.

"Not really," I said, scoffing. I stopped to think. "Well, actually, yeah."

He stepped back to take the photo. But I couldn't smile. At the last moment, I turned around to face the White House and threw both middle fingers up toward the sky. Omer chuckled and snapped the photo.

"Damn, honey, I love you! Alright... now let's get out of here before the security guards give us trouble." We shared a quick hug and took off running. It's still one of my favorite photos of myself: my strong, feminine, mixed-race form throwing up a gesture of defiance against a despicable symbol of racism and misogyny.

The wedding was a delight — a multi-day affair with rehearsal dinners, a private ceremony, a gorgeous vineyard reception, and a countryside after party featuring a band, fireworks, and a Turkish feast made by Omer's mother. Plus, the obligatory day-after brunch put on by the extended aunts and uncles to cure our inevitable hangovers.

I hadn't spent much time on the East Coast, and the family's charming property in Virginia was a woodland fantasy in which to be immersed. Several friends flew out from Portland for the occasion. I was finally introduced to the last few of Omer's East Coast friends from university, whose names I'd been hearing all year. It was a treat to see Eneas again (no making out this time), and to share stories and ambitions with Omer's closest friends. We ended the wedding night smoking a joint together around the happy couple's sparkly canvas glamping tent.

As much as I enjoyed being there, it felt very apparent to me that I was only bringing a part of myself into the setting. Surrounded by international city folk with multiple degrees and serious upper level careers, I felt like an alien. Single mom, hippie hemp farmer with her tattoos and muscles. Returning home felt good to me, like I could let all my sides out to play once again.

Natural

Later that week after we were back home, Omer and I spent an evening lounging in the living room by the fireplace. He listened as I rambled on about my fantasy of being an organic flower farmer with a massive, meandering garden of native plants, nestled up against the forest somewhere.

"And of course, I'll be doing my part for the bees, too," I said. "We need pollinators, you know. All that fruit you love to eat? It would be impossible without pollinators." I smiled at him and ran my hands through his hair.

"I love how much you love all this," he said, as though he didn't understand his own place in the natural world, like it was something one could opt into or out of. "It seems like a lot of your people care about these things, too."

"I mean... yeah. How could they not?" I asked. "Nature's the foundation of everything else. I can't imagine inviting someone into my life who doesn't get that." I said, not hearing the irony of proclaiming this manifesto to a supercomputing engineer with a very different relationship to the natural world.

He was quiet for a minute.

"I'm wondering how long you're going to be happy in this city," he said. "I couldn't live out in the country. If we're going to be here, it's important that you meet that need for nature one way or another. It's a big part of you. Otherwise... well, you'll wind up unhappy. And you probably won't be able to stay. I don't want that for us."

"Hmmm," I said. "I feel like I already *do* get that need met with people. I spend a lot of time outside and working in gardens. Wow. Actually, all my other lovers are super earthy. I never made that connection before. Calvin and Ari are both Virgos, earthy as hell and they're obsessed with plants. And mushrooms. And fresh air. Then there's Samuel, who... well you already know."

I didn't even consider the impact these words would have on him. And I didn't notice his reaction at the time. Yet, for Omer, seeing me hold so many others in such high regard made him feel invisible.

My whole life, I've grappled with the notion that my raw, unfiltered thoughts and emotions can be hurtful to loved ones. I can be self-protective and private, so I have always experienced the act of sharing candidly as an extension of trust and a tool for building intimacy. But I've been known to overshoot it, opting for radical truth in moments that call for nuance. Others have experienced this as tactlessness and insensitivity, even inconsideration.

Once, when I was 11, my mom stopped me mid-sentence:

"You know Bec, for every ten thoughts that come into that head of yours, you should probably only say one. Preferably one of the nicer ones," she told me, and I've been turning over that notion in my mind ever since.

30 Away

Weekend Magic

In early October, Ari and I had plans to attend a first-of-its-kind conference for women in cannabis. It was a weekend-long affair at a luxury ranch in central Oregon. She had been roped into speaking at a luncheon, and I'd been given a free scholarship, simply by being a fresh face in the industry and having a direct line to the right person to ask.

We were giddy to have so much time together, and the three-hour drive in her Prius sped past. She didn't like driving, but was very on board with being my co-pilot, which I found perfect. She could navigate, supply snacks, change the song, and all I had to do was drive. There was a charged energy between us that day which I hadn't fully tuned into before. I felt keenly aware of my desire to reach over and rest my hand on her leg.

She was feeling uneasy about the retreat and had almost stayed home. I listened as she told me about her wild history within the industry, about all the times she had been totally shafted by trusting someone powerful who wound up exploiting her creative prowess for their own personal gain. She felt called to leave the industry, but couldn't see a clear way out; her highly visible company was up and running.

On top of that, the organizers of the event were notoriously inconsiderate and difficult to work with. Ari had recent personal experience with the people in leadership that led to a negative falling out. She expressed skepticism at the organization's underlying motives. It was supposed to be a feminist-run, empowering women's retreat, but upon arriving we noticed that many of the speakers and virtually all of the investors present at the ranch were men.

When we reached the guest house, where Ari was meant to stay, she learned that no bed had been reserved for her and she'd have to sleep on the floor. I insisted that she come with me instead.

Over at my vacation house, our friend Sally, a high-profile cannabis educator, was already getting settled.

"What even is this place?!" she asked, hugging each of us as we entered. "Y'all, I was so close to not coming. I'm feeling creeped out by the whole thing."

We all stared at each other. *Right??* It was immediately obvious that we would be squadding up for the duration of the weekend.

We didn't go to any of the scheduled programming, aside from a nice workshop put on by a woman from Dr. Bronner's soap company about ethical business and Certified B Corporations. We all agreed that Dr. Bronner's should probably run the world.

That night, Ari and Sally shared the bed and I slept on the floor. A part of me was nervous at the thought of sleeping beside Ari — it seemed possible that I might make a half-conscious move toward her during the night which neither of us was ready for. The three of us slept in late and lazed the days away, wandering the winding pathways through hundreds of high desert acres.

The two of them shared stories with me and brought me up to speed on some of the shady and outright harmful things that had taken place within the industry. Selling out to corporate interests, for one, but also sexual harassment and assault. Blackmailing. Threats. Money laundering. All of it.

I felt like I was watching a documentary about the dark side of recreational cannabis, one that was playing out all around me. I shared about my experience on the sailboat. The whole industry, the very fact of it, left a sour taste in my mouth. I wanted to leave as fast as I had entered. We joked about all the powerful people, those we coined as "scary smart" and marveled at the odd array of seemingly benign villains Oregon's cannabis scene had attracted.

On Saturday night there was a banquet followed by a bonfire. I offered up that I'd brought some psilocybin capsules a friend had harvested and gifted to me. They were mellow; we could enjoy a nice micro-dose if we each took one.

Well, guess what? They were far stronger than I had recalled. By the time Nancy, the lead executive, presented her canned speech at dinner, all three of us had come up on mushrooms and were having a difficult time suppressing our giggles.

Shroomy

When I use mushrooms socially, I tend to become very theatrical and enjoy engaging with the people around me, exercising my comedic strengths. I felt especially rebellious as we listened to the speakers — Nancy introduced some tall, macho looking white man from the East Coast with one of the most pathetic "empowerment" speeches I'd ever heard. She kept repeating that we *needed* to work with men, we *needed* to work with people in power, if we were going to survive as women entrepreneurs. Then, with a wink and a wave she encouraged all the entrepreneurs in the room to introduce themselves to the investors and start making deals.

Ari looked at me across the table, wide-eyed and shroomy. "What. The. Fuck." She mouthed silently. I gaped back at her, then began looking around the room dramatically, feigning that I was an alien who had just crash landed at this event and was very confused at human behavior indeed. She left the table and I continued creating a comedic raucous. While Ari waited in the food line, the aforementioned macho white man investor approached her and inquired casually about buying her edibles company. She returned to the table in frustrated tears. She was sure Nancy had sent him her way.

Ari felt like she was being paraded around, once again, as the enticing "It Girl," the poster child of creative success in an emerging industry. She recognized it as a strategic move by Nancy to continue establishing herself as indispensable to the success of young founders. The fact that the three of us: Ari, Sally and myself, were all present free of charge, as were several other young leaders, only added to our suspicion that Nancy was more intent on putting on a show for investors than empowering women entrepreneurs.

"I need some fresh air," Ari muttered and wandered out to the open-air deck toward the fire pit.

Sally followed her out onto the lawn and I watched their silhouettes shrink into the distance, lit only by firelight. A few minutes later, I followed them out.

When I reached them, Ari was sobbing uncontrollably and trying to spit out words strong enough to convey the years of frustration, fear, hurt, and harm that had come her way because of people and forces like the very ones inside the banquet. I was amazed at her raw display of emotion. Psilocybin has a knack for bringing issues to the surface and triggering cathartic experiences that we may not be able to access otherwise. I stood and listened. Sally agreed and affirmed that her experiences had been very real and not okay.

"I just…. this is exactly everything that is wrong right now!" She pointed toward the banquet hall. "With cannabis, with business… with the world. Bad players like them taking advantage of the rest of us!"

We sat down on the lawn overlooking the dark hillside.

"I'm done. With all of this. I've known it for a while, but now it's obvious. This industry has drained so much out of me. It's not fucking worth it," she said.

We left the party and wandered the paths under the moon and stars. We stayed up late, tripping on mushrooms together and savoring all the heart-opening, laughter-inducing moments they brought our way.

On Sunday, we departed early without saying goodbye to our industry peers. The three of us shared a quick brunch together, and we had a sense that the deep hours of the night had bonded us for life. Sally then headed back to town, but Ari and I were in no rush to cut our weekend short; I was drinking in every moment of her presence. It was a gorgeous, sunny day, so we stopped at Smith Rock State Park for an afternoon hike. We paused along the path to watch some rock climbers, and she marveled at the fact that I actually found the activity fun, not terrifying.

"Who says it can't be both?" I asked.

She nodded in agreement.

"You've got a point there. Still, I'm just fine here on the ground."

The whole afternoon was like a blue-skied sepia dream. She brought that surreal quality with her wherever she went, like an intoxicating mist. We meandered slowly, taking our time to smell the desert sage and pocket little rocks that you're not supposed to bring home.

I looked at her, sparkling in her yellow tank top, her soft skin and strong torso peeking out. I resisted the urge to wrap my arms around her waist, unsure which of many factors was holding me back. There was the sheer power of my attraction to her, an intensity which I felt might frighten her off. There were old residues of homophobic programming still confused and trying to categorize her as a friend and not a romantic interest, as I had with many girl crushes over the years. And of course, there was the classic lovesickness that makes one feel almost intolerably good to the point of nausea.

When we departed, we sat silently for a mile or two listening to Manatee Commune playing lush downtempo beats over the speakers. We had a couple hours before arriving back in Portland. I slowly reached my hand toward hers. It felt so small in mine. Her fingers danced across my skin tenderly. I sighed.

"So. This is crazy," I said, glancing her way. She stared back, wide-eyed, somber.

"I know," she said.

"I did not see this coming. I feel like…" It was difficult to find the words. "You're just so familiar. I feel like you can feel the same things I feel in the world. Because we're the same in a hundred ways. I never thought I'd know someone like you. You're so YOU, and also like a fucking mirror, so can you see right through me. You're powerful and magnetic and warm and everyone seems to want a bite of you," I said.

"It's definitely felt like that at times…" she added.

"And on top of it, I have this weird sensation that, for the first time in my life… after all these relationships, I don't know who's in charge here," I said, motioning my hand between our two bodies.

Her eyes grew wide and she smiled.

"I *know*. It's like we've been best friends or sisters or rivals or….something… before," she said.

"I'm a little freaked out," I confessed.

"Me too, Becca. But I'm here for it," she said.

"So am I," I agreed.

We held hands for most of the drive home to Portland. I was in uncharted territory. I had dated women, had sex with women, but this… this was different than any connection I'd had with a person in this lifetime. She was soul family. I was insatiably attracted to her on every level. I was falling wildly in love with her, and with each new angle I witnessed her, my love expanded.

It was even more terrifying to me than my love for Samuel because this time, I couldn't find the fatal flaw.

Deeper

Sally's birthday was the week before mine; we were both Scorpio November babies. Ari booked us a vintage camper on the coast at a resort called the Sou'Wester. It was a rainy weekend and we holed up in our AirStream with snacks and paints and LSD. I truly felt like I was there with Ari; like we were a couple there celebrating our friend Sally.

On the first night, though, I volunteered to sleep on the couch again. I was keenly aware of the growing heat with Ari, and neither of us had named it aloud.

She had been at my house visiting that week while Omer was at work. In the midst of a long hug on the couch, I'd pulled her on top of me. We paused. I could practically feel the heat of her lips on mine as we held ourselves in suspension. We stayed like this for a very long time, syncing our breath, feeling the moment, and both watching to see what might happen next.

Finally, after a torturously long while, we kissed. It was the relief of a visceral tension which had been building for months. I was in a daze. She was pure magic to me. Magic and art. And we were meeting in the middle: she wanted to be there as much as I did.

So, with the knowledge of the heat a simple kiss carried, I hesitated to climb into bed beside her on Sally's birthday weekend.

We enjoyed a playful, deep and delightful time. I felt like we were three girls in a fort. We were the queens of heart to hearts and discussed everything: childhood, life plans and goals, art, society, capitalism, travel, memories. We played on the beach and wandered the town aimlessly. We ate an ungodly amount of snacks.

At one point during an afternoon of LSD journeying, we all curled up on the couch and stared at a single maple leaf, rainbowed with the hues of fall, for the better part of an hour.

"This leaf is... everything," one of us said.

"Seriously, though. Like.... *Everything*," said another.

"And there are basically an infinite amount of leaves like this on this planet...." we concluded. "Infinite everything."

We all looked at each other wide eyed, then burst out laughing. It was so true, yet so ridiculous.

After a day of cosmic coastal adventures only the three of us can fully appreciate, the day darkened into night. Ari and I lay curled on the couch while Sally painted with gouache. Lazily, we began a contact improv flow with our fingertips, then our hands and eventually our whole arms. We laid there, eyes closed, dancing with just our arms, never breaking contact, for a very long time, until finally I realized how deeply tired I was. I sighed, smiled, and got up to head to bed. By now, the effects of the LSD had muted down to a marvelous shimmer.

"Want some company?" Ari asked.

"Yes," I replied, without hesitation.

That was the first night we had sex. She glowed golden under the light cast by the amber lampshade above our bed. There was no more denying the chemistry and powerful pull between us. Being with her in this way felt at once totally right and totally foreign. She was so many things to me: a friend, a sister, an ally, a lover. To be naked together felt almost trite — like the pressure between our skin couldn't possibly bear the weight of everything that existed between us.

That didn't stop us from having a great time.

The next morning when I woke up, Ari was out of bed getting dressed.

"Hey," I said, pushing the hair out of my eyes sleepily.

"Hey, girl," she answered. "I'm kind of restless. I have a lot happening for me. I'm going to take a little walk." She leaned down and kissed me, then slid her fluffy orange beanie over her head and disappeared out the door.

When she returned, she was more settled and we checked in about the previous night. We agreed that what had taken place between us was a big deal, and that we also didn't know what it meant, and didn't need to sort out anything just yet. Still, we were both glad it had happened.

After that, the image of her in her honey glow haunted me whenever she was away, a welcome apparition to warm my coldest nights.

I told Omer about the weekend. He rolled his eyes at my use of LSD — I had recently expressed a desire to back off of tripping since the summer had been so drug heavy. I had justified that it was a special occasion in a perfect setting, the kind of personal, intentional moment for which I wanted to reserve these substances. I felt with some angst that he couldn't appreciate the fluidity and nuance of my decision-making process. To him, it looked like another impulse lined with excuses.

"Well, you can rationalize just about anything," he'd said.

He was less bothered about my having sex with Ari — in some predictable way, the absence of a penis made the situation less threatening to him. *(I'd had the same experience when I'd had sex with my friend June while I was with Jack.)*

AWAY

But I could feel the tension growing — Omer was questioning my ability to temper my attraction to Ari and maintain a balanced home life, and Ari could see the ways I was compromising myself to be with Omer, minimizing the parts of me that didn't fit the relationship. They'd never met, and I didn't plan on changing that. They were like earth and sky, better in their set places.

Breitenbush

I barely had a moment to myself these few months, in the midst of so much love and romance and work and mothering and cooking and rock climbing and trying to be a decent human and a good friend. There was so much time spent reflecting, communicating and coordinating with people. In the pie chart of my life was a huge slice dedicated to relationships. Though I didn't realize it at the time, the inner work I was doing was largely focused on my attachment style, and exploring all these different loves was teaching me about my gifts, my liabilities, and the sticking points that make it difficult for me to form lasting, loving relationships.

With all this happening, my weekend with Samuel came fast.

I took a Friday off from work for the occasion and dropped Moses with Keaton. We were bound for Breitenbush, a beloved spa and retreat center southeast of Portland. Samuel had been texting me sweetly all week to coordinate details. When I arrived, he was outside packing up the truck, his enthusiasm beaming and his music blasting.

"I'm so excited to spend the weekend with you," he said, taking me in his arms. "Oh, and...!" He turned and jogged over to the fig tree. "The second flush of figs just came in. Check these out." He pulled down handfuls of sopping, juicy green figs for me and I ate my fill while we loaded up the truck.

A part of me was actually fatigued from all the love I'd been swimming in during those months. I had Omer and his steadiness: our home rhythms, weekend trips and dinners with friends. I had Calvin's spacious, growing affection, plus kink and acro-yoga shenanigans. I had the deep bond of attraction and soul friendship with Ari. And then, there was this ancient and unspeakably rich thing with Samuel. I found my energy lagging, and as much as I wanted to match his enthusiasm, I felt aware that this was the glinting highlight of Samuel's week, and in mine, it was simply the next on the highlight reel of an immeasurably rich week.

"I spent some time yesterday looking at these maps," Samuel said. "I narrowed it down to two routes. They both have some beautiful roads I want to take you on." He drew his calloused fingertip over the soft paper. "Are you down for an adventure?"

"As much as I'll ever be," I told him with a grin. "I'm all yours."

We ate smoked salmon cheeks and garden pears as he drove us through the Mt. Hood National Forest, pulling over frequently to take photos and pick flowers for me. He picked a bundle of cloudy white Pearly Everlasting flowers, which I saved and hung in my bedroom to dry.

We were welcomed warmly when we arrived at Breitenbush.

"I'm going to make us a little home. You don't need to do *anything*," he said when we reached our camp site. This was an edge for me, the challenge of accepting generosity and acts of service without reciprocating or feeling guilt. He was someone who insisted on giving, and I set out to receive his extensions of love. So, I went on a little walk. When I returned, the inside of the truck canopy had been strung with lights and bedded down with a plush mattress. He'd made a little yard for us with a kitchen and hangout area and a covered place to set my things.

"Shall we go soak?" he asked. I nodded. A full circle moment, hearkening back to our first day together, soaking at Everett House.

We spent many hours that night at the pools. This pristine sanctuary overlooked rolling hills of unaltered land, nestled into a larger mountainside like a scene from a storybook. The three natural stone pools gradually increased in temperature, Goldilocks style.

Samuel had become someone with whom I could just be. We talked, sure, but mostly there was a sense of presence, speaking only when words would make the moment better than it was on its own. When we first met, this quality unnerved me, but as I became more comfortable with myself and with him, I'd begun to embrace the deep comfort of an easeful silence in the midst of a loved one.

Presence

The next morning, we woke early and soaked before the other visitors had roused themselves. We lay in the sun on the lodge's front lawn. We shared a feast of a lunch. We soaked again. In the afternoon, we took a lazy walk, arm in arm down to the river. We perched on a wooden swing, watching the bent birds reflected in smooth patches of water while frothy rapids rushed over boulders and logs. I felt like I was living someone else's life.

"It's so good to be here with you, Becca. I almost can't believe it," he said, squeezing me around the waist. He ran his hands through my hair playfully.

"I know. This is pretty perfect," I said. I felt a wave of emotion tug at me. "Ugh…" I added. I rubbed my eyes, as though this act would bring me more clarity.

"What is it?" he asked.

I stayed quiet for a while. I watched one of the birds take flight toward the trees.

"I just… I'm feeling very aware that this is so nice. And that you are leaving the country in a few weeks. And that I'm with Omer. I guess I'm just wanting to manage my expectations… and take in this perfect moment with you," I said. "What timing, huh?"

He sat there, quiet. I leaned my head onto his shoulder and stared out at the water, kicking the pebbles at my feet. The sweetness between us seemed to highlight the bitterness of the circumstances. His very presence called for presence. He was a reminder to me of life's most central lesson: that the present moment is truly all we have. In spite of my own stubborn resistance and my resolute feminism, he had unwittingly become one of my life's greatest teachers. I resolved to fully open myself to him for these last few days; no reason to hold back now. I didn't want to regret squandering the time we had to share.

Now though, there was more than just a willing presence. Our hearts were moving toward one another in a heavy new way. There was energy flowing between us that had been blocked in the past. It felt like a deeper love and understanding of one another, no longer held at a comfortable distance filled only with affection and tea and sex. I wanted to be seen and held, and I sensed that he did, too.

I felt fully loved and cared for out in the woods with Samuel. I knew that my most basic needs were met: I would be warm and dry and safe and sound. And I trusted that my heart's desires could be met, too. I could say anything to him and be heard. I could ask and he would answer. Again, without realizing it, just as he had before, he was tending to my inner child like a father would. Something in him just knew how.

There was an ethereal quality to that evening which moves me to tears whenever I think about it. It was like a sweet dream, almost too perfect for reality. It was truly one of the most touching nights of my life. We snuggled up under sparkling lights in our humble little truck bed and ate San Pedro cactus together. But first, he unhurriedly served me hot Kava tea. He rubbed my shoulders and burned sage and wrapped me in his arms and stared into my eyes for a long while. I saw love reflected back to me.

We wandered to the pools, hand in hand, and slowly undressed each other under the inky sky. No one was around. I turned toward the moon and let it wash me in its light, feeling the thrill of my bare skin against the cool night air and the heat of his eyes on my body, his hands tracing the bumps of my spine and the curves of my hips.

We slipped into the water, wordlessly, and soon found shallow platforms on which to rest on our backs. The hard stone held me up as I gazed at the stars, the San Pedro making them dance and flutter with elegant abandon. We must have stayed in that warm water for over an hour. We spoke in a meandering pace of everything and nothing. We laughed. We entwined our limbs in a bid to get as close to each other as we could while the laws of nature held us in two separate bodies. There was a pure peace, an untouchable bliss.

Once warm and dry in our bed, we gave ourselves over to each other and made love. For the first time, he wasn't just earnestly fucking me. It was more than a communion of pleasure. It was all love, embodied, start to finish. Seeing each other. Feeling each other. Heart to heart and soul to soul. Each stroke was charged with the words we hadn't said. After all was said and done, I pressed my hand into his chest.

"I love you," I said, unwavering.

We lay speechless and drifted sleepily between restfulness and invigoration. He ran a finger over my nose and lips, the bones of my cheeks and jaw and forehead, mesmerized.

"What are you thinking?" I asked him.

"I'm just feeling you. Letting you feel me," he said. "I've never let someone in like this. Not ever."

"Me either. It feels… wild," I agreed. I meant it. It was as deep and powerful as what I shared with Ari, but far off in some other direction, as if hearkening to an entirely different past life.

The last thing I remember was the taste of dark chocolate on my tongue and nestling into the crook of his shoulder with wholehearted contentment. When we woke the next morning, we had missed breakfast. We soaked one more time in the bright sunlight, smiling and winking at one another in silence.

"I'm starting to feel sad about the move. It's going to be lonely up in those mountains," he said as we ate lunch. He looked out the window at the tall Incense Cedar. "Would you come visit me? In Costa Rica?"

I didn't hesitate. "Of course I would." I took his hand in mine. "Like I've always said."

Sunday ended quickly and we had to return to society. I wasn't ready. I wanted more wordless nirvana with this man, my soul friend, my wildest, most unexplainable love. The trip had passed in a breath. There were no additional plans to be together before his departure.

When I arrived home that evening I was relieved to find the house empty. Omer was out at a show. It took me a few days to re-enter "normal" life after my time journeying with Samuel.

28

I received a lot of love on my birthday. To have four lovers, plus a sea of friends, old and new, was overwhelming. I chose not to have a party. Omer and I had plans to go to Maui for Thanksgiving, so we agreed that would be my birthday celebration.

On my actual birthday, Ari asked if she could have a few hours to spoil me. Moses was at preschool and I had finished my work early. Yes, of course.

She took me out for tacos on Division Street and I marveled at the simple thrill of taking a walk with her. It seemed the weather was always perfectly comfortable and something fantastical was always in bloom. Her company made my eyes wide open to beauty and art.

"Okay. I have a little surprise for you. Wanna come upstairs?" she asked when we returned.

I grinned and followed her up.

At the top, I resisted the urge to cry. Ari had transformed her bedroom into a dreamy fort space. She'd hung a sheer princess canopy over her bed, which was situated in the center of the room and piled with plush, furry, satiny textures. She had arranged a tray with mugs of cacao tea and a single flower in a bud vase. There was a card covered in confetti. It read,

> *"Becca, you are a chocolate cosmo. Happy Birthday. XO, Ari."*

I swooned and hugged her at least three times.

"Can we climb in?" I asked.

"Hehe, yes! That's the idea!" she replied.

She gave me a massage with sweet almond oil and we lazed the afternoon away in close embrace, with progressively less clothes until it was only our raw forms and heavy breath in the soft autumn light streaming through her window.

I felt so incredibly loved. This moment she had created, this tiny world within a world, felt like a peek into my soul that only she knew about. The dream of a life where we could just... be. Simple joy and aliveness, uncomplicated and totally within reach. *She* was the gift. These experiences were treasures for me to store up in myself.

That same night, Omer took me to a luxurious dinner at Le Pigeon and when we returned, he brought me out to the garage. He joked convincingly that he had bought me a sex swing and finally gotten it set up in the yoga space. He had me close my eyes.

I heard the familiar sounds of latches clicking.

When I opened my eyes, I saw a stunning sight: a beautiful Martin acoustic guitar adorned with a big red satin bow. I instantly began to cry, speechless.

"Do you like it?" he asked.

All I could do was nod and grin and try to pull myself together.

"I wasn't sure if it was an okay gift to get you. I know how much history you have with guitars, and I wanted to respect that. But, I also really want you to have one of your own again. Start a new chapter?" he said.

"I'm speechless. This is amazing, Omer. Thank you. Thank you." I said.

I spent the evening plucking its strings and pausing periodically to exclaim to Omer,

"This is amazing! You're amazing!"

Later that week, Calvin bought us tickets to Hump! Festival, Dan Savage's sex-positive, inclusive, humorous amateur porn film festival in Portland. I'd intended to go for several years; in fact, both Jack and Omer had mused about making films with me to enter into the contest. I was on board, with a hundred ideas, but we never had the timing quite right.

Calvin and I went together and had a roaring good time. It was entertaining, educational, and incredibly sexy. I've never felt so much sexual tension in a crowded theatre as I did during some of those scenes. You could practically feel everyone's hearts racing and pants tightening. That's a rare kind of community gathering, if you ask me.

There was one film that involved consensual non-consent. Basically, a rape fantasy scene. This was something I'd discussed with Calvin multiple times and felt very comfortable negotiating with him. I was sure it would happen eventually. He was more experienced with the world of doms and subs and had helpful questions about specifics that I'd never thought of.

Perhaps he'd lure me into an abandoned building on a random Sunday morning and stalk me through the house before tracking me down and taking me over. Don't ask me to explain why this turned me on so much; it just did. And the fantasy was specific to him, and our insane level of trust with each other. It was terrifying to think of someone else in his position. He squeezed my hand as we watched the scene. After it ended and we all cheered, I reached over, took his face in my hands, and kissed him hard.

"Love you, Calvin," I said. He grinned back and nuzzled into my neck, "Love you, B."

"That was hot," I added.

"… Yup," he replied.

Afterward, he brought me to Rimsky KorsaKoffee house. He bought me a banana split with a candle on top and sang me Happy Birthday. He told me hilarious stories of his youthful travels in Germany. Then he dropped me off at home and back to my default life.

I lay awake that night beside Omer, marveling at the life I'd found myself in. *How was it that in the span of just three years, I'd gone from a married Bible College graduate, starved for physical intimacy, to where I was now?* I was experiencing something I'd never fathomed as a Christian wife: I was in the midst of not one, two, or three… but *four* distinct and fulfilling love stories.

I felt completely saturated and along for the ride. Somehow, it was all working out. I felt balanced, fulfilled, and achingly grateful. There was no worry of what the future might hold; all I had space for was soaking up each moment with the abundance of people I loved.

31

Break

The Week of Three

Shortly after my love-soaked birthday, things took a heart-devastating turn.

Omer's mother was staying with us for a few weeks (which I enjoyed, and he mostly enjoyed). She offered to watch Moses the weekend after my birthday so that Omer and I could go out for a whole evening. He took me soaking at Everett House and then to Blossoming Lotus, a high-end vegan restaurant in the Lloyd District.

We sat across from each other, sharing salty cashew cheese nachos and spiced cocktails.

I was quiet, struggling to find anything to talk about that didn't involve one of my other lovers, who I'd been spending so much time with. They'd been occupying most of my mental space and free time for months. I tried to put them out of my mind. I asked him questions about work and how our friends were doing, and we chit chatted about our upcoming Maui vacation. He asked if I could help more with planning it, and I agreed.

"Honey, we need to talk," he said abruptly.

"…Okay. Talk to me," I replied.

"This is getting out of hand. I feel like you had all these light connections that were flirty and fun. They were basically friends who you played with sometimes. And now you're totally in love with several people? I don't know what to do with that. I don't know where I fit into your life," he explained.

I sipped my green tea and looked down. What could I say? It was true. I was swept up in love and confused where to go next.

"You're right," I said. "I never saw this coming. I knew I had a lot of love to give… but this isn't what I had in mind. They're each my friends, most of all, and they're really important to me. Think of how much you love your best friends. It's like that for me, too. Just… there's also sex involved."

"I feel like we're growing apart, Becca," he said. "I feel like you are more invested in these other connections than you are in us." There was pain in his eyes.

I could feel tears welling up in mine. I could see by my actions in recent weeks why he would feel that way. I'd been on autopilot in our relationship, content to make meals together, watch movies, go rock climbing and have sex. My passion and enthusiasm had been channeled toward my other lovers.

"Maybe I've been looking for the limits. Seeing how far I could take this and still have you. I've been testing your love for me. I think I haven't totally believed it could be true — to have our life together and still have the freedom I need."

He stared across the table. I could tell he was measuring his words, holding something back.

"I guess I'm going to be the one to say it. You're never going to," he said.

"Say what, babe?" I asked.

"I think you need to stop seeing these other people. At least for a while. We need to work on our relationship," he stated, plainly.

Silence. I held my breath. I turned to look out the window and Omer did the same. I was so relieved he wasn't ending our relationship in Blossoming Lotus on my birthday weekend. But I was stricken at the thought.

Ari.

Calvin.

Samuel.

These loves, these deep soul friends, each of whom I had a dimensional, thriving relationship with… out of my life? What would I say? How could I cope with that much loss all at once? Was it even worth it?

A tear streamed down my cheek. I nodded. I didn't really believe I had any choice in the matter. I could see he was hurting and frustrated. I didn't want to give up our life together.

"Okay... I, I think I can do that. It's going to be hard. Tell me more about what we need to work on."

We spent some time talking about our desire to bring more energy into our relationship — after he'd come back from the Burn and I'd moved in, we'd settled into a very comfortable home pattern with little newness or excitement. We were in a rut. I was preoccupied with my three earthy lovers, Omer had Jen and Aurelia, and our work schedules demanded a lot from us as well. We weren't even a year in, and we were in a cohabitating relationship plateau.

I took a moment to examine how rapidly things had changed. *How had this happened? Had this been inevitable all along? If I could go back, what would I have changed?*

Omer paid the check and we walked out. He stopped me by hand on the sidewalk and took me in his arms.

"I love you, honey. I want to make this work," he said.

Tears streamed down my face now, carrying countless emotions at once.

"I'm sorry," I said to him, about more than one particular thing. I resisted the compulsion to begin sobbing helplessly.

"I know. I am, too," he said.

"I guess I'll talk to everyone this week," I concluded. We drove home, and I went straight to bed rather than exchanging pleasantries with Omer's mother.

I lay awake that night imagining whether, and how, I would actually break it off with Ari, Calvin, and Samuel. Samuel had seemed inevitable, Calvin would be understanding, but Ari...

How, and why on earth, would I stop seeing Ari?

Heartache

Samuel and I had been talking all week. He was sending me sweet songs from Spotify and pictures of garden tools with a caption: "Should I sell this or put it in storage? Can't bring it to CR." Then there were the juicier, more explicit exchanges, which drew me back into our world of simple love.

A few days after my birthday talk with Omer, I took Moses to preschool and drove to Washougal for a morning hike with Calvin.

BREAK 415

On the way up, I confided in him about my struggles at work. I felt frustration with the patriarchal, all-male family of staff that, even on a good day, left me feeling very much like the black sheep. He empathized and validated my experience. We talked about life path and vision and paying our dues at challenging jobs.

When we reached the summit, he sat on a big log and pulled me onto his lap. It was a serene, cool day. We curled around each other and took in the pristine view. It had been a while since I hiked in the Gorge. For some reason, I remember he was wearing his vintage Levi's bell bottoms that only he could pull off. Why did he have to look, and feel, and… be… so easy to love?

I didn't want to say the words. He caught me before I was ready.

"Are you okay, Bee? You seem preoccupied," he inquired.

"Oh, no. Well, yes. Umm. Calvin, something's come up," I sighed.

"Talk to me," he said.

"I'm really struggling with Omer. We weren't prepared to be as non-monogamous as we became. We need to work on our relationship. Things have gotten really messy with all this love flying around and me not knowing where to land," I told him.

"Mmm-hmmm. That makes sense," he nodded. "It sounds like it has been a lot lately."

"I need to either take a break from seeing you or dial it way, way back," I said, beginning to cry. I wanted to launch into a soliloquy about how much I adored him and wished things were different and hoped that we could stay connected. But I opted for self-restraint, to spare us both the extra heartache of a long, desperate monologue that would change nothing.

His eyes welled up, too.

"You know, I've been in support of you and Omer since the beginning. I'll always be rooting for you two and your happiness. And you know where to find me if anything changes," he said. He took it all in stride, the most gracious man of them all. "I'm not sure what else to say right now. Just need some time to digest, I guess."

His grace and understanding took some of the sting out of a painful day. On the hike down, I felt like shit. It was an emotional marathon of a week, but I was determined.

Why

Omer had drawn a line, and it was my imperative to do what I needed to, to reign myself in and get right with him. I felt guilty. I felt I hadn't held up my end of our agreements, vague as they were, in forming a life with him. I wanted to be a good partner. I wanted to turn my shadows into something more acceptable. But what was my real motive — did I want to be monogamous and have a traditional relationship, or did I simply want to do what I must in order to be *seen* as a good partner?

At that time, I still entertained the idea that healing meant fundamentally changing the way I functioned in the world, and in love. Since then, I've come to believe that healing means acknowledging and integrating our histories and deepest desires, knowing them intimately and living our truths with self-awareness and integrity.

Omer's attitude toward my romantic life reinforced the notion that stability and traditional commitment were the more mature, evolved path forward. He implied that I needed to temper my wild heart and grow out of this insatiable drive to love everyone so fiercely and freely. It was the very quality he had spoken on with admiration that night at SOAK. But the theoretical experience of having a partner who loved everyone, and the daily reality of it, were quite different.

He wanted me to focus, to be less brazenly open to the world and its whims. He seemed to believe that I was trying to create an unconventional romantic life drawn from a fantasy. Well, maybe that part was true. I didn't have a clear end goal with Omer, besides avoiding the same mistakes I'd made with Jack and Keaton, and living more closely to my truth.

On some level, there was a conflicted dialogue within me compelling me to obey the rules of our culture. This was the third time I'd attempted non-monogamy and failed to make it work. After these years of peeling back layer upon layer of conditioning, I had finally hit a deep nerve: beneath everything was the reserved child who wanted to please people in authority in order to belong and be acceptable.

The daddy-daughter dynamic in our relationship wasn't hard to spot. Omer was older, male, stable, established, and financially secure. And then there was me: younger and wild-hearted and unpredictably fluid. He was setting a boundary and at once I wanted to please him and stay in his good graces.

Another side of me had a major urge to tell him he was out of touch with the times and he had known who I was when we got together. The same inner child that wanted to please her superiors also wanted to burn the rule book and fly in the face of everyone who had told her there was only one good way to live.

Adding to this complex dynamic between us was the ongoing conversation about our trajectory. Approaching 40 years old, Omer felt the push to settle down, travel less, get married and have kids. I had done all that already. At four years in, I was certain I didn't want to start over again with another child. We were on alternate paths — he was settling down, I was pursuing more freedom.

Sometimes I'd feel a whole rollercoaster of the heart in a single afternoon. I didn't feel clear at all. In non-monogamy I felt sincerely happier, more authentic and resilient, and understood by this variety of wonderful people who I'd chosen to be close with. But I also felt judged and dismissed by others in my life who couldn't make sense of it. Ari, Samuel, and Calvin all resonated with non-monogamy in their own ways and were on board with the nuance and fluidity of it.

Who was Omer, this man raised in a starkly different cultural and generational context, to tell me I was in the wrong? And how on earth were we going to meet in the middle? What might the middle even look like?

Clouds

A few days later, I had lunch with Ari at Fern Café after a yoga class.

She was getting ready for a four-month trip to Mexico. (I found it interesting that my lovers had roots in Central America. While I had felt called there since college, I had not yet been there.) She was subdued when she arrived. I vented to her about what was happening at home.

"So, I'm feeling pretty freaked out that he wants kids and I don't… and we're just not talking about it. Then last week at my birthday dinner, he asked me to take a step back from my other connections. Just sprung it on me." I slipped this in casually, hoping I could leave it and revisit it another time… or not.

I could tell that Ari had been keeping her mouth shut about Omer since the start. She wanted to be supportive and let me work out my own process. She trusted my sovereignty and my judgment. But also, she wasn't crazy about masculine energy in the first place, and it irritated her to witness the conditioned ways men operated in the world. Most of her inner circle was made of femme and non-binary queer folks.

"It's weird seeing you in such a straight crowd," she said simply. "Do you feel comfortable there? Sometimes, I feel like you're just repeating all the things that didn't work for you and Keaton, with someone new. Do you realize the first thing you told me about him was that he was a *kiteboarder*? What is inspiring you about this relationship?" she asked.

She had cut straight through my bullshit.

I stumbled over my words.

In truth, I wasn't sure. I hadn't spent enough time in my own element, embracing the reality of my own queerness, to know where I felt most myself.

Perhaps in this way I was still stuck in my own conditioned world. In cisgendered, straight communities I knew the rules and knew how to play along and navigate my way through. However, I felt a kindred spirit to the fluidity and freedom of the queer community. Yet I sometimes felt like an imposter; not queer enough. I was still very much immersed in a world of dudes and rock climbing and dancing at shows and, in spite of the Burner counterculture, traditional gender roles still reigned supreme.

Against men's bodies, mine knew what to do — I'd been forming those habits for 15 years. Every time I was with a woman, though, all bets were off. There was no script to follow. There was ultimate freedom to co-create, and all the risk that came with it.

As much as I hated to admit it, it was true: there were entire parts of myself I was withholding from Omer. I would wake before he and Moses every morning and sit alone by the fireplace to meditate. Then I would do my morning pages, creating freeform art a la The Artist's Way. I was very private about making my art, mostly sketches of plants or line drawings of landscapes.

I didn't let out my creative side around him. Or my masculine side. Or my "woo woo" side. The Becca living in that house was rational and feminine and straight.

As I struggled to form these thoughts into an answer, I realized I'd been seeking to preserve, even fight for, the more gender-bending part of me while living with Omer. I had funkier, more masculine swaths of my wardrobe that I didn't wear because they clashed with his aesthetic and made me feel out of place in our sophisticated home. Deep down, I felt like a fraud — like I was poorly playing the part of his demure partner in an upscale neighborhood of white folks and Volvos and wives and kids and dogs. And I felt like a fraud in the queer community, knowing I had a straight cis-male partner at home.

I watched as Ari picked at her burger.

"I don't want to eat this right now," she said, pushing it away.

"I feel like I just spent a lot of time bitching about Omer," I said, ashamed.

"I don't really know what to say…" she said. "I'm going through stuff here, too, Becca. We have this whole thing happening," she motioned between us. "And I feel like a little queer side piece to your regular life. And also, I'm leaving. And closing my business. And honestly…" her eyes grew blurry. "Things were hard enough before you came in. I just really didn't need this right now. It sucks knowing we have this connection that can't actually be a thing. I feel like I have this dark fucking cloud over me all the time."

I nodded. I could feel the pain in her words and I admired her uncompromising truth. What could I say? We sat and cried and tried to enjoy our annoyingly trendy turmeric lattes and mediocre salads.

We agreed to let things breathe for a while. We hugged and set off walking down the sidewalk in opposite directions. It felt wrong.

I was wrecked. I began to question what I was doing, and why. I couldn't see anything life-giving about cutting off these people who I loved and was loved by, who understood me and made different aspects of myself shine, who challenged me to be a stronger, softer, more courageous version of myself.

Samuel, Part V

I was feeling nothing short of depleted when I went to Samuel's house that weekend. He was chipper when I arrived. We savored a long kiss at his front door. He stared at me for a moment, a twinkle in his eyes, then turned and plucked a stem from the fuchsia plant on the porch where he allowed them to grow wild.

"This one reminds me of you," he said, handing it to me tenderly.

"Guess what?" he continued. "I have a new idea. You're going to love it."

"What's that?" I asked, refreshed by his upward energy. I was already forgetting the reason I'd come.

He waved his hands in front of me with a flourish. "Sprinter van," he beamed.

"Haha! Yes! Wait… you want to buy a sprinter van? But you're about to move out of the country," I wondered aloud.

"Oh, yeah. Well. I've been thinking…" He went back to pulling items out of his big shipping totes as he spoke. "I might want to keep more roots here in Portland than I thought. I'm not going to sell my truck. Or, maybe I'll sell it and get a Sprinter. I just want to be able to come back pretty often and have somewhere to stay. Wouldn't that be nice? We could see each other more," he smiled.

"Wow. That's a change. I mean… selfishly, I love that idea! But also, I am kind of surprised. When's your flight?"

"Oh. I haven't bought a ticket yet," he said, holding up two pairs of work gloves and debating which ones to pack.

"I thought you were leaving next week?" I pried.

"Well, I don't have to be… I'm not feeling inspired to rush off," he answered, looking long at me from the floor where he sat.

I was truly confused. He had seemed so certain this was a massive life change, finally a transition to living in those Pura Vida mountains where he'd been working for over ten years. Yet suddenly he had changed his whole tune.

We nestled onto the couch like we always did. I looked around the room, his art on the walls and jars of grains and beans and teas still on the kitchen counter. It didn't look like he was moving anywhere. I took in the sight of him, smiling at me sweetly, squeezing my hand in his. He was more open to me than he had ever been, and my desire to throw myself into him was almost unbearable.

"I can't wait for you to come visit. I'm going to miss you while I'm down there," he said to me.

"Samuel, I have to tell you something." I could barely look at him. The words made me sick. "I can't keep seeing you."

It felt almost ironic coming out of my mouth, as though I was playing an ugly prank. His stack of permaculture books in the corner caught my eye as they always did, and I recalled the evolution of our relationship inside this very room, the center of his humble home.

He furrowed his brow, confused, as if I was speaking a completely different language.

I spoke frantically as he stared on in silence.

"It's coming between Omer and I. We can't handle something this complicated. Here… I wrote you a letter." I pulled it from my bag. "I'm

BREAK

super confused being here right now. Just, read it okay? And call me later?" I stood up to leave.

"You're leaving, just like that? Wait, Becca. Hang on a minute," he said. "Let's talk about this."

I stalled by the door, one shoe in my hand. He continued.

"I'm so confused why you're saying this. Things are so good. Did Omer ask you to do this, or is this coming from you?" he asked.

"It's... both of us. I don't know..." I trailed off, choking back tears. I was so damn tired of crying.

"Becca. No. I don't accept this. This is a mistake. Please, don't leave." He took my shoe from my hand and set it back on the floor. "We need to talk about this. Come here." We sat back on the couch.

"Are you two really that happy? You're saying you want to be monogamous? Since when is that even you?" he asked.

I looked away. He was cutting straight through my bullshit, the same way Ari had.

"Do you really have it so good over there that you're willing to give this up? After everything? It doesn't seem like it. You know what it sounds like? It sounds like you're afraid." He was passionate, pleading, yet softer than usual.

He was right, and that angered me. I was afraid. Afraid of failing at another partnership on the heels of Keaton and Jack. I tried to explain the nuance of the situation, but my responses sounded trite. Confused as I was, I made only weak defenses against his fiery Aries love and determination to stay close to me. Truth is, I wanted that, too.

We went back and forth endlessly, talking in maddening circles, not hearing each other, before the emotional tension became so intolerable I had to tear myself away.

"Just... read the letter, okay? And then we can talk again. I can't stay here right now. It's too hard." I kissed him quickly and walked out the door toward my car. I stuffed the little flower he'd given me in my back pocket.

The Letter

I had drafted a letter in my phone and contemplated deleting it multiple times before actually putting pen to paper.

"Samuel,

It's been a wild surprise and a complete gift to share in this love with you. I honestly never guessed this would happen — I thought we'd always be friends who met on Tinder with a complicated history. Instead, you've built me a house of love and within it, you've made me feel wanted and at home. You've been generous, understanding, patient and kind. Thank you for our shared dreams. I can see trees and flowers and slow sunsets. Thank you for being vulnerable, for dropping into deep heart places with me and exploring the far reaches of the universe, too. I cherish the trust and friendship we have slowly built and the warmth that's bloomed out of it these last couple years.

Your love has been healing for me. You've reminded me of my best self, my deepest self, the roots of my soul where my passion for the earth and for people is pure and my visions are clear. You continue to inspire me just by being who you are. I see you. I feel you. You are truly good and your fire, courage, clarity and deep love are rare and so precious to me.

Loving you has felt freeing — like something strong and powerful, if a bit uncontrolled.

But I also have my own home where I am loved. It's a place where I'm finding healing every day. I believe I belong here. I have a partner whose love is healthy for me. It's one that balances my own fiery, passionate energy with steadiness, patience, and devotion. I've chosen to make a life with Omer, and to do what it takes to make it work.

I've made this choice because I believe it is right. I've been pushing my heart and my loved ones' too hard. It's not possible for me to be connected with multiple people who I love so intensely. It feels like a tightrope. It's better if you don't wait for me. I am here, committed to someone, and you are leaving, free as a bird.

The dreams you and I share are beautiful and moving. They're things I hold close to my heart. "Someday" is hard not to say because I am still so confused. All I know is that life has an uncanny way of inhaling and exhaling, of honoring the bonds we've made in this plane and others. Your deep soul love will always be a part of me. I already ache thinking of the unsatisfied distance that fills the space between us. This is fucking painful for me, and I hate that it is for you too. You've been brave in loving me and asking for what you want and I cherish your tenderness and passion.

For now, we need to let this breathe. I can't hold the love you're giving me. I wish I could. I wish I could have both of you and love you back as fully as you've loved me.

BREAK

I send my heart to you every day, no matter where you are. When you are alone in the mountains, or lonely, or filled with heartache and wanting, feel Big Love. You are inside of it and so am I. I'm there with you, just like we've been so many times before.

I believe we are held by a cosmic medicine that conspires for our good and our healing. Our meeting and our entire story has been synchronistic to the core. We've felt it. It's been a gift to meet you inside of that magic. It's something completely new to me. I've never gone into other realms with anyone like I have with you. Realms of the mind, of the body, of the heart. We can still rest on that Big Love. I believe we'll find each other there again.

Te amo, my querido. ¿Quién dice que no nos vamos a ver de nuevo?"

Who's to say we won't meet again?

Unwilling

Even as the letter flowed on, I had moved from complete resolve to live a life with Omer, to the belief that Samuel and I were not over; and rather that I was just doing what I needed to in that moment.

Later that night, we exchanged a messy series of texts. He felt totally blindsided. I felt it was unfair that he'd pretended I was fully available and allowed his heart to run wild, even though I'd tried over and over to slow us down and keep an eye on our expectations.

We were both frustrated with the other and hurt that we had allowed ourselves to tend to a love that simply couldn't grow where it was planted. He sent me a cascade of heart wrenching, disjointed messages:

"Becca, I want you to be happy and have a good life!"

"Right now I feel lied to by the person I trusted most. On Friday I felt more love for you than I've ever experienced. And now, this… you're just turning your back. I don't feel I can trust you anymore."

"I'm so caught off guard. I feel I am in some sort of shock. I feel like you are rushing into this big decision."

He kept fighting for me. The next week, he sent me a voice message.

"After all this talking, Becca, I guess what I've been thinking is this: are we okay not seeing each other? And not having this love and connection anymore? Is this something we want in our lives, or not?"

I'd never had someone fight for me the way he did.

He was actually *unwilling* to accept that I was walking away from something so good between us.

It was a love that had been brewing for several years and we had finally stayed still long enough to taste it, and damn, it was good. His level of clarity and fire frightened me. I've never in my life been as clear and specific as him on anything. I've just wanted to eat the whole world, on my terms and my timeline. I've wanted total freedom, and I've never known another desire as powerful as that one.

I was emotionally derailed. As I searched for a landing place after nearly tipping off my own edge, my friends lent their support and their questions. They talked me through it. Tess and Logan and Lori wanted to get to the bottom of it.

> *How did it feel to imagine bringing Moses to Costa Rica, or having a life with Samuel living here part time?*
>
> *How did I see that playing out, in reality?*
>
> *Was I truly happy with Omer and was that the life I wanted?*
>
> *Was it worth shutting the door on Samuel?*

They urged me to reflect on all the mystery beneath our connection. This frustrated me. It wasn't the support I wanted. I wanted to be told that I was making the right decision to stay with Omer, and that I really ought to slow down and stop making these love triangle shit shows for myself. Instead, my friends raised their eyebrows and marveled at the way he kept appearing in my life.

I didn't test myself by seeing him in person, but Samuel and I stayed in contact.

He began insisting to me that what we had was better and more lasting than the partnership I was in. He said that we both knew it.

I became defensive and closed off, carrying a "Who do you think you are?" attitude toward him.

But I didn't deny it.

We went through several tender weeks of back and forth until I became so confused that I chose to completely cut off contact with him. I wasn't sure what else I could do.

And then Omer and I left for Maui.

32

Vacation

Maui

I'd never been to Hawai'i before. We were to spend a week on Maui's north shore with two friends, Joe and Mariah, who were married. I was delighted to be going and felt that it would be a well deserved and rejuvenating reward for all the emotional labor I'd just undergone to make space for Omer in my heart again.

I was ready to connect with him.

Omer was tied up with work in the weeks after my birthday as the year's end loomed closer. He had patents to write and teams to manage, and felt that he needed to put his head down and work every minute he could, especially since we had two holiday vacations coming up: Maui for Thanksgiving and Mexico for Christmas.

I had arranged to take Moses for several weekends, since Keaton would be looking after him while I traveled. Omer offered to help me with the extra time, since it amounted to three straight weeks of parenting without a break. Instead, by the time the weekends came, he was so worn out from work that he needed to blow off steam by going dancing or rock climbing. I felt abandoned.

I was at home one Saturday night while Moses slept and Omer was out with our friends. I scrolled through photos in my phone from the previous months of unbridled adventures, poetic love and deep connection with Ari, Calvin, and Samuel. I allowed myself the pleasure of an erotic fantasy. Lying in Omer's bed alone, with my own hands between my legs, I recognized how quickly things had changed. In the space of two weeks, I'd gone from so much fullness to an emaciated shell of a relational life where I felt mostly alone much of the time.

I felt I had been duped.

It felt like a bait and switch to ask me to be monogamous so we could focus on repairing our relationship, and then become totally unavailable when it came time to make those repairs. Subtle feelings of resentment began to take root in me. I reminded myself over and over that ending these relationships were choices I had made because I wanted to be here. I had wanted to make things good with Omer. The frustrating part was, I still wasn't clear on whether any of this life *was* what I wanted. Less so now, than ever.

When we made it to Hawaii, I was able to set aside my heartache for the most part. It's hard to feel sad when wandering a tropical paradise under the gentle sun, beside a handsome, earnest partner.

He was intent on kiting Maui's North Shore and had researched the best locations. As usual, he and Joe planned the week's itinerary around the weather forecast. While he was on the water (I'd sworn off kiting by that point) I wandered the beaches and drew pen sketches of unknown flowers, shells and driftwood. That week, I filled half a journal with nature sketches, which only reminded me of the three beautiful souls I'd left in Portland.

Overall, it was a beautiful time. Wholesome and fun and drama free. And yet… I was discontent. I was bored. I found my time with Omer boring. I felt he had asked me to give up so much, and yet not offered much in its place.

I was deeply craving time alone on that island. I would wake before everyone else and sit out on the deck overlooking the property, pausing to breathe in the cool tropical morning air. I buried myself in my books and my sketchbook. I eased slowly back into comfort with Omer after the challenges we'd had. We savored long afternoons under the bright sunlight. We snorkeled with turtles on pristine beaches and Omer and Joe carted their gear to the windiest spots of the island for days at a time.

It was truly a paradise.

We saw natural wonders that left me speechless. There were alcove beaches of deep red sand, the summit of Haleakala mountain, sunsets on Little Beach, and driving the famed Road to Hana, which is still one of the most memorable, beautiful days of my entire life. Omer and I went on the adventure to Hana alone. It was the happiest day I'd ever shared with him.

The sun was bright but not sweltering. We bushwhacked in our swimsuits

VACATION

through muddy bamboo forests and hiked up waterfalls and swam up rivers to secret swimming holes. A few miles further, I couldn't contain my excitement within the Garden of Eden Arboretum. It was a fantastically abundant place bursting with life, as if the whole forest was stretching at the seams.

I've never seen so many giant, awe-inspiring trees! There were technicolor flowers as big as my torso and hundreds of rare plants nestled against the commonplace mango, jackfruit, papaya, bird of paradise, and what seemed to be thousands of others. I watched Omer "ooohh" and "ahhh" at the plants, joining in my excitement, like a parent joining a beloved child in a game of make believe. He was playing along, and I loved him for trying.

Later on, the others indulged me, and we spent an afternoon perusing the local farmers market. We bought more fruit than we could eat: coconuts, papayas, guayaba, and lilikoi. A beautiful woman, about my age, and her strong mother called shoppers over to the back of their big pickup truck, where they were hacking young coconuts open with machetes and serving them with giant straws.

On our last day there, we went to an extravagant birthday lunch at a ranch called the Mill House, celebrating two birthdays — Joe and myself. It was an airy and upscale restaurant and the food was hyper local and incredibly delicious.

There exists a photo from that meal. In it, I look beautiful in my fitted black Prana sundress, a big smile on my face and Omer's strong arm around my shoulder. The bright green mountains stand perfect against the cloudless sky, an immaculate, sparkling backdrop to a handsome, healthy couple.

I looked beautiful, but not at all like myself. I looked well-behaved and unremarkable. The woman in those pictures was a nice girl. She was the one who lived life by the guidelines, who slept in the nice house with the right car and the cute child and the dreamy vacations. She was destined to become a classy lady with dead eyes and a small life.

I couldn't shake the notion once it visited me: I was about to repeat the same mistake I had made with Keaton. I was about to choose security, again, over my fullest expression of self. Another bigger, but still small life. I'd already begun by sacrificing my deep and subversive heart connections with Ari, Calvin and Samuel. This relationship was a closer bet at success than my marriage, but at its core, it was not aligned with who I was and the unencumbered life I craved.

When Omer and I returned home from Maui, Ari was about to leave on a one-way flight to Mexico. I met her for a last-minute tea at Townshend's.

We talked, we cried, and we kissed on the mushy vintage couch in the big front window. I didn't care who saw us. I told her I was thinking hard about stepping out on my own, wondering what it might be like to live as a truly single person. She couldn't believe it. She was proud of me. We promised each other we'd meet again as soon as we could. I wished her safe travels and joked, yet again, about coming to visit.

SCUBA

One morning in early December, Omer burst into the kitchen, looking chipper.

"Honey. How do you feel about scuba diving?" he asked.

"Umm. Good," I said without hesitating. I smiled up at him. "Seems like fun. Why?"

"Great. Because we're going scuba diving in the Yucatan. I'll make some calls about getting you dive certified."

"Okay, then! Good talk!" I answered, laughing. What a life.

I felt good about learning scuba and I was elated to have the chance to witness some reefs firsthand. I'd seen the film Chasing Coral and knew that major coral bleaching and die-off events were happening at alarming rates due to rising ocean temperatures. Huge stretches of reef were turning completely barren. I wanted to see them flourishing while they were still there to be seen.

In life, most of my struggle with water has had to do with the edge where it meets the air. Water is deep and powerful, and its surface is often turbulent. My systems didn't know how to exist in the constantly shifting setting. I do not like holding my breath. The depth felt safer to me than the surface.

I pulled $700 out of an envelope of cash I had hidden behind a picture frame. It was money I'd been saving for taxes. Well, that had been the original plan. But I had to cover the cost of last minute private scuba lessons in a bougie fitness club, plus all my diving gear and a wetsuit. There was no internal debate. I was not willing to go all the way to Mexico with Omer and be unable to participate in the main activity while we were there.

I went through my two-day intensive crash course scuba training on my Moses-free days the following week. I spent the rest of my free time trying to get ahead on work to make my absence possible. The emotions I'd been experiencing in November before Hawaii were compounded. I'd been away from all my other lovers for a month. Samuel was back in Costa Rica, Ari was in Mexico, and Calvin had graciously returned to the friend zone.

One day, I took Moses on our routine afternoon walk. I let him stay up past sunset so he could see the Christmas lights brightening the whole neighborhood. It was just the two of us, since Omer was gone at a fitness class. I dressed Moses in his cozy gloves and boots and puffy coat. He asked me if we could have hot chocolate. I told him no, not tonight.

"Mom? Remember? Whenever we look at Christmas lights with Jack, we always have hot chocolate," he insisted. I sighed. I felt alone.

We wandered past entire blocks of inflatable Snoopy and Santa Claus characters beneath thousands of lights lining the rooftops. Moses chattered, content as we walked, and I thought back over all the love I had sacrificed in my life. *Why?* I wondered. Then, I had a realization.

For years, I'd been trading one person for another, constantly seeking someone who was closer to a good fit as a partner. Keaton wasn't right for me. Jack was closer. Omer was closer. Samuel was closer. Ari was closer.

I'd been looking for alignment *outside* of myself, an impossible aim.

Until that moment, it had never occurred to me that this was what I was doing.

As if I'd believed that only with a partner could I build a life that might somehow validate my existence. Someone to bring to life my deeply personal goals, dreams, successes and failures. Someone to make me feel safer in my own wild skin, as though it was impossible to provide that stability for myself. I wanted a sidekick so that if I failed, I wouldn't fail alone. If I came under fire, I wouldn't take the fall alone. I'd been looking for someone to be by my side because I hadn't learned to trust myself.

Damn. It was a tough pill to swallow.

Tulum

A few days later, Omer and I boarded another plane. It was almost Christmas. We had been on so many planes that year: San Francisco. Washington D.C. Hawaii. Mexico. I'd become accustomed to dozing beside him while we hurtled through the atmosphere. But this trip started off on the wrong foot. I was awake until 2:00 am packing. I'd had Moses with me for several weeks until dinner that evening, all while working full time and studying for my scuba certification. I felt totally exhausted and isolated.

As I gathered my bathing suit and sandals, I stood still for a moment. *Why was I going on this trip?* Things with Omer were a mess. We really hadn't found our stride since the upset six weeks earlier when he asked me to be monogamous.

Well, it's too late to back out now.

I hoped that perhaps we would be able to reconnect and clear the air while we were away (because international travel during the holidays is just the kind of low-stress activity that strained relationships need, right?)

Finally, I cinched my traveler's backpack and dragged my tired body upstairs to find Omer.

"Alright, honey. I'm packed. I'm going to bed. Remind me what time we're leaving for the airport?"

"The Lyft is coming in 20 minutes," he said.

Ugh. We didn't sleep at all. Our bodies were fatigued, and our moods were sour. Well, mine was. I had no energy at all to engage with him.

He had an earnest puppy dog appearance and kept glancing over at me, searching for some sign of goodwill. I was feeling cold and mean. The whole time we stood in line for check-in, I cursed his goddamned kiting gear. He always chose to travel with several options for boards and various sized kites, so the gear filled two massive golf travel bags. They were the size, shape, and weight of human body bags. I felt like I was dragging around the corpse of a grown man by the handle.

I hated lugging those bags around, even more so since I wasn't going to reap the recreational benefits of bringing them along. Airport trips took longer than usual because of special lines for oversized luggage. He'd been traveling with this gear for a decade and had it down to a science, but I still found the whole affair cumbersome and vowed I would never choose a sport that required that much equipment.

The following afternoon, after several flights, we landed in Cancun. Omer had slept for most of the flight. I had not, despite a promising cocktail of melatonin, kava, and CBD which made me extremely drowsy. I finally snapped at him while we waited in line for customs. I felt he was smothering me.

"How are you doing, honey? Do you need anything?" he asked for the third time.

"I need you to STOP asking me that. I haven't slept in 36 hours, Omer. I'm exhausted. I don't want to talk. Please, just let me be quiet and don't take it personally."

He was stung. He went silent. And then we stood together in line for customs for the next hour. It was terribly awkward.

We made it to Tulum late that night, and enjoyed a delicious beachside dinner. Before the food arrived, I apologized to Omer for being so terrible to him that afternoon. I treaded lightly, feeling that to pull at any thread of interpersonal conflict might prompt a deeper conversation and unravel us completely. He was gracious, yet looked at me throughout dinner as though I was an unpredictable and wild creature. After we'd slept, I finally felt like less of a monster.

The following morning, I went for a walk alone. Tulum was beautiful. It was a place in transition: formerly a bustling area serving mostly locals, it was fast becoming a destination for self-congratulatory yoga retreats and Instagrammable millennial beach parties. Once off the touristy main road, it hit me: I was in Mexico. *Mexico!* My homeland, for the first time. Locals smiled and waved as I passed. I felt safe there, not like an outsider invading someone's space, but like a welcome visitor with a shared sense of mutual respect and belonging.

"Buenas," they'd say. Good morning.

"Buenas," I'd reply.

I looked at the older men and I saw my dad. I noticed their laid-back demeanors as they went about their morning chores. Even their gait patterns and the way they gazed down at the sidewalk a few paces ahead of them was uncannily like my father's. Their mustaches, boots and cowboy hats adorned their sturdy frames as they cruised past on bicycles, hauling baskets of fruit or trailers with bricks and construction materials. Everyone seemed to be up to something. No one was stressed or rushed. My dad was everywhere.

Being there, in a place where his quiet way was the norm and my wound-up American way was unusual, I felt instantly like I understood him in a brand-new way. I wished, almost to the point of tears, that I could have been immersed in his culture, even briefly, as a young person. How might I have related to him differently all those years if I'd understood where he came from? Instead I simply saw him through my mother's eyes: as the man who had let us all down and couldn't seem to acclimate to social life in the white, Christian suburbs.

I wanted to stop someone on the street, anyone, and tell them, "I know I look Spanish, but my father is Rogelio Rodriguez Martinez and his family comes from northern Mexico and I am visiting his homeland for the first time and I feel like I finally understand the man who raised me."

Instead, when posed the simple question: "Como esta?" I simply replied, "Estoy bien. Si… muy bien."

When I returned to our hotel, I didn't feel I could share this breakthrough with Omer. I was still too guarded and angry to share something so tender. Feeling isolated had allowed me freedom to venture off alone, which was exactly what needed to happen. *I needed to be alone in Mexico.*

• • •

Eneas and Javier met us in Tulum, ready for a week of diving and kiteboarding. Taking a kiteboarding vacation together was Omer and his friends' Christmas tradition. We would be there for ten days total, enough time to explore Tulum and Isla Holbox.

On our second night, Omer and I finally had a blowout. I'd been hamming it up in the living room of our hotel suite with Eneas and Javi, happy to be reunited with Eneas again, laughing and telling jokes. More than once, Omer made jokes that I found to be in poor taste. I rolled my eyes. Later on, he chugged Eneas' entire margarita while Eneas was away from the table, just to fuck with him. I felt like I was watching these men revert into teenage boys, Omer most of all.

What are you doing here with these people? I thought to myself. I felt very alone, as though I was expected to play along with their dorm room antics or be perceived as an uptight bitch.

That night, Omer confronted me before we went to sleep. His lower lip was quivering.

"Do you even want to be here with me right now?" He stared at me. "I feel like you're disgusted with me and everything I do is irritating you."

It crossed my mind that we had another eight days together in Mexico. I attempted to soften. I sighed.

"I'm having a really hard time switching gears," I told him. "Things have been hard. And now we're in a new, beautiful place, but I'm feeling pretty raw. I'm holding a lot of resentment toward you and I don't know how to shake it," I told him, truthfully.

We had a clipped and unsatisfying discussion and agreed to give it some time. At the very least, neither of us wanted to have a shitty vacation.

The next day, we rose early for our diving trips. I completed my dive certification course on my own while my travel mates went out on a separate boat for a more advanced dive. I loved the group I was with. Nico, my instructor, was a young Venezuelan soccer player turned dive master. We had immediate rapport and the young, earthy Barcelona couple who came along were a welcome addition.

We dove in sparkling turquoise pools, called cenotés, and I felt I was in my element. It was such a contrast to the experience of learning to kiteboard. Under water, buckled into my scuba vest, I felt safe. I had the muscle memory down and was becoming comfortable with my breathing technique. Buoyancy is a wondrous thing — once you master it, you essentially feel weightless in the water. I entered into a trance-like state of calm, feeling how a deep inhale would cause me to float higher in the water, and a bubbly exhale would allow me to sink lower. I began to manage my depth simply by controlled breathing.

The underwater world was exactly that: another world. In the sea, the sound was different. Temperature felt different. It was a place indifferent to humans and bursting with a beauty and diversity we hardly deserve to witness. There was no speaking, no flapping about. We glided along in silent reverence, adding the occasional mermaid flip or twirl, just for the joy of it. I loved being weightless. It was likely the closest thing to flying I'll experience in this lifetime.

On my walk back from the dive shop, I called Ari. She answered on the second ring. I told her all about Tulum and my underwater adventure and my thoughts of my dad. We daydreamed about running into each other in the town square and sharing a plate of tiny tacos. She wished me a Merry Christmas.

When I reunited with the guys that evening, I was feeling like myself again. I was hopeful that Omer and I could find a good flow for the rest of the trip.

We traveled to the ruinas — both Tulum and Coba. These historical sites featured huge Mayan structures that are still intact, some deep in the jungle and some on the coastline overlooking the Caribbean. It was stunning. In an unfortunate sequence of events, Omer had guessed the wrong sunrise time and when we arrived at the site the sun was already climbing its ladder in the sky. None of us let him live it down.

The only thing detracting from what was otherwise a brilliant, beautiful morning in which to commune with this ancient and energetically charged place, was the number of done-up Instagram influencers and their photographer boyfriends treating every pathway and lookout point, every ancient temple and pyramid as their own personal photo backdrop.

"Wow. I know I'm a millennial, but I can't fucking stand millennials," I said, to no one in particular.

After the ruins, we spent a day at a beach resort called Papaya Playa, a place that hosted high-end beach parties for the local festival crowd. I drew in my sketchbook and wandered up and down the beach reading, while the guys rented kiteboards and skimmed over the shallow waters.

We all found a rhythm and I began to enjoy my time, though the lingering feeling of something wrong was tenacious as the tides, returning to torment me each evening as I lay awake beside Omer's sleeping body.

Deep Dive

Our big dive was two days before Christmas. It was an open water dive off the shore of the island of Cozumel. Our early morning was peppered with hot coffee and bright sunshine. We all crammed into Nico's little pickup truck and rode to the Cozumel ferry. It was a bustling, chaotic scene, as crowded as an amusement park, but with many more languages being spoken and crowds moving in all directions.

Once on the boat, I felt myself relax. The expansive waters were a rich bright blue, unlike any I'd ever seen before.

I was thrilled for my first open water dive, and happy to finally share a dive experience with Omer and Eneas. (Javier had stayed back in town and spent the day drinking and flirting with locals at Papaya Playa). Eneas had found a Santa hat and wore it on the dive, along with a psychedelic print wetsuit. He brought his GoPro and documented the whole excursion. Eneas stayed near me on the boat, while Omer milled around, fussing with gear and taking photos. More than once I leaned over to Eneas for a hug. I felt vulnerable. I wasn't feeling well, and this was worsened by the emotional unease I was facing with Omer.

I looked around the boat. There were ten divers in total. Eight were men in their forties and fifties, all European and experienced divers. Plus Nico, our dive master. Then there was me. A young, pretty woman alone on a boat in the Yucatan in a male-dominated world. They made glances my way as if to size me up and gauge whether I was up to the task.

On our first dive, the support staff strapped me into my gear and dumped me in the water first. I floated there, waiting, feeling relieved to be off the man boat. We all descended together and enjoyed a spectacular dive. It was like touring live scenes straight out of Blue Planet. We saw massive fish and eels and crabs the size of my head. The corals were otherworldly, still very much alive, reaching like Seussical sculptures toward the sky. I felt at peace down in the depths.

We all stayed close together, and I could sense that Omer was by my side. He was a certified dive master and had been an instructor in the past, so he walked the line between being totally confident in my capabilities, yet cautiously protective. It's so funny how we adults parent one another in this way.

We coasted along the ocean floor, about 30 meters deep. Eneas had the GoPro and was focused on filming a little school of clownfish when we saw a huge shadow looming in our periphery. We turned and saw an enormous black and white eagle ray gliding a few meters away. It must have been five meters across! I've never seen anything like it. It flapped its fins like aquatic wings, and with a few strokes it was off and away, up through the water toward the surface. I stared on in awe. Now, that was flying! The sweetest part was the pair of large fish riding beneath the eagle ray like content co-pilots. The whole scenario was straight out of *Finding Nemo*.

When we came out of the water, we gushed about the experience.

"Did you see that fucking huge thing?" said Omer.

"I know!! What was that? Some kind of sting ray?" I asked Nico.

"A Spotted Eagle Ray," he grinned.

"Wait, what?!" asked Eneas. Poor Eneas had missed the whole thing. We tried not to laugh.

"I hope it was worth your fish footage," Omer teased.

Sinking

The second dive was intense for me. We were diving in a strong current, along a steep reef that was basically an underwater cliff. All along the wall was habitat where we could see huge turtles, lobsters, schools of fish, eels and coral. I had a depth watch for the first time, and no one bothered instructing me on how to use it. I fiddled with it, but we were rushed, and I ultimately gave up and decided to just stay with the guys.

There was so much to keep track of for this dive. As a group, we had two separate plans based on our experience, dictating how deep we were allowed to go, and for how long. We would separate into two groups at a certain point in the dive, and each group was responsible for taking their safety stops at set times (this is a mandatory precaution to manage the nitrogen levels in your blood as you ascend to the surface).

The current was strong, and the lead weight belt the staff had given me was heavier than necessary, pulling me downward. I also had trouble with pressure in my ears during our descent, so I continuously had to stop and swim back up toward the surface and try to equalize the pressure. I couldn't get one of my ears to clear. It was a stressful situation, as we were in moving waters, trying to stay together, and we could only communicate nonverbally. I resolved not to panic. My entire focus was intent on staying with the group.

Once we entered the current, I settled into my breathing and became acclimated to where I was. But the current was taking me much faster than the guys. They were physically larger than I was and had more surface resistance, plus they had stronger technique in swimming perpendicular to the current to slow their movement. Not only was I moving rapidly downstream, I was also unaware that I was *sinking* gradually due to the extra weight on my belt. Once at a certain depth, everything looks the same. I heard beeping. The guys motioned to me. I didn't understand.

Nico swam down to me and inflated my vest to help me rise. He made a pleading motion and pointed toward the sky. He was asking me to please stay shallower in the water. He pointed to my watch. It showed that I'd gone down to 90 meters. A beginner diver is only certified to descend to 30 meters. Whoops! I nodded. We rejoined the crew.

Soon, the current caught us and we were cruising downstream again. The whole dive went by quickly, and although we saw many of the same beautiful sights, I was overwhelmed by the intensity of our drift and my sense of being very much out of control. It was an active exercise in staying present, breathing, and not panicking, under any circumstances.

Back on the boat, the guys teased me about my "beginner's confidence" and my eagerness to find the ocean floor. I promised that I was not trying to be rebellious; I was actually that clueless. And could someone please show me how to operate a damn dive watch? We all laughed it off. Omer was later mortified to learn that I hadn't been better prepared by my instructors for the dive.

"Becca, that was a tough dive," Nico said on the boat. "I dive all the time, and it was tough for me. Great job," he said. I took his words to heart.

The bright midday sun was now sinking toward the horizon and I peered off the back of the boat at the roiling expanse of turquoise ocean as we peeled off our wetsuits and headed back to Cozumel. I marveled at the mystery of life's unfolding. *How could I have imagined that I'd be scuba diving from a boat in the Caribbean with a Turkish engineer at the age of 28? And how could I have imagined that I'd find even this grand adventure unsatisfying and the sign of a small, limited life?*

True, vacations, travel, and new experiences were a piece of the satisfying life that I had been missing in my marriage. Omer had woken that up in me. He had coaxed my dancing out of me, and my athleticism, and my travel bug. There were also other things he had subconsciously coaxed back into hiding, which wanted to be released, once and for all.

My heart wanted something bigger.

I wanted to devour the whole world and embrace all the people in it. I wanted a life in which I felt free to love wildly, to my heart's content, in all the ways this might manifest, and to live on my own terms, true to my own integrity, free of guilt and shame.

Holbox

Javier, who had spent most of the trip happily day-drunk at Papaya Playa, parted ways with us when Omer, Eneas, and I headed north toward Isla Holbox. Holbox is an unbridged island on the very tip of the Yucatan Peninsula with no cars and a happily unbothered community of locals, European expats, and water sport enthusiasts. Golf cart taxis lined the streets and barefoot children ran around unencumbered.

The place was remarkable. The pristine beaches were the stuff of dreams: wide and flat with shallow turquoise waters, silvery velvet sand, and the occasional cabanas serving craft cocktails.

My debit card didn't work in Mexico, so Omer and I had agreed to just use our credit cards from his account for expenses while traveling. So once again, I was more or less dependent on him. He was the keeper of the cash. One day, while he and Eneas were kiteboarding, I spent a whole afternoon meandering along the shoreline. Later on, I wandered into a little shop and I swiped the card to buy myself a beautiful shawl of intricately woven silk threads in plum, rust and rose hues. Later, I discovered the perfect embossed Mexican leather bag. These became my keepsakes, relics from my first time in the homeland. *Thanks, Omer*, I thought as I emerged from the shop and onto the sandy road.

Despite the beauty that surrounded us, our room in Holbox was grimy, with tiny towels, linoleum floors, and brown curtains. We were underwhelmed. It was a strange place to spend Christmas.

On the night of Christmas Eve, Omer and I had basically been at each other's throats all afternoon. In spite of my attempts otherwise, I felt disgusted by everything he did — from his mannerisms to his quiet voice, which required me to constantly ask him to repeat himself. These things that used to charm me about him were now making my blood pressure rise. I don't think this aversion had so much to do with *him* as my own discomfort with this life I had unwittingly stepped into. The life he represented.

It was everything surrounding him. I watched myself from far away, as I cringed at his advances and rolled my eyes at his retorts. Our bed was uncomfortably small — especially compared to the California King to which we had grown accustomed, and the room was hot and damp. We weren't sleeping well. There was wet kiteboarding gear everywhere and Omer tried neurotically to manage the sand, which was intent on spreading into all our belongings.

One morning Eneas, seemingly unperturbed by our tension, went out to get coffees. Omer sat at the foot of the bed and looked at me.

"So," he said.

"….So," I replied. I knew it was time to start talking.

"What's up, honey?" he looked desperate.

I started to cry.

"Ugh. I don't know…. I feel weird. I feel lost. I feel like I'm losing myself," I told him.

He nodded.

"I don't think my heart is in this anymore," I continued. I pressed my palms over my eyes, trying to restrain the tears.

I was tempted to launch into a longer explanation, to express that I had really loved him, but that this didn't feel right and I wanted something different than the life we were in… but I felt I had already said enough.

He squeezed my foot.

"Yeah. I know," he said. "I've sensed that for a while." He looked distant and despairing.

VACATION

Silent tears continued to stream down my cheeks as I reclined there, staring at him. I felt more pity and guilt than heart wrenching pain, in contrast to other recent heartbreak experiences.

Why? What was my love for him made of? More than anything, I discovered, it was my wanting him to be loved.

I could see that the world hadn't given him enough of that. My love wasn't made of admiration or electricity or that deep karmic something. It was simpler, purer, more volatile, rooted in what I perceived as his need for love and acceptance. Something I had pulled from deep within myself like a rootless flower plucked from the garden of my soul. We watched as it withered before us, in the wake of me sacrificing all my other loves for the sake of this one.

To make matters worse, that evening I also got very sick. I mistakenly drank the ice water at a hipster smoothie bowl cafe. Rookie mistake. It wrecked my guts for the rest of the trip and I had to plan our outings based on guaranteed access to a restroom at a moment's notice.

Christmas morning, I stepped out onto the balcony and called Tess. I envisioned her curled up at our old house, the "Lodge Cabin" as we called it, playing Christmas carols on guitar while Matt sipped strong coffee and Martin cooked breakfast. I thought of our house-wide Christmas feast the previous year, "Wafflemas," and our lazy holiday spent on the couch watching Jack's favorite ski videos. I recalled the epic sex tape Jack and I had made that evening, the laughter and shared trust between us. I felt painfully homesick.

Tess didn't pick up. I called my mom. She didn't pick up. I called Keaton. He didn't pick up. I left them all voicemails, saying Merry Christmas and sending my love across time zones.

At least the wind was perfect.

Omer and Eneas spent the day kiteboarding. I wandered the island and talked with locals in my lousy Spanish. A young man tried to recruit me to be a tour guide. (Or was I about to be trafficked? I can't know for sure.) I sat on a bench in the town square and watched a legion of ants descend upon a sky blue lollipop melting near my feet.

Eneas found me at a bar on the beach. Omer was still out on the water, he told me. We chain smoked cigarettes and talked about life. He had heard about our split.

"But you guys have such a good thing going. Are you sure you aren't just going to change your mind in a week?" There was no sting in his voice; he sincerely wanted to know.

"I've been known to do crazier things," I laughed sadly.

He looked at me and raised his eyebrows with affection.

"It's not about it being good," I went on. "It just doesn't feel right. This isn't me, Eneas."

We had lobster pizza and margaritas for dinner. Omer was at the hotel cleaning up the kites.

"Well, maybe it's a timing thing. Maybe if you were a little older and in the same part of life," Eneas said lightly, reaching over to take my hand. "Becca, I know you're disappointed. It will get better. These things happen."

"I know… thanks," I said hollowly.

"In the meantime… there's still New Years! Let's do some drugs at Papaya Playa!" He let out his deep Greek laugh. I laughed back and lifted my margarita in resignation.

The hard conversation had actually softened Omer and I toward each other. There was a palpable relief between us, amidst the sadness and the questions of what would come next. I tried not to wonder where I would live, and with whom. I tried not to think of having to tell Moses that we were moving… again.

New Year

We loaded up our rental car and made the drive from Holbox back to Tulum for New Year's Eve. Papaya Playa had an exclusive all-night party that seemed like a festive way to end a complicated trip. We'd be flying home the next day. I couldn't believe we were considering attending when I learned that tickets were $190 USD each. I stared at the guys, incredulous.

They'd been in the East Coast club scene for decades and weren't especially surprised at the price.

"It's New Year's Eve," they reasoned with a shrug — as if that would make more sense to me.

"Alright… if you're sure you feel good about it," I said, knowing that Omer would certainly be footing the bill for my ticket.

We all got done up for the occasion. I wore my high-necked black velvet

VACATION **441**

mini dress and my funky maroon party boots. The guys wore their brightly colored leggings. Eneas' ensemble of artsy blue and pink flamingo leggings, my shaggy white fur jacket plus his European charm made him stand out from the crowd. Strangers approached us repeatedly, asking in Spanish if he had drugs to spare. He didn't.

The line to get inside stretched half a mile down the road.

As we searched for the back of the line I looked around at the people and felt embarrassed. This place was oozing privilege... obviously. What had I expected? Loud, rowdy Australian dudes were already drunk and feeling up the women in their group as they waited in line. The attire spanned from ornate Burning Man hippie garb to frat boy business casual, only with man buns. Each time the gate opened, people pushed forward aggressively in a bid to get inside before the venue reached capacity. It felt like a feeding frenzy.

Everywhere I looked, I found cell phones and purse flasks and superficial small talk. The vanity in that crowd rivaled the worst of Los Angeles. For the second time that week, I had a familiar thought:

Becca, what are you doing here?

Temps were cooling down as the hours ticked by. Omer and I stood in line, wrapped in each other's arms for a long time, nothing to say. Eneas had wandered off to smoke and perhaps fall in love with a foreign woman. We debated leaving, but it seemed a shame to waste the trip since we'd driven all that way and it was our last night. At 11:50 pm the skies cracked open and began dumping rain. Omer lifted his jacket over both our heads. These were the moments when he really shined. Even after all I'd put him through, he was caring and steady and protective.

We laughed as water poured down and soaked the sea of perfect pretty people, melting mascara and hairdos. We were thoroughly drenched when we heard the countdown from inside. "Cinco… Quatro… Tres…Dos… Uno….. FELIZ ANO!" Everyone cheered loudly, laughing and hugging. I took Omer's face in my hands and kissed him hard. He wrapped me up tight in his strong arms and kissed me back tenderly.

"I love you," I said, over the cheers.

"I love you too, honey," he said.

We stared at each other, rain dripping down our sad faces. We took in the scene around us and sighed. Tears joined the raindrops on my cheeks.

"I'm sorry for all of this," I told Omer, feeling crushed and confused.

"I love you, Becca. I'm not ready to give up," he shouted over the cacophony of tourists. "I don't want this to end."

"Neither do I," I told him, and in that moment, I meant it.

We finally made it through the gates, nearly $600 later, and the place was teeming with partiers standing around and shouting to each other over the DJ's music. Every person I saw had a drink in their hand. Every. Single. Person. I wanted to dance, but there was no room to move like there had been during our previous visit. I was also soaking wet in a velvet dress. The guys headed into the dance pit and I stayed back to take a moment to acclimate. Three different men approached me, trying to make small talk. I stared straight ahead, unavailable.

I squeezed through the crowd to the big fire pit near the shoreline to warm up. Even there, I saw very few people who seemed to be on my level: mostly sober, introspective, present. I made small talk with the handsome man tending the ceremonial fire. It was some comfort to have someone to talk to, but I still felt very alone.

Eneas came and found me after a while, trying to entice me to come dance. He offered to buy me a drink. But I didn't want to dance. Or drink. I didn't want anything related to this place. I told him I was a little overwhelmed and gave him my blessing to go on and have a good time.

"Okay, then..." he said in a sing-song voice with a wink. "Find me when you change your mind."

I leaned back on my plush beach cushion (this place had it all) and looked out toward the expanse of sky. The clouds were parting and I could see a few stars peeking through. I considered how big they all were, and how small we were. Then, I was distracted by countless petty conversations in the background and glanced around to find the voices. No one there looked particularly happy or seemed to be enjoying themselves.

These people are chasing something, I said to myself. *Even Eneas. And Omer. They're chasing something. You're not chasing the same things.*

"Hmm," I accidentally said aloud as it dawned on me.

I overheard an attractive woman demanding her friend retake a posed photo, proclaiming "We've got all night... we can do this until we get it right." It was like watching a real-life reality TV show.

For fuck's sake, I scoffed. *This is not my world.* The house music continued

VACATION **443**

its driving beat and a loud, visibly drunk couple nearly tripped over me as they passed.

None of this even looked fun to me. I'd seen too much contrast in the past few years to settle for these surface pleasures anymore. So much about my life with Omer had to do with curating experiences — sex and vacations and a beautiful home and party drugs and the company of people I only partially found interesting. It seemed like an easy habit to self-medicate or numb out with cheap thrills, forever looking outside of myself for peace. It reminded me of high school. Yet I saw it all around me, in people of all ages, here and at home.

I thought of the way I'd felt in the treehouse, alone with the mushrooms, or at Breitenbush, floating on the seas of San Pedro with Samuel by my side. The residual sense of deep, deep connection anchored me in myself, even now.

The contrast became clear that night.

I had once been insatiably curious and open-minded, a newly-divorced seeker, willing to play along at parties and festivals of all kinds, willing to talk with anyone about anything. Where I had once said yes to every Tinder date and run myself dry giving myself away to others, I now felt deeply rooted in my identity and clear about the company I wanted to keep. I had tasted what it was like to be around people who understood me, who left me feeling nourished, who craved soul connection and free play and memorable, wild experiences.

I knew I belonged in a very different environment than this one. For the first time in my life, I recognized the value of my own presence and the expansive, powerful, sensitive energy I carried. It wasn't recognized or valued in a harsh environment like this. There was no place for me here.

I envisioned things that moved me, things of substance like gardens and tea ceremonies, camping trips, art, music, playing with Moses and sharing with loved ones in the deep, satisfying work of the heart. These things formed the landscape of my inner world.

I walked over to the water and stepped into the lapping waves. The clear moon hovered over the horizon. She looked self-assured, as she always did. I let her illuminate my drenched, shadowy, exhausted form. A tear splashed down my cheek.

I'm opting out, I said to the silent sky. *I don't want any more of this chasing.* I thought to myself tiredly, over the pulsing music and the endless chatter behind me. *Better late than never. No more screwing around with this prevailing culture. It's not made for me.*

I dipped my hands in the cool saltwater and continued on, speaking silently to the Universe, the Divine, whoever might be listening.

I'm sorry I've been fighting it for so long. Life is simpler than I've been making it. I only want to have space for Big Love from now on. I'm ready to build my own life. Tomorrow, I'm coming home to myself. I'm choosing me: My garden. My wildness. Deep magic. Activism. I want to share these things with the people who can look me in the eyes and meet me there. Please help me find them throughout my life. I don't want to feel so alone.

I sighed loudly.

"Are you okay?" A security guard asked me.

"Oh. Yeah. I'm fine," I smiled, eyes still wet.

"Sorry ma'am, but we're not allowing anyone to get into the water tonight. Safety precaution," he said.

"Oh, sorry." I shook off my bare feet and I walked back to the fire, waiting for morning to come.

33

Home

Flight

We drove back to Cancun just before sunrise and dropped Eneas at the airport for his return to San Francisco. I was certain it was the last time I'd ever see him. He was Omer's best friend, after all. He squeezed each of us tight. Omer climbed into the car and turned up the music.

I stood in the parking lot with Eneas, shaking with sadness, unwilling to say goodbye.

"It's going to work out," Eneas said, taking my downcast face in his hands tenderly. He kissed me square on the lips, long and clear with nothing but pure friendship. "Take care of yourself," he said. Then he collected his bags and walked away. I climbed in the car with Omer and we watched as Eneas waved and blew us kisses, then disappeared through the sliding doors. Now, it was just us.

Back at the AirBnB, with a shared, unspoken understanding, Omer and I collapsed into separate beds in adjacent rooms.

On the flight home Omer slept fitfully beside me and I attempted to sketch in my notebook. No image would come. I wanted to write, but words were elusive. So finally, I gave up. I balled up my scarf into a pillow and rested my head on the window, watching the clouds go by.

Throughout my body, there was a sense of resolution. It felt like the ending to a significant season in my life; Omer was my third partner in three years. Each time, I'd been playing house. I hadn't recognized it. I was trying on different lives for size, convinced that with the right person, my life would feel right. With Jack and Omer, I'd found the intimacy and adventure I craved, in abundance, which I thought was the missing piece, but I still felt scarcely more free than I had in my marriage.

How did I get here, to my third failed partnership and a strikingly unconventional path? I had a cascade of realizations as the flight attendants wandered the aisles, handing out waters and pretzels. I felt kind toward myself, and finally willing to truly examine what had been happening beneath the surface. A few things seemed obvious.

I thought of my love life. I saw my heart's pattern of falling fast in love and giving my complete devotion to partner after partner.

It was a subconscious attempt to feel safe and tethered, to keep my wildness in check. I believed that for the "right person" I could be content abiding by social norms of monogamy and nuclear family. But once committed, I began to resent those who slept beside me as I tried to reclaim my personal agency and retroactively negotiate an honest outlet for my free spirit.

Wow.

I had been talking out of both sides of my mouth for years. I wanted stability and variety all at once, yet I was still developing the courage to radically ask for both and do the work it took to make that possible. I'd mostly been hiding from those I loved and diluting my desires into something agreeable.

I thought of my family. My inner child. There was still the daughter in me who wanted to reconcile with my father, to not be invisible to him. But he had disappeared back out of my life, with open-ended promises to see each other soon and a disconnected phone line, which left me resigned. So I subconsciously attached quickly and formed strong bonds with other, safer men. Then there was the angsty teen in me who wanted to break loose from my mother's grip, so I fiercely protected the personal freedom which she had withheld from me during my youth.

I thought of my loss of faith. The earnest child in me wanted to prove that I could be a "good person" without God. I had spent my relationships, and my life, allowing leaders, partners, and religion to set the standard for what was good and acceptable. I'd been trying to convince everyone, including myself, that I could behave, play nice, follow the rules. Maintain order.

What if my most deeply aligned self *wasn't* that nice? What if my role in this wild world was more of a disruptor, a catalyst, an agent of chaos and transformation and pushing the boundaries outward to make more space for what's possible? Could I finally be willing to fill a less understood, less adored place in the ecosystem, like a crow, a dandelion, a spider with her web? What if good didn't actually mean "good" in the way our culture saw it? Was I ready to reckon with my own shadows, and finally welcome them to be a part of me?

I thought of the psychedelics.

At my invitation, these medicines had blown my world wide open. They had shattered my belief that light and dark, chaos and harmony were separate forces at odds with one another. They had caused me to rethink the linear passage of time. They had carried me beyond my own self-involvement and given me a glimpse into a more universal wisdom that exists within all of life. They had reintroduced me to the world of Spirit that I had rejected with Christianity.

These medicines — LSD, mushrooms, MDMA, and San Pedro, among others — washed me in a deep love and a sense of place, a sense of belonging in the world that I'd been craving since birth. They invited me to meet the people in my life with the same compassion and belief in transformation that I desired. They had expanded my sense of what might be possible in the space of a lifetime.

They had provided me with reference points to return to again and again, reminders of what I inherently knew to be true: That everything was far outside my control. That I was a tiny speck in a huge Universe and needn't be so concerned with having a plan and getting everything right. That I was here, alive, but for a moment, and that the best thing I could do with that moment… is be fully alive and find ways to remove the barriers to that flourishing aliveness for others. They urged me to witness the pain and joy and art and suffering that makes up this world and go toward what calls for my soul's attention.

I thought of love and sexuality.

I had been conditioned by patriarchal church culture to believe a whole cascade of lies about what it meant to be a woman and to love. My heart was so obviously deviant from the picture they'd painted. I had been told by the Bible, youth pastors, and my own mother, that my big heart and wild openness were flaws. Liabilities. Not to be trusted. It took years to reclaim and embrace these double-edged gifts.

Even later on, in more progressive circles, I was often met with distrust and judgment for being a sex-positive woman (let alone *mother*) who was open to free sexual connection, and also open to lasting, intimate love. Times were changing gradually, but my true motive stayed the same: to find what was true for *me*, rather than be an advocate for non-monogamy or tell anyone else how to love.

As I looked back, I saw a great deal of heartbreak in my wake; not just my own. I had learned as a self-sufficient child to put my needs first. I had learned that others couldn't be trusted to offer support, presence, or care in my time of need. So, I had developed an inflated sense of self-importance and alienated myself from those who wanted to be close. In the awkward years of shedding these disorganized adaptations (which remains ongoing, lifelong work), I had welcomed partners and friends into my inner world, only to shut them out abruptly or sabotage the relationship when challenges arose or I was asked to make sacrifices for the health of the relationship.

In lectures and arguments, my mother had so often characterized me as a selfish storm passing through, leaving people in its wake. I feared that kind of power, and I also recognized it was something I wielded. Not only with my charming, inviting magnetism, but also with my forceful will, fierce wit, sharp tongue, and unwillingness to give others what they requested of me.

I wondered whether she was right. I had internalized the old saying:

> *"The difference between medicine and poison is in the dose."*

Had I really believed that was true of me? That it was possible for a woman to be safe only in small doses? Perhaps it had become a self-fulfilling prophecy. All my life, I'd been told I was too much: too opinionated, too disruptive, too magnetic. I was ashamed of these qualities, believing they were wrong, that they needed to be erased or transformed by the love of God. So, I'd concealed myself, trying to be smaller and more palatable, because I hadn't learned to trust my true nature or believe in a world that could value and hold space for it. In the shadows, these greatest strengths had mixed with resentment toward the world around me and become more forceful, enraged and uncompromising, even toxic.

It occurred to me that I could choose to embrace myself as a force of nature. That these old stories and subtly destructive habits didn't have to be a roadmap for the future unless I allowed them to be. I could hone my inner power as the gift it was. I could learn how to take up space without trampling others.

I unbuckled and stood to stretch my legs. In the airplane bathroom, I splashed my face with water and stared into the mirror. I looked tired, sun kissed, and strong. I looked like a woman with the world at her fingertips. When I returned to my seat, Omer sleepily kissed me on the shoulder and closed his eyes again.

HOME

Moses

I thought of my child.

The one who had woken me out of my sleep. I felt a deep, aching pride at the way I'd walked through motherhood.

It truly felt like he had chosen me. That wise, pure soul, blinking up at me from the water in those first moments like he'd known me all along. I considered the way he felt more like a comrade, a co-conspirator in life, and the way I'd known since his infancy to speak to him like a person, not a baby. He is someone who commands respect, who holds court, who causes people around him to pause. His presence, and later, his questions, caused me to examine everything. From my first honest doubts about religion while he was in my womb, to my deepest beliefs about love, justice, and activism, I had to contend with my own convictions in order to pass them on to him with integrity.

I recognized the way that society judges our mothers so hard. In my experience, this judgment came from the outside, mostly from church folk, who I didn't expect to understand me or my unconventional family. I imagined the existing condemnation in hushed tones, which would be multiplied if people actually knew the inner workings of my life: here was a brilliant mother who had chosen *not* to lose herself in motherhood, but to retain her identity as a woman.

A woman who traveled often, took many lovers of all genders, had a life of her own, used psychedelic drugs, and believed simply that healing, discomfort, and pleasure were central to a life well lived. A woman who had the audacity to know, in spite of her shortcomings and beyond all doubt, that she was a fantastic mother and worthy of love and respect.

In spite of all my wildness, I had maintained, with patience and heart, a deeply committed relationship with Moses for many years. I'd shown up for him in a way that I didn't know I could show up for someone.

When I thought of him, I saw a whole, vibrant, thriving child who was respected and allowed to be a child. Those around him saw it, too. I protected him fiercely, yet made space for his own autonomy. We argued. I changed my mind. He changed his mind. He was comfortable enough to tell me when I did something hurtful, and I was willing to listen. I apologized often. I let him play unsupervised. I evaluated risk differently than many mothers do. I let him meet my partners and form bonds with my special people, and I spoke well of all of them even after we'd parted ways.

I'd set myself aside over and over for him throughout the years, learning about sacrifice and healing by being the mother to Moses that I wished I'd had. And I'd also fought for the right to be a whole person, to have an identity beyond motherhood. New friends rarely realized I had a child when we first met, because it wasn't written all over me in the way I spoke, dressed, carried myself, and the things that occupied my mindscape. The relationship Moses and I shared was like soul family. He came into this world old and wise and witty. At age two he was calling me "Becca."

Our relationship was unconventional, cosmic and unique, like peers or travel mates. He has been my teacher as much as I am his. I recognize this and I remind him of it often.

Being Moses' mother has been a deeply profound element of my generational healing. On a daily basis, I've been breaking cycles and correcting course. I've refused to allow myself permission to pass along old traumas and emotional and energetic burdens that don't belong to him. At least, that's my goal. And I've been working hard at it since day one.

Shadows

I thought of my own shadows.

My shadow of perfectionism was so deeply, subconsciously afraid of failing, afraid of being wrong, afraid of being rejected altogether, that I surrounded myself with grounded and steady lovers to act as buffer zones between myself and the world. So my dreams were diluted into compromised, shared dreams. None of my partners wanted to start a permaculture food forest with me or become serial entrepreneurs or impact investors; those were my dreams. I was tempted to lure them in, just as I had pulled Keaton into the farm, into my dream, so I wouldn't be alone in the risk.

I was diluting and denying the very real power within me so the world around me would find me softer, acceptable and more realistic. Then I could pass for safe and well-behaved.

It occurred to me that I didn't actually have to do that.

I could do the things that scared me: I could be the expert of my own life and the gatekeeper of my own heart. I could abide by unyielding integrity toward myself and my path, as wildly unconventional as it was, rather than concerning myself with society's rules and expectations.

What would it feel like to be a truly single mother, truly devoted to my dreams and pursuits? To joyfully take responsibility for my own life, owning all the pride of my success and disappointment of failure? What if I truly held onto love with open hands, allowing it to flow over and through me, without attaching myself to any one person or bending to fit their path?

What if, for once, love didn't spell compromise? What if I was more like a rooted tree?

The thought of it seemed at first lonely to me; I'd become so used to being miserably enmeshed.

Then another thought occurred to me. I felt it deep in my hips and my belly and the cave of my chest: being fully in my own power, and fully loving and embracing myself, could be the starting point to a new way of navigating the world. This was the crucial piece I'd been missing. I actually could have it all.

I imagined a life where I chose every day to be radically honest with myself and with those I loved. I imagined gathering all the shadowy parts of myself that I often abandoned or hid within relationships, and bringing them with me wherever I went.

I thought of my "flaws." The things I'd been taught were unacceptable since childhood. I glanced over at Omer, who was still sleeping. I jotted down a list in my sketchbook.

> I love falling in love, and that is hard for some people.
>
> I am extremely sensual, and that is, too.
>
> I like to rebel and break rules. It feels good to me… like power.
>
> I take up a lot of space. I can fill a whole room.
>
> I am fluid and inconsistent.
>
> I can be secretive.
>
> I am a good liar, even to myself.

I'd always thought shadow work meant healing that which we perceive to be flawed or destructive, then transmuting it into something brighter and more whole. There had still been an air of perfectionism in my way of "doing the work."

Now, I realized, it was simpler than that: I could acknowledge and love my shadows. I could know them intimately. Hear what they were telling me. I could gather them up and give them a place to exist. Make sure they weren't doing harm by being repressed or squeezing out sideways.

I wrote the following in my journal.

Love your shadows

Gather them up

Again and Again

Each time they wander off to their hiding places

Like a mother hen

Gathers her chicks

The fluffy runts and rebels

All belong

Let them feel it.

New Nest

After we returned to Portland, I began looking for a new home. Omer and I were torn up at the impending separation and alternated between avoiding each other within the house and sharing sweet times that only made the aching worse. I told him I was resisting the push to leave. He asked me to please not drag it out. We had a few really messy arguments where he asserted that he had been more invested in the relationship than I had. At first, I was incensed at this notion. But the truth is, I had held back. I really hadn't allowed myself to fully decide anything about the future based on the fact that we were living together. I was constantly holding back, taking it moment by moment, and in that way, he had been more invested than I'd been.

For him, I was it. I was the Big Love. That was why he'd invited me to move in. He was wrecked by our parting. He gave me the rugs and the planters he'd paid for and as I packed, the house began to look bare and cold again. I was plagued with so much guilt for leaving him that I dwelled in a state of inner conflict for weeks. I really didn't know how he would recover.

Moses seemed unphased. "Well, at least all my toys and my books are already in the bins!" he said flippantly when I told him. He was most upset about leaving the cat behind. I was tempted to believe he was just dissociating from the situation, but the reality is that Moses had moved with me three times in three years. He and Omer were hardly more bonded than he was with my close friends and other lovers.

That week, I got in touch with my friend Indigo, a petite and vibrant massage therapist with a twinkle in her eye. She and I had met in the climbing gym that year while I was doing a CBD demo for climbers. She'd walked right up to my table in a frenzy, grinning, and said,

"Can I hug you??"

Um, of course she could! We laughed and hugged. She proceeded to tell me that she was a bodyworker and had been asking the Universe to guide her to a hemp farm that she could trust for products for her massage practice.

"And here you are!" she exclaimed.

Over the past year, we had become good friends. She'd visited the farm a few times — in fact, she toured the hemp fields with us the day I fell in love with Ari.

As I sat there on Omer's couch, petting his sleepy cat, I texted Indigo.

"Hey friend. Omer and I ended things over the holidays. You have a good network. Do you have any leads on good places on the East side?"

"Oh, I'm so sorry, Becca! Are you okay?" she replied. "I'm in the same boat. Been looking for places… I really want to live alone, but I'm not sure yet."

"I know, right? I'd live with just Moses in a heartbeat. But Portland's gotten so expensive."

"It sure has. Sending lots of support to you in this transition. Hugs…"

I didn't reply right away. A few minutes later, I took a chance.

"Hey, here's a thought. What if we lived alone…. together?" I asked.

"Ooh. Now I'm intrigued. Let's meet for coffee."

A week later, we were touring a lovely, gardened bungalow in the Alberta Arts District. She and I marveled at how smoothly everything had fallen into place, and I was at once surprised and also not at all surprised. Every time I had stepped out in courage and trusted what I deeply knew to be true for me, I felt the support of the Universe scooping me up and ushering me along like a big benevolent wave. Every. Single. Time.

That house we toured is our home now. Most of this book was written within its walls.

I moved in first. As he had before, Calvin offered to help me with the large furniture. He parked in Omer's driveway and we all exchanged cursory hugs. The three of us loaded my bookshelves and boxes into the van in relative silence, and when I came back inside for the last of my things, I found a stack of framed photos face down on the kitchen table.

"You should take these," Omer said. I held back tears as I gingerly placed the frames between my dresses and tapestries, cushioning the hard, fragile edges which held images of our fondest memories between their panes.

It was only a four-minute drive to my new house. (Portland is not a big place; I lived within three miles of Omer, Jack and Andrew, plus several other past and current lovers.)

In the new house there were two bedrooms. Attached to mine was a stairway leading up to a long, low ceilinged little loft: a perfect kid castle for Moses. The guys carried the heavy furniture inside, and written in his body language, I could tell that Omer felt out of place inside my new home. He left soon after.

"It's beautiful," he said to me with a cool kindness as he hugged me goodbye.

Calvin left for work. Moses was with Keaton for the weekend and Indigo still had a couple of weeks before her move-in date. I stood still in the empty living room and sighed. I smiled. I had arrived. It had taken three years since my marriage dissolved, but I was finally stepping into my own life.

I didn't unpack all the boxes full of practical items just yet. I began by watering my house plants, turning them just so, and hanging my gold-framed art on the walls. I tucked the photos from Omer in the back of my closet. I strung lights along the naked window frames. Unrushed, I arranged my teas and spices in their little drawers.

Then, I set up an altar in my bedroom, lighting a single sage leaf from a bundle I'd harvested in Samuel's garden. I felt alone. Alone… Alone. Only this time, it didn't torment me the way it had that day outside the teahouse with Keaton.

This time, alone felt like coming home.

HOME

# 34

Full Circles

After

The months after my move felt like a chaotic and delicious platter of smashed fruit. The shareable and seemingly relevant events kept unfolding. How does one know where to stop a story? Life has a way of marching on, quite unlike a book, so tidy and contained between its two covers.

After I moved, I created a personal website where I could write. I began assembling the pieces of this book, which I'd started in 2016 when Keaton and I first separated.

My first blog entry was titled "Polyamory."

> *January*
>
> I have four lovers, or is it five?
> Nestled around the world
>
> The strong Turkish engineer
> We climb, eat, hold each other close
> Through the night
> My safe place, we shared a home
> He was arms around me
> I ran away
>
> The sensual surfer
> We play acrobatics, whips & pops
> Feel the Earth in each other

Relish in society, universe, creation
He lovingly kneads my knots, entangles me, sets me free
I approach timidly

The light, bright artist
I've never craved a first kiss like this
She inverted my world then flew to Mexico
Our roots are intertwined
Two facets of one gem
I await her return

The fiery gardener
He's everything: dark, light, life, death
Even from the hills of Costa Rica
He burns me up, eats me alive, nourishes me
Tends my garden
No one has battled for me this way
I wonder of past lives

There's someone else
The passionate creative
She's here with me, my constant companion
I catch her eye in the mirror, I wink, I feel her rhythm
She holds my love
She is me.

Full Circle

I instantly loved my new home rhythms with Indigo and Moses. I felt closer to him than I had in years. Less distracted. Things with Omer had not ended in a clean break. It took months for us to wrest ourselves from each other, marked by deep grief and repeated attempts to simply redefine our relationship rather than cut each other off altogether.

Ultimately, not only did these attempts fail, they ended up doing a lot of damage to the love we were trying to salvage. We continued to see each other around town, often on dance floors, and it always felt speechless and raw.

Early on in 2020, at the height of the COVID-19 pandemic and more than a year after our heartbreak in Mexico, my simple request for a forgotten thermometer was the bridge back to our peace with each other. He dropped it on my porch and we shared smiles. During the lockdown, he and I organized our friends for a remote movie night and we laughed like old times at *Spinal Tap*, a movie Eneas had chosen. After that, Omer and I had a phase of sneakily dropping baked treats on each other's front steps, a belated and lighthearted peace offering to acknowledge that, after a year, we were moving on in peace.

Samuel

Samuel flew into town in January of 2019, shortly after I moved out of Omer's. He met me for tea at Townshend's, and I felt aware that I was only two blocks away from Ari's home, where so much had taken place. I also felt aware of how much I had changed since meeting Samuel three years earlier. And yet here we were, face-to-face yet again. We sat and stared at each other across a too-wide table.

We chatted about work and Costa Rica like usual, and finally stepped toward deeper themes.

"This feels really surreal," he said. "I'm sorry if I'm being distant, I just feel kind of… detached, I guess."

"Yeah. I get it.…" I paused. "There's a lot I want to say, but I don't know that it would be helpful."

"I'd like to hear," he said.

"Well, I've been thinking about how I handled things this fall," I said, pouring him some more tea from the pot. "I can see how I was careless. And… I was selfish."

"What do you mean?" he asked.

"I wanted your love. I tried to fit you into my life where there wasn't space. And then I left you high and dry." I looked over at him. "I'm sorry. I should not have shut you out like that."

He nodded.

"Thanks, Becca. It's crazy how feelings can change so much," he said. "I remember all that, it was pretty awful, but now I feel shut off from it. Like we were different people then. I met someone right after you left. She lives here in Portland."

I felt a sting in my heart, but overcompensated by acting supportive and interested in hearing about her. She was a gardener and they had a good, low-key flow. They weren't exclusive.

It wasn't an easy meeting, but it felt necessary, though there was no clear resolution. By this point I'd given up on ever assuming that things with Samuel were tidy and resolved. He texted me late that night.

"Want to soak on Saturday? 7:00 pm?"

"You know I do. I'll be there," I said.

We sat in the tearoom at Everett House for a long time and in some ways, it felt like rediscovering each other. We were uninhibited, seeing each other in a deeper way after all our love and conflict and the passage of time. Stakes were lower. There was less sexual tension and game playing than there had been in times past.

As we walked out, curse the gods, Omer was standing there in a towel, mid-spa session.

It was a hell of an awkward exchange.

After our soak, Samuel and I sat inside Guero, a hip little torta shop, eating carnitas and pineapple salad. Samuel reached across the table and took my hand in his.

"Becca. It's good to see you. Really," he said earnestly.

"It's good to see you, too. It always is," I told him with a shrug. "Feels different now. Less charged. I'm wondering what there is to salvage between us after everything."

"Me too. Thank you for reaching out. I'm glad we're connected. I think it will just take some time," he said.

We finished our food, smiling at each other cheekily. He nudged my foot under the table.

"What are you thinking?" I finally asked.

"I'm thinking you should come visit me in Costa Rica," he said.

I was shocked.

"Really?" I asked, eyebrows raised. "*After everything?*"

"Yeah. Do you want to?" he asked.

"Of course," I said.

The next week, I used my credit card and bought a round-trip plane ticket to Costa Rica that May.

FULL CIRCLES

Oaxaca

The dreary winter and persistent heartache was brightened by my regular FaceTime sessions with Ari. She was living in Mexico City, doing dance intensives and pancake pop-up brunches and generally just being a dream of a human. She invited me to come visit. I couldn't say yes fast enough. I looked online for plane tickets.

I sat at the kitchen table, making a fuss. I turned to Indigo. "Why am I hesitating?? Of course I want to go see her," I said.

"You've been through a lot this year," Indigo answered. "This is another big thing."

"Yeah… I know. Plus, maybe I'm feeling weird about taking my first trip without Omer… and going back to Mexico, no less."

"I think you're doing a brave thing Becca, and it's understandable that there's some hesitation," she said. "But you're going to have an amazing time with Ari."

"You're right. I'm going for it. Thanks," I replied.

I bought the tickets.

In February, I dropped Moses at Keaton's house again and boarded a flight toward Utah. By that evening, I'd traversed through the atmosphere, stopping in Salt Lake City, Mexico City, and Oaxaca. I felt largely at ease traveling alone and I smirked to myself as I boarded the plane with just my backpack, no luggage to check, no goddamned kiteboarding bags to fuss with.

I emerged from a tiny airport in Oaxaca and boarded a shuttle to the AirBnB to meet Ari.

Our week together was perfect. There was nothing at all we had to do. We stayed in humble, airy little bed and breakfasts that felt like palaces to me, with their outdoor kitchens and garden courtyards and walkability to the ocean.

There is truly nothing like spending time with Ari. We share a delightful cocktail of humor and depth, oscillating between deep talks about culture, privilege, art, and love… and making each other gasp for air with theatrically witty banter. Our flow has always been just that: flow.

A week in Oaxaca with nothing to do but enjoy life with my lover was about as perfect as one could imagine. It was marked with hot, sunny days swimming in the ocean, dusky evenings wandering in search of the best tacos, and languid mornings tangled up beside each other. I loved watching the way she shined in this foreign place: rattling off her perfect Argentine Spanish in a way that made locals do a double take at her fair features.

I carried the produce basket and the hotel keys and the money, and she navigated us around town and schemed our game plan each day. Morning coffee, beach walk, wander to the market for fruits and veggies, make a gourmet lunch at our place. We'd lounge away the hottest hours of the day in the shade discussing things like capitalism, food and Ayahuasca, and daydreaming about life plans.

Perhaps one day, I could be a sugar mama and fund every art installation and clever enterprise her brilliant mind could come up with. That's still the not-so-secret goal.

One morning I woke up and felt pure bliss. I needed to write, to capture the fleeting moment and preserve it in ink and paper.

Morning

>Birds chirp trailing trills
>Stray dog orchestra
>Imaginary tails wag
>
>Church music from afar
>Muffled by the breeze
>Piano
>A chorus of devotees
>
>Neighbors tromp past in calm conversation
>Beach and breakfast bound
>Lone truck rumbles by
>
>Washing machine outside my window
>Why?
>Swishes, splashes
>Sleepy rhythm
>
>Palm fronds rustling
>Abuelita sweeps the patio

The air escapes my lungs
My lover tosses in the sheets
A long, languid sigh
Contentment.

Last Night

Every evening, we sat on the beach in our wet swimsuits and watched the sun go down. Sunset was a community event in Zicatela, the little town where we were staying, just south of Puerto Escondido. Locals walked the beach selling bracelets, fresh coconut water, and home baked banana bread. We couldn't help but partake.

On our last evening together, Ari and I went out for a nice dinner of tacos de pescado.

"I can't believe it's our last night already," I said.

"Ugh, I know. Let's get dressed up!" she exclaimed.

I went into the courtyard to shake the sand from my belongings. When I returned, she was wearing a hilariously wacky polka dot clown dress that reached to the floor and setting her hair into French braids. To me, she looked just like a doll. God, I loved that woman.

"I really have to be in the right mood to wear this one," she said with a flourish.

We walked down the dark street holding hands, something we only did sometimes, and neither of us seemed to mind the stares. I felt more at ease with her than I ever had out in the world with another partner. It felt as natural as nature.

At dinner, we talked about family. She shared about the way she and her mother were bonded, like she had been brought into this Earth to be a light for her mom and help her find her way out of a dark time. That's exactly what she'd been doing for 28 years. I'd never seen a bond like the one between her and her mother. They owned a house together, ran a business together, and fought like lovers. They were soul family.

"It's kind of like my mom is my life partner," she said, setting down her taco. "Maybe that sounds weird."

I smiled wide. Tears of recognition welled up and streamed down my cheeks. She scooted her chair closer to mine and looked me square in the eyes.

"You're an amazing mom, Becca. I'm so amazed by you," she said.

I nodded, struck by the incredible parallels between her family and my own relationship with Moses.

"You understand something I've never been able to explain," I said. "But that's exactly it… Moses is my life partner. My friends with kids don't get it, people who I date don't get it. He's it. He's the one I committed to. He's the one who will be by my side, no matter what. I've had to be so good to him… better than I ever thought I could be." I wiped my blurry eyes with my scarf. "Ahhhh!" I said, laughing at my emotional display.

"He's so lucky, Becca. And you're going to have so much love in your life on top of that. You're starting a new chapter. I can't wait to see what you do next," she said.

I slept fitfully that night, thinking perhaps the emotions of leaving Ari were making my stomach turn.

When my alarm went off, it was still night. I got dressed in the dark and sleepily kissed Ari goodbye.

"See you soon, babe."

"See you soon. Love you."

We hugged five times.

On the private 6-seater flight from Puerto Escondido to Oaxaca, I felt a hot flush of fever and realized the worst: it wasn't just my emotions. I was sick… really sick.

I had one night to stay in Oaxaca by myself before my shuttle to the airport at 4:00 am the next morning. My intent had been to wander the city by foot and see the architecture, museums and botanical gardens.

But I was weak with fever.

My AirBnB host Nigel was a lovely Brazilian man about my age who provided me with unlimited water kefir and asked the house mates to be quiet while I rested. I was the sickest I have ever been in my life. I thought I might not make it home.

I had raging stomach sickness, and a fiery fever that compelled me to take a cold shower every couple of hours to try and lower my temperature. I was hallucinating. I felt like I was suffering in hell. I writhed in bed all day and all night, willing the hours to pass or sleep to come, but I was denied both.

Ari called me and told me she had the same thing happening. Thankfully, her mom was on her way to visit and she knew where to find the nearest farmacia.

I thought of the way that Omer had been the one to tend to me when I was sick. Now, I was alone in Mexico. I thought of being four flights away from my child, my family, my home, with no supportive partner to come home to. I felt hopeless and incredibly homesick.

Empty

I've finally made it home, after a grueling couple of days.

The house is silent this morning. It's Friday. I woke at sunrise, like I always do, sunlight streaming through the sheer drapes, but today, I am tired and hollowed out. I'm alone. This is a new level of depletion, emptiness, openness… I feel like my soul has been scrubbed clean. I didn't even know I needed it.

My life is changing, settling finally after three manic years, and even my body needed to make sure I am paying attention. I'm out of excuses and alternatives. It's been three years since my divorce — three years of running myself hard with distractions and sex and cleverly avoiding the start of my unbound, self-responsible, independent life.

I'm so hungry. I haven't eaten a proper meal since Monday. My plan to explore Oaxaca was replaced with the most agonizing 24 hours I've experienced since Moses was born. Bedbound. Bathroom bound. It was truly hellish — trapped in my own body, suffering without relief. I was alone in a strange place with no rest and the hours ticking away toward takeoff.

Since Monday, I've been on four planes and traveled from Playa Zicatela to Puerto Escondido, to Oaxaca, to Mexico City, to Los Angeles, and finally home to Portland. Land, sky, land, sky, land, sky… I've been hurled through the clouds and floated past thousands of people like an apparition. I felt other-worldly, almost ethereal, as I traveled. Just look at the way even food and water seemed to be denying my substance.

I could hold nothing inside of me, like pouring water into the mouth of a ghost and watching it spill onto the floor. I drifted through my travel days in a feverish haze, tethered to reality only by the knowledge of where the nearest toilet was and the weight of my traveler's backpack on my shoulders.

I made it home in some sort of altered state. Or as I see it, an "altared state." The sacred place where the veil has been lifted ever so slightly, where we have a chance to see ourselves, our world, and time itself in a different way. We don't always need psychedelics for that. In this state I could see myself, tired and worn out, like a child fighting rest, and replayed the three years I've spent avoiding owning my life. Flights and lovers and busy antics kept me focused on things other than knowing myself. I can see myself so much more clearly now, and with compassion.

I stand and wait for the tea kettle to whistle, closing my eyes and breathing deep. I'm empty. I'm tired. I'm weak. I've lost ten pounds in the past couple months since I left Omer.

I look at myself in the mirror.

My dry, sun-tanned skin wraps around sinewy arms and legs, over-defined and under-hydrated. My skin has taken on a rough, almost brittle quality. My hollowed belly has dozens of little brown spots, some sort of viral rash that came home with me from Mexico. The hollows under my eyes seem to pull my whole face downward and my hair hangs limply at my shoulders. The ridges in my sternum catch the light and I remember where my strong climber's chest used to be.

Wow, I'm tired. Tired of distracting myself in an attempt to fight the current of the Universe nudging me toward my highest good: agency and personal sovereignty.

There's finally so much empty space in my life for something new. What will I fill it with? Perhaps more importantly, how will I go about filling it? Will I distract myself again with romance and busyness, or will I step into a more settled and conscious way of moving through life? Can I just decide this once and make it a reality?

I doubt it. Life's rhythms are cyclical like rings on a spiral.

I sip my tea and stare across the glowing living room in its morning light. What a nest we've created here. It looks so inviting, it oozes calm and fullness. There's plenty of time for life. Slow your mania and settle your impulses, Becca. Look up from what you're doing. Smile. Feel the air dancing across your face. Be a little bug in the grass.

You're exactly where you need to be.

I'm beginning to remember how it feels to just be… me. The quiet, the pace. There's a richness I bring from my overflow when I'm living with compassion for my own needs.

I'm ready to begin filling myself back up.

FULL CIRCLES

Samuel, Part VI

Spring rode steadily on.

Omer and I finally cut ties for good in April. In May was my long-awaited trip to Costa Rica to visit Samuel at the eco-village. It was a trip resulting from a hot-and-cold, three-year lead up. I had no idea what to expect, and I attempted to have no expectations at all. We spoke only a few times in the weeks leading up to the visit. He sent me links to little AirBnB's in beach towns where we could spend a few days before heading into the mountains. He sent me photos, as he always had, of glistening jungle flowers engorged with nectar and dripping with morning dew.

In the LA airport, I called him to confirm my landing time that evening.

"Hey, Becca," he said gently.

"Hey! I'm at LAX. I'm at my gate eating trail mix. My flight is in a little while. How are you?"

"I'm good," he said. "Wow, it's crazy you're actually coming down. You just went for it," he said.

His tone was almost condescending. It implied that mine was the bold move, even after he had invited me close to ten times over the years and I'd bought the ticket months earlier. A seed of doubt entered my mind: Was I playing this up? Did he actually want me to come? If not, what was I doing? Why did this, again, feel unclear?

I put the doubts out of my mind and voraciously thumbed through my copy of *Braiding Sweetgrass* to help pass the time.

Reflection

In January, I wrote of four lovers, folks who held me close and who I cherished: Omer, Calvin, Ari and Samuel. Now it's May, and I'm more or less without them, by my choice. Omer and I have moved on. Ari and I are in silent suspension; I'm not even sure what country she's in now. I haven't reengaged with Calvin, although I see him often. And then there's Samuel. Or, there was. Still fire and depth and dark and light between us.

This year I've escaped my world for weeks at a time. Over and over, I've put a pause on my life, my family and my work, to become fully immersed in the worlds of my lovers. I've been a visitor, trying things on for size. Open minded, willing to explore, and driven by a desire to please my partners and share something meaningful together.

But I lost sight of my deep desire to exist dynamically in the overlap between two lives, and to grow the shared space. Instead, I compartmentalized their worlds and my own. For example, I lived and traveled with Omer for a year on his terms: his home, his festivals, his trips, culminating in Christmas in the Yucatan. I dove deep into my time with Ari in her alternative universe, both in Oregon and Oaxaca. I've loved these experiences, but I've also interrupted my life's flow time and again, instead of blending up something new and co-created with the people I love.

May 3rd

I'm playing casita with Samuel in Costa Rica. I'm actually here, fulfilling a years-long dream. We've been talking about me visiting since 2016 when he was still dividing his time between CR and Portland. But now that I'm here, I'm feeling ambivalent conclusion. I felt it within a few hours of arriving. The truck ride from the airport to the coastline was long and quiet, speckled with surface level chit chat, as though we didn't know each other as deeply as we do. A part of me wonders why I came, given all that's transpired between us, and I now realize that if I hadn't, I always would have wondered.

Of course, one major motive for coming is my interest in the eco-village and my desire to quiz Samuel on regenerative land management. On another level, I finally felt the freedom of choice. In this way, it was more of a saying goodbye to restrictive agreements, and to my life with Omer in finality, than it was saying a yes to my highest desires, or yes to Samuel, for that matter.

So here I am in the rainforest, a place bursting with life and motion, and rather than finding possibility, I sense ending. Completion.

It may have been mostly curiosity for Samuel, too. Things haven't been the same since I wrote that letter in October. I asked him to stop loving me, to stop fighting for me. I told him that the white-hot intensity of his love and pursuit were causing me emotional chaos and complicating my life with Omer. I was afraid of the power I felt between us, and I didn't have space to hold it. I knew it wasn't quite right. So we fought; fire and water, at odds. It dragged on and finally, I became exasperated. I slipped out and didn't look back.

Then he moved out of the country, and he landed here.

The karmic, weighty entanglement that we began three years ago has woven its thread through our lives, intensely for me, conveniently for him (it has seemed) and the loose ends feel tied up and ready to be trimmed. We've both moved on. That much is clear. We never really spoke about what happened; talking was never our strong suit. But some curiosity, or perhaps hope, or stubbornness hung in the air between us, a hazy smoke of a dream that might one day materialize.

So in January when we met for tea and he again invited me to visit, I bought a plane ticket. I still wondered about the remnants, the embers. Could something be revived? It took coming here to get my answer: the coffee has run low, the plants have seeded and been carried off by the wind. The fire's ash is now cold. I extinguished his love and now there's a cool wall in its place. It's clear that we are ready for other colors, new patterns, fresh hands on our skin. Something right and real. Something truly alive for each of us.

There has been an unrivaled spiritual and sexual power between us, and the extent to which this is unique is mirrored by our equally uncommon lack of emotional openness and ease. On the outside we might simply appear to be friends who sleep together. But with him I swing from high highs to low lows: feeling distant and guarded in our day-to-day exchanges, and impossibly intimate come nightfall. There's still a deep and incomplete connection; it hasn't changed. I only fully trust him when we're naked, and this is jarring for me.

It's a challenge here, as an affectionate extrovert to spend a week alone in the jungle with a man who doesn't much like to talk, or play, but gives a killer massage and sure knows how to make love during a lightning storm. I seemed to have forgotten this dual nature about him.

May 5th

This is the most time we've spent together. A week virtually alone. I am gaining a deeper understanding of who this beloved, frustrating man is to me.

He is fire. He is nonstop. Not in a frantic, manic sort of way that I can be, but in a slow burning, intense way that needs to use up fuel constantly, or risk spontaneously combusting and being consumed by the flames. He's a worker at his core. A doer. He is cut from the exact same cloth as my father, through and through. In fact, they share a birthday: April 1st. Aries. Triple fire sign, Samuel tells me. He is action, embodied. On the rare morning I wake and he is still in bed, he's been awake for hours choosing to stay put with his arm draped over me. He tells me his inner monologue is, "Get up. Get up. Get up."

We do find a flow when we are *doing* something together. Picking fruit. Driving somewhere. Making a meal. Being intimate. But the time in between action drags on like the melting desert scene in a Dali masterpiece. Nothing to say. Nothing to do. It's like even after three years, we no longer know what to do or how to be around each other. The ease has dissipated. There's no laughing or banter, no storytelling, no ease. Rarely a passing touch of affection. Just tasks. Give him a task and he will devote himself to it. Excel at it. Just this morning, he projected this emotion onto his earnest new farm dog, "Poochie," a scrappy little stray who wandered onto the farm a few weeks back.

"He just wants to know what to do," he said, picking green burrs out of the pup's beard. "He just wants to do good. Tell him and he'll do it."

He is an expert craftsman. He builds houses, paths and gardens and does so with a disciplined excellence and passion. He'd build a house that I could confidently live in. A lonely, sturdy home. I become my mother in his presence, watching my father. Longing for something more, something different from him. Three years of wondering.

I did glimpse more in him. More between us. For one weekend last year, I even felt him offer it up to me. Forty-eight hours of psychedelic openness and depth of heart at Breitenbush cracked our tightly held armors open. Talking. Sharing. Reflecting. Asking. Feeling into one another. After that trip though, he had begun to sort through his Costa Rica boxes and unpack things back into his closet. He hadn't bought his plane ticket yet. He was delaying his move, keeping his truck, and thinking about maintaining two home bases.

This scared me like hell. He just wanted me to let him love me, he said. He could make me happier than Omer could; that's what he said. I became uneasy and shut my doors just as he began to open his. And that was the week I extinguished the fire and broke his heart. Perhaps I had only let myself open up so much and received him so fully because I believed he'd be leaving soon.

The timing never lined up for us, not in three years. We were never fully available to be together.

Instead, we punctuated one another's lives when it was convenient, in lazy garden afternoons and weekend getaways between or on top of other relationships. Late night tea dates turned languid sleepovers. He told me that if he would have known, if he would have had the chance, he'd have pursued me sooner. He accused me of never being free long enough. There was a vein of truth in his words.

May 6th

I used to entertain us. I could tell him stories all afternoon and fill the air around us with a warm, gooey glow. I'd ask him bold or quirky questions insistently enough to garner a response. He played along.

But I've grown tired of his curt, distant answers. It no longer matters to me whether we talk or not. We've been in this loop for years now. I no longer ask him to share what he is passionate about, or to tell me about the friends he loves most. I no longer inquire why Immortal Technique is his favorite artist or whether he ever misses a cold beer now that he's sober. I'm not curious for any more glimpses into Key West life in the 80s. And he'll no longer stare off straight ahead as I stroke his hair or scratch his back in his favorite way, then shrug and answer, "I dunno. It's just how it is."

Sometimes I feel longing, other times I feel cold ambivalence. Sometimes, I shrink and grow silent in his presence, unsure of myself. Confused and tired of the invisible power dynamics fueled by his silence and his distance. Some moments I have felt afraid, like he is someone who could really hurt me if he wanted to. And do I trust him not to?

Responding warmly to my touch is no longer enough. His hands on my skin amidst seduction don't satisfy. The sex alone isn't worth the emotional weight of bridging our divide.

I no longer want to cultivate that space. His ground has grown hard. Mine is soft, but growing other things. For the first time since I've known him, it's obvious to me that our connection is done. The healing and revelations that have come over these three years feel complete.

To be fair, it's actually been good for me that he triggers the shit out of me. It's forced me to look hard in the mirror. There's the distance. The unpredictability, the coyness. The cold twinkly-eyed teasing and jabs. That sweet baby boy head on my lap that innocently charms and can do no wrong. He's at once my father, my mother, my brother, my child. He's man and god, union and conflict. Harmony and chaos.

Between us there's the whole of everything, just like I told Omer that day in the kitchen. Echoes of past lives, if there is such a thing. I've seen so much in us.

Archetypal masculine and feminine energies embodied. An absent husband and a neglected wife. We would have done well together out on the frontier. Me staring out the window, tending the home while he's away killing our dinner.

I see in us a loving, providing father and a cherished daughter. It was sparse and came only in flashes, but three times in three years I felt deep moments of healing and unwinding in his arms. When energetically clean, his presence has a rare effect on me.

So many other facets: A confident, powerful son and his adoring mother. Two lovers separated by war. Two siblings in an age-old rivalry. Fire and water trying to coexist.

The whole narrative is at once metaphor, and fully real. When we did San Pedro together I saw a glimpse of it, and as we rode the waves of DMT I saw it fully. We are archetypal. We have been working out generations of old stories together. But a new wave of healing is unfurling in me which requires no surrogate, no training wheels, no role playing or father figure for me to work out my energetic blockages on. Healing is integrating deeper and more subtly into my being as I form fresh, healthier ways of relating. Green shoots on sturdy branches.

And the story now is about my choice to walk away from something that drains and doesn't satisfy. Saying "no, thank you" to a connection not fully aligned with who I am now and who I am about to be. I've satisfied my stubborn, years-long curiosity and now I'm honest enough to admit I've had my fill.

35
Offering

Departure

A little talking, a little late.

We finally aired things out last night after a tense evening back from the mountains. Dinner was unfun. Once in our AirBnB we smoked some nice sleepy weed at the kitchen table. We locked eyes. Samuel asked me if I was mad at him.

"No, I'm not mad…" I said, straightening the place mats and fiddling with a stray thread. "Not much of anything, now," I answered honestly.

"I want you to know I'm here if you want to talk," he said. "I wasn't sure if…. maybe you were disappointed or had some expectations coming here."

I dropped my guard and chose to speak to him fully, unfiltered, realizing it was likely my last chance. Same country, same table, undivided attention, open lines. *Finally*.

In short: I told him our connection no longer satisfied me. It was clear we'd both moved on, and the chemistry that lingered was sexually electric, but left me feeling low. He recognized his inability to be emotionally present and apologized for not feeling differently. I told him there was no need.

I asked him to understand that I didn't want to sleep together when he comes stateside. I asked him not to call me for a date night as he had so many times before. At this, his eyes turned the table. He had trouble understanding my clear resolve. It's a conversation we'd had more than once before, and I remember talking in circles the last time. I chose not to drag it out.

Te Amo

Later in bed, I kept my pajamas on, ready to fall asleep fast.

"Goodnight," I whispered, and heard silence in response.

A minute later, through the dark: "Te amo."

"Hmm?" I asked, removing my earplugs.

"Te amo," he whispered.

I hadn't heard him.

"What'd you say, babe?" I asked again.

He turned toward me, "Te amo, Becca"

I let out an exhale. "Y te amo tambien."

We inched our backs closer to touching and I fell fast asleep.

When I woke in the morning, he was wide awake, staring down at me sadly with his dark hazel eyes. He gets so boyish when he's sad. We drank our coffee on the deck overlooking San Jose, me feeling clean relief with my honesty and him seeming weighted and regretful. He snapped photos of me curled up in my pajamas on the patio chair and doted over my beauty. I smirked and looked away.

The twenty-minute drive to the airport felt drawn out, him reaching out to touch me at every straightaway and stoplight, catching my eye every chance he could and sighing wistfully. It felt deeply familiar to my own memories of delivering him to the airport.

"How you doin' over there?" I asked, running my hands through his hair. I still couldn't resist.

"I'm wishing we would have connected more," he said. "I'm sad that this is over for you."

I didn't know what to say. I'd said it all, so I responded with silence.

How He Loves

I owe it to us both, to the very real love we shared and the healing we've received, to bear witness, now that all of the wondering is over. It matters to me to hear what has been said in the space between our hearts. He showed me love in his own way. In the way he knew how. Just as my father did all those years.

I am transported and immersed in memories of Samuel:

He sends me photos of flowers when we're borders apart. Vibrant, dewy, tropical treasures for me to wake up to. He sleeps with a club and a machete by his bed, prepared to defend against the actual threat of jaguars and thieves.

He whacks through the jungle with the same machete to clear a path for me. He knocks down a juicy green mango and then peels it slowly, feeding it to me, bite by bite. It's sour, like the lovechild of a mango and a green apple.

Further along the path he points out a fragrant ylang ylang tree. He veers from the trail and winks at me from up on the hill, then expertly slices through the stem as a bloom drops into his hand. He presses the fresh flower into my palm slowly. Intoxicating.

He builds a new fire for each meal, cooking me smoked trout eggs benedict with lemony braised chaya greens. He harvests ingredients around the property while I wash and chop vegetables. We devour yucca and pork stew. He saves me the best local chocolate and kneels beside me on the bed as we savor it.

He surrounds me with burning candles as I lie on the floor in the nest he's created. He gives me his undivided attention. Then he smudges me head to toe with Palo Santo, grazing me so closely that I can feel its warmth and trace its path across my skin. He spends an hour massaging my body with olive oil, then another hour making love to me while the rain pounds on the metal roof and the birds and insects sound their cacophony into the evening sky.

Only after this, as we lay entwined and he finally rests, collapsed beside me, can I recognize that this is who he is. This is how he loves. The fullness and the lack. And I choose not to punish him for it.

Acts of service. Tending to me and my garden. Three years of feeding me from his orchard and climbing trees to reach the sweetest fruit.

We pull up to the airport. I shed tears through our drawn out embrace. He shares sweet sentiments of love and longing, and I am washed clean with the saltwater from my eyes.

"We connected enough. In our own way," I say. "Thank you."

He grips my hand as I turn to walk into the airport. I pull it away. When I look out the window, his truck is gone.

I choose to let him be who he is, I choose to accept and as much as I can, understand him. And I choose to let our paths diverge as I board a plane, back to the place and people that are truly home to me.

My relationship to Samuel has always been powerful, yet built on complexity. Had the timing been more spacious, perhaps we would have tried to create something more commonplace. It's better that we didn't; I can't imagine trying to domesticate a tropical storm like us.

These experiences remind me how much I want, more than anything, to be the agent of my own life. How beautiful are the lives of my lovers, and how divergent from my own. I'm reminded how much I love the life I'm crafting for myself and my child: the specifics and the minutiae, the tone of the moment to moment, day to day flow, in the same way each lover adores their own life when they're feeling most aligned.

Each time I've crossed over to visit a lover's world, I've returned home seeing more clearly how aligned I am with my chosen life. Returning home feels like falling into the arms of my closest lover.

Edge of Decision

I settled back at home and tucked Moses into bed that first night, kissing his head a few extra times.

I burned the last of the sage Samuel had given me. I cleaned my altars and gathered up all the dried flowers, the feathers and stems, stones and shells I'd been collecting over the years, treasures that had been hand selected and given to me by the lovers who participated in shaping my life: Keaton, Cory, Jack, Andrew, Omer, Calvin, Ari, Samuel. I thought of all the people before and after these ones, who I'd have the chance to share love with in my lifetime because I'd made the courageous choice to love abundantly. Seeing all these treasures in one place and considering the beautiful souls they represented reminded me how fortunate I'd been in my life thus far.

It was clear I'd begun a new chapter: the making of my own life, tending to my own heartscape. I wanted to mark this transition. I looked at the artifacts of romance and thought of letting them go.

But I was resistant.

To let go felt like an edge, a decision, an irreversible action. I'd always loved keeping my options open. What if I changed my mind? What if I wanted to go back? What if I wasn't ready to be in charge of my life? I paused my spin-out and remembered that symbolism was just symbolism and healing would certainly not be linear.

Just burn the fucking potpourri, Becca.

OFFERING **475**

That night, I carried the bowl of remnants through my beautiful nest of a home and settled alone on the back deck. Kneeling at our fire pit, I prepared a fire, meticulously interweaving the twigs and kindling with the artifacts: flammable relics of a season that had broken, healed, and changed me.

It was an offering of gratitude. Atop the wood I added a single psilocybin mushroom and a sticky, sparkly cannabis flower, an ode to the medicines that had catalyzed this whole adventure. I owe them a debt of gratitude. I spent a moment reflecting on the wild, magical way my life had unfolded, thanks to some mysterious assembly of good fortune, bold decisions, resilience, community, and cosmic medicines.

I sat with my eyes closed for quite a while. Then Moses woke up crying from a bad dream.

"Mmooommmm!" I heard him call down the stairs.

Classic timing, Mo, I thought. I set the unlit match down and went upstairs to tend to him. I tucked him back into bed. Another kiss on the head. Ahh, mom life.

A while later, I returned to the fire. This time, I was ready to burn it. I tossed a match in and watched the remnants of my love and heartache transform into heat and light before my eyes. I felt at peace. For once, no tears came.

Thanks, Universe, I thought. *Thanks for this messy, edgy, beautiful life. I'm ready to begin again.*

36

Epilogue

As I assemble the last pages of this intricate rollercoaster of a book, I think about my notes to self. What do I want to take with me? And what would I like to leave you with, dear reader? I can't possibly synthesize and distill all the lessons and insights from a quarter-life crisis. I'm certain that much of it I won't fully understand until later in life. I know that you are intelligent enough to glean the elements that resonate with you.

I hope that you laughed, cried, and shared "Aha!" moments with me along the way. Here are some things I hope we'll both remember.

Healing and progress are not linear.

It's okay to learn things the hard way. I went through the same behavior loops numerous times within these pages. Sometimes, it takes repeating a pattern again and again to even recognize its presence and develop enough awareness to choose a different way.

It's not too late to apologize.

Time may take some of the sting away, but there is no substitute for owning the things that are my responsibility. Even after years, there are still apologies that would be welcome steps toward reconciliation in my life.

To that end: I am sorry to those I love who have been caught in the crossfire between me and my healing. To Keaton, Jack, and Omer specifically, thank you for being gracious partners. You deserve so much love. I am sorry that I made commitments I was unwilling to keep, that I lied to save face, and that I became defensive when called out. I am sorry for repeatedly putting myself first in our relationships. To Cory, Samuel, Calvin, and Ari, I am sorry for my inconsistency and carelessness with your hearts. I am sorry for showing up in ways that were convenient for me, without enough regard for how it tossed you around. I own the fact that I have work to do here.

I hope that if I had known better, I would have done better. I do know better now. I am committed to recognizing my shadows and the ways they manifest and taking responsibility for the impacts of my choices. I have a long way to go, and I understand that self-compassion does not negate accountability; they go hand in hand. Each day, each year, I am exploring how to live in radical honesty and integrity so I can better honor myself and the people who choose to be in relationship with me.

Live an examined life.

There is courage in questioning. Small deaths prevent big deaths. I believe that by taking the time to peel back the layers of my life and conditioning while I am young, I have chosen to exist in an ongoing state of expansiveness and evolution. I've cultivated a willingness to change as new experiences inform deeper understanding.

I've developed the practice of making subtle shifts and course corrections while still malleable, while the current of life is free-flowing. I believe this is much easier than reaching age forty, or sixty-five, and finding myself in a life that feels completely inauthentic, or worse, discovering that I am participating in harmful systems that make life worse for others. It's better to course correct early and often, rather than get all the way to Texas when I thought I was headed to New York.

Give permission to change.

I have witnessed such massive change in myself, my family members, and loved ones, that I've come to respect change as a constant force, steady as a river. Give yourself permission to ride the current, and give others that permission, too.

My brother had a baby boy last year. He was the first of my four siblings to become a parent. Moses and I went to the hospital to meet him. As I parked the car, I realized how fixed I'd become in my opinion of my brother. Of my whole family, for that matter. I'd pushed them away because of my memories and stories about them. In the meantime, I'd changed in major ways. Who was to say they hadn't also changed? In fact, they almost certainly had.

I sat in the hospital room holding his beautiful newborn son and tears welled up in my eyes. He spoke about the life-altering feeling of becoming a father.

"As soon as I held him, I realized that no one in the world is ever going to be as important to me as he is," he said. My brother, who I remembered as someone who fiercely centered himself at all costs, was transforming before my eyes.

I nodded in knowing agreement.

More recently, I was dropping Moses with my mom and we began discussing the George Floyd protests. She told me how our hometown was preparing for demonstrators. I explained to her that I'd been marching with Moses in Portland and talking with him about systemic racism.

I braced for inner frustration, recalling her words when I was a teen: "Don't go shopping at Lloyd Center unless you want to get shot by thugs and gang bangers."

Instead, I was amazed at the words that came out of her mouth next.

"I'm learning about white supremacy," she said. "I never really realized how deep it went. I'm reading books and watching videos. I know I'm late to the conversation… but I figure, it's never too late to learn."

This felt healing to me on a base level. We must believe that people can change, especially people closest to us, those who have hurt us. Don't pin people down to past versions of themselves. We must create space for the transformation of those around us and ask them to believe in our own transformation, too.

It is okay to evolve, even if it's not understood by others. Surround yourself with people who honor your evolution. Sometimes, all this inner change means we grow apart from people, communities, and vocations that we thought were woven into the fabric of our identities. That's okay. Let the change come. There's wisdom in it. We can fully embrace where we are, while honoring where we've been. Feel it all and let the waters carry you forward.

Become friends with discomfort and uncertainty.

I lost touch with my dad around the time Omer and I started dating. He just… stopped calling. I was unsurprised, but it still hurt. After all of that, gone again. I later learned that he had been living in his car during multiple attempts to escape a toxic relationship with his wife. As I sat with the news, I understood that his actions had everything to do with what was happening inside of his unique world, and were in no way a reflection of my worth or a lack of love for me.

Life is messy like that. It aches sometimes, leaving plotlines unresolved and relationships too heavy to hold. Life isn't a tidy movie with distinctly tragic or happy endings; it marches on. There's endless context and nuance. It's often uncomfortable to be alive. Let's see that as a gift and an opportunity for deeper resilience.

Self-awareness is a starting point.

As citizens of this shared world, we are responsible for what we contribute to it. There is no neutral. Lack of awareness and lack of action is not neutral; in fact, it reinforces existing paradigms. There is no activism, progress, or justice without us first looking hard in the mirror at ourselves and our personal histories: family background, relational blueprint, trauma, spiritual beliefs, cultural and racial conditioning, and so on. Deeper understanding enables us to understand the snags, the places that need attention and healing.

It's also important we don't get lost in a self-absorbed, self-help bubble forever. There's a world out here that calls for our active participation. We do the inner work so we can contribute to the outer work of transformation. We are each drops in the bucket. Looking inward is a lifelong practice of washing our eyes and cleaning our ears, removing as often as we can, the barriers of trauma, privilege, and numbness that prevent us from witnessing the realities around us.

Love takes many forms.

I have no business giving anyone relationship advice. My love life has more cautionary tales than success stories. Non-monogamy may be en vogue for the moment, and in many ways, it works for me at this time in my life. I prefer to be a free agent, focusing on open and authentic relating while I build my own life in integrity. But one thing is clear: life is fluid, change is constant, and the minute I think I KNOW something about myself or the world, the Universe laughs in my face and proves just the opposite.

When it comes to love, these are the questions I seek to answer:

> *Am I clear with myself about how available I am for a connection?*
>
> *Have I expressed myself clearly and made agreements I am willing and able to keep?*
>
> *Am I listening and asking as much as I am telling?*
>
> *Do I act in a way that demonstrates care and respect?*
>
> *Do I own my shit when it comes up?*
>
> *Where is the meeting point between the needs and desires of each person? That convergence is where healthy relationships can happen.*

What I have learned is that regardless of the open/exclusive relationship binary, there are some universals. All relationships, whether romantic, sexual, friendly, professional, or familial, stand on the same pillars: boundaries, communication, co-creation and respect.

These are the places to focus attention.

The rest is just specifics.

Perspectives

The following insights were provided by the real people who readers know as: Keaton, Jack, Logan, Tess, Ari, Calvin and Indigo.

Thank you to each contributor for your willingness and vulnerability.

Thank you to my family members, lovers and friends who were unable or chose not to participate, for your equally important role in my life. It is my goal to highlight the reality that in life, there are no tidy protagonists.

We each fill different and evolving roles for one another, and the cast of characters depends largely on whose lens is viewing the story.

I hope to honor alternate perspectives and lay bare the common threads where our lived experiences align.

Dear reader,

You know me as "Keaton." I can't speak for the entire book, but Becca has done a good job of keeping the facts accurate in this story as it pertains to our relationship. I'd only want to offer the reader my perspective on 5 things:

1) I think Becca gets you feeling sorry for her, playing the sexually deprived woman. I believe that she was — she is a woman with a healthy libido. Her story doesn't account for the emotional toll it had on me, being made to feel inadequate. From early on in the relationship I was aware that Becca had needs that I couldn't support. At first, I sincerely wanted to be able to satisfy her. As time went on, + felt that. It was out of my control, and we were too different, and I couldn't give her what she wanted/needed. Imagine you kept disappointing someone who you care about because of something you can't control and as a consequence they push you away. I was being punished for something I couldn't control/fix. We had this significant incongruence —

> I shut down sexually if I wasn't satisfied emotionally. She shut down emotionally if she wasn't satisfied sexually.

2) A lot of our issues in general stemmed from being young. I think we are still too young to be drawing final conclusions about our 20s. This is being written before either of us has turned 30.

Keaton's Perspective 485

3) Being a devout Christian greatly influenced my decision making. One example of this were my beliefs about sex: I did not value pleasure. I was taught in church that sex was an act of the flesh. Becca helped me begin to understand that it was OK to feel pleasure. I'm appreciative of that. I've been on my own journey to undo some of the harmful teachings that have permeated my entire life. My religiosity has haunted and inhibited me.

4) I love my family - Becca included. I've always done my absolute best in my relationships. I have loved Becca and my son well. I'm proud of the way I am co-parenting. I try to give my son unique, memorable experiences. I'm very proud of him and I love him more than anything else.

5) I have felt under-appreciated for what I have offered Becca. She has been afforded many experiences that you've read about because of my sacrifice and flexibility. I've been endlessly supportive.

She can be bad at showing appreciation, saying sorry or thank you. She can be self-absorbed. Becca has a lot of good qualities though. She's good at dreaming, making you feel like everything is possible. She tries to be aware of her blind spots too. I will attest to the fact that she has put a lot of heart and effort into reforming herself. And facing her past. It is an admirable quality. Probably my biggest takeaway from this narrative: Honest reflection and hard work leads to personal growth.

DEAR READER,

 I WANT TO START BY SAYING THAT I HAVE ABSOLUTELY NO IDEA HOW TO WRITE ABOUT AND EXPRESS THE COMPLEX, TURBULENT, EXTREME, WAVE-TRAIN OF EMOTION THAT WAS/IS MY RELATIONSHIP WITH BECCA. MY EXPERIENCE LIVING IN RELATIONSHIP WITH HER CHALLENGED THE FOUNDATIONS OF MY IDENTITY AND RESHAPED THE WAY I COMMUNICATE WITH ROMANTIC PARTNERS. IT SHOOK ME TO MY CORE AND MADE ME NEVER WANT TO TRUST ANOTHER HUMAN AGAIN; IT TAUGHT ME THAT LOVE CAN BE SO DEEP THAT IT WILL LEAVE YOU SHATTERED, LYING IN A POOL OF TEARS (ALONG WITH OTHER BODILY FLUIDS) OF PAIN AND JOY, UNDERSTANDING AND CONFUSION. IF I COULD TITLE THE BOOK OF OUR RELATIONSHIP, IT WOULD BE CALLED, <u>THE JOY OF REMEMBERING AND THE PAIN OF WANTING TO FORGET.</u>

 OUR RELATIONSHIP WAS FOUNDED ON THE TYPE OF FRIENDSHIP CREATED BY AN ORGANIC MEETING OF PEOPLE LIVING IN COMMUNITY WITH ONE ANOTHER.

Sharing the context of an intentional living space meant that there was an inherent foundation of transparent communication in regards to needs, feelings, and comfort. Our first real conversations were over the kitchen island, an informal setting to share life experiences and food. We were both getting over recent breakups and commiserated about lack of communication and clarity with past lovers. We shared our desire to find romance that was not built around concealment of emotions and the socioemotional games that seem foundational to relational norms in the millenial milieu. We also expressed mutual desire for physical fulfillment in the company of emotional intimacy, and shared growth. Our espoused desires for true partnership seemed incredibly compatible and these conversations often ended with prolonged eye contact that seemed to softly scream out an intent to act on our shared passions and relational values.

The natural progression of these conversations seemed obvious, even as I told myself that getting romantically involved with a "housemate" was quite ill-advised. The progression from platonic snuggle buddies to semi-celibate, sexually tense, incredibly attached and intimate snuggle buddies was rapid. We were quickly confronted with questions such as "How do we feel about sex in the bed you actively share with a three-year-old?", "Do we tell the housemates?", and "How do we feel about rope and butt plugs?" We began to develop a wonderful partnership founded on the co-creation of incredible food, hiking, music, costume parties, weekly bouldering sessions, long chats in the garden about our life plans, and lots of really really hot sex.

While this may seem pretty fantastic (and it was), our experience together was also influenced significantly by Becca's complex relational history. The more she shared about her past,

Jack's Perspective

489

The more it became apparent that she still had very complex, constantly shifting emotional connections to past lovers: one day she never wanted to hear from them ever again, the next week she would be explaining how important they were in her life, regardless of how they had hurt her.

It was a confusing time - I was (successfully, I feel) challenging and confronting any jealosy while holding space for her to process her feelings of connection and frustration for others. Processing was something I desired; we both expressed wanting an openness where we did not feel limited by our relationship but rather encouraged to explore the potential in other people we intersected with. However, in practice, this openness was restricted by Becca's interpretation of my desire to communicate as sabotage and her inconsistency with how much other people meant to her.

My desire for communication was partially due to my observations of

Becca's tendency to rapidly shift her evaluations of people and partially because of the opportunities to process emotions. In addition, there were practical considerations: we maintained a fluid-bond in our sexual relationship and I wanted assurance that her actions were not putting our health at risk. When she started dating another woman about a year into our relationship, I felt like access to some details of their coupling was a reasonable consideration. But it was always perceived as jealosy.

Looking back, this desire to know about her other relationships may have come partially from a deep insecurity and lack of trust in our relationship, something Becca later proved was not the least bit unfounded.

Although we had built our relationship on the foundational tenets of supported mutual growth, transparent communication, and openness to explore relational potential, the end of our romantic partnership was

Jack's Perspective **491**

brought about as Becca explicitly renounced these agreements. In one of our final parting conversations, she explained to me that she was no longer interested (and hadn't been for a while) in supporting my development as a person or engaging in any sort of relational "work". She stated that she had been withholding not only her feelings and emotions, but also truths about her actions. She said that she had been playing games with me. She expressed the need for space to come into her own as a woman and could not do that in a romantic relationship.

While I respected her desire for independent growth, I felt like she had cheated on me all over again, not sexually (although I have come to learn that this was part of it), but in the context of rejecting the fundamental premise of our entire partnership.

Our last night together was after we had already ended our relationship romantically but were still caught up in patterns of familiarity and attachment. It was Valentine's Day and I had just been offered the job of my dreams. In celebration, I bought two steaks and brought them over to Bella's house while she cooked them up (in lots of butter and caramelized onions — still to this day she prepares the best home-cooked steak I've ever had), I read my favorite books to Moses and put him to bed. We ate and reminisced (somewhat distantly) over wine and chocolate about the past and what the future might bring. I was excited to be out of graduate school and done with jobs; she was excited to have space to herself, out of her long pattern of relationships, a single woman who could focus on her own growth.

The next morning, her phone buzzed on the kitchen counter, showing a new picture message from her new lover. The next time I saw her, she was planning on moving in with him.

I once talked to a mutual friend who proposed that Becca uses the people around her (lovers, friends, her family, moses...) to fill holes in her life left by gaps in her upbringing and her development in the church and her family. Rather than working to make the holes smaller as she grows, she seeks to fill them full of whoever presents themselves as willing filler. She manipulates her relationships and her perceptions of those around her to fit into her life exactly as she needs, somehow balancing care + love with an incredible narcissism that can only come from an intense instinct for self-preservation.

STILL TO THIS DAY, BECCA IS THE ONLY PERSON WHO HAS EVER WRITTEN ME A LOVE SONG. THE ONLY PERSON (AT THE TIME) THAT I EVER CONSIDERED BUILDING A LIFE WITH. AND THE ONLY PERSON WHO HAS EVER TRULY BROKEN MY TRUST AND LOVE DOWN TO THEIR VERY CORES.

I STILL HAVE A PROFOUND LOVE AND APPRECIATION FOR BECCA, BUT THIS LOVE IS ACCOMPANIED BY AN EQUAL AMOUNT OF PAIN. TO ME, SHE IS THE MANIFEST-ATION AND EMBODIMENT OF PARADOX: LOVE AND ANGER, JOY AND SADNESS, PLEASURE AND PAIN. SHE IS ONE OF THE MOST BEAUTIFULLY COMPLEX AND DYNAMIC INDIVIDUALS I HAVE EVER MET.

ONE OF MY BIGGEST REGRETS IS THAT THE PAIN I FEEL HAS LIMITED MY ABILITY TO MAINTAIN A CLOSE FRIENDSHIP WITH HER (AND MOSES).

I TRULY WISH TO SEE HOW SHE HAS GROWN AS A PERSON AND WHO

she has become as she processes her past and builds a future for herself and her loved ones.

— Jack

Our story begins in the small town of Barlow at the church located on the edge of town. We were both new to town, just trying to find our place in a very close knit community. My mother had suggested that I should try and attend a church service which she had been told was very "alternative," since I wasn't much of a Christian, outside of family tradition and holidays. She thought maybe I'd be able to make some friends before summer was over. At 12 years old I was, for lack of a better word, 'precocious' and reluctant to go along with a culture based on ideas about what kids my age 'should be doing'. Becca understood this better than anyone. We met one evening in the parking lot where all the new ID students were socializing with the youth. From there, we had an instant connection and I relied on Becca as a mentor, a friend, and a safe place.

    One shared motive behind our heavy involvement in the church was the desperate desire to have community, a place where you knew you belonged and were loved. For many years, that

Logan's Perspective

Search was satisfied by the religious community. It's hard to describe in the same breath, the love and empowerment the church gave us, while also acknowledging that it was a time and place of shame and self containment. But it gave me Becca, and for that I am eternally grateful. To have found someone at such a young age who treated me like a peer, while also guiding me through some extremely traumatic times in my life, was so special and just the kind of person that she is; a beautiful woman of selfless love and undying loyalty.

    Two years later, when it came time for Becca to graduate from the IB program, I was overwhelmed with gratitude for having her as a mentor and friend to me, but at a loss for words to communicate the impact she'd had on my life. We were on our annual mission trip to Spokane, Washington with our church, crammed into a hotel conference room after a long day of community work. It came time for everyone to tell the graduating students exactly how much they had meant to us before we drove home and our beloved mentors and friends would be moving on. I felt an immense amount of pressure to say the perfect thing to my friend Becca, because everyone around us knew that we were thick as thieves, but I struggled to find the words. She didn't need me to stand up in front of everyone and explain how much she meant to me, but you could tell the expectations were high. All I remember is standing up with tears in my eyes, telling everyone I was lost for words. Finally, I just nervously blurted out, "I don't know what else I can really say, but Becca, you're like my soulmate". Of course the room snickered and gave me looks of confusion, but Becca just grinned, giggled, and whispered to me afterwards that it wasn't a silly thing to say and she knew exactly what I meant.

Post ID, our friendship continued to be close knit. I had moved quite a few times around the Barlow area and Becca had started dating Keaton and working outside the church. I was going through a pretty rough home life at the time, and Becca was there for me in ways that exceeded a normal friendship. The winter before she and

Keaton got married, I had been kicked out of my mothers home and it wasn't an option for me to live with my father. Becca took care of me like family; she got me to school, kept in contact with my parents, and made sure I felt safe. Once I was ready to go home, Becca made sure I knew her door was open to me whenever I needed it. Little 14 year old me couldn't have asked for a better sister figure in my life, and it was an honor to know that she loved me like family too. Later that year, I stood beside her as a bridesmaid in her wedding.

    Skip forward about 2 years. Both of us were living in Oak Grove. She was married to Keaton and I was 16, living with roommates and getting ready to study abroad for a year in Thailand. This time in our friendship was a strange little hiccup, a time when we weren't really able to relate to one another. I was a young woman of extreme curios- -ity for life experiences, the good, bad and ugly ones; Consequences in my life were something that I didn't avoid, but simply saw as a product of having an exciting life. I had grown out of the company of my peers and was ready for my life to expand as well.

I distinctly remember one conversation where I shared about some rebellious experiences I'd had recently and the many other things I wanted to do. In a few short months I was going to have the ultimate freedom, living abroad and finding all sorts of new ways to make trouble. A tone of judgment and fear washed over Becca like I had never experienced from her before. She expressed that my careless attitude and frivolous decisions were going to end up creating more hardships for me. I didn't dwell on this disagreement negatively, but I did feel confused.

    The conversation ended with an 'Alright, i'll see ya around I guess' attitude, and that lingered for a couple of years. It took time for me to realize that it was scary for Becca to hear this 'I'm gonna do whatever I want and just ride the wave of consequences' attitude, because it was like looking at her 16 year old self dead in the face. Care and concern from someone I saw as family was a pretty foreign feeling to me. She didnt want me to experience the same kind of pain she had experienced, but also wasn't sure how to express that in a way

I could understand. But our bond is like family; we may not always see eye to eye or even speak, but the unspoken bond of chosen family had, and will always hold us together.

Three years later, after my year in Thailand, I had settled back in Portland and our dialogue seamlessly reopened. Though our lives had lightly drifted apart, when we saw each other it was like no time at all had passed. We met in my neighborhood at my favorite market diner and we sat there catching up and reminiscing until the closed sign had been flipped over. We had to cover quite a bit of ground! But the conversation and gut wrenching laughter flowed on easily. We both had big new relationship changes: I had recently fallen in love with my new best friend, and Becca told me that she and Keaton had opened up their marriage.

I wasn't at all surprised when she told me. We had both radically grown away from the christian community by that point. Feeling unapologetic and free from that kind of burden really pushes you in the direction of the person you wanna be, so I was nothing but thrilled for Becca when she told me about this big shift. Sitting in this little market diner, Spring time had embraced us both with such a season of change. Before long everything had changed and I was helping her move out of her home and into an urban commune.

In just a few short months our worlds had been turned upside down and our asses kicked to the curb, it was honestly too much change to process while keeping our day to day routines, so we needed to get the hell outta dodge. I was distraught and heartbroken from a recent breakup to someone I was completely in love with. It was torture having to see him everyday at work and around our friends; I was starting to fall apart. Becca had just moved into the commune. Her divorce papers were being filed and she was coparenting and splitting time with Moses. Everything felt so raw at this time but fell exactly into place like it should.

So we decided to take a roadtrip to the deserts of Utah and Arizona, just far enough away from the noise of confusion and heartbreak back home, that it seemed like we'd be able to collect ourselves and move forward in those dusty orange lands. Our trip

Logan's Perspective

Started on a cold misty morning in November. I pulled up to the SE Portland commune in my little '98 Subaru, threw all our shit in the back, lit a cigarette, and got to driving.

Our first day driving was one so full of excitement and determination. It was also pretty comical. The goal was to drive from Oregon to Utah in one day, taking turns driving every couple of hours. Well... that didn't exactly end up being the case. Early on in our trip, we realized I may have underestimated exactly how strong my homemade brownies were, (since I am quite literally always stoned). Becca only lasted a solid hour behind the wheel. I just remember laughing my ass off while trying to keep calm as to not further scare the wicked stoned and frightened Becca behind the wheel. It was truly the perfect tone to start our trip. I cracked open a beer and drove for hours in the dark on the same never ending roads through Nevada, chain smoking and listening to an obscene amount of Led Zeppelin. It was easier to forget our pains and problems when we were mindlessly driving around in the middle of nowhere.

The next morning we found a BLM campsite sitting right on a Canyon near Zion, and so the exploring began. We hit all the classic spots in the area, from hiking Angels Rest to the crimson colored Hoodoos in Bryce canyon, our conversations flowed from dumb gossip to tearful reminders of just how frustrating and complex our realities were. We could go in circles for hours about where we came from to where we were going, trying to make sense of it all. We drove ourselves just crazy enough, surrounded by such great beauty, that the bitter taste in our mouths got a little sweeter. But we still needed a little help to let the floodgates open. So the next plan in our trip was to head to Arizona and trip on acid for two days during the super moon.

After setting up camp at Lake Powell we wanted to explore a bit outside the campsite before our 'big trip'. So we began to wander around the little town stopping at thrift stores and visiting Antelope Canyon, until we ended up at Horseshoe Bend. Looking into the vast beauty of this canyon absolutely brought us to tears.

We hoped that tripping on LSD would release our spirits from trauma that weighed on us. After wandering down to the water and losing our shit seeing the supermoon, we started a fire and the laughter as well as tears rolled late into the night. We talked for hours about forgotten memories, resentment held toward those who raised us, the men who had left a hole in our hearts, and the overwhelming confusion of being confident in our rugged independence. Our feet were restless and our minds moving a hundred miles a minute as we bounced around the fire laughing at how ridiculous we must have looked. But we couldn't care less, because we were unburdened and free in the cool desert night; in the desert we were able to accept our pain and begin to heal.

    Before we knew it our time of adventure had come to an end in Arizona, and it was time to head back North. Those two days specifically blossomed our friendship into a new territory of familial love, but more importantly brought us closer to our individual journeys of self love. It was the start of a new chapter in our lives.

Now here we are, in the year 2020, living 10 minutes down the road from each other, and still very much dear friends. I was extremely intimidated to be a part of Becca's book. I gave up a dozen times because nothing I wrote felt adequate enough in portraying our story and my undying admiration for Becca, but I finally had to buck up and get it done. If I have not successfully explained the impact she had on my life, I'd like to make it clear now.

    Becca has never given up on me, she has been patient and tender to me when I was so low in the dirt that I wouldn't care if I was forgotten about. Then stern and apologetically honest with me when I couldn't see through the bullshit clearly; she is a woman of true selfless love and strength. Grateful doesn't begin to cover how I feel to be a part of Becca's chosen family. No matter where we have gone in our lives, the months and years we haven't talked, the flame of our kindred spirits can't be extinguished; little 14 year old me said it best: Becca is my soulmate. We grew up together, and I truly would not be the person I am today without her.

I could go on forever like a sappy sentimental fool about Becca, but i'll close with this: Thank you Becca, I love ya, and here's to another decade with you.

—Logan

hello dear reader,

Tess here. I first met Becca in the summer of 2016 when we both moved into the Golden Hearth just two weeks apart. I don't remember our very first encounter like she does but I do remember our first "real" conversation.

She and Jack were beginning the dance of relationship in the wake of her divorce and heartbreak. I expressed to her how it was hard for me to watch this new relationship form. Not only because I was concerned with the consequences starting an inter-house relationship but because I also had a little thing for Jack and was feeling kinda second fiddle. I asked her to be gentle with me and with each other. It was something I'd never really done before- been totally honest like that. She listened, we talked, and that was the beginning of our fine friendship. and it continues to be the way I relate to her. She is someone I can fearlessly share my truth and experience with and someone I have compared myself to relentlessly.

Through our years of living together, we rode the natural ups and downs of cohabitation and friendship. Some tough stuff came up and we worked through it. Growing up, my family often let conflict go unaddressed until forgotten. So with Becca, I practiced authenticity and accountability. I could comfortably set boundaries or share my deepest thoughts. She was my closest confidant and dearest friend. And for all the changes she was going through, I think I served as a beacon of consistency and safety- a person she could turn to for care and encouragement. The same for Moses.

I welcomed them both with open arms. He and I developed a special bond through our weekly trips to the Farmer's Market and our time together, with and without Becca. She introduced me as her best friend and co-parent. We spent a lot of time together the three of us, working in the garden, playing outside, coloring and building. I observed Becca's

Tess' Perspective

gentle approach with Moses and marveled at what the world could be like if more parents were able to achieve the patience and respect that she exhibited towards him. She helped him deal with conflict, upset, and compromise with reason, kindness, and equanimity. We felt like a little family.

We also saw so much of our own mothers in each other and with that, for me, came the deep desire for her love and approval. In her constantly changing circle, I wanted to remain important and relevant. I witnessed people come in and out of her life, I feared that I was not enough.

At times I was jealous of her wildness and freedom. Sometimes I felt steady and righteous. Other times I was small and stagnant. Her boldness inspired me. I also made excruciating comparisons... watching her evolve and take risks was hard for me. I wrote a song about it later to process my feelings.

I judged her as she told me all the compliments the men on her path paid her in detail, often secretly cringing as she recounted all the swirly connections and new lovers she'd acquired, holding my own past in shame. I wondered what she was trying do or what she was trying to prove? Or if it was that at all. I finally figured that she was simply seeking the love and validation that only comes from within.

More recently, I think she has gotten in touch with that place. The place where one loves and accepts oneself. And now that I've tamed my jealousy, I can begin to learn my next lesson. As I watch Becca now from far away, I have found myself occasionally thinking, "who does she think she is to love so deeply and so recklessly? and to love herself like that?" And I realize she is my mirror. Like her, I want to take risks and learn by pushing the edges, loving myself and loving others fearlessly along the way. I have a feeling we will know each other a long time.

Scorpion Sister

I had never said to anyone just the way I felt but I let down my walls once & asked you for help. So much time has passed now & I've got a few doubts. I've been stayin in one place & you've been running around/ Scorpion Sister you live so free. Everytime I see you I want a different me. You're making it clear, so clear to me

My wild heart wants something new
my wild heart longs for broader views

because I've been green with envy, I've followed in your steps/ I have compared & dispaired & I haven't learned quite yet/ Scorpion Sister no I wont be stung. Do you see your shadow when you step into the sun? It stretches far & wide & puts a darkness over me. Scorpion Sister, I cant let that be. because

My wild heart longs to shine
I want your joy to be my joy
I want your joy to be my joy.

Even though I know were not that different there is something about you that makes me feel I'm missing/ missing out & missing pieces of a life i havent lived.
Scorpion sister somethings gotta give. somethings gotta give.

♡tess

Tess' Perspective

With some people its kinda hard, and with others its really easy. With Becca and I it has always been the latter, regardless of our unconventional start. We had what could be perceived as a complicated scenario for a typical beginning to a relationship — she had a serious partner, and I was preparing to travel indefinitely. But, we both knew these were just 'right now' things and weren't actually that important because we would be here for the long haul. It's never been easy in the boring way, quite the contrary.

We've had wild adventures from Oregon to Mexico and have shared some of our biggest cries; biggest laughs together. I believe we have a certain soul family that we're embodied here with to collaborate on our push forward in waking up to what our best lives can be. Light on the dark stuff. People that show up to accompany us through growth and to share many layers of love. We're that for one another.

I don't think of Becca as only an individual, but as a whole world. A way of thinking, a way of action, a way of living. A way of living in which pleasure and soul take the priority. A way of living in which each individual is uniquely evaluated, not based on the things they do of the clothes they wear, but by the way their heart pulses and their soul sings. Becca opened me up to a level of true love, one without attachment, yet one with stability and communication, and with ultimate freedom to grow. And the journey has just begun...

xo,
Ari

Ari's Perspective

For the Readers,

This is Calvin and the following is me in my own words as well as my thoughts on Rebecca and Edge Play.

I was in a line of students. Everyone was staring at their phones, at school pamphlets, the back of the heads in front of them, or staring blankly at nothing at all. I was scanning the small crowd wondering who my classmates would be in an intimate setting of massage therapy. My eyes met Rebecca's.

I have been through my 20's and around the block so to speak: married and divorced and have also parted from church and faith. I have had several relationships and experiences and learned a thing or two. It takes someone beyond ordinary to pique my interests. I probably knew at that moment by her glances, that she was beyond ordinary. I asked what classes she was taking. We had chosen opposite schedules, and our paths barely crossed.

Several months after making eyes, when we met on a grassy hill, and I shared some acro yoga with Rebecca, she introduced me to her child and boyfriend. Before leaving, she made it a very clear point to exchange numbers and insist we do more acro. During the acro there was unnecessary lingering in some of the touches and gentle falls. Hyper aware of such things, she struck me as bold. Who was this audacious and shameless beauty? If there is one thing in a romance that wins my acute attention, it is when a woman expresses confidence and gives a clear invitation. She had my attention, and I waited for an invitation I knew would come.

When she and Omar invited me to a party, I was honored. I am an introvert and normally shy away from gatherings larger than 3. Some time ago, I ended 5 social media accounts and laid my FOMO to rest. I prefer little attention unless it is direct one on one. I may be charming and entertaining in a group, but it leaves me energetically depleted sometimes for days; sometimes fatigue and disengagement hit me in the middle of social events, and I feel like a ghost. My enthusiasm to attend that gathering is a testament to how charming Rebecca and Omar had been together after we all briefly met.

Calvin's Perspective

I had no expectations or knowledge of their sexual orientations or relationship dynamics. But, I had intrigue, and I knew I would be surrounded by the finest people. The evening did not disappoint. A twighlight was late into the night outside when Rebecca nestled herself against me and Omer had a lady in his lap. Myself being mostly a stranger in this scenario, the atmosphere felt both exciting and somehow comfortable. The night ended in a mix of charm and intrigue that was pleasing, and I left feeling unusually energized.

I'm attracted to complexity but loathe ambiguity. One of the keys to this is communication. It is easy to communicate with Rebecca. Soon after the party, all my questions were answered.

Rebecca is extraordinary. I could chronicle her sensual delights with the passion of Neruda. Her mind, wit, and laughter make her pleasant company in any group or setting. Her communication and honesty flow without hesitation. She is easy to approach and willing to talk about anything. The force with which she flows is evident in her publication. She breaks the mold.

Her flaws: She has often said, "If I know you, I love you." At times her communication and directness are so sharp they feel as though they will cut you, but it is actually with a merciful and important truth (albeit the kind of truth that will cut a frail man's ego down to size if need be). She is a rebel with the sweetest face and a seductress who will be true to herself only and cannot be domesticated. She is wild, her soul is kindred, and I love her deeply for it all. Her love is not for the weak. Perhaps her only flaw is that she is an intrepid woman.

One thing that excited me about this book is the title, Edge Play. While edge play in BDSM circles entails extreme limits, I was introduced to the concept of consentually flirting with the edges of one's perceived safety. It is a trust-

Calvin's Perspective

building experience where there are opportunities for personal growth and connection through overcoming fear. The potential for gain is great and the possibility of damage is very real. You can edge play with yourself, but it is better to have a lifeline for support and aftercare when overwhelmed by the experience. I am attracted to providing such experiences where and when appropriate. One of our first times alone together, Rebecca and I had a swim that I won't forget. Power exchange can be an opportunity to let go, to trust and overcome irrational fear. Sexual chemistry for me can be about the mix of vulnerability, playfulness and cathartic release. It can also be about novel sensations - perhaps involving jute rope, a belt around the neck, a new way to orgasm, something dangerously public or simply offering sensual experience of eating sticky, vine-ripened figs off a new lover's thigh, or trying sour cream after sucking on a miracle berry.

When Rebecca informed me she needed to put the brakes on our sexy times to better focus on her and Omer's relationship, it was a very sad moment for me. We were at the top of a dramatic hike in the Gorge. The day was grey, and for some reason, there were rose petals littering the mud around the wind-worn log where we sat. She was sad too. I was proud of her for committing to Omer and decided to show support rather than loss. From that day on, our relationship has been more a fond friendship than anything. When her and Omer were seperating, I stepped back and maybe passed up invitations or opportunities that followed. I waited out the social and sexual extravaganzas but enjoyed hearing about them. I enjoy being in her presence every chance I have and listening to all her thoughts. She can move quickly and socially. I move comparatively slowly and stick to the sidelines

Calvin's Perspective

515

I hope to have her presence in my life until it ends.

Reading what I have so far, Edge Play is an accurate reflection of real-world relationships, fantastic sexual adventures in full fruition and the mind expanding tools we call psychoactive drugs. I am stoked to be a part of it all. It is not a fiction full of characters, but a story of real people, like the people we cross paths with in the street, at a festival, while taking classes or traveling to the coast. Maybe this can encourage more people to shed religious millstones, to test their edges and explore their fantasies in the real world with assertiveness. I sincerely desire that for all in need of liberation from shame or fear, for all who believe in life before death, and especially for the mothers out there who too often fall into the most critical of societal judgements. Who deserves life's pleasure's and exploration more!

Thank you readers for taking interest. Thank you Rebecca for sharing all your vulnerable, real and inspiring experiences with me and all the curious.

P.S. I still have plenty of rope...

Love,
Calvin

Our meeting, like many of Becca's introductions, warrants a retelling. Not only is it as whimsical and practical as she is, it encapsulates so much of the serendipity of what was to come. Here goes.

I sat in my parked car in front of the climbing gym, flustered after commuting through Portland traffic in the rain. Amidst the many things on my mind, I had been searching for a CBD company to use in my massage practice. I threw my arms up in the air and said, "Alright universe, I need a CBD company that I can trust. It needs to be organic, sustainable, local, and affordable. I let go of all control and ask that the right company finds its way to me."

With that settled I went climbing, and afterwards to dinner, where I realized in my flustered state I had left my wallet at the gym. After my dear friend paid for my meal I made my way back to get my wallet.

And there she was, with a big welcoming grin at a little table, giving out CBD samples. Magnets; I felt like two happy little magnets were swooped right toward eachother. Becca and I were instantly deep in conversation about CBD, the farm, healing + bodywork. Though our connection was initially planted in business, we quickly grew to be friends. As you well know by now, it's nearly impossible not to want to be friends with Becca.

The very same currents that drew us together that fateful night at the climbing gym directed us toward one another again nearly 8 months later. I was just beginning to THINK about moving out of my living situation and that week I got a text from Becca, kindly + thoughtfully asking her friends near and far if they knew of any available

Indigo's Perspective

housing for her and her then 5 year old son. Her relationship had recently ended with Omer.

My first impulse was to say, "Well wouldn't you know it, I'm thinking about moving soon myself. How about we chat about living together?" But an equally loud voice chimed in. I wanted to try living alone — in Portland. Which on my living wage was just insane, but I wasn't ready to let go of that desire just yet. There was also the fact that Becca and I had only really known each other for a short while. Although we were very friendly (we had in fact gone soaking at the local clothing optional spa together where we obviously chose no clothing) I didn't *really* know her. But something spoke even louder. She may be the only woman, close to my age, who when upon meeting her I immediately recognized that I did not feel the slightest hint of my own insecurity, comparison or jealousy.

Which to me is a big deal. In the short time I have known her, my little shadowy, comparison voices went quiet and the volume on my 'Inspired - Grateful - To - Be - Alive' voices got turned way the hell up. They have been ever since. Simply put, Becca leads with an open heart, radical self-respect, and a genuine desire to connect human to human.

Taking all of this into consideration, I reached back out to her the following to see if she had found any leads on living situations. The conversation turned from a sweet bubbling of sharing to a full boil of considering the possibilities of living together. That same day she came across the most charming bungalow in the Alberta Arts District and the very next day we were inside it, enchanted by it, and both equally working to enchant our future landlord; which we did.

During a brief but very direct heart to heart over breakfast we talked about what we needed from our soon to be shared home. I even brought a candle to set the mood ☺. Looking back I can't help but laugh imagining what Becca must have been thinking.

Indigo's Perspective

WE BOTH NEEDED PEACE FROM THE TURBULENT HEARTBREAK WE HAD BOTH RECENTLY ENDURED. WE NEEDED STABILITY AFTER SO MUCH CHAOS, BOTH GOOD AND BAD. WE NEEDED A NEST TO HEAL IN, TO FEEL OUR OWN STRENGTH + WISDOM.

I THINK WHAT I EXPERIENCED ON THE EVE OF SIGNING A LEASE TOGETHER IS WHAT MANY OTHERS HAVE EXPERIENCED WITH BECCA; TERROR AND EXCITEMENT. I ASKED THE UNIVERSE FOR WHAT I WANTED, SHE ARRIVED WITH A SIMILAR REQUEST, READY TO TAKE A LEAP INTO THE UNKNOWN TOGETHER, NEARLY 3 MONTHS EARLIER THAN I ANTICIPATED. HER WILLINGNESS TO TAKE THE PLUNGE WAS THRILLING AND ABSOLUTELY TERRIFYING. SHE WAS READY TO TAKE THIS CHAPTER CHANGE TOGETHER, WAS I READY?! CHANGE IS F*ING SCARY! NEARLY TWO YEARS LATER I CAN TELL YOU OUR NEST IS THRIVING. THE SERENDIPITY OF OUR MEETING HAS FOLLOWED US SHOWERING US BOTH IN STABILITY AND INCREDIBLE EXPANSION.

AT TIMES I HAVE HAD TO PINCH MYSELF TO SEE IF THIS PERPETUAL GIFT IS REAL; TWO INTELLIGENT WOMEN, LOVING, FIERCE WOMEN LIVING ALONG SIDE EACHOTHER, BOLSTERING ONE ANOTHER, LAUGHING LIKE MAD WOMEN WHEN WE ARENT PONDERING OR WEEPING.

I HAVEN'T EVEN MENTIONED MOSES. THE LOVE I FEEL FOR HIM IS IMMENSE. HE'S GROWN FAST. THEY'RE REALLY NOT KIDDING WHEN THEY SAY TIME FLIES RAISING KIDS. I HAVE NO DOUBT HE WILL BE A LIFE LONG FRIEND. WE'VE STARTED RECORDING HIS LITTLE MOMENTS OF WISDOM. LIKE HIS MOTHER HE IS ARTICULATE, DEEPLY LOVING, AND NO BS.

i HAD A MISCARRIAGE IN 2016 FOLLOWED BY A BRUTAL BREAK UP WITH MY FIANCE THAT SPANNED THE FOLLOWING 3 YEARS. TO SAY THAT LIVING WITH BECCA AND MOSES HAS BEEN HEALING IS AN UNDERSTATEMENT. MOSES' LAUGH RINGS THROUGH THE HOUSE AND MY HEART FEELS JOY ONLY A CHILD COULD FILL. IT'S BEEN TERRIFYING AT TIMES, TO THINK ABOUT THE NATURAL TENDENCY OF CHANGE AND HOW THE CURRENTS MAY CARRY OUR FREE SPIRITS INTO OTHER DIRECTIONS. I FINALLY FEEL LIKE I'VE FOUND SOLID GROUND AGAIN, HOME AGAIN.

Indigo's Perspective

EACH DAY IS A PRACTICE OF SAYING YES TO THE RICHNESS. A PRAYER TO REMAIN PRESENT AND GRATEFUL. I THINK FOR THE FIRST YEAR I RESISTED THE DEPTH OF THE JOY AND HEALING OUR HOUSE HAS BROUGHT.
I NOW LET THAT TWINGE OF "WHAT IF" INFORM A GREATER WISDOM TO SAY "HOW WONDERFUL".
HOW WONDERFUL WE GET TO SHARE IN THIS LIFE. IN THIS MOMENT. AND THAT WAS MADE EVER MORE CLEAR ON THE BACK DROP OF 2020.

WE COULD NOT HAVE IMAGINED WHAT 2020 WOULD BRING. THE SURREAL WAVES OF COVID-19 BROUGHT US EVEN CLOSER. OUR NEST STAYED AFLOAT AND BECAME A SANCTUARY TO TALK DEEP INTO THE NIGHT WITH TEARS IN OUR EYES ABOUT GEORGE FLOYD AND THE BLACK LIVES MATTER MOVEMENT. I AM A BETTER WOMAN FOR KNOWING BECCA, TALKING WITH HER. CRYING WITH HER. LAUGHING WITH HER.

SHE IS FIERCE. A FIERCE ACTIVIST, FRIEND, AND YES I HAVE HEARD HER FIERCE LOVE MAKING TO ;) THE WALLS ARE THIN OK?

BECCA IS A MASTER WEB WEAVER, A BRILLIANT NETWORKER AND COMMUNITY BUILDER. IT'S IN HER BLOOD TO BRING THE PEOPLE SHE LOVES TOGETHER. SHE IS GENEROUS WITH HER FRIENDSHIPS AND BROUGHT A BRILLIANT BOUQUET OF FRIENDS INTO OUR LIVES. YOU MAY HAVE NOTICED MY CHEEKY GARDEN METAPHORS AND THEY'RE NECESSARY BECAUSE DURING OUR TIME QUARANTINING AND TRIPPING ~~~~~~~~~~ OUT ON THE "NEW NORMAL", AND MAYBE A FEW MUSHROOMS, WE STARTED A FARM. REALLY ITS A LARGE GARDEN, A <u>VERY</u> LARGE GARDEN.

AS I FINISH MY LETTER WHICH HAS TAKEN FOREVER TO WRITE, SHE IS STEWING OUR MOST RECENT HARVEST OF TOMATOES IN OUR WARMLY LIT KITCHEN AS FALL CREEPS IN. EVEN NOW I PINCH MYSELF.

WHILE I PAINT A BEAUTIFUL SCENE HERE, ITS NOT ALWAYS MILK AND HONEY, OK MOSTLY ITS MILK + HONEY, BUT HER BOOK IS CALLED EDGE PLAY FOR A REASON.

BOY HAVE I COME TO LEARN ABOUT MY OWN EDGES AND DO SOME DEEP DIGGING.

COMING FROM A DIVORCED HOUSEHOLD MYSELF, I DON'T THINK I WAS PREPARED TO LIVE ALONG SIDE A SINGLE MOM, NOT BECAUSE LIVING WITH A LITTLE BOY CAN BE CHALLENGING, WHICH IT HARDLY EVER IS. SHE REALLY IS ONE OF THE MOST WELL BEHAVED KIDS I'VE MET. THE EMOTIONAL INTELLIGENCE AND DIRECT COMMUNICATION ON BECCAS PART HELPS. HE'S MORE ARTICULATE THAN I AM AT TIMES)

WHAT <u>HAS</u> BEEN CHALLENGING IS MY OWN CHILDHOOD BAGGAGE THAT COLORS THE JUDGEMENTS AND PROJECTIONS AROUND BECCA. TRIANGULATION, FEAR OF BEING INADEQUATE, ABANDONMENT, JUST ABOUT EVERY ISSUE OF MINE HAS BEEN BROUGHT TO THE SURFACE.

ALSO BEING MORE ON THE MONOGAMOUS END OF THE SPECTRUM I HAVE <u>DEFINITATELY</u> HAD TO WORK WITH MY OWN DISCOMFORT AROUND HER VERY DIFFERENT LIFESTYLE. IT'S SOMETHING I ADMIRE MOST ABOUT BECCA. SHE TELLS IT LIKE IT IS, NO B.S. WITH LOVE. IT'S WHAT ALLOWS ME TO TRUST HER, OVER + OVER AGAIN.

WHAT I'VE LEARNED LIVING W/ BECCA IS THAT WE SUFFER WHEN WE THINK WE CAN CHANGE SOME ONE ELSE, OR WHEN WE THINK WE CAN CHANGE FOR SOMEONE ELSE. WE SUFFER WHEN WE COMPROMISE ESSENTIAL <u>TRUTHS</u> ABOUT OURSELVES, AND WE SUFFER WHEN THOSE WE ARE IN RELATIONSHIP COMPROMISE THEIRS.

WHETHER ITS ROMANTIC OR NOT, THE RULES OF RELATIONSHIP APPLY TO EVERYONE. WHETHER WERE MONOGAMOUS OR NOT, LIVING IN A HEALTHY RELATIONSHIP REQUIRES US TO BE IN HEALTHY RELATIONSHIP WITH OURSELVES FIRST AND FOREMOST.

Indigo's Perspective

The people we surround ourselves with impact that vital relationship to self, and I am honored to have Becca's impact. Learning how different we can be as humans and maintain connectedness has been fundamentally life altering.

Living alongside Becca has lent itself to an intimate view into eachothers lives. There is no doubt that her medicine for others is often the alchemy of catalyzing change and working with edges. Whether the things she catalyzes are comfortable or not, pleasurable or not, seems inconsequential. The fact that she stirs something within people to acknowledge their own edges is what seems important. Really it's a long lasting gift. She has stared her mistakes in the face and humbly taken their lessons to heart, with open hands. Her integrity is stunning and organic as fuck.

I find myself looking to our relationship as a reference for my other friendships. Are we communicating well? Are we being respectful of one another? Am I owning mine and are they owning theirs? I have empathy for those who have been challenged by her scorpion nature. And I also have empathy for her tenderness and sweet sensitivity underneath her very capable and independent shell.

If it isn't already clear I have unyielding respect for Becca, eternal love for both her and Moses, and endless gratitude for their magic in my life. She shows the fuck up. Her very being is a sensual declaration of what it means to live an inspired

Indigo's Perspective

LIFE, TO FEEL LIFE IN ALL ITS FORMS; RADIANT AND MESSY, HEARTFELT AND HUMAN. HER LIFE IS ART IN MOTION, TO WHICH WE ALL HAVE THAT RIGHT. IF YOU TAKE ANYTHING LET IT BE THAT.

WITH LOVE,
Indigo ♡

THERE'S JOY ON THE EDGE.

I could have had a very different life if I had just stayed in my lane. I can see it clearly in the domestic lives of my church friends, with their kids, book clubs, essential oils and gushy online declarations of marital love. I could have lost myself in it; I almost did. For me, a curiosity about the world beyond my default settings and an openness to abundant life compelled me to ask more questions than I thought I could answer, to peer over the edge, the fences of right & wrong, in & out, sinful & holy that I had built around myself.

The world is far more weird, wonderful, and complex than I ever knew (or could possibly know). Living on the edge means saying YES! to life. It means opening the floodgates of possibility and trusting the challenging current of discovery, wonder, action, and expansion to rush over and through you, leaving you transformed like a seed becoming a forest.

meet you on the edge,
Becca

Rebecca Martinez

Dedication

Six months after the story in this book ended, I met a woman in need. Her name was Maya. She was a soft, vulnerably open woman with a childlike spirit, blowing about at the whims of her surroundings and looking for something, someone, solid to latch onto. I was that someone.

Maya, who was 44, had stage IV cervical cancer which, despite a summer of chemotherapy and radiation, had begun to spread throughout her body. To make things worse, she had no support system in Portland; she felt alone in the world.

We met during a meeting at the Waldorf School where our sons shared a kindergarten class. Raising her hand, she asked the teacher numerous parenting questions throughout the meeting. Afterward, I offered her a resource for bedtime meditations that my son Moses and I had been using, a simple extension of support from one mother to another.

I noticed the way other parents averted their gaze from her, the way one does at the discomfort of seeing a beggar on the sidewalk but has no time or change to spare. I felt ashamed at my own impulse to turn away, but I was deep in the throes of writing this book and my energy was maxed out.

The following week, Maya approached me after school and asked if I might be able to help her son with rides. She didn't have a car and she was spending hours on public transit each day. I imagined what that must be like, and it hit me just how fortunate I was to have a life with access to comforts and conveniences.

In true Becca form, I graciously said no. I had been learning to hold firm boundaries, you see, a skill I had been honing in recent years, and I had all but shut out the world so I could focus on my creative process. At this point in my life, I felt I had done enough hard things; I had paid my dues and I owed nothing to anyone. And yet, as she stared up at me with her big hazel eyes, nearly quivering with desperation like a wet, stray puppy that had wandered onto my doorstep, I felt compelled to respond.

"Let me think about it," I said, giving her my number.

I had no idea then, that I'd be lying beside her during her last days on this earth.

I began driving Maya's son, Lucian, to school with Moses. I wasn't used to making this level of sacrifice: waking up early, going out of my way, disrupting my own flow, to no personal benefit. I quickly learned that in order to get the boys to class on time, I must arrive fifteen minutes earlier than was agreed.

She struggled with the pace of practical life and had a propensity for making ordinary tasks extra challenging, sometimes to the extent that we had to laugh about it together. I learned she'd been walking several miles to and from the natural grocery store every few days with big glass jugs to refill them with filtered drinking water. How does anyone have time and patience for that? I wondered, and offered her a spare water filter, thus solving the issue.

"You're so capable. Life just seems so easy for you," she said sincerely. "I don't know why it's always been such a challenge for me."

In my mind, I thought, probably trauma. It's often trauma that blocks us from accessing our true potential.

I helped Maya get Lucian dressed in the mornings and put his lunches together. This familial support wasn't one sided though; she reminded me when we had class meetings and no-school days scheduled, something I was notoriously bad at tracking.

Soon, we became unlikely friends. I felt closed off to the world at that time and had become stringently selective about the company I kept. I'd resolved to surround myself only with people I sought to emulate, the crème de la crème. I was thriving in mutually supportive friendships with the best, brightest people I could find in Portland: entrepreneurs, creatives, activists.

And yet, there was something refreshingly raw and real in our friendship. We were both single moms. She came from a different world than I did, one with particular struggles and adversities I'd never experienced. She was intensely grateful for my help and expressed her appreciation often. She'd bring me little chocolate bars or send me loving text messages. She constantly attempted to give me gas money.

Maya was unemployed due to her health condition and offered to have Moses over for playdates several times a week. He is a child who seems to leave a trail of sunshine and calm everywhere he goes, and these playdates helped everyone. His company calmed her son and lifted Maya's spirits. This also gave me extra hours in the day so I could work on my book, take a walk with a friend, or blow off steam at the rock climbing gym. Countless pages in this book were completed thanks to her generosity.

I came to cherish her friendship.

We saw each other five days a week, more than I saw any other friend. She was my biggest fan and expressed often how much she admired my tenacity and believed in the work I was doing. When she asked how I was doing, I could tell she truly wanted to know. No bullshit.

After we took the boys to school, I'd drive her back and we'd share stories about our families, jobs we'd had, people we'd dated. We were both happy to have a friend and comrade.

The struggles thickened as the months went on, and our relationship required a great deal of energy. Her condition was declining, and her son's constant colds and ear infections necessitated a sort of parenting role, which I was able to fill. I never questioned whether I should be in this role; it was obvious that I shouldn't, but this was a moment, and a family, to which I felt called. I remember climbing out of a warm bed in the arms of a lover one evening to take Maya and Lucian to urgent care. When I arrived, he was holding his ear and screaming in pain. Another ear infection.

We drove to the clinic. Out on the sidewalk, I held the sweet pajama clad boy who was whimpering in pain as she spoke to the office staff inside. She came out defeated. Not only had she forgotten her identification, she also had the wrong kind of insurance for that clinic. With anyone else, I would have been extremely frustrated. But she brought out a deep patience and compassion in me. I just laughed in resignation and offered an alternative plan.

I didn't know such patience was possible until I felt it in my body. We drove all over Portland before they were finally set up with medical care and I could return, exhausted, to my sleeping lover in my own peaceful universe.

When it wasn't his health on the line, it was hers. She refused to go through treatment again; a summer of chemotherapy and radiation had ravaged her body and compromised her connection with her son. I watched as her body wasted and her symptoms worsened. She became unable to sleep.

She chose to rely on essential oils and beams of healing light planted in her by reiki-master shamans over the phone. She was reading new age books about faith healing. I suppressed my criticisms and tried to honor her path.

I monitored her pain levels, which she tended to minimize, and made it clear that I expected the truth from her. Each morning, after dropping the boys at school, we went inside her house so I could apply an elaborate essential oil protocol to the length of her spine. For a half hour every morning, I sat with her and massaged these fragrant oils over her fine bones. I'd drag my fingertips over her rapidly protruding vertebrae and hold back tears of grief as I witnessed the unspoken reality of a mortality that she couldn't yet admit to herself.

By Thanksgiving, the pain in her back left her unable to stand. It had become clear to me that she would not recover.

I cried in my mom's arms at Thanksgiving dinner as I realized that my friend was dying. That week, Maya requested that I drop her at the hospital to seek palliative care and they did very little for her. She was someone who skewed invisible; her airy energy made her prone to falling through the cracks of the medical system.

That night, as her son slept upstairs beside Moses, and I tossed and turned, waiting for her call, I wondered how on Earth I had become so entangled with this woman, her life and her chaos. Close friends questioned why I was helping her so much. How could I not? She had no one. All I knew was that I felt called, like my life was inextricably linked to hers, even if momentarily. Life had set her on the path right in front of me. What else could I do, turn my eyes away?

Perhaps it didn't appear so from the outside, but I needed her as much as she needed me.

After everything I'd been through in the past four years, I needed to believe in a world where anyone, regardless of their failures and flaws, their shortcomings and chaos, could still find love and belonging. I needed to believe that people could change — that I, someone who had learned early in life to put myself first at all costs, who had been called selfish by lovers, friends and family members, could set myself aside and put someone else first. Not just for a moment, but for a whole season of life. The challenge, the struggle, and the frustration were as healing for me as her friendship and love.

Maya was someone who cared.

In spite of her condition, she became actively involved in my life. We'd taken the boys trick-or-treating for Halloween and went to meet Santa during the holidays. She attended a pop up shop I hosted and got to know many of my friends. She was the first person to pre-order my book. We shared in the school's annual solstice walk with our homemade paper lanterns, winding through a sprawling city park and singing songs with our children about darkness and the promise of coming light.

Maya's days grew thin. After the holidays, it was clear she was running out of time. She couldn't be left alone and wound up sleeping on my couch while we attempted to sort out a plan. Her distant family and I rallied to raise funds for an alternative treatment in Mexico, which totaled over $30,000.

I tapped into my support network to help Maya and myself with housework, errands, and food coordination as I became immersed in supporting her. My mom, who I'd had a strained relationship with for so long, came over and cleaned my house while I worked from home one afternoon. She met Maya and Lucian and poured love on them in the way only moms know how.

I eventually passed the baton as decades-old friends in Los Angeles graciously took over her care.

It was a relief to have a taste of my own flow again. I began a new, demanding campaign job which absorbed the space I'd previously filled with caring for Maya. Winter melted rapidly into spring, and before long, rumors of a coronavirus reaching our shorelines were confirmed and the world as we knew it changed.

Friends helped Maya return to Portland. Sadly, her months of intensive treatments had been unsuccessful. By spring, the cancer had metastasized throughout her body and left her weak, with brittle breaking bones and rapidly declining faculties. This decline was familiar to me, having lost another loved one due to cancer a few years earlier.

In early May, Moses and I went to see her. COVID or no COVID, we were intent on sharing her last days with her.

"Have you seen her?" her friend asked in hushed tones when we arrived. Moses went outside to play with Lucian, just like he always did.

"I've seen recent pictures. It's okay, I can handle it," I replied.

I creaked the door open.

"Hey, Maya," I said with a smile. We hadn't seen each other in months. She

DEDICATION **529**

was smaller, hollowed out, a ghost of the woman I'd met in September. She beamed up at me, her childlike form cozy beneath piles of plush blankets and surrounded by greeting cards and bouquets of pink and purple flowers. Her bright eyes and huge smile were uncompromised.

"My friend!" she said with soft enthusiasm. "I'm so happy to see you."

There wasn't much to say. She asked me about my job and my book, and whether I'd had any exciting dates recently. She wanted to hear about it all. We laughed and cried. Her pain meds made her sleepy, but she urged me to stay as long as I could. So I did. The boys worked on a puzzle in the living room.

I lay beside her and she curled against me like a small baby nuzzles against the warmth of her mother. I tucked her blankets around her shoulders and ran my hands over her tenderly, holding her cool hand in mine and twiddling with the new growth on her recently buzzed hair.

As I looked at the photos pinned to her wall, I thought about what makes a life. I saw her young and healthy, traveling the world, making friends and magnetizing the love that she needed, wherever she went. The fact of mortality was so intimately present in the room with us. She dozed peacefully and as I held her close, I wondered what I'd be remembering at the end of my days.

What will I be leaving behind? What will I wish I had done? Who will I wish I had loved more intimately, forgiven more generously, and embraced more fully? What will I wish I had fought for, and what will I wish I had let go of sooner?

I came back every couple of days for a week, lying beside her quietly and promising to return again soon. She ordered Moses a scooter online and had it shipped to our house. She gave us her Instant Pot. She was unendingly thoughtful and generous.

"You two have a special bond," her caregiver said to us one day, as we wiped our eyes after a long and tearful, wordless exchange.

Maya wasn't speaking much by that point. There wasn't much left to say.

"Yeah," I agreed. I looked at Maya. "We came into each other's lives at just the right time."

She smiled at me sadly. Despite my attempts to be steady, I fell apart. I let myself feel it all, the deep ache of saying goodbye. Her caregiver slipped quietly from the room.

"This might be the last time I see you," I said to her, and the reality hit me as I spoke. My voice cracked. "Thank you for being my friend."

She squeezed my hand tightly, refusing to let go. Then she opened her eyes wide and looked up at me.

"I. Love. You. SO. Much." she said, clear as the evening sky.

Maya passed away the next morning. Friends from all over the country emerged online to share memories and celebrate her life. Her son went to be with his father. We saw her through her journey, watching from a distance as her earthen casket was tucked into the soil at the edge of a field where the grass meets the wild woods. Crows cawed and baby eagles called out as she was returned to the earth that loved her.

I drove home, emptied out, feeling her blessing to carry on with my life. Our work together was complete.

Maya was the kind of unlikely gift that would have been easy to miss out on. I could have said no that day at the school and carried on with my default life, uninterrupted. It was an attention to life that made it possible. A willingness to be surprised. A humble curiosity and an ability to navigate the edges of my comfort zone without abandoning myself.

The night Maya passed, Moses stood beside me as we picked flowers to create a bouquet in her honor. She was gone. The reality had been hitting me in waves. He watched the fat tears run down my cheeks and splash into the earth beside my zinnias and lavender.

"Mom, do you just want to think of how you felt before you knew Maya?" he asked. "Then you won't feel so sad."

I hugged him, appreciating his tender, sensitive heart.

"Well... I'm kind of happy that I'm sad," I told him.

He furrowed his eyebrows at me, perplexed at the obvious contradiction.

"My heart hurts right now, but I have a friend who I didn't have before. And I get to keep everything she taught me about life and remember the special times we shared."

He was quiet for a minute. I arranged stems of mint in the bouquet as he thought.

"Plus, I got a scooter," he said.

I nodded, and restrained my laughter.

DEDICATION

I met Maya at a time when I felt jaded. I'd been through loss and heartbreak, and had come to believe that sometimes, relationships just aren't worth the trouble. Maya's presence in my life softened me and revitalized my belief in the value of inconvenient, messy, whole, unrestrained love.

Witnessing the end of her life tore down my armor and helped me reckon with my own mortality. The satisfaction of supporting her and using my privilege to remove barriers to her wellbeing inspired me to stay open to the hidden opportunities in life, to avoid getting so absorbed in my flow that I miss what's going on in the world around me.

She reminded me of the growth that is possible when we break convention, step outside of ourselves, and move toward that which is challenging, uncertain and even misunderstood by others.

She inspired me to emerge from each new experience as someone softer, stronger, and more attentive to life.

Thank you for peering over the edge with me.

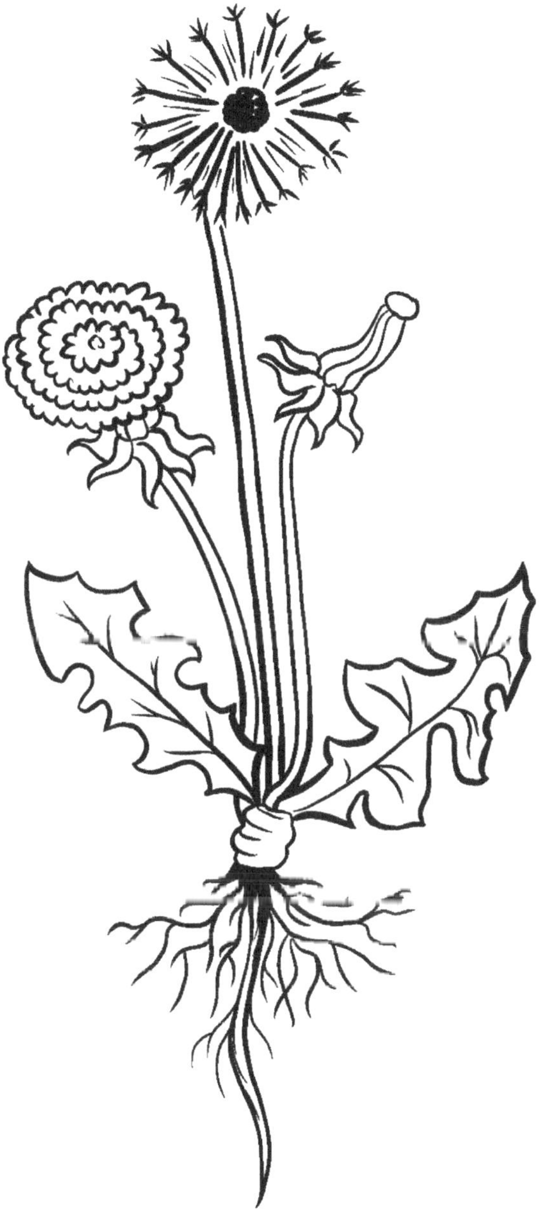

Reflections

Prompts for Book Club Discussion

Edge Play: (n)

An active state which requires curiosity, participation, and risk taking beyond the limits of one's comfort zone. The purpose of edge play is to promote liberation, resilience, awareness and healing.

In BDSM, the intersection of pain, pleasure and danger; an activity that challenges conventional boundaries of sanity and safety.

• • •

1. How did you feel reading Edge Play? Was the story challenging, cathartic, amusing?

2. If you could ask the author one question, what would it be?

3. What aspect of Rebecca's story could you most relate to?

4. What parts made you tear up, and what parts made you laugh out loud?

5. What character(s) did you resonate with the most? The least?

6. What did you already know about the subject matter (psychedelics, non-monogamy, Evangelical Christianity, the prison industrial complex) before reading Edge Play?

7. Did you learn something new from Edge Play? What questions do you still have?

8. Share a favorite quote from the book. Why does it stand out to you?

9. Themes of fire, water and blood appear throughout the story. What do you think each element represents through Rebecca's path? What elements would appear repeatedly in your own story?

10. Have you ever had a twin flame or soulmate, like Rebecca found with Samuel or Andi?

11. What is one scene you'd like to experience? What is one scene that made you cringe?

12. Consider the roles of Tess, Logan, Lori and other friends in the story. What responsibility do friends have to one another when going through crises? How would you have related to a friend like Rebecca during these events?

13. Being raised in an Evangelical, conservative setting shaped Rebecca and steered her trajectory. What forces helped shape you as a young person? Have you remained close to those beliefs, or moved away from them?

14. Rebecca experiences an out of body experience during childbirth. Have you ever had a cosmic experience like that?

15. Do you know any mothers as unconventional as Rebecca? What do you see as the core responsibilities of parenthood? Did this story challenge any of your attitudes or assumptions?

16. What were you taught about love and sex as a young person? What messages do you want to pass on to your own child or a young person in your life?

17. Discuss psychedelics as medicine. LSD pointed Rebecca back to her mother, psilocybin led to her father, and MDMA helped her return to her own heart. Is this a new concept? What other ways do you think Rebecca could have achieved these healing breakthroughs without psychedelics?

18. How did the author's relationship to aloneness change throughout the story?

19. Crows appear numerous times in Edge Play. What animals or natural environments have been your teachers in life, and what have they taught you?

20. What do you think the author's purpose was in writing this book? Did she achieve that purpose?

21. If you were to give Rebecca one piece of advice, what would it be?

22. What would you title a memoir from your twenties? What climatic event(s) would you include?

Made in the USA
Las Vegas, NV
08 December 2020